SHAIKH MUḤAMMAD AL-MUḤAMMAD AL-KASNAZĀN AL-ḤUSAYNĪ

A Life in the Footsteps of the Best of Lives

I0316206

Louay Fatoohi

SAFIS PUBLISHING
Birmingham – UK

Published in the United Kingdom by
Safis Publishing, Birmingham, UK.
www.safispub.com

ISBN 978-1-906342-25-8 (paperback)
978-1-906342-26-5 (ebook)

First Edition

Version Identifier: 20073101

Translation from Arabic: Madani Ramzan Sheikh and Louay Fatoohi
Cover design: Faiz Fattohi
Proofreading: James Newbury

The Passing of the Shaikh

We belong to Allah and to Him we will return (al-Nisā' 69)

It is with extreme sadness we report that Shaikh Muḥammad al-Muḥammad al-Kasnazān al-Ḥusaynī passed away in the first hour of Saturday 4th/July/2020 in Baltimore, USA, where he was receiving medical treatment. With his departure, Islam in general, and Sufism in particular, lost one of its greatest guides and good examples. Our Master spent his life calling people to Allah "with wisdom and good exhortation" (al-Naḥl 125), in word and deed, guiding numerous people.

O, Allah! Shower his tomb with Your light, bless his soul, and grant him a dwelling with those whom You have most favoured, "the prophets, the truthful, the martyrs and the righteous; excellent are those as companions" (al-Baqara 156)!

This book was already complete and in the process of publication when our absent-yet-ever-present Shaikh departed this world. Time constraints have prevented us from updating its content to reflect this saddest development.

Bismi Allāhi ar-Raḥmāni ar-Raḥīm (in the name of Allah, the Gracious, the Merciful)

Allāhumma ṣallī ʿalā sayyidinā Muḥammadi `l-waṣfi wal-waḥyi war-risālati wal-ḥikmati waʿalā `ālihi wa-ṣaḥbihi wa-sallim taslīmā (O Allah! Send prayer on our Master whose quality, revelation, message, and wisdom are most praised (Muḥammad), and on his lineage and companions, and salute him with a perfect salutation)

Write for the people of piety in the farthest cities,
about the Quṭb of Baghdad ʿAbd al-Qādir al-Ḥasanī
A full-moon that rose on the two rivers at a time
When darkness almost erased morning from time
Guidance poured out to all places no matter how far
As the soul's essence flows through the body
He exceeded walīs in knowledge and deed
The Quṭb of wonders in secret and in public
A great Ghawth whose stations are out of reach
No matter how much Allah's servants try
Stand in Ruṣāfa at our Master's, the Falcon
The best to answer if you call him when in need.

Martyred caliph ʿAlī Fāyiz (about Shaikh ʿAbd al-Qādir al-Gaylānī)

Unload the luggage, you have had enough sufferings
And kiss the sand of the ground and the doorstep
Unload the luggage for these are the quarters of our Shaikh
The station and the sought-after destination of seekers
And leave the camel caravan for you are not the first seeker
Of the way to salvation and the source of all means
How often you have gone around knocking on closed doors
Yet my the doors of my Shaikh's gardens are wide open.

Dr caliph ʿAbd al-Salām al-Ḥadīthī (about Shaikh Muḥammad al-Muḥammad al-Kasnazān)

The Author

Louay Fatoohi was born in Baghdad, Iraq, in 1961. He and his wife migrated to the UK in 1992. He lives in Birmingham, England. He obtained a BSc in physics from Baghdad University, Iraq, in 1984 and a PhD in astronomy from Durham University, UK, in 1998.

Originally from a Christian family, Louay reverted to Islam in his early twenties. He is one of the caliphs (representatives) of Shaikh Muḥammad al-Muḥammad al-Kasnazān. In addition to being his faith of choice and way of life, Islam is for him is a subject of deep intellectual interest. He is interested in Qur'anic and Islamic studies in general, but his main areas of research are as follows:

- Comparative study of history in the Qur'an, Jewish and Christian scriptures, and independent historical sources.
- Sufism.
- History of the Qur'anic text and revelation.
- Quranic Exegesis.

His publications in Islamic studies include:

- Authoring nine books in English, the latest of which is *The First and Last Revelations of the Qur'an.*
- Editing one book in English titled *The Wonders of Ṭarīqa Kasnazāniyya Brought to India.*
- Authoring eight books in Arabic, the latest of which is *Historical Miraculousness of the Concept of "Messiah" in the Noble Qur'an.*
- Editing one book in Arabic, *Fifteen Letters*, by Shaikh ʿAbd al-Qādir al-Gaylānī.
- Translating two books by Shaikh ʿAbd al-Qādir al-Gaylānī from Arabic into English, the latest of which is *Fifteen Letters.*
- Publishing many research papers and general articles in Arabic and English on various aspects of Islam.

Louay has also published fifteen research papers in cosmology and applied historical astronomy.

Photo 1: Shaikh Muḥammad al-Muḥammad in a session of songs of praise in the takya in Amman, Jordan (5th/January/2019). This is the front cover photo of the 2nd Arabic edition of this book.

Contents

Map 1: Iraq Governorates v
Map 2: Western Iraq and Eastern Iran vi
List of Photos vii
Preface 1
A) Sources 1
B) Methodology 3
C) Contents 5
D) Presentation 7
1 Ṭarīqa: The Way to Allah 11
1.1 Iḥsān 12
1.2 Ṣuḥba (Companionship) 15
1.3 Purification Ṣuḥba 22
1.4 Knowledge of the Self 28
1.5 The Muḥammadan Inheritor 32
1.6 Obedience in Ṣuḥba 36
1.7 The Spiritual Touch 42
1.8 Ṭarīqa and Sharia 51
2 The Ṭarīqa ʿAlīyya Qādiriyya Kasnazāniyya 57
2.1 The Shortest Way to Allah 57
2.2 Imām ʿAlī Ibn Abī Ṭālib 61
2.3 Shaikh ʿAbd al-Qādir al-Gaylānī 64
2.4 Shaikh ʿAbd al-Karīm Shāh al-Kasnazān 69
2.5 The Kasnazānī Shaikhs 80
2.6 The Chain of Shaikhs 85
3 Muḥammadan Karāmas 91
3.1 Muʿjiza 91
3.2 Karāma 97
3.3 The Function of Karāmas 103
3.4 Source of Karāmas 113
3.5 The Diversity of Karāmas and their Causes 118
3.6 Darbāsha 122
3.7 Spiritual Dispensation 125
4 Noble Lineage 133
5 In the Care of a Spiritual Father and a Pious Mother 141
6 Eduction and Self-Learning 153

7 Defending the National Rights of the Kurds 165
7.1 Shaikhs of the Ṭarīqa and Resistance to Injustice and Aggression...... 165
7.2 Historical Background of the Modern Kurdish Movement in Iraq.... 174
7.3 The Role of Shaikhs ʿAbd al-Karīm and Muḥammad al-Muḥammad in Launching the Kurdish Movement in Iraq 179
7.4 Shaikh Muḥammad al-Muḥammad's Military Activity 186
8 Family Life 209
9 Being Chosen for the Shaikhdom of the Ṭarīqa 215
9.1 Divine Appointment — Not Human Acquisition 217
9.2 The Designation of Shaikh Muḥammad al-Muḥammad al-Kasnazān 226
9.3 Shaikh Muḥammad al-Muḥammad's Designation of His General Deputy 237
10 Shaikh of the Ṭarīqa 245
10.1 Resuming the Shaikhdom of the Ṭarīqa 245
10.2 Karāmas That Confirm the Muḥammadan Inheritance 254
11 Muḥammadan Traits 261
11.1 The Necessity of Refined Manners for Spiritual Leadership 262
11.2 Prophetic Traits in Shaikh Muḥammad al-Muḥammad al-Kasnazān 264
11.2.1 Attractive Personality 264
11.2.2 Strategic Thinking 265
11.2.3 Multitasking 265
11.2.4 Working Hard 266
11.2.5 Modesty 266
11.2.6 Love for Children 268
11.2.7 Softheartedness 270
11.2.8 Helping the Poor and Needy 270
11.2.9 Charitableness Towards Orphans 271
11.2.10 Caring for the Mentally Ill 272
11.2.11 Compassion Towards Animals 273
11.2.12 Forbearance, Restraint, and Forgiveness 275
11.2.13 Cheerfulness of Countenance 276
11.2.14 Generosity 276
11.2.15 Giving Gifts 277
11.2.16 Interfaith Dialogue and Religious Tolerance 278
11.2.17 Loyalty 279
11.2.18 Joking 280
11.3 Promoting Prophetic Manners 281
12 Preaching 287
12.1 Increasing the Number of Caliphs, Training Them, and Sending Them to Preach 289
12.2 Delivering Sermons 292

12.3 Literature ... 295
12.4 Attributes of Kasnazānī Preaching ... 302
13 The Takya ... 309
13.1 The Ṭarīqa's Head and Heart ... 310
13.2 The Shaikh's Takya ... 315
13.3 Moving the Shaikh's Takya to Baghdad ... 317
13.4 Karāmas of Building Takyas ... 322
13.4.1 The Ramādī Takya in Iraq ... 322
13.4.2 The Khartoum Takya in Sudan ... 325
13.4.3 The Bangalore Takya in India ... 327
14 Dhikrs ... 335
14.1 The Means to Reach Allah ... 335
14.2 Specific Dhikrs ... 339
14.3 Kasnazānī Dhikrs ... 340
14.4 Kasnazānī Dhikrs in the Era of Shaikh Muḥammad al-Muḥammad 344
14.4.1 Perennial Dhikrs ... 344
14.4.2 Daily Dhikrs ... 346
14.4.3 Prayers of Peace and Blessings Upon the Prophet (PBUH) ... 350
14.4.4 Dhikr Circle ... 356
14.4.5 Temporary Dhikrs ... 359
14.4.6 Individual Dhikrs ... 360
14.4.7 Ḥizb al-Wāw ... 360
14.5 The Shaikh's Dhikrs ... 361
15 Riyāḍa (Spiritual Exercising) ... 365
16 Khalwa (Seclusion) ... 371
16.1 Al-Kasnazāniyya Khalwa ... 372
16.2 Shaikh Muḥammad al-Muḥammad al-Kasnazān's Seclusions ... 376
16.3 Supernatural and Spiritual Experiences ... 379
17 Political Persecution Against the Ṭarīqa in Iraq ... 387
17.1 The Spread of the Ṭarīqa and the Obedience of Dervishes to the Shaikh ... 389
17.2 The Ṭarīqa's Sources of Income ... 391
17.3 Harassment From the Authorities ... 395
17.4 Personal Persecution ... 400
17.5 Migration from Baghdad ... 407
17.6 Migration from Sulaymāniyya ... 412
18 Achievements ... 417
18.1 Reconstruction of Holy Sites ... 417
18.1.1 Visiting Holy Sites ... 422
18.2 The Muḥammadī Calendar ... 426

18.2.1 Converting Hijrī to Muḥammadī Dates 431
18.2.2 Converting Muḥammadī to Hijrī Dates 433
18.3 The Solar Date of the Birth of the Prophet (PBUH) 434
18.4 The Muḥammadī Shamsī Calendar 435
18.4.1 Converting Gregorian to Muḥammadī Shamsī Dates 437
18.4.2 Converting Muḥammadī Shamsī to Gregorian Dates 438
18.5 Al-Salām University College 440
18.6 Prophetic Odes 440
19 Interests 447
Epilogue 453
Biographical Timeline 455
Glossary 459
References 461
A) Classical and Old Works 461
B) Modern Works 465

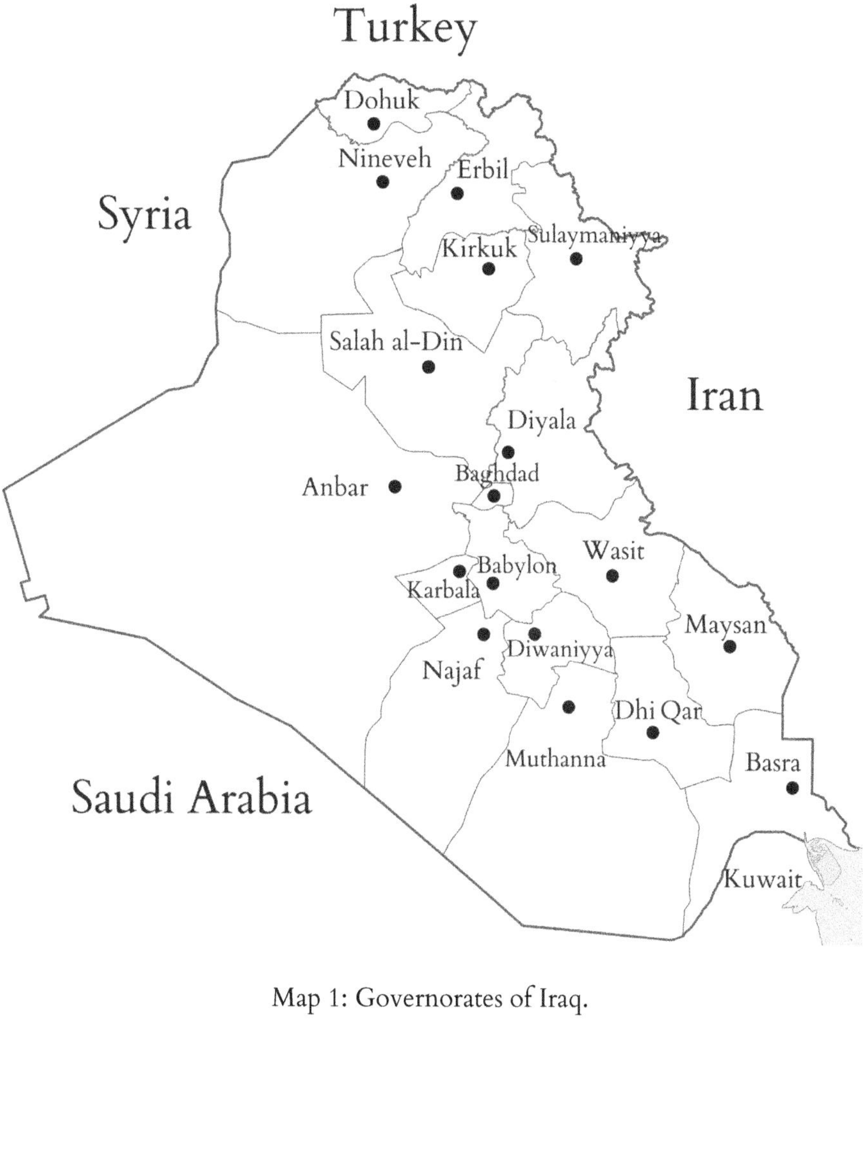

Map 1: Governorates of Iraq.

Map 2: Areas in northeast Iraq and northwest Iran mentioned in the book.

List of Photos

This is a listing of the photos in the book.

1: Shaikh Muḥammad al-Muḥammad in a session of songs of praise in the takya in Amman, Jordan (5th/January/2019). This is the front cover photo of the 2nd Arabic edition of this book.

2: Shaikh Muḥammad al-Muḥammad in a session of songs of praise in the takya in Amman, Jordan (24th/September/2015). This is the front cover photo of the 1st Arabic edition of this book.

3: Shaikh Muḥammad al-Muḥammad kissing a muṣḥaf in the takya in Amman, Jordan, on the day of celebrating the birth of Shaikh ʿAbd al-Qādir al-Gaylānī (20th/December/2018).

4: The hall of the shrines of the Kasnazānī Shaikhs in Karbchna, and the adjacent mosque behind can also be seen (19th/March/2016).

5: The shrine of Shaikh ʿAbd al-Karīm Shāh al-Kasnazān, and in the far left a part of the shrine of Shaikh ʿAbd al-Qādir al-Kasnazān can also be seen (19th/March/2016).

6: Shaikh Muḥammad al-Muḥammad in front of the hall of the shrines of the Kasnazānī Shaikhs in Karbchna (1981).

7: Shaikh ʿAbd al-Karīm in Kirkuk (2nd half of the 1970s).

8: Iranian police facilitating the movements of Shaikh ʿAbd al-Karīm in Sanandaj, Iran, because of the large number of welcomers (1962).

9: Shaikh Muḥammad al-Muḥammad with a group of dervishes in Penjwin on the border with Iran (1988).

10: Shaikh ʿAbd al-Karīm, second from right, and to his left is Shaikh Muḥammad al-Muḥammad during pilgrimage (1973).

11: Shaikh Muḥammad Al-Muḥammad, first from right, during pilgrimage (1973).

12: Shaikh Muḥammad al-Muḥammad in a public library in Baghdad (the 1990s).

13: Shaikh Muḥammad al-Muḥammad in his private room in the takya in Amman, Jordan, enjoying his favourite hobby of reading (2012).

14: Shaikh Muḥammad al-Muḥammad in a session of songs of praise in the takya in Amman, Jordan (24th/September/2015).

15: The meeting of Shaikh Muḥammad al-Muḥammad with Prime Minister ʿAbd al-Karīm Qāsim, and to his right Shaikh Ṭāhir, Shaikh Ḥusayn al-Kasnazān's oldest son. To Qāsim's left is Mullā ʿAlī Laylān then Mullā Muḥammad Amīn (1960).

16: Shaikh ʿAbd al-Karīm in the village of Halālāwa, on the border with Iran, after the withdrawal of Shaikh Muḥammad al-Muḥammad and the Peshmerga fighters after the battle of Darbandikhān (September/1961).

17: A number of Iranian officials visiting Shaikh ʿAbd al-Karīm in Iran on his way to meet the Shah of Iran in Tehran (1962).

18: Shaikh Muḥammad al-Muḥammad on the battlefront in Kurdistan, Iraq (first half of the 1960s).

19: Shaikh Muḥammad al-Muḥammad with his General Deputy and oldest son Shaikh Nahro in the takya in Amman, Jordan, on the night of the celebration of the birth of the Prophet (PBUH) according to the solar calendar (1st/May/2017).

20: Shaikh Muḥammad al-Muḥammad during the Friday prayer in the takya in Baghdad, and next to him is the martyred poet ʿAlī Fāyiz (middle of the 1990s).

21: Shaikh Muḥammad al-Muḥammad in a preaching session in the takya in Sulaymāniyya, Iraq (middle of the 2000s).

22: Shaikh ʿAbd al-Karīm in his last visit to the shrine of Shaikh ʿAbd al-Qādir al-Gaylānī, helped by Mullā Muḥammad Amīn (end of 1977).

23: Shaikh Muḥammad al-Muḥammad during the funeral ceremony of his father and Master of the Tarīqa before him Shaikh ʿAbd al-Karīm, in Kirkuk. Sadness and the heavy responsibility of the Tarīqa clearly show on him (February/1978).

24: Shaikh Muḥammad al-Muḥammad receives the Vatican ambassador to Jordan, Archbishop Giorgio Lingua, in the takya in Amman (March/2015).

25: Shaikh Muḥammad al-Muḥammad in the takya of Amman, Jordan (11th/December/2013)

26: Shaikh Muḥammad al-Muḥammad gives the pledge of the Tarīqa in his residence during his visit to London (2000).

27: Shaikh Muḥammad al-Muḥammad in one of his daily visits to the British Library during his stay in London. To his right is his General

Deputy and older son Shaikh Nahro and to his left his assistant Ḥājj Laṭīf (2000).

28: Shaikh Muḥammad al-Muḥammad, middle, in a session of songs of praise in the mosque of the takya in Baghdad (the 1990s).

29: Shaikh Muḥammad al-Muḥammad in a dhikr circle at the beginning of the construction of the main takya in Basra (1992).

30: Shaikh Muḥammad al-Muḥammad in the dhikr circle in the takya of Kirkuk (27th/August/1993)

31: The mosque in Karbchna; in front of it is the underground seclusion place of Shāh al-Kasnazān and Shaikh Ḥusayn. Shaikh Muḥammad al-Muḥammad has built a protective structure on it (19th/March/2016).

32: Shaikh Muḥammad al-Muḥammad in a session of songs of praise in the courtyard of the takya in Baghdad (1996).

33: The first seclusion of Shaikh Muḥammad al-Muḥammad in a cave at the foot of Mount Sagarma, which Shāh al-Kasnazān and Shaikh Ḥusayn also used for seclusion (1978).

34: Shaikh Muḥammad al-Muḥammad immediately after completing his first seclusion in Karbchna, followed by his assistant Ḥājj Muḥammad Maḥmūd (September/1978).

35: Shaikh Muḥammad al-Muḥammad before entering the hall of the shrine of Shaikh ʿAbd al-Qādir al-Gaylānī in Baghdad (1990s).

36: Shaikh Muḥammad al-Muḥammad in front of the shrine of Shaikh ʿAbd al-Qādir al-Gaylānī in Baghdad (1990s).

37: Shaikh Muḥammad al-Muḥammad on his farm in Dōra. The building behind him is today part of the al-Salām University College (1995/1996).

38: A page from the first printout of the Muḥammadī calendar, which was printed in its year of introduction (1991).

39: Shaikh Muḥammad al-Muḥammad in the middle of the dhikr circle in the takya in Baghdad (the 1990s).

40: Shaikh Muḥammad al-Muḥammad during the construction of the main takya in Baghdad (1981).

41: Shaikh Muḥammad al-Muḥammad in the mosque of Karbchna (early 1980s).

Photo 2: Shaikh Muḥammad al-Muḥammad in a session of songs of praise in the takya in Amman, Jordan (24th/September/2015). This is the front cover photo of the 1st Arabic edition of this book.

Preface

This book narrates the blessed biography of a prominent figure of Islam and a leading light in the sphere of Sufism and knowledge of Allah. Sayyid Shaikh Muḥammad al-Muḥammad is the Master of Ṭarīqa ʿAliyya Qādiriyya Kasnazāniyya, one of the biggest Sufi Ṭarīqas, which has followers throughout the world. Ṭarīqa Kasnazāniyya, as the name is usually abbreviated, traces its roots to the source of all Sufi ways, the Messenger of Allah, Muḥammad (PBUH). Our Shaikh is a descendant of the Prophet (PBUH) from both parental sides.

We will start the book with an introduction to its sources and methodology, followed by a brief overview of its content. We will conclude the introduction with an explanation of how the material is presented.

A) Sources

I have compiled the material of this biography from a variety of sources. I have taken the thought and opinions of our Shaikh directly from him. I have confined my sources in this case to his general lectures that I was fortunate enough to attend or obtain video or audio recordings of; his speeches and conversations in private sessions that he was generous enough to give me the opportunity to attend; and his published writings. When quoting from his lectures, I have converted the wording from the Iraqi dialect to standard Arabic and edited them, while carefully preserving the original meaning without any change.

I have taken the details of our Shaikh's biography, as well as a history of the former Kasnazānī Shaikhs, from a number of his relatives and followers who have accompanied him in the various stages of his life, before and after becoming the Shaikh of Ṭarīqa, as well as from his lectures, conversations, and writings. Concerning his relatives, my main sources were Shaikh Sāmān Maʿrūf, who is married to one of our Shaikh's sisters and whose sister is married to our Shaikh; Shaikh ʿAlī Ḥussein, his nephew; Shaikh Ghāndī, his second eldest son; and Shaikh Ridhā Karīm, his maternal cousin and brother-in-law, being married to one of our

Shaikh's sisters.

I have also taken information from several dervishes who accompanied Shaikh Muḥammad al-Muḥammad closely and have known him since his childhood. They were dervishes from the time his father, Shaikh ʿAbd al-Karīm al-Kasnazān, was the Master of Ṭarīqa. I would like to specifically name caliph Yāsīn Ṣūfī ʿAbd Allah. I would also like to acknowledge the help of caliph ʿImād ʿAbd al-Ṣamad in facilitating the collection of some of the material used in the book.

In the course of compiling material for this book, I was honoured to meet dervishes from the time of the Master of Ṭarīqa before Shaikh ʿAbd al-Karīm, his brother Shaikh Ḥusayn al-Kasnazān. Old age and poor health did not stop them from providing me with the historical information they have, being so keen to help document the lives of our noble Shaikhs. One manifestation of their love for our Shaikhs and commitment to Ṭarīqa is that they did not ask me to visit them at their homes, to spare themselves the effort, which is what I had intended. Instead, they came to meet me in the main Kasnazānī takya in the city of Sulaymāniyya, in Iraqi Kurdistan, even though some of them could not move without help. I would like to particularly mention the eldest of them, Hajj Sharīf, who is over a hundred years old. He said that in the days preceding our meeting he could not even turn in his bed without help, yet his desire to recount the history of the Shaikhs gave him on the day the strength to come to the takya with the help of two of his relatives. I would also like to mention caliph Karīm Mūryās who, despite his weak body and need for others to help him walk, gave me plenty of his time to recount some of the wonders and history of the Shaikhs.

The plan for the book, the methodology of research, and the selection and checking of information required indexing the large amount of material that I compiled from various sources. My brother Faiz conducted this task, which took a huge amount of effort and time. To make referring to our Shaikh's audio lectures and quoting them easier, it was necessary to transcribe them. My brothers Faiz and Duraid did that. Indexing and transcription made writing this biography significantly easier and faster.

To ensure the accuracy of the information and to make the book as good it can be, a number of my valued sources have reviewed drafts of the whole book or parts of it. The book has also benefited from the immensely valuable corrections and comments of my wife, Dr Shetha Al-Dargazelli, on more than one draft. Finally, several dervishes, in particular staff of the takya in Amman and the takya in Sulaymāniyya, provided me with most of the photos in the book.

Many other caliphs and dervishes helped one way or another in getting this book completed. May Allah reward all those who took part in this project. I would like to express all gratitude and appreciation. Without them, this book would not have come out in its current form.

I have carefully examined the historical details that I did not get directly from our Shaikh. I was instructed by our Shaikh to be particularly careful when examining accounts of supernatural feats of the Shaikhs of Ṭarīqa, to identify those that never happened and any inaccuracies in those that did take place. He asked me to check with him or with Shaikh Sāmān if need be. Many events are tens of years old, and human memory often forgets some details over time or even changes them inadvertently. Additionally, the narrators of some events did not witness them, but they conveyed what they had heard. I compiled and scrutinised these narratives with care, something that I was helped with by the multiplicity of sources. I did not include narratives that I could not feel confident of their authenticity and accuracy. At times, I could not verify certain details of a particular event, so I documented the details that I determined to be accurate and ignored the rest.

B) Methodology

This book presents the biography of Shaikh Muḥammad al-Muḥammad al-Kasnazān in a unique way. It recounts it in the context of explaining the Sufi method to get close to Allah, and it expounds Sufism, which represents the spiritual side of Islam, in the course of narrating the biography of our honourable Shaikh. In other words, the book explains Sufism through presenting our Shaikh's biography and, at the same time, recounts this blessed biography via introducing Sufism. This follows the didactic Qur'anic method of recounting narratives that presents biographies not only as histories, but also as lessons and motivational sermons:

> We narrate to you [O Muḥammad!] the best of narratives, by revealing this Qur'an to you; before it, you were one of the unaware. (Yūsuf 3)

Narrate to them stories that may reflect. (Al-Āʿrāf 176)

There is a lesson in their stories for the people of understanding. (Yūsuf 111)

This distinct method of narrating a biography can be used only when all aspects of the life of that person embody his beliefs. Only then, recounting the biography becomes an explanation of those beliefs and explaining them can be used for biographical narration. This is the case with Sufi Shaikhs where the life of each personified Islam, following in the footsteps of their great Master (PBUH), whose life was an explanation of his beliefs and his beliefs were the laws that governed his life. This method cannot be used for studying, for example, the greats of science, irrespective of their achievements and excellence in their respective disciplines. For as important and useful to humanity as these sciences are, they do not cover all aspects of the life of the scientists. A physicist may dedicate a large part of his life to physics, spending long years studying, conducting research, and writing. Physics, nevertheless, remains a natural science that does not touch most aspects of his life. No matter how much this scientist contributes and dedicates of his life to physics, this science would not determine how they deal with his family and people in general, shape his moral values, or form his personality and character in terms of generosity or greed, mercy or cruelty, truthfulness or dishonesty...etc. Islam, on the other hand, is a belief system that touches all aspects of a person's life. It is the *science of life*, not a temporary or limited occupation. This is why this book can be as much a biography of Shaikh Muḥammad al-Muḥammad al-Kasnazān as an explanation of Sufism.

Nearness to Allah grants every Shaikh of Ṭarīqa great, special blessings that are manifested in countless paranormal wonders. These "karāmas", as they are known, are the ink with which a large part of the Shaikh's life is written. Karāmas play a major role in the Shaikh's life, surrounding him even before becoming a Shaikh. Some karāmas point to him even before his birth, confirming Allah's selection of him for that spiritual leadership. Accordingly, we see wonders permeating all stages of the life of Shaikh Muḥammad al-Muḥammad al-Kasnazān. It is only natural, then, that this biography is full of paranormal feats.

As there are countless karāmas and they continue to occur all the time, no book, regardless of its size, can compile more than a tiny number of them. We have only mentioned in this biography wonders that have explanatory functions in their respective contexts. The biography of our Shaikh cannot be sufficiently covered without referring to the history, legacy, and karāmas of the Shaikhs of Ṭarīqa Kasnazāniyya who preceded him. We have, however, quoted only a small part of this blessed history, as required by the subjects and objectives of the book.

C) Contents

We have classified the subjects and ordered the chapters in a way that makes it possible for the book to introduce the biography of our Master and Sufism at the same time, following events in their chronological order as much as possible. We have compiled in this biography information about the various stages of his life and his diverse activities. This should give the reader a reasonably complete picture of his life, with its many challenges, sufferings, and achievements; with events that brought happiness and others that filled the heart with sadness. This biography has not confined itself to the history of our Shaikh after becoming the Master of Ṭarīqa at the age of forty, but we have also followed the different stages of his earlier life. We have also covered events that predated his birth that are relevant to studying his life. One thing that this comprehensive biography shows is the fundamental changes that happened to the character, personality, behaviour, and interests of our Shaikh after assuming the Shaikhdom of Ṭarīqa. After a life occupied by worldly interests — although Ṭarīqa still played a role in it, as he was the son of its Master and one of its dervishes — becoming the Shaikh of Ṭarīqa made the Ṭarīqa his first concern and calling people to Allah his main activity.

This is a brief overview of the contents of the book.

Chapter one introduces the concept of "Ṭarīqa" in the thought of Shaikh Muḥammad al-Muḥammad al-Kasnazān. It refers to the Qur'an and the life of the Prophet (PBUH), showing that Ṭarīqa is the "spiritual side of Islam", as our Master describes it. **Chapter two** focuses on the Ṭarīqa of our Shaikh, Ṭarīqa ʿAliyya Qādiriyya Kasnazāniyya, introducing its main Shaikhs. Due to the major role that karāmas play in the lives of the Shaikhs of Ṭarīqa, we have dedicated **chapter three** to introducing these paranormal feats that Allah honours his close servants with.

After these chapters that explain major Sufi concepts, the book focuses on the life of our Shaikh. **Chapter four** is about his noble pedigree, which goes back to the Messenger of Allah, Muḥammad (PBUH) from both parental sides. It also introduces the history of the Barzinjī sayyids in the north of Iraq to which he belongs. After chapter two's brief introduction to our Master's father, Shaikh ʿAbd al-Karīm al-Kasnazān, whom we learn more about in later chapters, **chapter five** discusses the spiritual home environment in which our Shaikh was brought up. The chapter gives special attention to the character and personality of his mother, Ḥafṣa, and her role as the wife of the Master of Ṭarīqa.

Shaikh Muḥammad al-Muḥammad was fond of studying from his childhood, so much so that his life is a continuous journey of learning. This is the subject of **chapter six**, which discusses his schooling and self-education. The Shaikhs of Ṭarīqa Kasnazāniyya have a long history of resisting injustice and aggression and defending the rights of the weak and oppressed. Our Shaikh spent around six years, 1961-1966, defending the rights of the Kurdish minority in the north of Iraq. This is discussed in detail in **chapter seven. Chapter eight** introduces the wife of our Shaikh and his children.

The Masterhood of Ṭarīqa represents spiritual succession to the Prophet (PBUH), not mere excellence at Islam's textual and intellectual sciences, which is why it is determined by Allah. After expounding how becoming a Shaikh of Ṭarīqa is an act of divine election, not human acquisition, **chapter nine** presents the history of electing Shaikh Muḥammad al-Muḥammad as Master of Ṭarīqa, succeeding his father Shaikh ʿAbd al-Karīm al-Kasnazān. **Chapter ten** continues this subject by detailing how he assumed the Shaikhdom of Ṭarīqa after Shaikh ʿAbd al-Karīm. It also recounts some of the karāmas that show his spiritual inheritance of the Prophet (PBUH). Being the representative of the Prophet (PBUH), the Shaikh of Ṭarīqa emulates the character of the Prophet (PBUH) and acquires his beautiful attributes. **Chapter eleven** focuses on describing the Muḥammadan traits of Shaikh Muḥammad al-Muḥammad al-Kasnazān, including his leadership qualities.

Our Shaikh considers calling people to Allah the greatest form of worship because causing Allah to love people and people to love Allah is the greatest of good deeds. **Chapter twelve** sheds light on his monumental preaching achievements throughout the world. The concept of "takya", which is the place of worship, learning, and meeting of the dervishes of Ṭarīqa, is then discussed in **chapter thirteen.** It explains our Master's exceptional efforts in establishing takyas in various parts of the world. **Chapter fourteen** first explains the importance of "dhikr" (remembrance of Allah) in the Ṭarīqa, before focusing on the changes made by Shaikh Muḥammad al-Muḥammad to the various dhikrs of Ṭarīqa Kasnazāniyya.

Chapter fifteen explains "riyāḍa" (spiritual exercising) in the Ṭarīqa and our Master's practice of it. **Chapter sixteen** then describes "khalwa" (solitude), the khalwas that he practised, and some of the spiritual experiences that he had when he was in solitude. The Ṭarīqa suffered considerable oppression by the Iraqi regime in the 1990s, which ultimately forced our Shaikh to emigrate from Baghdad to Sulaymāniyya, which he also had to leave later. This is the subject of **chapter seventeen.**

Chapter eighteen covers the religious, cultural, and social achievements and contributions of our Shaikh that were not covered in the previous chapters, such as the renovation of holy places. **Chapter nineteen** covers our Master's various interests, such as reading and collecting Sufi books and manuscripts. The last chapter is followed by a short epilogue.

Appendix A is a table showing major events in the life of Shaikh Muḥammad al-Muḥammad al-Kasnazān, listed in chronological order. **Appendix B** is a glossary of translated and untranslated technical and other important terms used in the book.

D) Presentation

To make it easier for the reader to follow the sources of the book, we have used footnotes to identify the sources of information and for marginal notes. In the case of our Shaikh's sermon, we identified sermons we have quoted by their respective dates. In the case of quoting from books, we mentioned the author's name, the book's title, and the page number. We have added to this information the number of the ḥadīth when quoting from a compilation of Prophetic traditions. We have compiled at the back of the book all of our written sources, including the details of every reference that we mentioned in the footnotes.

We have used a special font for writing the Qur'anic verses. We have identified exact quotes by including them inside quotation marks. At times, context requires using short exact quotes inside the body text, but most of the time we have placed exact quotes on separate paragraphs, which are laid out differently. Inexact quotes, which are often narratives from people, have been differentiated by putting them in separate paragraphs but without surrounding them with quotation marks.

We have translated most Arabic technical terms into English equivalents. The remaining small number of terms have been used without translation, as we felt that translating them accurately and succinctly is not possible. For easy reference, translated and untranslated terms have been compiled in a glossary at the end of the book.

The name of our Shaikh was "Muḥammad", but the Prophet (PBUH) honoured him in 2016 by adding one of his noble titles to his name, as we shall see in §9.1, so he became known as "Muḥammad al-Muḥammad". For consistency and to avoid confusion, we have used the name "Muḥammad al-Muḥammad" even when narrating the life of our Shaikh before that Prophetic gift.

Many Arabic names are usually abbreviated in the Kurdish language in daily use and unofficial contexts. For instance, "Muḥammad" is called "Ḥama", "Aḥmad" is "Aḥa", "Maḥmūd" is "Khula", and so on. For clarification, we have used the Arabic spellings of the names of the Kurds that are mentioned in the book.

We have Romanised the names of lesser-known people and places as they are pronounced in their original language. Conversely, we have spelled the names of well-known people and places as they are usually written in English. For instance, we have used the established English spellings of "Mecca" and "Medina", even though they do not represent how they are pronounced in Arabic.

For significant old dates, we have mentioned the Hijrī year followed by the Gregorian, to make it easier to place the event in its historical context in both calendars. For instance, our Shaikh was born in 1357/1938, that is, in the Hijrī year 1357, which corresponds to the Gregorian year 1938. If the day and month of a Hijrī date are unknown, it is not possible to determine which of the two Gregorian years that correspond to that Hijrī year is the one we need. In this case, we choose the earlier year. For instance, Shaikh ʿAbd al-Karīm Shāh al-Kasnazān was born in 1240 H, but we could not determine the day or even the month of the birth. Given that 1/1/1240 H corresponds to 25/8/1824 CE, the birth of Shāh al-Kasnazān may be in 1824 CE, if it occurred in the first four months of 1240 H, or 1825 CE, if he was born in the last eight months of the Hijrī year. When sources mention the Hijrī year but not the month or day, which is a common situation, we converted the Hijrī date to the Gregorian year assuming that the date was the first day of the first month, i.e. 1/Muḥarram, to avoid having to mention two Gregorian years. This means that the actual Gregorian year for any Hijrī date whose month and day are unknown is either the year we mentioned or the one that follows. Accordingly, the birth year of Shāh al-Kasnazān is mentioned as 1240/1824.

We have included in the book around forty photos of our Shaikh. When choosing those from the limited number of photos available to us, we have tried to cover different stages of his life, as well as various places and activities. We added to each photo a brief caption and, when possible, identified the place and date. We have numbered the photos sequentially for easy reference. The photos are of different quality, reflecting the varying quality of the originals. Some of them are very old and, unfortunately, we could not obtain high-quality copies.

We have added two maps showing areas that are mentioned in the book. The first map shows the governorates of Iraq. The second is of the northeast of Iraq and northwest of Iran, where we have marked the areas that were the focus of events mentioned in the book.

Finally, I must stress at the end of this preface that whatever I have succeeded to correctly and accurately present in the book is due to the favour of Allah (mighty and sublime is He), the blessings of my Master Shaikh, Muḥammad al-Muḥammad al-Kasnazān (may Allah sanctify his innermost being), and the help of all those who have generously helped me. I, however, take responsibility for any mistakes and inaccuracies.

"*Allāhumma ṣallī ʿalā sayyidinā Muḥammadi `l-waṣfi wal-waḥyi war-risālati wal-ḥikmati waʿalā `ālihi wa-ṣaḥbihi wa-sallim taslīmā* (O Allah! Send prayer on our Master, whose quality, revelation, message, and wisdom are most praised (Muḥammad), and on his lineage and companions, and salute him with a perfect salutation)"

The Ṭarīqa is the way of the noble Qur'an and the method of the Prophet (PBUH), as well as the people of his household and his Companions. In essence, it is the "straight path" that Allah Almighty mentions in the opening chapter of the Qur'an: "Guide us to the straight path — the path of those upon whom You have bestowed favour, not of those who have evoked Your anger or of those who are astray" (al-Fātiḥa 6-7). In essence, it is the way of truth and guidance, the way of Allah, the path that grants blessings and victory, in this world and the next, to those who remain steadfast upon it: "And [Allah revealed] that if they had remained straight on the way, We would have given them abundant provision" (al-Jinn 16).

Shaikh Muḥammad al-Muḥammad al-Kasnazān
(Al-Ṭarīqa al-ʿAlīyya al-Qādiriyya Kasnazāniyya, p. 73)

1

Ṭarīqa: The Way to Allah

The linguistic meaning of the term *ṭarīqa* is a "method" or "path" that leads to something or somewhere. As for the conventional Qur'anic meaning of the word, it refers to "the way to Allah":

> "[Allah revealed] that if they had remained straight on the way, We would have given them abundant provision". (Al-Jinn 16)

Using the exegetical approach of "the Qur'an interprets itself",[1] the concept of Ṭarīqa becomes unequivocally clear when linking the act of remaining straight upon it to the command to remain straight in other verses:

> "So remain straight [on the right path] as you have been commanded, [you] and those who have turned back with you [to Allah], and do not transgress. Indeed, He is Seeing of what you do". (Hūd 112)
>
> "So call [O Muḥammad] to that [religion of Allah] and remain straight [on the right path] as you are commanded". (Al-Shūrā' 15)
>
> "Indeed, those who have said, 'Our Lord is Allah' and then remained straight [on the right path] - the angels will descend upon them, [saying], 'Do not fear and do not grieve but receive good tidings of Paradise, which you were promised'". (Fuṣṣilat 30)
>
> "Indeed, those who have said, 'Our Lord is Allah', and then remained straight [on the right path] - there will be no fear concerning them, nor will they grieve". (Al-Āḥqāf 13)

Therefore, the Ṭarīqa is the "straight path" that Allah (mighty and sublime is He) refers to in several places in His noble book, as in this verse:

---

[1] Imām ʿAlī Ibn Abī Ṭālib described the Qur'an as follows: "Its parts speak through each other and they bear witness to each other" (*Nahj al-Balāgha*, pp. 469-470). In his interpretation of the verse "Allah has sent down the best of speech — a consistent Book" (39.23) in his exegesis *Jāmiʿ al-Bayān fī Tafsīr `Āy al-Qur'an*, Ṭabarī attributes to the Successor Saʿīd bin Jubayr (95/714) saying the following about the Qur'an when commenting on "a consistent Book": "Its parts are consistent with each other, its parts confirm each other, and its parts attest to each other".

> "Say, 'Indeed, my Lord has guided me to a straight path - a correct religion - the way of Abraham, inclining toward truth. And he was not among those who associated others with Allah'". (Al-Ān'ām 161)

This is the path to Allah. Specifically, it is the way of the magnificent Qur'an; the traditional way of the Seal of Prophets, our master, Muḥammad (PBUH); the path travelled upon by the noble people of his household and his Companions after him, and whosoever raised the banner of Islam after them, such as the Sufi Shaikhs — each one of whose lives were consumed with guiding people to the path of Allah and planting the love of Allah and His noble Messenger (PBUH) in their hearts.

1.1 Iḥsān

The path to Allah is based on three pillars: Islam, Īmān, and Iḥsān. The Prophet (PBUH) has further explained these three pillars of religion, describing "Islam" as follows: "[It is] to worship Allah and to never associate any partners with Him in worship, to establish prayer, to pay the compulsory charity (zakāt), and to fast the month of Ramaḍān". Describing "Īmān", he said: "To believe in Allah, and His angels, and His meeting, and His messengers, and to believe in the Resurrection". He expounded the strongest of the pillars of religion, "Ihsān", by saying: "[It is] to worship Allah as if you see Him; and if you cannot see Him, then verily He sees you".[2] Shaikh Muḥammad al-Muḥammad al-Kasnazān has summarized these pillars, saying: "Islam is obedience and worship; Īmān is light and sound belief; Iḥsān is the station of interior vigilance and observation".[3] Therefore, Islam comprises devotional practices, and Īmān is the confirmation of the thought that is the basis of these acts of worship. They are the two pillars that are familiar to all Muslims. As for Iḥsān, it is a special spiritual state that a believing Muslim experiences whenever Allah blesses him with spiritual unveilings that enable him to observe realities from the spirit world, which are out of the reach of those do not reach this state. By way of these spiritual unveilings, the worshipper who

---

[2] Bukhārī, *Al-Jāmi' al-Ṣaḥīḥ*, I, no. 50, p. 65.

[3] Shaikh Muḥammad al-Muḥammad al-Kasnazān, *Al-Ṭarīqa al-'Aliyya al-Qādiriyya al-Kasnazāniyya*, p. 75.

has reached the level of Iḥsān becomes always conscious of Allah. He becomes in constant presence with Him. He lives the reality that He Almighty is present in every place, and that nothing is absent from Him on the earth or in the sky: "He is with you wherever you are" (al-Ḥadīd 4). One of the daily dhikrs of the Ṭarīqa Kasnazaniyya reflects on the state of Iḥsān: "Allah is present with me, Allah is watching me, Allah sees me; Allah is with me, Allah is my Helper and He encompasses all things".[4]

Let us use an example to clarify the distinction between someone who has only acquired Islam and Īmān, and someone who Allah has also blessed with the state of Iḥsān. We know from the noble Qur'an and the Prophet's biography that in the second year after he migrated to Medina, Allah permitted the Muslims to arm themselves and defend their inherent right to worship Him and to follow the religion He chose for them, against the disbelievers who fought with the Muslims in every way and wanted to destroy them and deprive them of their right: "Permission [to fight] has been given to those who are being fought because they were wronged. Indeed, Allah is competent to give them victory" (al-Ḥajj 39). The Islam and Īmān that the fighters possessed was one reason that Allah granted them victory. We also know that one of the main aspects of this divine help that settled various battles in their armed struggle against their oppressors was the support Allah gave them through the angels:

> "[Remember] when you said to the believers, 'Is it not sufficient for you that your Lord should reinforce you with three thousand angels sent down?' Yes, if you remain patient and pious to Allah and the enemy comes upon you [attacking] in rage, your Lord will reinforce you with five thousand angels having marks [of distinction]". (Āl 'Imrān 124-125)
>
> "[Remember] when you asked for the help of your Lord, and He answered you, 'Indeed, I will reinforce you with a thousand from the angels, following one another'". (Al-Ānfāl 9)
>
> "[Remember] when your Lord inspired to the angels, 'I am with you, so strengthen those who have believed. I will cast terror into the hearts of those who disbelieved, so strike [them] upon the necks and strike from them every fingertip'". (Al-Ānfāl 12)
>
> "O you who have believed, remember the favour of Allah upon you when armies came to [attack] you and We sent upon them a wind and armies [of

[4] We will study the dhikrs of Tarīqa Kasnazāniyya in detail in Chapter 14.

angels] you did not see. And ever is Allah, of what you do, Seeing". (Al-Āḥzāb 9)

While all the Muslims believed in the promise Allah made to them, that He would support them through the angels, there was also a group among them who witnessed this angelic intervention. In other words, **all** of them believed in this intervening support from the spirit world in their struggle against the oppression they suffered, but only **some** of them saw this support with their own eyes. So the difference between a believing Muslim and one whom Allah has blessed with the station of Iḥsān, in addition to his Islam and Īmān, is like the difference between one who believed in the victory Allah granted to the Muslims through the angels without seeing them, and one whose faith was further empowered by his witnessing of the angels as they intervened in the fighting. Such proximity to the spirit world enables the believing Muslim to worship Allah as if he sees Him, as stated by the Prophet (PBUH). The Sufi does not stop at Islam and Īmān: indeed, his goal is to reach the station of Iḥsān.

Travelling the path to Allah does not merely grant a man intellectual knowledge. It also reveals to him spiritual secrets and realities that can only be discovered through direct experience. This is why Sufism is likened to tasting: the person who does not taste something by practising it cannot know its sweet taste; and he who does not practice it will never understand its reality, nor will he come to know its secrets, even if he were to study it all his life. The difference between the "study" of Sufism and the "practice" of Sufism is like the difference between reading or hearing about karāmas and directly witnessing these supernatural occurrences. It is like the difference between reading or hearing about the spirit world and its secrets and directly receiving spiritual openings. If we go back to our Qur'anic example above, it is like the difference between reading or hearing about the intervention of the angels in the fight against the disbelievers and seeing this intervention.

Even to one whom Allah has decreed that he will be a Shaikh of the Ṭarīqa in the future, and one to whom, and to others, hidden, yet clear, signals of this future decree have been revealed, the doors of the spirit world will not open to him until he begins to travel the Sufi path. In this regard, our Shaikh says that he read many books of Sufism during the time of his father, Shaikh ʿAbd al-Karīm, but those books did not give him anything besides knowledge from the outskirts of the world of

Sufism. However, after the passing of Shaikh ʿAbd al-Karīm, and after he assumed his place as the master of the Ṭarīqa and travelled on its path, the doors of the spirit world opened to him and its secrets began to be revealed to him.[5]

Since accessing these secrets is impossible except by way of travelling the Sufi path, some of its secrets cannot be divulged to anyone other than its people. A day may come where the traveller hears something, or sees something, from these secrets, and so he tells his Shaikh. His Shaikh may comment on it or add something to it. However, the Shaikh will never relate that secret to that dervish if he had not yet reached it by way of his spiritual travelling. Addressing the dervish in this matter, our Shaikh says: "I do not speak about the way to Allah to you for you to simply collect information. Rather, it is for you to put that knowledge into practice," i.e. it is for the disciple to travel upon the straight path. This journey cannot take place without accompanying a teacher to whom Allah has granted spiritual sciences, attributes, and gifts that enable him to assist those who wish to reach Him.

1.2 Ṣuḥba (Companionship)

The company one keeps has a tremendous and immediate effect upon a person, causing him to draw near to Allah or making him grow distant from Him. From what He (exalted and high is He) has said regarding ṣuḥba:

> "And the Day the wrongdoer will bite on his hands [in regret] he will say, 'I wish I had taken a way with the Messenger. Oh, woe to me! I wish I had not taken so-and-so as a friend. He led me away from the remembrance after it had come to me. And ever is Satan, to man, a deserter'". (Al-Furqān 27-29)
>
> "Close friends, that Day, will be enemies to each other, except for the righteous". (Al-Zukhruf 67)

From the words of the Messenger (PBUH) regarding the effects of fellowship upon a man: "A man keeps the religion of his friend. So let each one of you be cautious of who he befriends".[6] Several of the noble Prophetic ḥadīths have stressed the importance of keeping the company

---

[5] Shaikh Muḥammad al-Muḥammad al-Kasnazān, *sermon*, 22nd/June/2000.

[6] Tirmidhī, *Al-Jāmiʿ al-Kabīr*, IV, no. 2378, p. 187.

of the righteous in the journey to Allah. Among them is one in which he (PBUH) was once asked, "Who is our best companion"? He replied, "One whose sight reminds you of Allah, whose speech increases your knowledge, and whose deeds remind you of the hereafter".[7] Keeping the company of the righteous assists one in discovering one's faults and in rectifying them. To this effect, the Prophet (PBUH) has said, "The believer is a mirror to his believing brother".[8] This description applies to all believers. This is another of his ḥadīths regarding fellowship:

> "The example of a good companion and a bad one is that of the bearer of musk and of the one who blows the bellows. The bearer of musk either offers you some, or you buy it from him, or you find a pleasant fragrance emanating from him. And as for the one who blows the bellows, he either burns your clothes or you find a repugnant smell emanating from him".[9]

The sayings of the Prophet (PBUH) elucidate the importance of carefully choosing who a man associates himself with. This is because a person cannot help but be affected by the manners, behaviour, and temperament of the one he accompanies. This effect, which can be apparent and tangible or subtle and spiritual, causes a man to inherit some of the characteristics of his companion. These descriptions apply to any companionship in general. One of the clearest indications of the importance of fellowship, and that it has always been an essential means of getting closer to Allah, is found in the story of the prophet Moses when he accompanied Khaḍir, peace be upon them both. **Firstly**, Moses was accompanied by a youth who received knowledge from him and learned how to purify himself: "[Mention] when Moses said to his servant, 'I will not cease [travelling] until I reach the junction of the two seas or continue for a long period'" (al-Kahf 60). **Secondly**, the main lesson of the story is the fact that, directed by Allah, a prophet who speaks with God and is the bearer of the Torah went out in search of a particular man to follow and learn from. Despite the high status of this prophet and his proximity to Allah, there was someone whose fellowship he could benefit from. **Thirdly**, the sought-after companion must possess the qualifications

---

[7] 'Abd Ibn Ḥamīd, *Al-Muntakhab min Musnad 'Abd Ibn Ḥamīd*, I, no. 631, p. 482.

[8] Abū Dāwūd, *Sunan Abī Dāwūd*, VII, no. 4918, p. 279.

[9] Bukhārī, *Al-Jāmiʿ al-Ṣaḥīḥ*, III, no. 5332, p. 296; Muslim, *Ṣaḥīḥ Muslim*, IV, no. 2628, p. 2026.

required for this companionship, such as the description Allah gives of the qualities of Khaḍir: "A servant from among Our servants to whom We had given mercy from Us and had taught him from Us certain knowledge" (al-Kahf 65). Allah characterizes the man whom He sent Moses in search of by three attributes, the first of which being a servant who had fulfilled the conditions of servanthood [to Allah]. All of Allah's creatures are His servants against their will, hence His description of this man by his servanthood is an indication that he was a voluntary servant of Allah, not merely an unwilling one. The second special attribute is the fact that Allah granted him mercy, meaning a particular blessing he conferred upon this perfect servant. The third is the fact that Allah educated him with a form of special, godly knowledge. He described this knowledge using the place adverbial "ladun" rather than the similar word "'ind", both of which mean "from", in reference to Himself being the source of this knowledge. "Ladun" indicates more immense intimacy and special privilege than "'ind".[10] This knowledge, taken directly from Allah, is the reason why Moses sought Khaḍir's ṣuḥba: "May I follow you on [the condition] that you teach me from what you have been taught of guiding knowledge"? (al-Kahf 66). **Fourthly**, when Moses found the teacher he was in search of, he asked him to allow him to follow him. But through the knowledge Allah had directly conferred upon him, Khaḍir knew that Moses would not be able to uphold the conditions of the fellowship: "Indeed, with me, you will never be able to have patience" (al-Kahf 67). This was because Moses was not accustomed to accompanying one who surpassed him in knowledge, and so, Khaḍir's actions were immune to being understood or interpreted properly by Moses: "How can you have the patience for what you do not encompass in knowledge"? (al-Kahf 68). **Fifthly**, one of the conditions of fellowship is complete obedience because the one who is being accompanied knows the state of the one who is accompanying him better than him. This is why Moses vowed to submit his affairs to Khaḍir: "You will find me, if Allah wills, patient, and I will not disobey you in [any] order" (al-Kahf 69). Khaḍir's reply also affirms the importance of obedience: "Then if you follow me, do not ask me about anything until I make mention to you about it" (al-Kahf 80).

Travelling on the path to Allah is impossible without a guide who is

---

[10] Fatoohi, *Mafhūm 'Ladun' fīl-Qur'ān al-'Aẓīm*.

deeply familiar with it. This is why Allah (mighty and sublime is He) sent the prophets, peace be upon them all, and supported them with various kinds of knowledge and a light so that they would serve as guides, leading people to Him. Indeed, there was never a day when someone was able to journey upon the path to Allah without a companion illuminating the path for him and leading him on it. Even the Companions needed the fellowship of the greatest teacher (PBUH) in addition to the Qur'an. One indication that their companionship to the Prophet (PBUH) is among the greatest blessings conferred upon them by Allah is that they were distinguished with the title of "the Companions", meaning the companions of the Prophet (PBUH). Similarly, everyone who comes after them needs fellowship. To this effect, he (PBUH) said:

> "Indeed, I am leaving among you that which, if you hold fast to, you shall not go astray after me. One of them is greater than the other: Allah's Book, which is a rope extending from the sky to the earth, and my family, the people of my household. They shall not split until they meet me at the basin, so look after how you deal with them after me".[11]

Even the noble Qur'an does not obviate the need to accompany a guide for the one travelling upon the path to Allah. Although all matters of religion are outlined in detail in Allah's book, one needs a guide to help him practically, correctly, and accurately implement what the Qur'an commands and avoid what it forbids. In essence, he needs someone to help him transform the theoretical into practical application. The following well-known saying eloquently encapsulates the importance of a guide: "By Allah, no one who ever succeeded did so except by accompanying one who had succeeded".[12] The necessity of fellowship is another proof that iterations of the above Prophetic narration in which the people of the Prophet's (PBUH) household is replaced by his *Sunna* are fabrications because they ignore the need for

---

[11] Tirmidhī, *Al-Jāmiʿ al-Kabīr*, VI, no. 3788, p. 125. This ḥadīth is known as the ḥadīth of "ʿitra" or "thaqalayn", because one or both of these words occur in some of its forms. "ʿItra" means "descendants", "realives," and "clan", but in this ḥadīth it expressly refers to the descendants of the Prophet (PBUH). The word "thaqalayn" is the dual form of "thaqal", which means "something immensely valuable and important". It refers in this ḥadīth to "the Qur'an" and the "descendants of the Prophet (PBUH)".

[12] Ibn ʿAjība, *Īqāẓ al-Himam fī-Sharḥ al-Ḥikam*, p. 23.

fellowship.[13] The established practice of the Prophet both by word and by deed, or the "Sunna", is the explanation of the Qur'an, as our Shaikh says, not something added to it. So the reality of the distortion of this narration is not that it "adds" the concept of Sunna to it, but rather that it "omits" from it the role of fellowship and the fact that those whose fellowship Allah has obligated are the people of the household of prophethood.

Naturally, then, we find that the Shaikh of the Ṭarīqa also did not reach this spiritual rank except by his following a mentoring teacher. Therefore, when we read the history of any one of the Shaikhs of the Ṭarīqa, we find that he must have once accompanied a Shaikh to fulfil his need to be a student of a spiritual teacher. So, every teacher was once a student. Seekers who have reached Allah, Shaikhs of the Ṭarīqa included, achieved that by fellowship in the way of Allah, which began with the ṣuḥba of the Prophet (PBUH).[14]

We see in Moses' search for Khaḍir that he was prepared for the journey, however long or far, in search of the one whose fellowship would raise his current state, where he says to his young servant: "I will not cease [travelling] until I reach the junction of the two seas or continue for a long period" (al-Kahf 60). The sign of the end of the search, which Allah made known to Moses, was reaching the junction of the two seas. In his words, you see the determination not to stop before reaching that place, even if he were to remain a traveller for a long time. Similarly, the history of Sufism is rich with biographies of Shaikhs who travelled tremendous distances, in times when travelling was very difficult, in search of teachers they wished to accompany, and from whom they wished to learn, under their tutelage, the etiquette of the way to Allah. Shaikh ʿAbd al-Qādir al-Gaylānī, for example, migrated while still a young man from Iran to Iraq in search of a teacher.

The necessity of fellowship is not limited to knowledge of the spiritual path, rather it also includes sciences and disciplines of religion that necessitate transmission. For example, one cannot advance in the study

---

[13] Bayhaqī, *Al-Sunan al-Kubrā*, X, no. 20336, pp. 194-195. Bayhaqī also mentions immediately before this corrupted form of the ḥadīth its authentic wording (no. 20335), which has the historical expression "the people of my household" instead of "His Prophet's Sunna".

[14] Shaikh Muḥammad al-Muḥammad al-Kasnazān, *sermon*, last third of October/2013.

of the recitation of the Qur'an, Ḥadīth, and other religious sciences that are acquired by transmission without studying at the hands of those who excel in these disciplines. The tradition of travelling in search of teachers that will tutor a man in whichever discipline he desires is a well-established tradition among seekers of sciences that are gained by transmission throughout the ages. Indeed, even a seeker of intellectual sciences, religious sciences aside, needs to go to the experts in those sciences to learn from them.

The Prophet (PBUH) said, "Seek aid in every craft through its righteous people". Shaikh 'Abd al-Qādir al-Gaylānī connected this narration to the necessity of following a Shaikh who is well acquainted with Allah when seeking to reach Him Almighty:[15]

> "Worship is a craft, and its experts are those who are sincere in their deeds; those who are knowledgeable of the Law and have put it into practice; those who have bidden farewell to all creatures, having come to know them; those who have run away from their selves, their possessions, their children, and everything other than their Lord (mighty and sublime is He) on the feet of their hearts and their innermost beings. Physically, they dwell in populated places, in the midst of creatures; but their hearts are in the wilderness and deserts. They remain constant in this until their hearts grow and their wings strengthen, so they fly to the sky. Their spiritual determination increased, so their hearts flew and reached the True One (mighty and sublime is He). Thus, they became among those about whom Allah has said: "Indeed they are, to Us, among the righteous elect" (Ṣād 47)".[16]

The same way the seeker in search of Allah ought to accompany his spiritual teacher, it is incumbent upon the teacher to direct the disciple without the influence of any whims or flattery: "Know that among you is the Messenger of Allah. If he were to obey you in much of the matter, you would be in difficulty" (al-Ḥujurāt 7). Similarly, the Shaikh of the Ṭarīqa ought to direct the disciple upon the method of the Prophet Muḥammad (PBUH) without negligence. Just as the Prophet (PBUH) subjected himself and all aspects of his life to Islam, the Shaikh of the Ṭarīqa

---

[15] All quotes from the book *Jilā' al-Khāṭir* have been taken from the first edition of this manuscript, which was done by Shaikh Muḥammad al-Muḥammad al-Kasnazān. We also made use in some places of a later edition of the manuscript by two other researchers. Both editions are listed with the other references at the end of the book.

[16] Shaikh 'Abd al-Qādir al-Gaylānī, *Jilā' al-Khāṭir*, p. 16.

dedicates his life to teaching and serving the dervishes. This is why our Shaikh often talks about the importance of the dervish:

> "The dearest thing to the Shaikhs of the Ṭarīqa is all of you: the dervishes. Dervishes are more cherished than a son, are more beloved than a brother, are dearer than a father, are more beloved than anything because the Shaikh of the Ṭarīqa has dedicated his life to your service. The moment he sees you, he is like a gardener when he enters his garden in the morning and sees blossoming roses, and he smells their perfumed fragrance. He sees those beautiful roses in his garden and he is overwhelmed with joy. So when he sees you all, the Shaikh is happy like this, for he sees the fruits of his Ṭarīqa. He sees the roses — that blessed face, the face of Ṭarīqa. He sees his children, he sees his brothers, he sees part of his heart. He sees a cell from the cells of Shāh al-Kasnazān,[17] and he takes pride in you all. People possess money, but we possess the spirit. Your souls are a part of the spirit of Islam. All of us are spiritually linked to the Greatest Spirit. So, the dearest thing to the Shaikh is the dervish and the caliph.[18] You are all the most beloved thing to the Shaikh. The Shaikh does not possess anything that is more beloved to him than you all. No, by Allah. I have dedicated all my life in service to you all".[19]

This is how all Shaikhs describe their relationship with their disciples. This is, for example, what the master of our Shaikh taught him about the significance of the dervishes:

> "When I was a child, during the time of Shaikh ʿAbd al-Karīm, he would always inform me, and say to me, 'Be careful. Do not approach the dervishes; do not harm the dervishes; do not harm the caliphs, for they are beloved. The Shaikhs are not pleased when they are harmed. Be careful'. He would always caution me and say, 'The caliphs and the dervishes are beloved to the Shaikhs of the Ṭarīqa, more beloved than you, because they are my caliphs, they are dervishes. Do not approach them, do not harm them'. He would always teach us about the upbringing of a dervish, on the education and manners of the dervishes. He would say, 'The dervishes are beloved'. Even when madmen were brought into the takya, he would prevent us from approaching them,

---

[17] This is Shaikh ʿAbd al-Karīm Shāh al-Kasnazān, one of the most prominent Shaikhs of the Ṭarīqa. We will read about him in detail later.

[18] A "caliph" in Tarīqa Kasnazāniyya is a dervish whom the Shaikh has licensed to give people the pledge of the Tarīqa on behalf of the Shaikh. Being a caliph is not a spiritual status but an administrative one. Shaikh Muḥammad al-Muḥammad al-Kasnazān has a large number of caliphs in all parts of the world.

[19] Shaikh Muḥammad al-Muḥammad al-Kasnazān, *sermon*, 27th/September/2012.

and he would say: 'The dervish is dangerous, even when he is mad, he is dangerous. Do not draw near to him. Distance yourself from him. Do not harm him'. So the dervish is beloved, the dervish is a light, a mercy, a blessing for the Ṭarīqa. The dervish is a fruit of the Ṭarīqa. The dervish is an orchard of the Ṭarīqa".[20]

Shaikh ʿAbd al-Karīm used to instruct those who were nurturing our present Shaikh in his youth to prevent him from approaching the dervishes, for fear that he would unintentionally harm them, or affect their hearts that were permanently engaged in the dhikr of Allah and linked to their Shaikh's heart. The danger that Shaikh ʿAbd al-Karīm referred to is that the dervish that travels on the way derives spiritual energy from the energy of his teacher, so hurting him, even if unintentionally, could cause harm to the person who hurt him.

1.3 Purification Ṣuḥba

The path to Allah is not a physical one. It is, rather, a spiritual system. The role of the guide on this spiritual path is both inner and subtle, not only external and visible like the role of a guide to a physical roadmap. Allah has revealed this in His description of the role the Prophet (PBUH) plays in the guidance of the Muslims:

> "Just as We have sent among you a messenger from yourselves reciting to you Our verses and purifying you and teaching you the Book and wisdom and teaching you that which you did not know". (Al-Baqara 151)

In addition to Muḥammad (PBUH) teaching the Muslims from the various kinds of knowledge that Allah revealed to him, the verse also mentions another extremely important role of the Prophet (PBUH): the "purification" of the Muslims. Purification, or "tazkiya", is an internal, spiritual effect that differs from an external intellectual education. The traveller upon the path to Allah needs a guide who is well acquainted with the Qur'an and the Sunna of the Prophet (PBUH), which interprets the Qur'an, who directs him by what is morally correct and forbids him that which is wrong. The disciple also needs that guide to have the blessed ability to spiritually purify him, to help him in his internal struggle to cleanse his soul. This is the secret of the necessity of fellowship in Islam.

---

[20] Shaikh Muḥammad al-Muḥammad al-Kasnazān, *sermon*, 16th/December/2013.

Shaikh Muḥammad al-Muḥammad al-Kasnazān says in this regard:

"The practical way in which the soul is purified and acquires the best manners is through the fellowship of the Muḥammadan Inheritor and genuine guide. He is one who, by accompanying him, your faith, piety, and good manners increase. By being close to him and attending his gatherings, all your heart's diseases are cured and you get rid of the faults of your self. Your personality is affected by his, which resembles the perfect personality — the personality of the Messenger of Allah (PBUH)".

It is clear, thus, the mistake of one who thinks that he can cure his heart's diseases and free himself of the illnesses of his self by merely reciting the noble Qur'an and reading the ḥadīths of the Prophet (PBUH). The Book and the Sunna have gathered different kinds of remedies related to the illnesses of the heart and the self, so there must be a physician who accompanies these two to prescribe the correct medication for each sickness and describe the cure for each illness. The Messenger of Allah, Muḥammad (PBUH), used to treat the hearts of the Companions and purify their souls through his spiritual state and his words.

Then, our Shaikh cites what happened to the great Companion Ubay Ibn Ka'b:

"I was in the mosque when a man entered and prayed and recited [the Qur'an] in a style to which I objected. Then another man entered [the mosque] and recited in a style different from that of the first. When we had finished the prayer, we all went to the Messenger of Allah (PBUH) and I said: 'This man recited in a style to which I objected, and the other entered and recited in a style different from that of the first. The Messenger of Allah (PBUH) ordered them to recite and so they did, and the Messenger of Allah (PBUH) expressed approval of what they did. Internally, I fell into a sort of denial that did not occur to me even during the Days of Ignorance. When the Messenger of Allah (PBUH) saw how I was affected, he struck my chest, whereupon I broke into a sweat as though I were looking at Allah with deep fear".[21]

The Messenger's (PBUH) approval of the two different modes of recitation roused doubts in Ubay's heart to the point of rejecting him. The Messenger (PBUH) perceived what had occurred to him, so he struck him lightly upon his chest, whereby cleansing his heart from what had befallen it:

---

[21] Muslim, *Ṣaḥīḥ Muslim*, I, no. 820, p. 561.

"For this reason, the Companions of the Messenger of Allah (PBUH) could not treat [the illnesses] of their souls by merely reciting the noble Qur'an. Rather, they needed the Messenger of Allah's clinic (PBUH) because he was the one who could purify them, the supervisor over their upbringing, as Allah Almighty described him: 'It is He who has sent among the unlettered a Messenger from themselves reciting to them His verses and purifying them and teaching them the Book and wisdom — although they were before in clear error' (Al-Jumu'a 2). So purification is one thing, and teaching the Book is another. The meaning behind the Almighty's words "purifying them" is to grant them the state of purification. Therefore, there is a vast difference between the knowledge of purification and the state of purification, similar to the difference between the knowledge of fellowship and the state of fellowship. The combination of the two is perfection".[22]

The noble verse elucidates the fact that the ability to purify the self, as is the case with teaching Muslims the Qur'an, the Book, and wisdom, is not something that the Messenger (PBUH) acquired or bestowed on himself. Rather, it is a state and gift from Allah. People can study and teach the Qur'an and its sciences because they are sciences that are acquired by transmission, intellect, and talent. The ability to purify the self, however, is a purely spiritual matter that can be obtained only by keeping the company of one whom Allah has blessed with a special blessing. It is a blessing that is conferred on the companion from the accompanied person, increasing the latter's attachment to Allah and his love for Him. It makes him love drawing close to Allah and resent distancing himself from Him. It facilitates following Allah's orders and eschewing that which Allah has prohibited. The guiding Shaikh is the one who combines the knowledge of purification and the state of purification, addressing the disciple's intellect with this knowledge and treating his heart and soul with this state.

The noble Qur'an offers a subtle explication about the Prophet's (PBUH) role in reciting the Book to the people, in purifying them, and in teaching them the Book and wisdom. The noble Qur'an informs us of the supplication of the Prophet Abraham that was realised in Muḥammad (PBUH): "Our Lord, send among them a messenger from themselves who will recite to them Your verses and teach them the Book and wisdom and purify

---

[22] Shaikh Muḥammad al-Muḥammad al-Kasnazān, *Al-Ānwār al-Raḥmāniyya fil-Ṭarīqa al-ʿAliyya al-Qādiriyya al-Kasnazāniyya*, pp. 24-25.

them. Indeed, You are the Exalted in Might, the Wise" (al-Baqara 129). However, when Allah directly speaks in another three verses about this function of the Prophet (PBUH) in guiding mankind (al-Baqara 151, `Āl 'Imrān 164, al-Jumu'a 2), He mentions the act of purifying *before* the teaching of the Book and wisdom, as in this verse, for example: "It is He who has sent among the unlettered a Messenger from themselves reciting to them His verses and purifying them and teaching them the Book and wisdom – although they were before in clear error" (al-Jumu'a 2). We see here the emphasis that the Divine puts on the importance of the Muḥammadan purification in the spiritual nurturing of a Muslim. Spiritual purification, which does not occur except by way of fellowship, is among the most important functions of the Prophet (PBUH) and all those who spiritually succeed him.

The source of the spiritual blessings found in the fellowship of the Prophet (PBUH) is the light that Allah placed in him: "O People of the Book, there has come to you Our Messenger making clear to you much of what you used to conceal of the Book and forgiving much. There has come to you from Allah a light and a clear Book" (al-Mā`ida 15). This noble verse comprises two sections, each of which begins with the phrase "there has come to you", indicating the Prophet (PBUH) and the noble Qur'an. The first section mentions Muḥammad (PBUH) *explicitly*, in "Our Messenger," and the Qur'an *implicitly* because it revealed much from the previous revelatory scriptures, which were hidden by the people of the Book, as stated by His words "making clear to you much of what you used to conceal of the Book". Then the second section reiterates Allah's sending of the Prophet (PBUH) and the noble Qur'an, this time *implicitly* referring to the Messenger (PBUH) by the phrase "from Allah a light" and *explicitly* indicating the noble Qur'an by the phrase "a clear Book".

This light is the secret of the state of soul purification that Allah has granted His noble Messenger (PBUH). By inheriting this light, the Shaikhs of the Ṭarīqa inherit the state of soul purification that the dervishes who accompany them benefit from. Shaikh Muḥammad al-Muḥammad al-Kasnazān explains that the person who accompanies the Shaikh benefits from this light by four means: being near to the Shaikh; visiting the Shaikh; acquiring blessed things from the Shaikh; and entering into a state of internal observation with the Shaikh from afar, or, in other words, keeping the Shaikh in his heart. Accompanying the

Shaikh increases the light inside the disciple's heart, so he grows near to Allah. He begins to receive spiritual openings, experiences karāmas, and reaches to the rank of "wilāya", i.e. becomes a "walī": "Unquestionably, for the walīs of Allah, there will come no fear upon them, nor will they grieve" (Yūnus 62).[23] Thus, he attains what Shaikh ʿAbd al-Qādir al-Gaylānī refers to in this eloquent description: "What no eye has ever seen; what no ear has ever heard; what no heart of any man has ever before perceived",[24] with which the Messenger (PBUH) described what Allah (mighty and sublime is He) has promised for his righteous servants.[25] A "walī" is someone near to Allah on whom He has conferred spiritual blessings that at times manifest themselves in the form of supernatural feats. We will discuss the concept of "wilāya" in Chapter 3.

The following verse contains one subtle reference in the noble Qur'an that explains and confirms the importance of spiritual ṣuḥba: "When you are among them and lead them in prayer, let a group of them stand [in prayer] with you and let them carry their arms. When they have prostrated, let them be [in position] behind you and have the other group come forward that has not [yet] prayed and let them pray with you, taking precaution and carrying their arms" (al-Nisāʾ 102). Allah (exalted and high is He) commanded every group of the Muslims to pray with the Prophet (PBUH) because praying with him is not the same as praying with anyone else. If this were not the case, Allah would not have ordered them to pray in turn with the Prophet, which means that he prayed as many times as the number of groups he had to lead in the prayer, but a group of them would pray with him when he prayed while the rest of the groups would pray without him. This verse also explains the rewards of congregational prayers in general: by praying as a group, those who are spiritually weak benefit from those who are spiritually strong.

As Shaikh Muḥammad al-Muḥammad al-Kasnazān explains, spiritual fellowship, which begins with the spiritual touch of the initiation into the Ṭarīqa, is the basis by which one's faith ascends from being "traditional" to "authentic". Traditional faith is the kind of faith that one possesses without direct, experiential proof of its unseen foundations. Often, the person inherits this type of faith from his family and the culture

---

[23] Shaikh Muḥammad al-Muḥammad al-Kasnazān, *sermon*, 30th/June/2000.

[24] Shaikh ʿAbd al-Qādir al-Gaylānī, *Jilāʾ al-Khāṭir*, p. 27.

[25] Bukhārī, *Al-Jāmiʿ al-Ṣaḥīḥ*, II, no. 3136, p. 249.

in which he grows up. Some individuals also have intellectual arguments in its favour. As for authentic faith, one acquires it after witnessing, through direct experience, the unseen realities that his faith is based upon. In other words, our Shaikh's concept of "authentic faith" refers to the status of Iḥsān that the Messenger (PBUH) mentioned, which we discussed previously. One does not reach this status except by studying at the hand of a spiritual guide whose companionship leads him to supernatural, spiritual experiences that prove to him the truth of what he believes in. The true spiritual guide is near to and supported by Allah. Proximity to and support from Allah means that that person has the wisdom that answers and convinces the intellect, and he also possesses paranormal abilities that demonstrate to the intellect its limits and provide proofs of the unseen world that it has no way of reaching. What enabled the Companions to possess the kind of faith that they had was their companionship with the Messenger (PBUH), which enabled them to witness various miracles from him, day and night, including miracles that happened to them. Their faith was the faith of witnessing and observation, not merely based on blindly believing in what they had been informed of.

In the same vein, our teacher interprets the word "certainty (yaqīn)" in the verse: "Worship your Lord until there comes to you the certainty" (al-Ḥijr 99). Certainty is firm faith that is strengthened by directly experiencing karāmas and personal spiritual experiences, leaving no room for doubt in the heart or intellect of a believing Muslim.[26] In essence, "certainty" is "perfect belief in Allah".[27] He explains that "certainty" in this verse, as is the case with many Qur'anic words and verses, has more than one meaning. It also means "death", in which case the divine order means the obligation to the worship of Allah until death, meaning ceaselessly.[28]

Fellowship, then, is the gate to the status of Iḥsān.

---

[26] Shaikh Muḥammad al-Muḥammad al-Kasnazān, *sermon*, 28th/September/2012; 30th/October/2012.

[27] Shaikh Muḥammad al-Muḥammad al-Kasnazān, *sermon*, 4th/October/2013.

[28] Shaikh Muḥammad al-Muḥammad al-Kasnazān, *sermon*, 1st/April/2013; 18th/October/2013.

1.4 Knowledge of the Self

One major requirement for the purification of the self, which one attains through keeping good company, is knowledge of the self. Knowing one's self is a great blessing, hence the saying: "Allah has mercy on the person who knows the status of his self."[29] Self-knowingness is a basic requirement for knowledge of Allah, as in His words (PBUH): "Whoever knows himself has known his Lord".[30] Our Shaikh defines the meaning of "dervish" or "seeker" as "one who knows himself". As he knows himself, he becomes a "Lord-knowing".[31] This is why the title of "Allah-knowing" (*'ārif bi-llah*) that is bestowed upon the Shaikhs of the Ṭarīqa means "one who knows himself true knowledge", meaning "the perfected dervish". Self-knowingness means one knows the motives behind his actions and the reality of what he intends, his weak points that he must address, as well as the aspects of his power that he can use to benefit himself and others. One attribute of the person who knows himself is that he knows what knowledge he possesses what he does not. You may have seen people race to give a misguided opinion about something that seems easy to decide, while a knowledgeable person allows the matter to play itself out. As someone who knows himself, he realises that he does not have the knowledge related to that issue, so he does not join the people their involvement in matters that they are not knowledgeable of.

A self-knowing person knows the origins of his various conditions. He knows whether the source of a thought or feeling is a desire of the self or a spiritual state from his Shaikh, so he knows what course of action he must take and what he must avoid. This knowledge of the self and its

---

[29] Some think that this beautiful saying is a ḥadīth, i.e. a Prophetic saying, but we have not found a source that attributes it to the Prophet (PBUH).

[30] This ḥadīth has been quoted by many Sufis, including Shaikh Muḥyī al-Dīn Ibn 'Arabī, who wrote a book on this ḥadīth titled *al-Risāla al-Wujūdiyya fī-Ma'nā Qawlihi (PBUH) Man 'Arafa Nafsahu faqad 'Arafa Rabbāhu*; Shaikh Ibn 'Aṭā' Allah al-Sakandarī, who mentioned it in *Laṭā'if al-Minan*; Shaikh 'Abd al-Wahāb al-Sha'rānī, who mentioned it in *al-Ṭabaqāt al-Kubrā*; and others. However, even those who doubt or reject the attribution of this saying to the Prophet (PBUH) do not deny the fact that it is wise, as seen in the opinion that Suyūṭī has compiled in *Al-Qawl al-Ashbah fī-Ḥadīth Man 'Arafa Nafsahu faqad 'Arafa Rabbah.*

[31] Shaikh Muḥammad al-Muḥammad al-Kasnazān, *sermon*, 14th/November/2008.

innermost secrets enables the person to correct his faults that lead him to disobey and distance himself from his Lord. It helps him further develop his good attributes and acquire others, bringing him closer to good deeds and, consequently, his Lord. This is why knowing the Lord requires self-knowingness. Knowing the self is necessary for the struggle against the vagaries of the self, which the Prophet (PBUH) called "The greatest struggle".[32]

Iblīs' ignorance of himself overthrew from his position among the angels, becoming the accursed Satan. When Allah ordered the angels to prostrate to Adam, all of them did, except Iblīs, who refused to obey Allah's command and argued with his Lord: "I am better than him. You created me from fire and created him from clay" (al-Āʿrāf 12). Iblīs thought that the source of his refusal of Allah's order was "his knowledge" that was made of fire and, consequently, had a higher status than Adam, who was created from clay. Yet the origin of Iblīs' denial was not this alleged knowledge, as he thought. It was rather his ignorance of the pride within himself. Allah revealed the true cause behind his disobedience when He expelled him from his place and status: "Descend from Paradise, for it is not for you to be arrogant therein. So get out; indeed, you are of the debased" (al-Āʿrāf 13). The fact that it was arrogance that led Iblīs' to refuse to prostrate to Adam manifested itself even more evidently than in his first action, when he reacted to Allah's exposition of the cause of his disobedience. Instead of seeking mercy and forgiveness and joining those who prostrated to Adam, he insisted on his disobedience, until his spiritually fatal arrogance pushed him to threaten to deceive the new creation: "Because You have seduced me into error, I will surely sit in wait for them on Your straight path. Then I will come to them from in front of them and from behind them and on their right and on their left, and You will not find most of them grateful [to You]" (al-Āʿrāf 16-17). Then Allah showed him another aspect of the ignorance he had of himself and of the new creation when he announced: "Indeed, you will have no authority over My servants, except those who follow you of the seduced" (al-Ḥijr 42). Iblīs should have known that disobeying Allah could not stem from knowledge, but rather from ignorance of himself that made him see his arrogance as knowledge.

Ignorance of the self poses a tremendous danger to the person and to

---

[32] Bayhaqī, *Al-Zuhd al-Kabīr*, no. 373, p. 165.

others. At any moment and without his being aware, it can push him to err, and the mistake could be spiritually fatal, from which there can be no return, similar to what happened with Iblīs. Combining ignorance of the self with the insistence on this ignorance is a door to spiritual destruction. The more a person insists on his ignorance, the more his ignorance increases, as there are levels of ignorance, the same way there are levels of knowledge.

The story of the encounter between Moses and Khaḍir, peace be upon them both, emphasizes the importance and necessity of self-knowingness, as it was the subject of the first secret that Khaḍir revealed to Moses. Contrary to popular belief, the first secret that Khaḍir revealed to his companion was not the reason why he tore a hole in the ship, which is the presence of a king who was taking ships from their owners by force. Rather, the first secret was the reason why Allah ordered Moses to search for Khaḍir: Khaḍir knew Moses better than Moses knew himself! This was demonstrated in the first thing that he said to Moses in response to Moses' request to accompany him: "Indeed, with me, you will never be able to have patience". He went on to explain that Moses lacked patience over what he did not know: "How can you have the patience for what you do not encompass in knowledge"? Moses did not understand, in the beginning, the depth of Khaḍir's diagnosis and thought that it was something he could overcome by mere determination. Unconsciously, he confirmed the truth of what Khaḍir revealed since he promised something that he did not know he would fail to keep: "You will find me, if Allah wills, patient, and I will not disobey you in [any] order". Indeed, Moses repeated this false promise twice later on, but with decreased confidence. This decline in Moses' confidence in his self-knowingness is a subtle indication of an increase in knowing his self as a result of that companionship. The first promise that he made to Khaḍir showed extreme confidence that he would have the patience required to keep the companionship of this man who he hardly knew anything about: "You will find me, if Allah wills, patient, and I will not disobey you in [any] order". But his failure to pass the first test when he objected to the enigmatic behaviour of Khaḍir increased him in the knowledge of his self, and so he lost part of that misplaced confidence. Thus, his second promise was made with less confidence: "Do not blame me for what I forgot and do not cover me in my matter with difficulty". Not only did he acknowledge that he forgot what he had promised, but he also admitted that some of Khaḍir's could be more than he could bear. Then came his second objection, which revealed more to him about himself, until he almost acknowledged the validity of Khaḍir's diagnosis that he did not have the patience required to accompany him. So, he uttered his third and final promise with abundant sorrow, acknowledgement, and acceptance: sorrow over what he came to know about himself; acknowledgement of the superiority of Khaḍir's knowledge; and acceptance of the fact that things would turn out the way Khaḍir had promised they would: "If I should ask you about anything after this, then do not keep me as a companion. You have obtained, from me, an excuse". When he objected a third and final time, he became certain of his inability to accompany Khaḍir. He experienced an increase in his self-knowingness, which is why he did not try to argue with Khaḍir at all when the latter put an end to their educational fellowship with the words: "This is [a] parting between me and you". By accepting Khaḍir's decision, what Allah wanted from this extraordinary encounter came to pass: He raised Moses' level of self-knowingness. Moses was able to develop his self-knowingness because he did not *insist* on any ignorance he had about himself. He was sincere in letting the events teach him what he did not know about himself.

Khaḍir's self-knowingness allowed him to know his Lord, and for this reason, he understood Allah's orders, which were hidden from Moses, who thought that Khaḍir was behaving according to his whims. Self-knowingness gives the person knowledge of the human soul and people in general — even though there are levels to this knowledge, like all kinds of knowledge, as mentioned earlier. This is how Khaḍir knew the inner workings of Moses' self as soon as met him. Khaḍir did not reach the special knowledge that Allah describes as *of His own* except by way of knowing his inner self and its inner workings. The profound and fundamental lesson that Allah wanted to teach the prophet who speaks with him when sending him to meet Khaḍir is that a creature's knowledge of the Creator is related to his knowledge of himself. A man cannot increase his knowledge of his Lord except by increasing his knowledge of his self. There is no greater evidence of the importance of this fact than Allah's immortalization in the Qur'an of this historic encounter.

1.5 The Muḥammadan Inheritor

The Shaikh of Ṭarīqa inherits the spiritual states of the Prophet (PBUH) and his attributes, besides prophethood, which is a status that is not merited or inherited by anyone after the Messenger Muḥammad (PBUH). This is why he is known as the "Muḥammadan Inheritor" and it is said that "the Shaikh among his people is like the Prophet among his nation".[33] The Shaikh's role as a spiritual guide and teacher to his disciples, though he is not a prophet, is like the role of the prophet among his people. In §10.2, we will discuss some of the karāmas that demonstrate Shaikh Muḥammad al-Muḥammad al-Kasnazān's inheritance of the Messenger's state (PBUH), but here, we will mention one of these karāmas about Shaikh ʿAbd al-Karīm Al-Kasnazān, the master and father of our Shaikh. Indeed, every Shaikh of the Ṭarīqa Kasnazaniyya is a spiritual inheritor to the Messenger (PBUH).

Shaikh ʿAbd al-Wahhāb al-Tuʿma, imam and preacher of the mausoleum of Shaikh ʿAbd al-Qādir al-Gaylānī in Baghdad, used to harbour some questions and doubts regarding the Shaikhs of our Ṭarīqa. In 1996, he visited Shaikh Muḥammad al-Muḥammad and stayed as a guest for a night in Baghdad. In the early morning, Shaikh Al-Tuʿma related a strange vision he had seen to the caliphs in the takya. He saw the Messenger (PBUH) walking, followed by Shaikh ʿAbd al-Karīm al-Kasnazān. Whenever the Prophet (PBUH) would place his blessed foot in a certain place and then raise it, Shaikh ʿAbd al-Karīm would follow him and place his foot on the same spot. The Prophet (PBUH) would walk, and Shaikh ʿAbd al-Karīm would follow him in step. The vision clearly symbolized that the Shaikh was meticulous and exact in his following of the way of his forefather, the Prophet (PBUH). Shaikh Al-Tuʿma's heart was put at ease. Each step also signified a spiritual level reached by Shaikh ʿAbd al-Karīm. This vision reminds us of these words of Shaikh ʿAbd al-Qādir al-Gaylānī:

> "Every walī follows in the footsteps of a prophet, and I follow in the footsteps of my grandfather Muḥammad (PBUH). The Chosen One (PBUH) never raised his foot from a place except that I placed my foot in the place he

[33] Some sources have claimed that this is a ḥadīth but that is not true, even though the meaning of the saying is sound.

had raised it from unless it was a step taken from the steps of prophethood, as those steps cannot be taken by anyone other than a prophet."[34]

The ṣuḥba of the Shaikhs of the Ṭarīqa is unique, as Allah Almighty has blessed them with a special favour in making them inheritors to the Prophet (PBUH), making them the nearest means to reach Him: "Those whom they invoke seek means of access to their Lord, [striving as to] which of them would be nearest" (al-Isrā' 57). The Muḥammadan Inheritor possesses special spiritual insight that enables him to help the believer in seeing his hidden faults and assist him in remedying them. At times, this is done explicitly by word or by deed, and other times, by subtle indications; at times, through ordinary, familiar means, and other times, through paranormal means. Becoming a Shaikh of Ṭarīqa happens by selection by Allah, not by the people, and it is not a position attained by those who want it. It is possible for a person to do good, to succeed, and to reach high spiritual ranks, but the inheritance of the Prophet (PBUH) is a divine matter in which man has no hand, as is the case with prophethood. Allah chooses individuals for prophethood; prophethood is not attained by the deeds of the prophet. We will explore this subject in detail in Chapter 9.

Because the Muḥammadan Inheritor embodies the states, deeds, and words of the reverent Messenger (PBUH), he inherits various spiritual effects from him (PBUH). This spiritual blessing is among the signs of the Muḥammadan inheritance. The effects of the states of the Prophet (PBUH) show on the person who inherits these states just as the spiritual power of the Prophet (PBUH) was visible and palpable to all who accompanied him. Ḥanẓala al-Usayyidī, for example, who was one of the Companions who used to record the revelation in writing, relates an occurrence that demonstrates the spiritual effect of the Prophet's (PBUH) ṣuḥba. One day, Abū Bakr met him and asked him: "How are you, O Ḥanẓala"? He replied sorrowfully: "Ḥanẓala has become a hypocrite"! Abū Bakr was surprised by his answer and inquired further as to why he had answered this way. He replied: "When we are with the Messenger of Allah (PBUH), he reminds us of Hell and Paradise until it was as if we could see them. Then, when we leave the Messenger of Allah (PBUH), we are preoccupied with our spouses, children, and properties so we

---

[34] Al-Qādiri, *Al-Fiyūḍāt al-Rabbāniyya fīl-Ma'āthir wa-Wird al-Qādiriyya*, p. 85.

forgot much [of what we had talked about and how we had felt]". Abū Bakr concurred with his statement.[35]

The spiritual presence of the Prophet (PBUH) makes the remembrance of Allah and the Day of Judgement have a more powerful effect upon the soul. The verses of the noble Qur'an did not have as great an impact upon their believing reader or listener, regardless of the level of the piety of the reciter or listener, as they had when they were heard from the Messenger (PBUH). The voice of the Prophet (PBUH) unveils much more of the spiritual energy that Allah's words carry, which is an effect that the Companions used to feel.

The person who attends the gatherings of Shaikh Muḥammad al-Muḥammad al-Kasnazān can experience this matter directly. Often our Shaikh recounts in his talks verses regarding dhikr, such as: "Remember Me; I will remember you. Be grateful to Me and do not deny Me" (al-Baqara 152). A person may have read and heard this verse hundreds, if not thousands, of times, but hearing it from our Shaikh's lips allows the listener to find spiritual power in the verse that he did not feel when he heard it from anyone else, or if he were to read or remember it. The verse affects him in a way that it does not do when it comes from any other source. He perceives and feels its meaning more clearly. This unique experience does not change when one hears the verse again from our Shaikh. It happens each time he repeats it, as if each repetition lends itself to a unique experience, for in every repetition, the listener tastes a new form from the infinite beauty of the verse. It is the same with all words of guidance to the way of Allah: the moment they are spoken by the Shaikh who is well acquainted with Allah, his sincerity and the blessing of his nearness to Allah both cause the words to have a tremendous effect because they come from a heart full of Allah's light and dhikr, and not simply from a believer's intellect.

This spiritual effect is the reason why the shortest way to reach Allah Almighty is through the company of a Shaikh who acts in accordance with the way of the Prophet (PBUH). This effect also serves as proof, for the seeker, of the true Muḥammadan Inheritor. The teacher who affects the intellect without impacting the heart or soul can be a scholar who is erudite in religion, but he does not inhabit the station of inheriting the

---

[35] Muslim, *Ṣaḥīḥ Muslim*, IV, no. 2750, p. 2106-2107.

Messenger (PBUH). One can become a scholar by studying the ḥadīths of the Messenger (PBUH), and such scholar may become a practising one by following his honourable behavioural conduct (PBUH). But a practising scholar is not a Muḥammadan Inheritor until he inherits his purified spiritual states, that is, his spiritual blessing. The complete unique experience that one finds in the ṣuḥba of Shaikh Muḥammad al-Muḥammad al-Kasnazān is a result of the fact that he is an inheritor to the Prophet (PBUH), and so he embodies his honourable words, deeds, and states (PBUH).

The spiritual states of the Prophet (PBUH) cause their inheritor to be a source of paranormal occurrences, similar to the abundance of miracles that originated from the Messenger (PBUH). The spiritual effect that the Muḥammadan Inheritor has on the heart of the seeker is a kind of karāma. Many other kinds of paranormal occurrences originate from the Muḥammadan Inheritor to guide people to him and to strengthen their hearts on true faith. Such is the situation with all the Masters of the Ṭarīqa Kasnazaniyya. Each Shaikh's life was rich with karāmas, and these continued even after his parting from this world to the permanent abode. We will discuss the subject of karāmas in detail in Chapter 3. We will mention some of the karāmas of our Shaikhs in this book, but we will focus in particular on the karāmas of our present Master, Shaikh Muḥammad al-Muḥammad al-Kasnazān. Similarly, we will discuss some of the karāmas that demonstrate his being an inheritor to the Prophet (PBUH) in §10.2.

The Muḥammadan Inheritor is the authority in distinguishing between what is true, and what is false, in what has been said or written about the Messenger (PBUH). For example, some may doubt the authenticity of the above ḥadīth of Ḥanẓala al-Usayyidī, but the personal experience of the situation that is described in that narration in the ṣuḥba of Shaikh Muḥammad al-Muḥammad al-Kasnazān gives conclusive evidence of its authenticity. There is a karāma of our teacher that merits mentioning in this section.

In approximately 1994, Dr. ʿAdāb al-Ḥamsh, a specialist in Ḥadīth, regularly visited our Shaikh in Baghdad, like many scholars who would visit him and participate in discussions on various religious and cultural matters in his assembly. One day, he mentioned a ḥadīth that he considered authentic, but he was surprised when our teacher described it as fabricated. Dr. ʿAdāb said that he was certain that the ḥadīth was authentic, but our Shaikh insisted upon the fact that it was fabricated and suggested that he re-examine its authenticity. A week later, Dr. ʿAdāb came to visit our Shaikh, astonished, as he had discovered, after re-examination that the ḥadīth was falsely attributed to the Prophet (PBUH), as one of the men in the chain of narrators was known as a liar. When he asked our Shaikh how he knew that the ḥadīth was a fabrication, he replied by referring to the Shaikhs of the Ṭarīqa Kasnazaniyya: "My Shaikhs told me that this narration was fabricated; the Shaikhs do not speak other than the truth".

The Shaikh of Ṭarīqa is "a more reliable source of information than books" regarding the way of the Messenger (PBUH) because he acquires his knowledge from the Shaikhs and the Messenger (PBUH). This does not mean that one cannot learn from books. Yet, in religious and historical books in particular, including sources about the Sunna of the Prophet (PBUH), there is much information that is not easy to determine whether it is factual or at least accurate. Therefore, there is a continuous conflict about this information, being accepted by some and rejected by others. This is only natural, given that these books were compiled decades or centuries after the Prophet (PBUH) when means of documenting and authenticating documents were very basic. There are many unintentional errors in what has been written and many narrations that were fabricated for one reason or another. As for Shaikh Muḥammad al-Muḥammad, he received the Sunna of the Prophet (PBUH) from his Master Shaikh ʿAbd al-Karīm, who received it in his time from his Master Shaikh Ḥussein, and so on. Regarding this, our Shaikh says that he does not contradict the Sunna of the Prophet (PBUH) even by as much as a fingertip. The ṣuḥba of the Shaikhs and following them with sincerity confers piety, which is the key to knowledge: "Be pious to Allah, and Allah teaches you" (al-Baqara 272).

Therefore, the company of one of the inheritors to the Messenger's words, deeds, and spiritual states (PBUH) is the basis for reaching Allah.

1.6 Obedience in Ṣuḥba

The ṣuḥba on the path to Allah is a relationship with special conditions, the most important of which is the obedience of the companion to the one he is accompanying. Therefore, Allah ordered the obedience of the Muslim to the noble Prophet (PBUH) to be absolute:

> "Whatever the Messenger has given you — take, and what he has forbidden you — refrain from". (Al-Ḥashr 7)
>
> "It is not for a believing man or a believing woman, when Allah and His Messenger have decided a matter, that they should [thereafter] have any choice about their affair. Whoever disobeys Allah and His Messenger has certainly strayed into clear error". (Al-Āḥzāb 36)

Without this submission, the seeker does not reap all of the benefits of the ṣuḥba. Khaḍir, therefore, ordered Moses to submit: "Then if you follow me, do not ask me about anything until I make mention of it to you" (al-Kahf 70). When Moses failed to obey the order and objected three times to the actions of the one whose company he sought, the latter ended this fellowship: "This is [a] parting between me and you" (al-Kahf 78). Al-Nawawī said in his commentary on the story of Moses and Khaḍir:

> "In this story [we learn] about the etiquettes [one should have] with a scholar; the sanctity of the Shaikhs; [the need to] refrain from objecting to them and from interpreting that which one does not understand from their external behaviours and actions; [the need to] fulfil promises made to them; [the need to] apologize when one breaks their promise to them".[36]

Our Master says that the disciple must be in front of his guiding Shaikh as a dead person is in front of those who wash him. Just as the dead person does not resist the hands of those who wash him when they turn him over, the disciple should be like this in his obedience in following his Shaikh's orders, to benefit from his lead in his spiritual journey.

The obligation of obedience in the relationship of ṣuḥba is because the one who is being followed has godly knowledge that the follower has no access to. The actions of the one who is being accompanied, in terms of what he does and does not do, stem from this knowledge that is hidden to those who do not possess it: "I did it not of my own accord. That is the interpretation of that about which you could not have patience" (al-Kahf 82). This is the knowledge to which the noble Messenger (PBUH) alluded when he said: "I am the city of knowledge and 'Alī is its door, so whoever

---

[36] Al-Nawawī, *Ṣaḥiḥ Muslim bi-Sharḥ al-Nawawī*, XV, p. 137.

wants knowledge, let him enter through its door".[37] This honourable ḥadīth signifies that Imām ʿAlī Ibn Abī Ṭālib is the spiritual successor of the Prophet (PBUH). This spiritual succession and inheritance of godly knowledge was passed down through the chain of the Shaikhs of the Ṭarīqa, each of whom chose his successor through divine guidance. This spiritual succession will continue until the Day of Judgement.

Obedience in ṣuḥba is mandatory for everyone, as we observed in Allah's testing of Moses with Khaḍir. This is the case with every Shaikh of Ṭarīqa, who is obliged to follow what the Prophet (PBUH) and the Shaikhs of the Ṭarīqa direct him to do. Our Shaikh often describes himself as an "instrument" in the hands of the Shaikhs, who operate and direct him as they desire. One example that our Master gives to explain this to the disciple is saying that if the Shaikhs of the Ṭarīqa suddenly ordered him to travel somewhere, he would leave immediately and would not even stop to prepare for his travel. Among the examples of the perfected Shaikh of Ṭarīqa's obedience to his Masters is the following event that took place a short while after the passing of Shaikh ʿAbd al-Karīm. At the time, our Master had remained in the village of Karbchna in the Sulaymāniyya governorate for a relatively long time. One day, at about nine o'clock in the morning, he called the dervish who was responsible for the takya's kitchen, who was one of his sisters. He informed her that he, along with the family, guests, and visiting dervishes, would be leaving Karbchna for Kirkuk, which was where his permanent place of residence was at the time, and he requested that she prepare for the move. She, along with other workers who served the takya, prepared for the return to Kirkuk, including loading equipment for the kitchen, and other necessities, on cars for transportation. At about half-past eleven, our Shaikh called her again, this time to direct her to unload all the belongings and to prepare for lunch because the trip had been cancelled! The female dervish was surprised by this change, so she reacted spontaneously as she put her hands on her head in a gesture demonstrating the complicated position in which she found herself as she said: "How can I stop and prepare lunch at this late hour"? Our Shaikh's reply was only to put his hands on his honourable head also and reply: "What am I to do if they told me in the morning to return to Kirkuk and

[37] Al-Ṭabarānī, *al-Muʿjam al-Kabīr*, XI, no. 11061, p. 66.

now they advise me to remain in Karbchna"?

We see here our Shaikh's fulfilment of the orders of the Shaikhs without hesitation or even asking about the reasons behind them. Most of the commands from the Prophet (PBUH) and the Shaikhs of the Ṭarīqa from the spirit world to their representative in the world of appearances are private, spiritual imports that are not divulged by a Shaikh of Ṭarīqa, unless there is a necessity to reveal them.

Whoever closely accompanies our teacher witnesses much of such behaviours that embody his description of himself as an instrument in the hands of his Shaikhs, who move him as they like.[38] For example, sometimes he would be ready to travel to another city, with the cars, the belongings, and the escorts all also ready. They would be waiting for the command from our Shaikh who would also be sitting in wait for the order of the Shaikhs to travel. Sometimes the waiting period ends with the cancellation of travel and all associated plans! In the context of talking about the need for obedience, our Shaikh mentioned that after becoming the Shaikh of the Ṭarīqa, the Shaikhs ordered him one day to stop eating chicken thighs, so he did not go near them from that day on. He obeyed the command without asking for the reasoning behind it.[39]

These are some sayings by Shaikh ʿAbd al-Qādir al-Gaylānī about the importance of ṣuḥba and the necessity to couple it with obedience in the journey to reach Allah:

> "Listen and observe by your heart without doubts and you will see wonders. Relinquish your doubts about the people [of Allah], believe them, and believe in them, without asking 'why' or 'how'. They have allowed you to accompany them, accepted that you serve them, and gave you a share of what has been sent down to them. Favours and graces come down from heaven upon the hearts of the truthful, and the rewards of the innermost beings come down on their innermost beings, night and day. If you wish them to accept you for their service, you must purify your outward and your inward. Stand at the ready before them. Purify your heart from all heretical innovation, for the creed of the people [of Allah] is the creed of the prophets, the messengers, and the truthful, Allah's prayer and peace be upon them all. They follow in the footsteps of the righteous predecessors. Their doctrine is the doctrine of the elders. They do not claim anything unless they have

[38] Shaikh Muḥammad al-Muḥammad al-Kasnazān, *sermon*, 22nd/September/2016.

[39] Shaikh Muḥammad al-Muḥammad al-Kasnazān, *sermon*, 22nd/September/2016.

evidence for it."[40]

"O you who sits in your houses and cells with the self, inborn inclinations, passion, and little knowledge! Incumbent upon you is accompanying practising Shaikhs. Follow them and place your feet where they step. Be humble in front of them. Be patient with how they break you down until your passions have disappeared, your selves have been crushed, and the fire of your inborn inclinations has been put out".[41]

"O hermits and recluses, come and read my words, even if only a single letter. Accompany me for a day or a week so that you may learn something that benefits you. Woe to you! Most of you are in illusion, worshipping creatures in your cells. This matter does not come about by merely sitting in seclusion with ignorance. Woe to you! Walk in search of knowledge and scholars until no further walking is possible. Walk until nothing (in your body) obeys you".[42]

"When the seeker's accompaniment of the Shaikh becomes sound, the Shaikh feeds and provides him from what is in his heart of the food and drink of divine knowledge".[43]

Let us stop and take a look at Shaikh ʿAbd al-Qādir's words, "favours and graces come down from heaven upon the hearts of the truthful, and fountains of secrets descend on their innermost beings, night and day", to explain the meaning of the "sirr", or the "innermost being", which he distinguishes from the "qalb", or the "heart". This term refers to a hidden part of man that grows and develops by its nearness to Allah (mighty and sublime is He). The Shaikh explains in another place the particularity of the innermost being when he says that "the people of the innermost being were few in ancient times, and today they are the fewest of the few".[44] This means that the innermost being is not present, or is not as active, in every person's self as the rest of its components. Rather, it is a special entity that grows with proximity to Allah (exalted and high is He) and becomes a means of receiving special, divine unveilings and messages: "The believer remains in fear until his innermost being is given the book of safety. He conceals it from his heart and never reveals it to it. This

---

[40] Shaikh ʿAbd al-Qādir al-Gaylānī, *Jilā' al-Khāṭir*, pp. 10-11.

[41] Shaikh ʿAbd al-Qādir al-Gaylānī, *Jilā' al-Khāṭir*, p. 11.

[42] Shaikh ʿAbd al-Qādir al-Gaylānī, *Jilā' al-Khāṭir*, p. 8.

[43] Shaikh ʿAbd al-Qādir al-Gaylānī, *Jilā' al-Khāṭir*, p. 9.

[44] Shaikh ʿAbd al-Qādir al-Gaylānī, *Jilā' al-Khāṭir*, p. 11.

happens to only a few individuals."[45]

This term and concept is frequently mentioned, and its function distinguished from the heart, in the sayings of Shaikh 'Abd al-Qādir, as in these two examples:

> "Asceticism weighs heavily upon the body; divine knowledge weighs heavily upon the heart; nearness to Allah weighs heavily upon the innermost being".[46]
>
> "The believer has three eyes: the eye of the head, with which he looks at this world; the eye of the heart, with which he looks at the hereafter; and the eye of the innermost being, with which he sees the True One (mighty and sublime is He). The eye of the head expires in this world, the eye of the heart expires in the hereafter, and the eye of the innermost being remains with the True One (mighty and sublime is He) in this world and in the hereafter because it looks at Him in this world and in the hereafter".[47]

This innermost being is the meaning behind the Sufi expression "may Allah sanctify his *sirr*", which is exclusively mentioned after the names of great walīs. It declares that they are from "the people of the innermost being", meaning among the elite who have drawn near to Him (exalted and high is He). Thus, the phrase "may Allah sanctify his innermost being" is not like common, stock phrases such as "may Allah have mercy on him" or "may Allah bless his resting place", which can be applied to the majority of people as a prayer for them. Rather, it is an exclusive description that denotes a special place of nearness to Allah (exalted and high is He), indicating that Allah has purified and blessed the innermost being of that noble walī.

Whoever arrives at this level of nearness to Allah is blessed, similar to Allah's description of Jesus, peace be upon him: "He has made me blessed wherever I am" (Maryam 31). There are blessings in being near to and in the company of the people of the innermost being. This blessing even includes their personal belongings, as Allah taught us when restored the vision of a prophet by the blessing of another prophet's shirt: "Take this shirt of mine and cast it over the face of my father; he will become seeing. Bring me all of your family" (Yūsuf 93).

---

[45] Shaikh 'Abd al-Qādir al-Gaylānī, *Jilā' al-Khāṭir*, p. 26.
[46] Shaikh 'Abd al-Qādir al-Gaylānī, *Jilā' al-Khāṭir*, p. 24.
[47] Shaikh 'Abd al-Qādir al-Gaylānī, *Jilā' al-Khāṭir*, p. 47.

Among the most beautiful of what has been said regarding ṣuḥba and obedience to the Shaikh are these verses from the poem "Al-Nādirāt Al-'Ainiyya" by Shaikh 'Abd al-Karīm al-Jīlī, one of the grandsons of Shaikh 'Abd al-Qādir al-Gaylānī:

> Should the preordained or destiny lead you,
> to a true Shaikh who is well versed in the truth,
> Stand in his service and follow his objectives,
> and leave everything you used to do.
> Be with him as a dead person is with a dead washer
> who turns him about while he fully obeys.
> Do not object to matters of his that you are ignorant of,
> for objection is a form of disputing.
> Accept of him whatever you see even if
> Looked illegal, for looks may be deceiving.
> In the story of noble Khaḍir there is sufficient example,
> in his killing of the boy while Moses objected.
> When the morning dawned upon the night of his secret,
> and he unsheathed a sword of proof that would cut objections,
> Moses gave him an excuse, and so is
> the knowledge of the people [of the Allah] is full of novelties.[48]

The perfect obedience of the seeker to his Shaikh is the first of the three levels of annihilation, or "fanā'", in the way to Allah. This "annihilation in the Shaikh" leads to "annihilation in the Messenger (PBUH)", and annihilation in the Messenger (PBUH) leads to "annihilation in Allah (mighty and sublime is He)", which is the ultimate goal of Ṭarīqa. Obeying a Shaikh who is well acquainted with Allah enables the seeker to walk upon the path of the Prophet (PBUH), and travelling upon the path of the Messenger (PBUH) leads to complete submission to the One who sent him (mighty and sublime is He).

1.7 The Spiritual Touch

Travel on the Sufi path, by following a perfect Shaikh who inherited the spiritual states of the Messenger (PBUH), begins with a person taking an oath of allegiance at the hand of the Shaikh or one of his caliphs. The person seeking to take the oath repeats the vow of the Ṭarīqa after the

---

[48] Al-Jīlī, *al-Nādirāt al-'Ayniyya*, pp. 112-113.

Shaikh or caliph, in which he declares his taking of the present Shaikh of the Ṭarīqa, who represents the Messenger (PBUH) and the Shaikhs of the Ṭarīqa, as a guide. This oath of allegiance is an actualization of the pledge of the first Muslims to the Prophet (PBUH), which is described in the noble Qur'an:

> "Indeed, those who pledge allegiance to you [O Muḥammad] are pledging allegiance to Allah. The hand of Allah is over their hands. He who breaks his word only breaks it to the detriment of himself. He who fulfils that which he has promised Allah — He will give him a great reward". (Al-Fatḥ 10)
>
> "Certainly Allah was pleased with the believers when they pledged allegiance to you [O Muḥammad] under the tree. He knew what was in their hearts, so He sent down tranquillity upon them and rewarded them with an imminent conquest". (Al-Fatḥ 18)

Our Shaikh has introduced innovations to facilitate religious matters for people, following the noble verse: "Allah intends for you ease and does not intend for you hardship" (al-Baqara 185). One of these is that he has permitted the giving of the pledge by phone to whoever cannot find a caliph in his area to take the pledge from him by hand, or if travel is difficult for him. This also facilitates taking the pledge as soon as possible, as one does not know if he will have the opportunity to do so in the future were he to delay it. Although "the reward of deeds depends upon the intentions and every person will get the reward according to what he has intended",[49] as the Prophet (PBUH) has said, it is best to actualize every good intention at the closest available opportunity.

The pledge also represents a declaration of the disciple of his repentance, which is the first of the stations of Sufism. There is no travelling towards Allah without repentance. Among the educational karāmas that reveal the role of the pledge in purifying the disciple is that the hands of Shaikh Ismā'īl al-Wilyānī and Shāh al-Kasnazān used to sometimes blacken after they give the pledge, before returning to their original colour after a while as if the hand of the Shaikh had helped the disciple cast aside his sins in order for him to begin his journey to Allah. By taking the pledge the Muslim renews his Islam. Our Shaikh relates that sometimes the hand of his father Shaikh 'Abd al-Karīm al-Kasnazān would swell and turn black after he gives the pledge. We see this spiritual

[49] Bukhārī, *Al-Jāmi' al-Ṣaḥīḥ*, I, no. 1, p. 49.

sensitivity in the hand of a Shaikh of Ṭarīqa in other karāmas. One of these is that when some dervishes would kiss the hand of Shaikh ʿAbd al-Karīm, he would sometimes feel as though he had been bitten by a snake, or as if his hand had touched an electric current. But he would feel too embarrassed to prevent people from kissing his hand.

Shaikh Muḥammad al-Muḥammad al-Kasnazān calls the pledge of Ṭarīqa "the spiritual touch" because it spiritually connects the seeker of nearness to Allah to the present Shaikh, who is in turn spiritually linked to his Shaikh, and so on, passing through the chain of the Shaikhs of the Ṭarīqa to the Messenger (PBUH), who is spiritually connected to Allah. Our Shaikh emphasizes that a caliph cannot give the pledge to a person unless one of the Shaikhs of the Ṭarīqa is spiritually present during the process of the giving of the pledge.[50]

This spiritual connection between the Shaikh and the disciple is not an arbitrary relationship, but it is rather rooted in the spirit world. One incident that demonstrates this took place when two students wanted to take the pledge from the Shaikh Kāka Aḥmad al-Shaikh (1305/1887), yet he only gave the pledge to one of them. This dervish became the great walī Ḥasan al-Qara Chwārī. Meanwhile, he told the other seeker that he was destined to take the pledge from Shaikh ʿAbd al-Karīm Shāh al-Kasnazān, and not from him, or any other Shaikh.

When this one, who was also called "Ḥasan", went to Shāh al-Kasnazān in the village of Karbchna, the Shaikh did not give him the pledge. Instead, he told him that he would teach him something that would benefit him. He showed him a wild herb that sprouts in the spring and told him that rubbing hot copper with this grass converted it into gold. After returning to the village of Khawya where he lived, which is located at the foot of a mountain, Ḥasan went out one day intending to test what Shāh al-Kasnazān had told him. When he rubbed a piece of hot copper with that grass, the copper did indeed turn into gold. Yet, he was taken by the thought that he had not gone to Shāh al-Kasnazān to acquire gold and wealth. He rather sought from him the pledge of the Ṭarīqa, blessings and spiritual advancement. He realized that this was a test from the Shaikh. He closed his eyes and threw the piece of gold far away from the top of the mountain. He returned to Shāh al-Kasnazān and told him

---

[50] Shaikh Muḥammad al-Muḥammad al-Kasnazān, *sermon*, 1st/April/2013.

that he had not visited him in search of gold, but rather in search of nearness to Allah. The Shaikh laughed and gave him the pledge.

Shāh al-Kasnazān ordered his disciple to move and live in the village of Kānī Chnār, which is located between Chamchamāl province[51] and the village of Karbchna, in the Sulaymāniyya governorate. As a result, he became known as "Ḥasan Kānī Chnār". He was also known by the title of "Ḥasan the Caliph" because he was one of the caliphs of Shāh al-Kasnazān. Many karāmas appeared at his hand, among which is that these areas were known for large numbers of thefts. But shortly after him moving to live there, thefts ceased. The reason is that he would reveal the identity of the thief to his victim. Caliph Ḥasan became one of the great walīs.

Taking the pledge is a predestined affair. Circumstances must be facilitated for the person who is destined to take it, while it is impossible to ensure that it happens to someone who does not have the good fortune of being destined to take it. There are countless incidents throughout the history of Ṭarīqa that demonstrate this reality. A caliph named "Ṭāhā" was in his small shop where he sold home goods when the police arrested him on the pretext that he sold a bottle of milk at a price slightly above the official price. He was put in prison, where he met a man who had spent about two years in jail. The prisoner took to asking him questions about who he was and the circumstances of his imprisonment, as is usually the case when a new inmate arrives. During the conversation, Ḥājj Ṭāhā informed his companion that he was a caliph of Shaikh ʿAbd al-Karīm al-Kasnazān, at which point the prisoner surprised him by telling him that for close to six months he had been asking Allah to facilitate the means for him to take the pledge from Shaikh ʿAbd al-Karīm. The caliph realised that this was the reason for his imprisonment, and he gave the pledge to the prisoner. Caliph Ṭāhā spent only one night in prison, as he was released the following day without any explanation or legal prosecution. This incident reminds us of this saying of the Prophet (PBUH): "If a believer was on a mountaintop, Allah Almighty would appoint for him a scholar to teach him".[52]

---

[51] Administratively, Iraq is divided into Governorates each of which consists of a number of provinces, and each province consists of a number of districts.

[52] Shaikh ʿAbd al-Qādir al-Gaylānī, *Jilāʾ al-Khāṭir*, p. 47.

Many incidents demonstrate that some do not have the good fortune of taking the pledge. A caliph named "Muḥammad Maḥmūd" used to wish for a young cleric from his city, Chamchamāl, to take up the Ṭarīqa. He mentioned this to Shaikh ʿAbd al-Karīm al-Kasnazān more than once during his visits to him in Kirkuk, but the Shaikh would not comment. During one visit, he informed Shaikh ʿAbd al-Karīm that the religious cleric had requested that he convey his greetings to the Shaikh and that he promised to accompany him the next time he went to visit the Shaikh and would take the pledge. The Shaikh replied with something along the lines of: "O my son, there are people who do not have the good fortune of taking the pledge. Even if they go out in search of it, they will not take it". When caliph Muḥammad returned to Chamchamāl he heard that the cleric had been in a car accident that claimed his life! In his next visit to Shaikh ʿAbd al-Karīm, he told him about what had occurred, so the Shaikh reminded him of what he had told him, that the pledge was destined for some people, and that whoever was not destined to take the pledge would not take it, even if at one point he seemed determined to take it.

One type of incident that highlights this reality is that, sometimes, a person would put his hand in the caliph's hand and repeat the oath of the Ṭarīqa after him, until nothing is left except to say "I accept", to indicate his acceptance of the oath of the pledge. But then, he would withdraw his hand from the caliph's hand and refuse to complete the taking of the pledge by saying "I accept". Shaikh Muḥammad al-Muḥammad cites the following verse in explaining this matter: "Allah selects for His mercy whom He wills" (al-Baqara 105).[53]

One karāma that demonstrates the connection of the dervish with a particular Shaikh and that he is predestined to take the pledge of the Ṭarīqa is how Professor Dr Ḥasan Aḥmad Ḥāmid (may Allah have mercy on him), one of the great scholars in Sudan, took the pledge of the Ṭarīqa Kasnazāniyya. Dr Ḥasan was from a multi-generational family of Sufis of the Ṭarīqa Idrīsiyya, also known as the Ṭarīqa Aḥmadiyya, after Shaikh Aḥmad Ibn Idrīs (1758-1837), a Sufi Shaikh from Morocco. For whatever reason, Dr Ḥasan did not follow his ancestors in taking the pledge of the Ṭarīqa Idrīsiyya or any other Ṭarīqa. On one of the last nights of

[53] Shaikh Muḥammad al-Muḥammad al-Kasnazān, *sermon*, 8th/February/2016.

Ramadan in the year 1978, which might have been the Night of Power on the 27th, he had a dream. He saw Shaikh ʿAbd al-Qādir al-Gaylānī take him by the hand into Paradise, walking him around. This dream took place around six months after the passing of the Shaikhdom of the Ṭarīqa Kasnazāniyya to Shaikh Muḥammad al-Muḥammad, who at the time was in his first seclusion in northern Iraq. Dr Ḥasan had never heard of the Shaikh or even of the Ṭarīqa Kasnazāniyya.

Sixteen years later, that is in 1994, Professor Ḥasan saw Shaikh ʿAbd al-Qādir al-Gaylānī in his sleep a second time. The Shaikh appeared in a tremendous form and massive size, such so that his foot seemed to be the size of a pillar that supports a bridge. He said to him something along the lines of: "O my son! Take our Ṭarīqa and spread it in your country". Professor Ḥasan was puzzled by the meaning of the dream, especially because the Ṭarīqa Qādiriyya was widespread in Sudan. After three days, he went to see Professor Shaikh Muḥammad ʿAlī aṭ-Ṭarīfī, who was a follower of the Ṭarīqa Qādiriyya. Shaikh al-Ṭarīfī was dean of The College of the Holy Qur'an in The University of the Holy Qur'an and Islamic Sciences in Omdurman, where Dr Ḥasan was dean to The College of Sharia. Dr Ḥasan asked Professor al-Ṭarīfī to initiate him into the Ṭarīqa Qādiriyya because it had been indicated to him that he should invite people to follow it. Al-Ṭarīfī refused his request, telling him that his Ṭarīqa would not be from him and that it would reach him in its appointed time. After some time, The University of the Holy Qur'an and Islamic Sciences invited the renowned Iraqi reciter of the Qur'an, Ḥājj ʿAlā'u al-Dīn al-Qaisī (may Allah have mercy on him), who was head of the Islamic World Association of Readers and Reciters, to visit the university. When Ḥājj ʿAlā'u al-Dīn arrived at the university, the head of the university, Professor Dr Aḥmad ʿAlī al-Imām, was busy, so he asked Professor Ḥasan, as the dean of The College of Sharia, to welcome the guest on his behalf until he finished his engagements. When they together, Professor Ḥasan sensed the spirituality of Shaikh ʿAbd al-Qādir al-Gaylānī between them, so he asked Ḥājj ʿAlā'u al-Dīn if he was Qādiri. He confirmed that he was one the caliphs of Shaikh Muḥammad al-Muḥammad al-Kasnazān, Master of the Ṭarīqa ʿAlīyya Qādiriyya Kasnazāniyya, and that he had been charged by the Shaikh to give the pledge. Ḥājj ʿAlā'u al-Dīn presented a set of prayer beads to Professor Ḥasan, who stretched his hand out to take the pledge of the Ṭarīqa. Ḥājj

ʿAlāʾu al-Dīn gave him the pledge. As Shaikh ʿAbd al-Qādir al-Gaylānī ordered him to do, Professor Ḥasan played a major role in spreading the Ṭarīqa Kasnazāniyya, the Ṭarīqa of Shaikh ʿAbd al-Qādir al-Gaylānī, in Sudan. In §13.4.2, we will talk mention a karāma that occurred when establishing the first takya in Sudan.

The travelling seeker on the straight path of this spiritual touch sees for himself the tremendous reward that is referred to in the verse of the pledge, including the acquisition of spiritual openings. Our Shaikh says:

> "It is important that the caliph and the disciple abide by and preserve this blessing, this spiritual touch. Allah willing, during the spiritual journey, you will see with your eyes and feel with your souls — during times of worship, during times of supplication, during times of prostration and bowing to Allah (exalted and high is He) and during times of dhikr — the blessing of this spiritual touch".

Our Shaikh continues, likening the pledge to a spiritual plant that requires care and attention to grow and blossom:

> "This spiritual plant that is planted in your heart must be watered with the water of worship; watered with honesty; watered with truth; watered with the Muḥammadan Sharia; watered with prostration and bowing; watered with cleanliness, by avoiding injustice, by avoiding aggression, with worship, with applying Sharia because, for us, Sharia is the framework of Ṭarīqa. The Sharia is like a map, so it is necessary that you walk according to the Muḥammadan Sharia (PBUH), that you apply what the Messenger (PBUH) has commanded because he is commanded by Allah (exalted and high is He): 'Announce that which has been revealed to you' (Al-Māʾida 67)".[54]

He also says about the spiritual plant of the pledge:

> "The Shaikh of Ṭarīqa connects people to the Messenger (PBUH). The spiritual plant transfers from hand to hand, from the hand of the Shaikh to the hand of the caliph to the hand of the disciple. There is a spiritual plant that moves to the hand of the seeker from the respected Messenger (PBUH), from Allah (exalted and high is He). You do not see this plant externally, but when you become one of the people of the inward world you will see it. There is a light that moves from so-and-so to so-and-so to so-and-so to the hand of that disciple, and so that light descends into his heart. When he waters that light by the remembrance of Allah, by the remembrance of al-Raḥmān, it becomes

---

[54] Shaikh Muḥammad al-Muḥammad al-Kasnazān, *sermon*, 4th/March/2013.

like a good tree: 'Whose root is firmly fixed and its branches [high] in the sky'. This spiritual plant of light transfers from one Shaikh's hand to Shaikh, to Shaikh, to the present Shaikh, to the hand of the disciple, to his heart. This is what occurs in the spiritual realm. When the seeker waters this spiritual plant with the light of dhikr, it grows into a tree, as the Qur'an says: 'Like a good tree, whose root is firmly fixed and its branches [high] in the sky, it produces its fruit all the time, by permission of its Lord'".[55]

Our Shaikh stresses that even when one sees himself taking the pledge in his sleep, it is still necessary to realise his dream by taking the pledge in a state of wakefulness from the Shaikh. This means that following the Ṭarīqa demands to practise at the hand of a living Shaikh, for the disciple to take the pledge at his hand. It is not possible to follow a Shaikh who is present only in the spirit world. A person cannot claim that his Shaikh is Imām ʿAlī Ibn Abī Ṭālib, Shaikh ʿAbd al-Qādir al-Gaylānī, Shaikh Aḥmad al-Rifāʿī, or any Shaikh who is not present in the visible, physical world. Had this not been the case, the Messenger (PBUH) would have been the sole Master of all the Muslims, and there would not be chains of Shaikhs who are connected to him (PBUH). Just as it is not possible for a disciple to practise except at the hand of a living Shaikh, a Shaikh of Ṭarīqa cannot reach the level of Shaikhdom except by following a living Shaikh who appoints him as his successor as the Master of the Ṭarīqa.

One reason that the Shaikh must be living in the physical world is that the Shaikh's training of the disciple takes two forms: exterior and interior. As we have explained above, the interior training is the Shaikh's granting of the state of inner purification to the seeker through his spiritual influences. Some of the latter reaches the disciple no matter how far he may be from his Shaikh, as long as he is close to him in his heart. Other spiritual influences reach him through his visiting the Shaikh and observing him. Both kinds demand the existence of the Shaikh in the physical world.

The exterior training is delivered by the instructions and directions that the Shaikh gives to the seeker, through the language of the tongue and the language of subtle indications. These may be initiated by the Shaikh or are given in response to inquiries and requests of the disciple. In the case of exterior training, it is essential for the disciple to be able to

---

[55] Shaikh Muḥammad al-Muḥammad al-Kasnazān, *sermon*, last third of October/2013.

communicate with his Shaikh externally.

A disciple cannot travel upon the spiritual path without the Shaikh who he follows being present in the physical world. There are countless incidents throughout history in which we see a seeker travel vast distances to take the pledge at the hand of a particular Shaikh. We have previously referred to a similar situation in the journey of the prophet Moses in search of the righteous servant Khaḍir to take him as a teacher.

There are many Islamic behaviours, obligatory or desirable, that our Shaikh teaches the disciple externally. One example is his exceptional reverence for the glorious Qur'an. Muslims, in general, treat Allah's Book with all respect, not touching it if they are not on ablution, for example. One way in which our Master expresses his reverence for the noble Qur'an that is not known even among Muslims is standing out of respect for Allah's Book. When a person enters his gathering carrying a muṣḥaf (written or printed Qur'an), he stands out of respect for the Qur'an. He exhorts people regarding this matter, saying:

> "Is it permissible for any person to remain sitting when Allah's Words are brought and to not stand out of respect for it? Who is greater than Allah (exalted and high is He)? What is greater than Allah's Words, Glorified and Sublime is He? No one and nothing. You stand for your friend when he comes to you, so how can you not stand for the Qur'an? This is your scripture, your sanctities, your teachings, the Lord's Words, the Creator's Words, so upholding its sanctity is compulsory".[56]

When someone visits our Shaikh carrying a muṣḥaf, for example, to gift it to him, the dervish at his service informs him of this so that he can be prepared to stand out of respect for Allah's Book when the visitor enters. Here is a beautiful karāma that expresses this remarkable behaviour. Our Shaikh was once in the takya in Baghdad with many dervishes in his gathering when a seeker came in and walked towards him to greet him. Before the young man reached him, our teacher rose from his chair, and the assembly stood, not understanding the cause of his standing. The matter became clear when our Shaikh addressed the visitor: "O my son! How can you come to visit me when there is a muṣḥaf in your pocket"? It seemed that the disciple was either unaware of the Shaikh's etiquettes towards the magnificent Qur'an or that he forgot that

[56] Shaikh Muḥammad al-Muḥammad al-Kasnazān, *sermon*, 18th/September/2016.

a muṣḥaf was in his pocket. He apologised and completed his visit to the Shaikh. This is a didactic karāma, as perhaps there were others in the gathering who were unaware of this etiquette of our Shaikh. The karāma taught them that and demonstrated to them that the Muslim must show reverence to the Qur'an not only internally, but externally as well, and not just to the text of the Book of Allah, but to the muṣḥaf itself as well.

Revering the magnificent Qur'an is characteristic of all of our Shaikhs. Shaikh ʿAbd al-Karīm al-Kasnazān loved humbling himself before Allah's Book by placing his head beneath the muṣḥaf, usually after the sunset prayer, and would remain like that for a long time in a state of remembrance and humility. During that, he would not speak or listen to anyone. Our present Shaikh relates that he would sometimes visit his father, Shaikh ʿAbd al-Karīm, for whatever reason, only to find him in this state. He would leave and tend to other matters, sometimes for an hour or more, before returning to see the Shaikh, yet he would find him still in that posture of reverence for the Qur'an.[57]

1.8 Ṭarīqa and Sharia

Our Shaikh stresses the intimately integrated relationship between the Ṭarīqa and the Sharia. The Sharia specialises in the rules of worship, worldly transactions, and aspects of life in general. A person cannot be Muslim without adhering to the Sharia. Islam is an entity whose foundation is the Sharia and whose structure is the Ṭarīqa; it is impossible for a building to stand without a foundation, and the importance of the foundation derives from the structure built upon it. One symbolic expression used by our Master to explain the complementary relationship between the Sharia and the Ṭarīqa, and that the two represent the two sides of Islam, is his description of Sharia as the framework and Ṭarīqa as the core or the essence, and Sharia as the body and Ṭarīqa as the soul. This is what he said to the seekers in an assembly:

> "The Sharia is the foundation of every Sufi Ṭarīqa. Any dervish, any seeker, any Shaikh, any religious scholar, or any caliph that contradicts the

[57] Shaikh Muḥammad al-Muḥammad al-Kasnazān, *sermon*, 24th/September/2016.

Muḥammadan Sharia, even by a hair's breadth, contravenes his Ṭarīqa".[58]

"We are all soldiers of the Messenger (PBUH), soldiers of the Sharia, as it is our foundation. Do not contradict the Sharia of the Messenger (PBUH). Do not let others tempt you about what is permitted. We have the Sunna of the Prophet, the Book and the Sunna. We have the principles of the Ṭarīqa. Whatever is permissible in the Ṭarīqa is permissible in the Sharia. The Shaikhs do not have deviations because they follow the way of the Messenger. If we make any mistake, if we have any defect, they inform us. Your Shaikhs are true Shaikhs, not like one who falsely claims that he is a Shaikh of Ṭarīqa; no, by Allah".[59]

"Indeed, the foundation of your Ṭarīqa is the Messenger's (PBUH) Sharia. Anyone who has a deficiency in the Sharia has a deficiency in the Ṭarīqa. The Sharia is a crown on the seeker's head. We are masters of implementing the Messenger's Sharia (PBUH). We are soldiers of the Messenger (PBUH). We are soldiers of the Messenger's Sharia (PBUH). The Sharia is the foundation of the Ṭarīqa, and without the Sharia, there is no Ṭarīqa. The core of the Sharia is the Ṭarīqa".[60]

It is possible to conceptualize the Sharia as the boundary of the path to Allah. Without those boundaries, a person would not be able to remain on that straight path. At the same time, these boundaries are not the objective of the path, nor its destination: Allah is the ultimate goal. The Sharia ensures that the travelling person remains on the path to Allah, while the Ṭarīqa helps him to walk on the path and to increase in nearness to Allah (exalted and high is He). Hence, we find the Shaikhs of the Ṭarīqa most abiding by the Sharia, as in this well-known incident about Shaikh ʿAbd al-Qādir al-Gaylānī, which has been related by many people, including the following account by Ibn Taymiyya (728/1328):

"I was once engaged in worship when I saw a tremendous throne whereupon there was a light. It said to me: 'O ʿAbd al-Qādir! I am your Lord. I have made permissible to you what I have made forbidden for others'. I said to it: 'Are you Allah other than whom there is no God? Go away, O enemy of Allah'! That light ruptured and turned into darkness and said: 'O ʿAbd al-Qādir, you have saved yourself from me by your religious understanding,

---

58 Shaikh Muḥammad al-Muḥammad al-Kasnazān, *sermon*, graduation ceremony of caliphs, 2005.

59 Shaikh Muḥammad al-Muḥammad al-Kasnazān, *sermon*, 14th/November/2008.

60 Shaikh Muḥammad al-Muḥammad al-Kasnazān, *sermon*, on the night of ʿArafa, updated.

your knowledge, and the spiritual battles you went through in your various spiritual states. I have tempted seventy men by this tale'".

When Shaikh ʿAbd al-Qādir al-Gaylānī was asked how he had recognized the devil, he answered that he had recognized him by his words "I have made permissible to you what I have made forbidden for others". He went on to comment: "I knew that Muḥammad's (PBUH) Sharia cannot be abrogated or changed. Also, [I knew it was him] since he said 'I am your Lord' and could not say 'I am Allah, the One God other than Me there is none".[61] The accounts of this incident differ in many details, but they all agree on the Shaikh's statement that he recognized the devil from his claim to make forbidden matters permissible.[62]

The Sharia and the Ṭarīqa are both based on the noble Qur'an and the honourable Prophetic Sunna. However, legal rulings of the Sharia come from the intellectual reasoning of the Sharia scholars in interpreting these two sources. The particularities of the Ṭarīqa, meanwhile, come from the reasoning of its Shaikhs, and this reasoning is based on spiritual unveilings. Hence, the sciences of the Sharia are intellectual and transferable, meaning it is possible to transmit them, learn them, and teach them by way of books. The sciences of the Ṭarīqa, on the other hand, are spiritual. They cannot be acquired except by way of worship, piety, and keeping the ṣuḥba of those who possess this knowledge. It is the knowledge that Allah (mighty and sublime is He) describes in his noble words: "Be pious, and Allah teaches you" (al-Baqara 272). By combining the Sharia and the Ṭarīqa, Islam joins the intellect and the heart; it joins the transferrable, intellectual forms of knowledge and spiritual unveilings.

As such, it is not surprising that we find that the Ṭarīqa embraces the Muslim, regardless of the school of legal doctrine that he subscribes to. The Ṭarīqa does not differentiate between a Sunni and a Shiite, or a Hanafi and a Shafi, or followers any other schools of legal doctrine. This is the case with the Ṭarīqa Kasnazāniyya. Shaikh Muḥammad al-Muḥammad embodies this matter by word and by deed. He does not call upon the seeker to leave a certain school and follow another. You also see him doing his best to meet, invite, and honour Muslim scholars from

---

[61] Ibn Taymiyya, *Majmūʿ Fatāwā*, I, p. 172.

[62] Al-Tādifī, *Qalāʾid al-Jawāhir*, pp. 20-21.

different schools of thought.

The Ṭarīqa is a complete spiritual method that addresses all aspects of a person's life. What we have presented in this chapter is only a very brief introduction. We will address these matters in much detail in the context of studying the biography of Shaikh Muḥammad al-Muḥammad. Readers who desire even greater detail and depth in the study of Sufism may read our Master's books, which are mentioned in some detail in §12.3, and from which we have borrowed some quotes.

Photo 3: Shaikh Muḥammad al-Muḥammad kissing a muṣḥaf in the takya in Amman, Jordan, on the day of celebrating the birth of Shaikh ʿAbd al-Qādir al-Gaylānī (20th/December/2018).

"The Ṭarīqa is enjoining what is good and forbidding what is evil. Our Ṭarīqa is the Qur'an. Our Ṭarīqa is the purified Sharia. Our Ṭarīqa is based on the words, deeds, and states of the respected Messenger (PBUH)".

Shaikh Muḥammad al-Muḥammad al-Kasnazān al-Ḥusaynī
(Sermon, 6th/August/2013)

2

The Ṭarīqa ʿAlīyya Qādiriyya Kasnazāniyya

Now that we have examined the Ṭarīqa in general in the previous chapter, we will focus here specifically on the Ṭarīqa of our Master, Shaikh Muḥammad al-Muḥammad al-Kasnazān, which is one of the largest Sufi Ṭarīqas in the world.

2.1 The Shortest Way to Allah

There are numerous ways to Allah, which is why it is said: "There are as many ways [to Allah] as the number of creatures". These paths share the same goal, but they differ in the speed at which they deliver the seeker to Allah. The shortness of any path depends on the spiritual power present in the chain of Shaikhs of that Ṭarīqa: the stronger the spiritual power of its Shaikhs, the shorter the path. The lofty spiritual ranks that are reached by many seekers of the Ṭarīqa ʿAlīyya Qādiriyya Kasnazāniyya, one manifestation of which is the karāmas that occur to and through them, serve as one proof that it is one of the shortest ways to reach Allah. This is a matter that one cannot comprehend except by travelling on the path of the Ṭarīqa, that is, by taking the pledge to have a spiritual bond with his Shaikh, the other Shaikhs of the Ṭarīqa, all the way to the Prophet (PBUH), by committing to the commandments of the Sharia, and by persisting in the dhikrs of the Ṭarīqa. Only then will the seeker experience for himself the blessings of the Ṭarīqa. This personal experience then confirms the verity of the wonders of the spiritual states of the people of Sufism that he has heard or read about. One sign of the unique spiritual power in the Ṭarīqa ʿAlīyya Qādiriyya Kasnazāniyya is the karāmas that show new seekers acquiring spiritual unveilings and extraordinary occurrences as soon as they take the pledge. These are three such events.

In 2012, the deputy of Shaikh Muḥammad al-Muḥammad in India, caliph 'Imād 'Abd al-Ṣamad, was preaching in a village in Tamil Nadu in India when some Hindus, both men and women, accepted Islam at his hand and took the pledge of the Ṭarīqa. When they were taking the oath of the Ṭarīqa, one of the women took to weeping. After the completion of the pledge, the woman explained why she had wept. She had seen a falcon above the caliph's head whose head would reach the sky when it raised it and would rest atop the caliph's head when it lowered it. The falcon symbolised Shaikh 'Abd al-Qādir al-Gaylānī, as one of his most famous titles is "*al-Bāz al-Āshhab* (the Grey Falcon)". Notably, the other people who were taking the pledge with her did not see what she saw. The woman was singularly honoured with this spiritual unveiling. This karāma demonstrates the woman's move from disbelief to Īmān, not merely to Islam. This female seeker became a very active guide and brought many Hindus to the Ṭarīqa, including her three sisters and their husbands. She even brought Muslims who had previously dismissed and denied Sufism, the spiritual side of Islam.

The second karāma occurred in one of the takyas in the city of Basra in 1980. Government security forces were harassing the dervishes, who would cautiously gather to perform the dhikr and disperse as soon as they saw a security car close to the takya. One day, one person had just finished taking the pledge in the takya when he asked the dervishes sitting with him in wonder: "Why didn't you build walls for the takya, at least as shelter from the cold and the rain"? Then, with greater confusion, he added: "How does this ceiling stand without walls to support it"? Of course, the walls were fully built and intact, but he became suddenly able to see the street the takya looked out on and what took place there, as if the walls did not exist. While the disciples were still trying to make sense of what he said, he went on to alert them to security cars coming into the area. Then they realized that this was a karāma that enabled him to see a danger that they were unaware of. They dispersed before the security guards would arrive and discover their gathering in the takya.

Let us conclude this group of karāmas with one that occurred during the time of Shaikh Ismā'īl al-Wilyānī (1081/1670-1158/1745), one of the Master of the Ṭarīqa Kasnazāniyya. One night, a shepherd walked into the Shaikh's takya in the north of Iraq, attracting the attention of a group of dervishes there by his bulky body and heavy, shabby clothing. When they asked about what wanted, he replied that he had come to take the pledge from the Shaikh. The shepherd looked like a simple man, so one dervish wanted to tease him. He told him that taking up the Ṭarīqa was not that simple and that it had conditions. When the man asked for further information, he told him that he had to sit in the takya's reservoir until dawn and that the Shaikh would give him the Ṭarīqa after he offered the dawn prayer. It was wintertime and it was very cold, but the man's determination to take the Ṭarīqa made him sit in the cold water which covered a large portion of his body. He remained like this until dawn time when Shaikh Ismāʿīl al-Wilyānī came out and made his way to the place where ablution was performed before the congregational prayer. The shepherd heard the Shaikh ask a dervish if it was the time for the prayer. The dervish replied that he was not sure, at which point the shepherd answered from his place that the time for the prayer had come. Having noticed the man sitting in the reservoir, the Shaikh asked him why he was there. The man introduced himself and explained that he had come to take the pledge. The Shaikh asked him again why he was sitting in the takya's reservoir in that severe cold. The man replied that some dervishes had told him that one condition of taking the pledge was to sit in the takya's reservoir until morning when the Shaikh would come and give him the pledge. Then the Shaikh asked him how he knew that the time for the dawn prayer had come. The man said that he had heard the call to prayer in heaven! The Shaikh gave him the pledge. Shaikh Muḥammad al-Muḥammad al-Kasnazān has commented on this karāma: "Because of his strong belief, firm faith, proper focus, willpower, and submission, that seeker reached [high spiritual levels] in a single night",[63] even before his intention to take the pledge was fulfilled.

The karāmas that testify to the lofty spiritual ranks that are attained by seekers of the Ṭarīqa ʿAlīyya Qādiriyya Kasnazāniyya are also innumerable. For example, an elderly man came to the main takya in Kirkuk, where Shaikh ʿAbd al-Karīm al-Kasnazān lived. The man stood at the takya's entrance and greeted the dervishes who returned his greetings and invited him in. The man was poor and had lost his wallet, which contained everything he possessed. He did not want to ask for money from anyone, so he came to the takya seeking the help of the

---

[63] Shaikh Muḥammad al-Muḥammad al-Kasnazān, *sermon*, 19th/February/2015.

Shaikh, who was known for his karāmas, in finding his wallet. The man had been travelling on public transport to Sulaymāniyya when he took out his wallet and paid the fare, then put it back in his pocket. When boarded the vehicle to travel from Sulaymāniyya to Kirkuk, he discovered he had lost his wallet. While the man was speaking with the dervishes, Shaikh ʿAbd al-Karīm came out to the place where he receives the dervishes on the takya's second floor. The dervishes went up to greet the Shaikh and attend his assembly, and this man followed them. After the dervishes greeted the Shaikh and sat down, the man stood at the room's entrance and greeted him. Shaikh ʿAbd al-Karīm returned his greeting with clear affection. The man told the Shaikh that he was poor and had lost his wallet and asked him to help him find it by his blessings. Shaikh ʿAbd al-Karīm answered in Kurdish, "banā bakhwā", which means "we entrust our affair to Allah". It was a response that the disciples knew, from experience, meaning that the Shaikh was responding positively to the request. The man sat with the rest of the seekers.

After Shaikh ʿAbd al-Karīm delivered a sermon and the singers sang songs of praise, the Shaikh went to offer the midday prayer. The disciples descended to the ground floor to pray and to have lunch. In the takya, there was a walī called "Kāka ʿAzīz" (may Allah have mercy on him). In Kurdish, "Kāka" means "big brother". After lunch, Kāka ʿAzīz asked caliph Yāsīn Sūfī, who was sitting next to him, not to move while he slept for a short while. He laid down and covered his whole body, including his head, with a quilt, and remained like this for less than two minutes. He then lifted the cover and sat up, before folding the quilt, placing it on the ground between his back and the wall, and reclining against it. He asked caliph Yāsīn to call the man who had lost his wallet. Kāka ʿAzīz placed his empty hand inside the quilt that was behind his back, he then took it out holding a wallet. He asked caliph Yāsīn, who was fluent in Arabic and Kurdish, to ask the Arab man to describe the wallet he had lost. The man replied that it was a leather wallet, and he mentioned the number of each kind of banknote, as well as the coins that he remembered, inside it. He also said that the wallet had a pocket that contained a small pebble and a small piece of cloth that he carried for blessings. Kāka ʿAzīz opened his hand and gave the wallet to caliph Yāsīn to check its contents. He found it to be exactly as the man had described and returned it to him. When Shaikh ʿAbd al-Karīm came out in the afternoon to receive the dervishes, caliph Yāsīn informed him that the old man had retrieved his wallet. The Shaikh commented that jinn dervishes brought the wallet to Kāka ʿAzīz. Some Muslim jinns are dervishes:

> "When we heard the guidance, we believed in it. Whoever believes in his Lord will not fear deprivation or burden. (13) Among us are Muslims [in submission to Allah], and among us are the unjust. Whoever has become Muslim — those have sought out the right course. (14) As for the unjust, they will be firewood for Hell. (15) [Allah revealed] that if they had remained straight on the way, We would have given them abundant provision". (Al-Jinn 13-16)

There are just some of the karāmas that demonstrate the amount of spiritual power of the Ṭarīqa ʿAlīyya Qādiriyya Kasnazāniyya. They are proofs that it is one of the shortest ways to reach Allah. The Shaikhs of this Ṭarīqa are the source of this immense spiritual power. Every Master of this Ṭarīqa was the greatest of the Shaikhs of his time, our present Shaikh emphasizes. The name of the Ṭarīqa comes from three of the biggest luminaries of Sufism: Imām ʿAlī Ibn Abī Ṭālib (may Allah ennoble his face), Shaikh ʿAbd al-Qādir al-Gaylānī (may Allah sanctify his innermost being), and Shaikh ʿAbd al-Karīm Shāh al-Kasnazān (may Allah sanctify his innermost being). Imām ʿAlī is the Prophet's (PBUH) spiritual heir, and Sufi Ṭarīqas trace their spiritual lineage back to him. Shaikh ʿAbd al-Qādir al-Gaylānī and Shaikh ʿAbd al-Karīm Shāh al-Kasnazān were both revivers of religion. Thus, the Ṭarīqa carries their noble names. The rest of this chapter is an overview of these three luminaries of the Ṭarīqa, followed by an introduction to the three Shaikhs of Kasnazān who followed Shāh al-Kasnazān as the Masters of Ṭarīqa. The rest of the book will focus on our present Master and the fifth Shaikh of the Ṭarīqa Kasnazāniyya, Shaikh Muḥammad al-Muḥammad. There will be abundant digressions in different places in the book that reference the karāmas, words, and spiritual states of these Shaikhs.

2.2 Imām ʿAlī Ibn Abī Ṭālib

Imām ʿAlī was born 23 years before the migration of the Prophet (PBUH) (599 CE). When he was still a little boy, the Quraysh tribe was struck with famine. Muḥammad (PBUH) offered to raise ʿAlī to ease the burden of his uncle, Abū Ṭālib. From his childhood, ʿAlī was brought up with a unique upbringing under Muḥammad's (PBUH) care. After the revelation of the great Qur'an, many people were honoured by the company of the Messenger (PBUH). They were sincere with him and Allah blessed them with His favours, but Imām ʿAlī remained in that special standing with the Messenger (PBUH).

Imām ʿAlī was the first to accept Islam and the first to pray with the Prophet (PBUH). When the Trustworthy Prophet (PBUH) migrated, he left him behind to return the deposits that people had given to him as trusts. One sign of Imām ʿAlī's love for his Master and his willingness to sacrifice anything for his sake is that he laid in his bed the night of his migration from Mecca to Medina when the enemies of the Muslims from the Quraysh tried to kill him. After the migration, when the Messenger (PBUH) established brotherhood between the migrators from Mecca and the helpers from Medina, declaring every emigrant man from Mecca a brother to a supporter in Medina, he chose ʿAlī as his brother. He put his hand on his shoulder and told him: "You are my brother. You inherit me and I inherit you". The inheritance of the Prophet (PBUH) is unlike that of others. His bequest is knowledge, manners, and blessing. ʿAlī was the standard-bearer of the Messenger (PBUH) in every battle.

This is one example of how Imām ʿAlī described his unique status with the Messenger of Allah (PBUH):

> "You all know of my status with the Messenger of Allah (PBUH), of close kinship and special standing. He took me under his care when I was only a child. He used to press me to his chest and put me beside him on his bed, bringing his body close to mine and letting me smell his fragrance. He used to chew on something, then feed it to me. He found no lie in my speech, nor error in my deed…I used to follow him the way a young camel follows the footprints of its mother. Every day, he would show me one aspect of his manners, commanding me to follow its example. Every year, he used to go into seclusion in Ḥirā', where I saw him but no one else did. In those days, when there was only one house in which Islam existed, it was inhabited only by the Messenger of Allah (PBUH) and Khadīja, and I being the third of these two. I used to see the light of revelation and the divine message and smell the scent of Prophethood.
>
> I heard Satan's moan when the revelation descended on him (PBUH). I said, 'O Messenger of Allah, what is this moaning?' He said, 'This is Satan. He has despaired of being worshipped. You hear what I hear, and you see what I

see, except that you are not a prophet. But you are a vizier and you are surely on a good path".[64]

As Imām 'Alī was brought up under the care of the Prophet (PBUH), studied under his tutelage, and was the closest person to him in his life, he was also the last person to bid him farewell in this world. He rose to wash, enshroud, and bury his noble body. Imām 'Alī was the closest person to his Master (PBUH), physically and spiritually, in body and in soul.

The Messenger's choice (PBUH) to adopt 'Alī as a foster child and a close Companion for the duration of his life was not simply a coincidence. Rather, he chose him by way of insight and knowledge, fulfilling a divine order. Allah chose 'Alī to be the Messenger's (PBUH) spiritual caliph, and to be the spouse of his (PBUH) daughter, Fāṭima al-Zahrā`, to endow their progeny with the spiritual succession and the light of the Prophet (PBUH): "Allah intends to remove from you the impurity [of sin], O people of the [Prophet's] household, and to purify you with [extensive] purification" (al-Āḥzāb 33). In a famous incident, the Messenger (PBUH) gathered 'Alī and Fāṭima sat their two sons, Ḥasan and Ḥusayn, on his lap, and wrapped a garment around all of them. He then recited this verse, which is known as the "verse of purification", and described them as the people of his household.[65] This blessed lineage is the second of the two things that Allah granted Muḥammad (PBUH) to guide people, the first of which is the noble Qur'an:

> "Indeed, I am leaving among you that which, if you hold fast to, you shall not go astray after me. One of them is greater than the other: Allah's Book, which is a rope extending from the sky to the earth, and my family, the people of my household. They shall not split until they meet me at the basin, so look after how you deal with them after me".[66]

It is not surprising, then, that we find that the Messenger (PBUH) has described Imām 'Alī in many of his noble ḥadīths with unique descriptions that illustrate his special status as his spiritual successor. Imām 'Alī is the door to the city of prophetic spiritual knowledge: "I am the city

---

[64] Imām 'Alī Ibn Abī Ṭālib, *Nahj al-Balāgha*, pp. 469-470.

[65] Aḥmad, *Musnad al-Imām Aḥmad Ibn Ḥanbal*, XLIV, no. 26550, p. 173-174; Muslim, *Ṣaḥīḥ Muslim*, IV, no. 2424, p. 1883.

[66] Tirmidhī, *Al-Jāmi' al-Kabīr*, VI, no. 3788, p. 125.

of knowledge and ʿAlī is its door, so whoever wants knowledge, let him enter through its door".[67] The Prophet (PBUH) likened his status with ʿAlī to the status of Aaron, vizier to the prophet Moses: "Are you not pleased that you are to me as Aaron was to Moses"?[68] While returning from the farewell pilgrimage, that is about three months before his passing to the spirit world, when the Muslims reached Ghadīr Khumm, the Prophet (PBUH) announced that the guardianship of the Muslims was Imām ʿAlī's. He instructed that Imām ʿAlī must be obeyed, and he said that being loyal to ʿAlī derives from being loyal to him (PBUH). He prayed to Allah to ally with those who supported him and to wage war on those who opposed him: "O Allah! Whoever I have been a Master to, then ʿAlī is his Master. O Allah! Befriend those who befriend him, and be enemy to those who take him for an enemy; support those who support him, and forsake those who forsake him".[69]

Our Shaikh relates that when he was in Istanbul, early in the year 2000, he once heard minutes before the call to the dawn prayer, while awake, a deep voice from the sky slowly repeating this phrase three times: "Muḥammad is a light whose door is ʿAlī".[70] The voice was so loud and clear that it seemed to be heard in all parts of the city.

With the exception of the Naqshbandiyya Ṭarīqa, which traces its spiritual lineage to the Companion Abū Bakr al-Ṣiddīq, all Ṭarīqas of Sufism, which represents the spiritual side of Islam, trace their spiritual lineage back to Imām ʿAlī. He is the inheritor of the Prophet's (PBUH) spiritual sciences, and he was the one whom he chose to be his spiritual caliph, and then the purified people of his household after him.

2.3 Shaikh ʿAbd al-Qādir al-Gaylānī

This great Shaikh is the origin of the Ṭarīqa Qādiriyya in all its branches. Shaikh ʿAbd al-Qādir was born in 470 Hijri (1077 AD) to a father who traced his lineage back to Imām Ḥasan and a mother who descended from Imām Ḥusayn. Most older sources about his life state that his hometown

---

[67] Al-Ṭabarānī, *al-Muʿjam al-Kabīr*, XI, no. 11061, p. 66.

[68] Bukhārī, *Al-Jāmiʿ al-Ṣaḥīḥ*, II, no. 3580, p. 358.

[69] Aḥmad, *Musnad al-Imām Aḥmad Ibn Ḥanbal*, 1, no. 950, p. 262; no. 951, p. 263.

[70] Shaikh Muḥammad al-Muḥammad al-Kasnazān, *sermon*, 4th/March/2013.

was Gaylān in the north of modern-day Iran.[71] Some sources relate him to the village of al-Jīl on the shore of the Tigris near Madā'in.[72] Therefore, he is known by the title of "al-Gaylānī", "al-Jīlānī", or "al-Jīlī". The view that links him to Gaylān is supported by the claim that his mother tongue was Farsi, although he perfectly mastered Arabic by a miracle of the Messenger (PBUH).[73]

Shaikh ʿAbd al-Qādir migrated to Baghdad when he was 18 years old to complete his education and embark on a journey that was destined to be a unique spiritual journey. Baghdad was the capital of the Abbasid Caliphate and, more importantly, it was a major centre of knowledge and culture, teeming with various spiritual and intellectual activities. This time was also a period of political disturbances, with the Crusaders in Palestine, Syria, and Turkey, and Baghdad at the mercy of the Seljuk Sultans, whom the Abbasids sought the help of against regional threats.

In Baghdad, Shaikh ʿAbd al-Qādir first accompanied Shaikh Ḥammād ad-Dabbās (525/1131). He later accompanied Shaikh Abū Sa"īd al-Makhzūmī (al-Mukharramī) (513/1119) and took the pledge of the Ṭarīqa from him. Shaikh Abū Saʿīd had a school wherein he used to teach. Shaikh ʿAbd al-Qādir was put in charge of the school in 521/1127, becoming its sole teacher. He enlarged the school seven years later, so it became known after him. He would lecture three days out of the week. The number of those who attended his gatherings quickly increased until each sermon attracted thousands. He continued to teach in the school until he departed to the spirit world in 561/1165, and he was buried in his school. Due to the spiritual status of the Shaikh, his continued blessings, and his tremendous following, his tomb, and accordingly his school, has become one of the most sacred and highly visited Islamic landmarks.

Many students used to record Shaikh ʿAbd al-Qādir's sermons in writing, preserving his words for all time. Some of these discourses were compiled in three books, *Futūḥ al-Ghayb* (Revelations of the Unseen), *al-Fatḥ al-Rabbānī* (the Divine Revelation), and *Jilāʾ al-Khāṭir* (Purification

---

[71] Ibn Rajab, *al-dhayl ʿalā Ṭabaqāt al-Ḥanābila*, II, p. 189; al-Dhahabī, *Siyar Aʿlām al-Nubalā'*, XX, p. 439; Al-ʿUlaymī, *al-Manhaj al-Aḥmad fī-Tarājim Aṣḥāb al-Imām Aḥmad*, III, p. 216.

[72] Al-Shaṭnūfī, *Bahjat al-Asrār wa-Maʿdan al-Ānwār*, p. 115.

[73] Al-Tādifī, *Qalā'id al-Jawāhir*, p. 13.

of the Mind). The latter was edited and published by Shaikh Muḥammad al-Muḥammad al-Kasnazān in Baghdad in 1989. In addition to his discourses that were compiled by those who attended them, Shaikh ʿAbd al-Qādir penned other books, the most famous of which is *al-Ghunya li-Ṭālibi al-Ḥaqq* (Provisions for the Seeker of the True One), as well as poems, wirds, prayers, and supplications. There are other works that scholars have disagreed on their attribution to him.[74]

One thing that reflects Shaikh ʿAbd al-Qādir's spiritual status and the nearness to Allah that he has reached is his numerous karāmas. There has never been anyone in the history of Sufism who has had as many karāmas attributed to him as Shaikh ʿAbd al-Qādir. Karāmas were one means by which he called non-Muslims to Islam and guided Muslims and urged them to adhere to their religion. We will cite two karāmas that explain two of his more famous titles: "Muḥay al-Dīn" (Reviver of Religion) and "Sultan al-Āwliyāʾ" (Sultan of Walīs).

Shaikh ʿAbd al-Qādir recounts that when he returned to Baghdad from one of his spiritual journeys in 511/1117, when he was forty years old, he met a thin, sallow, sickly person laying on the ground who greeted him: "Peace be upon you, O ʿAbd al-Qādir". He returned the greeting. The ailing man requested that the Shaikh approach him, so he did. Then he asked him to help him sit up, so he sat him up. The sick man's body began to expand, improve in condition, and claim back its normal colour. Shaikh ʿAbd al-Qādir grew fearful. The man asked him if he recognised him, to which the Shaikh replied in the negative. The man went on to say: "I am religion. I was dead and buried but Allah resurrected me by you". After leaving the man, Shaikh ʿAbd al-Qādir went to a mosque where he met a man who helped him put his sandals on and addressed him: "O my Master, Reviver of Religion!". When the Shaikh went to pray, those who were praying took to kissing his hand and calling him by the title of "Reviver of Religion". He had never been called by this title before.[75]

The source of the title of "Sultan of Walīs" is that he was one day ordered to say "this foot of mine is on the neck of every walī of Allah". Every walī in every part of the world bowed, stretching their necks.

---

74 Zaydān, *ʿAbd al-Qādir al-Jīlānī*, pp. 89-104.
75 Al-Tādifī, *Qalāʾid al-Jawāhir*, p. 57.

These include Shaikh Abū Madyan al-Maghribī, Shaikh Abū Najīb al-Suhrawardī, Shaikh 'Abd al-Raḥīm al-Qināwī, Shaikh 'Alī Ibn al-Hītī, Shaikh Abū Sa'īd al-Qīlawī, Shaikh Baqā Ibn Baṭṭū, and others. Shaikh Aḥmad al-Rifā'ī, for example, was in his assembly in the village Umm 'Ubayda, southeast of the city of Wasiṭ in present-day Iraq, when he suddenly bowed his head and said: "And on my neck". When he was asked about this, he replied: "Just now in Baghdad, Shaikh 'Abd al-Qādir said 'this foot of mine is on the neck of every walī of Allah'".[76] Shaikh Muḥammad al-Muḥammad al-Kasnazān comments on this unique karāma: "The foot of Shaikh 'Abd al-Qādir is on the neck of every walī until the Day of Resurrection. There will not be anyone greater than him after him".[77] He is the sultan of the walīs of his time and the times that follow. Since the Shaikhs of the Ṭarīqa Kasnazāniyya are inheritors to Shaikh 'Abd al-Qādir al-Gaylānī, they are all referred to with the title of "Sultan", in addition to the title of "Shaikh", as each of them is the sultan of the walīs of his time. For example, Shaikh Ḥusayn al-Kasnazān is also referred to as "Sultan Ḥusayn al-Kasnazān", and so on.

It is impossible to exaggerate the role of Shaikh 'Abd al-Qādir in guiding Muslims and propagating Islam. The number of Sufi Ṭarīqas whose chains of Shaikhs connect to him largely exceeds the Ṭarīqas that connect to any other Shaikh. Accordingly, the number of followers of the Ṭarīqa Qādiriyya exceeds the number of followers of any other Ṭarīqa. Sufis in general, and Qādirīs in particular, have played an exceptionally immense role in spreading Islam throughout Africa and Asia.

Although every Sufi Ṭarīqa has a chain of Shaikhs that connects to the Master of all Sufi Ṭarīqas, the Prophet Muḥammad (PBUH), a tradition developed to name each Ṭarīqa after one, or at times more, of its greatest Masters. We believe that this tradition began with the name of Shaikh 'Abd al-Qādir, which is another proof of his tremendous status and being greater in worth that all walīs after him. The name "Ṭarīqa Qādiriyya" was the first of its kind. Other Ṭarīqas then adopted this method of naming. "Ṭarīqa Rifā'iyya", for example, is named after Shaikh Aḥmad

[76] Al-Yāfi'ī, *Khulāṣat al-Mafākhir fī-Manāqib al-Shaikh 'Abd al-Qādir*, pp. 35-37; al-Tādifī, *Qalā'id al-Jawāhir*, p. 25.

[77] Shaikh Muḥammad al-Muḥammad al-Kasnazān, *sermon*, 8th/May/2000.

al-Rifā'ī, Ṭarīqa Shādhiliyya after Shaikh Abū al-Ḥasan al-Shādhilī and Ṭarīqa Dusūqiyya after Shaikh Ibrāhīm al-Dusūqī. The names of all Ṭarīqas imitate the name of "Ṭarīqa Qādiriyya". Even when a Ṭarīqa is named after a Master who lived before the time of Shaikh 'Abd al-Qādir, research shows that this naming appeared after the naming of "Ṭarīqa Qādiriyya". "Ṭarīqa Junaydiyya", for example, takes its name from Shaikh al-Junayd al-Baghdādī, who lived about 250 years before Shaikh 'Abd al-Qādir. But this naming did not exist during the time of Shaikh al-Junayd and appeared only sometime after the appearance and prevalence of the name "Ṭarīqa Qādiriyya".

Similarly, were believe that the disciples of Shaikh 'Abd al-Qādir were the first seekers to be named after the Shaikh of their Ṭarīqa. Thus, the dervishes of Shaikh 'Abd al-Qādir became known as "Qādirī". In fact, it was Shaikh 'Abd al-Qādir who introduced this naming tradition, as a verse of his poem "al-Sharīfa" reveals:

> Be a sincere Qādirī all the time, sincere to Allah
> You will live happy and truthful in my love.[78]

Some people also adopted the title of "Qādirī" like a surname. Students of other Shaikhs followed this originally Qādiri tradition, so the disciples of other Ṭarīqas became known by titles such as "Rifā'ī", "Shādhilī" and "Badawī". We should emphasize again that the concept of Ṭarīqa and the need to follow a spiritual guide are as old as Islam itself, even if the practice of naming Ṭarīqas did not appear until the era of the Sultan of Walīs, Shaikh 'Abd al-Qādir al-Gaylānī.

We believe that this is also the history of the title of "Sultan of Walīs". It first appeared when people used it to refer to Shaikh 'Abd al-Qādir, as a result of his unique and famous declaration, "this foot of mine is on the neck of every walī of Allah", and all the walīs bowing their necks to him. Shaikh 'Alī Ibn al-Hītī, one of the many contemporary Shaikhs of Shaikh 'Abd al-Qādir who visited and served him, used to order his Companions to perform ablution and purify their hearts and thoughts when they would go to visit him because they were entering into the presence of "The Sultan".[79] Later, followers of other Shaikhs used "Sultan of Walīs"

---

[78] Shaikh 'Abd al-Qādir al-Gaylānī, *Dīwān 'Abd al-Qādir Al-Jīlānī*, p. 117.
[79] Zaydān, *'Abd al-Qādir al-Jīlānī*, p. 65.

as a title for their Shaikhs.

One title that is unique to Shaikh ʿAbd al-Qādir and was never used for anyone else is "al-Ghawth al-Āʿẓam", or "The Greatest Reliever". This title is found in the introduction to a treatise of his that lists spiritual imports from Allah. In it, he is repeatedly called by the title "Ya Ghawth al-Āʿẓam", hence the treatise is known as "al-Ghawthiyya".[80] It seems that the title of "Ghawth" also entered the language of Sufism after it became a title of Shaikh ʿAbd al-Qādir. It refers to a spiritual status that enables a walī to aid people in miraculous ways. But the title of "al-Ghawth al-Āʿẓam" remained unique to Shaikh ʿAbd al-Qādir.

The unique position of Shaikh ʿAbd al-Qādir in the history of Islam is not only due to his efforts to guide people and his karāmas throughout his life. But it is also the result of the continuation of his guidance and his karāmas to this day. The Shaikhs of the branches of the Ṭarīqa Qādiriyya followed in the footsteps of Shaikh ʿAbd al-Qādir in dedicating their lives to spread Islam. The karāmas of Qādirī Ṭarīqas throughout history are a continuation of the blessings of its Master, Shaikh ʿAbd al-Qādir, which in turn, are an extension of the miracles of the Prophet of Islam, Muḥammad (PBUH). The exceptional karāmas of the Ṭarīqa Kasnazāniyya, some of which are mentioned in this book, are living proof of the continuous blessing of al-Ghawth al-Āʿẓam.

2.4 Shaikh ʿAbd al-Karīm Shāh al-Kasnazān

The Ṭarīqa Qādiriyya reached Iraqi Kurdistan at the hand of Shaikh Ismāʿīl al-Wilyānī at the end of the 17th or beginning of the 18th century. Shaikh al-Wilyānī had taken the pledge of two Ṭarīqas, the Nūr Bakshiyya and the ʿAlawiyya, from his father, the great walī Muḥammad al-Nūdīhī. He liked to worship in seclusion, so he would spend most of his time worshipping far away from people until he received a command to start acting as a guide, which led him to Baghdad. There, he met Shaikh Aḥmad al-Iḥsāʾī and took the pledge of the Ṭarīqa Qādiriyya at his hand. He remained in his company for forty days before returning to Kurdistan, where he lived in the village of Qāzān Qāya before settling in the village of Wilyān. He was the first to introduce the Ṭarīqa Qādiriyya

[80] Shaikh ʿAbd al-Qādir al-Gaylānī, *Dīwān ʿAbd al-Qādir Al-Jīlānī*, pp. 203-230.

to northern Iraq.[81] Shaikh Ismā'īl al-Wilyānī is the third great grandfather of Shaikh 'Abd al-Karīm Shāh al-Kasnazān, the third of the luminaries of Sufism after whom the Ṭarīqa 'Alīyya Qādiriyya Kasnazāniyya is named.

This Ṭarīqa took the name of this venerable Shaikh because he was a reviver of religion. When his father Ḥusayn was a small child, his father, Shaikh Ḥasan, took him to visit a cousin of his, also named Ḥusayn, in Qāzān Qāya. The night the visitors stayed in the house of their relative, a daughter was born to Shaikh Ḥusayn. The latter addressed the child: "O Ḥusayn. If you stay here, I will give this newborn as a wife to you when you grow up. Your marriage will bear a son who will be a reviver of religion". Clearly, Shaikh Ḥusayn had a divine insight that enabled him to see this major future occurrence. When Shaikh Ḥasan heard his cousin's words, he ordered his son to kiss Shaikh Ḥusayn's hand and to tell him that he has accepted the gift. When the young girl grew up, Shaikh Ḥusayn married her. They had a child named 'Abd al-Karīm, who would later become Shaikh 'Abd al-Karīm Shāh al-Kasnazān. His father, Shaikh Ḥusayn, was also a righteous person. One of his karāmas was that people used to smell a distinctly pleasant scent in a place, sometimes for more than two days, after he had passed by it. He was known by the Kurdish title "būn khūsh", which means "the one who has a fragrant scent".

Similar to how the good tidings of the birth of the reviver of religion 'Abd al-Karīm came many years before he was born, karāmas followed that indicated the status he would achieve. Ma'rūf Kusta'ī, one of Shaikh Ismā'īl al-Wilyānī's children, was one of the people who prophesied Shaikh 'Abd al-Karīm's role in serving Islam. Shaikh Ma'rūf lived in northern Iraq in a village between the Chamchamāl province and the village of Karbchna, which is where Shaikh 'Abd al-Karīm was destined to live in the future. He had a takya there, and his shrine is there. He lived for about 130 years, and he did not leave any offspring. One day, when Shaikh 'Abd al-Karīm was a small child, he came with his parents to that area. When Shaikh Ma'rūf came to know of the arrival of his brother's grandson, he decided to go out to meet him. People tried to discourage him from doing this because of his old age, and because the custom was

[81] Al-Qāḍī, *Sirāj al-Sālikīn*, mentioned in Zakī, *Tārīkh al-Sulaymāniyya*, p. 217. See also Bruinessen, "The Qadiriyya and the lineages of Qadiri shaykhs in Kurdistan".

for the young to visit the elderly. They said that Shaikh Ḥusayn was supposed to visit his grandfather's brother. Yet, Shaikh Maʿrūf surprised them by replying: "I am not going out to welcome Ḥusayn, but the child that is with him. You do not know, but this child will become a reviver of religion. I am going to welcome ʿAbd al-Karīm". When Shaikh Maʿrūf reached the child's parents, they placed ʿAbd al-Karīm in his lap. Later, the place where Shaikh Maʿrūf carried the young ʿAbd al-Karīm, the future reviver of religion, became a site that people visited for blessings, and it still exists to this day.

Shaikh ʿAbd al-Karīm was born in 1240 H. (1824 CE) in the village of Do Pālān, which would later be known as "Kasnazān", named after him. It is a village of Qaradāgh in the suburbs of the Sulaymāniyya governorate in northern Iraq. Since his youth, he had turned himself away from the world, busy with the remembrance of his Lord. He would love to seclude himself in the mountains because that isolation with his Lord would facilitate the opportunity to meditate on His creation. His taking the pledge of the Ṭarīqa was a karāma that was one of the many indications of the lofty spiritual status Allah had written for him.

Shaikh ʿAbd al-Karīm went to the takya of his maternal uncle, the Master of the Ṭarīqa Qādiriyya of his time, Shaikh ʿAbd al-Qādir Qāzān Qāya. He was standing with a group of youths, observing the circle of dhikr, when he saw a hand reach out from the circle of dhikr and slap him on his cheek, causing him to faint. When he regained consciousness, he found his hand in the hand of Shaikh ʿAbd al-Qādir Qāzān Qāya, who was giving him the pledge of the Ṭarīqa. He reassured him of what had happened: "O my son! Do not fear what has taken place. The hand that you saw come out of the circle of dhikr was the hand of your grandfather Shaikh Ismāʿīl al-Wilyānī". This had not been a normal loss of consciousness, but rather it was what is known in the terminology of Ṭarīqa as "ḥāl". Let us pause for a moment to explain this concept, which will we come across many times throughout this book.

"Ḥāl" refers to various spiritual states that transcend the world of appearances that Allah bestows upon some of his servants. This is done through the Messenger (PBUH), who passes them down to the present Shaikh of the Ṭarīqa, who grants them to whichever seeker he wants. The ḥāl is not earned by the dervish, but rather, it is a grant from the Shaikh. Ḥāl is a spiritual power that takes different forms. It may last momentarily, such as an incident, feeling, or experience that happens to the dervish, or be a continuous matter. Some ḥāls are particular spiritual powers that the Shaikh gives the disciple according to the needs of the Ṭarīqa. In this case, the people of ḥāl would have certain roles in the Ṭarīqa. The effects of ḥāl sometimes appear in the form of karāmas that occur at the hand of those who have it. Such ḥāls are ranks gifted by the Shaikh to the seekers. Just as the Shaikh is the one who grants a seeker any particular ḥāl, he may change it to another ḥāl, the same way he may also deprive the seeker of the ḥāl if he no longer qualifies for that responsibility.

Shaikh 'Abd al-Qādir Qāzān Qāya then sent his nephew on a hunting expedition in the mountains. Shaikh 'Abd al-Karīm enjoyed hunting very much, to the extent that when he attended that circle of dhikr he was carrying a hunting rifle. The truth behind the Shaikh's order to his new disciple began to become clear when Shaikh 'Abd al-Karīm saw a gazelle on the mountain and moved towards it, intending to shoot it with his gun. He noticed that his approach did not make the gazelle move at all, so he became apprehensive and stopped. The gazelle turned and approached him, and spoke to him in the tongue of ḥāl: "Do not kill me. You have not been created to hunt". Then it left.

When he returned home, Shaikh 'Abd al-Karīm did not tell anyone about what happened. He feared that people would not believe him and make accusations against him, in addition to the fact that he did not understand what had happened to him. When he returned to the assembly of Shaikh 'Abd al-Qādir Qāzān Qāya, one of the disciples with ḥāl approached him and whispered in his ear: "It is your turn. Your time has come." These words reassured him. Then Shaikh 'Abd al-Qādir turned to him, smiling as he mentioned the incident with the gazelle and told him: "Follow this sign, my son". He sent him for seclusion in the mountains. Shaikh 'Abd al-Qādir's first order to Shaikh 'Abd al-Karīm to go the mountains was to teach him that he had not been created to hunt or any other worldly purposes, while his second order revealed to him that Allah (mighty and sublime is He) intended for him that he dedicate himself for worship.

Shaikh 'Abd al-Karīm went for a retreat on Mount Sagarma, which on one side overlooks the Qaradāgh province, and on the other side overlooks the Sangāw region, wherein lies the village of Karbchna, which he would later found and live in. The mountain was located on the then caravan route linking Baghdad, Sulaymāniyya, and Tabriz. The mountain's altitude is around 5,000 feet, and the hike from its base to its summit takes around an hour for those who are accustomed to climbing up mountains and more than twice that for others. It was over 20 kilometres away from the village where Shaikh ʿAbd al-Karīm lived, or about a four-hour walk. At that time, there were no villages in the surrounding area for several kilometres, as the area from Sangāw to Karbchna was uninhabited forests. The original name of the mountain was Sargarma, which means "hot head", before it became "Sagarma" over time. Shaikh Muḥammad al-Muḥammad has suggested that the depression in the mountain was most likely a volcanic opening in the past. It seems that at one time, the volcanic activity threw stones from the summit that fell on the side of Qaradāgh, as there is a rift, almost like a valley, on the Karbchnah side.

Shaikh ʿAbd al-Karīm's seclusion took place in a stone depression located under the highest peak of Sagarma called "Malās". The depression is known by the Kurdish name "Gaylān Āwā", which means the "Gaylāni Shelter", because it is believed that Shaikh ʿAbd al-Qādir al-Gaylānī went into seclusion there at some point during the twenty-five years that he spent in worship and continuous spiritual training in northern Iraq. The Gaylān Āwā depression was known to the locals, but it became more popular after Shaikh ʿAbd al-Karīm's return from his seclusion. The Gaylān Āwā depression is between two to two-and-a-half meters below the mountain's summit. It is around one-hundred meters long and fifty meters wide. Inside it, there is a cave and a small cold-water spring in solid stone. The spring was sufficient for the Shaikh's drinking and ablution. It should be noted that other sources of water on that mountain are a few hours' walk away.

There was no food, but just trees (mostly oak), stones, and clay. The place itself was terrifying, and there were many deadly wild animals in the area, such as bears, leopards, wolves, and boars. It is impossible to know of the existence of such a cave on the summit of a towering mountain such as Sagarma without climbing it, not to mention the difficulty of reaching it due to its rugged paths, as the area was completely cut off from people. The location of the cave is isolated from any residential area or commuter road, even today, despite its present renown and an abundance of modes of transportation, as well as the disappearance of many natural impediments, such as the forests that formed the surrounding areas in the past. It is evident that Shaikh 'Abd al-Qādir's having gone to that cave was by divine guidance, rather than the result of his search for a suitable place for seclusion. Similarly, Shaikh 'Abd al-Karīm's going to the same cave was by a command from Allah.

This is similar to Muḥammad's (PBUH) choosing of the Cave of Ḥirā` on Mount Nūr as the exclusive place for his seclusions. There are many caves and high hills and mountains in that area that could have accommodated the Messenger of Allah (PBUH). His choosing of the Cave of Ḥirā` looks even more strange due to the impossibility of knowing about its existence on the mountain's peak before climbing up to it. Indeed, a person who does not know it existed may fail to find it even when they are a few metres away from the mountain's summit! It is impossible to see it before reaching it, as getting there requires circling and hiking on a narrow road. Evidently, it was Allah (mighty and sublime is He) who guided Muḥammad (PBUH) to the Cave of Ḥirā`. Similarly, Shaikh 'Abd al-Karīm could find shelter in a mountain closer to his village and easier to get to than Sagarma, but many of the actions of the prophets and the walīs are guided, either expressly or subtly, by Allah.

Shaikh 'Abd al-Karīm remained cut off from everyone during his seclusion. Despite his family's efforts, they could not find him. His disappearance is why he became known during his absence by the Kurdish title "Kasnazān", which means "no one knows", as no one knew his fate. When someone would inquire as to what happened to him, the reply would be "Kasnazān". As for the Sufi explanation of this title, we find it in the words of the Shaikh later in his life: "Allah has granted me a network of secrets that no one knows of, save Allah and his Prophet (PBUH)". These secrets that no one knows of are the explanation of the unique title "Kasnazān".

The Shaikh's family despaired of finding him and lost all hope of his return. They concluded that wild animals had devoured him, so they did the funeral ceremonies for him. Shaikh 'Abd al-Karīm remained in consecutive seclusions for two years, during which he practised different spiritual exercises to purify his soul, elevate it, and bring it closer to its Creator. During this time, the Almighty Maker gifted him divine unveilings and bestowed the highest spiritual ranks upon him.

Then it was time for the Shaikh to return to people, to be a light that guides them to the way of his grandfather, the Messenger of Allah (PBUH). One day in the spring, his mother was offering her eldest son ʿAlī a plate of dolma that she had prepared when she took to weeping. When her son asked her why she was weeping, she told him that ʿAbd al-Karīm loved grape leaf dolma. Shaikh ʿAlī remembered his brother and also took to weeping and was unable to eat the food. That night, Shaikh ʿAbd al-Karīm appeared to his brother in his sleep and informed him that he was in seclusion in Gaylān Āwā. The dream woke Shaikh ʿAlī, but he thought that he had searched for his brother in that place several times and had not found him. He did not take the dream seriously and went back to sleep. Shaikh ʿAbd al-Karīm visited him a second time in his sleep and requested that he come to that cave, but he ignored what he saw a second time and went back to sleep. When the dream repeated itself a third time, he did not go back to sleep and decided to go to the place that his brother mentioned. He informed his mother of the three dreams, picked up a gun, and went in search of his brother.

When Shaikh ʿAlī arrived at the depression on the mountain's peak, he did not find his brother. He repeated the search, but to no avail. He decided to climb to the summit overlooking the depression. Then, he saw his brother standing inside Shaikh ʿAbd al-Qādir's place of seclusion, laughing. When Shaikh ʿAlī saw his brother, he unconsciously threw himself from that height, but he felt as if he was flying until he landed in front of the entrance to the place of seclusion. Shaikh ʿAlī embraced his brother and asked him about his two-year disappearance. The lengthy seclusion had left Shaikh ʿAbd al-Karīm thickly bearded, with long hair, and worn-out clothing. It is worth noting that the temperature in the cave during the winter falls far below zero; the cave is cold even in the summer. When Shaikh ʿAbd al-Karīm went for his seclusion, he did not take any provision or additional clothing with him. He only took his sword.

Shaikh Muḥammad al-Muḥammad al-Kasnazān explains that in Ṭarīqa, the sword has nothing to do with its function of the past as a combat weapon. It is a symbol that especially refers to "Dhu al-Fiqār", the sword that the Messenger (PBUH) gave to Imām ʿAlī, which in turn symbolizes Imām ʿAlī's spiritual deputyship of the Messenger (PBUH). Likewise, it symbolises the fight and strife against the self until death.

When one carries a sword, he must follow the Messenger (PBUH), then Imām 'Alī Ibn Abī Ṭālib, then the Shaikhs of the Ṭarīqa.[82] The sword is also used in seclusion to expel evil spirits, as we will see in Chapter 16, which deals specifically with seclusion.

Shaikh 'Alī wanted to take his brother back to his family, but Shaikh 'Abd al-Karīm told him that he still had one night left in his seclusion. He asked him to spend that night with him so that the two of them could return together the following morning. At the time of breaking his fast, Shaikh 'Abd al-Karīm gave his brother a piece of what looked like red clay, but Allah knows what it really was, mixed with fruit from a tree called "Aleppo oak", usually used in tanning leather. Shocked, he told him that this food was poisonous, but Shaikh 'Abd al-Karīm requested that he trust him and try it. When he ate this clay-like piece, he found incomparable delight in it, as well as a wonderful aroma he had never smelled the like of before. He did not feel hungry for more than a week afterwards. In his two years of seclusion, Shaikh 'Abd al-Karīm felt satisfied eating this mix of clay and plant and drinking water from the spring. It is impossible for a person to subsist under these circumstances, but the Divine Hand that led him to that isolated place and that complete seclusion assumed responsibility for his care and protection, the same way It spiritually nourished him and fostered his spiritual elevation. In the morning, Shaikh 'Abd al-Karīm returned with his brother to commence his decreed role in reviving the religion of his grandfather, the Prophet (PBUH). He became known by the title "Shāh al-Kasnazān", which means "Sultan of the Unseen". Thus, the Ṭarīqa became known after him "Ṭarīqa 'Alīyya Qādiriyya Kasnazāniyya", or "Ṭarīqa Kasnazāniyya" for short.

After his return from his seclusion, Shaikh 'Abd al-Karīm did not settle in the village of Kasnazān. Rather, he lived for a few years in a village called Fīkadara, about one and a half or two hours' walking distance from Kasnazān. He built a mosque there. When our Shaikh visited the village in 1967, the pillar of the mosque that Shāh al-Kasnazān used to recline on was still standing.

Shāh al-Kasnazān moved to a small village neighbouring the mountain Sagarma called Karbchna. He lived there for less than two years

---

[82] Shaikh Muḥammad al-Muḥammad al-Kasnazān, *sermon*, 14th/July/2000.

before permanently moving to an area about five kilometres away that, at the time, did not have other than two or three houses. The population of the village moved there with him, and the new place of residence became known as Karbchna (Map 2). The location of the old Karbchna was not attractive, and it was small and isolated. It seems that its first inhabitants chose it to provide them with natural protection against tribal wars.

With his cane, Shāh al-Kasnazān marked the building sites of a mosque, his house and the house of every family of the new village's population. Not only did he choose the location of the village, but he was also the first to plan and engineer its construction. The land of the new Karbchna was all forest, so each building was made from wood from the trees that covered its land. Water was readily available in the area through natural springs. Shāh al-Kasnazān built a takya in Karbchna and founded a religious school that became a hub for Sufi seekers and those seeking the truth. This is how Shāh al-Kasnazān established the village of Karbchna, which later became administratively affiliated with the township of Sangāw. The latter was previously affiliated with the governorate of Kirkuk but is now affiliated with the Chamchamāl province in the governorate of Sulaymāniyya. The village continued to expand, and it is said that by 1890 there were about 500 houses in it.

One of the karāmas of Shāh al-Kasnazān is his announcement that a body of water like the sea existed beneath Karbchna underneath a layer of rock. About thirty years ago, our Shaikh instructed for well to be dug in the village. The drilling continued deep without hitting water until it reached a stone layer that was about a meter thick. Once the drilling penetrated it, the water that Shāh al-Kasnazān had disclosed of came out. Water still comes out of the well to this day.

Shaikh ʿAbd al-Qādir al-Gaylānī blessed Karbchna when he chose a place of worship for himself on one of its mountains, then he chose it as a homeland for the Shaikhs of his Ṭarīqa. Over the years, the village has faced many difficult circumstances as a result of political and military conflicts in northern Iraq, as we will see later. Today, it is a sanctuary that houses the shrines and monuments of the Shaikhs of Kasnazān. One of these monuments is the "reservoir of Shāh al-Kasnazān". It is a place where sweet, pristine water gathers from a natural spring that Shāh al-Kasnazān and the dervishes used for ablution and drinking. He used to sit with his disciples there, usually from the time of the afternoon prayer until sunset. The Kasnazānī Shaikhs after him continued to frequent the spot and deliver sermons to the dervishes there. The reservoir is in a low place in an orchard whose trees were planted at that time by Shāh al-Kasnazān. Like every inch of the land of Karbchna, this reservoir has witnessed many karāmas by the Shaikhs. We will recount one of them.

A caravan that was going to visit the mosque of Kāka Aḥmad al-Shaikh passed near the reservoir of Shāh al-Kasnazān where the Shaikh was sitting. The travellers greeted him from afar, and he raised his hand, returning the greeting. There was a youth in the caravan named Faraj ʿAlī who thought that Shāh al-Kasnazān was arrogant because he had not stood for the caravan, only raising his hand. After the caravan had passed the place by about 200-250 metres, Shāh al-Kasnazān described the clothing and build of this young man to one of his disciples and sent him after the caravan to ask the young man to present himself before the Shaikh. When Faraj arrived, the Shaikh said to him: "O my son! I seek forgiveness from Allah that I should be arrogant. A Shaikh of the Ṭarīqa is not arrogant. Rather, I am currently using cupping therapy." Cupping requires the person to limit his movement. The young man wept after witnessing this spiritual unveiling by Shāh al-Kasnazān and became one of the dervishes of the Ṭarīqa Kasnazāniyya.

There is a karāma that kept happening at the reservoir of Shāh al-Kasnazān. There was a large boulder that would rise from the earth out of respect for the coming of Shaikh ʿAbd al-Qādir al-Kasnazān, who succeeded his father Shāh al-Kasnazān as the Master of the Ṭarīqa.

There are several different opinions regarding the origin and meaning of the village's Kurdish name. Shaikh Muḥammad al-Muḥammad opines that it is a modification of the name "Gul Bachna", which means a place for "picking roses". The mufti of Sulaymāniyya, Shaikh Muḥammad al-Qara Dāghī (may Allah have mercy on him), suggested that the origin of the name is "Qurb al-Janna" (near paradise). Another explanation is that the original name is "Karam China", where "karam" means "silkworm" and "china" is "weaving", so the meaning of the name is "weaving silkworm", due to the existence of a valley that has a large number of mulberry trees that silkworms inhabit.

There is another view stating that after the Islamic conquest of the area, the population requested there be someone who could teach them the Qur'an and religion. The caliph sent them a number of the Prophet's (PBUH) Companions. One night, some people acted treacherously against the Companions, murdering them. The village became known as "Kar Bachna", which means "take them quietly", where "kar" is "silence" and "bachna" means "cull them" or "kill them". There are Companions' graves east of the village, less than two kilometres away. The people in Kurdistan distinguish the tombs of the Companions by making them longer than other graves and letting trees around them grow and not cutting them. One charming expression of respect for the tombs of the Companions was seen when the nomadic Jāff clans there would temporarily go to another area where the climate is more favourable. They would leave any belongings they do not need to take with them near the graves of the Companions until their return at the beginning of the autumn. Not a single hand would touch their belongings out of respect for the Companions.

In addition to the two consecutive years that Shāh al-Kasnazān spent in Gaylān Āwā, he later entered other seclusions, equalling more than another two years. Sometimes he would seclude himself in Gaylān Āwā, and other times in another cave at the base of Mount Sagarma (photo 33). Other times, he would seclude himself in a pit in front of the mosque that he built in Karbchna. Our present Shaikh built a protective structure over the underground place of seclusion (photo 31). The number of seclusions that this devout Shaikh entered was forty, each of which lasted forty days, meaning that he spent 1,600 days in isolation with his Lord. That is more than four years and four and a half months.

Shāh al-Kasnazān lived a life that few have lived in the service of Allah (exalted and high is He) and by guiding people. Countless karāmas are attributed to him that have been witnessed by people in various parts of the world. The Sultan of the Unseen departed to his Lord's presence in 1320 H. (1902 CE) after establishing the pillars of the Ṭarīqa Kasnazāniyya, reviver of the Prophet's (PBUH) Sunna. Shāh al-Kasnazān's noble body is buried in the same spot as his chamber (photo 5), probably at his behest, similar to how the Messenger's tomb (PBUH) in Medina is located where his place of residence was. Every son and daughter of Shāh al-Kasnazān's was a walī, but he authorised the youngest of his sons, ʿAbd al-Qādir, to assume the Shaikhdom of the Ṭarīqa.

2.5 The Kasnazānī Shaikhs

Like his father, Shaikh 'Abd al-Qādir was pious and devout. He would always sit facing the direction of the Ka'ba in a state of constant dhikr, speaking little. The first World War was contemporaneous with Shaikh 'Abd al-Qādir. Alongside his disciples, he fought the Russian forces that invaded Iraqi and Iranian territories at the start of the war, and he resisted the British occupation of Iraq. As a result of the critical attacks in May 1919 that he and the fighters alongside him inflicted upon the occupational forces, the invaders sent a large squadron of British soldiers and local mercenaries to kill the Shaikh. They besieged and burned Karbchna, but only after the Shaikh had left the village with his family and took refuge in a cave in a mountain. Then the British army surrounded the mountain, but Allah rescued the Shaikh the way He had saved his grandfather (PBUH) before when he migrated from Mecca to Medina. He went to the west of Iran where he lived for the remainder of his life in the villages of Nijmār and Pīrān, in the Hawrāmān region, opposite Mount Sūrīn, which separates Iraq and Iran. "The Emigrant", as Shaikh 'Abd al-Qādir became known, passed away in 1341/1922.

As is the case with everything that happens to the Shaikhs of the Ṭarīqa, there was something great that Allah wanted from this migration. Shaikh 'Abd al-Qādir conducted extensive preaching campaigns in which he restored and spread the teachings of Islam. The Ṭarīqa Kasnazāniyya spread throughout Iran. One reason that the emigrant Shaikh had such great influence over people was his innumerable karāmas. Shaikh Muḥammad al-Muḥammad described the life of his grandfather Shaikh 'Abd al-Qādir as being all karāmas. He adds that probably no other Shaikh had more karāmas, other than Shaikh 'Abd al-Qādir al-Gaylānī.[83]

One sign of the piety of this extraordinary Shaikh was manifested when he settled in Iran in a village that had been extorted by one of its feudal landlords. He prohibited himself from using the water of the village for any of his daily needs because he considered its water as usurped from its legal owners. For the entire duration of his stay in the village, the Shaikh sufficed himself by using water from melted snow.

---

[83] Shaikh Muḥammad al-Muḥammad al-Kasnazān, *sermon*, 24th/September/2013.

Shaikh ʿAbd al-Qādir appointed his eldest son, Ḥusayn, who was born in 1306/1888 in Karbchna, as his successor to the throne of the Ṭarīqa. Alongside his father, Shaikh Ḥusayn fought the Russian forces and the British occupation forces after that, and he emigrated with him to Iran. Shaikh Ḥusayn brought his father's coffin to Karbchna and buried him next to his father, Shāh al-Kasnazān. He went back to Iran, but he returned to settle in Karbchna in the second half of 1923. Shaikh Ḥusayn rebuilt the village, the mosque, and the takya which the British army had all burned down. Before Shaikh ʿAbd al-Qādir emigrated from Karbchna in 1919, there were close to five hundred houses in it and it was the centre of Sangāw. Over time, however, and due to people moving away to cities, the number of houses decreased.

Shaikh Ḥusayn was fond of mountains and wandering there to the extent that he was known by the title the "Sultan of Mountains". He also led a life of unparalleled asceticism and struggle against the self. He frequently went to the mountains after midnight for worship, laying on thorny plants until the morning to tame his self. He would also at times withdraw into his grandfather Shāh al-Kasnazān's place of seclusion at the base of Mount Sagarma, and many other times in his grandfather's other place of seclusion in an underground pit in front of the Karbchna shrines. Likewise, he spent one summer in seclusion in Gaylān Āwā.

Sultan Ḥusayn was in a state of constant fasting in his final years. His food was limited to dry bread made from barley, and bitter wild gourds. He would often stop drinking water, even in the summer. His body reached such a point of weakness that a caliph would raise his hand for him when dervishes came to greet him. Once on the day of Eid, his mother, his brother Shaikh ʿAbd al-Karīm, and relatives came to him and begged him to agree to them bringing him a little bit of rice, gravy, and meat to eat, as it was Eid. The Shaikh agreed and washed his hands in preparation for the meal. But when he saw himself longing for the food, he said: "what a soul, like a dog! I swear by Allah, you will not eat; I swear by Allah, you will not eat. Take the food and distribute it to the poor". One of the many karāmas of Shaikh Ḥusayn is that people used to hear around him Muslim jinns performing dhikr of Allah.

Shaikh Ḥusayn al-Kasnazān was extremely generous. He would distribute whatever he had to those in need. He allocated monthly salaries to more than fifty families of orphans and the poor. One day towards the end of 1357/1939, his wife, sayyida Amīna, told him that the takya needed funding. He replied that he did not have anything to give her, but that they would receive a very large sum of money in a week. His wife asked him what he meant, to which he replied that he would depart this life after a week and there would be a considerable amount of money donated at his funeral. It was as he said it would be.[84]

As would have been the case during the life of Sultan Ḥusayn, this money also went to aiding those in need. The family went through difficult financial circumstances. Each week, they would send a few kilos of wheat to a mill located two kilometres from Karbchna. The bread they produced from this flour was all they could afford for their young and their old. This continued for a while after Shaikh ʿAbd al-Karīm assumed the Masterhood of the Ṭarīqa.[85]

Shaikh ʿAbd al-Karīm was born in 1330/1912 in Karbchna. He was brought up by two Masters of Ṭarīqa, his father Shaikh ʿAbd al-Qādir and his brother Shaikh Ḥusayn. Since his childhood, Muḥammadan attributes appeared in the young ʿAbd al-Karīm. He was selfless and compassionate, and he loved to serve the village's poor children and feed them from his food, preferring them over himself. Every now and then he asked his father for a lamb to be slaughtered and its meat to be distributed to the children of the village, all of whom were his friends. When some adults would intervene to dismiss the generous child, the Shaikh would order the implementation of his young son's will. He would say to those who objected that ʿAbd al-Karīm saw duties he has towards those children that the adults did not see. Signs of wisdom appeared in him from a young age. He used to act as an intermediary in resolving disputes and reconciling his friends.

When Shaikh ʿAbd al-Karīm grew up, he was very fond of horse riding and would go out to hunt on his horse. Because of his love of being alone and isolated, he was often unaccompanied. He was an ardent lover of the noble Qur'an and the Prophet's (PBUH) Sunna, adhering to them. Because of these good attributes and the spiritual capacity that Shaikh Ḥusayn saw in him, he loved him immensely. He would often take him with him when he went to the mountains at night to worship.

---

[84] Shaikh Muḥammad al-Muḥammad al-Kasnazān, *sermon*, 14th/September/2016.

[85] Shaikh Muḥammad al-Muḥammad al-Kasnazān, *sermon*, 20th/November/2018.

Shaikh ʿAbd al-Karīm would stay with his Master for days and nights, where he would be the only one to accompany him in his seclusion and stand at his service. When Shaikh ʿAbd al-Karīm was a young man whose facial hair was still not fully grown, Sultan Ḥusayn made him his representative for managing the affairs of the Ṭarīqa and the dervishes. Towards the end of his life, Shaikh Ḥusayn was in constant seclusion, so he made Shaikh ʿAbd al-Karīm the intermediary between him and the seekers. Shaikh Ḥusayn directed the disciples to their future Shaikh and informed them that all the affairs of the Ṭarīqa were now in his hands. The ascetic Shaikh remained withdrawn until he passed away.

Shaikh ʿAbd al-Karīm used to withdraw into a small private room. He would spend most of his day alone, praying, reading the Qur'an, and reciting his special dhikrs. He would offer supererogatory prayers in abundance, such that he would not raise his head from the prostration of sunset's supererogatory prayer until the call to the night prayer and would weep and moan He slept for a small portion of the night, and he supplicated much to Allah. He wept profusely and laughed little. He fasted for many days, confining himself to little water to drink. He ate little and did not consume much besides tea.

Political developments in Iraq, which we will discuss in detail in Chapter 7, led to Shaikh ʿAbd al-Karīm's emigration from Karbchna in 1959, residing in the village of Būbān in the Penjwin province, in the Sulaymāniyya governorate, on the Iraqi-Iranian border. In June of 1962, he entered Iran and resided for about a year in a bordering village located on a highland called "Mīrza Mīrā Shāh", between the villages of Khāwya and Mīrāwā. During this time, many seekers gathered there. He then dwelled in Sanandaj for a while, where he gave the Ṭarīqa to thousands of people and opened takyas. He went on preaching tours to Hamedan, Tehran, and Mashhad, meanwhile giving the Ṭarīqa to many. Thousands of dervishes and admirers followed him wherever he went until his roaming became difficult and costly (photo 8).

Shaikh ʿAbd al-Karīm returned to Mīrza Mīrā Shāh before leaving Iran in the first half of 1965, returning to Būbān. He permanently moved to Kirkuk at the end of that year (photo 7). The Shaikh travelled on several preaching tours around Iraq, including most governorates, such as Baghdad, Nineveh, Babylon, Najaf, Anbār, Tikrit, Erbil, and Sulaymāniyya. The Ṭarīqa spread widely during his time to different parts of the world, such as Iran, Afghanistan, Pakistan, India, and Zambia.

Shaikh 'Abd al-Karīm passed on to the Sublime Company in 1398 H. (1978 CE). He had appointed to succeed him as Master of the Ṭarīqa his son Muḥammad al-Muḥammad, the present Shaikh of the Ṭarīqa.

In Table 1, we have compiled the historic dates of birth and succession for each Shaikh of the Ṭarīqa Kasnazāniyya. We considered the date of the death of each Shaikh to be the date of his successor's assuming the Shaikhdom of the Ṭarīqa. This is only logical because there cannot be two Shaikhs at the same time in the Ṭarīqa Kasnazāniyya, the same way that the Ṭarīqa cannot be left without a Shaikh. We took these dates from the book *al-Ṭarīqa al-'Alīyya al-Qādiriyya Kasnazāniyya*, the book *al-Ānwār al-Raḥmāniyya*, and the *al-Kasnazān* magazine. We modified some dates, however, according to information that we have, as follows:

- **Shaikh 'Abd al-Qādir's death**: When detailing the events of November 1923, a senior official of the British administration in Iraq at the time, Cecil Edmunds, indicated that the Shaikh's death was in the previous year, i.e. 1922.[86]
- **Shaikh Ḥusayn's death**: We relied on two pieces of information in determining the year of Shaikh Ḥusayn's death. First, our Shaikh says that he was born the year of Shaikh Ḥusayn's death. Second, when Shaikh Ḥusayn was on his deathbed, hours before he departed from this life, he beckoned for his grandson, the infant Muḥammad al-Muḥammad, to be placed on his chest (refer to §9.2). Since Shaikh Ḥusayn's asceticism had left his body very thin, our Shaikh must have been younger than a year old at the time for him to have remained atop his body, even if only for a short while. Our Shaikh was born in the 14th of Ṣafar, 1357 Hijri, corresponding to 15th/April/1938 CE. Shaikh Ḥusayn's death must have been before the middle of April 1939, when our Shaikh was one year old. If we presume that the year in question in which our Shaikh was born and Shaikh Ḥusayn died is the Gregorian year, then Shaikh Ḥusayn's death was near the end of 1938. On the other hand, if the year in question was according to the Hijri

[86] Edmonds, *Kurds, Turks and Arabs*, p. 356.

year, 1357, then the death must have occurred before 20th/February/1939. The death must have occurred in the interval between the end of 1938 and the end of the second third of February 1939.

- **Shaikh ʿAbd al-Karīm's birth:** In calculating this date, we relied on three pieces of information. First, Shaikh ʿAbd al-Karīm's eldest son, Shaikh Ḥusayn, was born in 1927. Second, Shaikh Ḥusayn arranged the engagement of his brother Shaikh ʿAbd al-Karīm when he was a youth of about 13 years. This means that he married when he was approximately that age, as early marriage was the usual tradition at the time. If we assume that Shaikh ʿAbd al-Karīm's son Ḥusayn was born when he was approximately 15 years old, this would mean that he was born in 1912 CE. This is concurrent with the third piece of information we have, which is our Shaikh's saying that when Shaikh ʿAbd al-Qādir al-Kasnazān emigrated to Iran, Shaikh ʿAbd al-Karīm was a small child and that when he returned to Karbchna with Shaikh Ḥusayn in 1922/1923, he was around 10 years old.

2.6 The Chain of Shaikhs

The Ṭarīqa Kasnazāniyya has a continuous, unbroken chain of Shaikhs, meaning it has always had a living Shaikh: every Shaikh was handed the Masterhood of the Ṭarīqa hand-to-hand by his predecessor. As we have mentioned, this blessed Ṭarīqa goes back to the Prophet Muḥammad (PBUH), who bequeathed his spiritual knowledge to the Master of the Ṭarīqa after him, Imām ʿAlī Ibn Abī Ṭālib (may Allah ennoble his face). The Ṭarīqa continued from Imām ʿAlī in two branches.

Our Master calls the first "the Golden Branch" because it is the branch that comprises people of the prophetic household. It begins with Imām Ḥusayn, who passed it to the hand of Imām ʿAlī Zayn al-ʿAbidīn, to Imām Muḥammad al-Bāqir, Imām Jaʿfar al-Ṣādiq, Imām Mūsa al-Kāẓim, and from him to of Imām ʿAlī al-Riḍā.

Imām ʿAlī bequeathed the Ṭarīqa by way of its second branch to Shaikh Ḥasan al-Baṣrī. He passed it to the hand of Shaikh Ḥabīb al-ʿAjamī, who passed it to Shaikh Dāwūd al-Ṭāʾī. The two branches of the

Ṭarīqa Kasnazāniyya meet at Shaikh Maʿrūf al-Karkhī, who succeeded the Shaikhdom of the Ṭarīqa from Imām ʿAlī al-Riḍā and Shaikh Dāwūd al-Ṭāʾī.

The unbroken chain of the Ṭarīqa Kasnazāniyya Shaikhs continues from Shaikh Maʿrūf al-Karkhī to the hand of Shaikh Sarī al-Saqaṭī, to Shaikh Junayd al-Baghdādī, to Shaikh Abū Bakr al-Shiblī, to Shaikh ʿAbd al-Wāḥid al-Yamānī, to Shaikh Abū Faraj al-Ṭarsūsī, to Shaikh ʿAlī al-Hagārī, to Shaikh Abū Saʿīd al-Makhzūmī, to Shaikh ʿAbd al-Qādir al-Gaylānī, to Shaikh ʿAbd al-Razzāq al-Gaylānī, to Shaikh Dāwūd al-Ṭḥānī, to Shaikh Muḥammad Gharībullah, to Shaikh ʿAbd al-Fattāḥ al-Sayyāḥ, to Shaikh Muḥammad Qāsim, to Shaikh Muḥammad Ṣādiq, to Shaikh Ḥusayn al-Baḥrānī, to Shaikh Aḥmad al-Iḥsāʾī, to Shaikh Ismāʿīl al-Wilyānī, to Shaikh Muḥyī al-Dīn Karkūk, to Shaikh ʿAbd al-Ṣamad Galazarda, to Shaikh Ḥusayn Qāzānqāya, to Shaikh ʿAbd al-Qādir Qāzānqāya, to Shaikh ʿAbd al-Karīm Shāh al-Kasnazān, to Shaikh ʿAbd al-Qādir al-Kasnazān, to Shaikh Ḥusayn al-Kasnazān, to Shaikh ʿAbd al-Karīm al-Kasnazān, to the present Master, Shaikh Muḥammad al-Muḥammad al-Kasnazān, may Allah sanctify the innermost beings of them all.

Table 1: Historic Dates of the Shaikhs of the Ṭarīqa Kasnazāniyya

Master of the Ṭarīqa	Birth (H/CE)	Succession (H/CE)	Age at Succession	Death (H/CE)	Duration of Shaikhdom	Age at Death
ʿAbd al-Karīm Shāh al-Kasnazān	1240/ 1824	Unknown	Unknown	1320/ 1902	Unknown	78
ʿAbd al-Qādir al-Kasnazān	1284/ 1867	1320/ 1902	35	1341/ 1922	20	55
Ḥusayn al-Kasnazān	1306/ 1888	1341/ 1922	34	1357/ 1939	17	51
ʿAbd al-Karīm al-Kasnazān	1330/ 1912	1357/ 1939	29	1398/ 1978	39	68
Muḥammad al-Muḥammad al-Kasnazān	1357/ 1938	1398/ 1978	40			

Photo 4: The hall of the shrines of the Kasnazānī Shaikhs in Karbchna, and the adjacent mosque behind can also be seen (19th/March/2016).

Photo 5: The shrine of Shaikh ʿAbd al-Karīm Shāh al-Kasnazān, and in the far left a part of the shrine of Shaikh ʿAbd al-Qādir al-Kasnazān can also be seen (19th/March/2016).

"If you come to the Ṭarīqa with the objective of procuring karāmas, then this means that you have not come for Allah. Allah is the one who grants you karāmas. According to the principles of our Ṭarīqa, karāmas ought to seek out the seeker, not the other way around. You must seek the Creator of karāmas, the one who grants you karāmas: 'Indeed, the noblest of you in the sight of Allah is the most pious of you' (al-Ḥujurāt 13)".

Shaikh Muḥammad al-Muḥammad al-Kasnazān
(Sermon, 9th/June/2000)

3

Muḥammadan Karāmas

A supernatural feat that is performed by a walī is known as a "karāma" to distinguish it from a paranormal feat of a prophet, which is called "muʿjiza". Countless karāmas of Sufi Shaikhs have been recognized throughout history. These supernatural events touched the lives of innumerable seekers and other people. In fact, karāmas write a large part of the life the Shaikh of Ṭarīqa, even before he is born, as we saw with Shaikh ʿAbd al-Karīm Shāh al-Kasnazān and will see in our study of Shaikh Muḥammad al-Muḥammad al-Kasnazān's life. You see paranormal occurrences continuously overlap with normal events, so that every day of the Shaikh of Ṭarīqa's life is filled with evidence of his support from Allah Almighty, and consequently, of the truthfulness of his call, and his living in accordance with the noble Qur'an and the Messenger's (PBUH) Sunna. Karāmas are the ink that pens the biographies of the Shaikhs. Thus, it is necessary to examine the meaning of "karāma" before we study in the next chapters our Shaikh's life in detail. We will first touch upon the concepts of "muʿjiza" and "karāma" and the difference between them, and how karāmas are among the main manifestations of nearness to Allah.

3.1 Muʿjiza

Allah supported the prophets by paranormal occurrences that were linked to them in one way or another — some were performed by them, while others happened to them. Muslim scholars called any such paranormal event a "muʿjiza". The word is derived from the root word "ʿajaza", which means "he was unable", referring to the fact that the muʿjiza surpasses natural abilities, meaning that it cannot occur in normal circumstances. The derivatives of this root occur 17 times in the Qur'an, as in this example: "Indeed, what you are promised is coming, and you will not cause failure [to Allah] (*bimuʿjizīn*)" (al-Ānʿām 134). We will use the common translation of "miracle" for "muʿjiza".

Since miracles are impossible according to the laws of nature, the Qur'an presents them as proofs that the prophets are truly messengers of Allah, who has power over all things. They are signs indicative of the existence of Allah and the truthfulness of the message of the prophets at whose hands these miracles have appeared. Our Shaikh has this to say:[87]

> "What was the purpose of the miracles of the prophets? Their purpose was to confirm that that prophet was sent by Allah. The miracle is a proof confirming the existence of the Divine, confirming the existence of the One who is existent by necessity".[88]

Allah is the creator of the laws of nature and can stop or change them whenever He wills, as Shaikh ʿAbd al-Qādir al-Gaylānī says:

> "The belief of those who follow Allah's Book and His Messenger's (PBUH) Sunna is that the sword does not cut because of its nature, but it is rather Allah (mighty and sublime is He) cuts with it; that fire does not burn because of its nature, but it is rather Allah (mighty and sublime is He) who burns with it; that food does not satiate hunger because of its nature, but it is rather Allah (mighty and sublime is He) who satiates hunger with it; that water does not quench thirst because of its nature, but it is rather Allah (mighty and sublime is He) who quenches thirst with it. The same is true of all things of all kinds. It is Allah (mighty and sublime is He) who acts in them and with them, while they are only instruments in His hands with which He does whatever He wills".[89]

The Qur'an mentions many miracles performed by a number of the prophets. Moses, for example, was able to transform his cane into a snake and perform other miracles. These include parting the sea to make a dry path for the Children of Israel to travel on during their escape from Pharaoh and his army (Ṭāhā 9-79, al-Shuʿarā` 10-66). Similarly, Allah informs us that the Prophet Jesus spoke in the cradle and exhibited great wisdom, even while an infant. He also created birds of clay and then breathed life into them, healed the blind and the albino, revived the dead,

---

[87] Shaikh Muḥammad al-Muḥammad al-Kasnazān, *sermon*, 9th/September/2013.

[88] Philosophers use the term "existent by necessity" to refer to Allah (mighty and sublime is He), because His existence has no beginning or end: "He is the first and the last" (al-Ḥadīd 3). Creatures, on the other hand, are "existent by possibility", meaning that they may or may not exist.

[89] Shaikh ʿAbd al-Qādir al-Gaylānī, *Jilā' al-Khāṭir*, p. 31.

knew what people keep hidden in their homes, and caused a feast to descend from the sky (`Āl 'Imrān 45-48, al-Mā`ida 110-115, Maryam 23-33).

Some claim the Prophet Muḥammad (PBUH) did not perform miracles like those who came before him, and that the Qur'an is his sole miracle. The Qur'an is a unique miracle that testifies to Muḥammad's (PBUH) prophethood, but Allah's Book itself records several of the Messenger's (PBUH) miracles, including the following:

- **The Night Journey**: Allah (exalted and high is He) made the Messenger (PBUH) travel by night from the Ḥarām Mosque in Mecca to the Aqṣā Mosque in Jerusalem: "Exalted is He who took His Servant by night from the Ḥarām Mosque to the Aqṣā Mosque, whose surroundings We have blessed, to show him of Our signs. Indeed, He is the Hearing, the Seeing" (al-Isrā` 1).
- **The Ascension**: Allah raised the Prophet (PBUH) to the heavens: "By the star when it descends, (1) your companion [Muḥammad] has not strayed, nor has he erred. (2) Nor does he speak from [his own] inclination. (3) It is not but a revelation that is revealed, (4) taught by one who is powerful (5) One of soundness, and he rose to his true form (6) while he was in the higher horizon. (7) Then he approached and descended (8), so he became at a distance of two bow lengths or nearer. (9) He revealed to His Servant what he revealed. (10) The heart did not lie about what it saw. (11) So will you dispute with him over what he saw? (12) He certainly saw him in another descent, (13) at the Lote Tree of the Utmost Boundary (14), near it is the Garden of Refuge, (15) when there covered the Lote Tree that which covered [it]. (16) The sight [of the Prophet] did not swerve, nor did it transgress [its limit]. (17) He certainly saw of the greatest signs of his Lord". (al-Najm 1-18)
- **Knowledge of future events**: These verses illustrate that the Messenger (PBUH) saw in a vision his and the Muslims' entry to the Ḥarām Mosque as victors: "Certainly has Allah showed to His Messenger the vision in truth. You will surely enter the Ḥarām Mosque, if Allah wills, in safety, with your heads shaved and [hair] shortened, not in fear. He knew what you did not know, so He arranged before that a conquest is near [at hand]" (al-Fatḥ 27).
- **Knowledge of people's secrets**: This verse tells us that Allah revealed to the Messenger (PBUH) secrets people had: "When

the Prophet confided to one of his wives a statement; when she disclosed it and Allah made him aware of that, he made known part of it and ignored part. When he informed her about it, she said, 'who told you this?' He said, 'I was informed by the Knowing, the Acquainted'" (al-Taḥrīm 3).

- **The splitting of the moon**: The people of Mecca wanted the Messenger (PBUH) to show them a sign proving that he was indeed a messenger from Allah. He asked Allah to show them a miracle, so the moon split into halves. It is believed that these verses refer to that miracle: "The Hour has come near, and the moon has split [in two]" (al-Qamar 1)[90].
- **Supernatural throw**: During the Battle of Badr, the Messenger (PBUH) scooped dust and pebbles from the earth into his hand and threw them in the direction of the polytheists. He hit them, injuring and confusing them, which helped the Muslims achieve their first military victory: "You did not kill them, but it was Allah who killed them. You threw not [O Muḥammad] when you threw, but it was Allah who threw, that He might test the believers with a good test. Indeed, Allah is Hearing and Knowing" (al-Ānfāl 17).

Unique miracles, such as the Night Journey and the Ascension, demonstrate the Prophet's (PBUH) nearness to Allah. This nearness makes him a source of many miracles. Biographies of the Prophet and the Ḥadīth record a profusion of these supernatural occurrences, which began from his noble birth. The following are some of his miracles that occurred after his mission started:

- **Miracles of the Migration**: The Prophetic Migration from Mecca to Medina was accompanied by several miracles. **First**, the Prophet (PBUH) departed on the same night the polytheists had decided to assassinate him. **Second**, when the Messenger (PBUH) left his house, the assassins were waiting outside. He threw a handful of dust at them while reciting verses from the noble Qur'an, so they did not see him.[91] **Third**, when he (PBUH) and his Companion Abū Bakr hid themselves inside

[90] Bukhārī, *Al-Jāmiʿ al-Ṣaḥīḥ*, III, no. 4681, p. 131.
[91] Ibn Hishām, *Sīrat al-Nabī*, II, pp. 102-104.

the cave of Thawr on the way from Mecca to Medina, Allah aided the Prophet (PBUH) with invisible helpers: "If you do not aid him (the Prophet), Allah has already aided him when those who disbelieved had driven him out [of Mecca], as one of two, when they were in the cave and he said to his companion, 'Do not grieve; indeed Allah is with us'. Allah sent down his tranquillity upon him and supported him with helpers you did not see and made the word of those who disbelieved the lowest, while the word of Allah is the highest. Allah is Exalted in Might and Wise" (al-Tawba 40). Scholars and historians mention additional miracles related to this incident: a spider spun a web across the entrance of the cave,[92] a tree sprouted at the mouth of the cave and covered it, and two wild doves nested at the cave's entrance.[93] When the polytheists arrived at the cave, it seemed as though no one had entered it for a long while, so they did not inspect it.

- **Paranormal healing:** The Messenger (PBUH) miraculously healed various diseases. He blew on a blind child's eyes and restored his vision. His vision remained so sharp even when he was eighty years old that he could thread a needle. A woman brought a child whose arm had been burned after a hot cooking pot fell on his hand. He rubbed his saliva upon the injured arm causing it to heal immediately.[94]
- **Animals address the Prophet (PBUH) and acknowledge his prophethood:** There are many accounts of the Messenger (PBUH) speaking with animals. In some of these miracles, those present also understood the ensuing dialogue in Arabic. A bedouin once told the Prophet (PBUH) that he would not believe in him unless the male lizard he was carrying with him believed in him. When the Messenger (PBUH) addressed the animal, it replied and announced its belief in him, causing the bedouin to accept Islam. [95] In another miracle, a bird complained to the Prophet that his two chicks had been stolen

---

[92] Aḥmad, *Musnad al-Imām Aḥmad Ibn Ḥanbal*, V, no. 3251, p. 301; al-Ṭabarānī, *al-Muʿjam al-Kabīr*, XI, no. 12155, p. 407.
[93] Aṣbahānī, *Dalāʾil al-Nubuwwa*, p. 325.
[94] Aṣbahānī, *Dalāʾil al-Nubuwwa*, pp. 466-467.
[95] Bayhaqī, *Dalāʾil al-Nubuwwa wa-Maʿrifat Aḥwāl Ṣaḥib al-Sharīʿa*, VI, pp. 36-37.

from their nest. When he asked who had taken them, some people admitted that they had taken them. He ordered them to return them, and they did.[96]

- **The animals' reverence for the Messenger (PBUH):** A man complained to the Prophet (PBUH) that his camel had stopped obeying him, so he could not use it to water his palm tree, and became aggressive. He (PBUH) walked to the camel, who, as soon as it saw the Messenger (PBUH), proceeded to walk with its head between his hands, until it prostrated to him. He asked its owner to muzzle it and take it away, after which it returned to being obedient.[97]
- **The trunk of a palm tree's longing for him:** The Prophet (PBUH) used to lean against the trunk of a palm tree when addressing the Muslims. When he went to speak from a pulpit for the first time, the trunk moaned in longing for him (PBUH). He went to it and embraced it, so it calmed down.[98]
- **The gushing of water between his fingers:** The Prophet (PBUH) was travelling in the company of nearly fifteen-hundred Muslims when their water supply neared exhaustion, and the time to pray had come. The Messenger (PBUH) asked for water and poured it into a vessel. Then, he dipped his honourable hand into it, and water began to gush forth from his hand, so much so that all their needs were met.[99]
- **Prophesying future events:** Sayyida ʿĀ`isha said that in his final illness, the Prophet (PBUH) called his daughter, sayyida Fāṭima al-Zahrā`, and disclosed a secret to her, and she wept. When he saw her grief, he called her again and disclosed a second secret to her, and she laughed. When sayyida ʿĀ`isha asked her about what he had disclosed to her, she did not reveal the secret. When she asked her another time after his (PBUH) departure from this world, sayyida Fāṭima replied that he had first told her that he would not recover from his illness, which

---

[96] Bayhaqī, *Dalā`il al-Nubuwwa wa-Maʿrifat Aḥwāl Ṣaḥib al-Sharīʿa*, VI, pp. 32-33.
[97] Bayhaqī, *Dalā`il al-Nubuwwa wa-Maʿrifat Aḥwāl Ṣaḥib al-Sharīʿa*, VI, p. 28.
[98] Bukhārī, *Al-Jāmiʿ al-Ṣaḥīḥ*, I, no. 895, p. 266; Bayhaqī, *Dalā`il al-Nubuwwa wa-Maʿrifat Aḥwāl Ṣaḥib al-Sharīʿa*, VI, p. 66; Aṣbahānī, *Dalā`il al-Nubuwwa*, p. 399.
[99] Bayhaqī, *Dalā`il al-Nubuwwa wa-Maʿrifat Aḥwāl Ṣaḥib al-Sharīʿa*, VI, p. 11.

> made her weep. Then he informed her that she would be the first from the people of his household to die after him, so the glad tidings pleased her and made her laugh. The Prophet (PBUH) did not recover from that illness, and sayyida Fāṭima passed away about two months after him, having not reached thirty years of age.[100]

The Companions of the Prophet (PBUH) witnessed his ceaseless miracles; this eye-witnessing was necessary for them to have the tremendous faith that pushed them to sacrifice what was near and dear to them for the sake of Islam and its Messenger (PBUH).

3.2 Karāma

Performing, witnessing, or being the subject of supernatural feats is not limited to the prophets, as it is not particular to prophethood. It is rather a product of nearness to Allah. The noble Qur'an mentions individuals who were near to Allah who underwent similar experiences. One of them is Khaḍir (peace be upon him), who showed knowledge of hidden matters that were unknown even to one of the prophets of determination, to whom Allah had granted a book. In fact, Moses could not even understand these matters (al-Kahf 60-82). Another example is sayyida Maryam, whom Allah granted various paranormal occurrences. She would see Gabriel and the angels with her own eyes and converse with them (`Āl ʿImrān 42). Sustenance would miraculously reach her (`Āl ʿImrān 37), and she became pregnant without any man touching her (`Āl ʿImrān 45-47). Also, there are the People of the Cave, whom Allah put to sleep for more than three centuries, then roused from their slumber (al-Kahf 9-52).

The paranormal feats of those who are not prophets are known as "karāmas". This term is derived from His words "indeed, the noblest of you (*ākramakum*) in the sight of Allah is the most pious of you" (al-Ḥujurāt 13) because karāmas are linked to piety, which is the measure of nearness to Allah. Karāmas are associated with Allah's walīs in the Qur'an, as He calls the individual that is close to him "walī", which means "ally", i.e. "Allah's ally". We also see the sense of nearness in the term "walī" in its connection

---

[100] Bukhārī, *Al-Jāmiʿ al-Ṣaḥīḥ*, II, no. 3500, p. 336.

to the verb "yalī", which refers to what comes after something, some individual, or some situation without there being any gap between the two: "Unquestionably, [for] Allah's allies (*walīs*), there will come no fear upon them, nor will they grieve" (Yūnus 62).

The occurrence of karāmas to a person directly correlates to his obedience to Allah and his practice of spiritual exercises, such as fasting, that aim to control his instincts and materialistic tendencies. Shaikh Ibn ʿAṭāʾ Allah al-Sakandarī said: "How can natural laws be broken for you when you have not yet broken the natural habits of your self?".[101] This is one Prophetic ḥadīth about the walīs of Allah, narrated by ʿUmar Ibn al-Khaṭṭāb:

> "The Prophet (PBUH) said: 'There are people among Allah's servants who are neither prophets nor martyrs whom the prophets and martyrs will envy on the Day of Resurrection for their status with Allah.' They said: 'O Messenger of Allah! Will you tell us who they are?' He said: 'They are people who love one another for Allah's sake, without being blood-related or money ties. I swear by Allah, their faces glow in light and they walk in light. They have no fear when people have fear, and they do not grieve when people grieve.' He then recited this verse: 'Unquestionably, for the walīs of Allah, there will come no fear upon them, nor will they grieve' (Yūnus 62)".[102]

Naturally, as a result of following the Prophet (PBUH) and, consequently, their nearness to Allah, the laws of nature were broken for the Companions, their Successors, and other pious individuals. These are samples of the karāmas of the Companions and Successors:

- Caliph ʿUmar sent an army to Nahavand under the leadership of Sāriya Ibn Zanīm. When he was delivering the Friday sermon he suddenly stopped and shouted: "O Sāriya, the mountain! O Sāriya, the mountain! O Sāriya, the mountain!". ʿUmar himself, let alone those present, did not understand why he did that. The explanation came a few days later when the army returned from battle. Sāriya said that when the Muslim army was besieged, he heard ʿUmar's voice calling out to him: "O Sāriya, the mountain!" He ordered the army to take the mountain as a fort to protect it from the rear. This manoeuvre

---

[101] Sakandarī, *Ḥikam Ibn ʿAṭāʾ Allah*, p. 164.
[102] Abū Dāwūd, *Sunan Abī Dāwūd*, V, no. 3527, p. 386-387.

helped the Muslim army emerge victorious.[103]

- Usayd Ibn Ḥuḍayr and ʿAbbād Ibn Bishr left the Prophet (PBUH) after a visit on a very dark night. One of their canes lit up like a lamp, so they walked by its light. When they went their separate ways, the other cane lit up.[104]
- When the Companion Khubayb Ibn ʿAdiy was captured by the polytheists, he was seen while chained eating grapes, even though they were not available in Mecca at that time of year.[105]
- The Successor ʿĀmir Ibn ʿAbd Qays used to put whatever money he earned in his sleeve, and he would give some of it to anyone who asked him on the way. When he reached his house and gave the money that was left on him to his family, they would count it just to find out that it had not decreased from the original amount he had earned.[106] Another karāma of his is that he asked Allah to facilitate purification [i.e. the ablution] for him in the winter, so he would find the water for his ablution steaming hot.[107]
- When al-Āswad Ibn Qays claimed that he was a prophet in Yemen, he tried to force Abū Muslim Al-Khawlānī to believe in him. But this successor insisted on his belief in Muḥammad's (PBUH) prophethood and refused al-Āswad's claim. The latter grew furious and ordered that a huge fire be lit and threw Abū Muslim in it. The fire, however, did not harm him at all.[108]

Early Muslim scholars did not distinguish between the supernatural feats that are linked to prophets and walīs. They frequently used the term "`āya", which means "sign", because both are proofs from Allah that confirm the credibility of the message of the Prophet Muḥammad (PBUH). [109] For example, the compilation of ʿAbd al-Razzāq Ibn Hammām al-Ṣanʿānī (d. 211/826), one of the oldest books that compiled

---

[103] Lālikkā`ī, *Karāmāt Awliyā` Allah ʿAzza wa-Jall*, pp. 120-122; ʿAsqalānī, *Al-Iṣāba fī-Tamyīz al-Ṣāḥāba*, p. 533.

[104] Aṣbahānī, *Dalā`il al-Nubuwwa*, p. 561.

[105] Bayhaqī, *Dalā`il al-Nubuwwa wa-Maʿrifat Aḥwāl Ṣaḥib al-Sharīʿa*, III, pp. 324-325.

[106] Al-ʿAnqarī, ʿAbd Allah. *Karāmāt al-Āwliyā`*, p. 154.

[107] Al-ʿAnqarī, ʿAbd Allah. *Karāmāt al-Āwliyā`*, p. 155.

[108] Al-ʿAnqarī, ʿAbd Allah. *Karāmāt al-Āwliyā`*, p. 163.

[109] Al-ʿAnqarī, ʿAbd Allah. *Karāmāt al-Āwliyā`*, p. 24.

Prophetic Ḥadīth, includes a chapter named "Signs That are Hastened for the People of Certainty"[110] that narrates a number of the Companions' karāmas. As seen in the chapter's title, al-Ṣanʿānī links karāmas and faith. Al-Bukhārī, in his Ḥadīth collection, has a chapter that he named "Signs of Prophethood in Islam", in which he mentions many of the Prophet's (PBUH) miracles and two karāmas of two Companions.[111] It is evident from the titles of both chapters and their content that the two compilers of Ḥadīth considered the supernatural occurrences of the Companions as stemming from the Prophet's (PBUH) blessing. Hence, they serve the same function as muʿjizas in substantiating the divine source of his message. Similarly, books that compile the Messenger's (PBUH) miracles also mention Companions' karāmas, such as a book titled "Dalā`il an-Nubuwwa" (Proofs of Prophethood) by al-Āṣbahānī[112] and a book that has the same title by al-Bayhaqī.[113]

Some claim that a karāma cannot be the same kind as a muʿjiza, but this distinction between muʿjiza and karāma has no basis in the Qur'an. These scholars frequently cite Moses' muʿjiza of parting the sea, but this is a deliberate choice of a unique muʿjiza, while there are muʿjizas that have parallel karāmas. For instance, Jesus performed muʿjizas that demonstrated extraordinary powers of healing, and there are countless karāmas of this kind. The muʿjizas that cannot reoccur are those that are particular to the prophethood of a specific prophet, such as the scripture that Allah revealed to some prophets, because a walī, by definition, is not a prophet. In our Prophet's (PBUH) case, for example, the Qur'an is a miracle particular to his prophethood, so it is impossible for a walī, regardless of his status, to have something similar. This does not mean, however, that a walī may not receive any sort of revelation from Allah. This exclusivity is limited to the Qur'anic revelation, the likes of which cannot be sent down to anyone after Muḥammad (PBUH). Allah's revelation, however, comes in different forms. For instance, Allah inspired Moses' mother, even though she was not a prophet: "We inspired Moses' mother, 'Suckle him; but when you fear for him, cast him into the river

---

[110] ʿAbd al-Razzāq, *Al-Muṣannaf*, XI, no. 20541-20545, pp. 280-282.

[111] Bukhārī, *Al-Jāmiʿ al-Ṣaḥīḥ*, II, no. 3459, p. 327; no. 3491, p. 334.

[112] Aṣbahānī, *Dalā`il al-Nubuwwa*, pp. 557-563.

[113] Bayhaqī, *Dalā`il al-Nubuwwa wa-Maʿrifat Aḥwāl Ṣaḥib al-Sharīʿa*, VI, pp. 50-54, 77-80.

and do not fear and do not grieve. Indeed, We will return him to you and will make him a messenger'" (al-Qaṣaṣ 7). He informed her of a way to protect her child, and He revealed to her an extremely important piece of information from the Unseen, namely, that He would make her son a messenger. Our Master attributes to the Shaikhs of our Tarīqa saying that the only miracle that they would not perform, even though it is within their capability, is causing the birth of a child without a father, like the unique miracle of the creation of Jesus.

No evidence supports any differentiation between a muʿjiza and a karāma in terms of the nature of the paranormality involved. We also find an indication of this in these words of the Prophet (PBUH): "There may be a dishevelled person who is driven away from the doors [of houses and mosques] who, should he ask Allah for something, He would grant him his request".[114] This ḥadīth does not restrict what supernatural feats a righteous person may ask Allah for. This is confirmed by this Qudsī ḥadīth[115] that the Prophet (PBUH) conveyed from Allah, which explains the nature of paranormal powers that Allah may grant a walī:

> "I declare war on anyone who takes a walī of Mine for an enemy. The most beloved thing My servant draws near to Me though is what I have enjoined upon him. My slave continues to draw near to Me by performing supererogatory acts of worship until I love him. When I love him, I become his hearing with which he hears, his sight with which he sees, his hand with which he strikes, and his leg with which he walks. If he asks Me [for something], I will surely give it to him, and if he seeks refuge in Me, I will surely protect him".[116]

Given that the Arabic terms "muʿjiza" and "karāma" are not used interchangeably by scholars, then when using these Romanised terms, we will follow the same tradition of using the former exclusively for paranormal feats of prophets and the latter for paranormal feats of walīs. However, we are not going to extend this unjustified distinction into

---

[114] Muslim, *Ṣaḥīḥ Muslim*, IV, no. 2622, p. 2024.

[115] A Qudsī ḥadīth is a meaning without a specific wording that Allah revealed to the Prophet Muhammad (PBUH), so the Prophet (PBUH) expressed that meaning in his own words. It differs from the Qur'an in that the latter was releaved by Allah in meaning and in word. Naturally, Qudsī ḥadīths have a similar style to Prophetic ḥadīths whose meanings and wordings are both from the Prophet (PBUH).

[116] Bukhārī, *Al-Jāmiʿ al-Ṣaḥīḥ*, III, no. 6273, p. 493.

English by translating the two terms differently. Accordingly, either term may be translated as "paranormal act/feat", "supernatural act/feat", and "miracle".

As there are no qualitative or quantitative limits to Allah's power, there is no limit to the kinds of miracle that he grants to his servants. One who hears by Allah can hear any voice no matter how hidden or distant it may be, one who sees by Allah can see what is hidden in the sky and the earth, one whose hand strikes by Allah can do anything, and one who walks by Allah has space folded for him as though it does not exist.

Sufis refer to the various forms of miracle that Allah bestows upon his servants, removing all horizons to their senses and perception, by terms such as "elucidation of sight", "elucidation of hearing", and "elucidation of the heart". Allah grants whatever spiritual power He wills to one who draws near to Him, so the karāmas of walīs can take any form of the paranormal. This is something that is quickly discovered by the person who studies karāmas. This is how we should understand Shāh al-Kasnazān's words that Shaikh Muḥammad al-Muḥammad attributes to him:

> "Shāh al-Kasnazān showed me some things and said: 'Is this not impossible?' I replied: 'Indeed'. Shāh al-Kasnazān said: 'I make the impossible possible'".[117]

These things include one whereby Shāh al-Kasnazān inserted a container inside a much smaller one; a feat that is impossible according to natural laws.

The earlier Qudsī ḥadīth means that karāmas never stop occurring because the world would never be deprived of Allah's righteous walīs and nearness to Allah is the cause of karāmas. Many people believe in karāmas but their knowledge of them is confined to what they have read in history books and biographies. They believe that karāmas only happened to righteous people in the past. This misconception reflects ignorance of the reason behind the occurrence of karāmas: nearness to Allah. This blessed state is not limited to the people of a particular time. This misunderstanding also demonstrates unawareness of any of the countless miracles that have occurred and do occur at all times. Furthermore, this

---

[117] Shaikh Muḥammad al-Muḥammad al-Kasnazān, *sermon*, undated.

misconception reflects ignorance of the role of miracles. The role of karāmas ultimately necessitates the continuation of their occurrence, as we will see in the next section.

3.3 The Function of Karāmas

Scholars agree that a prophet's mu'jizas and a walī's karāmas are signs from Allah, confirming the prophet's call. The primary reason Allah allowed karāmas and did not limit miracles to mu'jizas is that people in every time and place are in need, in addition to logical proofs, of paranormal feats to attract them to religion and strengthen their faith. It is illogical to believe that people needed miracles to believe at the time of the appearance of a prophet but that subsequent generations did not have the same, if not greater, need for miracles to assure them of the validity of their belief. Before he announced his prophethood, Muḥammad (PBUH) was known in Mecca as "The Truthful, Trustworthy One". Yet this did not remove the need for miracles assuring the people of the authenticity of his claim that a Book from Allah was revealed to him and that he conveyed it to them as is. Thus, miracles had to be performed by him. The need for miracles did not become less in subsequent years than at the beginning of the call to prophethood. The Prophet (PBUH) was in a constant state of preaching to new individuals and peoples, hence his life was all miracles. Through miracles, Allah attracted great numbers of people, in the Arabian Peninsula and just outside it, who made a living by invading one another and, accordingly, shared history of enmity, hatred, and vengeance that goes back for decades. Allah made them brothers who would sacrifice themselves and their wealth for Allah:

> "Remember the favour of Allah upon you — when you were enemies and He brought your hearts together so you became, by His favour, brothers". ('Āl 'Imrān 103)
>
> "But if they intend to deceive you, then Allah is sufficient for you. It is He who aided you with His support and with the believers. He brought their hearts together. If you had spent all that is in the earth, you could not have brought their hearts together; but Allah brought them together. Indeed, He is invincible, wise". (Al-Ānfāl 62-63)

Our Shaikh emphasizes that, contrary to the claims of Islam's enemies, the Messenger (PBUH) did not propagate religion by force. The armed jihad of the first Muslims was out of self-defence against the hostile milieu that did not allow them to embrace and practice the religion that Allah chose for them, and so they chose for themselves. We must not forget that the Arabs before Islam were used to fighting and war. Any attempt to coerce them into entering Islam through armed force would not have made them truly embrace it, let alone permanently. Similarly, if Islam had spread in its nascency through violence and the use of arms, it would not have been more successful than other military campaigns that may be temporarily effective in achieving its objectives, before subsequent campaigns undo those achievements or wipe them out completely. Religious belief cannot be forced into the hearts of people, the same way it cannot be forced out of them. Hence, Allah has ordered that "there shall be no compulsion in religion" (al-Baqara 256). We see, for example, how for six decades the Soviet Union tried to turn its peoples away from religion and turn them into atheists. Yet, its attempts failed. It was the Union that dissolved and disappeared, while people retained their faith in their respective religions. The Messenger's (PBUH) muʿjizas and their extensions in the form of karāmas of the righteous people who followed Islam, as well as the powerful logic of its message and the attractiveness of its teachings, propagated Islam and firmly established it in the hearts of people.

The Prophet's (PBUH) muʿjizas were proof, to those who witnessed them, of the validity of his claim to prophethood. Being extensions of the Messenger's (PBUH) muʿjizas, karāmas play a similar role. They are proof, to those who did not live in his (PBUH) era and did not see his muʿjizas, of the historicity of the Muḥammadan muʿjizas and the truthfulness of his call. The lack of awareness among some Muslims today of the existence of karāmas causes them to deny some of the Prophet's (PBUH) muʿjizas that are documented in historical and Ḥadīth sources. They argue that these muʿjizas are not mentioned in the Qur'an and that these books combine what is historical and what is fabricated. The first argument is rejected by the Qur'an, which explicitly refers to some of the Messenger's (PBUH) muʿjizas, as discussed earlier. Additionally, it is an undisputed fact that the Qur'an did not document every detail of his (PBUH) life.

As for the second argument, there is no doubt that historical and Ḥadīth sources mix fact and fiction, but the scientific approach requires us not to reject all that is stated in them, the same way it demands that we do not accept everything they mention. It is impossible to track the origin of every claim in these books about the Prophet's (PBUH) miracles to check whether it is historical or not, due to the unavailability of sources and means of auditing incidents that occurred this long ago. The solution, however, comes from another source: karāmas. Karāmas are historical incidents that are amenable to scientific validation because they occur in every era. Although karāmas do not directly or specifically substantiate every mu'jiza of the Prophet Muḥammad (PBUH) mentioned in Ḥadīth and historical sources, they confirm that all those types of miracles may have occurred. For instance, sources state that he miraculously healed the sick. Karāmas of healing the sick, which occur in every era, validate those statements in general terms, and so on.

Naturally, karāmas played a leading role in spreading Islam to different parts of the world, attracting people to it and fortifying their belief. They convinced them that the message of Prophet Muḥammad (PBUH), which the preachers carried, was the truth. They also proved to them that this religion was truly from Allah because such limitless spiritual power could only have originated from Allah, the Omnipotent, who has power over all things. For example, Shaikh 'Abd al-Qādir al-Gāylānī's exceptional role in spreading Islam, during his lifetime and up to today, is owed to his countless miracles. Paranormal occurrences, in the way of mu'jizas and karāmas, facilitate the acceptance of Allah's call, but they do not rob a person of their volition and force him to do so. Many people rejected the prophets' messages, despite the miracles that testified to the veracity of their claims. Allah has confirmed this in many verses in the Qur'an:

"Even if We opened to them a passage into heaven and they continued to ascend through it, they would say, 'Our eyes have only been dazzled. Rather, we are a people affected by magic'". (Al-Ḥijr 14-15)

"Even if We had sent down to you [O Muḥammad] a book written on a page and they touched it with their hands, the disbelievers would have said, 'This is not but obvious magic'". (Al-Ān'ām 7)

"If their evasion is too difficult for you, then if you are able to seek a tunnel into the earth or a stairway into the sky to bring them a sign, [then do so]. Had Allah willed, He would have united them upon guidance. So never be of the ignorant". (Al-Ān'ām 35)

There is no remedy for the person who insists on rejecting what his senses perceive to this extent!

Karāmas also make people recognise the true Shaikhs who guide people to Allah. Anyone who behaves following the way of the Qur'an and the Prophet's (PBUH) Sunna, by word and deed, acquires a portion of his light and inherits his spiritual states. Paranormal feats then happen to him and because of him. The nearer that devotee draws to Allah, the more karāmas appear near to him and far away, night and day. They acquaint people with his status with Allah and invite them to follow him to reach their Lord. Hence, there are those to and from whom miracles rarely appear, while there are those who experience them every day, in sleep and in wakefulness. The seeker's adherence to the Ṭarīqa's dhikrs and his Master's instructions kindles the love of the Shaikh in his heart. This love, in turn, leads to love of the Messenger (PBUH), and love of the Messenger is the means to Allah Almighty's love. Karāmas are the fruits of the finest kind of love that Allah created and facilitated for His servants. Every true love is a positive force whose effects appear to the lover in different facets of his life. Nevertheless, the finest fruit of love — the love of Allah and His Prophet (PBUH), as well as the Shaikhs of Ṭarīqa — reflects the status of the beloved, hence the fruits of divine love are unequalled.

A person's claim that he is a Shaikh of Ṭarīqa and that the Prophet (PBUH) and the Shaikhs have chosen him as a representative of theirs cannot be true if he does not have karāmas that testify to its validity. A Shaikh cites the karāmas of righteous predecessors to instil faith in people's hearts and strengthen it. The degree of his impact on people, however, comes from the karāmas that appear at his hands and are witnessed by seekers, both in their lives and the lives of others. These miracles prove to people that this Shaikh is of the same class as the servants of Allah that he speaks about, and that he is their inheritor. They demonstrate his connection to the Muḥammadan Light, which is the source of these karāmas. They testify that following him to follow in the true Prophetic Sunna, which leads to Allah. Since the Shaikhs of the Ṭarīqa Kasnazāniyya inherited the Prophet's (PBUH) states and spiritual knowledge, there are countless karāmas in the life of each one of them. Miracles cause people from everywhere, every race, every culture, and every social background to gather in the Ṭarīqa. There is no practising seeker who has not witnessed and experienced themselves the Ṭarīqa's karāmas.

Countless karāmas have attracted individuals who previously had no interest in the Ṭarīqa or even made it close to the hearts of those who used to be enemies of it, its Shaikhs, and its followers. For instance, some seekers of Shaikh ʿAbd al-Karīm's went to Khoshnāw, in the Shaqlāwa province in the Erbil governorate in northern Iraq, to preach and call people to the Ṭarīqa. A man named "Aḥmad" who lived in this village harboured an intense hatred for the dervishes. His wife, however, loved to learn about the Ṭarīqa. She took her baby and went with relatives to attend the dervishes' dhikr without telling her husband. But her husband came to know of this and grew furious. When she came back home, he refused to open the door until she told him where she had been. When she did, he insulted her and refused to allow her and their son into the house. Despite his parents, who lived in the same house, pleading with him, Aḥmad refused to allow his wife and baby into the house, forcing them to stay in a relative's house.

That night, the husband saw in a dream a man he did not know insulting him, calling him a "fool". The man extended two fingers towards his eyes and threatened to take them out. The man then pulled his hands back, at which point Aḥmad felt as if the fingers touched his chest. He woke up terrified and found himself completely paralyzed. He did not call out to his parents, hoping that things would go back to normal. He did not want to mention the vision, which was clearly related to his hatred of the Ṭarīqa and ill-treatment of his wife that night.

His condition did not improve, and it was not something that could be kept secret for long. In the morning, his parents discovered their son's sudden loss of mobility, the cause of which he claimed to be ignorant of. Due to the gravity of his condition, his brothers and relatives quickly gathered around him. He insisted that he did not know what had happened to him until the repeated questioning made him claim that the day before he fought with a man who wrestled him to the ground, and the fall on his back led to his paralysis. When his family brought that man, he confronted Aḥmad and denied his having seen him at all in the past few days. Aḥmad remained in that condition, with his family in extreme grief, not knowing what had happened to their son or how to help him.

After two months, Aḥmad's brother visited him with a group of the village's dervishes. They urged him to go with them to Kirkuk to visit their Master, Shaikh ʿAbd al-Karīm al-Kasnazān, that Allah may listen to the Shaikh's prayer for him. Aḥmad disclosed his dream to them and promised to take the pledge from their Shaikh if he turned out to be the man who had visited him in his sleep. By merely intending to go with them, Aḥmad began to feel better. He asked them to let him take a shower and get changed first.

When Aḥmad arrived at the takya in Kirkuk with the dervishes, he saw Shaikh ʿAbd al-Karīm from afar, sitting in the courtyard. He immediately recognized him as the same man who had visited him in his dream. When he approached him and held his hand to kiss it, the Shaikh told him, "From now on, be sensible", before giving him the pledge. The Shaikh asked a caliph called "Mullā Jabbār" to also make the new dervish a caliph! Mullā Jabbār asked the dervish what his name was to write it on the caliphate certificate. He said, "Aḥmad". He asked for his father's name, but before he could reply, Shaikh ʿAbd al-Karīm said "Mām Ḥusayn". The word "Mām" in Kurdish means "Uncle", which was indeed the name of Aḥmad's father. Caliph Aḥmad still has the caliphate certificate showing his name as "Aḥmad Mām Ḥusayn", as Shaikh ʿAbd al-Karīm said.

When thinking about the impact of karāmas on people, we can understand our Shaikh's saying that they have a unique role in transforming a person's faith from "traditional" to "true", citing this verse: "Worship your Lord until there comes to you the certainty" (al-Ḥijr 99). Traditional faith is what a person inherits from his family, culture, and upbringing. Such faith is driven more by habit, imitation, and indoctrination than acquisition and free learning. This faith remains limited in its firmness even when the person increases his knowledge of religion and strengthens the intellectual foundations of his faith. The reason is that a large part of religious belief comprises matters that belong to the unseen, so they are not possible to intellectually prove or refute. For instance: it is not possible to use reason to verify the existence of the Day of Resurrection, as it is a future event that is impossible to infer from present events and cannot be proven using logic. Similarly, the intellect cannot ascertain the world of angels because it is completely different from our world and cannot be reached by our senses or the available means of exploration. The same goes for the jinns and spirit world. No matter how brilliant one is in establishing his belief, which is often inherited and sometimes acquired, on strong intellectual foundations, these would not be enough to support all aspects of religious belief. Here is where karāmas come in, to provide proofs to substantiate religious belief, including what is unseen, replacing doubt with certainty: "Worship your Lord until there comes to you the certainty" (al-Ḥijr 99). Miracles are proofs in the visible world of the unseen world whose source is "Knower of the unseen and the visible" (al-Ān'ām 73). Miracles strengthen faith in the unseen aspects of religious belief. The goal of karāmas is to transport the devotee to the state of Iḥsān: "To worship Allah as if you see Him; and if you cannot see Him, then verily He sees you".[118]

The purifying ṣuḥba is the way to witness miracles directly, which itself is the path to Iḥsān. However, as already mentioned, the good one gains and karāmas one experiences from the companionship of Allah's people depend on giving this ṣuḥba its due. That right is worshipping Allah Almighty and upholding religious commandments and prohibitions. Our Shaikh says that when the seeker fosters the Ṭarīqa pledge, which he likens to a spiritual plant, with the care it deserves, Allah grants him various miracles:

> "When the seeker tends to and waters this plant — that is, by the light of dhikr, the light of worship, the light of purity, the light of cleanliness, the light of Sharia, the light of the Qur'an — Allah (exalted and high is He) illuminates his heart. He sees whatever he wants to see buy Allah's permission. Allah illuminates whatever He wants for him because He said about Himself: 'His command is only when He intends a thing that He says to it, 'Be', and it is' (Yāsīn 82)".[119]

There is a big difference between hearing or reading about something and witnessing it for oneself, because direct experience is the source of certainty about that thing. This applies to all things in general, including karāmas. Anyone who follows the right path will inevitably see with his own eyes the signs of that truth in the form of miracles in which the laws of nature are nullified and the extraordinary overcomes the ordinary. In his assemblies, Shaikh 'Abd al-Qādir al-Gaylānī used to reiterate that reaching Allah causes one to witness "what no eye has ever seen, what no

---

[118] Bukhārī, *Al-Jāmi' al-Ṣaḥīḥ*, I, no. 50, p. 65.

[119] Shaikh Muḥammad al-Muḥammad al-Kasnazān, *sermon*, last third of October/2013.

ear has ever heard, and what and has never occurred to any human being".[120]

There is another very important reality of karāmas. Some miracles are special gifts that the receiver must conceal. Some of the miracles that result from nearness to Allah are meant to be public signs for people, as the purpose behind them is to guide and call people to Allah. Other miracles are special, so they must be kept secret and not be revealed to the public. The Prophet Muḥammad (PBUH) performed many miracles that people witnessed. These were of the public category of miracle, whose function was to be proof of the divinity of his message. Indeed, Allah ordered him to announce every manifestation of the favours He blessed him with, including public miracles: "As for the favour of your Lord, speak about it" (al-Ḍuḥā 11). Naturally, the Messenger (PBUH) had countless special spiritual paranormal experiences, during his worship, for example. It is illogical to assume that he spoke publicly about all of them.

This also applies to karāmas. Some karāmas occur publicly, while some are revealed by their possessors so that they may indicate the continuation of the message and blessings of the Prophet Muḥammad (PBUH). These guide people to the way to Allah, in addition to confirming the righteousness of those to whom these miracles are attributed. In the case of preaching, it is permissible, or even at times necessary, to reveal karāmas. But the individual who is near to Allah also experiences special karāmas that are meant for him alone. This noble verse speaks of special karāmas that happen to the virtuous person:

> "Indeed, those who have said, 'Our Lord is Allah' and then remained on a right course — angels will descend upon them, [saying], 'Do not fear and do not grieve but receive good tidings of Paradise, which you were promised. (30) We are your allies in this life and the Hereafter. You will have therein whatever your souls desire, and you will have therein whatever you request, (31) as accommodation from One who is forgiving and merciful'". (Fuṣṣilat 30-32)

Our Shaikh emphasizes that since these karāmas are special grants to the devout seeker, he must not reveal them to others, though he may inform his Shaikh of them. Announcing special karāmas can cause pride and vanity in the disciple's heart, negatively affecting his spiritual state.

---

[120] Shaikh ʿAbd al-Qādir al-Gaylānī, *Jilā' al-Khāṭir*, p. 27.

Being special gifts to the individual that reflect his spiritual state, he must not share them with others. Disclosing them may cause them to stop from occurring because one of their requirements is concealment. In the course of teaching in parables, our Master says that the dervish's keenness to hide the karāma must be like the keenness of a weak, elderly, and poor woman to hide a piece of a gold coin that she owns, fearing that someone might steal it or that she might lose it.

While many karāmas of the Shaikhs of Ṭarīqa with which they help their disciples and people in various matters are public, at times, some of these paranormal occurrences take place without one's perceiving them. In the 1970s, the attendees of an assembly of Shaikh ʿAbd al-Karīm al-Kasnazān in Kirkuk — including our present Master, Shaikh Muḥammad al-Muḥammad — were speaking about different karāmas of the Kasnazānī Shaikhs that had happened to them and that they had witnessed. One speaker, a grandchild of Shāh al-Kasnazān, related karāmas of his grandfather. His brother thought to himself that he was the only person who was not talking about Shāh al-Kasnazān's karāmas because the Shaikh had not graced him with any. When this man came to the assembly the following day, he informed the attendees of his thought and his mistake. He told them that he saw Shāh al-Kasnazān that night in a dream who reminded him of an incident that occurred to him in Kirkuk: "Remember the day you were crossing the street and two cars came from opposite directions, one from the city of Mosul and the other from Kirkuk, and you found yourself between the two cars. How did you suddenly find yourself on the other side of the street?" Then the man realised that it was his grandfather Shāh al-Kasnazān who saved him in that situation without him being aware. This miracle shows that many karāmas come in the form of spiritual assistance from the Shaikhs of Ṭarīqa to people. Our Shaikh comments on this fact saying that the spiritually aware seeker recognizes such spiritual interventions when they occur, but the Shaikhs help the seeker even if he is not conscious of this aid.[121]

Our Shaikh stresses that the dervish must never make witnessing or experiencing a karāma a goal. The devotee's goal must be nearness to Allah for his devotion to be purely for Allah's sake. As for karāmas, they

---

[121] Shaikh Muḥammad al-Muḥammad al-Kasnazān, *sermon*, last third of October/2013.

will come as a result of this nearness:

> "If you come to the Ṭarīqa with the objective of procuring karāmas, then this means that you have not come for Allah. Allah is the one who grants you karāmas. According to the principles of our Ṭarīqa, karāmas ought to seek out the seeker, not the other way around. You must seek the Creator of karāmas, the one who grants you karāmas: 'Indeed, the noblest of you in the sight of Allah is the most righteous of you' (al-Ḥujurāt 13).[122]

A devotee has the right to ask to see what strengthens his faith, as the Prophet Abraham requested: "when Abraham said, 'My Lord, show me how You give life to the dead'" (al-Baqara 260). But this differs from making witnessing miracles a goal of worship. The objective of worship is annihilation in Allah Almighty's love.

Since receiving and performing karāmas is linked to the person's nearness to Allah, the more a servant draws near to Allah with the performance of dhikr and righteous deeds, the more the miracles he is granted. Our Shaikh relates that a dervish asked a caliph to pray to Allah to fulfil a need of his. The caliph promised that he would. The situation repeated itself several times, with the caliph promising all dervishes that he would pray for them. At night, the caliph saw the Shaikhs in a dream, asking him reproachfully: "What worship did you perform today that you guaranteed the dervishes all these promises to fulfil their needs?" Allah (mighty and sublime is He) says: "Call on Me; I will respond to you" (Ghāfir 60). He has promised us a positive response when we call on Him, and calling out to Him means worshipping Him. Our Shaikh likens this to a person who goes shopping whose money limits what he can buy.[123] Allah's gifts to His servant are commensurate with the status of his worship, even though Allah's mercy and favour exceed the servant's merit.

Karāmas also have a role in the spiritual education of the seeker. Through karāmas, spiritual secrets and knowledge are revealed that cannot be attained intellectually. The Ṭarīqa's dhikrs are a fruit of such spiritual revelations, whereby the Shaikhs receive devotions that have spiritual benefits that suit the needs of the dervishes' spiritual development in specific times and places. The Shaikhs then make these revelations part

---

[122] Shaikh Muḥammad al-Muḥammad al-Kasnazān, *sermon*, 9th/June/2000.

[123] Shaikh Muḥammad al-Muḥammad al-Kasnazān, *sermon*, 15th/April/2016.

of the devotions of the Ṭarīqa.

Karāmas are a fruit of worship and nearness to Allah Almighty. They have four primary benefits for anyone who performs them, whom they happen to, and who witnesses them. In addition to their unique role in promoting his faith from traditional to true, they show him who truly lives according to the Messenger's (PBUH) way. They are also a means through which Allah helps His servants with their various needs. Finally, karāmas are a source of spiritual education and knowledge.

The goal of karāmas is not material gain in this life — a fact that is highlighted by many karāmas. Shāh al-Kasnazān went with a few others to the village of Khāwya to bring wheat for the takya. On the way, his daughter asked him why they needed to go to that village to bring wheat, instead of getting what they need by way of a karāma from him, such as causing gold liras to come out of the earth. The Shaikh moved with his cane a rock on the road, unveiling gold liras underneath. His daughter was happy and wanted to take the gold, but the Shaikh push the rock back in its place, hiding the liras. He went on to tell her: "We do not want gold. Had we wanted it, it would not have been so accessible to us. It is better for us to get the wheat from Khāwya than take these liras".

3.4 Source of Karāmas

We have mentioned that the source of the seeker's karāmas is the spiritual power of the Shaikhs of Ṭarīqa. This, in turn, is a gift from the Prophet (PBUH) and an extension of the spiritual power that Allah has given him. The karāmas of every Shaikh and his disciples reflect his spiritual status. The miracles that one Shaikh performs may not be possible for another Shaikh. This also means that the Shaikh's miracles change and vary with his spiritual development.

The occurrence of karāmas to the seeker depends on the level of his love for the Shaikh, the Prophet (PBUH) and Allah Almighty, and on submitting his affairs to the Shaikh to lead him on the Muḥammadan Way to Allah. But it is still essential for the seeker not to feel a sense of conceit when he experiences karāmas, and not to forget that his connection to the chain of Shaikhs of the Ṭarīqa, through the pledge, is the cause behind this blessing. If he becomes cut off from them, this blessing is immediately cut. The seeker's practice of Sufism is the "means" by which karāmas appear. The "source" of these miracles, however, is the spirituality of the Shaikh of Ṭarīqa, which is derived from the spirituality of the Messenger (PBUH), to whom Allah (mighty and sublime is He) granted that which He did not grant to anyone. The spiritually aware dervish, therefore, does not attribute the karāmas that he performs to himself but rather to his Shaikh. As the disciple's spiritual status and blessing increase, the humbler he grows and the more insistent he becomes on describing himself as the lowest and simplest dervish.

The behaviour of our Shaikh provides us with a great lesson here. The attendees of an assembly of our Master often recount karāmas attributed to him that they witnessed or had happened to them or to others, such as our Shaikh appearing to an ailing person in a dream and curing them of their sickness. When these karāmas are mentioned in front of him and are attributed to him, he says "I seek forgiveness from Allah", and follows that by saying, "this is a result of the Messenger's (PBUH) blessing", "these are karāmas of the Shaikh", or other phrases that distance himself from the reported miracles and attribute them to his Masters. Shaikh ʿAbd al-Karīm did exactly the same thing when his karāmas were mentioned in front of him. This utmost etiquette is characteristic of all Shaikhs of the Ṭarīqa. If the Shaikh of Ṭarīqa feels embarrassed to attribute a karāma to himself, even though those who witnessed it saw him perform it with their own eyes, then what about the Shaikh's disciples when he experiences a karāma?

A dervish's vanity when experiencing karāmas and attributing them to himself instead of his Shaikh spiritually harms him. If he does not redress himself and correct his mistake, he loses that blessing. Indeed, he can even lose his faith. Generally speaking, the disciple's disobedience to the Shaikh and opposing his orders leads to the dispossession of the dervish's blessing because it is from his Shaikh, and the Shaikh enjoins only what is good and forbids only what is wrong. There are many such instances in the history of Sufism. One of these happened to a caliph named Riḍā, a contemporary of Shaikh Ḥusayn, and then Shaikh ʿAbd al-Karīm after him. This dervish had tremendous blessings, such so that when he went to preach in the city of Sulaymāniyya in northern Iraq, beating the dhikr drum, he and the dervishes with him would be followed by wild animals, including wolves, foxes, and others, in every area they passed by. He would be seen with 200-300 dervishes and a number of these wild animals that would accompany them as if they were also hearing his preaching and listening to him. On caliph Riḍā's way back from a preaching trip, the animals would leave him in the area that they had joined him in. One of the manifestations of the blessing that the Shaikhs of Ṭarīqa gave to Riḍā was that his prayer would be answered when he was engaged in preaching. Many sick people were healed by his prayer, and other miracles happened at his hands that brought people to the Ṭarīqa and made it beloved to them. Most residents of the Shahrizor region became Kasnazānī disciples at his hands.

This blessing was a result of Riḍā's love for his Shaikh and his sincerity with him. When he would come to visit him in Karbchna, where Shaikh 'Abd al-Karīm resided at the beginning of his Masterhood, he would begin to crawl from its outskirts on his hands and knees out of love and respect for the Shaikh. Nonetheless, vanity gradually infiltrated his heart and he forgot that he was a dervish, so whatever blessing he had was from the Shaikh. Vanity seized him until he began to write supplications for people, even though the Shaikh did not authorise him to write supplications, as the Ṭarīqa Kasnazāniyya has special dhikrs that contain all a person needs of blessing, as we will see later. He also tempted himself into embezzling some of the donations people gave to the Ṭarīqa. He thought that the blessing that showed on him was essentially his, so it had no relation to the Shaikh of Ṭarīqa, and that he was the cause of those donations, which justified this greed to himself.

One afternoon, Shaikh 'Abd al-Karīm saw his Shaikh, Sultan Ḥusayn, in a dream. The latter informed him that caliph Riḍā was on the way to visit Karbchna, and that he had a specific amount of money belonging to the Ṭarīqa, but that he had embezzled some of it. He disclosed to him that the money that he was bringing to the takya was in a red napkin, and he informed him of the number of each kind of banknote. He ordered him to return the money to Riḍā and to expel him from the Ṭarīqa. When Shaikh 'Abd al-Karīm woke up, he asked if Riḍā had come, but he was told that he had not. At that time, in those remote, mountainous villages, there were no means of communication enabling people to know if someone from another area was coming unannounced. Shaikh 'Abd al-Karīm went to Shāh al-Kasnazān's orchard and performed the afternoon prayer there. After the prayer, he asked if Riḍā had arrived. The answer was, again, in the negative. Shortly afterwards, the sounds of the drum of visiting dervishes were heard from atop the mountain overlooking Karbchna. Word came that the one who was beating the drum was caliph Riḍā, whose arrival the Shaikh was anticipating.

When greeting the Shaikh, Riḍā told him that he had brought a donation for the takya, but the Shaikh refused it and told him to hold onto it. The Shaikh revealed the sum of the amount that he had brought and the amount that he had stolen from peoples' donations to the takya. He informed him that the proof of what he was saying is that he had placed the money in a red napkin, and he disclosed the number of each kind of note in it. Shaikh ʿAbd al-Karīm then expelled this dervish, and this was his last visit to the Shaikh. Riḍā's faith was taken from him and all the blessing that he had was pulled from him. After enjoying a great status among the people, he ended up dying on the street, and his grave site remains unknown. Even his widow forgot him, just as the people did, and married after him. No information remains about him other than the details of his deviation from the Ṭarīqa and his unfortunate end.[124]

Let us cite another example from Shaikh Ḥusayn's time. There was a sergeant major by the name of Ḥasan working as a commander of the police station on Mount Sagarma. At the time, there were police stations on the caravan route. One morning, Ḥasan was hunting on the Karbchna side of the mountain when he saw a fox climbing up the mountain, coming from the direction of the village. When the fox got close, he noticed a large piece of honeycomb in its mouth. The fox dropped the honeycomb there and left. Ḥasan descended to where the honey was. He saw that it was clean, and it seemed appetizing to him. He ate some of it and carried the rest with him to the station.

After a short while, a special state overcame the sergeant major that made him unaware of his actions. He left the station, without his weapon, and began to climb down the mountain towards Karbchna. When his comrades at the station asked him what he was doing, he did not respond. Ḥasan went to visit Sultan Ḥusayn. When the Shaikh asked him why he had come, he replied that he did not know. The Shaikh gave him the pledge and instructed him to go into seclusion for forty days. After he completed it, the Shaikh ordered him to seclude himself for another forty

---

124 Shaikh Muḥammad al-Muḥammad al-Kasnazān, *sermon*, 22nd/September/2016; 4th/December/2013.

days. Ḥasan delayed visiting his family in Kirkuk, his wife began to inquire about him. The news reached her from the station that her husband had gone to Karbchna and had not returned.

She took her children and went to Karbchna where she found Ḥasan in his second seclusion. She tried to persuade him to return to his post, afraid that he would be imprisoned, expelled from the police, and lose his source of income. He refused to return and said that, with Allah's permission, his salary won't be stopped and she would continue to receive it. The wife went to Sangāw to receive her husband's two salaries, which were paid in full. Officials also told her not to worry about the salary and that they hoped Ḥasan would return. Then she returned to Kirkuk. The following month, the wife went a second time to Sangāw to get the salary, she then visited Karbchna to see her husband, who had finished his second seclusion. The Shaikh made him a caliph and instructed him to return to his family and his post in the police. After some time, Ḥasan left his post in the police and continued to preach as a caliph.

As a result of his struggle against his self and his proper Sufi conduct, Ḥasan reached spiritual levels, had blessings, and became famous. When people would ask him to give them something, such as a specific kind of food, he would put his hand on a wall and say "gul Ḥusayn" and the food would appear in his hands. The Kurdish word "gul" means "rose". He would use this call for spiritual support from Shaikh Ḥusayn. Unfortunately, after a while, Ḥasan deviated from the straight path. His blessing was taken away, and people forgot about him and did not know what happened to him.[125]

Our Shaikh has a wise saying that describes the state of the people who perform karāmas or witness them yet they still stray from the path:

> "There are people in the Ṭarīqa whom the Shaikhs immerse in karāmas yet none of these karāmas sticks to them. Their likeness is like a flint stone that absorbs no water when immersed in it".

The main error of these caliphs was that they were beguiled by the karāmas that appeared at their hands, becoming ignorant of themselves after being self-knowing: "When adversity touches man, he calls upon Us; then when We bestow on him a favour from Us, he says, 'I have only been given it because of [my] knowledge.' Rather, it is a trial, but most of them do not

---

[125] Shaikh Muḥammad al-Muḥammad al-Kasnazān, *sermon*, 22nd/June/2000.

know" (al-Zumar 49). After realizing that every blessing they had received was not of themselves but was rather ḥāls and spiritual levels that the Shaikhs of Ṭarīqa bestowed on them, conceit replaced this knowledge with ignorance and misguidance. When they lost their knowledge of themselves, they lost the way and were no more travellers on the path. The dervish is "one who knows himself". This self-knowingness is a prerequisite for the person to become "Allah-knowing": "Whoever knows himself has known his Lord". If arrogance had not caused them to err, each one of them would have preserved his knowledge of himself, and thus his knowledge of his Shaikh, and therefore his knowledge of his Lord.

It is necessary to stress here that a mistake committed by a person who has experienced many karāmas and has seen with his own eyes what cannot be described by the tongue or comprehended by the intellect have worse consequences than the same mistake when committed by a person who has not had such spiritual openings from the Shaikhs. Also, the cases of the withdrawal of blessings that we mentioned, which ended with the disciples going astray, share something important. The sinful dervish insisted on his mistake and did not retract. The cause of their misguidance was not a momentary lapse or a mistake that they rectified as soon as they were aware of it, but rather, it was pride and insistence on the error until it ultimately took them to perdition.

3.5 The Diversity of Karāmas and their Causes

In the Qur'an, Allah mentions different kinds of muʿjizas of the prophets, indicating that they take countless forms. This is also the case with karāmas, as they are an extension of muʿjizas. Even any one kind of these divine miracles can appear in countless forms, as Allah (mighty and sublime is He) is capable of breaking all laws of nature. Let's consider, for example, how the Almighty transformed the nature of fire and made it cool for prophet Abraham when his people threw him in it: "We said, 'O fire, be coolness and safety for Abraham'" (al-Ānbiyā` 69). The cause of breaching the norm is divine intervention. Since this intervention can occur through any means, there is no limit to the forms that muʿjizas and karāmas can take.

The Shaikh may cure an irremediable illness by prescribing the diseased person to eat some honey or to drink water that he has blessed. But if the patient decided to eat whatever honey he wanted or drink as much water as he liked, they would not cure him of his illness because it is not in the nature of honey or water to remedy these incurable diseases. It is the spiritual power of the Shaikh that made that honey or water a cause for a miracle. This blessing that Allah has conferred upon the Prophet (PBUH) and the Shaikhs of Ṭarīqa can make anything a cause for the breaching of any norm. There is no limit to the kinds of muʿjiza and karāma.

The reason for the occurrence of one karāma in a certain form and second in another is known only to those who know such secrets. It is evident, however, that the occurrence of a paranormal act in a certain way is not random. Whoever studies muʿjizas and karāmas can only conclude that there are hidden laws that determine how each of these miracles occur. They are not laws of the natural world, however. Let us compare, for example, three karāmas of paranormal healing by our Shaikh, where we can see that the curing of the illness differed in every case. The first karāma occurred in 2005 or 2006 to the dervish Aḥmad Sharīf Pāshā from India, who recounts here what happened:

> I was struck with hemiplegia about sixteen or seventeen years ago. At the time, an English doctor treated me, and I achieved eighty per cent recovery. I was left with partial paralysis of the face, as my mouth remained permanently twisted towards the right side. This prevented me from speaking properly. For example, I could not pronounce the letter "f."
>
> At some point after taking the pledge of the Ṭarīqa, I went to work in Saudi Arabia. One day, after performing the dawn prayer, I stood in front of a photo of Shaikh Muḥammad al-Muḥammad al-Kasnazān to talk to him directly, and I said to him: "In the past, I did not pray and used to talk badly. Nevertheless, before being struck with hemiplegia, I did not have any speech impediment and could speak freely. Yet, I am now a practising dervish, observing the prayer and dhikrs, but I cannot enunciate properly; why are you not helping me?" I was talking with some anger.
>
> When I slept that night, I had a strange dream. I was in a hospital that was unfamiliar to me. There was a doctor there who had come from China. He was wearing a surgical mask. He told me that he was going to cure my facial paralysis. I lay in bed and the doctor started treating me with acupuncture. The treatment lasted about half an hour, during which time he inserted needles into various parts of my body. When he finished, the doctor said to

me: "Your treatment is now complete. You are 98% cured." I asked him: "Sir, who are you?" He removed his mask, and I realized that it was Shaikh Muḥammad al-Kasnazān.

I woke up scared. It was about three o'clock in the morning. I performed my ablutions and the dawn prayer. I then looked into the mirror and saw that my facial paralysis had completely gone away. My mouth was now normal. The other 2% that the Shaikh mentioned in the dream concerns a little issue I still have at times when I swallow food and I am not careful. All I need in such cases is a drink of water.[126]

The second karāma took place in India in 2012. A woman came to caliph ʿImād ʿAbd al-Ṣamad and complained to him, crying. She had a medical issue with her nose, which had been severely blocked since birth, but her condition had worsened. The doctors said that she needed surgery. The procedure was extremely costly, and she and her unemployed husband were barely able to feed themselves. The caliph gave her the Ṭarīqa's pledge and asked her to start reading the Ṭarīqa's dhikrs. A week later, this dervish came to visit the caliph. Looking happy, she told him that she saw in a dream Shaikh Muḥammad al-Muḥammad cut her stricken nose and replace it with another. He spoke to her in her language, Urdu. When she woke up, she found drops of blood and mucus on her nose and the pillow and her ailment had gone away. She visited her doctor, who did not believe her story. Nonetheless, he also could not explain what had happened, as he had taken X-rays of her diseased nose just a few days, and it was now sound. The caliph asked her if she had seen a picture of our Shaikh, and she said that she had not. When he showed her the Shaikh's picture, she jumped up and started kissing it. She confirmed that he was the man who cured her in her sleep.[127]

The third karāma happened to the poet, Dr ʿAbd al-Salām al-Ḥadīthī. On an ordinary day in 1991, a severe dust storm struck Baghdad. Someone informed our Shaikh that this would adversely affect the health of caliph ʿAbd al-Salām as he suffered from asthma. When he visited our Shaikh that night, he asked him about it and what the doctors were doing about it. He replied that he was struck with this severe asthma when he was studying in Italy in 1983, and despite many doctors having examined

---

[126] Fatoohi, *The Wonders of Ṭarīqa Kasnazāniyya Brought to India*, pp. 28-29.
[127] Fatoohi, *The Wonders of Ṭarīqa Kasnazāniyya Brought to India*, pp. 17-18.

him there and in Iraq and his use of various remedies, his condition had not improved. Our Shaikh asked him about the use of honey as a remedy. Caliph ʿAbd al-Salām replied that he had tried that, before adding that he did not believe anything could cure him besides our Shaikh's spiritual influence. Our Shaikh answered him immediately: "It is the Messenger's spiritual influence". Dr ʿAbd al-Salām had to take the asthma medication Ventolin every night before going to bed and after waking up in the morning. When he went to bed that night, however, he did not feel the need to take it, as was usually the case. Nonetheless, he decided to take it just in case. When he woke up in the morning, he again noticed that he did not need it. This time, he decided not to take it. He never suffered from an asthma attack after that. He was cured of his illness ever since he asked for a cure through the Shaikh's blessing.

There are clear differences in the way the three cases were cured. In the first two karāmas, the cure came via a dream, while in the third one, the cure was administered in an awakened state. The first cure was through Chinese acupuncture, the second through surgery, and the third through supplication. In the first karāma, 2% of the disease was left, whereas in the other two cases the cure was complete. The paranormal healing in the first two karāmas occurred while the afflicted individuals were thousands of kilometres away from our Shaikh, while the healing in the last karāma occurred in his presence. If we compare these karāmas to others, we will find even more differences between them.

Reflecting on these differences reveals that the world of karāmas has specific laws, so it is not a random world where things happen haphazardly. There are spiritual reasons for the occurrence of one karāma in one way and another in a different way. These reasons are among the secrets of karāmas.

There are karāmas characterized by a very high degree of complexity and detail. Each one of these karāmas consists of many interconnected events that include multiple people, occur over a long time, and cover different places that are far from each other. Such a karāma is, in fact, a chain of interlinked karāmas. In that sense, a compound karāma seems like a cinematic film; it is indeed a film directed by the Almighty Creator. Such karāmas illustrate, without a doubt, that they were created and orchestrated by Allah's hand because they reflect an amazing power and control over people, time, and space. We will come across a number of these karāmas in the book.

3.6 Darbāsha

There is a special kind of public karāmas in the Ṭarīqa Kasnazāniyya known as "darbāsha", clearly derived from the Farsi word "dervish". Darbāsha denotes specific paranormal feats that the Shaikh permits some dervishes to perform to reassure people that the Ṭarīqa has a tremendous spiritual power to facilitate their believing in it. When the person travels the Sufi way, they encounter direct, special spiritual experiences. In the beginning, the darbāsha feats that a person sees and the karāmas that he reads or hears about are all the miracles of the Ṭarīqa that he is familiar with. But when he follows the Ṭarīqa, he starts experiencing, in wakefulness and sleep, karāmas that are specific to him. Darbāsha is a means, not an end, by which individuals are attracted to the Messenger's (PBUH) way. It is important to note that practising darbāsha is not a requirement of following the Ṭarīqa. The vast majority of dervishes do not practise darbāsha. Nonetheless, it is a preaching means available to those who prefer to use it.

Darbāsha includes a variety of feats:

- Inserting sharp objects, such as skewers and swords, into various parts of the body, including the cheek, tongue, base of the mouth, arm, pectoral muscles in the chest, and various parts of the abdomen. Disciples use metal instruments of varying thicknesses and widths in these feats. In the case of thin body parts, such as the cheek and base of the mouth, some disciples use pointed wooden skewers instead of metal skewers because it is possible to insert a wooden skewer into these areas without it breaking. Wooden instead of metal skewers are used because they are supposedly more painful and dangerous since they tear body tissue more than their metal counterparts. Wooden skewers often have relatively rough surfaces and irregular diameters.
- Inserting daggers into different sides of the skull, as well as the clavicle, using wooden mallets. The disciple may hammer the dagger into his head himself, or another disciple might do it for

him. Sometimes the dagger is inserted in so deep that it cannot be pulled out by hand, getting stuck in the skull's bones. In this situation, the attempt by someone else to pull the dagger out may result in a separation of the handle and blade, causing the dagger's blade to remain inside the head. When this happens, the disciple usually leaves the dagger in his head for a few minutes, after which the dagger begins to gradually come out of the head, at which point it becomes possible to pull out by hand. It may automatically come out if left alone.

- Chewing and swallowing unused razors, as well as shards of broken glass from glass cups and fluorescent light tubes. There is an additional danger when using light tube glass because the mercury inside the tube is poisonous.

The miraculous nature in these feats is that the dervish remains completely unharmed, even though the wounds caused and the body parts involved make these feats extremely dangerous. The dervish suffers no pain or, at times, feels a small prick when the sharp object pierces his body. He does not bleed, even though, under normal circumstances, these wounds usually cause severe bleeding. The wounds do not get infected even though the darbāsha equipment is unsterile. At times, the dervish deliberately dirties the equipment to further emphasize the miraculous nature of the feat.

The paranormal nature of darbāsha is not limited to immunity against pain, bleeding, and infection. The healing process of wounds is another amazing breach of the laws of nature. All wounds heal almost immediately after the object is removed from the body, at times leaving a small scar, and sometimes not leaving any mark at all. There is more than one aspect of paranormality in this kind of healing. The speed at which the wounds heal contravenes the fundamentals of medical theory and has absolutely no natural explanation whatsoever. The very healing of the wound, regardless of how fast, is supernatural because many of the wounds inflicted by darbāsha are the kinds of wounds that, under normal circumstances, cannot heal automatically without medical intervention. Leaving them untreated, in fact, can have dangerous consequences and could be even fatal. It is important to stress that the healing of the entry wound is accompanied by the healing of any additional bodily damage that could have been caused by the instrument. Finally, the ultimate proof of the miraculous nature of darbāsha is that dervishes can repeat them as many times as they like, meaning the success rate in performing feats of darbāsha is 100%.

Darbāsha includes other paranormal feats that dervishes perform:

- Exposing body parts to fire without getting burned. A piece of cloth wrapped around a wooden dowel or metal rod is typically used for this. The cloth is immersed in a flammable substance, such as oil, then ignited, which dervishes use to expose their face, hands, and feet to the flames. Immunity against fire may also be demonstrated by the dervishes by carrying with their bare hands metal plates heated to the point of redness. They may also hold the hot plates clenched between their teeth. At times, dervishes hold red-hot coals in their bare hands and put them in their mouths. In this case, immunity against gas poisoning is also demonstrated.
- Dervishes expose their hands to poisonous snake bites and scorpion stings. They also deliberately expose their tongues to snake bites. Dervishes sometimes eat snake heads or devour scorpions. The supernatural aspect of these feats is the immunity to poison. A similar karāma of the Companions was performed by Khālid Ibn al-Walīd. He was warned that foreigners wanted to give him poison to drink. He asked for the poison to be brought to him. He said "in the name of Allah", and drank it. He was not harmed at all.[128]
- Dervishes expose their bodies to a dangerous alternating electric current for several minutes.

These are the most common feats of darbāsha that dervishes perform, but there are other feats that some dervishes sometimes practice. They may hit their head forcefully against a large rock, a wall, or the ground, without sustaining any injuries. They may pass a sharp blade over their tongue several times, causing deep wounds that heal instantly. They may even pierce their neck with a skewer. They perform other feats of darbāsha.

---

[128] Aṣbahānī, *Dalā'il al-Nubuwwa*, p. 445.

Unlike similar feats performed by individuals who follow other religions and spiritual philosophies that have no relation to the Ṭarīqa, dervishes do not undergo any sort of special training to acquire these skills. Rather, disciples are capable of performing feats of darbāsha as soon as the Shaikh of Ṭarīqa permits them to do so.

The practice of darbāsha has only one goal: to guide people to the Ṭarīqa. Hence, the Shaikhs of Ṭarīqa stress that these feats must not be used for any other purpose.

3.7 Spiritual Dispensation

Karāmas can happen to anyone, not just to those who accompany a person who is near to Allah, because they are a means by which Allah confers his favours upon whomsoever He desires. Allah confers favours on anyone He desires, whether that servant deserved it or not. For instance, a sick person may see the Messenger (PBUH) in a dream where he cures him of his illness. A person may visit a blessed place, such as the Ka'ba or a walī's shrine, in a time of need. While there, something supernatural may happen to him by which Allah fulfils his need. These gracious miracles, however, occur with low frequency. They happen to a small number of people, and they rarely happen to someone more than once in their life. Such miracles do not necessarily indicate the merits of those to whom they occur, in the same way that the majority of favours any person receives are a grace of Allah's mercy rather than obtained on merit: "Were you to count Allah's favours, you would not be able to enumerate them" (Ibrāhīm 34).

A devotee may acquire karāmas and blessings as a result of his worship and piety. This is something that an individual can acquire even if they have not taken the pledge of the Ṭarīqa. However, there are spiritual ranks that allow a servant to direct matters in the world of spirits. These cannot be reached without following the Ṭarīqa. The ranks of walīhood — such as "Ghawth", "Quṭb", "Watad", and "Badal" — are specific roles assigned by the Shaikhs of Ṭarīqa to a certain number of accomplished seekers, for these walīs to aid the Shaikh, under his supervision, in managing the Ṭarīqa's spiritual affairs. It is impossible to reach any rank of walīhood without taking the pledge from a living Shaikh who represents a continuous chain of Shaikhs tracing back to the Prophet

(PBUH). The following incident clarifies this issue.

A relative of our Shaikh used to worship abundantly. Once, he retired to his room for six months, locked the door and wrapped himself in a cloak. He did not see anyone or any light, remaining in constant worship. His family would leave for him water and a small amount of soup by his door. One day, at dawn, his worship caused him to hear a voice above his home, announcing that he had become a Quṭb. At the end of the announcement, the voice ordered him to go to Shaikh ʿAbd al-Karīm Al-Kasnazān in Karbchna. The voice was so loud and clear that it seemed to this devotee that everyone in Chamchamāl, where he resided, heard the announcement. He was happy with what he had heard, but his pride refused to allow him to visit Shaikh ʿAbd al-Karīm and take the pledge from him.

Afterwards, the man decided to go to Baghdad to visit the shrine of Shaikh ʿAbd al-Qādir al-Gaylānī and stay there for worship. The accommodation that those in charge of the honourable shrine provided him with was not comfortable. In his heart, he asked for Shaikh ʿAbd al-Qādir's help. The Shaikh visited him in his dream and instructed him to go to a person named "Fattāḥ", who seems to have been the administrative officer of the shrine, and tell him that Shaikh ʿAbd al-Qādir was sending him his regards. He was to tell him that the Shaikh was ordering him to provide accommodation for him. To help the man prove the veracity of his claim, the Shaikh told him that every day Fattāḥ would take for his family the best cut of the meat donated to feed the shrine's guests.

In the morning, the man went to Fattāḥ and conveyed what Shaikh ʿAbd al-Qādir said. When he heard the Shaikh's words, Fattāḥ fell unconscious to the ground. After those present helped him recover, he admitted the truth of what Shaikh ʿAbd al-Qādir had said about him, and he repented. He provided comfortable accommodations for the man. The latter persisted in worship until he reached the point of being confirmed as a Quṭb, the rank that had been granted to him in Chamchamāl. Shaikh ʿAbd al-Qādir came to him a second time and repeated what the previous voice had already told him, that he would find what he was looking for in Karbchna, so he must go there. This devout man's pride remained obstinate with regard to visiting Shaikh ʿAbd al-Karīm.

When the man's stay ended, he left Baghdad and returned to his family. On the way between Chamchamāl and Karbchna, he stopped by the village Kānī Kawā and read the Qur'an in front of the shrine of Shaikh Ma'rūf Kawsta`ī, son of Shaikh Ismā'īl al-Wilyānī. While reciting the Qur'an, he heard a voice emanating from the shrine ordering him to go to Karbchna. He raised the Qur'an in his hand, drew closer to the shrine, and addressed it, saying: "For the sake of this Qur'an answer me, is this your voice, or is there an intruder between us?" He wanted to confirm that the voice did not belong to someone masquerading as Shaikh Ma'rūf to mislead him. An answer came from the shrine confirming that the speaker was Shaikh Ma'rūf, and it repeated the order to go to Karbchna. The man's pride prevented him, once again, from carrying out the order. The blessing he had was taken from him because of his arrogance, as he reported.

One day, he saw the hand of a man entering his back and coming out of his belly. He could even see the hair on top of the hand. The hand then was withdrawn, removing with that withdrawal all the blessing that he had. He lost the rank of Quṭb, which he would have qualified for had he fought his self and assented to taking the Ṭarīqa pledge from Shaikh 'Abd al-Karīm Al-Kasnazān. These spiritual posts do not exist outside of the Ṭarīqa. One subtle point to note is that this man reported the story of his loss of the walīhood when he visited our present Shaikh, who became the Master of the Ṭarīqa after succeeding Shaikh 'Abd al-Karīm — whom the man could not bear to visit!

The following is another incident in this regard, which happened while our Shaikh was in his first seclusion in mid-1978, six months after he had become the Master of the Ṭarīqa. One afternoon, he glanced towards the Shaikhs' shrines in Karbchna and asked them to give the dervishes ḥāls and spiritual dispensation, to help him manage the affairs of the Ṭarīqa. That night, our Master saw Shaikh 'Abd al-Qādir al-Gaylānī greet a dervish named Maḥmūd in his place of seclusion, which was three meters below our Shaikh's. Our Shaikh heard this dervish say that from now on, he would only seek spiritual support from Shaikh 'Abd al-Qādir al-Gaylānī. In other words, he thought that his relationship to Shaikh 'Abd al-Qādir no longer passed through the chain of Shaikhs that his present Master connected him to. When our Shaikh saw this dervish's complacency with a vision of Shaikh 'Abd al-Qādir, he faced the Shaikhs' shrines again and addressed them that, from now on, he would never make such a request; that he would let them do as they pleased, as they knew better. As for Maḥmūd, his ignorance of the fact that Shaikh 'Abd al-Qādir's visit was only in answer to our Shaikh's request made him complacent. Later, he tried to change the wording of a dhikr that our Shaikh gave to dervishes in seclusion (see §14.3). He persisted in his arrogance until he was expelled from the Ṭarīqa. Unfortunately, there are other similar cases of dervishes whom the Shaikhs of Ṭarīqa had granted blessings but Satan made them forget that these blessings had reached them by way of their Shaikhs. They deviated from the straight path.

The Shaikhs' granting of a rank of walīhood to a dervish means that a spiritual line of communication is opened between him and the seeker, regardless of the spatial distance between them, through which the Shaikh communicates what he wants the disciple to do for the Ṭarīqa. The following is a karāma of our Shaikh that pertains to a great walī called Aḥmad Muḥammad Amīn (may Allah have mercy on him). In the early 1990s, our Shaikh travelled from his place of residence in Baghdad to Kirkuk. Some of the dervishes from northern Iraq, who were in the main takya in Baghdad visiting him, went with him. When he was in the main takya in Kirkuk, he was invited to a celebration of the Prophet's (PBUH) birth the next day in the city of Dōr, which is 150 kilometres away. That afternoon, he asked one of his aides to choose about ten dervishes to accompany him in attending the celebration. At the time of the dhikr known as "Wird al-'Aṣr",[129] our Master delivered a sermon about spiritual affairs in the Ṭarīqa in which he said: "There are dervishes that can call out to dervishes in Shahrizor from here, and they would hear the call". The distance between Shahrizor in the Sulaymāniyya governorate and the takya in the Kirkuk governorate is about 200 kilometres.

The next morning, Aḥmad Muḥammad Amīn came to the Kirkuk takya. He found there a dervish that he knew, named Qādir Muḥammad Maḥmūd. The latter was one of those who accompanied our Shaikh from Baghdad to Kirkuk and attended the sermon of at the time of Wird al-'Aṣr. Aḥmad trusted that Qādir would not reveal the secret, so he asked him, in a hushed voice, whether something had happened. Qādir asked him to clarify the vague question, so Aḥmad answered:

---

[129] Wird al-'Aṣr is one of the dhikrs of the Ṭarīqa (see §14.4.2).

"Yesterday, I was in Baghdad with the Shaikh, before taking his leave to return to my family in Sulaymāniyya when he travelled to Kirkuk. Yet, after I arrived in Shahrizor, he called out to me three times in the afternoon, saying: "Come, O Aḥmad"! There must be something, but I could not come yesterday because the road closes in the evening. [This was due to the then conflict between the central government and the Kurdish rebels in Iraqi Kurdistan]. I waited for the morning, took the first available public transport, and came to see what the Shaikh wants from me."

Having understood the question, Qādir replied that our Shaikh wanted to take some dervishes to a celebration of the birth of the Prophet (PBUH) that day, so it seems that he wanted Aḥmad to be one of them, which is why he called him. The similarity of this karāma to the karāma of caliph 'Umar Ibn al-Khaṭṭāb's call to the army commandant Sāriya is remarkable.

The history of the Ṭarīqa Kasnazāniyya has a countless number of karāmas that caliphs and dervishes have performed or that had happened to them. These demonstrate the high spiritual ranks and posts that they reached. This, in turn, shows the high and unique status of the Ṭarīqa Kasnazāniyya Shaikhs. We have gone over, for instance, the karāma of Kāka 'Azīz' having found money that a man had lost in an unknown location. We need to to stress that ranks of walīhood in the Ṭarīqa are not limited to men, but rather they are accessible to women as well. All of Shāh al-Kasnazān's children, for example, both the boys and the girls, were walīs.

Because of Allah's love for His walīs and their status with Him, He is an enemy of anyone who shows enmity to them. We have already seen the Qudsī ḥadīth in which Allah states: "I declare war on anyone who takes a walī of Mine for an enemy",[130] before He goes on to detail the miracles that He can bestow on His walīs. Therefore, ignorance of Allah's walīs and being distanced from them is safer for a person from nearness to them while harbouring enmity for them, in public or in secret. There are innumerable karāmas that confirm the Lord's words, and we will mention one of them here as an example. Late one summer night, Shaikh 'Abd al-Qādir al-Kasnazān was sitting in the Karbchna mosque's yard, accompanied by a relative, when he suddenly called his servant

[130] Bukhārī, *Al-Jāmi' al-Ṣaḥīḥ*, III, no. 6273, p. 493.

Muḥammad Amīn and asked him to bring coal tongs and a lantern. Sultan ʿAbd al-Qādir pointed to his foot, so Muḥammad brought the lantern down to his feet and saw a large, dead scorpion. The Shaikh asked him to throw it away. Then, he turned to his companion, commenting: "Anything that approaches walīs wanting to harm them only harms itself".[131]

As we mentioned at the beginning of this chapter, karāmas are the ink that records many details of the Shaikhs of Ṭarīqa's biographies. Studying the life of a Shaikh of Ṭarīqa means growing familiar with his karāmas. In addition to the already mentioned karāmas of Shaikh Muḥammad al-Muḥammad al-Kasnazān, we will discuss other karāmas in different chapters as we study his honourable life. We will recount them in the context of the topics that are relevant to their respective details.

---

[131] Shaikh Muḥammad al-Muḥammad al-Kasnazān, *sermon*, 18th/December/2018.

Photo 6: Shaikh Muḥammad al-Muḥammad in front of the hall of the shrines of the Kasnazānī Shaikhs in Karbchna (1981).

"Our actions and our movements are all with the spiritual influence of the Messenger (PBUH), the people of the prophetic household, al-Karrār (Imām 'Alī), Imām Ḥusayn, our Master al-Gaylāni, and our Master Shāh al-Kasnazān, may Allah sanctify their innermost beings. We walk with their spiritual influence, their power, their blessing, and their supervision".

Shaikh Muḥammad al-Muḥammad al-Kasnazān
(Sermon, 7th/January/2010)

4

Noble Lineage

The lineage of sayyid Shaikh Muḥammad al-Muḥammad al-Kasnazān traces back to the Prophet Muḥammad (PBUH) from both his father's and mother's side.

His father is sayyid 'Abd al-Karīm, son of sayyid 'Abd al-Qādir; son of sayyid 'Abd al-Karīm Shāh al-Kasnazān; son of sayyid Ḥusayn; son of sayyid Ḥasan; son of sayyid 'Abd al-Karīm al-Khāwī; son of sayyid Ismā'īl al-Wilyānī (1158/1745); son of sayyid Muḥammad an-Nūdīhī (who is known as "the Red Sulphur"); son of sayyid Bābā 'Alī al-Wandarīna; son of sayyid Bābā Rasūl al-Kabīr; son of sayyid 'Abd al-sayyid al-Thānī; son of sayyid 'Abd al-Rasūl; son of sayyid Qalandar; son of sayyid 'Abd al-sayyid; son of sayyid 'Īsā al-Aḥdab (941/1534); son of sayyid Ḥusayn; son of sayyid Bāyazīd; son of sayyid 'Abd al-Karīm al-Awwal; son of sayyid 'Īsā al-Barzinjī; son of sayyid Bābā 'Alī al-Hamadānī; son of sayyid Yūsuf al-Hamadānī (who is known as "the Shooting Star of Religion"); son of sayyid Muḥammad al-Manṣūr; son of sayyid 'Abd al-'Azīz; son of sayyid 'Abd Allah; son of sayyid Ismā'īl al-Muḥaddath; son of Imām Mūsā al-Kāẓim (183/799); son of Imām Ja'far al-Ṣādiq; son of Imām Muḥammad al-Bāqir; son of Imām 'Alī Zayn al-'Ābidīn; son of Imām al-Ḥusayn; son of Imām 'Alī Ibn Abī Ṭālib (may Allah ennoble his face) and sayyida Fāṭima al-Zahrā`, the daughter of the Messenger of Allah, the Seal of Prophets and Messengers, Muḥammad (PBUH).[132] Each one of our Shaikh's ancestors was a paragon of piety who had numerous karāmas attributed to him, testifying to his nearness to Allah (mighty and sublime is He).

The mother of Shaikh Muḥammad al-Muḥammad al-Kasnazān is sayyida Ḥafṣa, daughter of sayyid 'Abd al-Qādir Gulanabar; son of sayyid

[132] One source in which the early ancestors of our Shaikh are listed is al-Najafī, *Baḥr al-Ansāb*, p. 62.

Muḥammad Ṣāliḥ; son of sayyid ʿAbd al-Qādir Qāzānqāya; son of sayyid Ḥusayn Qāzānqāya; son of sayyid Maḥmūd Klīsa; son of sayyid Ismāʿīl al-Wilyānī, the sixth great-grandfather of Shaikh Muḥammad al-Muḥammad al-Kasnazān from his father's side.

Just as Allah blessed our Shaikh with an exceptional father — a Master of the Ṭarīqa — He also blessed him immensely with a mother who was an exemplar of piety and obedience to Allah. As we will see later, it was Shaikh Ḥusayn al-Kasnazān who chose sayyida Ḥafṣa as a wife for his brother and the Shaikh of the Ṭarīqa after him, ʿAbd al-Karīm: "So that Allah might accomplish a matter already destined" (al-Ānfāl 42). Those who saw sayyida Ḥafṣa frequently cite that she was always in a constant state of worship.

Thus, Shaikh Muḥammad al-Muḥammad comes from a most noble lineage. He was raised by parents whom Allah had graced with piety and nearness to Him. Ten of Shaikh Muḥammad al-Muḥammad's ancestors from his mother's side were also Masters of the Ṭarīqa ʿAlīyya Qādiriyya Kasnazāniyya, which shows the blessing in his noble lineage. They are his father sayyid Shaikh ʿAbd al-Karīm al-Kasnazān, his grandfather sayyid Shaikh ʿAbd al-Qādir al-Kasnazān, and his great-grandfather, after whose spiritual secrets the Ṭarīqa takes its name of "Kasnazāniyya", sayyid Shaikh ʿAbd al-Karīm Shāh al-Kasnazān. Another Master of the Ṭarīqa is sayyid Shaikh Ismāʿīl al-Wilyānī, the first person to bring the Ṭarīqa Qādiriyya to Iraqi Kurdistan. Then there are the six Imāms of Mūsā al-Kāẓim, Jaʿfar al-Ṣādiq, Muḥammad al-Bāqir, ʿAlī Zayn al-ʿĀbidīn, Ḥusayn, and ʿAlī Ibn Abī Ṭālib (peace be upon them all). Two of our Shaikh's ancestors from his mother's side, sayyid Shaikh Ḥusayn Qāzānqāya and his son sayyid Shaikh ʿAbd al-Qādir, were also Masters of the Ṭarīqa.

Persecution forced many descendants of the Messenger of Allah (PBUH) to emigrate from the Arabian Peninsula, which was the homeland of their greatest ancestor, the Prophet Muḥammad (PBUH). One of these descendants, named "Yūsuf", emigrated north to the city of Hamadān, in present-day northwestern Iran, so he acquired the title of "al-Hamadānī". This emigration was apparently harmful to emigrants but, on a deeper level, it was actually a source of mercy for the inhabitants of the areas where the emigrants went, guiding people to the way of their forefather, our Master Muḥammad (PBUH). Sayyid Yūsuf al-Hamadānī was a scholar, a Sufi, and an ascetic, and he was well-versed in Islamic jurisprudence. As a result of his piety and knowledge, thousands of people gathered around him to learn about Sufism and other religious sciences. This is why he is known as "the Shooting Star of Religion".

To avoid getting mixed up, we should clarify that the sayyid Yūsuf al-Hamadānī we are referring to is not Shaikh Abū Ya'qūb Yūsuf al-Hamadānī, who was a contemporary of Shaikh 'Abd al-Qādir al-Gaylānī. Abū Ya'qūb said to Shaikh 'Abd al-Qādir: "It's as if I see you [in the future] in Baghdad, sitting on the preaching chair, addressing the public, saying: 'this foot of mine is on the neck of every walī'. It's as if I see the walīs in your time bowing their necks out of reverence for you".[133] Sayyid Yūsuf al-Hamadānī, on the other hand, came about two centuries after Shaikh 'Abd al-Qādir.

Sayyid Yūsuf had a son named Bābā 'Alī who was a prominent scholar and Sufi. He had three sons: Mūsā, 'Īsā, and Muḥammad. The three brothers went to perform the pilgrimage and to visit the Messenger (PBUH). Returning via Iraq, they headed north until they reached the area that later became known as "Barzinja", where they decided to stay for some time. One night, 'Īsā saw the Prophet (PBUH) order him to permanently settle in the area and to build a mosque there. His elder brother Mūsā stayed with him, while his younger brother Muḥammad returned to Hamadān, before settling in Afghanistan.

Sayyid Mūsā and sayyid 'Īsā carried out the Prophet's (PBUH) order to build a mosque and reside in the area. They served Islam, preaching to people. Sayyid Mūsā married the daughter of a well-known Shaikh there. A short while after marrying her, he went to preach in a nearby area, where he was assassinated by an extremist group of the Nuṣayriyya sect.[134] Sayyid 'Īsā brought his corpse and buried it in Barzinja. He married his brother's widow, Fāṭima, and Allah blessed them with twelve children. Sayyid Mūsā did not have any children, so all Barzinjī sayyids, including our Shaikh's family, are descendants of sayyid 'Īsā. Both shrines of sayyid 'Īsā and sayyid Mūsā exist today close to the mosque they

---

[133] Al-Hītamī, *Al-Fatāwā al-Ḥadīthiyya*, p. 316.

[134] Nuṣayriyya is another name for the "Alawis" or "Alawites".

built.[135]

The history of the Barzinjī sayyids, in general, shows that they inherited an indescribable blessing from their forefather (PBUH). We see this in the great number of walīs that have come from this blessed lineage and in their countless karāmas. Their offspring are found all over the world. Shaikh Muḥammad al-Muḥammad al-Kasnazān describes his forefather sayyid ʿĪsā al-Barzinjī as the "Reviver of the Family and Religion".

Sayyid ʿĪsā al-Barzinjī is also known with the title "Nūr Bakhsh", which means "Giver of Light", because light would appear on the face of anyone who took the pledge from him. The Messenger (PBUH) kissed him just above his forehead, so he would drape his turban just above his forehead so that the light would not blind its beholder.

Establishing our Shaikh's relation to the noble Muḥammadan family tree is of utmost importance because, as we mentioned in the previous chapter, the Messenger (PBUH) said:

> Indeed, I am leaving among you that which, if you hold fast to, you shall not go astray after me. One of them is greater than the other: Allah's Book, which is a rope extending from the sky to the earth, and my family, the people of my household. They shall not split until they meet me at the basin, so look after how you deal with them after me".[136]

This ḥadīth has a clear instruction that following Allah and the Prophet (PBUH) means following the magnificent Qur'an and the people of the prophetic household. Allah (exalted and high is He) made his noble Prophet's (PBUH) progeny the nearest of His creation to Him and the most in preaching to people and calling to His way. The people of the prophetic household are inheritors of his (PBUH) spiritual states. This ḥadīth above, known as the "Ḥadīth al-ʿItra" (Ḥadīth of the Family), explains His words: "Allah intends only to remove from you the impurity [of sin], O people of the [Prophet's] household, and to purify you with [extensive] purification" (al-Āḥzāb 33).

Some accounts suggest that the Prophet (PBUH) said these words a

---

[135] Al-Mudarris, *ʿUlamāʾunā fī-Khidmat al-ʿIlm wal-Dīn*, pp. 421-422. There are a number of different narratives in varoius sources about how sayyids ʿĪsā and Mūsā settled down in Barzinja, such as the version in Edmonds, *Kurds, Turks and Arabs: Politics*, pp. 68-71.

[136] Tirmidhī, *Al-Jāmiʿ al-Kabīr*, VI, no. 3788, p. 125.

few months before his passing from this world. According to the way it is narrated in *Saḥiḥ Muslim*, before the Messenger (PBUH) stated the "Ḥadīth al-Thaqalayn" (Ḥadīth of the Two Weighty Things), he said, "I am only a man who is about to receive my Lord's messenger [i.e. the Angel of Death]",[137] which confirms that the ḥadīth was stated just before he departed from this world. Muslim also mentions that the Prophet (PBUH) delivered the sermon at the watering-place of Khumm, which means that it is likely the same sermon in which Imam ʿAlī's authority over the Muslims was declared: "O Allah! Whoever I have been a Master to, then ʿAlī is his Master. O Allah! Befriend those who befriend him, and be enemy to those who take him for an enemy; support those who support him, and forsake those who forsake him".[138] It is evident from the ḥadīth's text that it was a "final will", meaning that it is likely one of the last things he ordered. This, in turn, confirms its importance and clarifies its meaning and significance.

---

[137] Muslim, *Ṣaḥīḥ Muslim*, IV, no. 2408, p. 1873.

[138] Aḥmad, *Musnad al-Imām Aḥmad Ibn Ḥanbal*, I, no. 950, p. 262; no. 951, p. 263.

Photo 7: Shaikh ʿAbd al-Karīm in Kirkuk (2nd half of the 1970s).

Photo 8: Iranian police facilitating the movements of Shaikh ʿAbd al-Karīm in Sanandaj, Iran, because of the large number of welcomers (1962).

Photo 9: Shaikh Muḥammad al-Muḥammad with a group of dervishes in Penjwin on the border with Iran (1988).

"Shaikh ʿAbd al-Karīm al-Kasnazān would not sleep at night. After leaving his assembly with the dervishes, he would pray the night prayer and remain in a state of dhikr until he would complete the morning prayer, the Sunna prayer, and his other devotions. Then, he would sleep. Even when he was extremely ill, he would continue to recite the Qur'an".

Shaikh Muḥammad al-Muḥammad al-Kasnazān
(Sermon, 24th/September/2016)

5

In the Care of a Spiritual Father and a Pious Mother

Among Allah's favours on our Shaikh is that he was brought up under the care of a father who was a Master of the Ṭarīqa, possessing Muḥammadan attributes. His spiritual and biological father, Shaikh ʿAbd al-Karīm, was the primary influence on him. He learned the best traits and virtues from his Master, and this influence shaped his personality and behaviour tremendously. Our Shaikh loved his father immensely and deeply revered him, so much so that he could not bring himself to sit in his presence until he permitted him to do so. He often avoided sitting in Shaikh ʿAbd al-Karīm's presence even after he permitted him to do so. He would be ashamed to ask him a question or ask him for anything, and he would not approach him unless he had summoned him for whatever reason, or to ask for his thoughts on matters in which he needed his opinion.

As was the case with all of Shaikh ʿAbd al-Karīm's family, our Shaikh would call his father and refer to him as "Shaikh". Although he was his biological father, he was his spiritual father in the spirit world before that. The seeker's soul is connected to his Shaikh's soul ever since the day Allah created souls. Despite the significance and sanctity of a paternal relationship, the seeker's relationship to his Shaikh has a greater effect on his life. Generation by generation, this blessed family inherited this respect and reverence for the Shaikh of the Ṭarīqa. Today, for example, we see that the family of our Master only calls him and refers to him as "Shaikh". Our Shaikh's children would only stand in his presence, except for Shaikh Nahro, who our Shaikh has ordered to sit in his assembly, being his General Deputy. Our Shaikh's spiritual relationship with Shaikh ʿAbd al-Karīm was unique; it was not merely a relationship of a disciple and his Shaikh. Rather, it was also a relationship of a Shaikh of Ṭarīqa in the making with his teacher and Shaikh of the Ṭarīqa before him. We will go over many details of this unique relationship. In §2.5, we briefly discussed Shaikh ʿAbd al-Karīm's life, and we will learn more about him in the chapters to come.

Allah increased His favour on our Shaikh by giving him a mother who was another exemplar of religious devotion and piety. Sayyida Ḥafṣa's lineage traces back to the Prophet (PBUH) from both her father's and mother's side. Her parents were themselves brought up by Sufi families known for their piety. As we mentioned before, her ancestry from her father's side goes back to sayyid Maḥmūd Klīsa, son of sayyid Ismāʿīl al-Wilyānī. Sayyid ʿAbd al-Qādir, sayyida Ḥafṣa's father, was a caliph of Shāh al-Kasnazān. Although he was sometimes called "Guptapa", which was the name of the village he resided in, in the district of Sangāw, he was known as "Gulanabar", which means "bulletproof". One day, Shāh al-Kasnazān placed his blessed hand on sayyid ʿAbd al-Qādir's back and told him that bullets would not kill him. Despite the many battles he entered — some against the Russians who invaded northern Iraq via Iran at the beginning of World War I, and later against the British — and the slight traces of bullets on his body, he did not die because of any shots that hit him. He lived to be approximately ninety years old. Our Shaikh's mother recounts that when her father would return from fighting the Russians, he would undo the belt on his Kurdish clothes, and bullets that hit him without harming him would fall from the belt. This was so well known that even a staff member of the British administration in Iraq at the time mentioned that sayyid ʿAbd al-Qādir was famed for being "bulletproof".[139]

One of the miracles of Shāh al-Kasnazān in this regard is that some people told him that Kāka Aḥmad al-Shaikh had a "gula bard", an amulet that made a person bulletproof, and asked him to give them something similar. Shāh al-Kasnazān tore off a piece of the fur rug he was sitting on with his blessed hand and said: "This is gula bard for you". In other words, he did not need to make a special amulet for protection against bullets. A small piece of the fur he was sitting on was enough to do the job.

A while after Shāh al-Kasnazān passed away and his relatives had inherited his personal belongings, no one knew where the rug had ended up or who had it. One night, our Shaikh's niece dreamt that a piece of

---

[139] Edmonds, *Kurds, Turks and Arabs: Politics*, pp. 340-341.

Shāh al-Kasnazān's rug and another piece of the belongings of Shaikh ʿAbd al-Qādir Kasnazān were inside a pillow that was in the possession of her paternal aunt. When she woke up, she opened the pillow and found what she had seen in the dream.

There are many miracles attributed to our Shaikhs in the way of protecting dervishes from bullets. In 1983, some Iranian dervishes, accompanied by caliph ʿĀrif Faraj (may Allah have mercy on him), wanted to visit Shaikh Muḥammad al-Muḥammad in Karbchna. As the Iran-Iraq war was at its height, the border between the two countries was closed, so the dervishes crossed the border on foot. They beat dhikr drums and tambourines and hoisted the Ṭarīqa's banners to identify themselves. When they reached Shānadarī, near Shahrizor province, Iraqi soldiers on the hills opened fire at them. Some of the shots hit their bodies but did not harm them. The soldiers noticed the strange situation and that the dervishes did not fire back at them. They ceased firing and approached them to investigate the situation. One dervish became angry and tried to strip a soldier of his weapon, so the soldier shot him in the thigh. When the soldiers became confident that these dervishes had come in peace, and after they had witnessed how the shots had not harmed them, they left them to complete their journey. The dervishes reached Karbchna, each carrying bullets that had hit his body without harming him. Caliph ʿĀrif felt too ashamed to inform our Shaikh what had happened with the dervish who was hit, so another dervish informed the Shaikh to ask him to pray for the dervish's recovery. Our Shaikh took a napkin and put a bit of his saliva in it to be given it to the wounded dervish to place it over his wound. He criticised the dervish's attempt to attack the soldier and said that had he not done so, the Shaikhs would have protected him the same way they had protected his fellow dervishes.

As for sayyida Ḥafṣa's mother, she is sayyida Khadīja, daughter of sayyid Muḥyī al-Dīn al-Qarachwārī, son of sayyid ʿAbd al-Karīm, son of sayyid ʿAbd al-Qādir Qāzānqāya, grandfather of sayyid ʿAbd al-Qādir Gula Nabar. When sayyida Khadīja passed away, sayyida Ḥafṣa was a little girl of no more than two or three years old. Her father put her under the care of her maternal uncle, Shaikh ʿAbd al-Karīm Qādir Karam, until she grew older and was returned to her father. When she was with her uncle, she learned the Qur'an under Mullā Muḥyī al-Dīn, who was the family's cleric. After marrying Shaikh ʿAbd al-Karīm, she completed her studies under the great Azhar Shaikh ʿAbd al-Ḥalīm Maḥmūd's wife, when the two visited Sultan Ḥusayn and stayed in Karbchna for a while. Likewise, Shaikh ʿAbd al-Karīm studied the Qur'an under Shaikh ʿAbd al-Ḥalīm. The latter completed his university studies in Egypt and became a scholar in 1932. He then joined the Azhar mission at the Sorbonne, France, at the end of 1937 and stayed there until he received his doctorate in 1940. Since Sultan Ḥusayn departed to the spirit world early in 1939, we can narrow Shaikh ʿAbd al-Ḥalīm's visit to Karbchna to some time between 1932-1937. His decision to pursue a doctorate in Islamic Sufism, specifically on the renowned Sufi Ḥārith Ibn Asad al-Muḥāsibī (243 H.), points to the influence his visit to Shaikh Ḥusayn al-Kasnazān had on him. ʿAbd al-Halīm Maḥmūd became Shaikh of al-Āzhar in 1973, and he held the position until his passing in 1978.[140]

Sayyida Ḥafṣa was chosen as Shaikh ʿAbd al-Karīm's wife by divine decree. Her brother Musṭafā was a childhood friend of Shaikh Ḥusayn. He loved Sultan Ḥusayn deeply, and the Shaikh loved him dearly as well. They also fought together against the British army in northern Iraq, as we will see in §7.4. Musṭafā offered Shaikh Ḥusayn his sister Ḥafṣa in marriage, but the Shaikh did not want to marry. About two years after returning to Karbchna from his emigration to Iran, Shaikh Ḥusayn spoke to Musṭafā of wedding the young woman to his brother, ʿAbd al-Karīm. Shaikh Musṭafā consented to this great honour. Sultan Ḥusayn fetched his brother, at the time a boy no older than thirteen. When the child heard his elder brother and Shaikh of the Ṭarīqa's decision, he began to cry and ran away, as children are wont to do. Sultan Ḥusayn told him that he had his reasons for ordering that this marriage takes place. He knew that the marriage of his brother and the Shaikh of the Ṭarīqa after him to that young woman would produce Shaikh ʿAbd al-Karīm's successor to the Masterhood of the Ṭarīqa. The young woman was five years older than Shaikh ʿAbd al-Karīm, which was contrary to the prevalent tradition of having an older husband and younger wife. This contradiction confirms that there must have been a secret purpose behind their marriage.

Shaikh ʿAbd al-Karīm married sayyida Ḥafṣa early in his youth. They had their first son, Ḥusayn, in 1927, and in 1937, the first of their four

---

[140] ʿAbd al-Raḥmān, Saʿīd. *Shuyūkh al-Āzhar*, V, pp. 15-16.

daughters, ʿĀʾishā, was born. Then, at dawn, on Friday 15th/April/1938, Allah gifted them the secret behind their marriage: the child whose paternal uncle and Master of the Ṭarīqa, Sultan Ḥusayn, named "Muḥammad", and who was destined, after about eighty years, specifically in 2016, to have the Messenger (PBUH) augment his name with his noble name, becoming called "Muḥammad al-Muḥammad". Less than a year after this blessed birth, Sultan Ḥusayn left this world, leaving his brother, Shaikh ʿAbd al-Karīm, as the Master of the Ṭarīqa. Sayyida Ḥafṣa also provided Shaikh ʿAbd al-Karīm with their daughters, Kāfiya, Ḥalīma, and Salmā.

Our Shaikh also has six half-brothers: Halgurd, Pishwar, ʿUqayl, ʿĀzar, Murtaḍā, and Kūshash. He also has six half-sisters, all younger than him: Zaynab, Sarwa, Shanū, Mahnāz, and Faraḥ.

The young Muḥammad al-Muḥammad grew up in a spiritual household in which the remembrance of Allah never stops. His father was the Muḥammadan Inheritor and Master of the Ṭarīqa; his mother was an exceptionally devout woman who was always in a state of dhikr and who constantly maintained her ablution. Our Shaikh relates that he only saw her doing three things: praying, reciting the Qur'an, and reading either dhikrs or the book *Dalāʾil al-Khayrāt*, which is a compilation of prayers of peace and blessings upon the Prophet (PBUH). Everyone who saw sayyida Ḥafṣa mentions that she was always in a state of remembering her Lord. She never suckled her children without being in a state of ablution. This was also the case of Sultan Ḥusayn's wife with her children.

Early in 1956, sayyida Ḥafṣa's eldest son, Ḥusayn, died from an incurable disease. From then on, until she passed away in 1994, she was in a constant state of spiritual retreat. She stopped eating meat and became a vegetarian; she would not eat fat or oil, and she would not go near gravy or rice. She even forbade herself from eating certain kinds of fruit, such as oranges or sugary fruit. She refrained from eating all the foods her deceased son used to enjoy. Most of the time, she only ate thin pieces of bread with soup.

As was the case with the wives of the Messenger (PBUH), wives of the Shaikhs play important roles in helping them fulfil their duties in service to Allah's way. A Shaikh's life has special demands that his wife is more suited to tend to, such as ensuring the conditions of cleanliness, purity, and permissibility in his drink, food, belongings, and places of sitting, worshipping, and sleeping; knowing what foods the Shaikh can and cannot eat, and preparing the Shaikh's food while in a state of ablution. The Shaikh maintains a tremendous level of pious restraint, so his wife, as well as all who serve and manage his household, must care for that.

The Shaikh of Ṭarīqa's wife bears part of the burden on her shoulders. The Shaikh of Ṭarīqa's household is not an ordinary home. Rather, it is one of Allah's homes, established in service to all who travel on the path to Allah. It is an open-doored takya that people from all over constantly flock to for different needs. Hence, the housework is managed around the clock. The Shaikh's house is among the houses that Allah (exalted and high is He) describes in his noble Book: "In homes that Allah has ordered to be raised and that His name be mentioned therein; exalting Him within them in the morning and the evenings [are] men whom neither commerce nor sale distracts from the remembrance of Allah and performance of prayer and giving of charity" (al-Nūr 36-37). While the Shaikh is responsible for all affairs of the Ṭarīqa and its dervishes, his wife helps manage the affairs of this house of dhikr. This includes supervising the preparation of food for guests, who come and go at any time, ensuring the takya is well kept and so on. Sayyida Ḥafṣa was an exemplary wife who she spent her life helping Shaikh ʿAbd al-Karīm serve the Ṭarīqa and its dervishes.

As there are male caliphs in the takya who are responsible for preaching to men, there are also female caliphs in the women's takya who teach women. Sayyida Ḥafṣa often sat in the women's takya to receive visitors, give them the pledge, listen to their needs, and advise them, as she was very knowledgeable in religious matters. She would also bless water and give to those in need or pray for them. She had a special room where she would receive those with private needs that could not be addressed in front of other women. While the Shaikh of Ṭarīqa must serve the Ṭarīqa and its dervishes, his wife must help him in this undertaking. Sayyida Ḥafṣa carried out this duty in the best possible way and was a real help to Shaikh ʿAbd al-Karīm. She persisted in serving the Ṭarīqa and its female disciples after Shaikh ʿAbd al-Karīm's departure, when her son, Shaikh Muḥammad al-Muḥammad, took over as Shaikh of the Ṭarīqa. Our Shaikh's wife assumed her responsibilities after her.

Sayyida Ḥafṣa was a walī whose karāmas were witnessed by many people. During her burial ceremony, attendees noticed that her foot was sticking out of her shroud. Before they could touch the foot to push it back inside, she pulled her foot in as if she were still alive.

Sayyida Ḥafṣa had a special standing with Shaikh ʿAbd al-Karīm. He would listen to her opinions on things. The following is an incident that reveals her special status with the Master of Ṭarīqa. One night in 1973 or 1974, some dervishes were preaching in a remote area near ʿẒaim in the Diyālā governorate. During the presentation of some feats of darbāsha, a caliph named Qāsim recklessly inserted a sword inside a dervish's belly. This caused a bigger and deeper wound than usual, so much so that some of the dervish's internal organs came out. The caliph tied the dervish's belly with a large bandage, asking the Shaikhs for support to help the man recover. Contrary to what usually happens to those who practice feats of darbāsha, the preaching and dhikr ended and the wounded dervish did not recover. The caliph had no recourse other than to take the injured dervish to the Shaikh in Kirkuk.

At the time, and in that remote area, there were no taxis, so they had to wait until dawn when a dump truck came to deliver building plaster material to a resident of the area. The driver agreed to transport the wounded dervish and placed him in the back of the truck. The truck was far from being as clean as it needed to be for a wound, not to mention one as serious as this one. Since most of the road in that area was unpaved at the time, the injured dervish was constantly exposed to bumps on the road.

At about six in the morning, the dervish arrived at the takya, unconscious but breathing. Any doctor would assert that even though he was still alive, he would not live much longer and that it was useless to attempt to treat him because of the seriousness of the injury. Shaikh ʿAbd al-Karīm sent for our Shaikh, who was resting at home. When our Shaikh came, he found Shaikh ʿAbd al-Karīm very angry. He pointed to the dervish lying on the ground with his internal organs out. The purpose of practising darbāsha was not to expose the body to extremely dangerous stunts, but rather to provide what would suffice as proof to onlookers that since the dervish's body did not suffer what the body naturally suffers when performing these feats, the Ṭarīqa has spiritual power. The more dangerous the act the greater the spiritual energy needed to protect the dervish. Hence, the dervish is not supposed to use more spiritual energy than he needs.

In his anger at the caliph's recklessness, Shaikh ʿAbd al-Karīm refused to intervene. He told those present to take the injured dervish to the hospital and to take the caliph to the police. At that moment, sayyida Ḥafṣa intervened, reproaching Shaikh ʿAbd al-Karīm, reminding him that he was Master of the Ṭarīqa and remained responsible for the welfare of the dervish, even if the caliph had made a mistake. Besides, the wounded dervish was now in his house, so he could not abandon him and send to the hospital. Likewise, the caliph could not be sent to the police. Shaikh ʿAbd al-Karīm calmed down, listened to sayyida Ḥafṣa's request, and backed down from his decision.

Obeying Shaikh ʿAbd al-Karīm's command, a dervish opened the bandage. It had dried and was stuck to the wound as a result of the amount of blood and secretions that had leaked out, as well as the length of time the wound had remained untreated. The bandage made an audible sound when it was taken off. The afflicted area was contaminated with plaster during transport. With the help of two other dervishes, the dervish forcefully pushed the stiff, swollen bowels back into the wounded dervish's belly using a headwrap as a bandage that they wrapped around his belly. They did this with no medical knowledge, using their bare hands and without sterilisation. This is extremely dangerous in normal circumstances since it contaminates the body's internal organs. This circumstance, however, was supernatural because it involved the spiritual intervention of the Shaikhs. Then, Shaikh ʿAbd al-Karīm instructed them to put dust from Shāh al-Kasnazān's shrine on the dervish and place him in the middle of a circle of dhikr. The dhikr was performed by those who were in the takya at the time, around seven, including our Shaikh.

During the dhikr, the injured dervish's face began to gradually gain colour, and he began to regain consciousness. After the dhikr ended, Shaikh ʿAbd al-Karīm asked that the dervish be left alone to sleep. Our Shaikh returned to his house and the rest of the dervishes went their separate ways. After about six hours, the dervish woke up and felt hungry. He asked for soup. After eating, he suddenly felt the need to use the facilities. Medically speaking, a bowel movement indicates the proper functioning of the intestinal organs. The dervish made a complete recovery.

This incident of Shaikh ʿAbd al-Karīm complying with sayyida Ḥafṣa's suggestion reminds us of situations where wives of the

Messenger's (PBUH) helped him by giving him their views on certain issues that he took on board. One example happened with the Treaty of Ḥudaybiyya. After the Messenger (PBUH) and the polytheists agreed to the treaty's terms and wrote them down, he ordered his Companions to proceed with the necessary slaughtering of sacrifices and shaving of their heads of performing the lesser pilgrimage. Some Companions objected, however, because they thought that the treaty's terms were not in the Muslims' best interest. As such, they did not carry out the Prophet's (PBUH) command, even though he repeated the order three times. When he went to his wife, Umm Salmā, he told her what had happened. She suggested, "O Prophet of Allah, do you like it [i.e. the treaty]? Go, and don't say a word to any of them until you slaughter your goat and call your barber to shave your head". He came out and did not speak to anyone. He slaughtered his goat and had his head shaved. This reminded the Companions that the actions of the Messenger (PBUH) are driven by divine decrees, there was wisdom behind them, even if that wisdom escaped them, and that he could not disobey Allah's command, even if it was disapproved by those near and dear to him. One by one, the Companions began to slaughter their animals and shave their heads.[141]

Naturally, sayyida Ḥafṣa also had a special standing with her son, Shaikh Muḥammad al-Muḥammad. We see evidence of this in a similar karāma that took place on a winter day in the mid-1980s. A dervish was injured while performing a feat of darbāsha in Mosul, so he was brought to the main takya in Baghdad. He was wrapped in a blanket full of dried blood, as it takes more than five hours to get to Baghdad from Mosul. Shaikh Muḥammad al-Muḥammad was very angry with what this dervish had done and did not want to intervene to cure him. Sayyida Ḥafṣa reminded her son of the similar incident that had happened during his father's time and requested that he help the dervish. Our Shaikh instructed the dervishes to recite a poem composed in the Iraqi dialect in praise of Sultan Ḥusayn al-Kasnazān, "Niʿmaen Abū Ṭāhir Yā Rāʿī al-Shāra". The word "niʿmaen" is a word of praise; "Abū Ṭāhir" is a title of Sultan Ḥusayn, where "Abū" means father and "Ṭāhir" is the name of his eldest son; "rāʿī al-shāra" means "of the sign", meaning the one who leaves a sign when he spiritually intervenes, such as answering a seeker's request

[141] Bukhārī, *Al-Jāmiʿ al-Ṣaḥīḥ*, II, no. 2644, p. 119.

for aid. Shaikh Muḥammad al-Muḥammad lowered his head during the ode's recitation. He then gently struck the dervish's leg with his blessed foot, and the dervish moved. Afterwards, they took the dervish to the hospital where he was given a large amount of blood. The doctors in the hospital could not understand how this person was still alive!

In 1994, sayyida Ḥafṣa departed to her Lord in Baghdad and was buried near the Kirkuk takya in the Shaikh Muḥyī al-Dīn Karkūk cemetery, one of the Masters of the Ṭarīqa Kasnazāniyya. Our Shaikh's wife, sayyida Kažāl, assumed her responsibilities in the takya after her.

Thus, our Shaikh had the best upbringing, under the care of a father who was a Shaikh of the Ṭarīqa and excellent educator, and a devout, pious mother who spent her life helping her husband, Shaikh ʿAbd al-Karīm, serve the Ṭarīqa and seekers of proximity to Allah. Our Shaikh was nurtured with an ideal Islamic upbringing that gave him the best qualities and traits. When Allah wants to make someone a means of guidance, He chooses those who nurture him so that he is brought up according to His plan.

Photo 10: Shaikh ʿAbd al-Karīm, second from right, and to his left is Shaikh Muḥammad al-Muḥammad during pilgrimage (1973).

Photo 11: Shaikh Muḥammad Al-Muḥammad, first from right, during pilgrimage (1973).

"We do not instruct the seeker to abandon knowledge, because it is through knowledge he worships his Lord. Knowledge makes the person understand the act of worship because knowledge is light: 'Are those who know equal to those who do not know?' (al-Zumar 9). We instruct the disciple to perform righteous deeds. We instruct the disciple to study, to read, to go to school, to learn, to become educated, and to worship. How beautiful it is when a seeker is well-educated!".

Shaikh Muḥammad al-Muḥammad al-Kasnazān
(Sermon, 29th/January/2010)

6

Eduction and Self-Learning

Shaikh Muḥammad al-Muḥammad inherited his forefathers' love for learning in general and for studying the sciences of Sharia in particular. As a child, he entered Karbchna's religious school, which was founded by Shāh al-Kasnazān. There, he studied under grand scholars and jurists of the time, such as Mullā Kāka Aḥmad Sayf al-Dīn, the encyclopaedic scholar who authored many books, and who mastered several disciplines, including history, sociology, mathematics, and physics. In his diaries, he mentions that he decided to go teach in Karbchna's religious school because the spiritual influence and power of the Karbchna Shaikhs gave him a tremendous ability to serve the students. Our Shaikh also studied under Mullā Saʿīd Zamnākū, who authored an entire Qur'anic exegesis, and Mullā ʿAlī Musṭafā, also known as "ʿAlī Laylān".

Since Shaikh Ḥusayn was about eleven years older than Shaikh Muḥammad al-Muḥammad, he was keen on caring for his younger brother, especially since their father was busy managing the Ṭarīqa's affairs. Shaikh Ḥusayn was known for his refined knowledge, vast social influence, and physical strength. He preferred that his brother join a secular school and study medicine, instead of continuing his education in a religious school. At the time, secular universities accepted graduates from religious schools, as long as they passed a special exam. Shaikh Ḥusayn hired a special teacher, "Karīm Zindī" (may Allah have mercy on him), to teach his younger brother, who was around 12 years old at the time, the subjects that are taught in secular schools, such as history, science, English, and mathematics, to prepare him for the special exam. Zindī taught our Shaikh for four years.

Our Shaikh passed the exam in Kirkuk and was accepted in the sixth grade, which he completed. He then completed secondary education in a school located near the historic Kirkuk Citadel. Shaikh ʿAbd al-Karīm would leave Karbchna with his family during the winter and reside in the takya within the citadel. In the latter half of the 1940s, Shaikh ʿAbd al-

Karīm bought a tract of land in the citadel, upon which he founded a takya, which was the first main takya in Kirkuk. In Sultan Ḥusayn's time, one of his caliphs managed a takya in the Kirkuk Citadel, near the land where Shaikh ʿAbd al-Karīm later built a takya. Sultan Ḥusayn would live in the old takya whenever he visited Kirkuk.

During his years of study in Kirkuk, our Shaikh would stay in the takya there to continue his studies when Shaikh ʿAbd al-Karīm returned to Karbchna, or when he went to the village of Hawmārāmān in Qaradāgh in the Sulaymāniyya governorate. Shaikh ʿAbd al-Karīm would rotate his place of residence between Kirkuk, Hawmārāmān, and Karbchna.

Shaikh Muḥammad al-Muḥammad completed secondary education and entered high school, which at the time took two years to complete. Towards the end of 1954, his brother, Shaikh Ḥusayn, became ill by a disease that doctors failed to diagnose. The disease gradually worsened until it rendered him bedridden. After Shaikh Ḥusayn's second operation in the al-Imam Hospital in Baghdad, it became clear that he had cancer. The disease prevented Shaikh Ḥusayn from helping his father, so Shaikh Muḥammad al-Muḥammad was forced to abandon his studies to be close to his father and his ailing brother. In early 1956, Shaikh Ḥusayn passed on to Allah's mercy in the Kirkuk Citadel takya. He was twenty-nine years old. He was buried next to his paternal uncle's shrine, Sultan Ḥusayn, in Karbchna.

Our Shaikh thought to resume his studies, but after the death of his brother, there was a need for him to serve his father, the Shaikh of the Ṭarīqa, so he erased the thought. He had to take on the responsibility of managing the many social and tribal relations and overseeing his farms. His father bought him a Jeep for transport for his new responsibilities. Since his childhood, our Shaikh was active and full energy and enjoyed taking on responsibilities.

In 1956, our Shaikh had to perform compulsory military service, but he only stayed in the army for about forty days. At the time, the man could pay one hundred dinars in lieu of performing mandatory military service, which our Shaikh paid.

After he abandoned his secular studies and returned to Karbchna, our Shaikh enrolled in the town's religious school once again and received certification as a religious scholar from Mullā ʿAbd Allah Muḥammad

ʿAzīz al-Karbchnī (may Allah have mercy on him), who was one of Shaikh ʿAbd al-Karīm's caliphs. The military coup that overthrew the monarchy in 1958 and his interest in defending the rights of the Kurdish minority in Iraq led to his migration, along with Shaikh ʿAbd al-Karīm, to the village of Būbān in the Penjwin province on the Iraqi-Iranian border in early 1959. He then joined the armed Kurdish movement for six years beginning in September 1961 — a period we will read about in Chapter 7. He could no longer continue his studies, which required stability, dedication, and persistence.

In addition to his religious and secular studies, our Shaikh never stopped teaching himself. For instance, from 1959 to 1960 in Penjwin, he studied Farsi under Qāḍī Raḥīm, the Qāḍī of Mahābād in Iran and a caliph of Shaikh ʿAbd al-Karīm. His interest in learning Farsi was due to the great number of dervishes in Iran. He was an avid reader and would read as much as he could despite his limited free time. After retiring from politics in the second half of the 1960s, whenever he visited Baghdad, he would frequent the city's bookstores daily in search of books of interest. He was interested in books of religion, history, politics, and psychology; he had no interest in novels or books of poetry.

The following is a karāma that demonstrates our Shaikh's effort to learn. In 1976, Shaikh ʿAbd al-Karīm gave caliph Yāsīn Ṣūfī fifteen dinars to buy a copy of Fakhr al-Dīn al-Rāzī's *al-Tafsīr al-Kabīr* (The Great Commentary). He told him that the commentary consisted of sixteen parts. When the caliph returned to his place of residence in Ramādī, he asked its two bookshops, but they did not have the book. He went to one of Baghdad's biggest bookstores, but he could not find it there either. The store owner told him that it was unlikely that he would find it. Yet, when he asked for it in a small bookstore nearby, he found what he was looking for. The shopkeeper brought the book, but it turned out that it was written in eight volumes. The caliph said that he had been told that it would consist of sixteen parts, so the shopkeeper assured him that every volume contained two parts, so that is sixteen in total. The commentary was an old lithograph edition dating back eighty-three years. Caliph Yāsīn asked about the price, and the seller said that it was fifteen dinars — the exact amount Shaikh ʿAbd al-Karīm had given him. He said that he wanted to purchase the commentary, on the condition that he could return it if it turned out not to be the same commentary wanted by the person who had sent him. The shopkeeper told him that the commentary originally belonged to a deceased Shaikh of Ṭarīqa and that the Shaikh's family had asked him to sell it to them. He said that if he did not return the book within ten days, he would give the money to the family of that Shaikh. They agreed.

When the caliph went to Kirkuk and entered Shaikh ʿAbd al-Karīm's assembly with the commentary in hand, the Shaikh stood, out of reverence for the magnificent Qur'an, and motioned for him to place the commentary on a table. The caliph explained that even though the commentary was in eight volumes, it was, in fact, sixteen parts and that it was an eighty-three-year-old edition. Shaikh ʿAbd al-Karīm leafed through the book, confirming that it was the one he was looking for. At that moment, the caliph was thinking to himself why the Shaikh would need this specific commentary. Shaikh ʿAbd al-Karīm looked at him and said, "My son, I do not need this commentary. However, Kāka Muḥammad (meaning our Shaikh) has read twenty-two Qur'anic exegeses, which is something no one knows, including his wife and mother. I want him to read this one as well".

In the latter half of the 1970s, our Shaikh wished to complete his university studies. He took permission from Shaikh ʿAbd al-Karīm to study at al-Āzhar University in Cairo. He travelled to Cairo towards the end of 1977 and obtained the university's approval to study as an off-campus student residing in Kirkuk and to travel to the university every year for the necessary exams, but only after obtaining an initial certificate from the university. Our Shaikh stayed in Cairo for 42 days, in which time he obtained that certificate and returned to Kirkuk. About two months after his return, in early February 1978, Shaikh ʿAbd al-Karīm passed away. Our Shaikh succeeded him as Master of the Ṭarīqa, so he was forced to abandon any thoughts of completing his studies.

Our Shaikh continued to read and educate himself, focusing primarily on books of Sufism. While he lived in Baghdad in 1982-2000, he visited bookshops nearly every day. He would familiarize himself with what they had in stock and with any new releases, and he would pick up whichever books aroused his interest. He would visit nearly every day the massive bookshops in Bāb al-Sharqī, whereas he would visit al-Mutanabbī Street bookstores on Fridays, where books from personal libraries were sold. It was possible to acquire rare and very old books this way. He would also check to see what mobile vendors were offering from the books they displayed on the ground.

After becoming Shaikh of the Ṭarīqa, our Master added ancient Sufi manuscripts, including those that specialised in dhikrs and supplications, to the list of books he took interest in. Beginning in the early 1980s, until he migrated from Baghdad in 2000, our Shaikh would spend most of his morning, usually two to five hours, visiting libraries that contained manuscripts and books on subjects that were of interest to him (photo 12). These included the "Iraqi House of Manuscripts", once named "Saddam's House of Manuscripts", which contains more than 45,000 manuscripts; "The al-Āwqāf Library"; and "The al-Ḥaḍra al-Gaylāniyya Library". He did not limit his visits to the manuscript libraries in Baghdad; he also visited libraries in Mosul and Sulaymāniyya. In addition to directly familiarizing himself with all of these manuscripts, the immense scale of such a task required that he take several assistants with him. He would tell them what he was searching for, and they would then present what they found to him. In his efforts, he was more like the head of a research institution than a single researcher. This effort was the start of a massive project to write "The Kasnazān Encyclopaedia", the only encyclopaedia of Sufism in the world, that we will touch on in §12.3, although our Master did not publicly announce this project at the time.

Even the deterioration of his eyesight and his need for a magnifying glass did not diminish his interest in manuscripts and in reading. For example, in the second half of February 2000, he spent two weeks in Istanbul waiting to complete his travel arrangements to London, where he would receive treatment for his eyes. Instead of resting his eyes and taking a break from reading, he would visit the famous Süleymaniye Library daily. The library contains more than 67,000 manuscripts. He would choose certain manuscripts from the library's four indexes and familiarize himself with them. He would also visit the Atatürk Library in the same city. He kept this practice up during his six-month stay in London, March-September 2000, during which time he underwent two eye operations. He would go, on an almost daily basis, to the British Library, which contains a large number of ancient Arabic manuscripts (photo 27). He would choose specific manuscripts from the indexes and scan through them. When he found something of interest, he would mark the pages he wanted to copy, but he would sometimes ask for the entire manuscript to be copied. When he came to London, he had already compiled more than 5,000 entries of the encyclopaedia of Sufism, that is more than half of its contents. This unique encyclopaedia was completed and published less than five years after his return from Britain.

Our Shaikh also visited the Library of Congress in the United States of America. He travelled there for medical examinations and treatment in 2003 and 2004, and then 2010 when he underwent a kidney transplant in early August. He returned in 2014, 2016, and 2019 for periodic evaluations and treatment.

In recent years, now in Amman, his body can no longer stand walking through libraries, so librarians have started to send new arrivals in areas of interest to him to the takya. He would look them over and decide whether he would like to purchase or return them. The severe weakening of his eyesight has made it difficult for him to read, except when the writing is very large (photo 13). His personal assistant would read the index and, sometimes, specific topics of our Shaikh's choosing, of each new book, before deciding whether or not to keep that book. Most days, our Master chooses topics from certain books and asks his assistant to read them to him. His deteriorating health in general, and his weakening eyesight in particular, have not affected his interest in reading books. Not a day goes by without him reading through some books. One of the fruits of our Shaikh's interest in books and manuscripts is that, over the years, he has amassed a tremendous, fully indexed personal library that includes tens of thousands of books and thousands of manuscripts.

One aspect of his general interest in education and culture is that after he retired from politics, his assembly in Kirkuk became a daily forum for prominent scholars and intellectuals. Various religious and philosophical issues and books were discussed and debated. These discussions included critiquing anti-religious philosophies that were popular among intellectuals, such as atheism and materialism, and defending Islamic and Sufi thought. He would purchase various newly published books that he and his assembly would read and discuss.

This intellectual assembly continued after our Shaikh became the Master of the Ṭarīqa and moved to Baghdad. Famous intellectuals, academics, writers, and artists would frequent this assembly, such as sociologist Dr ʿAlī al-Wardī, linguist Dr Ḥusayn ʿAlī Maḥfūẓ, historian Dr Ḥusayn Amīn, historian and archaeologist Sālim al-`Ālūsī, archaeologist Dr Bahnām Abū al-Ṣūf, astronomer Dr Ḥamid M. al-Ni'aymī, preacher of Sulaymāniyya and president of the Scholars of Northern Iraq Association Shaikh Muḥammad al-Qaradāghī, expert and reciter of the Iraqi maqam Hāshim al-Rajab, and many others. Our Master's daily assembly attracted great minds and hosted broad and extensive discussions. 'Abd Allah Sallūm al-Sāmurrā'ī, one of the most prominent thinkers of the then ruling Ba'ath Party who frequented our Shaikh's assembly, described it as a place where "one could breathe intellectually and be spiritually enriched". At times, these intellectual assemblies lasted well past midnight, possibly as late as two in the morning.

Our Shaikh constantly stresses the need to acquire knowledge and that it is a door to faith and approaching Allah. He also mentions that knowledge is a form of power, citing the noble prophetic ḥadīth: "The strong believer is better and more beloved to Allah than the weak believer". [142] Just as he encouraged and welcomed intellectuals and academics, opened his assembly to them and provided them with an atmosphere in which they could exchange ideas and opinions, he constantly reminds the disciples of the necessity to acquire as much knowledge as possible:

> "We do not instruct the seeker to abandon knowledge, because it is through knowledge he worships his Lord. Knowledge makes the person understand the act of worship because knowledge is light: 'Are those who know equal to those who do not know?' (al-Zumar 9). We instruct the disciple to perform righteous deeds. We instruct the disciple to study, to read, to go to school, to learn, to become educated, and to worship. How beautiful it is when a seeker is well-educated".[143]

Our Master encourages the completion of a university degree and to continue onto postgraduate studies if possible. He also allows students to temporarily stop reading the Ṭarīqa's dhikrs during exams, while continuing to perform the obligatory prayers, and to try to make up for what they miss once on holiday. Just as he encourages disciples to acquire the highest academic qualifications, he urged his children to excel in their studies and to at least obtain a basic university degree. All of his sons

---

[142] Muslim, *Ṣaḥīḥ Muslim*, IV, no. 2664, p. 2052.

[143] Shaikh Muḥammad al-Muḥammad al-Kasnazān, *sermon*, 29th/January/2010.

completed their undergraduate studies, some of them completed postgraduate studies, and his daughter graduated from a teachers' college.

In 2003, our Shaikh's efforts to promote learning and science and to encourage people to get as much education as possible led him to establish an educational institution in Baghdad, a university called "Shaikh Muḥammad al-Kasnazān University College", later renamed the "al-Salām University College". The college grants baccalaureate degrees in several subjects in science and humanities.

One important achievement of our Shaikh was that he has increased the dervishes' degree of awareness and understanding of the Ṭarīqa's thought and practices. He has published books and literature dealing with various aspects of the Ṭarīqa, and he regularly delivered lectures. He has urged dervishes to study and acquire what was easily available to them in the way of different types of knowledge. He has also attracted many intellectuals, academics, and those with higher university degrees to the Ṭarīqa. Shaikh Muḥammad al-Muḥammad has made the educational development of the Kasnazānī seeker one of his constant concerns.

Our Shaikh also organized three intensive courses for a large number of caliphs, where they were taught by qualified academic scholars who specialise in various areas of Islamic studies. The participants received official certifications. The study covered several subjects, such as Sharia, Sufism, creed, jurisprudence, and even foreign languages. The first course was held in 1994, at the Institute of Imams and Preachers in Baghdad. The second course was held in the summer of 1996, in the main takya in Baghdad, and the third in 2005, in the main takya in Sulaymāniyya.

Our Shaikh's interest in education and the dissemination of knowledge amongst disciples and people has manifested itself in his authoring of a number of books, including the only encyclopaedia on Sufism. He compiled in the latter opinions of Sufi Shaikhs throughout history on various Sufi terms and concepts. In May 2006, he was awarded the "Arab Historian Medal" and the "Arab History Certificate" by the Union of Arab Historians, in recognition of the large role he has played in Islamic and Arab education.

Photo 12: Shaikh Muḥammad al-Muḥammad in a public library in Baghdad (the 1990s).

Photo 13: Shaikh Muḥammad al-Muḥammad in his private room in the takya in Amman, Jordan, enjoying his favourite hobby of reading (2012).

Photo 14: Shaikh Muḥammad al-Muḥammad in a session of songs of praise in the takya in Amman, Jordan (24th/September/2015).

"We are called 'The Messenger's Nation', so what is the difference between a Shi'ite and a Sunni? A Kurd and an Arab? A Persian and anyone else? We are all the Messenger's Nation. There is no difference between an Arab and a non-Arab, except in piety:[144] 'Indeed, the noblest of you in the sight of Allah is the most righteous of you' (al-Ḥujurāt 13)".

Shaikh Muḥammad al-Muḥammad al-Kasnazān
(Sermon, 2nd/November/2013)

---

[144] The Prophet (PBUH) said in his Farewell sermon: "O people, your Lord is one and your father Adam is one. There is no superiority for an Arab over a foreigner, nor for a foreigner over an Arab, and neither for a white-skined person over a black-skined, nor for a black-skined over a white-skined, except by piety: 'Indeed, the most noble of you in the sight of Allah is the most pious of you' (al-Ḥujurāt 13)" (Bayhaqī, *Shu'ab al-`Īmān*, IV, no. 5137, p. 289).

7

Defending the National Rights of the Kurds

The Messenger (PBUH) loved worshipping and being alone with his Lord even before the Qur'an was revealed, but he was never cut off from society. Rather, he combined worshipping Allah alone and having a fully integrated social life. He was a mecca for those who wanted to trust something and was sincere in dealing with people. He was known as the "Truthful, Trustworthy One". The Messenger (PBUH) did not change after the Qur'an's revelation; he loved worshipping, standing in prayer at night and being alone with his Lord. He would also call people to Allah constantly. The need to defend and spread religion caused him to combine his roles as a prophet and messenger of Allah to people with his political and military leadership of the Muslims in defending them.

7.1 Shaikhs of the Ṭarīqa and Resistance to Injustice and Aggression

As was the case with the Messenger of Allah (PBUH), the responsibilities of the spiritual leadership of the Ṭarīqa and their many practices of worship did not keep the Shaikhs of Ṭarīqa away from people. Rather, they lived in the heart of society, enjoining people to do good and forbidding evil, changing what displeases Allah by hand, tongue, and heart: "If anyone sees an evil, let him change it with his hand; if he is not able to do so, then [let him change it] with his tongue; and if he is not able to do so, then with his heart — and that is the weakest of faith".[145] For instance, Imām ʿAlī Ibn Abī Ṭālib had an unparalleled record of armed jihad with the Prophet (PBUH) against the polytheists who wanted to deprive the Muslims of their right to choose their religion, as

[145] Muslim, *Ṣaḥīḥ Muslim*, I, no. 49, p. 69.

well as after the Messenger in defence of the great principles of Islam against those who wanted to undermine them under the name of Islam. Likewise, Imām Ḥusayn wrote one of the finest stories of self-sacrifice when he confronted those who betrayed the will of the Prophet (PBUH) and tried to exploit Islam for personal gain.

The Greatest Ghawth, Shaikh ʿAbd al-Qādir al-Gaylānī, also did not distinguish between guiding people to Allah and rectifying worldly issues, such as standing against injustice and aggression. Instead, he combined the two duties. He distanced himself from rulers and people of power to be completely free and independent in guiding people, unlike many clerics of the time, who were tools used by rulers for worldly gain. Yet, he did not hesitate to intervene in politics when the public's best interest so required. In 541 H (1146 CE), for example, the Abbasid caliph al-Muqtafī li-Āmr Allah appointed Yaḥyā Ibn Saʿīd, known as Ibn Marjam, as a judge. He was unjust and accepted bribes without anyone being able to confront or stop him. Shaikh ʿAbd al-Qādir took advantage of al-Muqtafī's presence in the mosque one day and addressed him from the pulpit, saying: "You have put the worst tyrant in charge of the Muslims. What will you say tomorrow, before the Lord of the Worlds?" The caliph dismissed that unjust judge.

Similarly, the Shaikh's school in Baghdad was a preparation centre for Muslims fighting against the Crusaders, as he was contemporary to the two leaders ʿImād al-Dīn Zinkī and his son Nūr al-Dīn Zinkī:

> "The news of the school indicates that it played a key role in preparing the generation that confronted the Crusader threat in the Levant. The school would receive the sons of those displaced when they fled the Crusader occupation. It would prepare them and then return them to the areas of confrontation under Zinkī leadership. Later, some of these students became famous, such as Ibn Najā the Preacher, who later became a political and military adviser to Saladin; al-Ḥāfiẓ al-Rahāwī; Musā Ibn al-Shaikh ʿAbd al-Qādir, who moved to the Levant to partake of the intellectual activity there; Muwaffaq al-Dīn, the author of *al-Mughnī* and one of Saladin's advisors; and his relative, al-Ḥāfiẓ ʿAbd al-Ghanī. The last two attended ʿAbd al-Qādir's school after their family was displaced from Jamāʿīl in the Nablus area, in

Damascus".[146]

After Ibn Najā completed his studies with Shaikh ʿAbd al-Qādir and asked for his permission to travel to Egypt, the Shaikh told him that when he arrives in Damascus, he would find Nūr al-Dīn Zinkī's forces ready to invade Egypt, which was under Fatimid rule at the time. He asked him to tell Nūr al-Dīn's commanders that they would not succeed in this campaign and that they would succeed in the second campaign. They did not heed Shaikh ʿAbd al-Qādir's advice, however, and attacked Egypt, so the campaign failed. Nūr al-Dīn prepared a second campaign, and this time, he succeeded in conquering Egypt and uniting it with the Levant. So Shaikh ʿAbd al-Qādir's prediction came to pass.[147]

The success of the Abbasid caliphate in restoring its authority and power after its decline in the Seljuk period, including the resurgence of the Abbasid ministry office, contributed to the victories of Nūr al-Dīn Zinkī and Saladin al-Āyyūbī against the Crusades. The Qādiri school and its great Master also played a big role in raising the awareness of and mobilising the public:

> "ʿAbd al-Qādir al-Gaylānī's movement is considered an important tributary in the jihad and resistance movement led by Nūr al-Dīn. It was particularly so at the grass-roots level and in Baghdad, the capital of the Abbasid Caliphate. He influenced society by his call, preaching, and advice".[148]

Shaikh ʿAbd al-ʿAzīz, one of Shaikh ʿAbd al-Qādir's sons, fought against the Crusaders. He took part in Saladin al-Āyyūbī's conquest of Ashkelon in 583 H (1187 CE), then he went to Jerusalem.[149] Shaikh ʿAbd al-ʿAzīz settled in northern Iraq, where his tomb is located, in the Aqra province of the Dohuk governorate.

The Kasnazānī Shaikhs fought invaders and aggressors and emigrated when they needed to, just as their grand Master, the Prophet (PBUH), emigrated and fought before them. Shaikh ʿAbd al-Qādir Kasnazān stood against Ottoman oppression when a Turkish commander wanted to

---

146 Gaylānī, *Hākathā Ẓahara Jīl Ṣalāḥ al-Dīn wa-Hākathā ʿĀdat al-Quds*, p. 170. See also pp. 249-255.

147 Shaṭnūfī, *Bahjat al-Asrār wa-Maʿdan al-Ānwār*, pp. 297-298.

148 Ṣallābī, ʿAlī Muḥammad. *Al-Dawla al-Zangiyya*, p. 640.

149 Tādifī, *Qalāʾid al-Jawāhir*, p. 43; Gaylānī, *Al-Shaikh ʿAbd al-Qādir*, p. 273.

recruit villagers from Karbchna by force during a notorious campaign called "Seferberlik" (public conscription or mass deportation), so that they would be fuel for a war that had nothing to do with them. The gendarmerie commander retreated out of fear, empty-handed, without recruiting any of the villagers. Just as Shaikh ʿAbd al-Qādir al-Gaylānī encouraged his children to fight against the Crusader occupation, Shaikh ʿAbd al-Qādir pushed his son Shaikh Ḥusayn to combat the occupants of Muslim land in Kurdistan.

Shaikh ʿAbd al-Qādir Kasnazān released a fatwa that called for armed jihad against the Russian forces that invaded Iranian, then Iraqi, lands in the beginning of World War I, massacring and abusing many women, children, and elderly people and mutilating their bodies. Hundreds of disciples responded to the call and gathered in Karbchna, volunteering for jihad. The Shaikh assembled an army and placed his son, and Shaikh of the Ṭarīqa after him, Ḥusayn, and his nephew Riḍā, as its commanders. Tribal chieftains and people of influence organized under this blessed leadership. The famous Kurdish rebel, Maḥmūd al-Ḥafīd, led another army of mujahedin. The two local forces met and entered into a fierce battle against the Russian army that lasted for days in an area bordering the Iraqi city Penjwin and the city of Bāna to the north, which is currently located within the Iranian border. With the visible support and spiritual influence of Shaikh ʿAbd al-Qādir, who was staying in Penjwin, the small number of lightly-armed mujahedin defeated the large Russian army, which was heavily armed with various kinds of weapons, causing many deaths and taking many prisoners. The fighters followed the remnants of the vanquished army to Lake Urmia in Iran, which is close to the borders with Turkey, Armenia, and Azerbaijan.[150]

Shaikh ʿAbd al-Qādir al-Kasnazān also declared jihad against the British occupation. In 20th/May/1919, Maḥmūd al-Ḥafīd captured Sulaymāniyya, appointing a new governor, taking control of the government records and treasuries and cutting off telegraph communication with Kirkuk. The British mobilized an army from the Kifrī region to Sulaymāniyya to break the siege. When Shaikh Maḥmūd came to know of this, he sent for help from Shaikh ʿAbd al-Qādir al-Kasnazān to repel the British forces. On 22nd of May, at Shaikh ʿAbd al-

---

[150] Alī Ḥusayn al-Kasnazān, *Al-Mujāhid al-Akbar al-Shaikh ʿAbd al-Qādir al-Kasnazān.*

Qādir's behest, Shaikh Ḥusayn and Shaikh Riḍā led an army from the north; Shaikh ʿAbd al-Qādir Gulanabar — father of sayyida Ḥafṣa, future wife of Shaikh ʿAbd al-Karīm Al-Kasnazān — and his son Musṭafā led an army from the south. The two forces drew the British into an ambush between the villages of Karbchna and Kchan. The mujahedin achieved a swift victory, killing some of the British and capturing others. They also disarmed the convoy and seized the cash it carried and their horses.[151]

Among the prisoners they took were a Captain Marr, the commander of the British forces, who had been wounded in the battle, and an officer named Schofield. The prisoners of war were released after some time, and the rebels buried the dead of the invading forces in Karbchna. It should be noted that Sangāw, where Karbchna is located, was of strategic importance because it was on the trade route between Sulaymāniyya and Baghdad.

Less than a month after their defeat in the battle of Sangāw, the British mobilized a large army supported by planes and tanks from Kirkuk to Chamchamāl to end Shaikh Maḥmūd al-Ḥafīd's control over Sulaymāniyya and to hunt down the leaders of the battle of Sangāw, including Shaikh ʿAbd al-Qādir al-Kasnazān, Shaikh Ḥusayn al-Kasnazān, and Shaikh ʿAbd al-Qādir Gulanabar. On 18th/June, the mujahedin and the British forces clashed in a great battle in the Bazyān Pass. The large difference in the number of troops favoured the invaders. Maḥmūd al-Ḥafīd was wounded in the battle and was taken as a prisoner of war, alongside his brother-in-law, Muḥammad Gharīb. Shaikh Musṭafā, Shaikh Ḥusayn al-Kasnazān's maternal uncle, was among those who were wounded. The British army chased the commanders of the mujahedin and headed towards Karbchna, burning it down in retaliation. It failed in its attempts to arrest Shaikh ʿAbd al-Qādir and his son, who headed towards the villages of Khāwya and Kasnazān, where many disciples and relatives lived. They then stayed one night in the village of Kānī Sīf on Mount Surin, on the Iraqi-Iranian border. The villagers placed food for the hungry migrants on rocks, instead of pots, thinking that they were gipsy nomads, who were considered dirty. The Shaikh's relatives were saddened by this situation and cried. The harsh conditions they experienced as a result of migration were exacerbated by the cruelty

---

[151] Bell, *Review of the civil administration of Mesopotamia*, pp. 64-65.

of mistreatment, having become used to being respected by people. The Shaikh comforted them, saying: "Don't cry. You will see what I will do for you when we get to Iran". One karāma that accompanied this blessed migration happened when the Shaikh, his family, and those with him took refuge in a mountain cave. The British soldiers failed to find them, even though they came very near to the cave. Soldiers even left shoe marks on the dresses of some migrant women but did not see them.

The discontent of British administration in Iraq against Shaikh ʿAbd al-Qādir can be seen in his description by one of its high-ranking officials, Cecil Edmonds, as a "turbulent and dangerous agitator". It is worth mentioning that Edmonds mentions Shaikh ʿAbd al-Qādir only twice, in passing, in his famous book about his time of service in Iraq. Yet the only time he mentions him directly and describes him with the above description, he also mentions a karāma of the Shaikh, related to Edmonds by Shaikh ʿAbd al-Karīm Qādir Karam. The karāma demonstrates the Shaikh's prescience of his hour of death and how he prepared for it by gathering his children and appointing one of them, meaning Shaikh Ḥusayn, as Shaikh of the Ṭarīqa after him. Shaikh ʿAbd al-Qādir was so famous for his karāmas that even when an enemy of his — a British politician — mentioned him in passing in his political book, he could not help but mention one of his miracles. Interestingly, after his account of the karāma, Edmonds admits that the high esteem in which the narrator of the karāma held Shaikh ʿAbd al-Qādir contravened his image of a "turbulent and dangerous agitator" according to the British. Edmonds ends his comment with the adage "God knows best"![152]

Shaikh ʿAbd al-Qādir's departure to the spirit world was accompanied by miracles, as his life was rich with miracles, but Edmonds' account is inaccurate. We will recount here the details of the death as narrated by one of its witnesses, Ḥājj ʿAbd al-Karīm Ḥājj Ṣāliḥ, whom Sultan ʿAbd al-Qādir raised since he was a young orphan and kept him by his side. He also fought alongside Shaikh Ḥusayn. The day he died, the Shaikh seemed to be in good health. After the night prayer, however, his body began to heat up. The Shaikh lay down, facing the Kaʿba, surrounded by his family, including his four sons: Ḥusayn, Kāka Muḥammad, ʿAbd al-Karīm, and Muḥammad Ṣāliḥ. It seemed from the gathering of his family

---

[152] Edmonds, *Kurds, Turks and Arabs*, p. 356.

around him, despite his illness not looking serious, that the Shaikh had told them that the time of his departure had come. The Shaikh was in a state of dhikr and would not speak, as was usually the case. There was a small opening in the room for ventilation and light, as was common at the time. There were luminous candles in each of the room's four corners. Suddenly, a small green bird entered through the ventilation hole and flew to each candle and extinguished it. When those present relit the candles, they found that the Shaikh had departed to his Lord's presence; they did not see the moment he left this life.[153] The Shaikh's illness lasted less than an hour. This reminds us of the words of the Greatest Ghawth, Shaikh ʿAbd al-Qādir al-Gaylānī, which states that the way the Angel of Death takes a human soul reflects its good or bad state in this world and the hereafter:

> "If you see the Angel of Death (prayers of peace and blessings be on our Prophet and on him) come to you laughing, with a relaxed face, and you see his assistants likewise, greet you and take your soul gently, as he took the souls of the prophets, the martyrs, and the righteous (Allah's prayer and peace be on all of them), then expect good on the Day of Resurrection. The first day will show you the second day and its details. If you see good [on the first day], then [you will see] good [on the second day]; if you see bad [on the first day], then [you will see] bad [on the second day]. The Angel of Death came to Moses (prayers of peace and blessings be on our Prophet and on him) holding an apple in his hand. He let Moses smell it and took his soul in that smelling. Similarly, anyone who is near to Allah will have the Angel of Death take his soul in the easiest, most beautiful way possible".[154]

Karāmas also happened when the body of Shaikh ʿAbd al-Qādir was being repatriated to Iraq for burial next to his father, Shāh al-Kasnazān, in Karbchna. Dervishes covered the coffin to protect it from the unceasing rain and then carried it on their shoulders. At some point inside the borders of Iraq, they approached a bridge on a valley that they needed to cross. But when they became very close to the bridge the coffin starting feeling heavier, until they had to quickly offload it and place it on the ground. They tried to carry it again without success. In fact, it became too heavy to even move. Dervishes realised that this was

[153] Shaikh Muḥammad al-Muḥammad al-Kasnazān, *sermon*, 28th/October/2013.

[154] Shaikh ʿAbd al-Qādir al-Gaylānī, *Jilā' al-Khāṭir*, p. 106.

supernatural. They starting performing dhikr hoping that it will return the coffin to its normal condition, but nothing changed. At this point, a dervish who possesses ḥāl intervened. He explained that Shaikh ʿAbd al-Qādir had said when migrating from Iraq that he would not tread on land that was under British occupation. This bridge had been built by the occupying forces, so the Shaikh would not cross it even after his death. The dervish then sat next to the Shaikh's head in the coffin and spoke to him. He said that they realise that he does not want to cross this bridge because it was built by the British, so they are going to carry the coffin through the valley, even if they would drown. The dervish was referring to the fact that the rain that had been falling for several days had filled the valley with water, so it was too deep to cross without a karāma by the Shaikh.

After the dervish's words with the Shaikh, the dervishes tried to lift the coffin and found that it had returned to its normal weight. The valley was full so that the horses could barely keep their heads above water. Strangely, the water only reached the knees of the pedestrian dervishes who were carrying the coffin and accompanying it. The dervishes were able to get the coffin to the other side of the valley without using the bridge or drowning. Caliph Mulla ʿAlī, who was one of the those who transported the coffin, noted that the continuous falling of the rain for seven days meant that when the Shaikh's coffin reached Iraq, the rain had not left any trace of the boots of the occupying soldiers.

The dervishes continued to carry the coffin until they reached a junction that leads into two directions. One led to Karbchna, where the dervishes wanted to burry the Shaikh. They found caliphs and dervishes from another village to which the other road led. These had learned that the coffin was passing from there to Karbchna, so they came to try and take the coffin for burial in their village instead of Karbchna, to have blessings of the Shaikh. The other dervishes argued that Karbchna is also where Shāh al-Kasnazān is buried and that it is where Shaikh ʿAbd al-Qādir was born. But that did not convince the villagers, who insisted on taking the coffin to their village, even if they had to do it by force. At this point, the dervish who possess ḥāl who spoke to the Shaikh before crossing the valley intervened and spoke to the Shaikh once again. He told him that they wanted to take lay him in Karbchna but that the other group of dervishes wanted to take him to their village. He asked the

Shaikh to signal to them where he would like to be taken. As soon as the caliph ended his question, the coffin, which was on the ground, turned to face Karbchna and then moved in its direction abound three metres without anybody touching it. The villagers then conceded that Karbchna should be the Shaikh's burial place and they accompanied the other dervishes in their journey to it.

A number of Shaikh ʿAbd al-Qādir's karāmas appeared to Maḥmūd al-Ḥafīd, one of which we will mention here. After the latter fell into the hands of the British in the Battle of the Bazyān Pass, and after he recovered from his wounds, he was sentenced to death by a British military court. The sentence was later reduced to ten years in prison. In 1921, he was exiled to India to spend his sentence there. His brother-in-law, Muḥammad Gharīb, was also with him in his prison in exile, as he was sentenced to five years in prison. Al-Ḥafīd had a dream in which Shaikh ʿAbd al-Qādir informed him that he would be released, return home, and be appointed governor. He gave him a sign that at sunrise, a strong gust of wind would uproot a tree in the prison's courtyard. As foretold, the British released their prisoners, after which Maḥmūd al-Ḥafīd spent some time in Kuwait. Then the British returned him to Iraq to install him as governor of Iraqi Kurdistan in September 1922. In November, he called himself "King".[155]

It is important to note that the political and military contributions the Kasnazān Shaikhs made were always within the framework of their primary responsibility — the good of the Ṭarīqa — rather than for any secular gain. Their actions clearly reflect this absolute priority. For example, caring for the Ṭarīqa required that Shaikh ʿAbd al-Qādir and Shaikh Ḥusayn emigrate, rather than remain in northern Iraq in a state of ongoing jihad against an occupying army far superior in number and wherewithal to any resistance army that could be assembled from local fighters. As the Kasnazānī Shaikhs' participation in and withdrawal from jihad and the political action front reflect their prioritizing of the Ṭarīqa's spiritual leadership duties, it is no surprise that they are mentioned very little in writings of political and revolutionary history.

---

[155] Edmonds, *Kurds, Turks and Arabs*, p. 301.

7.2 Historical Background of the Modern Kurdish Movement in Iraq

The collapse of the Ottoman Empire in the First World War presented the Arabs and Kurds with the opportunity to get rid of the oppressive Ottoman power that treated them, and other non-Turkish nationalities, as second-class citizens for four centuries. However, they were not prepared to replace the unjust Ottoman rule with British occupation. As we saw in the jihad of Shaikh 'Abd al-Qādir and his son Shaikh Ḥusayn, the Kurds in northern Iraq resisted the British occupation forces during the First World War and after the fall of the Ottoman Empire. Shaikh Maḥmūd al-Ḥafīd led more than a thousand Kurdish volunteers, and other Kurdish leaders led other volunteers, and both joined the Ottoman forces and informal Arab fighters in the Sha'aiba area in southern Iraq in mid-April 1910, in fighting invading British forces that were trying to extend their control north.[156] The efforts of the resistance did not succeed, however, so the British forces continued to head north until they entered Baghdad in 1917. After Britain completed occupying Iraq in 1918, the relations between its forces and Iraqi Kurdistan politicians and fighters in the subsequent four decades went through different phases, ranging from agreement and cooperation concerning devolved administration of some cities — that is, giving the Kurds some kind of autonomy — to the Kurdish armed uprising and British military repression when differences surfaced about principles or implementation of mutual agreements. Some Kurdish aghas and tribes supported the British and maintained friendly relations with them.

Despite the importance of the many political and military developments and events in the Iraqi Kurdistan region during the British occupation that followed the collapse of the Ottoman Empire, this period is not directly related to this chapter's subject matter. We will skip past those events and move to the military coup that took place on 14th/July/1958. In this section, we will very briefly address the circumstances created by that coup that led to Shaikh Muḥammad al-

---

[156] Zakī, *Khulāṣat Tārīkh al-Kurd wa-Kurdistan min Aqdam al-'Uṣūr al-Tārīkhiyya ilā al-`Ān*, p. 274; Aḥmad, *Kurdistan fī-Sanawāt al-Ḥarb al-'Ālamiyya al-`Ulā*, p. 186; Juwayda, *Al-Ḥaraka al-Qawmiyya al-Turkiyya wa-Nash`atuhā wa-Taṭawwuruhā*, p. 308.

Muḥammad al-Kasnazān's involvement with politics. In the next two sections, we will focus on our Shaikh's political and military activity.

The 14th/July coup was one of the most important turning points in Iraq's modern history. A group of army officers seized power and killed King Faisal II and the royal family. They abolished the monarchy and replaced it with a republican system. Brigadier General ʿAbd al-Karīm Qāsim became in charge of the country, holding the posts of Prime Minister, Minister of Defence and Commander-in-Chief of the Armed Forces. The second in command was Colonel ʿAbd al-Salām ʿĀrif, who held the posts of Deputy Prime Minister and Minister of the Interior. Qāsim gradually turned himself into the state's sole leader and took over all powers after relieving ʿĀrif of all of his posts in 1959. One aspect of his dictatorship is that he cancelled the license for founding political parties that ʿĀrif had issued, allowing only a dissident faction of the Iraqi Communist Party led by Dā`ūd al-Sāyigh to operate. Just as Qāsim is credited for the Iraqi government improving relation with the Kurds at the start of the revolution, he was also responsible for its subsequent deterioration, as we will see.

Initially, the Kurds did not have a unified response to the 14th/July military coup. Two groups of power among the Kurds had two completely different positions. The first side was represented by leaders and politicians who welcomed the coup, which they saw as a source of hope for achieving their national goals. This hope was particularly raised two weeks after the coup when its leadership declared a provisional Iraqi constitution whose third clause of its first section stated the following:

> "The Iraqi entity is based on the cooperation of all citizens, by respecting their rights and safeguarding their freedoms. Arabs and Kurds are considered partners in this country. This constitution recognises their national rights within the unity of Iraq".

This clause made the Kurds partners in Iraq and recognized their national rights as the second-largest nationality that comprised the Iraqi population. Another important indication that the coup's leadership was serious in its concern to improve relations with the Kurds is that the first government established by the coup made Bābā ʿAlī, Shaikh Maḥmūd al-Ḥafīd's son, Minister of Transport and Works, while the Presidential Council included another Kurd, Khālid Naqshbandī. Additionally, a number of Kurds were appointed to various high-level government positions.[157] The Iraqi government also released all Kurdish political prisoners.

Kurdish political leaders' hope that the coup would bring positive change for Iraqi Kurdistan was further manifested when the Kurdistan Democratic Party (KDP) supported the coup. This party, which was founded in 1946 and had an honorary president, Mullā Musṭafā Barzānī, also sent a delegation from different regions of Kurdistan, headed by party secretary Ibrāhīm Aḥmad, to Baghdad to offer congratulations to the coup's leaders. Qāsim invited Barzānī to return to Iraq, as he had spent 11 years as a refugee in the Soviet Union. Barzānī arrived in Baghdad in October 1958 and was welcomed by the public. Qāsim generously received him and allocated monthly salaries to both him and the refugees who returned with him.[158] Qāsim also allowed the publication of the "Khabāt" (The Struggle) newspaper, the KDP mouthpiece.

There was a second group of influential Kurds — namely, aghas and feudal lords — who saw the coup as a curse. Over the years, the large clans were represented in the governments and parliaments during the monarchy era, but this privilege ended after the coup. Unlike the KDP, clan chieftains did not congratulate the coup's leaders. The largest evidence that the coup was bad for them came on 30th/September/1958 when the government issued what became known as the "Agrarian Reform Law No. 30 of 1958". It limited one person's ownership of agricultural land to one thousand dunams of land irrigated by free-flowing water or by artificial means and two thousand dunams of rain-irrigated land. The property of any individual beyond this amount was to be distributed to farmers. This meant the distribution of half the agricultural land to farmers who worked for landowners and gave ten per cent of the crop to the landowner as wages for farming their land.[159] However, this law, which included all areas of Iraq, failed to take into account the specifics of the situation in Kurdistan, whose agricultural lands depended mainly on rain rather than irrigation. The landowners in

---

[157] Juwayda, *Al-Ḥaraka al-Qawmiyya al-Turkiyya wa-Nash`atuhā wa-Taṭawwuruhā*, pp. 659-661.

[158] Aḥmad, *Al-Ḥaraka al-Kurdiyya fīl-'Irāq*, pp. 147-149.

[159] Mcdowall, *A Modern History of The Kurds*, p. 306.

Kurdistan did not have the means of production available to the Arab farmers. Thus, the owner of a thousand dunams of irrigated land in the central and southern regions was considered an average owner, while in Kurdistan, he was considered a very large feudal lord.[160]

The implementation of the Agrarian Reform Law began in 1959, but the failure of the state to plan and oversee the implementation of the law led to a serious collapse in the agreements, relations, and systems of agricultural work in Kurdistan, which had existed for decades between agha landowners and feudal lords, on the one hand, and farmers, on the other. Some landowners abandoned land that they thought the law would deprive them of, whereas some farmers began to forcibly take lands, with some using violence. Fearing for their lives, some landowners had no option but to leave Iraq for Iran.[161] A state of chaos ensued that paralyzed the movement of agriculture in Kurdistan and had a significantly negative impact on the entire region, as agriculture was the field most people worked in and their only source of livelihood.

The dispute of the feudal lords with the government reached its climax in June 1961, when the government refused to meet with their delegation to discuss their demands to abolish the land tax introduced by the Agrarian Reform Act and to amend that law and end the turmoil in the region created by Qāsim's policy. The government's disregard of the delegation led the feudal lords to refuse to pay the new tax. This, in effect, signified their disobedience and rebellion against the government, including refusing to implement the Agrarian Reform Law. Ironically, most farmers, who were supposed to benefit from agricultural sector reforms, supported the landowners in their conflict with the government. This demonstrated the strength of clan loyalty in the region.

Meanwhile, the relationship between Qāsim and Barzānī was also beginning to falter at the beginning of 1960. Barzānī wanted more rights for the Kurds than Qāsim was prepared to give. Specifically, he could not agree with Barzānī's and his party's view of the Kurdish cities in Iraq, Turkey, Iran and Syria as a unified Kurdistan. When Barzānī applied for permission for the KDP, the Iraqi government demanded a change in the party's name and approach so that it would be less threatening to Iran and

---

[160] Barazānī, *Al-Barazānī wal-Ḥaraka al-Taḥarruriyya al-Kurdiyya 2*, p. 66.

[161] Barazānī, *Al-Barazānī wal-Ḥaraka al-Taḥarruriyya al-Kurdiyya 2*, pp. 66-67.

Turkey. Both countries were troubled by Barzānī's ambitions and the potential effects of the party in fuelling the nationalist feelings of their Kurdish populations, who exceeded the Iraqi Kurds in number. After the amendments were made, the party obtained a license to officially operate in February. Three months later, Ibrāhīm Aḥmad angered the government by cancelling most of these changes. In October, he further exacerbated the situation by publishing an article in Khabāt opposing the second clause of the first section of the interim constitution, which states that "Iraq is part of the Arab community". He considered this description as non-applicable to the Kurdish people. This, in addition to other negative developments and the growing suspicion between the two sides about the other side's true goals and intentions, led to increased tension between Qāsim and Barzānī. This reached a point that made the latter feel unsafe in Baghdad, so he left it for Barzān in March 1961. The government considered Barzānī's departure from Baghdad as a declaration of estrangement. It launched a campaign of arrests that targeted members of the KDP in Baghdad, closed its branches and discontinued the party newspaper and other Kurdish publications.[162]

Although Mullā Musṭafā and the leaders of the KDP on the one hand, and the aghas and feudal lords on the other, had two completely different reactions to the coup d'état of 14th/July, they became partners in their open hostility towards Qāsim's rule in the latter half of 1961. This rapprochement of interests was facilitated by Barzānī's plans of action being "a blend of tribalism and nationalism".[163] Still, some Kurds, such as the Zībār clan, remained loyal to the government.

As the situation between the government and the Kurds worsened, the army grew more active in the area and began to prepare for combat. Some clan fighters began to cut the army off from roadways, including the Darbandikhān and Bazyān straits. On 6th/September/1961, the party declared a general strike that paralyzed all life in Kurdistan. The next day, Shaikh Muḥammad al-Muḥammad al-Kasnazān led an armed force that attacked and occupied a police station on the road between Penjwin and Darbandikhān and seized its weapons to secure the supply route between the two areas. This was one of the first military operations of the Kurdish

---

[162] Aḥmad, *Al-Ḥaraka al-Kurdiyya fīl-ʿIrāq*, pp. 169-177.
[163] Mcdowall, *A Modern History of The Kurds*, p. 310.

revolution.

Qāsim responded two days after the sit-in and attack on the police station by shelling the gatherings in Darbandikhān with artillery and aircraft. The military tension between the Kurdish forces and the army escalated, reaching a peak on 11th/September — the date considered as the beginning of the Kurdish revolution. Government aircrafts bombed rebel groups in the Bazyān strait and opened the road between Kirkuk and Sulaymāniyya. The army indiscriminately bombed villages across a large area that included Barzān. This led to an alliance between the Mullā Musṭafā forces and many aghas against the government.

After this historical introduction to the Kurdish movement in Iraq, in the next two sections, we will follow the political and military activity of Shaikh Muḥammad al-Muḥammad al-Kasnazān in the movement. Because our focus here is the biography of our Shaikh, rather than the history of the Kurdish movement, we will focus on his activities even if they take us away from the main developments of the Kurdish revolution. We have gathered in these two sections is a brief, rather than a detailed, account of our Shaikh's role in the Kurdish movement, to help us achieve the goal of this book in providing a complete picture of his life in general, including an era that played a role in shaping his character. We leave the detailed recording of this stage of his life to others.[164]

7.3 The Role of Shaikhs ʿAbd al-Karīm and Muḥammad al-Muḥammad in Launching the Kurdish Movement in Iraq

Shaikh Muḥammad al-Muḥammad entered the political arena by the permission and blessing of his father, and Master of the Ṭarīqa at the time, Shaikh ʿAbd al-Karīm al-Kasnazān. It ought to be remembered that a Shaikh of Ṭarīqa is not a politician, so he is not politically motivated. He has the Ṭarīqa's best interest at heart at all times, as the Shaikhs of Ṭarīqa

[164] We have complied the details of the history of Shaikhs ʿAbd al-Karīm and Muḥammad al-Muḥammad in the Kurdish movement from two sources: Shaikh ʿAlī Ḥusayn al-Kasnazān, our Shaikh's nephew, who witnessed some of these events while living with his grandfather Shaikh ʿAbd al-Karīm; and Shaikh Riḍā Karīm, our Shaikh's maternal cousin and brother-in-law, who was one of those who fought alongside him.

have entrusted him with the responsibility of serving the way to Allah. Hence, he does not contribute to or support any political or military activity that does not agree with the Ṭarīqa's principles and objectives. Any direct or indirect role that the Master of Ṭarīqa plays, and any activity that he condones, must be understood within the context of his being a representative of Allah on Earth, whose primary responsibility is spreading the Ṭarīqa and helping people draw near to Allah. This is the lens through which one should view the Shaikh of Ṭarīqa's agreement with certain politicians and military personnel, and his disagreement with others.

The majority of landowners were feudal lords. They had large expanses of farmland. Most of the returns and benefits of these lands accrued to them, their families and relatives, so they grew wealthier on top of the wealth they already had. Meanwhile, farmers were poor because of the limited crops they gained from feudal lands. The economic gap between the two classes widened. The Agrarian Reform Law was intended to end the monopoly of a small number of feudal lords had over a majority of agricultural land to distribute it to a large number of poor farmers and raise their standard of living.

There was a small number of landowners who were not aghas put in place and given land by the Ottoman Empire, nor tribal chiefs because of their social positions in their tribes, nor feudal lords who traded land and collected it. The Kasnazānī Shaikhs were of this small, distinguished group. They used their land and its resources in the service of the takya, Muslims, the poor, and calling people to Allah. Their land was closer to being a religious endowment than a personal possession. Although belonging to the Shaikh of Ṭarīqa in the eyes of statutory law, these lands actually belonged to the Ṭarīqa in the eyes of divine law, as is the case with everything the Shaikh has. A Shaikh of Ṭarīqa must put all that Allah has given him in the service of religion, whether the source of that livelihood is paid work, trade, voluntary charity, or compulsory charity. The Ṭarīqa's primary sources of income and property are the compulsory and voluntary charity that the dervishes give, which are used in Allah's way. This money belongs to Allah, not to any individual, and it is for Allah, not for worldly purposes. Here are some incidents that illustrate this.

During Shaikh ʿAbd al-Qādir al-Kasnazān's stay in Iran, the king of

Sanandaj's wife, Mulūka Khān, sent him the deeds to ten villages as a present. This lady was from a large, wealthy Kurdish family that owned many villages and a lot of land in the Marivan region of Iran and Hawmārāmān in Qaradāgh, Iraq. The migrant Shaikh graciously refused the gift, saying that he was a dervish and did not need villages. When his son, Shaikh Ḥusayn, intervened to convince him to accept the gift, he told him: "My son, this does not benefit us. Our drum and tambourine are better than villages", referring to the drum and tambourine of dhikr. Shaikh Ḥusayn alluded to a well-known Sufi family in Sulaymāniyya that owned a lot of lands. The Master of Ṭarīqa replied that the property would end up in the hands of many bad grandchildren, which is actually what happened, and Shaikh ʿAbd al-Qādir repeated what he had said: "Our drum and tambourine are better than villages".

We also find that the growth of the Ṭarīqa's property during the Shaikhdom of Sultan Ḥusayn as a result of the donations of dervishes did not change his asceticism, which grew day by day. In the last years of his life, he even abandoned food, drink, and all worldly pleasures to devote himself fully to worship. The purpose of increasing the Ṭarīqa's wealth is to serve the Ṭarīqa not the Shaikh as the Shaikh himself is a servant of the Ṭarīqa.

Let us cite another incident that shows the different role possessions play in the life of a Shaikh of Ṭarīqa, as opposed to the materialistic role they play in the life of a feudal lord. As we have mentioned, the prevailing practice was that the farmer would work the land and give its owner a tenth of the harvest to pay for their use of the land. However, when Sulṭān Ḥusayn bought the villages of Karbchna and Žālā, he told the farmers that he would not take the usual tenth of the crop they used to pay as rent to the owners of these lands. Rather, he would accept the payment as charity (zakāt) for the takya, or in other words, he would consider it as money that would only be used in Allah's way: "Charity (zakāt) is only for the poor; for the needy; for those employed to manage it; for those whose hearts are brought together; for freeing captives [or slaves]; for those in debt; for Allah's cause; and for the [stranded] traveller — an obligation [imposed] by Allah. Allah is Knowing and Wise" (al-Tawba 60). It also meant that the farmer could work the land for free because zakāt is obligatory anyway, even if the landowner collected rent from the farmer. In fact, Sulṭān Ḥusayn completely reversed what the landowners used to do, buying several villages and distributing their lands to their respective farmers. A while after his death, Sulṭān Ḥusayn's family subsisted on only a limited amount of bread, as a result of his having given away everything that came his way for Allah's sake. Sufi Shaikhs had customarily protected peasants from those who tried to exploit since the time of the Ottoman Empire:

> "The Sufi Shaikhs of various Ṭarīqas defended the farmers' interests and tried to limit the exploitation and tyranny caused by the aghas. They became the Kurd's centre of attention because they defended their interests with the Ottoman government and with the administrations in Kurdish areas which tried to impose taxes that burdened the farmers and also imposed mandatory military service".[165]

However, the chaos that prevailed with the Agrarian Reform Law's debut in 1959 did not distinguish between an ordinary landowner and a Shaikh of Ṭarīqa — between personal belongings and money belonging to the Ṭarīqa. As a result of the disorder and encroaching instability, in addition to his divine foresight of the political and military developments that were to come, Shaikh ʿAbd al-Karīm al-Kasnazān decided to leave the takya in the Kirkuk Citadel for Karbchna. In early February 1959, he left Karbchna to live in the village of Būbān in the Iraqi city of Penjwin, on the Iraqi-Iranian border, northeast of Karbchna. The dervishes there built a takya for the Shaikh in preparation of his arrival, which all the disciples in Iran were looking forward to. The dervishes in Karbchna, as well as others, tried to persuade Shaikh ʿAbd al-Karīm to stay there. Some disciples laid in front of the Shaikh's car before his departure from Karbchna, trying to dissuade him from leaving the village. This migration, however, was something that Allah wanted in His divine wisdom. One facet of this wisdom was for Shaikh ʿAbd al-Karīm to complete the preaching efforts initiated by his father, Shaikh ʿAbd al-Qādir al-Kasnazān, when he emigrated to Iran in mid-1919 after the British army entered Karbchna. Shaikh ʿAbd al-Karīm's migration resulted in a new, massive preaching tour that, this time, reached deep into Iran, including the capital, Tehran.

This was not the first time Shaikh ʿAbd al-Karīm travelled to that area. In 1946, a powerful earthquake struck Penjwin and aftershocks persisted

---

[165] ʿAlī, *Al-Ḥaraka al-Kurdiyya al-Muʿāṣira*, p. 27.

in the area. Terrified, its inhabitants left the city and their homes and camped out in tents. There were many dervishes in Penjwin and in nearby cities, as a result of Shaikh ʿAbd al-Qādir al-Kasnazān's preaching. The residents sought out Shaikh ʿAbd al-Karīm, reasoning that his blessed presence would cause the aftershocks to stop. The Shaikh went to Penjwin and stayed there for a while, and the aftershocks stopped after his arrival. Since that year, Shaikh ʿAbd al-Karīm would often spend the summer in a mountainous passage called Nawshākhān about three kilometres away from Būbān in Penjwin, where his son, Shaikh Muḥammad al-Muḥammad, would be responsible for taking care of the farmland that Shaikh ʿAbd al-Karīm owned.

In the early 1950s, during one of Shaikh ʿAbd al-Karīm's summer stays, ʿAbd al-Karīm Qāsim — perhaps a lieutenant colonel at the time and in charge of a regiment stationed in Penjwin — visited the Shaikh with officers in his regiment. He asked for Shaikh ʿAbd al-Karīm to pray for him, and possibly took the Ṭarīqa from him.

After Shaikh ʿAbd al-Karīm's migration in 1959, Shaikh Muḥammad al-Muḥammad began to enter the political arena. In addition to being the Shaikh of Ṭarīqa's son, his extensive social relationships helped him rise quickly. He was treated as if he was the head of a clan, despite his young age. He had leadership qualities that made him trustworthy to others, including being brave, and did not fear anyone or anything. He always had a military force under his command to protect the takya from aghas and other people of power and influence who might be tempted to harm the Ṭarīqa. He also provided support to the oppressed, some of whom sought refuge in the takya in Būbān. These include Sulaymān Muʿīnī, secretary of the Iranian KDP, and Ḥamad Khaḍr Pasha, a member of parliament in the monarchy era who fled to Iran after the coup led by ʿAbd al-Karīm Qāsim.

Due to his status with the public, Shaikh ʿAbd al-Karīm's migration to Būbān played a large role in making people aware of the challenges created by the growing differences between Qāsim's government and the Kurdish political, tribal, and spiritual leaderships. One main reason behind these differences was Qāsim's transformation into a dictator and his dealing with all challenges he faced in with a purely militaristic mentality. Qāsim lacked the political leadership skills that are indispensable when dealing with different sides with diplomacy, flexibility, and prudence.

In 1960, Qāsim heard that Shaikh ʿAbd al-Karīm had left Karbchna and moved to Penjwin because of the developments caused by the misapplication of the Agrarian Reform Law and the way he was dealing with Kurdish national rights. He wanted to mend the situation and please Shaikh ʿAbd al-Karīm, so he sent one of his Kurdish advisers to him to invite him to Baghdad to meet him in person. The Shaikh thanked the envoy for the invitation, which he graciously declined. Instead, he sent his son, Shaikh Muḥammad al-Muḥammad, as his representative, along with his nephew, Shaikh Ṭāhir, the eldest son of Shaikh Ḥusayn al-Kasnazān; Mullā ʿAlī Laylān, who was a teacher in the religious school in Karbchna before Shaikh ʿAbd al-Karīm left the village; and Mullā Muḥammad Amīn, a resident of Karbchna who was a close associate of the Shaikh (photo 15).

Qāsim expressed his reverence and appreciation for Shaikh ʿAbd al-Karīm to the delegation and asked if there was anything the Shaikh wanted. Our Shaikh spoke to him about a privately-owned village that the state had confiscated, so he ordered that it be returned. However, this did not take place. He also informed the delegation about his intention to hold parliamentary elections and his hope that Shaikh Muḥammad al-Muḥammad would become a representative. Qāsim hosted the delegation for seventeen days, during which time the state covered the costs of their stay. He gifted them hunting rifles and ammunition and ordered the Director of National Security to issue permits allowing them to carry weapons and to provide them with any assistance they needed. Yet, Qāsim's generosity with the delegation did not solve the fundamental issue that caused Shaikh ʿAbd al-Karīm to leave Karbchna, and this exceptional treatment of the Shaikh's delegation did not reflect a change in Qāsim's policies in his relationship with the Kurds in general. The relations and trust between the government and the KDP and Kurdish tribal heads continued to deteriorate.

Tribal chieftains began to gather around certain leaders to unite their ranks and efforts. Among the most prominent of these leaders were Shaikhs ʿAbd al-Karīm al-Kasnazān and his son, Muḥammad al-Muḥammad. In the latter half of 1961, tribal chieftains assembled in the village of Tapī Safā, in the Khormāl district, Halabja province. They swore on a muṣḥaf in the presence of Shaikh ʿAbd al-Karīm, and under his auspices and religious backing, to work together and not to betray one another or the cause.[166] Prominent Kurdish politicians — including Nūrī Shāwīs, Mullā Rasūl, and Colonel Nūrī Aḥmad Ṭāhā, members of the Political Bureau of the party — visited Shaikhs ʿAbd al-Karīm and Muḥammad al-Muḥammad in Būbān, which shows their status and role in supporting and strengthening the Kurdish movement. The visit of Jalāl Ṭālabānī, also member of the party's Political Bureau, to Būbān was his first meeting with the Shaikhs.[167] A historical testimony in this regard came from Mīrzā Siddīq al-Penjwinī, a member of the local party committee in Penjwin. In an interview with "Kurdistan TV" in the late 1990s, he said that no other place could have accommodated this great gathering of tribes other than Shaikh ʿAbd al-Karīm's takya in Būbān.

Early on, the Kurdish movement heavily relied on support from tribal chieftains and aghas, as the KDP played a smaller role in the development of events. As time passed, the party grew and its role in leading the Kurdish movement increased. This reflects the nature of the Kurdish people at the time; the clan was its basic societal unit, so tribal affiliation was stronger than political or partisan affiliation. It was only surpassed by the Sufi affiliation of some followers of Sufi Ṭarīqas. Our Shaikh played a big role in enabling the party to have a significant impact in advancing the Kurdish movement. He influenced tribal chieftains and disciples of the Ṭarīqa, and he also put the military force under his command in the service of the objectives of the party.

It is important to stress that Shaikhs ʿAbd al-Karīm al-Kasnazān and Muḥammad al-Muḥammad supported the Kurdish movement to secure the national rights of the Kurds within a unified Iraq. The Kasnazān Shaikhs always stood against any proposal to divide Iraq, whether on national, sectarian, or any other grounds. Shrines of Shaikhs of the Ṭarīqa Kasnazāniyya bless the country of Iraq from north to south, and east to west. Our Shaikhs reject any attempt to separate between these holy shrines.

---

[166] Shawkat Ḥājj Mushīr, member of the Political Burue of the Patriotic Union of Kurdistan, which had not been formed at the time of this event, mentioned in his autobiography that this meeting was in the house of his uncle, Ḥājj Muṣṭafā.

[167] Barazānī, *Al-Ḥaraka al-Taḥarruriyya al-Kurdiyya wa-Ṣirāʿ al-Qiwā al-Iqlīmiyya wal-Duwaliyya 1958-1975*, p. 92.

7.4 Shaikh Muḥammad al-Muḥammad's Military Activity

The Būbān assembly was responsible for the bloc between Penjwin, Darbandikhān, and Shāhrūz. Shaikh Muḥammad al-Muḥammad, a young man of twenty-three years, was their field commander, under the supervision of Muḥammad Rashīd Khān, an experienced commander who had been involved with leading the armed Kurdish movement in Iran since 1946. Ḥājj Ibrāhīm Charmaga, a caliph of Shaikh ʿAbd al-Karīm Al-Kasnazān and tribal chieftain of the large, renowned Ismāʿīl al-ʿUzayrī clan, led the movement from Bazyān.

As we have seen, the attack on a police station between Penjwin and Darbandikhān led by Shaikh Muḥammad al-Muḥammad on 7th/September/1961 was one of the first military operations of the Kurdish movement. After the army attacked on 11th/September, the Bazyan group resisted for less than a day before the army entered the area. The Darbandikhān group continued to defend for six days, despite being insufficiently armed in comparison to the army. Then Nūrī Aḥmad Ṭāhā arrived and informed them of the party's decision to retreat because the army would soon intensify its operations. The fighters wanted to stand their ground, especially having thus far succeeded in repelling the army, but they fulfilled the party's command and withdrew.

That night, the fighters went their own separate ways. About twenty combatants stayed with Shaikh Muḥammad al-Muḥammad. There were eight members of the party's local committee in Penjwin, some with their families. Shaikh ʿAbd al-Karīm had his family with him, as well as his brother, Muḥammad Ṣāliḥ, and his nephews, Laṭīf, Qādir, and Ismāʿīl and their families. All left Būbān before the army's arrival and went to the bordering Iraqi village called Halālāwa, about a kilometre away from the Iranian village of Khān Mashīkhān, as it was far more difficult for the government's forces to reach it (photo 16). They stayed there for a few days, and the fighters positioned themselves in preparation to fight the army in case they followed them to that area. The combatants included dervishes and refugees from the Iranian KDP.

Someone came from Penjwin carrying an order, probably issued by the General Military Commander Aḥmad Ṣāliḥ al-ʿAbdī, to pardon the tribal chieftains, including Muḥammad Rashīd Khān. The pardon, however, excluded Shaikh ʿAbd al-Karīm, Shaikh Muḥammad al-Muḥammad, and those with them in Halālāwa. There seemed to be two reasons behind this exclusion. First, Shaikh ʿAbd al-Karīm was the spiritual leader under whose auspices and religious backing the rebellious clans had allied themselves. Second, Shaikh Muḥammad al-Muḥammad had led one of the earliest military operations of the Kurdish revolution on 9th/September/1961.

Our Shaikh prepared the fighters to face the army in case the army tried to reach them. Shaikh ʿAbd al-Karīm said that he would fight with them and promised to kill a soldier with every shot he took. Still, Shaikh Muḥammad al-Muḥammad was careful to spare the Shaikh of Ṭarīqa from combat. He told his father that he would kill himself if he did not retreat to a safe place. Shaikh Muḥammad al-Muḥammad swore that, if necessary, he would fight to the death, alongside the combatants that were with him, including his cousins, dervishes, and party members.

As for the Iranian government, they first informed Shaikh ʿAbd al-Karīm and those with him that it would remain neutral, and it asked that they do not cross the Iranian border. This stance improved somewhat, thanks to the intervention of Iranian disciples, specifically an influential Kurd named Amīn Mukrī who served as military commander for Marivan, who had a good relationship with our Shaikh. Before the armed Kurdish movement, an Iranian soldier under Mukrī's command fled to Iraq. He had a modern American rifle with him, and smuggling these kinds of weapon into Iraq was a major offence at the time. Mukrī sought Shaikh Muḥammad al-Muḥammad's help in retrieving the rifle. After inquiring about the fugitive soldier and discovering his whereabouts, our Shaikh purchased the rifle from him and returned it to Mukrī. Because of this one favour, Mukrī intervened with Iranian authorities to help in the difficult circumstances that Shaikh ʿAbd al-Karīm and the families that were with him were experiencing.

One night, a senior Iranian officer, accompanied by military officers, crossed the border and visited Shaikh ʿAbd al-Karīm. The military personnel exhibited deep respect for him and kissed his hand. They told him that, as a humanitarian initiative, women and children could enter Iran and live in an encampment away from any aggression from the Iraqi army. However, because of agreements and relations with Iraq, and to prevent Iran from getting involved in the conflict, men were not allowed to enter Iran. The women and children entered Iran and stayed there for more than two months.

Meanwhile, the army, which had entered the area of Penjwin, went every now and then to the border area where Shaikh Muḥammad al-Muḥammad's troop was located, but without coming into contact with it. The army did not know the exact size of the force, and its positions were also well fortified, so it was capable of causing the army to incur casualties. The army planes continued to conduct exploratory flights in search of the rebels.

In October 1961, a delegate from the administrator of the Penjwin province arrived with a letter addressed to Shaikh ʿAbd al-Karīm. The administrator's letter tried to persuade the Shaikh to return to Penjwin and it assured him that the government wanted to pardon everyone and to make amends. The government initiative was driven by its concern about a rapprochement between the Iranian government and Shaikh ʿAbd al-Karīm, his influence over dervishes in Iraq, his growing influence in Iran, and the fact that some Iranian KDP members turned to him. The government also wanted to end the confrontation with Shaikh Muḥammad al-Muḥammad's force because, while still small then, it wanted to prevent the force from growing. This was particularly concerning because the deterioration of the relationship between the government and the Kurds threatened to cause many Kurds to join the Kurdish rebels, whether tribal or partisan.

Then came Ḥājj Rasūl, Garmag the deputy to the administrator of Penjwin, along with others, to persuade Shaikh ʿAbd al-Karīm to return to Penjwin. Initially, he refused the request, and so did Shaikh Muḥammad al-Muḥammad, who accused the delegate of being traitors who collaborated with the government and could not be trusted. Rasūl affirmed Shaikhs ʿAbd al-Karīm and Muḥammad al-Muḥammad of the respect and esteem he had for them. He told them that they Shaikhs and the families with them did not have to live in such harsh conditions and that they could all return safely to Būbān. In the end, the two parties agreed to allow Shaikh Muḥammad al-Muḥammad's forces to carry their weapons as long as they returned the weapons they had seized from the army and police. Everyone returned to Būbān in November 1961. One factor that influenced the Shaikhs' decision to return to Būbān was the harsh, snowy winter that would soon arrive in the areas inhabited by the families and fighters.

In few months after the return to Būbān, in early 1962, the KDP changed its style of direct armed confrontation with the government to hit-and-run guerrilla warfare. The Kurdish forces — known as "Peshmerga", stemming from two Kurdish words that mean "in front of death" — used ambushes from time to time to attack military targets, such as an army or police troop moving from one area to another. They would flee before government forces could identify the individuals or groups that carried out those operations. The government could not organize any kind of effective military activity against the fighters because it could not identify who they were. The main purpose of these operations was to seize weapons because the Peshmerga had limited, worn weapons that were no match for the government forces' weapons.

In early March, our Shaikh thought to capture Penjwin, but this bold plan required greater military strength than he had at his disposal. In the same month, Jalāl Ṭālabānī and the large troop that he commanded seized control of police stations in the Shahrabazār province and even controlled the Chwārta district, the province's capital.[168] Shaikh 'Abd al-Karīm sent Shaikh Riḍā, his son-in-law, and an individual from the KDP to Ṭālabānī in Shahrabazār to ask him to join forces with our Shaikh in capturing Penjwin. The operation would be carried out in the Spring, when it was warmer. The two parties agreed.

At the end of March, the Penjwin district administrator, Rūbītān al-Jāf, who secretly sympathized with the Kurdish rebels, informed the Peshmerga of the movement of a police squad, originally belonging to a border post in Penjwin, from one point to another. A group of fighters under our Shaikh's command set up an ambush for the police force, which consisted of about ten individuals. In addition to the squad's weapons, the rebels also took hold of a wireless radio. Due to the usefulness and scarcity of radios at the time, the Peshmerga considered the device very important booty.

In early April 1962, after attending a gathering where the Fātiḥa was read for a relative of his in Hawmarāmān, our Shaikh headed towards Karbchna with a large Peshmerga troop. They sneaked through backways to avoid army control points, and they stayed there for three

---

[168] Muhammad, *Akrād al-'Iraq Tahta Ḥukm 'Abd al-Karīm Qāsim 1958-1963*, p. 166.

days. He spoke to people about the expanding Kurdish movement, and he told them that there was a plan to take control of Penjwin. A messenger came from Būbān carrying a letter from Jalāl Ṭālabānī informing our Shaikh that his forces were en route to Penjwin. The letter asked him to return to Penjwin to carry out the plan to seize the province that he had agreed to in early March. Our Shaikh returned the very same day. The two forces blockaded the road to Penjwin and besieged the province's capital for about fifteen days. While this was happening, the Iraqi army mobilised a brigade to Penjwin to break the siege, but another Peshmerga troop kept the army busy and delayed their arrival. The rebels eventually managed, with the help of some tribal chieftains and people, to force the government troops to surrender, so they entered the centre of Penjwin on the night of 20th/May/1962. The rebels acquired about two hundred firearms, including fully automatic assault rifles. The spring of 1962 marked a period of setbacks for the Iraqi army, which suffered several defeats at the hands of large and small groups of Kurdish rebels.[169]

After this successful attack, it was only a matter of time before the army's forces reached Penjwin. During the Kurdish forces' siege of Penjwin, Shaikh ʿAbd al-Karīm returned to the bordering village of Halālāwa. He, as well as migrants who were with him, wanted to enter Iran. This time, the Iranian government allowed them to enter its lands and stay there on the basis that they were civilian refugees, not combatants. A female dervish donated undeveloped land located on a highland in Iran called Mīrza Mīrā Shāh, nestled between the villages of Khāw and Mīrāwā. The dervishes there quickly built a takya for the Shaikh and houses for the migrants with him. In July 1962, the Shaikh moved into the takya, and those who were with him and their families moved into their respective homes so that they would no longer burden the villagers there. Shaikh ʿAbd al-Karīm remained in Iran until his return to Būbān in 1965, as we will see later.

As for the combatants, al-Ṭālabānī left for Chmī Rīzān with his forces, and the aghas of Penjwin all returned to their respective safety areas. Our Shaikh and his forces headed to the bordering village of Kānī Sīf located on Mount Surin on the Iraqi side. It was difficult to reach the mountain,

---

[169] Barazānī, *Al-Ḥaraka al-Taḥarruriyya al-Kurdiyya wa-Ṣirāʿ al-Qiwā al-Iqlīmiyya wal-Duwaliyya 1958-1975*, p. 201; Aḥmad, *Al-Ḥaraka al-Kurdiyya fīl-ʿIrāq*, p. 189.

and it featured a thick canopy of trees and grooves that made it easy to hide from the army and overhead planes. Also, climbing the mountain from the village was extremely difficult, as the path was very bumpy and filled with sharp, injurious rocks that tore clothing and flesh. Shaikh ʿAbd al-Qādir al-Kasnazān and his family, as well as those who were with them, spent a night in that village while emigrating from Iraq to Iran. This village also featured a cave that Shaikh Maḥmūd al-Ḥafīd sought refuge in for a while.

The scarcity of food and water made life in Kānī Sīf extremely harsh. The fighters tried to get some food from the villagers, but many of them were hostile to the Peshmerga because they saw fighting the government as an unnecessary problem. When planes bombed the area, civilians were killed. The combatants could barely get hold of bread, which they would eat dry, sometimes spoiled. At one point, hunger and lack of food forced them to hunt a bear and consider eating it.

A short while after taking Penjwin, our Shaikh sent a letter with a fighter to Nūrī Shāwīs, a member of the party's Political Bureau, who was hiding in Sulaymāniyya. In the letter, he presented a bold idea of heading towards Qaradāgh to seize it and encourage its inhabitants to participate in the Kurdish movement, or, at the very least, to show more support for it. Shāwīs, however, was warned against this plan because it was difficult to implement, particularly because of how active the Communist Party was in the area. This response did not deter our Shaikh, especially since there were many relatives, tribal chieftains, and Kasnazānī disciples in Qaradāgh who could help the fighters. He decided to proceed with his plan.

After spending thirteen days in Kānī Sīf, the fighters left the town at night, as one of them knew a way to the city of Shahrizor that did not pass by Iraqi army checkpoints. They travelled in secret until they reached the villages of Grīza and Banājūt, where many dervishes lived. Ḥājj Fattāḥ Grīza and Ḥājj ʿAzīz, both of whom were caliphs of Shaikh ʿAbd al-Karīm, hosted them there and kept quiet about their presence. There the fighters had their first proper meal after more than two weeks. They stayed there for three nights. Then, a guide led them by night to ʿArbat, Shahrizor, where many inhabitants of the villages there were dervishes, until they reached the house of Shaikh Karīm, one of Shaikh Ḥusayn al-Kasnazān's sons, who is a paternal cousin of our Shaikh. The

Shaikh slaughtered and prepared a sheep for them. They stayed there for one night before being hosted by caliph Tawfīq Ḥājj Faraj. They knew the way to Qaradāgh from there, so they went to the village of Hawmarāmān, where they stayed for more than a week to rest.

Shaikh Muḥammad al-Muḥammad went to Qūpī Qaradāgh and established a base in Dārī Zard. Despite the existence of a police station in the centre of the Qaradāgh province, the police did not dare try to attack the rebels stationed in the mountains. The Shaikh was surrounded by many relatives, tribal chieftains, dignitaries, dervishes, and party members. He educated the inhabitants there about the Kurdish movement and its goal of obtaining Kurdish national rights, including Kurdish autonomy.

He began planning to capture the centre of Qaradāgh. He set up a checkpoint in Gula Zarda to prevent the arrival of military reinforcements from Sulaymāniyya, thus isolating the province's centre, where there were about 70 policemen. Peshmerga forces surrounded the centre and demanded that the besieged police surrender. The police refused, however, hoping that the army would save them in response to their request for backup from Sulaymāniyya. Meanwhile, army aircraft began bombing Peshmerga groups and headquarters. The siege continued for seventeen days without the army being able to send any reinforcements, at which point the besieged police forces were forced to surrender on 22nd/September/1962. The Kurdish fighters acquired a large number of arms, including 75 rifles and two automatic guns.[170] This victory expanded the combatants' reach of influence from Penjwin to Ṭūz Khūrmātū and Kifrī via Qaradāgh.

This humiliating victory for the rebels angered the government. They rushed to retaliate against villages inhabited by the relatives of the attacking Kurdish force's commander, Shaikh Muḥammad al-Muḥammad al-Kasnazān. Fighter planes bombed Karbchna, Žālā, Drūzna, Dār Parū, Hanjīrā, and Bānī Mūrd. These bombings were not aimed at the Kurdish rebels. Rather, they were random bombings whose targets were civilian victims that did not have anything to do with the Kurdish forces' attack on Qaradāgh.

Our Shaikh sent a telegram to the party's Political Bureau and the

---

[170] Mankūrī, *Bah Sah Rhātī Syāsī Kūrd*, p. 50.

headquarters of Barzānī informing them of the victory in Qaradāgh. Jalāl Ṭālabānī visited him to congratulate him. Party organizations, Peshmerga groups, and headquarters were established in the area between Qaradāgh to Kifrī. This enabled the Kurdish forces to carry out hit-and-run guerrilla operations against army troops. Our Shaikh commanded the operations of that large front from his headquarters in Qaradāgh. He also educated the Kurdish people, including farmers, about the Kurdish movement to increase the number of those who joined the cause directly, as well as those who supported it indirectly and provided moral support.

Meanwhile, because of his spiritual status and the significant impact he had on the Kurdish nationalist movement in Iraq, whose impact could expand into Iran, in the latter half of 1962, Shaikh ʿAbd al-Karīm received an invitation to meet the Shah of Iran, Mohammad Reza Pahlavi (photo 17). He was accompanied by influential Kurdish personalities, including Dawūd Bīk al-Jāf, a chieftain of the Jāf clan and a parliamentary member in the royal era, who was also one of his disciples. In the meeting, the Shah agreed to aid the Kurdish movement by treating wounded and ailing Peshmerga fighters but not by supplying them with arms or equipment. He also promised to allow the dervishes in Iraq to visit the Shaikh in Iran.

Shortly before the military coup that overthrew him, ʿAbd al-Karīm Qāsim announced that the Kurdish movement was in decline and had all but died out. To refute this propaganda and show that the Kurdish revolution was growing and becoming more powerful, our Shaikh, along with Major Kamāl Muftī, led a daring attack on the Kirkuk-Baghdad train line in Sulaymān Bīk, near Ṭūz Khūrmātū, on 5th/February/1963. This military operation was dangerous and difficult for many reasons. Accessing the train from Qaradāgh, specifically when departing from the village of Wārānī, near Zīnāna, required that they walk along certain roads so that government forces would not detect them. Most of the route was open rather than mountainous, so it was not easy to stay hidden. It was also necessary for the fighters to reach the train station before the train passed through it. Not only that, but they also had to be careful not to arrive too early before the train's arrival because the longer they stayed there, the more likely it was that government forces would detect them and their operation would fail. Also, being discovered would make it extremely difficult for them to withdraw unharmed. The fighters needed to return to safe havens where government forces could not reach them and keep them hidden even from enemy aircraft. Accurate calculations and adherence to these times were essential to the operation's success, keeping it under wraps and preventing any loss of life. The time between leaving the rally point, executing the attack, then returning to the rally point took about eighteen hours.

The attacking forces subdued a group of police in the railway station and seized the weapons that were on the train. The train had passengers and prisoners. The rebels explained that they were not targeting civilians, but rather they were conducting these military operations to force the Iraqi government to return their stolen rights. They released the passengers.

Three days after the attack on the train, on 8th/February/1963, ʿAbd al-Salām ʿĀrif and the Ba'ath Party succeeded in leading a military coup in which they deposed the government and executed ʿAbd al-Karīm Qāsim. Interestingly, shortly before the coup, an old dervish of Shaikh ʿAbd al-Qādir al-Kasnazān called Rashīd visited Shaikh ʿAbd al-Karīm, who at the time was not feeling well. The dervish arrived after the night prayer and went on to mention his awareness of Shaikh ʿAbd al-Karīm's anger at Qāsim before telling him about a dream he had had the previous night. He saw Qāsim being laid on a carpet before it was fully rolled over his body several times. The carpet became like a cylinder with Qāsim's body trapped inside. The carpet was then unrolled and Qāsim was found to have died. Caliph Rashīd commented that Qāsim was finished, which is indeed what happened shortly afterwards.

Instead of turning a new page of peace and entering into dialogue with the Kurds, ʿĀrif persisted in using Qāsim's repressive methods, perhaps because of his inclination towards Arab nationalism. Four months after the coup, on 9th/June/1963, the National Council for the Command of the Revolution issued a communiqué that disparaged the Kurdish movement and threatened to eliminate its "insurgent" leaders and the movement as a whole if they did not lay down their arms. The following day, the government forces commenced their military campaign.

Our Shaikh led a Peshmerga troop from Qaradāgh in occupying police stations and a National Guard headquarters in Kifrī. On their way to Kifrī, news reached the fighters that the government was sending a force from Jalawlā` under the command of Ḥammād Shihāb, who in a few years was to become Secretary of Defence after the coup of the Ba'ath Party on 17th/July/1968. After it became clear that the government forces had nearly surrounded Kifrī, our Shaikh and the military leaders met and concluded that an attack on Kifrī would be a major risk and could potentially cause heavy casualties among the Kurdish rebels. Instead, they decided to attack the Baghdad-Kirkuk train. That night, government forces attacked nearby Kurdish villages, looting their livestock and property and burning them to the ground. When the Kurdish forces came to know of the crimes the army had committed against the civilian inhabitants, their leaders decided that they had no other choice than to return to the original plan of attacking the army, despite its great risk. They considered it better to die than to fail to respond to what the army had done. In 24th/August/1963, Peshmerga combatants set up an ambush against the army, but the army discovered the plan and attacked the backup force that was behind the Kurdish troops. Despite the resistance of the Kurdish forces against the army, which outnumbered and outgunned them, and causing it losses, they lost twenty-seven Peshmerga fighters, and the army captured one of the combatants.[171]

After this battle, our Shaikh decided in September to visit his father in Marivan to reassure him that he was safe. Due to his preoccupation with military activity, he had not visited him since he had left for Iran. Some fighters accompanied him on this visit. They entered Iran in secret at night, as the Iranian government did not allow Kurdish fighters, let alone a prominent military commander, to enter its lands, fearing that the Kurdish movement in Iraq would extend to Iranian Kurds. The Iranian government also did not want to get involved in the conflict between Iraq's Kurds and the Iraqi government. The next day, the Iranian Sultan became aware that a group of armed Kurds were visiting Shaikh ʿAbd al-Karīm. A team from Iranian intelligence, SAVAK, surrounded the takya. They arrested four fighters, but they did not find our Shaikh, who hid, with three of his companions, in a room they did not search. During the interrogation, the detainees said that they did not enter Iran as combatants, but rather as dervishes coming to visit their Shaikh, and the

[171] For more details, see Karīm, *Sha Ri Qāta Kānī Kifrī.*

security officers released them. The respect that even SAVAK officers had for Shaikh ʿAbd al-Karīm likely played a big role in their release. The fighters returned to Iraq completely unharmed.

On 18th/November/1963, ʿAbd al-Salām ʿĀrif staged a coup against the ruling Ba'ath Party — his partners in the coup against ʿAbd al-Karīm Qāsim — due to deep internal conflicts within the party's leadership. ʿĀrif believed in a military solution to the Kurdish problem, but recent conflicts, as well as consecutive military and political assassinations, weakened the army. Army morale was also very low as a result of losses incurred in the war with Kurdish forces. ʿĀrif exploited his elimination of the Ba'athists from power, so he changed the military-solution policy and attempted to peacefully resolve the Kurdish problem through an open dialogue.[172] He opened channels of communication with Barzānī in December of 1963, and the two sides reached an agreement on 10th/February/1964.

The Political Bureau of the KDP, however, rejected the agreement between the government and Barzānī because it did not guarantee the Kurds sufficient rights. This resulted in a major split in the Kurdish movement. Barzānī replaced Peshmerga leaders who were party members, and the party responded by stripping Barzānī of his party powers. In June, Barzānī called a party conference and issued a decision to dismiss all members of the party's Central Committee and replace them with his supporters. The vast majority of the Peshmerga and the clans sided with Barzānī, who represented the tribal side of the Kurdish movement and always saw himself as greater than the party. The party cadres, on the other hand, supported the party's Political Bureau. In cooperation with clans, Barzānī launched an armed attack on the Political Bureau. The latter, which included Jalāl Ṭālabānī and Ibrāhīm Aḥmad, along with approximately 400 armed followers, was forced to take refuge in the Iranian city of Hamadān.[173]

Our Shaikh was more inclined to side with the party. His relationship with the Political Bureau members was far stronger than his relationship

---

[172] Barazānī, *Al-Ḥaraka al-Taḥarruriyya al-Kurdiyya wa-Ṣirāʿ al-Qiwā al-Iqlīmiyya wal-Duwaliyya 1958-1975*, p. 281; Daza yī. *Aḥdāth ʿĀṣartuhā*, p. 75.

[173] Ṭalabānī, *al-Ḥayāt*; Barazānī, *Al-Ḥaraka al-Taḥarruriyya al-Kurdiyya wa-Ṣirāʿ al-Qiwā al-Iqlīmiyya wal-Duwaliyya 1958-1975*, pp. 186-287.

with Barzānī. Even though he belonged to the tribal side of the movement because of his origin and status, he was inclined to the party because it represented the movement's ideology, and he was particularly influenced by Ibrāhīm Aḥmad and Nūrī Shāwīs. When the fight between the two sides broke out, he did not support one side over the other because both represented the Kurdish movement. He put his offensive operations against government forces on hold, while remaining prepared to defend against army attacks on Kurdish forces in his front.

Whenever our Shaikh visited Barzānī, the latter would attack Jalāl Ṭālabānī and Ibrāhīm Aḥmad and charge them with allegations. On one visit, Barzānī called him to abandon the party leaders and follow him instead. Our Shaikh replied that he had not become a Peshmerga fighter because he followed a particular person, but rather because of his faith in the cause of Kurdish national rights. He added that he did not follow anyone besides his father, Shaikh ʿAbd al-Karīm al-Kasnazān, the greatest person who merited following. Barzānī seconded what he said, saying: "By Allah, I testify that there are a thousand men like Barzānī who eat and drink in Shaikh ʿAbd al-Karīm's takya".

Barzānī also tried to buy an alliance with our Shaikh. He sent him with Kūkhā Ismāʿīl, Shaikh of the Jāf tribe in Dūkān, with a sum of money hoping that our Shaikh needed it. Our Shaikh thanked Barzānī for his offer, but he refused the money and told the messenger that he was capable of funding himself and the Peshmerga who were with him. He added that should he need any money, he would ask the Political Bureau for it. This was another confirmation from our Shaikh to Barzānī that the party was nearer and dearer to him.

Two months later, Barzānī tried once again to persuade our Shaikh to support him in his dispute with the party. He sent to him in Qaradāgh a delegation of senior clan chieftains, including Shaikh Ḥusayn Būskiyan, ʿAbbās Māmand Aghā, ʿAbd al-Karīm Shaikh, Raʾūf al-ʿAskarī, and Kāka Muḥammad Shadala. The delegation also included two Arab military officers in the Kurdish revolution — Salīm Fakhrī, Director of Radio and Television in the era of ʿAbd al-Karīm Qāsim, and Raʾīs Mūsā, as well as ʿAzīz Muḥammad, secretary of the Communist Party of Iraq. The communists allied with Barzānī after ʿAbd al-Karīm Qāsim staged a coup against them in mid-1959. The delegation conveyed Barzānī's request for our Shaikh to visit him in Rānya so that he could declare his support for him in his struggle with the party. Our Shaikh wanted to express his refusal to Barzānī face to face and to tell him that he had joined the Kurdish movement because he believed in its cause, and not because he followed him or anyone else. However, he agreed to the suggestion of some of the fighters who were with him, who proposed that they visit Barzānī on his behalf and convey his position on the matter. They feared foul play from Barzānī, who might have arrested the Shaikh when he informed him of his refusal to ally with him against the party's leaders.

As for Shaikh 'Abd al-Karīm, after residing in Iran in mid-1962, his preaching campaigns and karāmas quickly caused his reputation to spread far and wide. People began to enter the Ṭarīqa in large numbers. Efforts of calling people to Allah took him to Hamadān in eastern Iran, Tehran in the north, and even Mashhad in the far northeast. His reputation preceded him wherever he went. A large crowd of people would come out to greet him; sometimes they would even lift his car on their shoulders. The police sometimes had to intervene and break up the Shaikh's welcomers to facilitate his movement (photo 8).

Yet, the Shaikh of Ṭarīqa was being increasingly harassed by the authorities. Due to SAVAK reports and the incitement of adherents of other Sufi Ṭarīqas, the Iranian government offered several times to move him to the town of Malayer in Hamadān, where the migrant leaders of the KDP were located. By moving the Shaikh to that region, deep in Iran, the authorities wanted to distance him from the Iraqi border and cut the link between him and the Kurdish movement in Iraq, which the Iranian government feared would extend into the Kurdish region within its borders. He had to either comply with what his hosts wanted, in which case it seemed like he worked for the Iranian government, living away from the majority of disciples in Iraqi Kurdistan, or he had to leave Iran and return to Iraq. He decided to return to his country. In April 1965, Shaikh 'Abd al-Karīm left Iran and lived in an encampment near the bordering Iraqi village of Halālāwa. The party's leaders supported his position and his return to Iraq, as they saw it as being in the best interests of the Kurdish cause. He did not return to Iran after this.

'Abd al-Salām 'Ārif's administration exploited the dispute between the KDP and Barzānī, and the fact that Shaikh Muḥammad al-Muḥammad had put his military operations against the army on hold. The administration pardoned Shaikh 'Abd al-Karīm and his son and sent a delegation to the former to inform him that the government welcomed their return to any part of Kirkuk. At first, Shaikh 'Abd al-Karīm returned to Būbān, then at the end of 1965, he permanently moved to Kirkuk. The Kirkuk Citadel takya no longer sufficed for the family's needs, so he first rented two homes in `Āzādī. He would receive dervishes in a takya near Imām Qāsim that he had asked the dervishes to build before he left for Iran. In 1967, he moved into a rented house opposite the takya. This enabled him to supervise the construction of a takya and two houses for him and his family in nearby Imām Qāsim. After its completion, he moved there in 1968. He permanently resided there until his departure from this world in 1978. As for the Kirkuk Citadel takya, it was demolished in the 1980s, along with historical residential houses, when the government declared the entire Kirkuk Citadel area a historical site in which no one could reside.

As a result of a cabinet reshuffle in the Iraqi government, a military commander was put on the head of the new government. Air force General 'Ārif 'Abd al-Razzāq supported the resumption of fighting against the Kurds. In early April 1965, the army launched a new, massive military campaign against Peshmerga posts. The party leaders in Iran took this opportunity to try and reconcile with Barzānī. Meanwhile, our Shaikh was staying in Chwisa in Penjwin when he received a letter from his friend Laṭīf al-Ḥafīd, son of the revolutionary Maḥmūd al-Ḥafīd, who had good relations with both Barzānī and the party's leadership. The letter informed him that Jalāl Ṭālabānī was with Laṭīf in the village of Syāgwīz, Penjwin, and invited him to have lunch with them the next day. Our Shaikh had a special appreciation for Shaikh Laṭīf and would not reject a request from him. The next day, he went with his uncle Shaikh 'Abd al-Qādir to the meeting. Ṭālabānī informed him that the party's leadership wanted to make amends with Barzānī and resume military operations. The internal conflict in the Kurdish movement made our Shaikh decide against taking up arms once again. The old party leaders offered to resume fighting under Barzānī's command, and he agreed. Ṭālabānī, Ibrāhīm Aḥmad, and others returned from Iran to Iraq.

In early April 1966, the army decided to launch a new, massive attack on Barzānī's forces. Such attacks were often accompanied by reprisals and led to large casualties among innocent civilians who had nothing to do with the fighting, in addition to their displacement and loss of property.

Someone suggested asking Shaikh ʿAbd al-Karīm to act as a mediator between the Kurdish rebels and the government to prevent the imminent attack and to try to find a radical, peaceful solution to the conflict. Our Shaikh liked the idea. He went from Penjwin, where he was staying, with Shaikh ʿAbd al-Qādir Chawisa, to visit Muṣṭafā Barzānī in the village of Sāwchī, Marivan, and present the idea to him. The latter supported the proposal. Our Shaikh wrote a letter to his father in Kirkuk, informing him of the Kurdish movement's leadership's desire for him to represent the party in peace talks with the government, with which Shaikh ʿAbd al-Karīm agreed.

Shaikh ʿAbd al-Karīm was accompanied on his visit to Baghdad by Shaikh Riḍā Karīm, our present Shaikh's cousin and brother-in-law; Mullā Muḥammad Amīn; and Shaikh Muḥammad Ṣāliḥ, our Shaikh's uncle. The latter was an old friend of ʿAbd al-Raḥmān ʿĀrif, Chief of Staff of the army and brother to President ʿAbd al-Salām. They visited ʿAbd al-Raḥmān in his office and asked for his help in facilitating a meeting for Shaikh ʿAbd al-Karīm with the president to try and find a peaceful solution to the Kurdish conflict. He expressed support for the initiative, immediately contacted ʿAbd al-Salām, and secured a date for them to meet with him the following day. He asked them to come to his office before the meeting to have them transported to the president's office in his car.

ʿAbd al-Salām welcomed Shaikh ʿAbd al-Karīm and his entourage and served them coffee. The Shaikh said that he had come to visit the president in his capacity as a Shaikh of Ṭarīqa who favoured peace. He stressed that the fighting in Kurdistan had harmed many Kurds, Arabs and Kurds were brothers, Allah had created all men as equals, and Muslims should not kill each other. He asked the president to cease all military operations to spare innocent civilians and their lands and possessions harm and enter peace talks with the Kurdish rebels. ʿAbd al-Salām answered inflexibly that the Kurdish rebels were the ones causing harm to people. Shaikh ʿAbd al-Karīm replied that the inhabitants of Kurdish areas had been damaged by army operations. He added with some firmness that the army had even burned his home, takya, and mosque in Būbān, including muṣḥafs and religious books. ʿAbd al-Salām expressed his appreciation for Shaikh ʿAbd al-Karīm's initiative and said that he would issue an amnesty for the Kurdish rebels and allow them to return to their homes, posts, and jobs. But it was clear that he was unwilling to enter into a dialogue with the rebels, completely ignoring the question of Kurdish national rights, which was the crux of the conflict.

The car returned Shaikh ʿAbd al-Karīm and his entourage to ʿAbd al-Raḥmān, who expressed his regret over the meeting's failure to yield more positive results than the amnesty. He promised to try and persuade the president to change his mind. He also said that he would ask the prime minister, ʿAbd al-Raḥmān al-Bazzāz, to try and influence ʿAbd al-Salām. Bazzāz was a civilian who leaned towards a peaceful solution to the Kurdish conflict, unlike the army chiefs.

A few days after ʿAbd al-Salām refused Shaikh ʿAbd al-Karīm's request, before the army commenced its massive offensive in Kurdistan, the Divine Hand intervened. On 13th/April/1966, the president was on his way to Basra when his helicopter crashed, killing all those on board. What happened to ʿĀrif became commonly described by Iraqis in this saying, which rhymes in Arabic: "he went up as meat (*laḥm*) and came down as charcoal (*faḥm*)"!

Shaikh ʿAbd al-Karīm went to extend his condolences. When Bazzāz saw him, he asked an officer to escort him from the hall that received general mourners to a private room. Bazzāz sat by the Shaikh's side and promised to open the door for a dialogue between the government and the Kurdish movement's leadership. It was clear that ʿAbd al-Raḥmān ʿĀrif had talked to him about the matter, as he promised, and Bazzāz seemed optimistic that the Kurdish problem could be resolved after ʿAbd al-Salām's death.

Three days later, Major General ʿAbd al-Raḥmān ʿĀrif was appointed President of the Republic, succeeding his deceased brother. Although the new president, like Bazzāz, inclined towards peacefully resolving the Kurdish conflict, pressure from military personnel caused him to keep the same militant approach as his predecessor. This included launching the comprehensive attack the army had planned. In early May 1966, a pro-government Kurdish force occupied the strategic mountain of Hendren and handed it over to the Iraqi army. Ten days later, the Peshmerga bombed the government forces on the mountain with heavy artillery, and they followed that with an attack by Kurdish rebels, mostly members and supporters of the Communist Party. The attack inflicted serious damage on the government forces. This battle was one of the Kurdish rebels' biggest victories against the Iraqi army. The defeat angered the army's leadership, and Shaikh ʿAbd al-Karīm's fears became a reality. The army poured their anger out on civilians and their planes bombed indiscriminately, with vengeance.[174]

The Battle of Mount Hendren underscored to the Iraqi government, once again, the impossibility of a military victory over the rebels. The government wanted to stop the fighting, which was something that Barzānī was also interested in. He wanted to pre-empt the negotiations that had begun between the government and his Kurdish enemies under Ṭālabānī's leadership and to cut them off. This would also enable him to focus on fighting the party. The government and Barzānī reached an agreement on 29th/June/1966, which recognized the national rights of the Kurdish people.[175]

The fierce fighting between Barzānī's forces and the party continued. Each side wanted to control the largest possible area of Kurdistan to be the legitimate representative of the Kurdish revolution. The army did not take sides in this conflict. Our Shaikh led the party's forces in Penjwin, where he lived, but his apathy towards armed action was growing because the struggle against the government for Kurdish national rights had turned into an internal struggle between the two wings of the Kurdish movement. The disillusionment with the Kurdish movement evolved into a decision to retire from armed action as a result of a particular incident. In a battle that our Shaikh participated in, Fattāḥ Aghā, who was part of Barzānī's troop, was wounded. Aghā was a friend of our Shaikh, and his father and grandfather were followers of the Ṭarīqa Kasnazāniyya. Our Shaikh did not know that he was with Barzānī's troop. When he came to know what had happened, he was deeply affected. He decided that this was a sign that the nature of military action had changed, and that it was high time he retired.

The party's leadership respected our Shaikh's decision and understood the reasons for it. They remained on good terms with him. Barzānī also welcomed his retirement as it meant that his rivals were losing one of

---

[174] Daza yī. *Aḥdāth ʿĀṣartuhā*, p. 118.

[175] Barazānī, *Al-Ḥaraka al-Taḥarruriyya al-Kurdiyya wa-Ṣirāʿ al-Qiwā al-Iqlīmiyya wal-Duwaliyya 1958-1975*, pp. 289-295.

their most courageous and brilliant leaders. In his assemblies, our Shaikh continued to call for reconciliation between the Kurds.

During his years of military action, our Shaikh was exposed to many dangers. Yet, divine care kept all harm away from him. For instance, he mentions that during one battle, the army shelled them with artillery from a mountaintop in Ṭūz Khūrmātū, and he thought that dust caused by the shelling hit his body every now and then. When he looked closer, he saw that whatever dirt he had on him was, in fact, shell fragments. Shaikh ʿAbd al-Karīm would reassure our Shaikh's mother and his family about his welfare during his years of involvement in the Kurdish movement, saying: "He will not be killed. I will not let any harm come his way".[176]

Our Shaikh wanted to return to and live in Hawmarāmān, Qaradāgh, which was under Barzānī's forces control. Barzānī ordered his troops not to harass him, in respect for his religious or social status, so he settled there. Through 1968-1971, he was preoccupied with managing his father's farmlands, which produced wheat, barley, rice, and other crops. It was the main source of income for the Ṭarīqa and main takya in Kirkuk, where Shaikh ʿAbd al-Karīm lived. As a result of the perpetual internal conflict within the Kurdish movement combined with our Shaikh's history with the party, his freedom of movement remained limited. When he wanted to visit his Master and his family in Kirkuk from time to time, he would inform Barzānī's forces before going on his trip, so that they would not think that he was re-establishing contact with the party's leadership or contacting the government. He was subjected to attempted attacks by those who had not forgiven him for once being a part of the faction that opposed Barzānī. He decided to move to Kirkuk, where he lived in a house opposite Shaikh ʿAbd al-Karīm's takya, in the safe area of Imām Qāsim.

Because of our Shaikh's work with the party and his rejection of Barzānī's attempt to individually control the Kurdish movement, the latter restricted his freedom of movement four or five times. At times, this restriction of movement was close to house arrest. This restriction lasted at times for several weeks.

In early 1970, Ṭālabānī visited Kirkuk and wished to meet our Shaikh.

---

[176] Shaikh Muḥammad al-Muḥammad al-Kasnazān, *sermon*, 18th/June/2018.

At the insistence of General Kamāl Muftī, head of the party's military wing, who, alongside our Shaikh, led the Kirkuk-Baghdad train attack in 1963, our Shaikh met Ṭālabānī at the party's headquarters. Their relationship had weakened as a result of our Shaikh's withdrawal from military activity in the past four years. The meeting was an opportunity to rejuvenate the relationship, but Ṭālabānī wanted our Shaikh to return to the Kurdish movement. Later, he invited our Shaikh to visit him in Sulaymāniyya. They met in his headquarters in Bakrajū. He asked him to resume his military and political activities, but our Shaikh turned down the offer.

A short while later, on 11th/March/1970, an agreement was signed between the Iraqi government and Mullā Musṭafā Barzānī that granted autonomy to the Kurds. The agreement recognized the national rights of the Kurds, including making Kurdish, alongside Arabic, an official language in Kurdistan, allocating a special budget for the region, establishing legislative and executive councils there, and other things as well. Although the Iraqi government and Barzānī signed the agreement, a major point of contention remained between them. Barzānī wanted the Kirkuk governorate to be considered as part of the autonomous region, while the Iraqi government's stance was that its affiliation with Kurdistan should be determined by the results of a census. The two parties agreed to work to resolve this dispute within four years, after which they would be ready to put the agreement into effect. However, the two sides failed to reach an agreement, as Barzānī insisted that Kirkuk in its entirety was part of the autonomous region. This failure was directly facilitated by the support Barzānī received from Iran, the United States, and Israel, mostly through SAVAK, Mossad, and the CIA.[177] These countries considered solving the Kurdish problem to not be in their best interests because continued fighting was weakening the Iraqi army and shaking the stability of Ba'ath Party rule, which was what they wanted.

Relations between the government and Barzānī were formally cut off on the fourth anniversary of the autonomy accord, on 11th/March/1974. The Iraqi government unilaterally declared the implementation of the autonomy accord. Barzānī responded by retaking up arms against the

---

[177] Barazānī, *Al-Ḥaraka al-Taḥarruriyya al-Kurdiyya wa-Ṣirāʿ al-Qiwā al-Iqlīmiyya wal-Duwaliyya 1958-1975*, pp. 401-492.

government. The army followed suit, and so the peace between the two parties ended. Iran began stepping up its military support for Barzānī, including sending anti-aircraft guns, which negatively impacted the Iraqi army. Iran's true motive, however, was not to support the Kurdish revolution, which it feared would extend to its own large Kurdish population. It intervened to secure certain concessions from Iraq, which it eventually succeeded in getting. On 6th/March/1975, Saddam Hussein and the Shah of Iran, Mohammad Reza Pahlavi, signed an agreement in Algeria, in which Iraq gave half of the Shaṭṭ al-'Arab to Iran in exchange for ending its support for Barzānī's forces. Within days, Barzānī was forced to announce the cessation of the armed Kurdish movement and to seek refuge in Iran himself. Following the collapse of the Barzānī movement, Jalāl Ṭālabānī founded the Patriotic Union of Kurdistan (PUK) on 1st/June/1975.

After announcing the implementation of the autonomy agreement, the Iraqi government resorted to Kurdish leaders, including well-known figures in its history of struggle with the Kurdish movement, that saw in the autonomy agreement a real chance for the Kurds to obtain their national rights within the unity of Iraq. It sought practical support of these individuals for the autonomy agreement. Shaikh Muḥammad al-Muḥammad was one of these leading figures, becoming a member of the Legislative Council of the Autonomous Region in its second cycle in 1977. He put his membership in the council on hold, however, after Shaikh 'Abd al-Karīm's death, to dedicate himself to the Ṭarīqa. Assuming the position of Shaikh of Ṭarīqa marked a radical turning point in all aspects of his life.

Shaikh Muḥammad al-Muḥammad struggled for human rights and struggled against injustice, just like the Shaikhs of Ṭarīqa Kasnazāniyya before him, his grandfather, Shaikh 'Abd al-Qādir; his uncle, Shaikh Ḥusayn; and his father, Shaikh 'Abd al-Karīm. Those six years of jihad (1961-1966) played their role in building his character and shaping his development. They were a phase in the formation of a spiritual Master for whom Allah had decreed greatness.

Photo 15: The meeting of Shaikh Muḥammad al-Muḥammad with Prime Minister ʿAbd al-Karīm Qāsim, and to his right Shaikh Ṭāhir, Shaikh Ḥusayn al-Kasnazān's oldest son. To Qāsim's left is Mullā ʿAlī Laylān then Mullā Muḥammad Amīn (1960).

Photo 16: Shaikh ʿAbd al-Karīm in the village of Halālāwa, on the border with Iran, after the withdrawal of Shaikh Muḥammad al-Muḥammad and the Peshmerga fighters after the battle of Darbandikhān (September/1961).

Photo 17: A number of Iranian officials visiting Shaikh ʿAbd al-Karīm in Iran on his way to meet the Shah of Iran in Tehran (1962).

Photo 18: Shaikh Muḥammad al-Muḥammad on the battlefront in Kurdistan, Iraq (first half of the 1960s).

"Shaikh Nahro is my heart; he is my liver. He is your servant — a servant of your Ṭarīqa. I, my children, and everything we own are in service to the Ṭarīqa. We are servants to your Ṭarīqa. We are all soldiers of the Messenger (PBUH), soldiers of Sharia because it is our foundation".

Shaikh Muḥammad al-Muḥammad al-Kasnazān
(Sermon, 14th/November/2008)

8

Family Life

Towards the end of 1957, Shaikh Muḥammad al-Muḥammad al-Kasnazān married his paternal uncle's daughter. At the time, he lived in Karbchna. This marriage resulted in a son, who later died, and a daughter. This marriage, however, was not destined to last. Our Shaikh's involvement in 1961 in political and military activities, in defence of Kurdish national rights, made reconciling the new commitments and his family responsibilities impossible. His work for the Kurdish movement required him to not have a fixed address and to be in a state of constant movement. He divorced his wife that year.

A few years, after he retired from the Kurdish movement, our Shaikh decided to remarry. Out of the love he had for his mother, and the confidence he had in her judgement, he let her choose his wife, if Shaikh ʿAbd al-Karīm would bless her selection. Sayyida Ḥafṣa chose a young woman named Kažāl as a wife for her son. She is from a well-known family that is related to our Shaikh's family. She is the daughter of Shaikh Maʿrūf, son of Shaikh ʿAbd al-Karīm Qādir Karam, a maternal uncle of sayyida Ḥafṣa who took care of her after her mother died when she was a little girl.

There was a strong relationship between the two families, even when Shaikh ʿAbd al-Karīm's family was in Karbchna and Penjwin before they settled in Kirkuk, where sayyida Kažāl's family lived. Sayyida Ḥafṣa had a lot of love for her cousin and her milk-brother, Shaikh Maʿrūf, who was also a close friend of her son, Shaikh Ḥusayn, and who later became Shaikh ʿAbd al-Karīm al-Kasnazān's lawyer for issues related to farmland in Sangāw. Shaikh ʿAbd al-Karīm also had a lot of love for him. In 1959, Iraqi authorities sentenced Shaikh Maʿrūf to death for political reasons, and the sentence was carried out in 1963 during the reign of ʿAbd al-Salām ʿĀrif.

Shaikh Muḥammad al-Muḥammad married sayyida Kažāl in early 1969. At the time, he lived in Hawmarāmān, Qaradāgh. He used to move between Hawmarāmān and Kirkuk, where Shaikh ʿAbd al-Karīm lived, but in 1971, he permanently moved to Kirkuk, next to his father's house. After a while, he built an additional parlour in front of his house to receive guests.

He was blessed with his eldest son, Nahro, on 12th/December/1969, and after about a year and a half, Ghāndī was born. Our Shaikh's two eldest sons were named after the eminent leaders of the Indian independence movement, Mahatma Gandhi, who led India to independence in 1947, and Jawaharlal Nehru, Gandhi's political successor and the first prime minister of independent India. Our Shaikh's choosing of these two names reflects his admiration for these two leaders and what they did for their people. The word "Nahro" in Kurdish also means "small river".

Our Shaikh wished to have many children. In 1972, when he only had Nahro and Ghāndī, a dervish named Maḥmūd Gulāl, who had ḥāl, said to him: "Would you be satisfied with seven? I guarantee that you will have seven children". Afterwards, our Shaikh indeed had five more children so that the number of his children became seven! In 1973, he had Malās, whose name means "prepared" and "vigilant" in Kurdish. It is also the name of the highest mountain in Karbchna. He next had Bresh, whose name is that of a mountain summit near Karbchna. He then had ʿAmmār, Junayd and, finally in 1983, ʿAbd al-Karīm. As we have mentioned, our Shaikh has a daughter from his first marriage.

Our Shaikh's children, like all children of the Shaikhs, were raised in the arms of the Ṭarīqa since their youth. Like all dervishes, they treat their father as the Shaikh of Ṭarīqa. He is also their spiritual father, just as he is the spiritual father of all the disciples. They refer to him as "Shaikh" and not by the traditional title of a father. A sign of the respect they have for him is that they do not sit in his assembly unless compelled to do so. They do not speak before him or speak in his assembly, unless he speaks to them, or when they have something they need to tell him.

Just as the Shaikh of Ṭarīqa asks the seekers to serve the Ṭarīqa and selflessly devote themselves to calling people to the way of the Messenger (PBUH), he demands the same sincerity and sacrifice of his children, and he directly teaches them the Ṭarīqa's etiquettes. He also appoints those who educate them in this regard. For example, Shaikh ʿAbd al-Qādir al-Kasnazān gave one of his elder cousins, Shihāb, the responsibility of educating his children about the Ṭarīqa. He would say to him: "Teach the children to be close to the takya and the dervishes. The cobbler teaches his son his craft from an early age". Our Shaikh asks his children to make all their work a service to the Ṭarīqa. Whether someone is working in business, politics, or any other field, he asks him to do his job in service of the Ṭarīqa. The following is one of our Shaikh's comments in this regard:

> "My only concern is guiding people. Everything I have is in service to you. Even my children are at your service, in service to the Ṭarīqa. My soul is in service to you and the Ṭarīqa. I am a servant to the Ṭarīqa and its dervishes. I am proud of this title because my forefathers referred to themselves in writing as 'Servant of the Poor".[178]

The Arabic origin is translated as "the Poor" here is "Faqarā`", which is the plural of "faqīr". The latter literally means "poor person", but this term is figuratively used for those who seek nearness to Allah, i.e. the followers of the Ṭarīqa. Here, our Master refers to the fact that the Kasnazānī Shaikhs would refer to themselves as "Servant of the Poor" and would seal their letters with this title. We also see this immense modesty in Shaikh ʿAbd al-Qādir al-Kasnazān's usage of the shoemaking profession in the analogy he gave.

The same way our Shaikh urges disciples to attain the greatest degree of knowledge they possibly can, he has made sure that each of his sons at least obtains a university degree. Despite the copious amount of work in the Ṭarīqa, he followed his children's progress in their studies since their youth. When his youngest child, ʿAbd al-Karīm, was a small boy, he did not like going to school, and at times, would manage to stay at home. When our Shaikh would see him in the house when school was still in session, he would ask someone to take him to school, even if there was not much time left in the school day. Our Shaikh also appointed a close relative to follow up on the details of their studies closely.

All of our Shaikh's sons succeeded in obtaining a basic university degree. Shaikh Nahro obtained a bachelor's in Accounting, then completed his doctorate in Islamic History; Ghāndī holds a BA in Law and an MA in Media; Malās holds a BA and an MA in Architecture; ʿAmmār holds a bachelor's degree in Medicine; Brish holds a bachelor's

---

[178] Shaikh Muḥammad al-Muḥammad al-Kasnazān, *sermon*, 22nd/December/2005.

degree in Dentistry; Junayd holds a bachelor's degree in Pharmacology; and ʿAbd al-Karīm holds a bachelor's degree in Medicine. Our Master let his sons choose whatever fields they wanted to study, but he particularly liked medicine because medicinal fields provide a great service to people, and a doctor has a greater understanding and appreciation of the supernatural feats of the karāmas of darbāsha. It is obvious that our Shaikh's preference influenced his children, with the predominance of medical fields in their choices of study.

Shaikh ʿAbd al-Karīm also wanted his grandson, Qalandar, son of the late Shaikh Ḥusayn, to study medicine. When it was time for him to enrol in university studies, Shaikh ʿAbd al-Karīm had already departed from this world, and he wanted to study engineering instead. Our Shaikh intervened to fulfil Shaikh ʿAbd al-Karīm's wish, so Shaikh Qalandar completed his studies in medicine.

As we mentioned earlier, the Shaikh's wife has special tasks that help her husband in managing the affairs of the takya. After the death of our Shaikh's mother, sayyida Ḥafṣa, these tasks were passed down to sayyida Kažāl. One of the beautiful attributes that sayyida Kažāl has is that she never gets angry, even in the most difficult, most irritating circumstances.

Photo 19: Shaikh Muḥammad al-Muḥammad with his General Deputy and oldest son Shaikh Nahro in the takya in Amman, Jordan, on the night of the celebration of the birth of the Prophet (PBUH) according to the solar calendar (1st/May/2017).

"Ascending to Shaikhdom is, according to the people of Ṭarīqa, a heavenly selection — a heavenly designation — that takes place by the command of Allah (blessed and exalted is He) and the command of His Messenger, our Master, Seal of Prophets and Messengers, Muḥammad (PBUH)".

Shaikh Muḥammad al-Muḥammad al-Kasnazān
(Al-Ṭarīqa al-ʿAlīyya al-Qādiriyya Kasnazāniyya, p. 161)

9

Being Chosen for the Shaikhdom of the Ṭarīqa

Allah Almighty explains in his noble Book that prophethood is not something that is earned, but it is rather something that is conferred. None of the prophets became prophets by their attempts and efforts. Rather, Allah chose whoever He wanted from his elite servants for this exceptional mission and its responsibilities. Hence, Allah ordered his noble Prophet (PBUH) to respond to the disbelievers' objections to his mission by saying: "I am not something of a novelty among the messengers" (al-Āḥqāf 9). When the disbelievers supported their refusal of the Prophet's (PBUH) message by arguing that he had not come from the greatest of people, "They said, 'Why was this Qur'an not sent down upon a great man from [one of] the two cities?'" (al-Zukhruf 31), Allah clarified the foolishness of this objection and responded to it with several arguments, such as: "Is it they who distribute the mercy of your Lord?" explaining "It is We who have apportioned among them their livelihood in the life of this world and have raised some of them above others in degrees (in status) that they may make use of one another for service" (al-Zukhruf 32). If a person cannot gain from this world more than what Allah has apportioned for him, then there is no doubt that the greatest mercy — which is the mercy of sending Muḥammad (PBUH), "We have not sent you [O Muḥammad] except as a mercy to the worlds" (al-Ānbiyā` 107) — is a divine selection. Allah (mighty and sublime is He) also describes his favours upon the noble Messenger (PBUH) as follows, "Ever has the favour of Allah upon you been great" (al-Nisā` 113), referring to what favours He has chosen for him, including the message, revelation, manners, and so on.

This is another verse that reproaches the disbelievers for their protest against the prophethood of Muḥammad (PBUH) and points out that there are secrets behind the selection of any prophet that people can not perceive:

> "When a sign comes to them, they say, 'Never will we believe until we are given like that which was given to the messengers of Allah'. Allah knows best where He places His message". (Al-Ān'ām 124)

Being a Shaikh of Ṭarīqa means spiritually inheriting from the Messenger (PBUH), and not just memorizing texts and learning intellectual sciences of his religion. It is, therefore, ultimately a matter decided by Allah. One proof that Allah Almighty is the one who chooses the Shaikh of Ṭarīqa is that there are Shaikhs of the Ṭarīqa that do not leave a successor, as a result of their being a lack of someone among the Shaikh's followers who is qualified for the post. The chain of Shaikhs of that Ṭarīqa is, thus, cut. In this case, it is incumbent upon the disciples of that Ṭarīqa to renew their pledge at the hand of a living Shaikh. One requirement of a guiding Master is that he must be alive in this world so that seekers can benefit from him, as previously explained. For example, before passing away, Shaikh 'Uthmān Byāra, Shaikh of the Ṭarīqa Naqshbandiyya in northern Iraq, declared that there would be no Shaikh of his Ṭarīqa after him. His disciples had to follow another Shaikh after his death.

Allah enabled those He so desired, among those he had granted knowledge to, to see the signs of prophethood in our Master Muḥammad (PBUH) even before his mission, as was the case with Baḥīra the Monk in Buṣrā, Syria. This hermit was worshipping in his cell, not paying attention to passersby. But when one day a trade caravan passed him by, he saw indications that the long-awaited future prophet was in this caravan, even though Muḥammad (PBUH) was very young. The monk looked after the caravan and its people until he met the boy and was blessed by this meeting.[179] Similarly, the Almighty enables those He so desires, among those he has granted knowledge to, to recognize the future Shaikh of Ṭarīqa before Allah puts him in this position, even if he is a small child, and sometimes even before he is born, as we will see in this chapter.

---

[179] Ibn Hishām, *Sīrat al-Nabī*, I, pp. 236-238.

9.1 Divine Appointment — Not Human Acquisition

Shaikh Muḥammad al-Muḥammad al-Kasnazān writes that the Ṭarīqa's Shaikhdom is "a Divine mandate. Not every scholar is a guide. The Shaikhs of Ṭarīqa have Divine permission". He cites these noble verses:

> "One who invites to Allah, by His permission, and an illuminating lamp". (Al-Āḥzāb 46)
> "He whom Allah guides is the [rightly] guided, but he whom He leaves astray — never will you find for him a protecting guide". (Al-Kahf 17)
> "I made you for Myself". (Ṭāhā 41)
> "Indeed, I will make upon the earth a successor". (Al-Baqara 30)
> "We have enumerated all things in a clear register". (Yāsīn 12)

Then he goes on to say:

> "The Shaikh of Ṭarīqa is one who has permission from Allah Almighty. He is a guiding walī, one of those who are specially made, Allah's caliph on earth, a possessor of spiritual secrets, sequentially connected to our Master, the Chosen One (PBUH), through the spiritual chain of the Shaikhs of Ṭarīqa, may Allah sanctify each of their innermost beings".[180]

The appointment of a Shaikh of the Ṭarīqa is a direct order from the Messenger (PBUH), so it is by Allah Almighty's order, and not by the reasoning of someone. The present Shaikh of Ṭarīqa informs the disciples and people in general about who will succeed him. For instance, Shāh al-Kasnazān handed the Ṭarīqa's Shaikhdom over to his youngest son, ʿAbd al-Qādir. Shaikh ʿAbd al-Qādir, however, made the eldest of his four sons, Ḥusayn, his successor. As for Shaikh Ḥusayn, he did not grant the Ṭarīqa's Shaikhdom to any one of his many sons, but he rather chose his brother ʿAbd al-Karīm. Shaikh ʿAbd al-Karīm then chose the eldest of his seven sons, Muḥammad al-Muḥammad. Thus, the person who becomes Shaikh of the Ṭarīqa is not necessarily the youngest or oldest, the closer relative to the previous Shaikh, the more versed with textual or intellectual sciences, or the one who better matches any such external criteria. Choosing the Shaikh of Ṭarīqa is a divine matter that is based on special wisdom, so it is designated by the Messenger (PBUH).

---

[180] Shaikh Muḥammad al-Muḥammad al-Kasnazān, *al-Ṭarīqa al-ʿAliyya al-Qādiriyya al-Kasnazāniyya*, p. 85.

Countless karāmas have demonstrated that the appointment of Shaikh of Ṭarīqa is a decision from the spirit world, not an intellectual decision or a status that a person can acquire through their deeds. We saw, for example, the Prophet (PBUH) chose Imām ʿAlī, rather than any other companion, as his spiritual caliph. We have also seen what was revealed to the Shaikhs of Ṭarīqa regarding Shaikh ʿAbd al-Qādir al-Gaylānī years before it became reality. Similarly, we mentioned in Section 2-4 karāmas about the designation of Shāh al-Kasnazān as Master of the Ṭarīqa. We will now explore one karāma about the appointment of each one of the three Kasnazānī Shaikh after him before we devote the next section to the appointment of the fifth Shaikh of Ṭarīqa Kasnazāniyya, our present Master, Shaikh Muḥammad al-Muḥammad.

When Shāh al-Kasnazān was in his final sickness, many people came to visit him in Karbchna, including his relatives from Khāwya and Kasnazān. He was in his room the night of his demise, and his youngest son, ʿAbd al-Qādir, was sleeping, along with relatives, in another room in the takya. One of them, named "Ḥasan", was lying down but not asleep yet when he saw Shāh al-Kasnazān spiritually appear there. Ḥasan watched as Shāh al-Kasnazān began to turn Shaikh ʿAbd al-Qādir and massage him from the top of his head to the bottom of his feet, all over his body, as though he were preparing him for something. Shaikh ʿAbd al-Qādir did not wake up or show any sign of being aware of what was happening. Shāh al-Kasnazān glanced over at Ḥasan and gestured to him to keep quiet about what he had just seen. Early the next day, Shāh al-Kasnazān seemed to be in good health, so the visitors began to return to their villages. A short while after their departure, however, a villager followed them to inform them of Shāh al-Kasnazān's passing, so they returned to Karbchna. What Shaikh Ḥasan had seen was Shāh al-Kasnazān preparing Shaikh ʿAbd al-Qādir to be Master of the Ṭarīqa after him.

Shāh al-Kasnazān had several children, some of whom had high social and tribal status, but he chose their youngest to become the Master of the Ṭarīqa. The eldest, Aḥmad, wanted to contest his brother for the Ṭarīqa's Shaikhdom after their father's demise. He did not accept the decision of his father, thinking that he was better qualified to succeed him. One day, Shaikh Aḥmad was sitting in Shāh al-Kasnazān's seat when Shaikh ʿAbd al-Qādir passed in front of him and greeted him. Shaikh Aḥmad returned the greeting. After a few seconds, he saw his youngest brother pass by him again in the same direction and greet him, so he returned the greeting. The situation repeated itself tens of times. Shaikh Aḥmad was taken aback. He understood the implication of this karāma: the Shaikh of the Ṭarīqa has special knowledge that allows him to identify the person that deserves to succeed him. That person then becomes subject to attention and care from the Shaikhs of Ṭarīqa and receives spiritual power from them that is not available to others. Shaikh Aḥmad admitted he was wrong in contesting his brother, and he realized that Shaikh ʿAbd al-Qādir was Shaikh of the Ṭarīqa after their father, Shāh al-Kasnazān.

This karāma also shows the appearance of the Shaikh of Ṭarīqa spiritually in many places at once, which is a well-known phenomenon attributed to the grand Shaikhs of Ṭarīqa throughout history, including the Kasnazānī Shaikhs. For instance, Ḥājj Fattāḥ, who stood in service to Shaikh ʿAbd al-Karīm al-Kasnazān during his assemblies, says that he would sometimes see a copy of Shaikh ʿAbd al-Karīm come out of his noble body while he was sitting, preaching to the seekers. The copy would pass by and gently press its noble thumb on his shoulder and say, "Fattāḥ, watch out", and it would do the same when it returned. Ḥājj Fattāḥ would sometimes count close to forty copies of Shaikh ʿAbd al-Karīm leaving his body.

The following karāma emphasizes Shaikh Ḥusayn's designation as Shaikh of the Ṭarīqa. After Shaikh ʿAbd al-Qādir al-Kasnazān's death, some caliphs rejected Shaikh ʿAbd al-Qādir's appointment of his son Shaikh Ḥusayn as Shaikh of the Ṭarīqa and claimed that they were Shaikhs of the Ṭarīqa. This grave sin was made easier to commit by the fact that Shaikh ʿAbd al-Qādir had spent the last three years of his life as a migrant in Iran and passed away there, far away from Karbchna. Shaikh ʿAbd al-Qādir had a caliph named Muḥammad Bāwa, nicknamed Ḥama Gada, who was a great walī from Girmayān, south of Kirkuk. He went to Karbchna in the company of three-hundred dervishes and the set up their tents there. The caliph then went to visit the shrine of Shaikh ʿAbd al-Qādir, whose son Shaikh Ḥusayn had returned his noble body to the village from Iran to be with his father, Shāh al-Kasnazān. At the time of the visit, Shaikh Ḥusayn was visiting farmers of his outside the village.

The shrine of Shaikh ʿAbd al-Qādir is in the same hall as the shrine of Shāh al-Kasnazān. Between the two, there are shrines of the other children of Shāh al-Kasnazān. At the time of the visit, a relative of Shaikh ʿAbd al-Qādir called Salām was sitting in front of Shāh al-Kasnazān's shrine reciting the Qur'an softly. Caliph Salām, who later documented what happened during this visit, was among those who rejected Shaikh Ḥusayn's succession of Shaikh ʿAbd al-Qādir. He was sitting in such a place that made him invisible from the door that led to the hall hosting the shrines, so caliph Muḥammad did not see him or sense his presence when he went in. Muḥammad greeted the recumbent walīs from the entrance to the shrine, and he heard Shaikh ʿAbd al-Qādir answer him from his resting place: "Allah's peace and mercy be upon you, caliph Muḥammad". Caliph Salām was one of Shaikh ʿAbd al-Qādir's cousins and caliphs and he accompanied him for many years, so he recognized his voice and manner of speech. He stopped reciting the Qur'an and remained silent, listening to what was happening. Caliph Muḥammad said: "Dear Shaikh, the dervishes have split after you. For Allah's sake, for the Messenger's sake (PBUH), for the sake of Shāh al-Kasnazān, tell me, who is your deputy? Who is the Shaikh after you?" Shaikh ʿAbd al-Qādir answered: "My dear son, Ḥusayn is my deputy. Go to Ḥusayn". Once Shaikh ʿAbd al-Qādir answered, caliph Salām felt the irrepressible need to cough. When he coughed, Shaikh ʿAbd al-Qādir went quiet, as did caliph Muḥammad. He left the blessed place and caliph Salām followed him.

They saw Shaikh Ḥusayn from a distance, returning to the village on his horse. They remained standing in front of the shrine's door until Shaikh Ḥusayn arrived. Caliph Muḥammad approached him and held the bridle of his horse and spoke to him about the Ṭarīqa's Shaikhdom. Shaikh Ḥusayn said that there were caliphs who wanted to be Shaikhs of the Ṭarīqa and that the dervishes could go to them. The caliph replied: "Sulṭān ʿAbd al-Qādir has just told me, 'Ḥusayn is my deputy'. You are his deputy". When Shaikh Ḥusayn heard this, he dismounted from his horse. After this karāma, dervishes who deviated returned and pledged their allegiance to Shaikh Ḥusayn as Master of the Ṭarīqa, especially since Salām, who heard Sulṭān ʿAbd al-Qādir for himself, had been opposed to Shaikh Ḥusayn's succession to the Shaikhdom of the Ṭarīqa.

A similar karāma occurred after Shaikh Ḥusayn informed the disciples that the Shaikh of Ṭarīqa after him was his brother, ʿAbd al-Karīm. Shaikh Ḥusayn had entered about a hundred seekers into seclusion, including a relative of his called Shaikh Faraj sayyid ʿAlī, whom we met when discussing Shāh al-Kasnazān's karāma that made him become a Kasnazānī dervish (§2.3). One day, Shaikh Faraj saw from his place of seclusion Shaikh ʿAbd al-Karīm riding on his horse. The latter was dressed handsomely, surrounded by companions and accompanied by hunting dogs, heading towards a prairie to hunt. Shaikh Faraj doubted that this man, who was preoccupied with hunting and worldly pursuits, was qualified to succeed Sulṭān Ḥusayn, who was an unparalleled ascetic. He remained in a constant state of fasting in the last four years of his life, and he did not even drink water for six months, sufficing himself with tea. It was as if he had remained in permanent seclusion. Shaikh Faraj was cast into doubt when he saw that the deputy's condition differed completely from the state of the Shaikh who had appointed him.

Shaikh Faraj did not make mention of these doubts, as he was in seclusion, but Shaikh Ḥusayn sent for him, requesting that he present himself in the takya. After Shaikh Ḥusayn finished supplicating, he turned to the dervish and said: "Leave ʿAbd al-Karīm alone"! Afterwards, Shaikh Faraj returned to his seclusion. Three or four days later, the same thought occurred to him, as he questioned how Shaikh ʿAbd al-Karīm, who is preoccupied with the world, could succeed the ascetic Shaikh Ḥusayn. Shaikh Ḥusayn sent for him a second time and told him: "Didn't I tell you to leave ʿAbd al-Karīm alone"? On the tenth day of seclusion, the dervish was, once again, overcome with doubt regarding Shaikh ʿAbd al-Karīm's qualification as the successor to Shaikh Ḥusayn. Shaikh Ḥusayn sent for him a third time, this time telling him: "Shaikh Faraj, by Allah, by Allah, by Allah, the matter is not for me to decide. The Messenger (PBUH) is the one who appointed ʿAbd al-Karīm for this post". At that moment, Shaikh Faraj's heart was purged of all doubt, and these thoughts did not occur to him again.

Allah looks at the Shaikh of Ṭarīqa with the eye of special providence from his birth. He inundates him with attributes that enable him to carry the trust of such a post, similar to what the Almighty told Moses: "[So] that you would be brought up under My eye" (Ṭāhā 39). The eye of divine providence continues to follow the Prophet's (PBUH) spiritual successor throughout his life, just like Allah said to Muḥammad (PBUH): "You are in Our eyes" (al-Ṭūr 48). Allah always cares for those He chooses, but this divine providence takes on new dimensions when the new Shaikh takes up this position, causing his condition to begin to transform. Whoever objects to the Shaikh's appointment of his deputy does so because of knowledge he thinks he has about that deputy. The truth is that this kind of objection is not based on knowledge, but rather on twofold ignorance. First, he is ignorant of the deputy's spiritual condition before Shaikhhood, which is something internal, invisible. Second, he is ignorant of the fact that Allah transforms the deputy's internal state when he becomes Shaikh of the Ṭarīqa.

The Shaikh of Ṭarīqa has unique attributes and a distinct character that cause him to rise above others. Consequently, any individual he chooses to succeed him as Shaikh of Ṭarīqa cannot match him in the beauty of his qualities. No matter how praiseworthy the deputy may be, there remains a big difference between his praiseworthy attributes and the distinguished attributes of the Shaikh of Ṭarīqa. When a dervish forgets that Allah's choosing of an individual as Shaikh of Ṭarīqa means that this individual has spiritual capabilities, even if they have yet to be fully realized, and that Allah is responsible for his spiritual development and ensuring that he turns out the way He wants him to, then he may fall into the error of objecting to this choice.

Also, the deputy chosen by the Shaikh may be preoccupied with many worldly affairs that make him seem like he is unqualified for the Ṭarīqa's Shaikhdom. For instance, Faraj objected to Shaikh Ḥusayn choosing Shaikh ʿAbd al-Karīm as Shaikh of the Ṭarīqa because he saw that he had worldly interests, while Sulṭān Ḥusayn was an ascetic in every regard. Similarly, Shaikh Muḥammad al-Muḥammad's life as a military commander in the Kurdish movement in northern Iraq did not provide any indication of his future as a spiritual leader of Ṭarīqa with disciples, both human and jinn, everywhere. The extremely important fact that many people do not realise is that when a deputy becomes Shaikh of the Ṭarīqa after his Master's death, his states and his actions begin to transform. The secrets behind the Prophet's (PBUH) choice begin to show on him. Even though every Shaikh of Ṭarīqa is destined to hold this post even before he is created, his external appearance before ascending to this post may not foreshadow his internal state after doing so, even though his life before Shaikhdom is not free of subtle indications that are perceived by people who possess spiritual ḥāls and sound understanding. As soon as the Prophet (PBUH) and the Shaikhs of Ṭarīqa put him in the position of Shaikhdom, his state begins to change, traces of Allah's hidden knowledge about Him begin to show on him, and the secret of him being chosen as Shaikh of the Ṭarīqa becomes clear to everyone. We also see this, for example, in the new Shaikh's transformation into the principal source of the karāmas of the Ṭarīqa, after the late Shaikh.

The same way the internal state, outward conduct, and overall qualities of a person who Allah has decreed to become a Shaikh of Ṭarīqa transform when he assumes that position, his spiritual development also continues. This is what happens to the prophets whom prophethood moves to a completely new internal state, and it then takes them on a perpetual spiritual journey from one spiritual phase to the next. The Ṭarīqa's Shaikhdom is not prophethood, as Allah sealed prophethood with our Master Muḥammad (PBUH), but a Shaikh of Ṭarīqa is also in constant spiritual development. Given that the Shaikhs of Ṭarīqa continuously progress to higher spiritual levels, the Shaikh of Ṭarīqa's spiritual states in his latter days are not the same as they were at the beginning of his Shaikhdom. This progression is even mirrored in the nature of the karāmas that occur at the hands of the Shaikh of Ṭarīqa, as well as in the grants that he receives from the Messenger (PBUH) and the Ṭarīqa's Shaikhs.

On 18th/May/2016, our Shaikh announced one of the special gifts that the Prophet (PBUH) granted him that reflects the ascension of his spiritual status. He distinguished and honoured our Shaikh by adding one of his noble titles to our Shaikh's name, changing his name from "Muḥammad" to "Muḥammad al-Muḥammad". "Muḥammad al-Muḥammad" means "Muḥammad of the Prophet Muḥammad (PBUH)". It is a name that expresses how the Prophet (PBUH) has chosen our Shaikh as if the Messenger (PBUH) described him as "Muḥammad who belongs to me" or "Muḥammad whom I have chosen for myself".

Through this karāma, the Messenger (PBUH) also revealed his choice of a new title for himself: "al-Muḥammad". The addition of the definite article to the name "Muḥammad" indicates exclusivity, making "al-Muḥammad" a unique title that points to one Muḥammad: the Prophet (PBUH). This is the case with other titles that the use of the definite article makes exclusively refer to him. For instance, the noble Qur'an describes Muḥammad (PBUH) by the titles of "the Prophet", "the

Messenger", "the One Who Cloaks Himself" and "the One Who Covers Himself". He (PBUH) has also mentioned other titles of his:

> "I am Muḥammad; I am Aḥmad; I am al-Māḥī (the Effacer), the one by whom disbelief is effaced; I am al-Ḥāshir (the Gatherer), with whom mankind will be gathered; I am al-'Āqib (the Last to Come), [after whom no prophet will come]".[181]

Scholars have mentioned other names of the Prophet (PBUH) derived from his attributes and deeds, such as al-Shāhid (the Witness), al-Mubashshir (the Bearer of Glad Tidings), al-Sirāj al-Munīr (the Illuminating Lamp), al-Hādī (the Guide), and other names. He also used to be called "al-Ṣādiq" (the Truthful One) and "al-Āmīn" (the Trustworthy One) even before his mission. Each of these descriptions can refer to various individuals when it occurs with the indefinite article, but when mentioned with the definite article, the description refers to Muḥammad (PBUH) in particular. It is worth mentioning that scholars have traditionally referred to the Messenger's (PBUH) "titles" and "epithets" as "names" because his names are "all epithets [of praise], not mere labels used only for identification. Rather, they are names derived from attributes he possesses that necessitate praise and distinction for him".[182] The same is true for Allah's attributes, which are referred to as "the Beautiful Names".

A vision that our Shaikh saw on the 17th/Ramadan/1437 H, which corresponds to 22nd/June/2016, also reflects his spiritual ascension. He saw himself visiting the shrines of the Ṭarīqa Kasnazāniyya Shaikhs in Karbchna with green flags waving for his arrival. He was standing in front of Shaikh 'Abd al-Qādir al-Kasnazān's shrine, and he and the Kasnazānī Shaikhs were all immersed in a dense unique light. Shaikh 'Abd al-Qādir was standing in front of the door, holding a book he read from. He said to our Shaikh, who was standing in front of him: "You are a caliph". Our Shaikh replied: "Yes, my beloved". Shaikh 'Abd al-Qādir repeated more assertively: "You are a caliph". Our Shaikh replied, once more: "Yes, my beloved". Then Shaikh 'Abd al-Qādir sharply repeated the phrase a third time, emphasizing the declaration he read from the book: "You are a caliph". This austerity seems to have been in response

---

181 Muslim, *Ṣaḥīḥ Muslim*, IV, no. 2354, p. 1828.

182 Ibn Qayyim al-Jawzīyya, *Zād al-Ma'ād fī-Hadyī Khayri al-'Ibād*, I, pp. 84-85.

to the shyness and modesty our Shaikh was overcome with as a result of this bestowal and because of where he was. Our Shaikh responded a third time: "Yes, my beloved". This vision indicates that our Shaikh is "Allah's representative on earth".[183] These two karāmas, for example, took place more than thirty-eight years after our Master became the Shaikh of the Ṭarīqa. They demonstrate the continuation of his spiritual ascension and attainment of more high spiritual ranks.

The tremendous spiritual power that Allah grants a Shaikh of Ṭarīqa, that causes countless miracles, is testament to how Allah assumes responsibility for a Shaikh once he assumes Shaikhdom. Shaikh Muḥammad al-Muḥammad al-Kasnazān explains this wondrous phenomenon:

> "Shaikhdom is something that is related to spiritual power, which is beyond the limits of matter, which is the realm of human ability. It is not a worldly, materialistic, or tangible post that people can compete for. The spiritual power that is granted to the Shaikh who is chosen for Shaikhdom is a divine outpouring — divine power that is far beyond visual perception. Belief in this power comes by way of seeing what it does, not by touching it like one would touch physical matter, as it transcends that".[184]

The Ṭarīqa's Shaikhdom is intrinsically linked to the Prophet (PBUH). The greatest Shaikhs of Ṭarīqa are from the pure, prophetic household, regarding whom Allah (mighty and sublime is He) has said: "Allah intends only to remove from you the impurity [of sin], O people of the [Prophet's] household, and to purify you with [extensive] purification" (al-Āḥzāb 33). Hence, the spiritual successor of the Messenger and Master of the Ṭarīqa after him (PBUH) was Imām ʿAlī Ibn Abī Ṭālib, and after him the Imāms who are his children and grandchildren.

The Shaikhdom of Ṭarīqa Kasnazāniyya has been exclusive to this blessed family. This is substantiated in the will of Ghawth sayyid Shaikh Ismāʿīl al-Wilyānī, Shāh al-Kasnazān's third great-grandfather:

> "In no way is it possible, until the Hour of Resurrection, for the Ghawth to be cut from my sons and grandsons from subsequent generations over the years and throughout the ages. The rank of being a Ghawth will remain

---

[183] Shaikh Muḥammad al-Muḥammad al-Kasnazān, *sermon*, 1st/February/2018.

[184] Shaikh Muḥammad al-Muḥammad al-Kasnazān, *al-Ṭarīqa al-ʿAliyya al-Qādiriyya al-Kasnazāniyya*, pp. 161-162.

present within them in particular".[185]

We see this fact in Shāh al-Kasnazān's promise with Allah Almighty:

"Allah (blessed and exalted is He) has promised me that the Shaikhdom will remain present among the people the Ṭarīqa and that it will never depart from them. Even if no one from the Kasnazānī family remains except for a blind old woman, who assumes the Shaikhdom and leads people by it, Allah, Blessed and Sublime is He, would facilitate the means for her to do so and would support her as long as she adheres to the Ṭarīqa and travels the path of guidance".[186]

9.2 The Designation of Shaikh Muḥammad al-Muḥammad al-Kasnazān

As is the case with all Shaikhs of Ṭarīqa, Shaikh Muḥammad al-Muḥammad was appointed to the Shaikhdom of the Ṭarīqa by divine decree and communication by the Messenger (PBUH). Allah Almighty designates whomever He wills to represent His noble Messenger (PBUH) even before his birth. The Omnipotent Creator chooses his father and mother, thus selecting his genes and biological composition. We saw this in the marriage of Shāh al-Kasnazān's parents, and we saw this a second time when Shaikh Ḥusayn chose for his brother and successor, Shaikh ʿAbd al-Karīm, the wife who was to have his son and successor, Shaikh Muḥammad al-Muḥammad. This is a manifestation of divine subtlety whose secrets remain hidden until they are realised and become public, which is when eyes see, ears hear, and the intellect understands them. One of Allah's beautiful names is "al-Laṭīf", which means "the Subtle One", i.e. the one whom senses cannot perceive. He described Himself saying: "Vision perceives Him not, but He perceives [all] vision; and He is the Subtle, the Acquainted" (al-Ānʿām 103).[187] Who saw Joseph's brothers' throwing him down a well as a cause leading to Allah raising him to the seat of government and the highest levels of divine proximity? Therefore,

---

[185] Shaikh Muḥammad al-Muḥammad al-Kasnazān, *al-Ṭarīqa al-ʿAliyya al-Qādiriyya al-Kasnazāniyya*, p. 162.
[186] Shaikh Muḥammad al-Muḥammad al-Kasnazān, *al-Ṭarīqa al-ʿAliyya al-Qādiriyya al-Kasnazāniyya*, pp. 162-163.
[187] Fatoohi, *The Prophet Joseph in the Qur'an, the Bible, and History*, p. 230.

after Joseph (peace be upon him) mentioned how Allah graced him and his family — "O my father, this is the interpretation of my vision of before. My Lord has made it come true. He was certainly good to me when He took me out of prison and brought you [here] from bedouin life after Satan had induced [estrangement] between me and my brothers" — he closed his speech with this profoundly wise statement: "Indeed, my Lord is Subtle in what He wills. Indeed, it is He who is the Knowing, the Wise" (Yūsuf 100). Similarly, Allah's choosing and His leading of the Shaikhs of Ṭarīqa contain many divine subtleties that can be understood only by whomever Allah wills from those He has blessed with spiritual revelations and knowledge of the unseen.

There are innumerable karāmas and spiritual unveilings that illustrate that Allah chose Shaikh Muḥammad al-Muḥammad for the Shaikhdom of the Ṭarīqa. One of these karāmas occurred before his birth. When Shaikh ʿAbd al-Qādir was informed of the birth of his son ʿAbd al-Karīm, he asked that the newborn be brought to him. There were several dervishes present in his assembly. When the baby was placed before him, the Shaikh moved his cane above the child to and fro and said: "What Allah wills, what Allah wills. Allah will guide many Arabs at the hands of the son of this man to the true path". In Shaikh Muḥammad al-Muḥammad's time, especially after the main takya in Baghdad was built and he permanently moved from Kirkuk in the north to Baghdad in 1982, a vast number of Arabs actually took the Ṭarīqa's pledge.

In the 1950s, a walī and disciple of the Ṭarīqa Kasnazāniyya, named Ṣāliḥ Muḥammad Amīn (may Allah have mercy on him), saw a vision that prophesied that event. He saw the Shaikhs taking the Ṭarīqa's banners from northern Iraq to Baghdad in the centre of the country. Even though he implored them to keep the Ṭarīqa's banners in the north, they only left a small banner and took the rest south. In 1973 or 1974, Shaikh ʿAbd al-Karīm revealed that the Shaikhs' gaze and the Ṭarīqa's blessing were oriented towards the Arabs in the south. In 1975, Shaikh ʿAbd al-Karīm was in Karbchna overseeing renovations of the roof of the shrines' hall and the mosque when the walī Aḥmad Muḥammad Amīn spoke to the Shaikh about seeing in ḥāl something similar to what his brother Ṣāliḥ saw about twenty years before. He saw the Ṭarīqa's banners, canes, and prayer rugs being loaded into a car to transport them to the south. He tried to prevent this, but he only succeeded in taking some of the canes.

Sayyida Shamsa (may Allah have mercy on her), Shaikh Ḥusayn's daughter, relates what happened the blessed night our Shaikh was born. At the time, she was ten years old. When the Shaikh Ḥusayn learned that the wife of his brother ʿAbd al-Karīm went into labour at night, he kept walking back and forth between the house's entrance and patio, reciting "Yā Hū, Yā Hū", waiting for the newborn's delivery. Shaikh Ḥusayn did not calm down and sit until he was told of the delivery at dawn, Friday, 15th/April/1938.[188] Our Shaikh was not the first child of Shaikh ʿAbd al-Karīm and sayyida Ḥafṣa. Their son Ḥusayn was born eleven years before our Shaikh, and they were blessed with their first daughter, ʿĀ`ishā, one year before him. Thus, Sulṭān Ḥusayn's interest in our Shaikh's birth specifically is exceptional.

When Sulṭān Ḥusayn sent for the newborn, a number of his children, some of whom were very young, were in his assembly. When the Shaikh extended his hand to greet the swaddled newborn, an aged dervish told him that this would make his children jealous. Yet, the Shaikh took the child, placed him on his lap, and began praising him: "This is the reviver of the religion, this will benefit religion, this will live a long life". It was also Sulṭān Ḥusayn who named him "Muḥammad", following the prevalent tradition of the Shaikh of Ṭarīqa choosing names for newborns. Clearly, Shaikh Ḥusayn saw a future Shaikh of Ṭarīqa in his nephew, just as his father, and Master of the Ṭarīqa before him, Shaikh ʿAbd al-Qādir, said of him.

When Shaikh Muḥammad al-Muḥammad was about two to three months old, he became so ill that his parents thought that he would not survive. They took him to his uncle, Sulṭān Ḥusayn, who had isolated himself from people and the world. The Shaikh of Ṭarīqa, who knew that Allah had a future and tremendous spiritual role written for the child, told them not to worry about their baby for he had Guardians protecting him. They were, thus, assured that he would be fine.

There is a similar karāma that happened to Shaikh ʿAbd al-Karīm when he was a small child in the cradle. His mother, sayyida Raḥīma, would see cats sharing his cradle with him. She would chase them away, fearing they would harm him, but they would return after a while. One day, when she shooed them, one of the cats admonishingly spoke to her:

---

[188] Shaikh Muḥammad al-Muḥammad al-Kasnazān, *sermon*, 10th/February/2016.

"Why do you shoo us away? We are here, by the Shaikh's order, to protect ʿAbd al-Karīm". After that, she left them to their business.[189]

This divine protection since childhood reminds us of how Allah protected Moses as a child when He said to his mother: "Suckle him; but when you fear for him, cast him into the river and do not fear and do not grieve. Indeed, We will return him to you and will make him a messenger" (al-Qaṣaṣ 7). He was in grave danger because Pharaoh was killing every child from the Children of Israel. Allah's plan to rescue him also seemed extremely dangerous, but "Allah is predominant over His affair, but most people do not know" (Yūsuf 21). Indeed, Allah saved the future prophet from every danger and fulfilled His promise to his mother: "So We restored him to his mother that she might be content and not grieve and that she would know that the promise of Allah is true. But most people do not know" (al-Qaṣaṣ 13).

One event that embodies Sulṭān Ḥusayn's exceptional love for his nephew took place when this ascetic Shaikh was on his deathbed, hours before his departure from this world. Shaikh ʿAbd al-Karīm and his wife were sitting close to the Shaikh, weeping over his imminent departure from them and this world. Their child, who was less than a year old, was in the company of a guardian. When Shaikh Ḥusayn saw him while lying on the bed, he motioned for the baby to be brought to him. When they brought the child to him and placed him on his chest, he began kissing him and sniffing his neck, as if he could smell the pleasant fragrance of the Ṭarīqa he was destined to take care of forty years later. Those present began to cry more when they witnessed this moving scene. Then, Shaikh ʿAbd al-Karīm came and lifted the child off the Shaikh's chest, whose asceticism and seclusions over the years had taken their toll, so that the baby's weight would not hurt him. This was the last good omen from Sulṭān Ḥusayn before he departed from this world about the lofty status that the young Muḥammad al-Muḥammad would have in the future.

Naturally, the future Shaikh of Ṭarīqa receives indications and has experiences that tell him that Allah has destined an important future for him. In the spring of 1957, when he was a youth of nineteen years of age, Shaikh Muḥammad al-Muḥammad would sit on a small hill in the morning, overseeing the planting of rice in farmland that he had in Hawmarāmān, Qaradāgh. He used to take advantage of his time alone to

---

[189] Shaikh Muḥammad al-Muḥammad al-Kasnazān, *sermon*, 28th/October/2013.

memorize the Qur'an. One night, he was sitting on his bed, reclining on cushions between his back and the wall, facing the Ka'ba, so he was facing towards Karbchna, where Shaikh 'Abd al-Karīm lived. He was reciting the chapter of Yāsīn from the Qur'an when he closed his eyes. He saw a white light like the moon approaching him from afar. The whiteness of the light was like no other white and indescribably beautiful. He knew that it was the honourable Messenger (PBUH): "There has come to you from Allah a light and a clear Book" (al-Mā`ida 15). The light continued to draw near to our Shaikh until it entered into his eyes, mouth, ears, nose, neck — all over his body. The light had a unique quality of delight, and it was so dense that he could feel the light move through his body. After the prophetic light had entered our Shaikh's body, he felt as if his body was not there anymore, and he was overcome with a spiritual state of crying accompanied by a feeling of pleasure that he had never experienced before.[190]

Shaikh 'Abd al-Karīm had hinted to individual dervishes in private that "Kāka Muḥammad", which is how he used to refer to Shaikh Muḥammad al-Muḥammad, would succeed him as Shaikh of the Ṭarīqa. Still, for many long years, our Shaikh's role in serving the Ṭarīqa remained limited to meeting the takya's needs and helping disciples with their worldly needs. He did not have any role in the spiritual matters of the Ṭarīqa or its dervishes. That, began to change, however, when Shaikh 'Abd al-Karīm decided to perform the pilgrimage to Allah's sanctified House in 1971. In that year, the pilgrimage was at the beginning of February. Shaikh 'Abd al-Karīm gave our Shaikh the Ṭarīqa's pledge with his noble hand and appointed him as his General Deputy, which is his successor for the spiritual, not only worldly, matters of the Ṭarīqa. Our Shaikh asked his Master to give him comprehensive permission in spiritual sciences, and Shaikh 'Abd al-Karīm granted him his request. Before his travel, Shaikh 'Abd al-Karīm informed the dervishes who visited him in Kirkuk that Shaikh Muḥammad al-Muḥammad was his General Deputy and that he would take his place while he was away. One thing told them: "As of today, you do not know the real Kāka Muḥammad. The day will come, however, when you, and everyone in

---

[190] Shaikh Muḥammad al-Muḥammad al-Kasnazān, *sermon*, 10th/February/2016; 22nd/September/2016.

the world, will know his reality". Our Shaikh stayed in the takya, representing his Master during his pilgrimage to Allah's sanctified House.

Shaikh ʿAbd al-Karīm would attend dhikr circles on Monday and Thursday nights in the main takya in Kirkuk, so this became one of his General Deputy's tasks for as long as the Master was on the pilgrimage. One night, the winter cold was brutal, as usual, but it was hot inside the takya because it was filled with dervishes and because of the heating system. The takya's door was open and our Shaikh was standing in front of it, covering a part of the door's opening. When the disciples were chanting the first dhikr that is accompanied by drums, "Ḥayy Allāh, Ḥayy Allāh", our Shaikh felt a cool breeze enter from outside, touch his body, and enter the centre of the dhikr circle in the takya. The breeze had a unique fragrance, similar to that of a damask rose, which our Shaikh recognised as the Messenger's (PBUH) special scent. This pleasant fragrance remained for days on the left side of his body, where the prophetic breeze had touched him.

Our Master says that every Shaikh has a special fragrance, the same way every flower has a special scent. Spiritually conscious dervishes recognize a Shaikh's spiritual presence even before they see him because of his distinct fragrance. When a Shaikh presents himself somewhere, dervishes who possess ḥāls smell that Shaikh's scent in that place, even if they visit that place after the Shaikh has left because that Shaikh's scent remains for a while after he is gone. The noble Qur'an confirms this reality when it describes the muʿjiza of the Prophet Jacob smelling his son's scent, the Prophet Joseph, from afar: "When the caravan departed, their father said, 'Indeed, I find the smell of Joseph, if you did not think me weakened in mind" (Yūsuf 94). The noble verse indicates that Jacob smelled Joseph's scent when the caravan departed, that is when it left Egypt, which means that he smelled it when Joseph's shirt was still days away. He must have spiritually sensed the scent, i.e. by way of a muʿjiza.[191]

A karāma that expresses this reality happened during Shaikh ʿAbd al-Karīm al-Kasnazān's final visit to Baghdad. In 1976 or 1977, he travelled from Kirkuk to Baghdad with two of his relatives, one of whom was driving the Shaikh's car. As was his habit when he visited Baghdad,

---

[191] Fatoohi, *The Prophet Joseph in the Qur'an, the Bible, and History*, p. 221.

Shaikh ʿAbd al-Karīm stayed at the Ḥakīm hotel on al-Rashīd street, near Wathba square in the Hafez al-Qāḍī district. A walī, Aḥmad Muḥammad Amīn, who we have previously mentioned, decided to visit the Shaikh in Baghdad, even though he did not know where the Shaikh was staying, had never visited Baghdad before, and did not speak Arabic. When the dervish got off the public transport vehicle that gave him a lift from Kirkuk to Nahḍa Square in Baghdad, he walked to Shaikh ʿAbd al-Qādir al-Gaylānī's shrine, less than kilometre away, hoping that he would find there a Kurdish dervish that could help him locate the Shaikh. However, he did not find anyone there that could help him. While still unsure what to do, he suddenly smelled Shaikh ʿAbd al-Karīm's scent. He began to follow the scent until he reached the hotel, which was about half a kilometre away from the shrine. When he continued past the hotel's entrance, the scent disappeared. He realised that the Shaikh was in the hotel. He went up the hotel's stairs and found him there. After greeting him, one of the Shaikh's companions, who were amazed by his arrival, especially since he was completely unfamiliar with Baghdad, asked how he was able to find them. He told them what had happened.

Indeed, it is even possible to smell the Shaikh's scent in his belongings and his children. Shaikh Ṭāhir, Sulṭān Ḥusayn al-Kasnazān eldest son, was working as a teacher in a village in the Dāqūq province of Kirkuk. One day, he was with some teachers in a carriage that was taking them from Dāqūq to their village when a man going in the opposite direction passed by. Shortly after passing them, the man ran back to them and asked that they stop the carriage. He asked them: "Which one of you is Sulṭān Ḥusayn al-Kasnazān's son?" The men were astonished by the question, but suspicious of what the strange man wanted, they denied that any of his sons were among them. The man, however, swore that one of Shaikh Ḥusayn's son was with them and that he would not let them pass until they informed him who it was! They asked him how he could be so sure of what he claimed. He replied that when they crossed paths, he saw his Master, Shaikh Ḥasan al-Qarachawārī, point to their carriage and he smelled Shaikh Ḥusayn's scent! He went on to say that all he wanted was to kiss the hand of Shaikh Ḥusayn's son and smell his scent, and then he would let them go on their way. At that moment, Shaikh Ṭāhir admitted that he was Sulṭān Ḥusayn's son. We have mentioned how people used to refer to Shāh al-Kasnazān's father with the title "būn khūsh", which means "the one who has a fragrant scent", because of his distinct, pleasant scent that could sometimes be smelled in a place for more than two days after his passing.

Returning to the subject of Shaikh ʿAbd al-Karīm's appointment of our Shaikh as Master of the Ṭarīqa after him, he would confirm to dervishes and caliphs that Shaikh Muḥammad al-Muḥammad was his successor by statements such as "I do not want anyone who does not want Kāka Muḥammad" and "I do not love anyone who does not love Kāka Muḥammad". He would even say: "If the light of my eyes that I see with does not want Kāka Muḥammad, then I do not want it"! These decisive words that leave no room for negotiation prove that Shaikh Muḥammad al-Muḥammad's designation was a prophetic order that could not be objected to or even debated over: "Whatever the Messenger has given you — take" (al-Ḥashr 7).

Shaikh ʿAbd al-Karīm had a special love for Shaikh Muḥammad al-Muḥammad that was unlike his love for anyone else. Shaikh ʿAbd al-Karīm would always ask about our Master and inquire about his condition when he was not around. He would also give him the most precious and most beautiful gifts that were presented to him. This was not a result of the usual love and care that a father gives his son. Rather, this love and care was both unique and special because it was the love and care of a Shaikh of Ṭarīqa for his successor, for the Muḥammadan Inheritor after him. Our Shaikh reciprocated this special spiritual love for his Master. We see the same situation in Shaikh Muḥammad al-Muḥammad's love and attention for his General Deputy, Shaikh Nahro. Our Shaikh loves and cares for all of his children, but his love and care for Shaikh Nahro are particularly unique. They are not a result of his being the eldest of his children, but rather because he is his General Deputy, whom our Shaikh has announced will succeed him as Master of the Ṭarīqa. Anyone who has witnessed the relationship between Shaikh ʿAbd al-Karīm and Shaikh Muḥammad al-Muḥammad recognises that the relationship between Shaikh Muḥammad al-Muḥammad and Shaikh Nahro is of that same kind of unique spiritual bond.

Those who possess ḥāls are often spiritually attracted to the future Shaikh of Ṭarīqa, even before he assumes its Shaikhdom. Dervishes who possess spiritual unveilings knew that Shaikh Muḥammad al-Muḥammad would succeed his father to Shaikhdom, even before Shaikh ʿAbd al-

Karīm announced it. In the early 1960s, about fifteen years before our Shaikh became the Master of the Ṭarīqa, a dervish named Majīd from Khurmāl, Sulaymāniyya, who had spiritual ḥāl, said that a day would come when dervishes of "King Muḥammad", as he liked to refer to Shaikh Muḥammad al-Muḥammad, would come to visit him by plane. At the time, dervishes would exclusively travel by land to visit Shaikh ʿAbd al-Karīm, as air travel was not as common as it is now. He would also describe "King Muḥammad's" future dervishes, saying that the majority of them would be bareheaded. He said this at a time when the majority of people, including disciples, whether Arab or Kurdish, would cover their heads.

Also in the 1960s, when our Shaikh was still involved in the Kurdish movement, he met an aged female dervish in the company of her grandsons. When our Shaikh greeted her, the elderly woman returned the greeting and added, referring to her grandsons: "These are your dervishes". This happened a few years before Shaikh ʿAbd al-Karīm appointed our Master as his deputy. There are many examples of these unveilings. The Messenger (PBUH) also told some dervishes that Shaikh Muḥammad al-Muḥammad would succeed his father as Shaikh of the Ṭarīqa.

Three or four years before our Shaikh became Master of the Ṭarīqa, three accomplished disciples — Uncle Ḥusayn, ʿAlī Fshān, and Ibrāhīm Galālī — sometimes liked to leave Shaikh ʿAbd al-Karīm's assembly and would go stand at the door of our Shaikh's assembly hall. Our Shaikh would be annoyed, sometimes to the point of being upset, and would ask them to go to Shaikh ʿAbd al-Karīm's assembly, as he was the Shaikh of Ṭarīqa, to whom they were spiritually linked. Also, our Shaikh did not like anyone to remind him that Shaikh ʿAbd al-Karīm would one day depart from this world, but the dervishes would reply that they liked to be near his assembly. One day in 1973 or 1974, Uncle Ḥusayn and ʿAlī Fshān made a crown out of metal wires and, along with Ibrāhīm Galālī, brought it to our Shaikh's assembly. When he saw them carrying it, he understood what they intended to do and became upset. He asked them to leave, but they placed the crown in his assembly hall and then left.

As the present Shaikh of Ṭarīqa's death and the advent of the new Shaikh draw near, dervishes who possess ḥāls begin to sense this imminent change. Where there was once only love for the present Shaikh in their hearts, love for the next Shaikh begins to grow in their hearts, so they start feeling drawn to him. About five or six months before Shaikh ʿAbd al-Karīm's departure, our Shaikh noticed an increase in dervishes with ḥāls who would come close to him. He was anxious about this because he knew what it meant. They began, for instance, to come to his assembly after Shaikh Abd al-Karīm leaves his assembly and goes to his private room for worship. Our Shaikh would try his best to dismiss them, but the dervishes' inclination towards him was not their choice. It was, rather, a divine intervention as Allah directed their hearts towards the person whom He had chosen to succeed the present Shaikh. This paranormal intervention was necessary because, otherwise, a dervish's heart cannot love any other Master beside his present Master.

The intervention of the Prophet (PBUH) and the Shaikhs of Ṭarīqa in moving the dervishes' hearts is demonstrated in the visions and spiritual experiences that dervishes witness that reveal the future Shaikh's imminent assumption of the Shaikhdom of the Ṭarīqa and attract their hearts to him. A few months before Shaikh ʿAbd al-Karīm's departure, for example, Aḥmad Muḥammad Amīn visited our Shaikh and told him about a vision he had seen. He saw the honourable Messenger (PBUH) take one of two outfits from a bundle of clothes and give it to our Shaikh. About two months later, another walī and caliph called Ḥājj Mullā ʿAbd Allah visited our Shaikh and told him that he saw the Messenger (PBUH) ask for a cane then give it to our Shaikh. Visions and spiritual unveilings like these confirmed to our Shaikh the imminence of the departure of his Master, and that he would assume the Ṭarīqa's Shaikhdom. A dream of the Prophet (PBUH) is always a true dream because he (PBUH) has said: "Whoever sees me [in a dream] then, indeed, he has seen the truth, as Satan cannot appear in my form",[192] and, "Whoever sees me in a dream has really seen me, as Satan cannot impersonate me".[193]

Karāmas and spiritual indications that confirm what the Shaikhs of Ṭarīqa have said about Shaikh Muḥammad al-Muḥammad's designation for the Ṭarīqa's Masterhood continued to happen and still happen today. They include our Shaikh taking the pledge directly from the Prophet (PBUH). Less than two months before Shaikh ʿAbd al-Karīm's death, our

---

[192] Bukhārī, *Al-Jāmiʿ al-Ṣaḥīḥ*, III, no. 6749, p. 603.

[193] Bukhārī, *Al-Jāmiʿ al-Ṣaḥīḥ*, I, no. 109, p. 82.

Shaikh was blessed with meeting the Messenger of Allah (PBUH) in a dream. He (PBUH) was sitting with his blessed back reclined against Shaikh Sulṭān Ḥusayn's head in his shrine in Karbchna. He was facing the Ka'ba, almost in the direction of Kirkuk, where Shaikh 'Abd al-Karīm lived. He had a light beard and seemed sad. As soon as our Shaikh saw him, he rushed towards him and fell to his knees before him. With complete subservience and submission, he extended his hand, which was balled into a fist. His fist met the Messenger's (PBUH). Our Shaikh's fist seemed like a child's fist in comparison to the Prophet's (PBUH) fist.[194] Our Shaikh's joy in meeting with the Messenger (PBUH) was mixed with concern over what the vision indicated. When he told his Master about the dream, however, Shaikh 'Abd al-Karīm remained silent and did not comment. Our Shaikh knew what his Shaikh knew: this dream meant that Shaikh 'Abd al-Karīm would soon be leaving this world and that the Ṭarīqa's Shaikhdom would be transferred to him. This taking of the pledge at the Prophet's (PBUH) hand explains our Master's words about his noble palm: "Whoever touched this palm has touched the Prophet's (PBUH) palm".

Sulṭān Ḥusayn also visited Shaikh Muḥammad al-Muḥammad and placed his nephew's hand in his hand and gave him the succession of the Ṭarīqa. Shaikh 'Abd al-Karīm then gave the Ṭarīqa's caliphate to our Shaikh by hand. Progressively, he gave him all the permissions and spiritual Sufi matters he had from the Shaikhs of Ṭarīqa. These include permission to write supplications that Kāka Aḥmad al-Shaikh gave to Shāh al-Kasnazān, even though our Shaikhs only used them in exceptional cases. Our present Shaikh sometimes gives certain caliphs special supplications to use temporarily while on preaching tours, to cure specific diseases, for example. However, Ṭarīqa Kasnazāniyya's daily and perennial dhikrs contain enormous spiritual energy. By consistently performing them, a dervish can obtain all kinds of karāmas, spiritual grants, and whatever he needs. Shaikh 'Abd al-Karīm also handed to Shaikh Muḥammad al-Muḥammad the responsibility of the takya and told him that his time was up.

The notification came once more during Shaikh 'Abd al-Karīm Al-

---

[194] Shaikh Muḥammad al-Muḥammad al-Kasnazān, *sermon*, 10th/February/2016; *al-Ṭarīqa al-'Aliyya al-Qādiriyya al-Kasnazāniyya*, pp. 163-164.

Kasnazān's last visit to the honourable shrines of the Shaikhs in Karbchna. After staying there for a few days, our Shaikh came from Kirkuk to visit him. When Shaikh ʿAbd al-Karīm decided to return to Kirkuk, he went to visit the shrines as a farewell. This visit, however, was not like previous visits. When he came out of the hall of the shrines, he sat on a chair near the door with a joyous expression, and he addressed the large crowd of caliphs and disciples that were present:

> "My children! My dervishes! From this day forth, sayyid Shaikh Muḥammad is your Shaikh. This is our Master's order. Whoever obeys him has obeyed us, and whoever loves him has loved us. Whoever disobeys him has disobeyed us".

Then he turned around, looked at the shrines, and said:

> "I am saying my farewell to you now. This is my last visit to you. This is your deputy whom you have entrusted".[195]

Our Shaikh began to cry. He took his Master's hand and kissed it, saying: "You are in good health. You have broken our hearts". Those present also began to weep because of the gravity, majesty, and sadness of the situation. After returning from Karbchna, Shaikh ʿAbd al-Karīm entrusted his son and General Deputy with the administration of the Ṭarīqa's takyas. Shaikh ʿAbd al-Karīm passed away about two months after his last visit, and Shaikh Muḥammad al-Muḥammad succeeded him. Before his demise, Shaikh ʿAbd al-Karīm also made final farewell trips to holy shrines in Baghdad, Karbala, and Najaf.

9.3 Shaikh Muḥammad al-Muḥammad's Designation of His General Deputy

Following the way of the Prophet (PBUH) and Shaikhs of Ṭarīqa, our Master designated a Shaikh of Ṭarīqa after him and communicated this to disciples and people in general. Since the end of the 1990s, our Shaikh indicated from time to time that his eldest son, Nahro, was his deputy and has treated him with distinction (photo 19). For instance, our Master called a large number of caliphs and dervishes for a meeting on

---

[195] Shaikh Muḥammad al-Muḥammad al-Kasnazān, *Al-Ānwār al-Raḥmāniyya fīl-Ṭarīqa al-ʿAliyya al-Qādiriyya al-Kasnazāniyya*, p. 1.

22nd/December/2005 in the main takya in Sulaymāniyya where he lived. In that meeting, named the "Meeting of the Lovers", our Shaikh said about "Caliph Nahro": "Allah willing, he is the future Shaikh; your Shaikh, your brother, your servant and the Ṭarīqa's servant".[196]

Granting the inward and outward deputyship of Ṭarīqa Kasnazāniyya deputyship to Shaikh Nahro was officially announced in the "Address of the Pledge". Our Master gave this sermon to hundreds of caliphs and dervishes on 14th/November/2008 in the takya in Sulaymāniyya. This is what he said in that announcement:

> "The Shaikh has a General Deputy, and caliphs are deputies among you. However, the General Deputy is Shaikh Nahro. Any instruction from Shaikh Nahro is an instruction from the Shaikh. He is the Shaikh's eldest son and deputy. No one besides Nahro represents the Ṭarīqa after Shaikh Muḥammad al-Muḥammad. He is the one who represents the Ṭarīqa after the Shaikh. Be mindful of this. He is your little brother, but he is also the Shaikh's deputy. When the Shaikh is present, he is a small dervish in your midst, but when the Shaikh is absent, he is the Shaikh's deputy. Protect yourselves from anyone who wants to cheat you in the name of the Ṭarīqa, in the Shaikh's name, or in the Kasnazāniyya name. Be ready and see what your little brother Shaikh Nahro needs from you. Help him, Allah willing, because he is my successor, the Shaikh after me. As of now, no one represents me other than Nahro, because he is the Shaikh's General Deputy. His instructions are the Shaikh's instructions, so it is obligatory to obey him. Allah willing, all he wants is what is best for you. He works for your best interests, and he is sincere with you, sincere with your Ṭarīqa.
>
> The Shaikhs do not designate an unqualified person to preside as Shaikh. The Shaikh does not choose by himself but, it is rather, they — from the Messenger (PBUH) to sayyid ʿAbd al-Karīm — who choose. They are the ones who appoint the Shaikh's General Deputy. The Shaikh needs deputies. After Shaikh Nahro comes the caliphs, who are the Ṭarīqa's deputies. Shaikh Nahro does not command you to do wrong. He commands you to do good. He commands you to do what is right and forbids you from doing what is wrong. Obeying Shaikh Nahro derives from obeying the Shaikh, and obeying the Shaikh derives from obeying the Messenger (PBUH): 'Obey Allah and obey the Messenger and those in authority among you' (al-Nisāʾ 59).
>
> You must not follow any words besides those of the trustworthy caliphs who have taken these words from the Shaikh or Shaikh Nahro. There may be

[196] Shaikh Muḥammad al-Muḥammad al-Kasnazān, *sermon*, 22nd/December/2005.

someone who comes and claims that he was told such and such a thing in a vision. You must not rely on him. There is the Shaikh and there are the caliphs. The present is not like the past. Wherever you are, you can inquire about any matter from the Shaikh's office or from Shaikh Nahro, as he represents the Ṭarīqa after the Shaikh. Protect yourselves from hypocrites who claim that Shaikh Nahro is one thing and the Shaikh is another. This is not true. Shaikh Nahro is my heart; he is my liver. He is your servant and a servant of your Ṭarīqa".[197]

Long before this, our Shaikh, like some disciples with ḥāls, knew that Shaikh Nahro was his successor. For example, in late 1981 or early 1982, when Shaikh Nahro was a child of around twelve years, our Shaikh was having breakfast one morning with his brother-in-law, Shaikh Sāmān. He was filled with joy as he shared with him a dream he had seen the night before. He saw Sulṭān Ḥusayn al-Kasnazān take someone off a chair and put Shaikh Nahro in his place. The chair here refers to the position of Shaikhdom. The visionary dream illustrates that the Shaikhs of Ṭarīqa chose Shaikh Nahro as our Shaikh's successor as early as a few years after he assumed the Ṭarīqa's Shaikhdom.

When Shaikh Nahro was almost a year old and could finally sit, he would move his head up and down, similar to a movement done during dhikr. Shaikh 'Abd al-Karīm would reassure Shaikh Nahro's mother and his family that the child was fine and that there was no need to worry about him, but the continuous, rapid nature of the movement made his mother fear that he had some sort of disease or that his neck would be damaged. She took him to several doctors, including in Baghdad, but they did not find anything wrong with his body and could not explain the cause of this movement. This dhikr movement is a manifestation of the obvious blessing that Shaikh Nahro has had since his youth. He was born and grew up in the takya, surrounded by the sound of dhikr drums. He would attend the dhikr circles daily ever since he was very young. Shaikh Nahro still continuously moves his head in this spontaneous way, though the movement is not as fast and visible as it used to be.

The General Deputy has a special place in the Shaikh of Ṭarīqa's heart since he represents the Ṭarīqa's future. The Shaikh cares for him with exceptional care and carries special love for him because he will carry the

[197] Shaikh Muḥammad al-Muḥammad al-Kasnazān, *sermon*, 14th/November/2008.

Ṭarīqa's banner and responsibilities. We saw how our Shaikh had a special place in Shaikh ʿAbd al-Karīm's heart. Similarly, Shaikh Nahro has a unique status with Shaikh Muḥammad al-Muḥammad. Shaikh ʿAbd al-Karīm also exhibited special care for his grandson since his childhood. He would every day be brought to his grandfather, the Shaikh of Ṭarīqa, who would embrace him and pray for him. He would often sleep in the Shaikh's lap while repeating the dhikr "Yā Wadūd".[198]

We see the special status that Shaikh Nahro has with our Shaikh in a dream our Master had of the Messenger (PBUH) in 1998. Our Shaikh wanted to organise the Ṭarīqa's traditional annual celebration of the noble Prophetic birth, which fell in early July that year. However, the presence of thousands of the Ṭarīqa's disciples would worry the Iraqi government, which was growing increasingly strict and harsh on the Ṭarīqa due to its widespread popularity. It was particularly so given that that the Interior Minister had warned against organising the celebration, as we will see in greater detail in Chapter 17. While hesitating over hosting the celebration, our Shaikh saw the Messenger (PBUH) in a dream. He and a few individuals were visiting the Prophet (PBUH), who was sitting in an old-style home in a room whose door was open. In front of the room, there was a courtyard with a column. Our Shaikh sat beside the Prophet (PBUH). A man was standing near the Messenger (PBUH), and there was also someone named ʿAlī, who probably represented Imām ʿAlī, sitting in front of the Messenger (PBUH). He was reciting poetry to the Prophet (PBUH) that he hoped would bring joy to his noble heart. The Prophet (PBUH) was looking at him, happy with what he was hearing. A while after this lengthy sitting, lunch was brought. The loaves of bread were old-fashioned; each was a red circle. After they finished eating lunch with the Messenger (PBUH), our Shaikh saw the Messenger's noble hand (PBUH) reach into his chest, take out a muṣḥaf with a zipper on it, and place it on the table spread in front of him. He repeated this movement several times, extracting several muṣḥafs from his noble chest. The Prophet (PBUH) wanted to send these muṣḥafs as gifts to people in different parts of the world. This scene reminds us of the noble verse: "There has come to you from Allah a light and a clear Book" (al-Mā`ida 15). The Messenger (PBUH) is Allah's light through which He

[198] Shaikh Muḥammad al-Muḥammad al-Kasnazān, *sermon*, 2nd/May/2018.

sent the clear Book.

The Prophet (PBUH) stood up, so our Shaikh wanted to ask for permission to leave. He looked at the Messenger (PBUH) and implored him: "For Allah's sake, Nahro; for Allah's sake, Nahro". He was asking the Messenger (PBUH) to keep Shaikh Nahro under his care. Asking the Messenger (PBUH) to take care of Shaikh Nahro, but not asking the same for anyone else, including himself, demonstrates the extent of our Shaikh's love for Shaikh Nahro. The Prophet (PBUH) continued to look at our Shaikh without saying anything. The man standing next to the Prophet (PBUH) said that Nahro was the Shaikh's eldest son. The Prophet (PBUH) ordered our Shaikh and his companions to sit so that he could give them something for blessings. He told the standing man to bring a pair of scissors to gift them some hair from the front of his noble head. He placed a towel on the ground to protect the hair from falling on the ground and began cutting the Prophet's (PBUH) hair. Our Shaikh could hear the sound of the hair being cut. The intense blackness of the hair made it reflect colours. After a tuft of hair was cut, it grew in length. When it was given to our Shaikh, he put it around his neck, held its ends in his hands, began to cry tears of joy and started saying that he would take it to his children and would not give any of it to anyone else. The standing man mentioned that ʿAlī, our Shaikh's nephew, who was in Sulaymāniyya, was sick. He was suffering from a heart condition, had lost a lot of weight, and was depressed. The doctors were unable to help him. The Messenger (PBUH) positively responded to the request, and the patient was cured immediately.[199]

---

[199] Shaikh Muḥammad al-Muḥammad al-Kasnazān, *sermon*, 26th/May/2000; 10th/February/2016.

Photo 20: Shaikh Muḥammad al-Muḥammad during the Friday prayer in the takya in Baghdad, and next to him is the martyred poet ʿAlī Fāyiz (middle of the 1990s).

Photo 21: Shaikh Muḥammad al-Muḥammad in a preaching session in the takya in Sulaymāniyya, Iraq (middle of the 2000s).

"I am like you. I belong to the takya; I belong to the Shaikhs. I am one of your brothers — a dervish. However, the Shaikhs have assigned special obligations to me. They have placed me in Shaikh ʿAbd al-Karīm's position. This is an order from Allah, from the honourable Messenger (PBUH), from the Shaikhs. I am one of you in the Ṭarīqa, but I have more obligations, as they have placed me in the place of the honourable Messenger (PBUH)".

Shaikh Muḥammad al-Muḥammad al-Kasnazān
(Sermon, 1st/February/2018)

10

Shaikh of the Ṭarīqa

As we have seen, the present Shaikh of Ṭarīqa announces who his successor will be before his departure from this world so that there is no doubt in the matter. The Shaikh's appointment is by the Prophet's (PBUH) choice, which is a spiritual designation that people cannot intellectually infer. For example, a few years before his demise, Sulṭān 'Abd al-Qādir announced that his son Ḥusayn would succeed him. Sulṭān Ḥusayn entrusted his brother 'Abd al-Karīm with many responsibilities of the Ṭarīqa and its dervishes when he was younger than eighteen, that is, about eight years before Shaikh Ḥusayn passed on to the spirit world. He also told the dervishes, years before his demise, that Shaikh 'Abd al-Karīm would succeed him to the Ṭarīqa Shaikhdom. As for Shaikh 'Abd al-Karīm, he revealed his successor seven years before he departed this world. When he went for hajj in 1971, he made Shaikh Muḥammad al-Muḥammad his deputy, leaving him in charge of the affairs of the takya and the dervishes. Our present Shaikh has followed suit by designating his eldest son, Nahro, as his General Deputy and Shaikh of Ṭarīqa after him.

The present Shaikh may entrust his General Deputy with some of the Ṭarīqa's responsibilities, such as managing the takya, but he remains the only Master of the Ṭarīqa, as the Ṭarīqa cannot have more than one Shaikh at a time. The General Deputy is the future Shaikh, but while the Shaikh is alive, he is just another one of the Ṭarīqa's disciples. After the Shaikh's passing, however, the General Deputy becomes the Shaikh of Ṭarīqa and all of its spiritual and worldly affairs are transferred to him.

10.1 Resuming the Shaikhdom of the Ṭarīqa

Shaikh 'Abd al-Karīm suffered from a heart condition, and Shaikh Muḥammad al-Muḥammad made arrangements take him to Britain for treatment. On Wednesday morning 1st/February/1978, he was in poor health. While sitting on a chair at home, he felt a pain in his chest. He wanted to go to our Shaikh's house next door when he suddenly fell to the ground. Someone phoned our Shaikh, and he hurried over to find Shaikh ʿAbd al-Karīm sitting on the floor with the help of an assistant. Our Shaikh took him to the Republican Hospital in Kirkuk and kept him company, staying in a room opposite his Master's room. One karāma of Shaikh ʿAbd al-Karīm that astonished medical staff in the hospital is that a machine for treating heart conditions that had been in disuse for a while began working again when it was needed to treat the Shaikh.

Shaikh ʿAbd al-Karīm stayed in the hospital for three days, during which doctors injected him with sedatives. As soon as he would wake up from the coma and open his eyes he would ask for a prayer mat, even though his health prevented him from doing so, before going back into the coma. At 9:50 PM on Saturday 4th/February/1978, the Shaikh of Ṭarīqa passed on to his Lord's presence.

Strangely, all four Kasnazānī Shaikhs died of a heart attack, each living for a short while after the attack before passing on to the eternal realm. Shāh al-Kasnazān remained for one night, Sulṭān ʿAbd al-Qādir for one hour, Sulṭān Ḥusayn for three days, while Sulṭān ʿAbd al-Karīm remained for three days.[200]

After washing and shrouding the noble body and reciting the Qur'an over it, our Shaikh wept, saying: "For years I have been crying over this hour, not only now". These feelings reflect not only the tremendous grief that our Shaikh felt at the loss of his Shaikh but also the Ṭarīqa's heavy burden that was now on his shoulders. Overbearing grief remained visible on our present Shaikh throughout the mourning (photo 23).

A group of dervishes prepared a grave for Shaikh ʿAbd al-Karīm in the hall of the shrines of the Shaikhs in Karbchna, which was being renovated at the time. His noble body was transferred to Karbchna on Sunday morning, with the burial ceremony completed at 1:30 PM. Villagers stood all along the road between Kirkuk and Karbchna, which was more than a hundred kilometres long, to bid farewell to a Shaikh whose reputation spanned the horizon. The passing of a Shaikh of Ṭarīqa is not a mere move from the material world to the spirit world because the Shaikhs of Ṭarīqa are alive with Allah, receiving provision. Their karāmas

---

[200] Shaikh Muḥammad al-Muḥammad al-Kasnazān, *sermon*, 8th/May/2000.

that perpetually continue after their departure from this life attest to this fact. With the passing of Sulṭān ʿAbd al-Karīm, his General Deputy, Shaikh Muḥammad al-Muḥammad, succeeded him to the Ṭarīqa's Shaikhdom.

Condolences were accepted at a mosque in the Iskān area and in a large tent near the Shaikh's house in Kirkuk. Due to Shaikh ʿAbd al-Karīm's reputation and large number of dervishes, people who loved him, and others who wanted to offer their condolences, our Shaikh continued to welcome mourners for many days after the death of the Shaikh. This was necessary because many dervishes lived in remote areas where there were no quick means of communication or transportation, so it took some time for the news of the Shaikh's passing to reach them. The Iraqi President, Aḥmad Ḥasan al-Bakr, sent a representative on his behalf to attend the funeral reception. The Iraqi government also issued a decree allowing incoming mourners from Iran, where there is a large number of dervishes, to enter the country through the Sulaymāniyya governorate without needing to obtain a visa.

When a Master of Ṭarīqa passes on to the spirit world and his successor assumes the Ṭarīqa's Shaikhdom, his dervishes must pledge their allegiance to the new Shaikh. This pledge does not involve taking the Ṭarīqa's entire pledge anew. Rather, it includes the seeker accepting that the new Shaikh is now his Master. The following beautiful incident demonstrates the fact that the Shaikh of Ṭarīqa's designation is a spiritual affair that everyone must comply with. On the third day of mourning in our Master's guest house, Shaikh Muḥammad Ṣāliḥ, one of Shaikh ʿAbd al-Karīm's brothers, stood up and announced that he would be the first to pledge his allegiance to Shaikh Muḥammad al-Muḥammad as Master of the Ṭarīqa after Shaikh ʿAbd al-Karīm. Our Master addressed Shaikh Ṭāhir, Sulṭān Ḥusayn's eldest son, who was about seventy years old at the time, and said something along the lines of: "You are Shaikh Ḥusayn's son. If you wish to be Shaikh of Ṭarīqa, I am prepared to serve you as I served Shaikh ʿAbd al-Karīm". Shaikh Ṭāhir knew, however, that the Ṭarīqa's Shaikhs had chosen Shaikh Muḥammad al-Muḥammad as their successor. He replied that our Shaikh was the most qualified for this trust. He then gathered his brothers, children, and grandchildren and led them to kiss our Shaikh's hand and to pledge their allegiance to him. Our Shaikh officially assumed the Shaikhdom on the third day of mourning.

All the caliphs and dervishes who were present pledged their allegiance to the new Shaikh of Ṭarīqa by saying: "I accept you as my Master and my guide in this life and the hereafter". That pledge took about three hours to complete because of the tremendous number of disciples who were present. Still, caliphs and dervishes kept coming to pledge allegiance to the new Shaikh for more than a week afterwards.

When a new Shaikh assumes the Ṭarīqa's Shaikhdom, the hearts of some disciples find it difficult to accept the new Shaikh as a successor to the departed Shaikh. This difficulty arises as a result of a combination of the extreme love for the late Shaikh that over the years grew in the seeker's heart, especially if he accompanied his Shaikh for a long time, and the tremendous pain that he feels as a result of separating from that Master. The disciple may suffer, for example, when he finds someone else sitting on his late Shaikh's chair or uses any of his belongings, even if it is the new Shaikh who was appointed by the late Shaikh, because the love of the disciple for his Shaikh is unique. However, by way of a karāma from the Shaikhs, the disciple's love for his departed Shaikh quickly expands to include the new Shaikh, occupying the unique place of "the present Shaikh" in the disciple's heart. It is impossible for any true lover of the departed Shaikh to not find love for the new Shaikh invading his heart so that he finds that he sees, loves, and treats his new Master the same way he saw, loved, and treated the late Shaikh. In the previous chapter, we saw that dervishes who possessed ḥāls begin to feel attracted to the future Shaikh a while before the present Shaikh's demise, and they also see spiritual unveilings in dreams and wakefulness that assure their hearts and minds of the transference of the Ṭarīqa's Shaikhdom and make them accept it. Thus, they became disciples of the new Shaikh as they were once disciples of the departed Shaikh.

Whatever love for the Shaikh that appears in the disciple's heart is a facet of what Allah Almighty refers to in his words: "I bestowed love upon you from Me" (Ṭāhā 39). Our Shaikh uses an analogy to describe how love for the new Shaikh enters the disciple's heart, saying that the Shaikhs of Ṭarīqa make their new successor a receptacle for their honey, so anyone who loves that honey is attracted to him. Anyone who loved the Messenger (PBUH) as a Master and a guide found the same love in his heart for Imām ʿAlī after the Messenger's (PBUH) departure, as he is his spiritual heir. Likewise, love for the new Shaikh appears and grows in the disciple's heart.

It is well known that some disciples would have questions or doubts about the new Shaikh's eligibility to succeed the previous Sheikh. The personal history of the new Shaikh at the time of assuming the Shaikhdom is often dominated by worldly preoccupations, bereft of karāmas and spiritual exploits like those of the departed Shaikh. If the disciple does not remember that this normal situation is the case with almost every new Shaikh, then he may doubt the eligibility of the new Shaikh to the Shaikhdom. The reality, however, that ought to remove all doubt concerning the new Shaikh's qualification is that the late Shaikh chose him, which means that he is chosen by the Prophet (PBUH) and all the Shaikhs of Ṭarīqa.

Many karāmas occur that confirm the new Shaikh's entitlement to the Shaikhdom to help doubtful dervishes, who have forgotten the late Shaikh's will, come back to their senses. Just as there were karāmas and spiritual unveilings regarding Shaikh Muḥammad al-Muḥammad's succession that occurred while Shaikh ʿAbd al-Karīm was alive, many miracles occurred after our Shaikh assumed the Shaikhdom of the Ṭarīqa. One of these instructive karāmas happened to a dervish named Fu`ād Jāsim from the city of Ramādī. He had a firm belief in Shaikh ʿAbd al-Karīm, having witnessed many of his karāmas. About three weeks after the Shaikh's death, this dervish visited caliph Yāsīn Ṣūfī and told him that he had a question he hoped would not upset him. He went on to explain that he believed that Shaikh ʿAbd al-Karīm was the Master of the Ṭarīqa and Sultan of walīs, but he did not know anything about Shaikh Muḥammad al-Muḥammad. It was clear that Jāsim doubted the new Shaikh's succession of his predecessor. Caliph Yāsīn replied that whatever applied to Shaikh ʿAbd al-Karīm was equally true of his successor. He explained that the present Shaikh does not assume the Shaikhdom because he so desires or because he chooses to do so. Rather, this happens according to the Prophet's (PBUH) order, as well as with the approval of all of the Ṭarīqa's Shaikhs. He alerted the dervish that questioning the present Shaikh's eligibility was no small matter.

The next day, dervish Jāsim visited the caliph a second time and told him the following:

> When I visited you yesterday, my heart was not at ease with Shaikh Muḥammad al-Muḥammad's succession of Shaikh ʿAbd al-Karīm. Your

> words reassured me, but not completely. When I went to bed last night, I was still thinking about this issue. In a dream, I saw that I was in Medina, near the al-Salām Gate, which people enter through to visit the Prophet (PBUH). I heard the sound of the Kasnazānī dhikr drum and the voices of dervishes chanting "Ḥayy Allāh, Ḥayy Allāh". Then I heard a voice saying: "Shaikh Muḥammad al-Muḥammad al-Kasnazān has come with Kasnazānī dervishes to visit the Messenger (PBUH)". My heart rejoiced at this. I wanted to visit the Messenger (PBUH), but I thought that since our Shaikh's son and Ṭarīqa's disciples had come, I would wait to visit with them.
>
> Then I saw Shaikh Muḥammad al-Muḥammad walking in front of a large, unending crowd of dervishes who were raising the Ṭarīqa Kasnazāniyya banner that exists in the main takya in Ramādī. The Shaikh entered from the al-Salām Gate, and I entered behind him. The Shaikh walked until he was facing the Messenger's (PBUH) resting place, and I was behind him. I saw the door to the noble prophetic resting place open like a sliding door, and then the door to the Messenger's (PBUH) shrine also opened like a sliding door. The Messenger (PBUH) came out and embraced Shaikh Muḥammad al-Muḥammad, taking in his scent, while the Shaikh kissed the Prophet's (PBUH) hand. While the Prophet (PBUH) embraced our Shaikh, he looked at me and said: "O Dervish, I am the one who put him in Shaikh ʿAbd al-Karīm's place".

Caliph Yāsīn warned the dervish that if his heart turned away from the Shaikh again, faith may never settle in his heart afterwards.

Something similar happened with another caliph and a cleric, Ḥājj sayyid Ṭāhā, from the Dibis province in the Kirkuk governorate. After Shaikh ʿAbd al-Karīm's departure, this dervish thought that no one could take Shaikh ʿAbd al-Karīm's place, so he did not visit Shaikh Muḥammad al-Muḥammad to pledge his allegiance to him. After a while, he had a dream where he saw several of Shaikh ʿAbd al-Karīm's caliphs whom he knew trying to open a closed door. They failed to open the door no matter how hard they tried. Then, Shaikh Muḥammad al-Muḥammad came and easily opened the door for them. The dream's meaning was clear, so he visited our Shaikh and pledged his allegiance to him. When our Shaikh asked him why he had delayed the visit, he related the dream to him.

On the eighteenth day of his having assumed the Ṭarīqa's Shaikhdom, our Shaikh was sitting in the morning in the takya's courtyard. Those who came to offer their condolences for Shaikh ʿAbd al-Karīm's passing had already left. After a while, an elderly man walked in and greeted the caliph standing at the Shaikh's service, who returned the greeting. The man asked the caliph about "sayyid Muḥammad". The caliph asked him if he was a dervish, and he answered in the affirmative. The caliph reproached him, asking him how he could be a dervish and not know who his Shaikh was, as our Shaikh was sitting in the courtyard. The man replied:

> My father and uncles would travel on foot from Hawīja,[201] where we lived, to visit Sulṭān Ḥusayn. When I was a small child, I asked to go with them to visit the Shaikh. My father tried to dissuade me from travelling with them because the trip took days to complete on foot, but I insisted on visiting the Shaikh. In Karbchna, Sulṭān Ḥusayn called me over to him and gave me the pledge. I haven't visited the Shaikh since then.

The caliph asked him, in wonder, why he had come to visit Shaikh Muḥammad al-Muḥammad a short while after he had assumed the Shaikhdom, even though he never visited Shaikh ʿAbd al-Karīm during his forty years of Shaikhdom. The man said that Sulṭān Ḥusayn came to him in a dream the night before. Looking upset, he ordered him to go to Shaikh Muḥammad al-Muḥammad. At that moment, our Shaikh intervened and asked the caliph what the man wanted. He told him about the conversation they just had. Our Shaikh instructed the dervish to begin a "khatma" of "*lā ilāha illallāh* (there is no god but Allah)", and then "*Allāh*", which are the first two dhikrs of the Ṭarīqa Kasnazāniyya's nineteen perennial dhikrs. He also instructed him to continue to visit now and then. A "khatma" of any dhikr in the Ṭarīqa Kasnazāniyya means reciting that dhikr one hundred thousand times. When the dervish realised that the one who was sitting on the chair and speaking was the Shaikh, he approached him and greeted him.

A karāma that relates to Shaikh ʿAbd al-Karīm's death came to light on the third day after his departure to the spirit world. A caliph from the Gambia named Ibrāhīm ʿAbd Allāh Jāllū came to the funeral reception. He had taken the Ṭarīqa's pledge years ago when he was receiving an education in Islamic studies in Ramādī. Before his death, Shaikh ʿAbd al-Karīm appeared to the caliph and instructed him to attend the funeral reception in Kirkuk. The dervish immediately began making travel

[201] The Hawīja district is in Kirkuk, about 160 kilometres from Karbchna.

arrangements, and he arrived on the third day of the funeral reception.

Ibrāhīm had witnessed a karāma of Shaikh ʿAbd al-Karīm many years earlier, even before becoming a dervish. After taking the Ṭarīqa's pledge in Ramādī's main takya, he asked the caliph who gave him the pledge about a majestic man in a picture on the wall. The caliph told him said that it is Shaikh ʿAbd al-Karīm, Master of the Ṭarīqa. When this dervish heard this, he said "Praise be to Allah" three times, then reached into his pocket and pulled out a small book, that could almost fit into the palm of your hand. It was "Burda al-Madīḥ", Imām al-Būsīrī's famous poem in praise of the Prophet (PBUH). He went on to tell the caliph the following:

> When I was in my third year of secondary schooling, this man came to me (he pointed to Shaikh ʿAbd al-Karīm's picture) in a dream and showed me this book. He said: "My son, take this book. When you finish your secondary schooling and come to study in Iraq, come visit me in Kirkuk". At the time, I was living in my brother's house because my school was far from my family's home. The next morning, on my way to school, I visited a bookstore on my route. I found the book that the Shaikh showed me in the dream on display. When I wanted to buy it, the shopkeeper told me that I would not benefit from it because it was in Arabic, but I bought it anyway.
>
> About a month later, someone told me that my brother's house had burned down. The news shocked and disturbed me. I kept thinking about the book. When I reached the house, I found that the fire had rendered it into ashes, as it was made from wood, like all houses there. I went to the room where the bookcase was and reached into the ashes that covered the ground hoping to find the book. I found it intact — the fire had not touched it, unlike the rest of the books.

During the ceremonies of the fortieth day after Shaikh ʿAbd al-Karīm's death, our Shaikh was sitting in the shrines' outside courtyard in Karbchna, facing the mountain, when he advised to the dervishes who were present, saying something along the lines of:

> O Dervishes! Look after your behaviour as dervishes and preach. Shaikh ʿAbd al-Karīm was a piece of light from Allah. I am not Shaikh ʿAbd al-Karīm. Shaikh ʿAbd al-Karīm was Master of the Ṭarīqa for forty years, while I have only completed forty days as of today. Those present should tell those who aren't, and if there is anyone among you that do not see me, (he rose from the chair and stood so that all the disciples could see him), know that none of you will see any blessing from me, even by this much (he pointed to his fingertip),

except by way of hard work and merit.

Shaikh Muḥammad al-Muḥammad's statement represented a change in granting spiritual gifts. Shaikh ʿAbd al-Karīm used to grant spiritual power to many caliphs and dervishes, even if they were not exceptional worshippers; the blessing was mostly gifted, rather than earned. As for our present Shaikh, he emphasizes the need for the disciple to earn spiritual power from the Shaikh through worship.

Sometime after the ceremonies of the fortieth day ended, our Shaikh decided to perform ʿumrah. He went to Karbchna to visit the shrines. Some dervishes, who were accompanying him on the visit, entered the shrines with our Shaikh. Three of them would go with him for ʿumrah. After greeting the Shaikhs and reading the opening chapter of the Qur'an for them, he asked Shaikh ʿAbd al-Karīm for permission to perform ʿumrah. At that moment, the Shaikh's tomb began to shake, and it continued to do so for more than a couple of minutes. The vibration was visible to all who were present. It was so intense that it even tilted the covering on the shrine to one side until it fell. In addition to accompanying Shaikh ʿAbd al-Karīm for ḥajj in 1973 (photos 10, 11), our Shaikh also performed ʿumrah once in the first half of 1978.

All the Kasnazānī Shaikhs wore Kurdish clothing, and such is the case with our Shaikh, although the design of his clothing differs slightly from Shaikh ʿAbd al-Karīm's style of dress. About two or three months after our Shaikh assumed the Ṭarīqa's Shaikhdom, he was visiting the Shaikhs in Karbchna when a caliph, who had served Shaikh ʿAbd al-Karīm, approached him, carrying an outfit similar to the clothes Shaikh ʿAbd al-Karīm used to wear. He asked our Master to wear what he called "the clothes of Shaikhdom" during his visit to the shrines. This request upset our Shaikh, who answered: "Shaikhdom is not tied to clothes. Even if I wore European clothing, I would still be the Shaikh of Ṭarīqa". True Islam and nearness to Allah are not based on one's external looks, including what they wear. Rather, it is based on the love and consciousness they have for Allah in their heart. Our Shaikh often wears the Arab cloak over his Kurdish clothes when receiving guests.

10.2 Karāmas That Confirm the Muḥammadan Inheritance

Many karāmas and spiritual unveilings foretold Shaikh Muḥammad al-Muḥammad's succession of Shaikh ʿAbd al-Karīm as Master of the Ṭarīqa. We have also seen a number of miracles that occurred after our Shaikh assumed the Ṭarīqa's Shaikhdom. Here we will recount other karāmas that confirm his state of being an inheritor to the Prophet (PBUH).

On 10th/October/2012, a car broke down in front of the takya's land in Saraipalya, Bangalore, India before the takya was built. Three men got out of the car, one of whom turned out to be a businessman, another an engineer, and the third a professor of Sufism named Ḥaydar ʿAlī. Having noticed the takya's flag, when they entered, they inquired about the place. Caliph ʿImād ʿAbd al-Ṣamad told them that it was a takya of the Ṭarīqa ʿAlīyya Qādiriyya Kasnazāniyya, whose Master was Shaikh Muḥammad al-Muḥammad al-Kasnazān al-Ḥusaynī.

The caliph offered the pledge to the professor and explained how it was necessary to take the pledge at the hand of a perfected Shaikh. He explained the qualities of a perfected Shaikh. The words had an impact on the professor's heart, who expressed his desire to take up the Ṭarīqa. The caliph told them that their car would start after they took the pledge, as Allah would have fulfilled the good that He wanted for them in having the car break down in front of the takya. The professor said that they would see if what he promised was true, and they all took the pledge.

The professor asked if the car would now start, and caliph ʿImād answered in the affirmative. They wanted to open the bonnet of the car to examine the engine, but the caliph dissuaded them from doing so, as he had promised them that the car would start. He asked them to get into the car, close the doors, and start the engine. The car started, and they were happy with the karāma. The professor got out of the car, kissed the hands and feet of the caliph, and donated a sum of money to the takya. Amazed at what had happened, the professor said that his house was near the takya so he would stay in touch with the caliph.

The next day, the professor came with five or six people. He knelt at the takya's door before entering. After introducing his friends, he said that he wanted to relate something that happened to him the day before. Caliph ʿImād thought that the professor wanted to recount to his friends the karāma of the broken car starting without repair. He surprised, however, with what he had to say:

> After I left yesterday, some doubts arose in my heart. I thought to myself: "I am a professor of Sufism, so how can this person teach me, give me the pledge, etc.?" I felt envious. When I arrived home, I was tired, so I slept. I had a dream in which I saw this takya, and you were sitting in this exact place in the same position. I gradually got closer to you, but I was surprised when I found that the face was not yours; it was of an older person. That man called to me, so I sat beside him. He started to tell me the same things you told me. I said: "My Master, I heard these words yesterday from someone who was sitting here. He was wearing clothes a green shawl similar to yours, but his face was different". The person replied: "Yes, that was Shaikh Muḥammad al-Muḥammad al-Kasnazān's caliph. I am the Messenger of Allah's caliph, ʿAlī Ibn Abī Ṭālib. When you put your hand in the hand of Shaikh Muḥammad al-Muḥammad's deputy, you put your hand in ours".

The professor began to cry, and those present were overcome with awe. Then he went on to say that Imām ʿAlī Ibn Abī Ṭālib added:

> We, the family of the prophetic household, have authorised our inheritor Shaikh Muḥammad al-Muḥammad ʿAbd al-Karīm al-Kasnazān to speak on our behalf.

The very same day, caliph ʿImād phoned our Shaikh's assistant in Amman to tell him about this karāma. The latter informed him that the night before, Shaikh Muḥammad al-Muḥammad said that he has permission to speak on behalf of the prophetic household.[202]

The following vision that our Shaikh's caliph in India saw in Bangalore, on 11th/September/2013, confirms that our Master promotes the Messenger's (PBUH) way:

> While I was waiting for the time of the afternoon prayer, I fell asleep. I had a dream in which I saw myself in Medina, peace and blessings be upon its owner. I was standing at the end of a long queue of people. We were waiting for the Prophet (PBUH) to come out from his resting place under the green dome so that we could visit him. Suddenly, everybody turned to me and said: "Come, the Messenger (PBUH) is asking for you". I also turned around to see if these people were addressing someone behind me, but there was no one. At that moment, the line of people split in two, allowing me to walk through the

---

[202] Fatoohi, *The Wonders of Ṭarīqa Kasnazāniyya Brought to India*, pp. 47-49.

middle. I walked with extreme shyness. I saw the Messenger (PBUH) standing near the door. He looked tired and was leaning on Shaikh Muḥammad al-Muḥammad al-Kasnazān for support. Our Shaikh's right hand was behind the Messenger's back, under his noble armpit on the right. He (PBUH) had his left hand on Shaikh Muḥammad al-Muḥammad's shoulder. I said: "Allah is the greatest! The Messenger (PBUH) is tired? Why?" The Shaikh gestured with his noble head to come closer. Before I got closer, I could see some of the Messenger's (PBUH) features, but as I moved closer, thick clouds gathered around both of them, so I could only see the Shaikh's face. When I was close, I heard the Messenger (PBUH) say: "He is the only one who lifted me", meaning the Shaikh.[203]

Let's cite another of the many karāmas that speak of Shaikh Muḥammad al-Muḥammad's succession to the Prophet (PBUH). A man from Egypt took the Ṭarīqa Kasnazāniyya pledge a long time ago, but instead of committing to its methods and dhikrs to see proof of the way to Allah, he went from Shaikh to Shaikh. He was unaware that he needed to adhere to the Ṭarīqa's method, rather than go to a new Shaikh now and then, to see its blessing so that his heart would gain certainty. This is the karāma as related by this dervish:

I am a man who worships a lot. I am a lover of the prophetic household and of righteous people. I used to always think about the chief walī of this time, and I would often ask Allah to guide me to and acquaint me with him. I would always visit Imām Ḥusayn. On my last visit, I begged him to tell me who the chief walī and Muḥammadan Inheritor of this age was. I saw a dream in which I was in a large sacred place. The Greatest Messenger (PBUH) was present in the form of a tremendous light, sitting on a luxurious throne. All the members of the prophetic household were to his right and left, all with absolute poise, in an atmosphere of tremendous spirituality. I approached him with reverence, with my head and gaze cast downward. I crawled over to him and kissed his noble feet. I heard him say: "My child! My inheritor and my son in this era is from Iraq. He is Shaikh Muḥammad al-Muḥammad al-Kasnazān, and he is the Pole of Guidance (*quṭb al-irshād*) in this age". when I raised my head up towards his noble face, I saw Shaikh Muḥammad al-Muḥammad al-Kasnazān himself sitting on the throne, with Imām ʿAlī Ibn Abī Ṭālib sitting on his right. The Imām stood up and hugged Shaikh Muḥammad al-Muḥammad al-Kasnazān out of happiness and delight and

---

[203] Fatoohi, *The Wonders of Ṭarīqa Kasnazāniyya Brought to India*, p. 51.

said: "He is my son, my soul, he is from my flesh and blood".

The man renewed the Kasnazānī pledge at the hand of a caliph of our Shaikh in Egypt.

In §9.2, we saw the karāmas where the Messenger (PBUH) named our Shaikh "Muḥammad al-Muḥammad" and where the Ṭarīqa's Shaikhs told him that he was Allah's representative on earth. Both of these point to our Master's being an inheritor to the Prophet (PBUH). Countless karāmas have illustrated that Allah and his noble Messenger have chosen the Shaikhs of the Ṭarīqa ʿAlīyya Qādiriyya Kasnazāniyya and Shaikh Muḥammad al-Muḥammad al-Kasnazān to occupy the Ṭarīqa's Shaikhdom and the deputyship of the Prophet (PBUH).

Photo 22: Shaikh ʿAbd al-Karīm in his last visit to the shrine of Shaikh ʿAbd al-Qādir al-Gaylānī, helped by Mullā Muḥammad Amīn (end of 1977).

Photo 23: Shaikh Muḥammad al-Muḥammad during the funeral ceremony of his father and Master of the Tarīqa before him Shaikh ʿAbd al-Karīm, in Kirkuk. Sadness and the heavy responsibility of the Tarīqa clearly show on him (February/1978).

"The dervish must have the manners, etiquette, and behaviours of the Messenger (PBUH). The dervish must emulate the honourable Messenger (PBUH). Anyone who hurts his family, his kin, or people in general, is not a dervish. The dervish must apply the noble ḥadīth to himself: 'The best of people are those who benefit others'.[204] He must be among the best of people".

Shaikh Muḥammad al-Muḥammad al-Kasnazān
(Sermon, 22nd/January/2010)

---

[204] Bayhaqī, *Shu'ab al-Īmān*, VI, no. 7658, p. 117. This ḥadīth also occurs in the form "the best of people are those who are most beneficial to people" (Ṭabarānī, *al-Mu'jam al-Āwsaṭ*, VI, no. 5787, p. 58).

11

Muḥammadan Traits

A prophet's muʿjizas are necessary for people to believe in his message. Prophethood is a call related to the unseen, so for those who live in the visible world to believe in it, they need evidence of its belonging to the unseen world is needed. Paranormal events are proofs of the reality of the unseen world that prophethood speaks of, as they are a window in the natural world into the supernatural world. Their originating from a prophet also proves that that particular prophet has been sent by Allah Almighty, the Knower of the seen and unseen. Muʿjizas humble the intellect and assure it of the messenger's truthfulness. Religion presents a unique, consistent interpretation of life and the universe, both its visible and hidden aspects. Supernatural occurrences are proofs of this understanding.

Yet, faith is more than just an intellectual conviction. It is also a state of the heart. Faith is a combination of conviction of the intellectual and love in the heart. A person's actions are not solely driven by their intellectual convictions. In fact, the role of rational arguments and logic is limited in comparison to the role of emotional drivers. Feelings play a bigger role in a person's actions, even if people are tempted to believe that their actions are more rational than emotional because this belief makes them feel like their actions are closer to being right. A person often justifies their actions, including their mistakes, using rational arguments and logic, when it is clear to others that their actions are emotionally driven. Hence, rational conviction does not suffice as a method to mend a man's actions to align them with religion's requirements. A person needs to have love in their heart that inclines them towards good deeds and diverts them from doing bad. If mental conviction comes from the logic of prophethood and its miracles, then what is this love in the heart and what is its source?

11.1 The Necessity of Refined Manners for Spiritual Leadership

This love is the love for Allah (mighty and sublime is He). Its origin is love for the one whom Allah sent as a guide to Him. No human being knew the Sender (mighty and sublime is He) except by way of a messenger from Him. Hence, the messenger must reflect the beautiful attributes of the Sender so that love for the messenger and, consequently, love for the Sender can grow in the heart of the person to whom the messenger was sent. Allah blessed our Master Muḥammad (PBUH) by showering him with the most beautiful of traits. He addressed him in His noble Book, praising his noble qualities: "Indeed, you are of a great moral character" (al-Qalam 4). One of the great character traits that our noble Prophet (PBUH) has is his mercy and compassion for believers:

> "There has certainly come to you a Messenger from among yourselves, grievous to him is what you suffer, concerned over you is he, to the believers he is kind and merciful". (Al-Tawba 128)
>
> "Among them are those who abuse the Prophet and say, 'He is an ear'. Say, '[It is] an ear of goodness for you that believes in Allah, believes the believers, and is a mercy to those who believe among you'. Those who hurt the Messenger of Allah — for them is a painful punishment". (Al-Tawba 61)

The noble Qur'an shows us how the Prophet Muḥammad's (PBUH) mercy and softheartedness were necessary for the success of his mission:

> "So by mercy from Allah [O Muḥammad!] you have been lenient with them. Had you been rude, harsh in heart, they would have disbanded from about you. So pardon them, ask forgiveness for them and consult them in the matter. When you have decided, then rely upon Allah. Indeed, Allah loves those who are reliant". (ʿĀl 'Imrān 159)

It is evident that the noble verse is referring to those who were physically close to the Messenger (PBUH), that is "the Companions". If the Prophet (PBUH) did not show mercy, softheartedness, and tenderness, which are opposite to harshness, coarseness, and incivility, even his closest Companions would have left him. It is clear from the command to the Prophet (PBUH) to pardon and forgive them that he treated them with mercy and softheartedness, rather than rudeness or harshness, even when they made mistakes.

There is great wisdom in this divine revelation: even the revelation of the magnificent Qur'an in their midst over the years and their direct and continuous witnessing an abundance of miracles of the Prophet (PBUH) would not have been enough to prevent his Companions from deserting him, had Allah not combined them with the putting exceptional mercy and deep tenderness in his (PBUH) heart. This mercy was behind many of his miracles that helped people with their needs, thus helping them in both religious and worldly matters. The secret behind Islam's continuous spreading is not solely the Qur'an, as those who wish to belittle or limit the role of the Messenger (PBUH) claim, nor it even the Qur'an and miracles alone. The secret is a combination of the Qur'an, the miracles of the Qur'an's possessor (PBUH), and his wholesome traits of mercy, softness, and compassion.[205]

Wholesome character traits are a necessity of prophethood. This way, the prophet — that is, any prophet — can be an exemplary role model, as Allah (exalted and high is He) has described our noble prophet: "There has certainly been for you in the Messenger of Allah an excellent pattern for anyone whose hope is in Allah and the Last Day and [who] remembers Allah often" (al-Āḥzāb 21). Following any prophet means taking him as an exemplar, so he must exemplify the qualities that Allah wants people to have. Admirable traits also attract hearts, the same way loathsome traits repel them. It is, thus, incumbent upon every prophet to be of an elevated moral character. Hence, Allah Almighty commends our Master Muḥammad's (PBUH) moral character beyond all praise: "Indeed, you are of a tremendous moral character" (al-Qalam 4). The Messenger (PBUH) said: "I have not been sent except to perfect the best of conduct".[206] He (PBUH) also directly linked Īmān with moral character: "The most perfect of believers are those best in character".[207]

In addition to an elevated moral character, there are abilities and talents that any position of leadership, including spiritual leadership, requires. These elevated manners and leadership qualities met in the Messenger Muḥammad (PBUH). He was the best messenger and the best of mankind.

---

[205] Fatoohi, *Ṣifāt Qiyādiyya Lil-Nabī Muḥammad (PBUH).*

[206] Bayhaqī, *Al-Sunan al-Kubrā*, X, no. 20782, p. 323; Aḥmad, *Musnad al-Imām Aḥmad Ibn Ḥanbal*, XIV, no. 8952, p. 513.

[207] Ṭabarānī, *al-Mu'jam al-Ṣaghīr*, I, no. 605, p. 362.

11.2 Prophetic Traits in Shaikh Muḥammad al-Muḥammad al-Kasnazān

Since the Ṭarīqa's Shaikhs are representatives of the Prophet (PBUH), who selected them from among people, Allah has bequeathed his states to them. The same way karāmas happen at the hands of a Shaikh of Ṭarīqa because they are an extension of the Prophetic muʿjizas and ceaseless proof of these miracles, the Shaikh also inherits the Prophet's (PBUH) moral character. There are countless and endless karāmas of Shaikh Muḥammad al-Muḥammad al-Kasnazān that make sound minds recognize his inheritance of the way and blessing of the Messenger (PBUH). He has Muḥammadan traits that attract the living heart and assures it that he is a Muḥammadan Inheritor.

In §9.2, we mentioned that Allah gazes upon whom he chooses as Shaikh of the Ṭarīqa with the eye of special providence and nurturing, even before his birth. He provides him with the means that grant him whatever attributes He wants for him. When he assumes the Ṭarīqa's Shaikhdom, his internal state, conduct, and qualities begin to transform and evolve, rapidly and tremendously, to reflect the requirements and responsibilities of the General Deputyship of the Messenger (PBUH) among people. We will review some of the Muḥammadan traits that Shaikh Muḥammad al-Muḥammad al-Kasnazān has.

11.2.1 Attractive Personality

Allah graced our Shaikh with an attractive, uniquely wholesome personality that endeared him to people since he was a child. This personality was one of Allah's favours that is related to his future role as Master of the Ṭarīqa: "I bestowed love upon you from Me" (Ṭāhā 39). The blessing of the Shaikhdom of the Ṭarīqa multiplied this wholesomeness, causing love for him to spontaneously and directly enter the hearts of all who saw him. This effect is not something that only dervishes feel, but it extends to people in general. Often, people who have met him for the first would mention his endearing personality. This helped our Shaikh succeed in establishing a wide range of social relationships with different people, old and young, rich and poor.

This charisma made him naturally sociable, always surrounded by people, and his assembly never free of visitors. Even when he would go out for whatever reason, he would always like to have others accompany him. This trait is adorned by an interest in and awareness of different kinds of knowledge, as well as an exceptional ability to engage with people and exchange views on various scientific, cultural, and political subjects.

His attractive personality, leadership qualities, and the people's trust in him gave him, since his youth, great social standing among tribal chieftains and community elders. They would listen to what he had to say and often turn to him to resolve their problems and disputes. They would treat him like a clan chieftain while he was still just a young man.

His love for defending the oppressed made him a mecca for the weak. Many would turn to him and live in his village, under his protection, escaping from those who oppressed and harmed them. He was brave and unyielding when confronting any oppressor, and he was not afraid of blame when standing for what is right.

11.2.2 Strategic Thinking

So that he could be the Prophet's (PBUH) representative in leading the Ṭarīqa and shouldering the responsibility of spreading it far and wide, Allah blessed our Shaikh with leadership qualities and a strategic outlook that enabled him to see into the future and perceive what the majority of people would fail to see. Sometimes he plans something or does something that people do not understand at the time, and many years pass before its benefits appear. He also can make decisions and do things that involve a fair amount of risk, but these are calculated risks and far from being reckless or inconsiderate. An example of this is his historic decision after he became Master of the Ṭarīqa to move the centre of Ṭarīqa from Kirkuk in northern Iraq to the capital of Baghdad, despite the sensitivity of government authorities at the time to religious movements and organizations in general. Besides, he was seen as a Kurd, despite descending from the Prophet (PBUH), at a time when the state and the Kurdish nationalist movement were in a state of unstable peace.

11.2.3 Multitasking

Another leadership quality of our Shaikh is his ability to simultaneously manage several responsibilities, completely different from one another, with clear vision and efficiency. Within a very short period, he may discuss details of building a takya in any given country, propose solutions to certain agricultural problems on his farm, prescribe dhikrs and herbal remedies to diseased dervishes who have come to visit him, check out new book releases to choose what he would like to read, discuss sending a preaching delegation of caliphs to any given country, and other tasks that completely differ from one another. Managing these responsibilities not only requires the ability to understand the details of each case adequately and make the right decisions but also to be able to do all this very quickly. A large number of responsibilities means that there is limited time to manage them all. Managing different responsibilities requires special talent that is a necessity of our Master's position of leadership.

11.2.4 Working Hard

Managing many responsibilities at the same time requires the person to be hardworking and willing to dedicate as much time and effort the different tasks need. Since his childhood, our Shaikh has been diligent and assiduous and has disliked laziness. When he was at school, he enjoyed his studies and was an assiduous student. He was only eighteen years old when his older brother Ḥusayn died, so he took over the many tribal and social responsibilities of his father and Shaikh of Ṭarīqa. He also managed his father's agricultural lands. Had not had excellent work ethics, he would not have joined the Kurdish movement and lived six years of extreme hardship and austerity.

Throughout his life, our Shaikh continued to work hard. You would see him, for example, in one day visiting a manuscript library looking for works of interest; overseeing agricultural work on his farms; receiving various visiting guests, caliphs, and dervishes; discussing projects for building and renovating takyas; and other tasks. Our Shaikh always urges dervishes to work hard and diligently. He often repeats the well-known saying: "There is a blessing in moving". Only advancing in age and deterioration of his health gradually limited his ability to work.

11.2.5 Modesty

One of the Muḥammadan traits that our Shaikh has is modesty that manifests itself in his every word and deed. A sign of this deep modesty is that he avoids attributing any karāma to himself, ascribing it instead to the Prophet (PBUH) or Shaikhs of the Ṭarīqa. Even when the karāma includes clear evidence of his involvement, where he is seen by the person who saw the karāma or had it happen to them, our Shaikh avoids relating it to himself. He repeats the phrase "I seek forgiveness from Allah" when any karāma is mentioned in front of him that is attributed to him, and, instead, ascribes it to the Ṭarīqa's Shaikhs.

Another manifestation of this prophetic modesty is that he describes himself as "Servant of the Poor" — a title that the Ṭarīqa Kasnazāniyya Shaikhs have proudly bestowed upon themselves. The sanctity in which disciples see him and their great reverence for him, being the Master of the Ṭarīqa, do not prevent our Shaikh from describing himself as "Servant of the Poor" and repeating the adage "the people's master is their servant". He gives disciples a striking lesson in humility, obeying Allah's command: "Lower your wing to the believers" (al-Ḥijr 88). We find an explanation of the saying "the people's master is their servant" in the Messenger's (PBUH) ḥadīth: "Most beloved to Allah (exalted is He) are those who benefit people most".[208] Our Shaikh has many beautiful, moving words in this regard:

> "I would cherish that I every day clean the takya myself, wash the takya, and clean the dervishes' shoes. It is an honour for me to clean the shoes of the dervishes who come to the takya seeking Allah's Face because the takya is Allah's house (exalted and high is He): 'In homes that Allah has ordered to be raised and that His name to be mentioned therein' (al-Nūr 36). I am a Shaikh, but I am a servant; I am a Shaikh, but I am the smallest person in the Ṭarīqa. The Shaikh must be a servant, and he must teach his brothers, the caliphs, and his sons, the dervishes, about service".[209]

A sign of our Shaikh's modesty and his service to disciples is his concern for every seeker that visits him and how he allocates time for them, regardless of their social, economic, or cultural standing. Many people of high social standing love to visit him and spend time with him, so if our Shaikh wanted to, he could spend most of his time allocated for visitors with them. While giving attention to society's elite, he spends the

---

[208] Al-Ṭabarānī, *al-Muʿjam al-Kabīr*, XII, no. 13646, p. 453.

[209] Shaikh Muḥammad al-Muḥammad al-Kasnazān, *sermon*, 22nd/December/2005.

majority of his time with people in following up matters relating to dervishes, preaching to them, asking about them, and listening to their needs. A moving situation that our Shaikh's visitors often see is his patiently and attentively listening to the details of the needs of the simplest dervishes, some of whom had just taken the pledge. In addition to praying for the one in need, he may, depending on the need, prescribe a specific dhikr for him, advise him, or direct one of his helpers to give him what he needs — such as preparing herbal medicine for an illness he has, providing him with information he was unaware of, directing him to someone he needs to connect with, helping him by giving him money from the takya fund, and so on. The number of visitors with needs does not dissuade him from demonstrating such concern.

11.2.6 Love for Children

Our Shaikh loves children a lot. He loves playing with his grandchildren and he devotes attention to the children of dervishes when they visit him with their families and speaks to them with tenderness and prays for them. When he goes to the marketplace, he sometimes asks his companions to bring some chocolates or treats to give to children who meet them in the market. Our Shaikh is even affected by the sight of children going to school on foot, and he says that if he could, he would provide a car for every child to take them to and from school.

As our Shaikh's house in Karbchna is located on a small hill, and the number of the houses in the small village does not exceed sixty, the night there is perfectly quiet, so he can hear any relatively loud sound at night. While worshipping at night, the sound of a crying child sometimes reaches him and pains his heart until he finds it difficult to continue his dhikrs or worship. He would ask one of his aids to go to the child's house, enquire why the child is crying and ask the family to try and satisfy the child's need to stop the crying. If they cannot, the aid tries to help them in fulfilling that need.

A karāma of our Shaikh that demonstrates his love for making children happy took places during his visit to the United States at the end of 2014. He was in a Walmart in Virginia when he passed by a small child in a pushchair that was whining and crying. Shortly after passing the child, our Shaikh turned to his companions and asked them to get a nice toy. They selected a toy and brought it to him, but he pointed to a plane on one of the shelves instead, and he asked one of them to buy it for the child. The companion took it to the child's mother and pointed to our Shaikh, who was standing somewhat far away, and told her that he had heard the child crying so he wanted to gift him the toy. The mother was surprised by this strange offer from an elderly man that she did not know, but she agreed. Our Shaikh approached the child and fondly spoke to him. The companion gave the toy to the child, who stopped crying as soon as he got hold of it.

After our Shaikh and his companions went shopping, the companion who purchased the toy remembered that he had forgotten to give the mother the purchase receipt that she needed to present when she left as proof of having paid for the toy. He went back and gave her the receipt. This time, having had the time to reflect on this strange offer, she asked him about the man who had purchased the gift. The companion told her, very briefly, that he was the Master of a big Sufi order in the Middle East and that his name was Muḥammad al-Muḥammad al-Kasnazān. The mother began to cry and said that the child was fatherless and that she had promised him that she would buy him that exact aeroplane, but it was more than she could afford. Although she had roamed around the store with the child, he would not forget the toy and would not stop crying and asking for it. One aspect of this karāma of our Shaikh is his having chosen the same toy that the mother had promised to buy for her child. The mother asked our Shaikh's companion to convey her thanks to him again.

After the companion joined our Shaikh again and told him what the mother had said, Shaikh Nahro wanted to offer the mother financial help, but he rejected the idea to avoid the possibility that the woman would misunderstand this initiative. After our Shaikh finished shopping and headed with his companions towards the casher, they found the child's mother there, paying for simple, basic home necessities. Shaikh Nahro saw this as a sign supporting what he previously thought. He gave his companion a sum of money to pass on to the mother as another gift for the child. He informed her of the wish of our Shaikh's son to gift a sum of money to the child. Flustered, he added that he did not know the reason behind the gift and then handed her the sum. This time, she sobbed uncontrollably. He asked her why she was crying, and she told him that the first time they pleased her son and this time they pleased her because she was badly in need of financial assistance. She said that she could not pay her electricity bill and that this money had come just in time!

11.2.7 Softheartedness

Shaikh Muḥammad al-Muḥammad has a heart that is extremely soft and sensitive, and he is thus inclined to weeping. He quickly bursts into tears when he hears the remembrance of Allah, the Messenger (PBUH) and Shaikhs of the Ṭarīqa. Our Shaikh is particularly sensitive to any mention of Imām Ḥusayn, peace be upon him, and the injustice he and his family suffered. Every year, he hosts a gathering in remembrance and praise of the Messenger (PBUH) and his honourable family in commemoration of Imām Ḥusayn's martyrdom in the battle of al-Ṭaff and for what this unique sacrifice represents in terms of meaning and lessons that will survive to the Day of Judgement.

This softness of his heart is also seen in his interactions with disciples and people in general, and in his response to the hardships and difficult circumstances they face, whether they affect them individually or as groups. The Servant of the Poor is extremely generous with the poor and needy. Many families depend entirely on the assistance of our Shaikh. In recent years, difficult circumstances in Iraq caused by ISIS terrorist activities, which have led to the displacement of many people, have made our Shaikh care for thousand displaced families. He charged his deputy Shaikh Nahro with the responsibility of housing and feeding these families, in addition to looking after their health and the rest of their needs. Our Shaikh ordered that his farm in Dōra, Baghdad, be converted into a massive encampment to shelter displaced disciples of the Ṭarīqa and others, without exception. The number of displaced individuals in the encampment reached thirty-five thousand. The main takya in Sulaymāniyya also received large numbers of those who were forced to leave their homes. Our Shaikh assumed responsibility for their accommodation and living costs.

11.2.8 Helping the Poor and Needy

Our Shaikh considers poverty and destitution as holding serious consequences for the individual and society as a whole. He always reminds dervishes that every Muslim is obligated to help the poor and needy. The following is one of his many sayings in this regard:

> "When people are poor, they turn to impermissible deeds. But if I, you, and others help them, then they will not resort to what is forbidden. Then, the poor person will say: 'Allah has provided for me. My Muslim brothers, my dervish brothers, my good brothers help me; why should I turn to what is forbidden?'"[210]

Our Shaikh cites the noble verse, "cooperate in righteousness and piety" (al-Mā`ida 2), as a reminder that helping the poor and needy is one facet of cooperating in righteous deeds that this noble verse obligates. Our Shaikh also says that this help is one of the responsibilities of the Muslims that the Prophet (PBUH) commanded in his ḥadīth, "Every one of you is a guardian, and every one of you is responsible for his subjects".[211] This responsibility is also a manifestation of the love, compassion, and sympathy that this honourable ḥadīth mentions: "In their mutual love, compassion, and sympathy, the believers are like a body. When a part of it suffers, the whole body responds to it with wakefulness and fever".[212]

Our Master often mentions the noble verse, "spend out of what We have provided for them". The fact that is mentioned in Allah's Book six times (al-Baqara 3, al-Ānfāl 3, al-Ḥajj 35, al-Qaṣaṣ 54, al-Sajda 16, al-Shūrā 38) is a testament to the importance of what it commands. He stresses that the majority of people have misunderstood this noble verse, thinking that it means to provide help to the poor and needy with what exceeds one's need for sustenance. He explains that it urges the Muslim to spend from his daily sustenance, from what he eats and drinks, thus helping the needy from what he spends on himself and his family: "This way he is rewarded. You attain the reward when you think of the poor and orphan children as you think of your children".[213]

11.2.9 Charitableness Towards Orphans

Our Master shows special tenderness towards orphans, whom Allah Almighty singled out for mention in many noble verses. This is also a

---

[210] Shaikh Muḥammad al-Muḥammad al-Kasnazān, *sermon*, 16th/September/2013.

[211] Bukhārī, *Al-Jāmi' al-Ṣaḥīḥ*, I, no. 872, p. 261.

[212] Muslim, *Ṣaḥīḥ Muslim*, IV, no. 2586, p. 1999-2000.

[213] Shaikh Muḥammad al-Muḥammad al-Kasnazān, *sermon*, 11th/August/2013.

trait that all Kasnazānī Shaikhs have had. The following is an incident of our Shaikhs that demonstrates the extent of their love and care for orphans. Sulṭān ʿAbd al-Qādir al-Kasnazān was walking from Shāh al-Kasnazān's reservoir to Karbchna's mosque when he saw two orphans. He reached into his pocket to give them some money, but he did not find any. He asked the dervishes that were with him if they were carrying any money, but they also did not have any. The Shaikh lifted the orphans onto his shoulders and walked until they laughed, then they hopped off him. When people asked why he had done so, he replied that the displeasure of these two orphans would lead to Allah Almighty's being displeased with him. He wanted to give them something to make them happy, and since he did not have any money, he carried them on his shoulders to please them. Shaikh ʿAbd al-Qādir al-Kasnazān would also set aside food from the takya and go out at night to distribute it to orphans himself.

In another exploit of our Shaikhs in this regard, a woman came to meet Sulṭān Ḥusayn al-Kasnazān, but his attendants told her that he was preoccupied with worship. She insisted that they tell the Shaikh that a widow with orphans wanted to greet him. The Shaikh granted her permission to visit him. After greeting him, she said that she was a mother of orphans and did not want to beg people for money, so she was asking for his help. The ascetic Shaikh did not have any money that he could give her, but he did not want to send her back empty-handed either. He pulled a golden tooth he had out of his mouth and gave it to her so that she could sell it and support herself and her orphans.

11.2.10 Caring for the Mentally Ill

Another aspect of our Shaikh's exceptional care for the vulnerable in society is his care for the mentally and psychologically ill, as well as those with special needs. Decades ago, when society lacked the awareness to treat these people with dignity and respect, our Shaikh would care for them, look after their needs, and recommend that they are treated well. When Iraq was under the weight of harsh economic embargoes after its occupation of Kuwait, someone told our Shaikh that there were cases of deaths among inpatients of the al-Rashād hospital for mental health due to a lack of food. These patients suffered from a scarcity of food more than others because they were from the vulnerable groups of society that received the least attention from the government and people in general. Our Shaikh had the main takya in Baghdad send food daily to the hospital. It reached a point where happiness would pervade the hospital's patients as soon as they saw the Kasnazānī emergency aid vehicle. After a while, the government, which treated the Ṭarīqa and everything it did with caution and suspicion, told our Shaikh to stop this humanitarian initiative.

Mentally and psychologically ill patients, as well as those with special needs, sometimes come or are brought to the takya seeking blessings and a cure. Our Master's instruction is to treat them well, even those who suffer from behavioural problems, and to be generous in feeding them.

In the 1980s and 1990s, a retired policeman named ʿAbd Allah (may Allah have mercy on him) with special needs frequented the main takya in Baghdad daily, often for long hours. He had no family that could care for or look after him. Our Shaikh would recommend that he is looked after well, and he treated him with special kindness and chatted with him now and then to teach dervishes to treat this vulnerable group of people with dignity and leniency. When ʿAbd Allah was afflicted with a severe illness, our Shaikh asked a caliph to accompany him for as long as he stayed in the hospital and to donate blood to him. When ʿAbd Allah passed to Allah's mercy, our Master instructed dervishes to bury him, as his family would have done.

11.2.11 Compassion Towards Animals

Our Shaikh's wholesome nature, compassion and softheartedness are not limited to people only. Rather, they encompass all creation, including animals and plants. This is the disposition of all Shaikhs of the Ṭarīqa who inherited softheartedness and sympathy from the traits of their praiseworthy Master (PBUH). The greatest teacher (PBUH) told his companions the following story:

> "A man was walking when he became thirsty. He went down a well and drank from it. As soon as he came out, he came upon a panting dog eating mud out of thirst. He said: 'This dog is suffering from the same thirst I was suffering from'. He [went back down into the well], filled his shoe [with water], gripped it with his teeth, climbed back out and gave the dog water. Allah thanked him and forgave him".

The companions asked him: "O Messenger of Allah, is there a reward for us in serving animals?" He said: "There is a reward in every living thing".[214]

There are many events and karāmas that demonstrate the sympathy of the Shaikhs of Ṭarīqa towards animals and their care for them. We will recount some of these. In the 1990s, the Shaikhs of Tarīqa informed our Shaikh that his fish on his farm in Dōra were hungry. After enquiring from the people in charge of the farm, he learned that the fish had been left without food for three days. He personally went to the farm and fed the fish. The way the fish competed for the food showed how hungry they were.[215]

One day in October 2008, Shaikh Muḥammad al-Muḥammad phoned a caretaker of the Sulaymāniyya takya from Amman and told him that that night, the Shaikhs had informed him that the takya's dogs were hungry and asked him to look after them. When Ḥājj Laṭīf went out looking for the dogs, he found them all gathered in one place as if they were waiting for him! He signalled to them, so they followed him to where he had the food.[216] Our Shaikh would also remind the takya's caretakers now and then of the necessity of feeding the takya's dogs.

A similar karāma occurred one morning in 2014 or 2015. From Amman, our Master contacted a caretaker of his farm in Sulaymāniyya and told him that the Shaikhs had informed him that the dogs were hungry and asked him to feed them. It turned out that those in charge of the farm did not have anything with which to feed the dogs for four days.

Having compassion for animals is a trait shared by all of our Shaikhs. In his youth, Shaikh ʿAbd al-Qādir al-Kasnazān was hunting rabbits when he let the hunting dogs chase one. Unexpectedly, the rabbit ran towards the Shaikh, before jumping onto the saddle of the horse he was riding and sitting in front of him. The rabbit looked up at the Shaikh and tears began to stream from his eyes. When Shaikh ʿAbd al-Qādir saw this supernatural situation, he also began to cry and took what had happened as a sign. He asked his companions, who also witnessed this karāma, to

---

[214] Bukhārī, *Al-Jāmiʿ al-Ṣaḥīḥ*, II, no. 2292, p. 16.

[215] Shaikh Muḥammad al-Muḥammad al-Kasnazān, *sermon*, 29th/10/2019.

[216] Shaikh Muḥammad al-Muḥammad al-Kasnazān, *sermon*, 14th/November/2008; 29th/10/2019.

tie the hunting dogs up and take the rabbit somewhere too far for them to reach it. As a result of this incident, Shaikh ʿAbd al-Qādir abandoned hunting completely.[217]

In spring, a large number of starlings migrate to Iraq. Some people make a business out of hunting, caging, and selling them. When Shaikh ʿAbd al-Karīm al-Kasnazān would see these birds, he would buy all the birds the seller had. He would then reach into the cage and release the birds one by one, smiling.[218]

Mercy towards all of creation is a noble, prophetic trait: "We have not sent you [O Muḥammad] except as a mercy to the worlds" (al-Ānbiyā` 107). Mercy and softheartedness are characteristics that our Shaikh particularly acquired a great deal of after he assumed the Ṭarīqa's Shaikhdom.

11.2.12 Forbearance, Restraint, and Forgiveness

Shaikh Muḥammad al-Muḥammad is forbearing and patient, controls his anger, and is very forgiving. If something upsets him, his anger is fleeting: "Those who spend [in the cause of Allah] during ease and hardship and who restrain anger and who pardon the people. Allah loves the doers of good" (`Āl ʿImrān 134). A beautiful facet of this Qur'anic verse is that it commands us to be charitable and forgiving towards everyone, without discrimination, meaning not only towards Muslims. There are many instances of people hurting our Shaikh one way or another — because of grudge, envy, or enmity towards the Ṭarīqa — with him responding to that harm with patience, restraining his anger, and even showing forgiveness and generosity. These are from the noble prophetic attributes that Allah instilled in his honourable prophet (PBUH) when he ordered him to: "Repel [evil] by that [deed] which is better; and thereupon the one whom between you and him is enmity will become as though he was a devoted friend" (Fuṣṣilat 34). Allah goes on to reveal that this immensely refined moral character can only be attained through much patience, but it is also a door to great good: "But none are granted it except those who are patient, and none are granted it except one having a great portion [of good]" (Fuṣṣilat 35). For instance, in the Ba'ath Party era in Iraq, there were many

---

[217] Shaikh Muḥammad al-Muḥammad al-Kasnazān, *sermon*, 3rd/May/2018.

[218] Shaikh Muḥammad al-Muḥammad al-Kasnazān, *Al-Ṭarīqa al-ʿAliyya al-Qādiriyya al-Kasnazāniyya*, p. 201.

individuals whom government agencies charged with spying on our Shaikh and the Ṭarīqa. They wrote confidential reports that sometimes harmed and led to problems for our Shaikh, the Ṭarīqa, and dervishes. When that regime came to an end, our Shaikh did not try to take revenge on those spies, even when he knew who they were. Some of them even started to consistently frequent the takya and at times visit our Shaikh, who would not blame them for the past, and would never even mention it.

Alongside our Shaikh's forgiving nature and tolerance towards those who harm him and his family, as well as towards those who attack the Ṭarīqa from the outside, he is absolutely firm with any disciple that harms the Ṭarīqa, by word or by deed, by bringing its name into disrepute. Enemies of the Ṭarīqa would particularly use whatever disciples do to attack the Ṭarīqa. The Ṭarīqa's reputation and image is a responsibility the Messenger (PBUH) and the Shaikhs of Ṭarīqa entrust the Shaikh of the time with. It is incumbent upon the Shaikh of Ṭarīqa to protect and defend its purity. However, our Shaikh forgives the erring disciple when he apologizes, reforms his ways, and repents.

11.2.13 Cheerfulness of Countenance

Our Shaikh has a cheerful disposition, always welcoming people with a smile on his handsome face. You could see on his illuminated face this description of a Companions of the Prophet (PBUH): "I never saw anyone smile more than the Messenger of Allah (PBUH)".[219] This description embodies the Messenger's saying (PBUH): "Smiling at your brother is an act of charity".[220] Many an individual meets our Shaikh with inward or outward enmity, but our Shaikh's smile and cheerful disposition cleanses their hearts of all feelings of malice and enmity, filling it instead with amity and goodwill.

11.2.14 Generosity

Our Shaikh's every action reflects unparalleled generosity. He puts himself, his family, and all of the Ṭarīqa's resources in service to seekers and people in general. The Ṭarīqa Kasnazāniyya is a mecca for the poor,

---

[219] Tirmidhī, *Al-Jāmiʿ al-Kabīr*, VI, no. 3641, p. 30.

[220] Tirmidhī, *Al-Jāmiʿ al-Kabīr*, III, no. 1956, p. 506.

those in need, orphans, and the indigent — Muslim or otherwise. Even when experiencing financial hardship, he does not stop looking after the large number of people he has assumed responsibility for and looking after those who knock at the takya's door asking for help. His generosity is manifested in his behaviour, both inwardly and outwardly. The following beautiful incident is an example of this. While walking in the markets of Amman, our Shaikh wanted to buy something that he saw, even though it seemed like he did not need it. He asked one of his companions to enquire about its price. The seller demanded a price that was way above market value. He asked his companion to offer the seller a lower price, but the companion told him that the price he was offering him was still very high, only to be surprised by the reply: "I know, but I want to help this seller out"! At times, he buys things that are overpriced to benefit the seller, perhaps because the seller is low on income or spends in Allah's way by helping the needy.

11.2.15 Giving Gifts

One facet of our Shaikh's generosity is that likes to present gifts to people. He does not hesitate to gift rare or expensive things that he owns. His love for giving gifts to people is not only a feature of his generosity, but it is also application of the Prophet's (PBUH) ḥadīth: "Give gifts, for it causes you to love one another".[221]

One peculiarity of our Shaikh's behaviour is that at times he buys a thing that he does not need and he has no need to purchase it. Later, it turns out that he knew it would be of benefit in the future, often as a gift for someone. In early 2015, he was visiting a shop in Amman that sold prayer rugs when he asked his companion to purchase a prayer rug that had a picture of the Prophet Jesus on it and another that had the picture of his mother, Mary, peace be upon them both. The companion asked himself what the Shaikh of the Ṭarīqa wanted getting these sorts of prayer rugs that Christians usually bought. He was visibly confused, so our Shaikh told him to get the prayer rugs and not to worry himself about the matter. About two months later, in early March, the Vatican ambassador to Jordan, Archbishop Giorgio Lingua, visited our Shaikh in the takya. Our Shaikh sent for the prayer rugs and gift them to the visitor

---

[221] Mālik *Muwaṭṭa` al-Imām Mālik*, V, no. 3368, p. 1334.

(photo 24)!

11.2.16 Interfaith Dialogue and Religious Tolerance

This meeting demonstrates how our Shaikh is keen on bringing religions together and encourages respecting different beliefs and cultures. He opened the doors of the Kasnazānī takyas to those of other faiths who would like to learn about Islam and observe how Muslims worship. In addition to his refusal to make a distinction between Muslim schools of thought, he is doubly keen on cultivating a spirit of cordiality, respect, and constructive dialogue between Islam and other religions. In this, he also embodies the conduct of his magnificent grandfather (PBUH), who used to welcome People of the Book, debate with them in a friendly manner, and honour them, in an age when religious tolerance was not unheard of.[222] Indeed, one of the first things our noble Prophet (PBUH) did after he migrated to Medina was to create what would later become known as the "Constitution of Medina". It laid out the bases of peaceful coexistence — cooperation, even — between Muslims and People of the Book and recognized their religious and civil rights.[223] This document, also known as the "Charter of Madina", is considered the first civil constitution of its kind in history.

The Shaikh's of Ṭarīqa followed in the footsteps of the Prophet (PBUH) in respecting other faiths and urging their followers and people, in general, to not ridicule the beliefs of others. This made people of other faiths look at the Ṭarīqa Shaikhs with love and respect. For instance, there was a Jewish cleric named Saʿīd who loved visiting Shaikh Ḥusayn al-Kasnazān. One aspect of his respect for the Shaikh is that he would not sit in the Shaikh's assembly, despite the Shaikh's repeated request to him to take a seat. His typical reply was that seeing the Shaikh was enough to make him happy. Khawaja Saʿīd even asked for a letter that had received from Shaikh Ḥusayn to be placed under his head when he dies as an object of blessings. Also, when our Shaikh was in the Kurdish movement, he would send to his father in Iran from time to time a list of medications that he needed. Jews who frequented Shaikh ʿAbd al-Karīm were the

---

[222] Ibn Hishām, *Sīrat al-Nabī*, I, pp. 489-490.
[223] Ibn Hishām, *Sīrat al-Nabī*, II, pp. 126-130.

ones who sourced those medications.[224]

Naturally, Muslim clerics who criticised Sufism or were not inclined towards it did not attend Shaikh ʿAbd al-Karīm's assembly. Our Shaikh, however, has strived to establish relationships with them, showing generosity towards them when they visit the takya or when he meets them anywhere else. At times, he would send delegations of caliphs to religious clerics who attack the Ṭarīqa in their assemblies or from pulpits, to show them, through respect and dialogue, the error in what they say and in creating an unjustified schism between Muslims. His efforts have succeeded in reducing the hostility of these clerics towards the Ṭarīqa Kasnazāniyya, in particular, and Sufism, in general. He has also reduced tension between Sufi groups and others. This also reflects his extraordinary ability to successfully establish cordial ties with various people, including those of different beliefs.

11.2.17 Loyalty

Shaikh Muḥammad al-Muḥammad is incredibly generous with the needy, poor, indigent, and orphans whom he does not know and does not make it known that he is the source of this generosity. It is not surprising, then, that he is tremendously loyal towards those who serve and aid the Ṭarīqa. He does not forget a person's help, no matter how small a gesture or how long ago, and he does not hesitate to lend a helping hand to him when he is in need. He often inquires about the families of deceased dervishes and of their condition and if they need any assistance.

Loyalty is an attribute of Allah (exalted and high is He), hence "The Loyal One" is one of his beautiful names.[225] Scholars have identified noble verses that contain derivatives of the word "*wafāʾ*" (loyalty), such as: "That Day, Allah will pay them (*yuwaffīhim*) in full their deserved recompense" (al-Nūr 25). Our Shaikh has added the following noble verse that does not contain the word "*wafāʾ*" but demonstrates most beautifully Allah's loyalty towards his believing servants: "As for the wall, it belonged to two orphan boys in the city, and there was a treasure for them beneath it, and their father had been righteous. So your Lord wanted that they reach maturity and extract their treasure, as a mercy from your Lord. I did it not of my own accord"

---

[224] Shaikh Muḥammad al-Muḥammad al-Kasnazān, *sermon*, 26th/October/2019.

[225] Al-Qurṭubī, *Al-Asnā fī-Sharḥ Asmāʾ Allah al-Ḥusnā*, I, pp. 422-423.

(al-Kahf 82). In loyalty to the orphans' father, who was a righteous man, Allah made Khaḍir fortify the wall for them, which was on the verge of crumbling, to hide their treasure until they grew up and found it and could make use of it.[226]

Even though there is a massive number of people — dervishes and others — who have served the Ṭarīqa, our Shaikh remembers all of them, which is a testament to his powerful memory. At times, an ordinary person or someone who is not well known comes to visit our Shaikh after a long time of not seeing him, but the Shaikh surprises his assembly's attendees by remembering that person and a service they did decades ago, including details from the distant past of the nature of the service that no one thought was possible to remember. He often takes the initiative of remembering those who have distanced themselves from the Ṭarīqa and sends someone to call and ask about them, perhaps because of some help that person gave one day. Shaikh Muḥammad al-Muḥammad's exceptional loyalty is not limited to those who are close to him. It even includes those who helped him or the Ṭarīqa in a small way.

The strength of our Shaikh's memory is also seen when he is forced to cut his conversation with someone as a result of receiving an urgent phone call or dealing with an emergency, which may take several minutes to resolve. As soon as he finishes dealing with the issue, he resumes his conversation with that person from where they stopped as if he had been reading a book and had marked where he had left off!

11.2.18 Joking

Alongside our Shaikh's seriousness and firmness in managing the affairs of the Ṭarīqa and its dervishes, and his keenness on adhering to the commands and prohibitions of Sharia and the Ṭarīqa, he likes to joke when the time is right. At times, he likes to make light, humorous conversation with a dervish who is clever and witty, and he also enjoys listening to stories of funny pranks. Managing the Ṭarīqa's affairs and challenges that arise place the Shaikh of Ṭarīqa under constant psychological stress, so laughter plays a healthy role in relieving stress. The Companion 'Ikrima described the Prophet (PBUH) as follows: "The

---

[226] Shaikh Muḥammad al-Muḥammad al-Kasnazān, *sermon*, 16th/June/2018.

Prophet was a bit of a jokester"[227]. When Ibn ʿAbbās was asked if the Prophet (PBUH) joked, he replied: "The Prophet (PBUH) would joke".[228] The Companion Nuʿaymān Ibn ʿAmrū al-Ānṣārī often joked and laughed, and the Prophet (PBUH) enjoyed his jokes and humour.[229]

Here is a lovely story. Caliph Yāsīn Sūfī was joking with some dervishes in the Baghdad takya when a caliph named "Ṭāhā" called him and advised that he stop joking in the takya. Even though caliph Yāsīn knew there was no harm in joking with the dervishes, he stopped joking out of respect for this older caliph. While the two conversation's topic changed, our Shaikh's servant came to inform Yāsīn that the Shaikh wanted to see him in his lounge. He was surprised when our Shaik told him that earlier that day he obtained a book that compiled all reports of the Messenger's jokes (PBUH)! Then he called his wife and asked her to bring the book and lend it to the caliph to read. Before the latter left, our Master related a joke from the book.

After leaving, caliph Yāsīn went to Ḥajj Ṭāhā and asked him, smiling, what he had said to him before he went to see our Shaikh. He replied that he had advised him not to joke in the takya. Yāsīn told him that our Master had sent for him so that he could give him a book that compiled the Prophet's (PBUH) jokes and banter! Ḥajj Ṭāhā was stunned by the Shaikh's precisely timed intervention, and he realized that his objection to joking had no basis in the Prophetic Sunna. One detail about this karāma is that the book was not in our Shaikh's hands at the time of the incident, but he had to send for it. It is evident that he knew what had happened between Yāsīn and Ṭāhā, so he called the former and then sent for the book to lend it to him.

11.3 Promoting Prophetic Manners

The same way the Shaikhs of Ṭarīqa inherited and embodied the manners of the Prophet (PBUH), they persisted in reminding disciples to follow the example of the noble prophetic character. Our Shaikh always orders caliphs and dervishes to abide by wholesome moral character traits and

---

[227] Aṣbahānī, *Akhlāq al-Nabī wa-`Ādābuh*, I, p. 495.
[228] Aṣbahānī, *Akhlāq al-Nabī wa-`Ādābuh*, I, p. 487.
[229] Ibn ʿAbd al-Birr, *Al-Istīʿāb fī-Maʿrifat al-Aṣḥāb*, pp. 1526-1530.

distance themselves from evil conduct. The following are some of his words to disciples, advising them to uphold the Messenger's (PBUH) moral character and to abandon all evil attributes and actions:

"Islam is refinement. Islam is good manners. Look at the pure Sharia — all of it is good manners: no killing; no oppression; no eating what is forbidden, no aggression, no adultery, no spying on others, no disloyalty, no lying, no usurping people's wealth, no showing aggression to them. These transgressions are mentioned in Sharia. All of these are good manners. Ṭarīqa is good manners, the Messenger's manners: dhikr is one of the Messenger's manners, reading the Qur'an is one of the Messenger's manners, prostrating and bowing are among the manners of the Messenger, repenting and seeking forgiveness are among the manners of the Messenger, bearing witness to Allah's oneness is one of the Messenger's manners. Where do we get all of these manners from? From the honourable Messenger (PBUH)".[230]

"A person who does not have manners is not suitable for dervishood. A dervish must strengthen the Ṭarīqa's pillars, not harm them! Any person lacking manners is not a dervish. We have nothing to do with him, and his way is false. Ṭarīqa comes with manners: 'Indeed, you are of a great moral character' (al-Qalam 4). A dervish must learn the Messenger's manners and apply them to himself, in the way he treats his family, his wife, his children, people, his mother, his father: 'Say not to them [so much as] 'fie' and do not rebuke them' (al-Isrā` 23). Otherwise, how can you be a believer? The dervish is a believer, and Īmān is following the Messenger's (PBUH) example, implementing the Muḥammadan Sharia. Anyone who hurts a dervish is not a dervish. Anyone who hurts people is not a dervish. Anyone who does not have manners is not a dervish. If someone hurts people, creates problems for people, lies to people, usurps their money, usurps their wealth, commits aggression against them, defames them and behaves hypocritically among disciples, then this person is a hypocrite. This is not a dervish. Allah, the Messenger and the Shaikhs have nothing to do with him".[231]

Our Shaikh explains how a shortfall in manners leads to losing one's faith:

"The dervish belongs to the people of dhikr, the people of knowledge: 'Be pious towards Allah, and Allah will teach you' (al-Baqara 282), 'Indeed, Allah is with the pious and those who are doers of good' (al-Naḥl 128). He belongs to the people of Iḥsān, and Iḥsān is 'to worship Allah as if you see Him; and if you

---

[230] Shaikh Muḥammad al-Muḥammad al-Kasnazān, *sermon*, 4th/December/2013.
[231] Shaikh Muḥammad al-Muḥammad al-Kasnazān, *sermon*, 22nd/January/2010.

cannot see Him, then verily He sees you'. Then, O disciple, how can you lie? How can you hurt people? How can you speak ill of people? This means that your faith is incomplete. You have not yet reached the stage where you worship your Lord as if you see Him.

Why else would you sit here now, motionless in front of the Shaikh, believing in the Shaikh, yet outside Shaikh's assembly (where you misbehave) there is someone who bigger than the Shaikh looking at you: 'He is with you wherever you are' (al-Ḥadīd 4). He is with you: 'Does he not know that Allah sees?' (al-'Alaq 14). The disciple must have faith in Allah (exalted and high is He) that he is under the Most Merciful's gaze, as he is 'of all things, encompassing' (Fuṣṣilat 54). You must repeat the following dhikr after your prayers so that you may take a lesson from it: 'Allah is present with me, Allah sees me, Allah is a witness on me. Allah is with me, Allah is my helper, and He is of all things, encompassing'".[232]

About the purity and excellence of the manners of the dervish, our Shaikh says that he must be like "pure honey" that is flawless. He always reiterates that a real dervish does not even hurt an ant, meaning he does not cause harm to any of Allah's creation, no matter how small or insignificant. A true dervish must embody his Shaikh's manners, who in turn embodies the great moral character of the greatest of Allah's creation: our Master Muḥammad (PBUH).

[232] Shaikh Muḥammad al-Muḥammad al-Kasnazān, *sermon*, 22nd/January/2010.

Photo 24: Shaikh Muḥammad al-Muḥammad receives the Vatican ambassador to Jordan, Archbishop Giorgio Lingua, in the takya in Amman (March/2015).

Photo 25: Shaikh Muḥammad al-Muḥammad in the takya of Amman, Jordan (11th/December/2013).

"The most important thing that you can spend your time and effort working on is preaching. For us, preaching is the greatest worship. Preaching is the greatest deed in Ṭarīqa. Enjoining good and forbidding evil is the most important thing because you teach people to worship, direct them towards Allah (exalted and high is He), implement the Muḥammadan Sharia (PBUH). You are educators: learn and teach people. You take your knowledge from the Shaikhs and the Muḥammadan Sharia and convey it to people and teach them".

Shaikh Muḥammad al-Muḥammad al-Kasnazān
(Sermon, undated)

12

Preaching

The Prophet's primary concern was conveying Allah's message: "O Messenger, announce that which has been revealed to you from your Lord. If you do not, then you have not conveyed His message" (al-Mā`ida 67). Allah Almighty reiterated this command in the Qur'an in many places, such as this: "Call to the way of your Lord with wisdom and good exhortation and argue with them in the best way" (al-Naḥl 125). The Messenger (PBUH) spent his life calling people to Allah, and he constantly reminded Muslims of the importance of preaching and urging them by it. This is expressed in the following noble ḥadīth, which demonstrates the status of a preaching Muslim:

> "Shall I not inform you of a people who are not prophets, nor martyrs, whom the prophets and martyrs will envy on the Day of Resurrection because of their place with Allah (mighty and sublime is He), on pulpits of light upon which they will stand?"

When the Companions asked him about them, he said: "Those who make Allah's servants beloved to Allah, and who make Allah beloved to His servants. They walk the earth as advisers". The companions asked him how they make Allah's servants beloved to Him, so he replied: "They order to love Allah and forbid them" — meaning to forbid them from what Allah dislikes — "when they obey, Allah will love them".[233]

Following in the footstep of their grandfather, the Messenger of Allah (PBUH), the Kasnazānī Shaikhs spent their lives calling to the way to Allah and, sacrificing what was precious and dear for this purpose. Just like all of the Masters of Ṭarīqa before him, Shaikh Muḥammad al-Muḥammad never stops, even for a day, reminding disciples of the necessity of preaching and supporting them with everything they need to convey Allah's words, His remembrance and the Prophet Muḥammad's (PBUH) message to people all over the world. Preaching

---

[233] Bayhaqī, *Shu'ab al-Īmān*, I, no. 409, p. 367.

is not limited to inviting non-Muslims to Islam and urging negligent Muslims to strongly hold on to religion. Rather, every action in the way of enjoining good and forbidding evil is an act of preaching, even when preaching to those who are committed to Allah's Book and His way. Our Shaikh says:

> "It is impermissible to stop preaching. One must preach daily, even to his family, extended family and relatives. Preaching is of utmost importance".[234]

Our Shaikh goes on to say: "My every concern is the Ṭarīqa and preaching". Another one of his saying about preaching that he reiterates is, "Through preaching, obligations are enjoined".[235] Preaching leads non-Muslims to Islam and teaches them its obligations of praying, fasting, almsgiving, and performing hajj, and it also reminds heedless Muslims of them. Preaching is the way to Islam and the way of reminding of it. Embracing Islam means upholding its obligations. Hence, "Through preaching, obligations are enjoined".

In extolling the virtues of preaching and giving the pledge, our Shaikh relates that upon returning home, his father, Shaikh ʿAbd al-Karīm, would sometimes be asked about his apparent joy. He would say that he was happy because he had just given the pledge to someone.[236] This situation reminds us of a piece of advice that the Messenger (PBUH) gave to his spiritual caliph, Imām ʿAlī Ibn Abī Ṭālib, the day he sent him to conquer Khaybar: "If one person is guided through you, it would be better for you than getting red camels".[237]

After Shaikh Muḥammad al-Muḥammad assumed the Ṭarīqa's Shaikhdom, the preaching of Ṭarīqa Kasnazāniyya expanded like never before. When he became the Master of the Ṭarīqa in early 1978, there were three small takyas in Baghdad. When he migrated from Baghdad at the end of 2000, the number of its takyas had reached about 135, despite the severe constraints of the then government and its security services to limit the Ṭarīqa from spreading, which included ordering the closure of the majority of takyas in Baghdad, as we will see in detail in Chapter 17.

---

[234] Shaikh Muḥammad al-Muḥammad al-Kasnazān, *sermon*, 22nd/December/2005.
[235] Shaikh Muḥammad al-Muḥammad al-Kasnazān, *sermon*, 2nd/March/2013.
[236] Shaikh Muḥammad al-Muḥammad al-Kasnazān, *sermon*, 22nd/December/2005.
[237] Bukhārī, *Al-Jāmiʿ al-Ṣaḥīḥ*, II, no. 2846, p. 173. Arabs considered red camels as the most precious property that a person can have.

The main takya in Baghdad was bursting with disciples every day, and wherever you looked, you would see people taking the pledge. On days of the major dhikr on Monday and Thursday nights, the attendees in the takya would number in the hundreds.

On days of religious celebrations, the takya could not accommodate all of the disciples. On days of Eid, there would be a long queue of disciples, each waiting for half an hour or more before it was their turn to greet the Shaikh. In 1998, our Shaikh hosted the last celebration of the Prophetic birth before he migrated from Baghdad in his orchard in Dōra, as the main takya could no longer accommodate the thousands of people who attended.

Our Shaikh expanded the extent of preaching efforts in the various activities of calling people to Allah, including:

- Increasing the number of preaching caliphs, training them, and sending them to preach all over the world.
- Continuously giving sermons.
- Authoring and publishing books and encouraging caliphs to write about the Ṭarīqa.
- Opening takyas.
- Facilitating the study of darbāsha karāmas by international scientific research institutions.

We have talked about karāmas in Chapter 3, and in Chapter 13 we will examine in detail our Shaikh's massive achievements in building takyas, having founded a large number of them in different countries around the globe. In this chapter, we will focus on the other three areas of preaching: developing caliphs, giving sermons, and authoring and publishing books. We will conclude the chapter by reviewing the characteristics of Kasnazānī preaching.

12.1 Increasing the Number of Caliphs, Training Them, and Sending Them to Preach

In the Ṭarīqa Kasnazāniyya, every dervish must preach because calling people to Allah has always been one of the most important duties of the Muslim since the time of our Master Muḥammad (PBUH). However, this is an even greater duty for dervishes that have been given formal permission to preach, i.e. the caliphs. In addition to their responsibility to invite people to the Ṭarīqa, caliphs are authorised to give the Ṭarīqa Kasnazāniyya pledge on behalf of the Shaikh. Hence, our Shaikh's focus on preaching has made him greatly increase the number of caliphs. He began to give formal permission to preach to all who can call people to Allah and the desire to do so. Our Shaikh always reiterates that the best caliphs and dervishes are those that preach the most.

Our Shaikh organised intense educational courses for some active caliphs to raise their level of knowledge of the Ṭarīqa and Sharia, so that they could preach to people in the best way possible. The preacher who speaks about Islam and the Ṭarīqa with knowledge and expertise can answer people's questions with wisdom and can respond to ignorant and biased individuals who attack Sufism. Kasnazānī dervishes, in general, have become more knowledgeable and have a greater understanding of Sufism.

Our Shaikh is very keen on training every caliph and dervish so that they can be true representatives of the Ṭarīqa. He always mentions the importance of following the example of the Prophet (PBUH), "There has certainly been for you in the Messenger of Allah an excellent pattern for anyone whose hope is in Allah and the Last Day and [who] remembers Allah often" (al-Āḥzāb 21), who has the highest moral character: "Indeed, you are of a great moral character" (al-Qalam 4). This way, people can follow their example:

> "We, Kasnazānī dervishes, must be the cleanest of people in society, so that they may follow our example, so that they may follow the lowest Kasnazānī dervish".[238]

Our Shaikh always advises disciples and caliphs, and he also intervenes to solve problems that arise among them and advises those who have erred. He always tries to mend relations between dervishes when there is a disagreement or conflict. He wants them to be brothers who are affectionate to each other for Allah's sake and always prepared to move past the mistakes they make with one another. In his preaching assembly, he often says that if it were not for envy, aversion, and other ill feelings between caliphs, "the Ṭarīqa would span from east to west". He often

---

[238] Shaikh Muḥammad al-Muḥammad al-Kasnazān, *sermon*, 22nd/January/2010.

reminds disciples of the prophetic ḥadīth: "Believers are like bricks: they each support one another",[239] and the Prophet (PBUH) laced his noble fingers together when he said this. He also mentions his (PBUH) ḥadīth: "In their mutual love, compassion, and sympathy, the believers are like a body. When a part of it suffers, the whole body responds to it with wakefulness and fever".[240]

Our Master is a teacher with a big heart that tolerates anyone who errs, confesses their mistake, and rectifies their behaviour. However, at the same time, he is never lax with anyone who insists on distorting the image of the Ṭarīqa with damaging words or actions. Individuals have been dismissed from the Ṭarīqa because they became a source of harm for the Ṭarīqa and people in general.

He has sent preaching caliphs to Islamic countries and others. They have given people the Ṭarīqa's pledge in different parts of the world, from the largest, most modern and wealthiest cities of the developed world, to the smallest, oldest, and poorest villages in the third world. He has sent preachers to India, Malaysia, Sudan, Kenya, Benin, Togo, Comoro Islands, Britain, Germany, the Former Soviet Union, the United States of America, and other countries. He has also permitted giving the pledge over the phone and the internet to those who cannot find a caliph near their place of residence or who for whom travelling for that purpose is difficult.

A great preaching achievement of his is having established a prominent presence of the Ṭarīqa Kasnazāniyya in India. In 1994, he sent caliph Yūsuf Ḥusayn (may Allah have mercy on him) to preacher there. With Allah's permission and the blessings of the Ṭarīqa's Shaikhs, the Ṭarīqa Kasnazāniyya gained a large number of disciples. In 2011, he sent caliph ʿImād ʿAbd al-Ṣamad to continue the preaching efforts. Today, there is a large number of dervishes and caliphs in different areas and cities in India, as well as takyas, with more under development.

Reflecting the reality that Allah gave women the same share he gave men in religion, and recognizing their significant role in developing individuals and society as a whole, our Shaikh has increased the number of female caliphs as well. There is now a large number of female preachers

---

[239] Bukhārī, *Al-Jāmiʿ al-Ṣaḥīḥ*, I, no. 471, p. 171.

[240] Muslim, *Ṣaḥīḥ Muslim*, IV, no. 2586, p. 1999-2000.

in the Ṭarīqa to teach women about Islam and its spiritual side:

> "O Kasnazānī dervishes! Convey your message to everyone, to every individual in society, men and women, young and old. Convey the Muḥammadan message because the Ṭarīqa belongs to everyone. The Ṭarīqa enjoins good and forbids evil".[241]

12.2 Delivering Sermons

Since his ascension to the Shaikhdom of Ṭarīqa, and in keeping with the conduct of his Master, Shaikh ʿAbd al-Karīm, and the Shaikhs of Ṭarīqa before him, our Shaikh has always been keen to speak to disciples about religious affairs and remind them of their obligations to Allah, their families, and society. Before his health forced him to attend circles of dhikr less frequently, he would lead seekers in Wird al-ʿAṣr every day, missing it only when preoccupied with other Ṭarīqa affairs.

He would also always attend the dhikr circle held on Monday and Thursday nights and, of course, the celebrations of Eid and other religious occasions. Along with attending Wird al-ʿAṣr, our Shaikh sometimes delivered a sermon before or after the dhikr. As for Monday and Thursday nights, he usually gave a sermon after the dhikr ended and before the singing of hymns began. After moving from Sulaymāniyya to Amman, due to the nature of the building of the takya and his health, he no longer attends dhikr circles and assemblies of hymns. He only attends the latter when they are hosted in his assembly in the takya. He does not stop preaching and delivering sermons to dervishes and others who visit his private assembly.

Shaikh Muḥammad al-Muḥammad is in a constant state of preaching, whether his assembly is attended by disciples who come to visit him and listen to his words that remind them of Allah and his Messenger (PBUH) or people who come for any particular reason, and whether the attendees were in the hundreds or a few individuals. The way to Allah, religious issues, and the state of Muslims are always topics for sermons, conversations, and dialogues, even in his private assembly. For example, when he went to Moorfield Hospital in London on 11th/May/2000, to have a procedure done on his eyes, a few dervishes, including the author

---

241 Shaikh Muḥammad al-Muḥammad al-Kasnazān, *sermon*, 22nd/January/2010.

of this book, accompanied him as aides. When our Shaikh was sitting on a bed waiting to be taken to the operating theatre, he was not talking about the surgery or anything related to it, nor did he show any signs of anxiety, as an average person would. Instead, he was teaching his companions about pious restraint (*wara'*) in Sufism, and the need for the Sufi seeker to not take the concessions of Sharia, but rather, to demand the greatest degree of commitment from himself. He talked about the need to avoid backbiting and be vigilant in observing the heart's thoughts and repelling satanic whispers. He spoke about the types of dhikr drums and using them along with tambourines in performing dhikr, the immortality of the spirit in the Ṭarīqa, and other religious matters.

This was also the case when he was in The Johns Hopkins Hospital in Baltimore, Maryland, in the USA, for a kidney transplant. During his stay in the hospital, he was always preaching to the medical staff there. Such instances illustrate his unique disposition and his dedication of his entire life to preaching and serving Islam, Muslims, and people in general.

The Shaikh of Ṭarīqa's preaching, just like the rest of his affairs, is directed by the Shaikhs. One day in 1981, our Shaikh left his home in the Baghdad takya and headed towards the takya's mosque, accompanied by the engineer in charge of building the takya. While they were crossing the takya's courtyard leading to the mosque, his companion asked him to deliver a sermon to dervishes urging them to work, noting that some had not been helping enough in the building work. Our Shaikh smiled and replied that the matter was out of his hands; when the Shaikhs wanted him to speak, he spoke with ease and fluency, but when they did not want him to speak, he was unable to speak. This reminds us of Shaikh 'Abd al-Qādir al-Gaylānī's words that explain the difference between the speech of a self-appointed preacher and of one whom Allah makes to speak, having drawn him near to Him and made him well-acquainted with Him:

> "The Prophet (PBUH) has said: 'The tongue of the one who knows Allah becomes exhausted',[242] meaning he becomes mute. The tongue of his self, his desire, natural inclination, habits, lies, slander, and falsehood becomes silent. The tongue of his inward state speaks, the tongue of his heart, innermost being, essences, truthfulness, and purity speaks. The tongue of his falsehood

[242] Al-Rāzī, *Mafātīḥ al-Ghaib: Al-Tafsīr al-Kabīr*, XV, p. 113.

becomes silent, and the tongue of his truth speaks. The tongue of his talking about things that are of no concern to him becomes silent, and the tongue of his heart speaks about things that are relevant to him. The tongue of seeking his self becomes silent, and the tongue of seeking the True One speaks.

At the beginning of knowingness, speech is cut off and a person's entire existence melts. He is rendered effaced to himself and to others. Then, if the True One (mighty and sublime is He) wills, he resurrects him. If He wants him to speak, He creates a tongue for him with which He enables him to speak. He causes him to say what He wants of words of wisdom and secrets. His speech becomes a medicine within a medicine, a light within a light, a truth within a truth, a rightness within a rightness, and a purity within a purity because he speaks only at the command of Allah (mighty and sublime is He), through his heart. If he speaks without being commanded to do so, he perishes. He does not speak unless commanded, in response to something that overcomes him".[243]

Most of our Shaikh's sermons are in Arabic because the majority of attendees are usually Arabs. Sometimes, he delivers lectures in Kurdish when most attendees are Kurds. When he preaches to those who do not speak Arabic or Kurdish, such as English speakers, a disciple translates. Our Master uses simple language that makes his words, which are deep in meaning, easy to understand by even the simplest of people. Hence, our Shaikh usually delivers sermons in the vernacular, using Modern Standard Arabic only when necessary.

There is a striking resemblance between our Shaikh's words and the sermons of the al-Ghawth al-Āʿẓam, Shaikh ʿAbd al-Qādir al-Gaylānī, who would deliver them in his school in Baghdad. As we have mentioned in our description of the Muḥammadan Inheritor's words, they are words that do not solely address the intellect. Rather, they also touch the inner depths of hearts. The words of a Shaikh well-acquainted with Allah stem from a heart brimming with Allah's love, hence they contain light and spiritual energy. They penetrate the barriers of the seeker's self and the barriers of his worldly interests to impact his heart.

The Shaikhs of Ṭarīqa do not use sermonizing as a means to flaunt their religious or spiritual knowledge because their speech is directed by Allah and is in His cause. The focus their words on what increases the seeker's determination to perform dhikr and to do what Allah wants him

---

[243] Shaikh ʿAbd al-Qādir al-Gaylānī, *Jilā' al-Khāṭir*, p. 103.

to do. Hence, our Shaikh limits his preaching to particular topics that remind seekers of the requisites of travelling on the path to Allah, citing noble verses; honourable ḥadīths; the Messenger's (PBUH) deeds, states, and manners; and the conduct, words, and karāmas of the Ṭarīqa's Shaikhs. When he cites Allah's words or the Prophet's ḥadīths, the listener finds a special delight in them and effect on the heart every time they are mentioned, which are not lessened by them being repeated. This is something that anyone who listens to his words experiences directly. Our Shaikh says:

> "We always reiterate verses, ḥadīths, and sayings of the Shaikhs: 'So remind, if the reminder should benefit' (al-Āʿlā 9). This is so that you may benefit, O seeker! So that you may reflect once again on the Shaikh's sayings, the sayings of the Shaikhs, because the words of the Shaikh and the Shaikhs are consistent with the Sunna and the Book".[244]

Our Shaikh says the following in regards to what he focuses on in his exhortation:

> "Some say, 'the Shaikh repeats himself'. Of course, I repeat myself for the disciple, so that I may teach him and make him understand. I tell him the same thing every time, I even repeat it a thousand times. If you do not follow what I say, what am I to do? Of course, the Shaikh repeats himself because he speaks from what he has. He is like a shopkeeper who sells what he has in his shop, nothing else! My shop [sells] worship, my shop [sells] good conduct, my shop [sells] my dhikrs and my wirds. I speak about my dhikrs and my wirds. I speak about my Ṭarīqa. I speak about my conduct. I talk about what I have, about what I can talk about. I don't have anything else. These are my goods".[245]

There are many videos and audio recordings of our Shaikh's lectures on the internet.

12.3 Literature

Shaikh Muḥammad al-Muḥammad has published four books in Arabic, including a unique Sufi encyclopedia that educates the inquirer of the way to Allah about the fundamentals of the Sufi way in general, and the Ṭarīqa Kasnazāniyya in particular. It teaches the seeker about the

---

[244] Shaikh Muḥammad al-Muḥammad al-Kasnazān, *sermon*, 11th/January/2014.

[245] Shaikh Muḥammad al-Muḥammad al-Kasnazān, *sermon*, 18th/September/2013.

requisites of the Ṭarīqa, namely, refined manners, conduct, and various forms of worship. Some of these books have been translated into other languages. All of these publications are available for download, free of charge, on the internet.

The following is a summary of Shaikh Muḥammad al-Muḥammad's published books in order of their date of publication:

1) **Title**: *Al-Ānwār al-Raḥmāniyya fīl-Ṭarīqa al-'Aliyya al-Qādiriyya al-Kasnazāniyya* (Lights of the Merciful One on the Ṭarīqa 'Aliyya Qādiriyya Kasnazāniyya)

Place and Date of Publication: This book was first printed in Baghdad in 1988. It was then published a second time in Cairo in 1990 by Madbouly Bookshop.

Introduction: The Shaikh dedicated his first book to be a detailed presentation of the historical and ideological fundamentals of Sufism and the seeker's code of conduct on the Sufi path. In addition to noble Qur'anic verses, the Messenger's (PBUH) ḥadīths, and the author's views, the book cites the views of a large number of Sufi Shaikhs and scholars to illustrate the fact that not only is Ṭarīqa an indivisible part of Islam, but that it is also its spirit, and to emphasize that practising it is at the core of Islam. The book contains various information about the Ṭarīqa Kasnazāniyya, including its Shaikhs, dhikrs, and devotional practices.

Contents: The book contains an introduction to Sufism and the Sufi and presents different stations, states, and practices of Sufism, including repentance, companionship, love, spiritual bonding, listening to devotional singing, dhikr, internal strife, silence, vigil, isolation, seclusion, inner thoughts, fear, hope, truthfulness, sincerity, patience, satisfaction, gratitude, asceticism, pious restraint, and reliance.

The book also covers the proper etiquettes the disciple must have when attending the Shaikh's assembly, inside the takya, being with his fellow dervishes, eating food, sleeping, how to dress, how to sit, and when on the road, and the ruling on travelling and visiting his Shaikh. It also addresses important Sharia issues such as purity, ablution, and prayer.

The book explains the karāmas of walīs and how they stem from the mu'jizas of the Prophet Muḥammad (PBUH). It discusses Sufi practices that are often objected to by those who are ignorant of their reality and origins in Sharia, such as asking for the intercession of walīs, asking for spiritual support, and kissing the hands of righteous people and paying homage to them. Additionally, the book touches on some of the dangerous mistakes that some people who practice Sufism make, such as following a deceased Shaikh instead of a living Shaikh or taking more than one Shaikh. It also looks at the lives of the Shaikhs of Ṭarīqa Kasnazāniyya and provides a commentary on its dhikrs, methods of giving pledge, seclusion, and spiritual exercises.

2) **Title:** *Jilā' al-Khāṭir Min Kalām al-Shaikh 'Abd Al-Qādir* (Purification of the Mind: From Shaikh 'Abd al-Qādir's Words)

Place and Date of Publication: Baghdad, 1989.

Introduction: This is a manuscript containing forty-five lectures from Shaikh 'Abd al-Qādir's preaching assemblies in his school in Baghdad. Our Shaikh edited the manuscript, relying on three source texts from the Qādiriyya Shrine Library, the Iraqi Museum Library, and the al-Āwqāf Library in Baghdad. This was the first time the manuscript was edited and published.

Shaikh Muḥammad al-Muḥammad did not publish the forty-five lectures as separate chapters in the book, as they occur in the manuscript and as is the tradition of editing manuscripts, including editing manuscripts of Shaikh 'Abd al-Qādir's lectures. He employed a creative technique to help those who read about, practise, and teach Sufism to better benefit from the words of al-Ghawth al-Ā'ẓam. He divided the contents of the lectures into forty chapters, each covering a particular Sufi subject, such as "patience", "forgiveness", and "annihilation". He compiled passages from Shaikh 'Abd al-Qādir's lectures on every subject and put them in their respective chapters. This clever thematic organization makes it easier for the reader to study and remember Shaikh 'Abd al-Qādir's sayings about each of these important themes, which would have been difficult otherwise.

Contents: Our Master prefaced the book with an introduction to the exceptionally devout life of Shaikh 'Abd al-Qādir al-Gaylānī. The chapters of the book are as follows: the etiquette of accompanying shaikhs; repentance; seeking a means to Allah; love; reliance; asceticism; fear; patience; sincerity; truthfulness; grief; satisfaction; piety; striving against the self; the blessings of dhikr; works of the heart; the saints' knowledge; putting knowledge into practice; spending on the poor; isolation; seclusion; the definition of a Sufi; annihilation; forgiveness; the light of the believer; denouncing the world; the fruit of knowledge;

denouncing hypocrisy; the benefits of the month of Ramadan; the benefits of mercy; prohibiting injustice; neglecting what is of no concern; humility; denouncing pretence; envy; curtailing hopes; death; thinking well of others; having a sense of shame; and enduring affliction.

3) **Title:** *Al-Ṭarīqa al-ʿAliyya al-Qādiriyya al-Kasnazāniyya* (The Ṭarīqa ʿAliyya Qādiriyya Kasnazāniyya)

Place and Date of Publication: Baghdad, 1998

Introduction: There are common themes between this book and *al-Ānwār al-Raḥmāniyya*, but this book addresses these themes differently, adds to the topics of the earlier book, and covers many new topics. This book does not replace *al-Ānwār al-Raḥmāniyya*, but rather, it completes it. It clarifies some of the issues that cause controversy and disagreement between scholars. The book is primarily based on noble verses, the Messenger's ḥadīths (PBUH), and perspectives and sayings of Shaikhs and scholars.

Contents: Like *al-Ānwār al-Raḥmāniyya*, this book also addresses stations of the Ṭarīqa: repentance; reliance; fear; hope; truthfulness; sincerity; patience; pious restraint; asceticism; satisfaction; and gratitude. It also covers the history of the Shaikhs, dhikrs, and etiquettes of Ṭarīqa Kasnazāniyya. It discusses in detail the greatness of the Messenger (PBUH) and the noble Qur'an, the status of the people of the prophetic household, and the symbol that Imām Ḥusayn embodies. The book also discusses the status of Imām ʿAlī as the bearer of the Ṭarīqa's knowledge after the Messenger (PBUH). It also looks into the meaning of the Shaikh's being a Muḥammadan Inheritor. It discusses the subject of karāmas, including the proof of their validity in the Qur'an and Sunna, as well as the karāmas of the people of the household of the Prophet (PBUH), the Companions, and the Ṭarīqa Kasnazāniyya.

The book devotes an entire chapter to the subject of intercession and seeking a means to Allah, due to its significance and because it is the biggest objection some people raise against Sufism. Citing the noble Qur'an and the honourable prophetic Sunna, the book demonstrates the validity of seeking the intercession of the Prophet (PBUH) and the people of his household, believing in intercession, visiting the shrines of walīs, and seeking blessings through relics of the Messenger (PBUH) and righteous people. The book also touches on the permissibility of listening to devotional songs.

4) **Title:** *Mawsūʿat Al-Kasnazān Fīmā Aṣṭalaḥa ʿAlayhi Ahl Al-Taṣṣawuf wal-ʿIrfān* (Al-Kasnazān Encyclopedia of Terms Coined by the People of Sufism and Gnosticism)

Place and Date of Publication: Damascus, 2005, Dār al-Maḥabba.

Introduction: The encyclopedia consists of twenty-four volumes. It is a unique work that is the first of its kind. There is at least one encyclopedia for every kind of branch of knowledge, but this work is the only encyclopedia specializing in Sufism. In preparing it, Shaikh Muḥammad al-Muḥammad used hundreds of sources, including one hundred and fifty manuscripts that had not been edited before, such as *Jawāhir al-Āsrār wa-Laṭāʾif al-Ānwār* by Shaikh ʿĪsā son of Shaikh ʿAbd al-Qādir al-Gaylānī. As we have mentioned before, in preparing the encyclopedia, our Shaikh used manuscripts from a large number of libraries, including manuscript libraries in Iraq, the Süleymaniye Library and Atatürk Library in Istanbul, and the British Library in London.

Compiling an encyclopedia of such breadth requires a full team of experts in various sub-sciences to take on such a comprehensive task, but our Shaikh conducted this enormous research project and compiled this monumental encyclopedia with the help of a handful of dervishes who assisted him in finding manuscripts and printed sources that he would look over and select material from that he wanted for the encyclopedia. They would also make copies of photographs he wanted to keep from sources and would sometimes look through sources for whatever he asked them to search for.

Working on this monumental project took more than a quarter of a century. In the beginning, our Shaikh did not declare that the goal was to produce an encyclopedia of Sufism. He would speak about collecting perspectives of Shaikhs on various Sufi terms, but later, he began referring to the idea of compiling an encyclopedia.

In its preface, our Shaikh mentions the objectives behind developing this quantitatively and qualitatively enormous work:

- To shed light on the history of Islamic Sufism since its inception to the present era, especially in this time where the world is spiritually famished.
- To fill the need that the Islamic library has for this kind of lexical Sufi work, in a time where it abounds with

encyclopedias and dictionaries for various other religious sciences.

- To shed light on the origins, principles, phases, and criteria of Sufi terminology within a modern framework of lexical mapping.
- To uncover meanings of the sciences, primary sources, and doctrinal foundations of Sufis; also, to unveil their spiritual stations, ranks, states, inner experiences, and stations of nearness to Allah Almighty that they have been granted.
- To reveal the interdependence between the past and the present of Sufi terms and their shared objectives, despite the multiplicity and diversity of their Ṭarīqas.
- To make Sufi terminology easy to understand.
- To provide a comprehensive Sufi reference that is sufficient for researchers and students of this field so that they do not have to refer back to books and libraries.
- To facilitate tracking terms throughout history in chronological order, which makes it easier to analytically and comparatively study them.[246]

Contents: This encyclopedia contains thousands of terms that Sufis have exclusively used in their books and sayings, in addition to terms that were not only used by them but that they ascribed Sufi meanings to, such as Allah's beautiful names and the names of the Messenger (PBUH). The encyclopedia also includes common words, such as "house" and "tree", that Sufis use as symbols and metaphors, which has given technical meanings. The encyclopedia mentions the various meanings of each term according to various Sufis.

For any given term, the encyclopedia first introduces its linguistic meaning in the dictionary, followed by the places where it appears in the magnificent Qur'an, then its instances in the honourable Sunna, if at all, before covering its meanings according to Sufi Shaikhs. One innovation of the encyclopedia is that it organises the perspectives of Shaikhs in chronological order, making it easier to track the development of each term and its transformation over time. For further benefit, the

---

[246] Shaikh Muḥammad al-Muḥammad al-Kasnazān, *Mawsū'at Al-Kasnazān Fīmā Aṣṭalaḥa 'Alayhi Ahl Al-Taṣṣawuf wal-'Irfān*, I, pp. 12-13.

encyclopedia refers to the perspectives of some researchers that have reported the views of Sufi Shaikhs and have commented on them. The encyclopedia also mentions the meaning of any given term according to the Ṭarīqa Kasnazāniyya Shaikhs.

The first term in the encyclopedia is the letter "alif" and the last is "the Grand Days". The number of terms and words exceeds ten thousand. The terms fill twenty-two volumes, and the twenty-third volume is dedicated to biographies of influential Shaikhs, scholars, and researchers whose views are covered in the encyclopedia. The twenty-fourth and final volume contains several indexes, including an index of terms and an index of words and encyclopedia sources.

Scholars and academics who have reviewed the encyclopedia have praised its uniqueness, importance, and comprehensiveness. They unanimously agree that it is a precious addition to Sufi literature in particular, and Islamic literature in general.

Our Shaikh has also compiled two books of supplications for the Ṭarīqa Kasnazāniyya disciples:

Title: *Al-Ṣalawāt al-Kasnazāniyya* (Kasnazānī Prayers (on the Prophet (PBUH))).

Place and Date of Publication: Baghdad, 1990.

Contents: This book contains a compilation of the most beautiful and powerful prayers of blessings upon the Prophet (PBUH). Prayers of blessings upon the Messenger (PBUH) have a special status in the Ṭarīqa Kasnazāniyya dhikrs, as we will see in detail in §14.4.3. Our Shaikh printed this book in the 1990s when it was compiled, but collecting prayers of blessings upon the Prophet (PBUH) is a continuous project under his supervision. As of now, the number of blessed prayers that have been collected exceeds ten volumes when published.

2) **Title:** *Ḥizb al-Wāw*

Contents: This unique dhikr, which was communicated to our Shaikh in 2013, consists of every Qur'anic verse that starts with the letter "wāw" in the order in which they occur in the muṣḥaf. Our Shaikh says that this wird came about "by Allah's command to the honourable Messenger (PBUH), to the Shaikhs, and the Shaikhs communicated it to me".[247]

Our Master oversees the production of the Ṭarīqa's educational literature in the form of brochures and booklets, such as the booklets of *The Concept of Ṭarīqa in Islamic Sharia* and *The Dhikrs of the Ṭarīqa ʿAliyya Qādiriyya Kasnazāniyya*. Shaikh Muḥammad al-Muḥammad has several other books in preparation.

Our Shaikh's General Deputy, Shaikh Nahro, published two books in 2007 based on his father's, the Master of the Ṭarīqa's, perspectives: *Visions and Dreams: A Sufi Perspective* and *Miraculous Sufi Healing and Modern Medicine*. In 2006-2014, under Shaikh Nahro's management, our Shaikh also issued *Al-Kasnazān Magazine*, which deals with Sufism in general.

12.4 Attributes of Kasnazānī Preaching

The Shaikhs of our Ṭarīqa urge Muslims to call others to Islam. Calling people to Allah was incumbent upon the Messenger (PBUH) so, consequently, it is incumbent upon every Muslim: "O Messenger, announce that which has been revealed to you from your Lord" (al-Mā`ida 67). They also stress that preaching in the Ṭarīqa Kasnazāniyya is based on the two foundations of calling to Allah in the Qur'an: wisdom and good exhortation. Calling people to Allah must be based on logical arguments vested in knowledge, respect, and kind words: "Invite to the way of your Lord with wisdom and good exhortation and argue with them in the best way. Indeed, your Lord is most knowing of who has strayed from His way and He is most knowing of who is [rightly] guided" (al-Naḥl 125).

A facet of the Qur'anic description of preaching is peaceful coexistence with other religions and respecting people's rights in choosing their religion and belief. This is a right that the Qur'an endorsed and commanded by in a time when this was unheard of — more than a thousand years before it was adopted by human-made law:

> "There shall be no compulsion in religion". (Al-Baqara 256)
>
> "Say, 'O disbelievers, I do not worship what you worship. Nor are you worshippers of what I worship. Nor will I be a worshipper of what you worship. Nor are you worshippers of what I worship. For you is your religion, and for me is my religion". (Al-Kāfirūn 1-6)

---

[247] Shaikh Muḥammad al-Muḥammad al-Kasnazān, *sermon*, 12th/September/2013.

"Do not insult those they invoke other than Allah, lest they insult Allah in enmity without knowledge". (Al-Ān'ām 108)

"The servants of the Most Merciful One who walk upon the earth easily, and when the ignorant address them [harshly], they say [words of] peace". (Al-Furqān 63)

Hence, our Shaikh has always strongly condemned all extremist groups that try to force people to accept a particular religion or doctrine, including extremist and terrorist movements that try to hide their reality under the name of Islam and use coercion and violence against Muslims and non-Muslims:

"In the Ṭarīqa, there is no compulsion in religion, for any group, any nationality, any doctrine, or any religion across the globe. We spread love: 'If they incline to peace, then incline to it [also]' (al-Ānfāl 61). We spread mercy; we spread brotherhood and love; we spread equality; we spread peace between people in the world.

We are not killers; we are not terrorists; we are peacemakers. We spread mercy, brotherhood, and love. We spread true Islam, not like those false claimants who kill people, blow people up, and hurt people. This is out of the fold of Islam. The religion of Islam is a religion of mercy: 'We have not sent you,' O Muḥammad, 'except as a mercy to the worlds' (al-Ānbiyā` 107). To all the world: to the Kurd, to the Arab, to the Indian, to the Chinese, to the English, to the American, to the African, to the Jew, to the Russian — to all. We are humanitarians. We treat people with humanity. In fact, we do so even with animals. Being kind towards animals is Islamic teaching, as is being kind towards everything. You are the people of kindness, people of love, people of brotherhood, people of peace, people of prostrating and bowing to Allah".[248]

Our Shaikh goes on to emphasize that Islam is based on peace and brotherhood and denounces the campaigns that distort the Prophet Muḥammad's (PBUH) message by extremist and terrorist groups in their pursuit of goals contrary to Sharia and the Ṭarīqa:

"Allah says: 'If you love Allah, then follow me and Allah will love you' (`Āl 'Imrān 31). How will Allah love you? Through your love for people, your service to people, your camaraderie with people, your being in harmony with people; through brotherhood, through love, through protecting people's honour, and through protecting people's lives.

The view that says, 'He is English, so kill him', or 'He is Russian, so kill

[248] Shaikh Muḥammad al-Muḥammad al-Kasnazān, *sermon*, 11th/January/2012.

him', or 'He is Jewish, so kill him', does not exist in Islam. You must not try to kill someone who is not trying to kill you. You must resort to kind words: 'Call to the way of your Lord with wisdom and good exhortation and argue with them in the best way' (al-Naḥl 125). You must not behave as though you 'tear the earth apart' or 'reach the mountains in height' (al-Isrā` 37). Rather, with brotherhood, love, and Islam, bring them to Islam. Through Islam, treat them as though they were your father, your son, your sister, your brother, and your daughter. Islam enjoins good and forbids evil".[249]

True preaching in Islam is based on respecting others and showing mercy to everyone:

"We welcome the poor disbeliever. We welcome the diseased disbeliever. We welcome the orphaned disbeliever. We serve all of mankind. Islam does not distinguish between people; it serves all of mankind. The Messenger (PBUH) is the Messenger of Mercy: 'We have not sent you [O Muḥammad] except as a mercy to the worlds" (al-Ānbiyā` 107). When a Christian orphan comes along and you serve him, he may become a Muslim. When a poor Christian comes to you and you serve him, and he sees that you are Muslim and that you serve the poor, his heart may incline towards Islam so he becomes a Muslim. Our actions must attract people to Islam. We must be sympathetic towards the poor, the needy, orphans, and widows because the Messenger (PBUH), our Master Abu Bakr, our Master 'Umar, our Master 'Uthmān, and our Master 'Alī did not turn away a Jew, a Christian, or a Zoroastrian. They did not drive them away; rather, they served them as they served Muslims. They have their religion and we have ours".[250]

The same way our Shaikhs teach us through their words, they guide us through their deeds. An elderly Christian lady in need used to come to the takya in Baghdad asking for food, so the takya's caretakers would give her what she needed. Once, one of them told our Shaikh that this woman's dress was indecent and unbefitting of the takya. He told him to leave her alone and not prevent her from coming to the takya, so that Allah may guide her.

The following incident demonstrates what our Shaikh means when he speaks of the role of tolerance and mercy in guiding people. Our Shaikh was present in a dhikr circle when a visibly drunk person joined the circle. The caliph in charge of managing the circle allowed him to

[249] Shaikh Muḥammad al-Muḥammad al-Kasnazān, *sermon*, 11th/January/2012.
[250] Shaikh Muḥammad al-Muḥammad al-Kasnazān, *sermon*, 14th/July/2000.

participate in the dhikr. After the dhikr ended, this man went to the caliph and told him that he was drunk and asked him to show him where he can shower and do ablution so that he could take the pledge afterwards. Had the man been driven away from the dhikr, he would not have changed. The tolerance and patience with which the Ṭarīqa treated him led him to forgiveness and guidance.

Many non-Sufi Muslim clerics and non-Muslim clerics visit our Shaikh. He welcomes and honours them, and he discusses various topics and exchanges views with them. Our Shaikh's efforts reflect his desire to guide people to Islam, preserve good relationships with adherents of various Islamic schools of thought and adherents of other religions, and promote and spread a spirit of tolerance, peace, and dialogue throughout society.

Our Shaikh reiterates his instructions to disciples to stay away from "injustice, disloyalty, spying on others, and killing" because these actions are "forbidden in Islam, forbidden in the Ṭarīqa".[251] He also encourages "serving the poor, orphans, the needy, the disabled, one's country, and not resorting to destruction, injustice, killing, disloyalty, and crimes, as they are prohibited in the Ṭarīqa".[252]

---

[251] Shaikh Muḥammad al-Muḥammad al-Kasnazān, *sermon*, 5th/September/2012.
[252] Shaikh Muḥammad al-Muḥammad al-Kasnazān, *sermon*, 5th/December/2012.

Photo 26: Shaikh Muḥammad al-Muḥammad gives the pledge of the Tarīqa in his residence during his visit to London (2000).

Photo 27: Shaikh Muḥammad al-Muḥammad in one of his daily visits to the British Library during his stay in London. To his right is his General Deputy and older son Shaikh Nahro and to his left his assistant Ḥājj Laṭīf (2000).

"The takya is a spiritual school that prepares a disciple to be a worshipper, a seeker, and a righteous person and reformer in society. We want a Muḥammadan (PBUH) society, a society like the society of the Companions of the Messenger (PBUH): 'The forerunners, the forerunners (10) — they are the ones that are brought near [to Allah]' (al-Wāqiʿa 10-11). We want their moral character: 'Indeed, you are of a great moral character' (al-Qalam 4). May Allah (exalted and high is He) send His blessings and peace upon you, O my Master, O Messenger of Allah".

Shaikh Muḥammad al-Muḥammad al-Kasnazān
(Sermon, 22nd/January/2010)

13

The Takya

The takya has a critical role in the Ṭarīqa because it is the house of worship and knowledge, as well as the place where disciples convene with their Shaikh and meet one another. Hence, Shaikh Muḥammad al-Muḥammad al-Kasnazān has made building takyas a foremost effort of his in delivering the spiritual message of the Messenger (PBUH) to the greatest number of people possible, Muslim or otherwise. He established new takyas in various cities in Iraq and expanded those that were no longer spacious enough to accommodate attendees.

Our Shaikh's moving to Baghdad in 1982 led to a major increase in the number of people who were attracted to the Ṭarīqa. The number of takyas in Baghdad increased from three before he moved there to one hundred and thirty-five by the time he migrated from Baghdad at the end of 2000. He visited many of the new takyas that were opened in Baghdad, where a celebration of the Messenger's (PBUH) birth would be hosted followed by the blessed Kasnazānī dhikr to bless the new takya.

The same way the establishment of the main takya in Baghdad was directed by our Shaikh, he also instructed and supervised the construction of the main takya in Basra in southern Iraq, which was built in 1992 (photo 29). From time to time, he would visit the main takyas in various governorates and would almost directly supervise them because the main takya in each city is the preaching hub and means for the instructions of the Shaikh of Ṭarīqa to be disseminated to secondary takyas, and consequently to all disciples, in that city. He stopped these visits of his after he migrated to Sulaymāniyya and then Amman after that, and also because of his health, in addition to the unstable political and security situation throughout Iraq.

With the spreading of takyas in various governorates of Iraq and numerous Arabs taking the Kasnazānī pledge, Shaikh ʿAbd al-Qādir al-Kasnazān's revelation, when he looked at his newborn son, ʿAbd al-Karīm, who was swaddled, was realised: "What Allah wills, what Allah wills. Allah will guide many Arabs at the hands of the son of this man to the true path".

Kasnazānī takyas also spread during the era of our Shaikh in different countries around the world, thus exceeding hundreds worldwide. Even his old age and poor health have not diminished his resolve in this domain of preaching. He still does what he can to encourage and support caliphs and dervishes in building takyas.

13.1 The Ṭarīqa's Head and Heart

The Farsi and Kurdish origin of the word "takya" is "tāk kāh". The first word means "one" or "singular", and the second means "place" or "venue", so "tāk kāh" means "the house of oneness", meaning "the house of 'there is no god but Allah, and Muḥammad is the Messenger of Allah'", as our Shaikh explained the etymology of the name.[253] Other common traditional names for the takya include "khāniqah", "zāwiya", and "ribāṭ". It is a place where disciples gather for prayer, to perform congregational and individual dhikrs, to learn and teach religious principles, to remember words and karāmas of the Ṭarīqa's Shaikhs, and to study and teach the Sufi way of life. It is a place that is frequented by all who wish to learn about the Ṭarīqa and by those who are contemplating taking the pledge. It is a place where religious learning, in general, is obtained. Our Shaikh described the takya as "a spiritual school that prepares a disciple to be a worshipper, a seeker, and a righteous person and reformer in society".[254] It is a place where a seeker learns the principles of the way to Allah and the method of walking upon it, beginning with the fundamentals of Sharia.

In describing the takya's importance for seekers, our Shaikh likens a disciple without a takya to a homeless person because the takya is a shelter for the seekers of the way to Allah. It is very difficult for the number of disciples to grow in an area where there is no takya. He urges any group of disciples that do not have a takya in their area to establish one, even if a temporary one, even if there are only five of them. He always mentions that even if there are thousands of disciples in any given area, the

---

[253] Shaikh Muḥammad al-Muḥammad al-Kasnazān, *sermon*, 27th/September/2012.

[254] Shaikh Muḥammad al-Muḥammad al-Kasnazān, *sermon*, 22nd/January/2010.

inexistence of a takya where they may gather for dhikr, study, receiving and transferring the Shaikh of Ṭarīqa's teachings and instructions, and coordinating preaching activities greatly limits the spreading of the Ṭarīqa as well as the learning of dervishes. The development of a dervish's spiritual learning remains very limited in the absence of a takya where he may continuously meet with other dervishes. Hence, our Shaikh says that without a takya, there are no disciples and no Ṭarīqa. It is a must for a seeker to have love in his heart for the takya, love for serving it, and love for expanding it.[255]

Often the first takya in an area is merely a single room in the house of a dervish that he dedicates to the Ṭarīqa's observances, but the goal is to establish a takya in a property specially reserved for it. Even though takyas that are a part of dervishes' homes serve the Ṭarīqa and its dervishes, they cannot serve as a full-fledged takyas.

The takya features services to seekers of nearness to Allah that are not available in traditional mosques. In addition to having a mosque for establishing obligatory and voluntary prayers, dhikrs, and even retreats, it also has a kitchen to provide food and drink to seekers, the needy, and passers-by. It also has a sleeping place for disciples who come from far away, and it acts as a shelter to those who need it. Those who are sick frequent the takya in search of blessings and healing. Shaikh Muḥammad al-Muḥammad describes it as a "spiritual and mental school and hospital" because the Ṭarīqa's Shaikhs are doctors and scholars of the soul. It also serves as a school to study religious matters. Thus, the takya's functions are broader and more varied than those of a mosque.[256]

It is important to note that even though the takya's primary function is religious, it also has humanitarian, social, and educational functions for people in general, Sufi or otherwise. For example, the takya's kitchen feeds dervishes who are present in the takya for dhikr, and it also provides food for the needy who come to the takya. We have mentioned how the main takya in Baghdad would send food to a mental health hospital.

The takya is also a place people turn to when resolving disputes and seeking reconciliation. It is also a place where good is enjoined and evil is forbidden, where people are helped to improve themselves, and where

[255] Shaikh Muḥammad al-Muḥammad al-Kasnazān, *sermon*, 7th/July/2000.
[256] Shaikh Muḥammad al-Muḥammad al-Kasnazān, *sermon*, 7th/July/2000.

people are educated about new challenges arise and how to confront them. It participates directly and actively in educating society and in cultivating its culture. We have talked about how Shaikh ʿAbd al-Qādir al-Gaylānī's school in Baghdad, which was comparable to a takya, played a crucial role in preparing a generation of mujahedin who stood against the Crusaders. These students included luminaries who played important roles in this jihad. In various Islamic countries, takyas played extremely crucial roles in pitting Muslims against colonization and urging them to enter into jihad.[257] Some of the most famous mujahedin commanders were Sufis, such as ʿAbd al-Qādir al-Jazāʾirī (1883) and ʿOmar al-Mukhtār (1931).

Kasnazānī takyas have played an active role in tackling one of the biggest challenges facing Muslims and non-Muslims today, which is the rise of extremist, takfiri, and terrorist ideologies and movements. Kasnazānī takyas combat these ideologies by clarifying their deviation from Islamic thought, exposing their history and the circumstances that led to their appearance, and dismantling the illegitimate objectives of movements that adopt these deviant ideas. In recent years, many takyas in Iraq were attacked by terrorist groups, such as ISIS, which completely or partially blew up, razed, or burned around forty Kasnazānī takyas in the governorates of al-Ānbār, Nineveh, Salaḥ al-Dīn, Diyāla, and Baghdad. They have also killed hundreds of dervishes and abducted scores of them.

The Shaikh of Ṭarīqa appoints a caliph to manage each takya, and this caliph is helped by other caliphs and dervishes. There is usually more than one takya in any given city when it is a large city and there is a relatively large number of disciples. In this case, the Shaikh of Ṭarīqa designates a takya as the main takya in that city. The caliphs in charge of serving the main takyas have added responsibilities of communicating the Shaikh's instructions and any other administrative directives to the other takyas.

When there is no building specially reserved as a takya in an area, usually due to a sparsity of dervishes or a lack of means, as a temporary measure, a place is rented to be used as a takya for dhikr and special occasions. Alternatively, one or more dervishes reserve a separate room in their homes as a takya. Even when there are buildings specially

---

[257] Jab Allah, "Dawr al-Ṭuruq al-Ṣūfiyya fil-Mujtamaʿ al-Jazāʾirī".

reserved as takyas, some disciples like reserving a room in their homes to function as a takya, for blessing or to facilitate the performance of the Ṭarīqa's dhikrs without having to go to the designated takya, which may be relatively far away. When a takya does not occupy a building dedicated to it, however, it cannot provide all the services that designated facilities do.

The takya is a house that the Mighty and the All-Knowing One has described as: "In homes that Allah has ordered to be raised and that His name be mentioned therein; exalting His name within them in the morning and the evenings (36) are men whom neither commerce nor sale distracts from the remembrance of Allah and performance of prayer and giving of zakat" (al-Nūr 36-37). There are special etiquettes involved with visiting and being inside a takya. Unsurprisingly, while there, it is impermissible to do anything that contravenes religious commandments. It is also improper to engage in worldly matters inside it, in word or deed. The full focus must be placed on worship, as well as teaching and learning about religious matters. The seeker must also preserve the takya's cleanliness and order, just as he would his own home.

Since it is a house of dhikr, worship, and remembrance of righteous people, the takya is a blessed place where Allah's light descends upon His servants, as Almighty said in a Qudsī ḥadīth: "I accompany the one who remembers Me".[258] The Prophet (PBUH) also described circles of dhikr as "gardens of Paradise".[259] Being a place of dhikr, the takya is described by our Shaikh as a "piece of Paradise on earth".[260] The takya is blessed with the presence of the souls of the Shaikhs of Ṭarīqa and the descent of angels because of its being a place of Allah's dhikr. For all these reasons, our Shaikh emphasizes the takya's sanctity.

This blessing is what has made takyas destinations for those who suffer from various diseases, including those that are medically untreatable. The diseased person may be asked to sit in the middle of the dhikr circle, lie down in the takya's resting area, drink water from the takya, or sweeten his tea with sugar that was blessed by having been placed in the middle of the dhikr circle. There are countless karāmas of miraculous cures for

---

[258] Bayhaqī, *Shu'ab al-Īmān*, I, no. 680, p. 451.

[259] Tirmidhī, *Al-Jāmi' al-Kabīr*, V, no. 3510, p. 488.

[260] Shaikh Muḥammad al-Muḥammad al-Kasnazān, *sermon*, 7th/July/2000.

various illnesses by way of being blessed by things from the takya.

In describing the takya's blessing and the reward for serving it, Shaikh Muḥammad al-Muḥammad al-Kasnazān says:

> "I wish I could clean and wash the takya with my own hands every day, as a great number of our Shaikhs used to do. They would clean the mosque and the takya with their beards for Allah's sake, to please Him, because the takya is a holy place. The takya is mentioned in the Qur'an: 'In homes that Allah has ordered to be raised and that His name be mentioned therein' (al-Nūr 36). This is Allah's house, the Messenger's (PBUH) house".[261]

In explaining the duty a seeker has to continuously visit the takya to attend dhikr circles and participate in congregational dhikrs and prayers, our Shaikh says:

> "The takya is the Ṭarīqa's head; the takya is the Ṭarīqa's heart; the takya is the Ṭarīqa's brain. When you abandon the takya, you abandon the Ṭarīqa. When you are committed to visiting the takya, you are committed to the Ṭarīqa, righteous deeds, Īmān, and dervishood for Allah's sake, for the Ṭarīqa's sake. Anyone who abandons the takya abandons Allah (exalted and high is He)".[262]

Our Shaikh continues, advising seekers:

> "When you go to the takya, you renew your involvement with the Ṭarīqa, your covenant, your pledge, your Īmān. The Messenger of Allah said (PBUH): 'Renew your Īmān'. They said: 'How do we renew our Īmān?' He said: 'Repeat abundantly the phrase 'There is no god but Allah''.[263] When you go to the takya, you remember Allah (exalted and high is He): 'The remembrance of Allah is greater' (al-ʿAnkabūt 45)".[264]

On Eid al-Fiṭr 2012, the Ṭarīqa's Shaikhs informed our Master that when a dervish visits the takya, joins the dhikr circle, and participates in the session of praise, he leaves the takya completely free of sins.[265]

---

[261] Shaikh Muḥammad al-Muḥammad al-Kasnazān, *sermon*, 27th/September/2012.
[262] Shaikh Muḥammad al-Muḥammad al-Kasnazān, *sermon*, 7th/January/2010.
[263] Aḥmad, *Musnad al-Imām Aḥmad Ibn Ḥanbal*, XIV, no. 8710, p. 328.
[264] Shaikh Muḥammad al-Muḥammad al-Kasnazān, *sermon*, 7th/January/2010.
[265] Shaikh Muḥammad al-Muḥammad al-Kasnazān, *sermon*, 5th/December/2012.

13.2 The Shaikh's Takya

The Shaikh dedicates his entire life in service to the Ṭarīqa, Islam, and Muslims, even when he is with his family. Hence, his house is a takya. The Shaikh's takya is the Ṭarīqa's main takya worldwide and its headquarters.

Along with the seeker's need to continuously visit the takya near his home, there is exceptional importance in visiting the Shaikh's takya because it has special spiritual benefits. In addition to the blessing of it being a house of Allah's dhikr, the Shaikh of Ṭarīqa's permanent presence therein adds the blessing of it being a place of one of Allah's closest servants. There is an immense blessing in a seeker's visiting of the Shaikh's takya, even when he is not fortunate enough to see the Shaikh.

As mentioned earlier, ṣuḥba is the Ṭarīqa's foundation and the means to reach Allah. The one who is accompanied, i.e. the Shaikh, is the means by which the one who accompanies him, that is the seeker, is connected to Allah: "O you who have believed, fear Allah and seek the means [of nearness] to Him and strive in His cause that you may succeed" (al-Mā`ida 35). A seeker's visiting of the Shaikh as much as he can is one of the fundamental pillars of his Sufi conduct. The Shaikh purifies the seeker internally and externally: "Just as We have sent among you a messenger from yourselves reciting to you Our verses, purifying you, teaching you the Book and wisdom, and teaching you that which you did not know" (al-Baqara 151).

One manifestation of the blessing of the takya wherein the Shaikh resides is that it is constantly blessed with the presence of the Messenger (PBUH) and the Ṭarīqa's Shaikhs because he is the one they appointed to their deputyship. Some disciples were visiting Shaikh Ḥusayn al-Kasnazān when they told him about their desire to visit Shaikh Ismā'īl al-Wilyānī's shrine. The Shaikh smiled and permitted them to do so. When they left, the Shaikh said: "They don't know that our Master Ismā'īl al-Wilyānī was just here".[266] In a similar incident, some dervishes visited Shaikh 'Abd al-Karīm al-Kasnazān and expressed their wish to visit some shrines of righteous people, which he granted. After they returned from their trip, he asked them: "What have you got from the stones and walls?" They replied: "Nothing, O Shaikh". The Shaikh told them: "My sons,

---

[266] Shaikh Muḥammad al-Muḥammad al-Kasnazān, *sermon*, updated.

everyone you want to visit is present here. When you come here, you visit all of them".[267]

This is logical and natural because the Messenger (PBUH) and Shaikhs of the Ṭarīqa are the ones who made Shaikh ʿAbd al-Karīm their deputy among people. The Shaikh did not want to dissuade the seekers from visiting the shrines of righteous people, but he wanted to teach them that a dervish's desire to visit any given shrine while he is visiting his Shaikh reflects a lack of awareness that his Master represents all of the Ṭarīqa's Shaikhs and that his takya represents their shrines.

Kāka Aḥmad al-Shaikh, a great walī, son of Shaikh Maʿrūf an-Nūdīhī, son of Shaikh Musṭafā, son of Shaikh Aḥmad, Shaikh Ismāʿīl al-Wilyānī's brother, one of Shāh al-Kasnazān's ancestors, said something similar. On his way back from hajj, he visited Shāh al-Kasnazān in Karbchna. He addressed those present, advising them: "Whoever cannot visit the Greatest Ghawth, Shaikh ʿAbd al-Qādir al-Gaylānī in Baghdad, this cousin of mine, Shaikh ʿAbd al-Karīm Shāh al-Kasnazān, stands in his place. Visiting him is the same as visiting Shaikh ʿAbd al-Qādir".[268] In this statement, this great knower of Allah's also acknowledges Shāh al-Kasnazān's spiritual merit. It is noteworthy that Kāka Aḥmad was more than thirty years older than Shāh al-Kasnazān.

The same way there are exceptional blessings in the Shaikh's takya, seeing the Shaikh causes a seeker to receive his lights and overflowing spiritual bounty, which purify him and help him draw nearer to Allah. In addition to these internal spiritual benefits, there are immense external benefits in meeting the Shaikh. Representing the Prophet (PBUH), the Shaikh only says things that remind a seeker of Allah, of what He revealed in the noble Qur'an, and of the Messenger's sayings, deeds, and states (PBUH). His assembly is a place where good is enjoined and evil is forbidden. In the Shaikh's assembly, there is continuous remembrance of Allah and constant reminders of Him, the Prophet (PBUH), the Shaikhs of Ṭarīqa, and righteous people: "Remind, for indeed, the reminder benefits the believers" (al-Dhāriyāt 55). Our Shaikh says: "Visiting the Shaikh increases your faith and love, strengthens your faith, and spiritually

---

[267] Shaikh Muḥammad al-Muḥammad al-Kasnazān, *sermon*, 22nd/December/2005.

[268] Shaikh Muḥammad al-Muḥammad al-Kasnazān, *sermon*, 22nd/December/2005.

relaxes you".[269] In describing the benefits of visiting the Shaikh, he adds:

> "By visiting the Shaikh, you receive benefits; you earn purification of the soul; you earn nearness to the Shaikh. You take blessing from the Shaikh, listen to the Shaikh, and follow him...When you have a problem, whether internal or external, you present it to him because he is your Shaikh, internally and externally. When you have an internal illness in the Ṭarīqa, he is the doctor who cures you. When something external happens to you in the Ṭarīqa, your Shaikh is your role model, the one you listen to and implement his words".[270]

In visiting the Shaikh, there is also the "renewal of the Ṭarīqa's covenant; renewal of faith; renewal of loyalty; renewal of the seeker's spiritual sonship of the Shaikh; renewal of the spiritual bond with the Shaikh; renewal of a seeker's pledge to Allah".[271] Our Shaikh cites Shaikh ʿAbd al-Qādir al-Gaylānī's words about how a seeker must visit his Shaikh at least once a year, and that a caliph must visit with more frequency. When our Shaikh was in Baghdad, he expressed the need for caliphs of takyas in Baghdad, as well as caliphs of takyas in neighbouring governorates who could, to attend the official dhikr on Thursday night in the main takya.

13.3 Moving the Shaikh's Takya to Baghdad

When our Shaikh became the Master of Ṭarīqa in early 1978, Iraq's main takya, meaning the Shaikh residence, was in the district of Imām Qāsim in the city of Kirkuk in northern Iraq, where Shaikh ʿAbd al-Karīm al-Kasnazān settled down in 1968. Our Shaikh expanded the takya, added an adjoining house to it, made a takya for women, vacated his house adjoining the takya where he used to live during his father's Shaikhhood, and turned it into a takya for dervishes as well.

One of the most important preaching steps Shaikh Muḥammad al-Muḥammad took in building takyas was his decision, shortly after assuming the Ṭarīqa's Shaikhdom, to move the main takya to Baghdad; that is, he moved his place of residence from Kirkuk to Baghdad. This

[269] Shaikh Muḥammad al-Muḥammad al-Kasnazān, *sermon*, 22nd/December/2005.
[270] Shaikh Muḥammad al-Muḥammad al-Kasnazān, *sermon*, 19th/September/2012.
[271] Shaikh Muḥammad al-Muḥammad al-Kasnazān, *sermon*, 26th/October/2012.

led to the quick spread of the Ṭarīqa like never before. When he became the Master of Ṭarīqa, there were only three small takyas in Baghdad: one in the al-Raḥmāniyya quarter, which was a room in a house; another one in the al-Ārdharūmlī quarter; and a third near the al-Gaylānī Shrine. There was only one caliph in Baghdad, named "Bāqir" (may Allah have mercy on him), who managed the al-Raḥmāniyya takya, the city's first Kasnazānī takya.

When our Shaikh visited Baghdad early in his Shaikhhood, staying in the Ibn Khaldūn hotel, near the al-Ṣarrāfiyya Bridge, he spoke to a dervish named Kāmil Shihāb (may Allah have mercy on him), who used to manage the al-Ārdharūmlī takya, about the necessity of establishing a takya in a dedicated building. There, the Shaikh would meet disciples, and disciples would practice dhikr, worship, and preach. He directed him to search for suitable land to build the main takya upon, after giving him an idea of the kind of place to look for. After checking out potential sites, Hajj Kāmil proposed a plot of land in the district of Ḥayy al-Qudhāt in central Baghdad with an area of 1,365 square metres. As the land was in the suburbs of Baghdad, some Arab and Kurdish disciples thought that it was far from the city's centre and that it would not be easy to access. When our Shaikh visited it, however, he saw the future takya there and decided that it was the required land.

The land was surrounded by a fence, but neighbouring houses dumped their rubbish on it. The land was owned by the state, and the authorities were considering more than one plan for using the land, but they had not made a final decision. A karāma facilitated the Ṭarīqa's acquisition of the land. A large number of disciples, filling around seven large buses, went to visit Shaikh Muḥammad al-Muḥammad in Karbchna, where he was supervising the renovation of the Shaikhs' shrines. Hiding among the visitors, there was a young man named ʿAlī from the security department of the National Command of the ruling Ba'ath Party in Iraq. He had been sent by security agencies to spy on the Ṭarīqa. The Ṭarīqa had always been a source of concern for the government, which did not understand that it was a spiritual organization, not a worldly one. Its concern was further heightened by the fact that the Ṭarīqa's Shaikh was a Kurd, as were many of its dervishes, because the central authorities were in conflict with Kurdish political and armed wings. When the visitor was among hundreds of disciples in

Karbchna near the Shaikhs' shrines, our Shaikh was sitting with guests in his house, which is located on a hill about 250 metres away from the tombs. Our Master suddenly summoned caliph Muḥammad Maḥmūd (may Allah have mercy on him), who served as his administrative deputy among caliphs and dervishes, described that man to him, and told him to deliver a message to him.

When caliph Muḥammad found the man, he took him aside and delivered our Shaikh's message to him: Karbchna was a safe zone, so there was no need for the pistol he was hiding. Also, there were Peshmerga fighters in surrounding areas that could cause trouble for him if they knew that he was armed. Muḥammad asked him to give him the pistol so that he could keep it as a trust. He would accompany him on the way back after the visit ended and he would return it to him in Sangāw after he and the rest of the dervishes crossed the danger zone and entered the total safety zone, where there were no Peshmerga fighters. The man's face changed to reflect the magnitude of shock he was in. He initially denied that he was carrying a weapon, but when he found Muḥammad absolutely confident in the Shaikh's revelation, he confessed to the validity of what he had said and gave him his pistol. He asked him to take him to see the Shaikh. When our Shaikh received him, he repeated what he had said before, that Karbchna was safe, and that it was best not to carry a weapon in this area since Peshmerga fighters might misunderstand and hurt him if they came to know that he was armed. He reassured him once again that the caliph would return his weapon to him in Sangāw on the way back. He told him that the Ṭarīqa was not hiding anything that would require spying on it, and that the main concern of the Shaikh and dervishes is to remember and worship Allah. He asked him to write an accurate, detailed report to whoever sent him of what he saw when he returned. He also asked him to come and see him again afterwards.

'Alī became a sincere disciple. He used his connections to secure the approvals needed for building the takya on the land in Ḥayy al-Qudhāt. By a karāma of the Shaikhs, this man was turned from a spy on the Ṭarīqa into one of its good disciples. He appeared at the perfect time to provide an important service for the Ṭarīqa, helping to expedite the building of the main takya in Baghdad. The takya's land was registered in 1979, about a year after our Shaikh assumed the Shaikhdom of the Ṭarīqa, and its construction began in 1980 (photo 40). Our Shaikh would constantly visit Baghdad to oversee the construction work. In the beginning, he would stay in a hotel, but when his visits became longer, he rented a house. The takya was opened in 1982, so he visited it more frequently until he moved with his family in the same year to permanently reside in his home in the takya. Baghdad became the Ṭarīqa's preaching hub.

The takya was designed and built under our Master's direct supervision. He asked the lead engineer to make the dhikr yard large. The engineer said that he had also asked him to make a mosque that could accommodate those who prayed and performed dhikr, a hall for dervishes, some of whom would be staying in the takya, and a house for the Shaikh, which would also not be free of visitors. Thus, it was difficult to make the dhikr yard large. The engineer's thinking was influenced by the size of the small dhikr yard in the Kirkuk takya, saying that he did not believe that there was a need for a large yard because it would not be filled. Our Shaikh said that the Ṭarīqa's Shaikhs bring as many disciples as a takya can accommodate: the bigger the takya is, the more the disciples' number. He asked him to make the dhikr yard as big as possible. Thanks to continuous preaching, dervishes started to fill the takya's yard on Monday and Thursday nights, when dhikr circles are held. Our Shaikh said the same thing when critiquing the building of the orchard in Dōra, which the Ṭarīqa started to use for some religious celebrations when the main takya could not accommodate attendees.

Our Master asked for a special hall for women to be made, where female preachers could teach female dervishes and seekers of knowledge about the Ṭarīqa. Therein, his mother would also receive those who wanted to visit her, seeking her prayer or advice. When the dhikr circle is established on Monday and Thursday nights, the sleeping room, which overlooks the takya's courtyard where the dhikr is held, is also reserved for women, so that they may participate in the dhikr.

Our Shaikh made the door of the takya's mosque a replica of the new door that was designed for the Shaikhs' shrines in Karbchna. The work was carried out by skilled workers in Isfahan. Dervishes also brought an enormous samovar from Isfahan that was placed in front of the takya's mosque. Amazingly, both the door and the samovar were transported on foot from Isfahan to Baghdad because at the time the border between Iraq and Iran was closed because the two countries were at war. This required travelling a rugged, dangerous mountain route to stay hidden from authorities in both countries.

When the takya's mosque, which is 22 metres long and 17.65 metres wide, was being designed, our Master did not want to use pillars inside its hall. Shaikh Sāmān Maʿrūf, the lead engineer, said that the mosque's huge dome was made out of reinforced concrete and its peak was 17 metres above the mosque's floor, so its weight and weight of its covering needed to be supported by pillars, according to engineering laws. Our Shaikh, however, repeated his request that the mosque must not have any pillars inside it. Sāmān said that even though engineering laws required building supporting pillars, he would make the dome without pillars, relying on our Shaikh's spiritual influence. Two days after casting the dome and putting up temporary wooden pillars to allow the building materials to harden, the caliph who was supervising the construction noticed that one of the wooden pillars had tilted. Shaikh Sāmān reiterated that the dome was supposed to be supported by pillars, but expressed no concern for it since it did not collapse during the casting process. After the mosque's completion, a huge, very heavy chandelier was also hung from the dome's roof (photo 28)!

After the dome was covered from the outside and a crescent moon was placed on its peak, Shaikh Sāmān had a dream where he saw Shaikh Ismāʿīl al-Wilyānī's hand supporting the dome. One day, when a group of engineers asked our Shaikh how the dome of the takya's mosque stood without supportive pillars, he replied: "Shaikh ʿAbd al-Karīm's hand is supporting it until the Day of Resurrection". Even large explosions near the takya as a result of aerial bombardments during the Gulf War did not affect the mosque's dome — another proof of its being under the protection of the Ṭarīqa's Shaikhs.

It is dervishes who build takyas because they are Allah's houses and they are places wherein they gather and establish dhikr circles. When establishing a main takya in any given city, not only disciples from that city participate in building it, but also disciples from other cities come to help. This is how, for instance, the main takya in Baghdad was built.

In one of the karāmas that accompanied the building of the main takya in Baghdad, our Shaikh, who was in Kirkuk at the time, sent caliph Aḥmad Ḥusayn and another named Muḥammad to a factory in the city of Erbil to buy marble for the takya. He specified the type of marble to them, its colour, dimensions, and the required amount. The factory's manager apologized and said that what they wanted was unavailable. Our Shaikh asked them to once again go to the same factory and ask for the marble. Hesitant, Aḥmad said that the factory's manager told them that the marble was unavailable, but since this was the Shaikh's wish, he would go again. Our Shaikh patted him on the back encouragingly and said: "Go Kasnazānī, Kasnazānī". When they reached the factory, Muḥammad felt too embarrassed to ask for the marble again, so Aḥmad went to the manager's office alone. He told those present in the office that he knew that they had already told him that they did not have this kind of marble, but that he had returned to check once again to be sure, in deference to the Shaikh's wish. The manager restated that they did not have that kind of marble, but an employee there who was writing something put his pen aside and asked the caliph to follow him to the storehouse because he was reminded of the possibility that such a kind of marble was available. The employee removed a cover that revealed the marble that the Shaikh wanted. The available amount matched the desired quantity. Stunned, the employee said: "Your Shaikh knows our factory better than us". This karāma reminds us of a mu'jiza of Jesus, peace be upon him, which was that he knew what people stored in their homes: "I inform you of what you eat and what you store in your houses" (`Āl 'Imrān 49).

13.4 Karāmas of Building Takyas

Since takyas are places of Allah's dhikr and have a special blessing, there are always karāmas that accompany the process of choosing their location and building them, as we saw in the case of the Baghdad takya. We see this phenomenon in particular with main takyas, as we shall see in three examples from Iraq, Sudan, and India.

13.4.1 The Ramādī Takya in Iraq

The main takya in the city of Ramādī is the first large takya that was built outside northern Iraq.

In early 1966, the army summoned those who were enlisted for compulsory military service that year, which included caliph Yāsīn Ṣūfī. The city in which he would do his military service was Ramādī, west of Baghdad, in the Anbār governorate. The caliph was hesitant about serving in the military and going far away from Shaikh ʿAbd al-Karīm in Kirkuk and from his family in the governorate of Erbil in northern Iraq. He visited Shaikh ʿAbd al-Karīm and asked him about the matter. Shaikh ʿAbd al-Karīm first told him not to go, but after ten minutes, he called him and told him to go and that Allah willing, good would come from his going. He advised him to preach.

About a month after he settled in Ramādī, Yāsīn rented a house to act as a takya where dervishes could perform dhikr and call people to the Ṭarīqa, as Shaikh ʿAbd al-Karīm directed him to do. The Ṭarīqa Kasnazāniyya began to spread in that city.

In mid-1970, the decision to demobilize caliph Yāsīn's unit came. He bade farewell to the dervishes in Ramādī to go back to live in northern Iraq. He went to visit Shaikh ʿAbd al-Karīm in Kirkuk. Before even getting the chance to kiss his hand, the Shaikh ordered him to return to Ramādī and settle there, telling him that this was Sulṭān Ḥusayn's order.

The small takya did not offer all the services and activities of a specialized takya. Dervishes were also harassed for performing dhikr and conducting preaching sessions in a house that was originally reserved for living, not in a takya or a mosque. One day, Yāsīn wished in secret that the Ṭarīqa would have a building specially reserved as a takya. The following day, a tribal chief in Ramādī, Hajj Qāsim al-Ṣaffār, phoned him and asked him to come to see him for some reason. After the caliph arrived, Hajj Qāsim contacted a person named Najam Ḥāmmād and asked him to come. Then, he explained the situation to the caliph. The man who was coming was not religiously observant and paid no attention to what was and was not permissible. His ailing wife had had a dream in which she was told that her only cure was to place the palm of a Kasnazānī banner near a source of water that she uses to wash in a clean place so that the used water did not mix with dirty water. The palm of a Kasnazāni banner is a piece of iron placed on top of a wooden column around which a flag bearing the Ṭarīqa's name is wrapped. Flags are placed in takyas and are also customarily carried by dervishes when they go on preaching trips. The woman did not tell her husband about the vision at first, but she had the same vision again the following night. Having noticed that she was distrait, her husband asked her what was bothering her, so she told him about the dream. She warned him that if they wanted to contact Kasnazānī disciples for this purpose, they would ask them to take the pledge. When the husband came to Hajj Qāsim's house, caliph Yāsīn informed him that he and his wife had to take the pledge and that he would pass them the palm of a Kasnazānī banner. They took the pledge and the wife did what she had seen in the dream, and she was cured immediately.

The next day, the couple sent for caliph Yāsīn. The wife told him that she had vowed to donate 300 dinars when she was cured. She presented the sum to him so that he could purchase land for the takya, even though she did not know that a few days earlier he prayed to be able to build a takya. The caliph thanked her and asked her to keep the sum with her until he needed it. He searched for land in the same area as the existing takya. Someone took him to see a tract of land that he liked. When he asked about it, it turned out that it was owned by the father-in-law of the woman who had been cured by a karāma of the Ṭarīqa! The caliph went to the landowner, who also took the pledge, and mentioned that he heard that he was selling some land and asked to view it with him. There were parcels of land in that area, so the caliph wanted to confirm that the land he wanted was the land that the man owned. Indeed, the owner took him to the same piece of land. The caliph told him that he wanted to purchase it and that his son would pay its price. The landowner said that he had been offered 200 dinars for the land, but he had refused the offer. However, since the land was being bought to build a takya, he would sell it to the caliph for 150 dinars. The takya was fully constructed in 1971.

There is a related karāma that happened years before this, i.e. before there was even any talk about this takya. A dervish who possessed ḥāls named Majīd, whom we have mentioned in a karāma in §9.2, visited caliph Yāsīn in Ramādī. The two were walking on a path near the land that was destined to be the future takya's location. Majīd was holding a cane that had an iron hook handle that he usually used for certain needs, such as uprooting plants. Every now and then, he would stop to remove a stone from the path. Yāsīn asked him to walk faster because of the heat of the summer sun. Majīd told him that Shaikh ʿAbd al-Karīm would one day pass by this road. He walked a little further before stopping again and saying "this is an enemy", removing a stone with his cane. He looked like symbolically paving the road that Shaikh ʿAbd al-Karīm would travel upon years later. Once more, Yāsīn asked him what he was doing. Majīd swore and reiterated what he had said before: a day would come when the caliph would see Shaikh 'Abd al-Karīm pass by that road. Shaikh 'Abd al-Karīm indeed passed by that road when he visited the main takya in Ramādī after its completion.

Shaikh 'Abd al-Karīm visited Ramādī twice, in 1970 and then in 1972 after the main takya was built. Two other takyas were built in Ramādī during Shaikh 'Abd al-Karīm's lifetime. Shaikh Muḥammad al-Muḥammad completed what Shaikh 'Abd al-Karīm had started. He dedicated so much effort to preaching in Ramādī, including visiting it many times after he settled in Baghdad. The number of takyas there greatly increased and many of the city's inhabitants took the Ṭarīqa Kasnazāniyya pledge.

13.4.2 The Khartoum Takya in Sudan

One of our present Shaikh's karāmas in building takyas accompanied the founding of the first Kasnazānī takya in Sudan.

After the Iraqi reciter of the Qur'an Hajj 'Alā' al-Dīn al-Qaysī (may Allah have mercy on him) returned from an official trip to Sudan in 1944, he informed our Shaikh that he had given the Ṭarīqa's pledge to Professor Ḥasan Aḥmad Ḥāmid and told him about Shaikh 'Abd al-Qādir al-Gaylānī's order to Professor Ḥāmid to spread the Ṭarīqa al-Qādiriyya in Sudan. Our Shaikh sent caliph Ṭāhā 'Ubayd al-Ṭā'ī to Sudan and told him that he would find that the Shaikhs had prepared what he would need to preach.

Ṭāhā arrived, in the company of two other caliphs, in Khartoum on Tuesday 11th/January/1994. They headed straight for Professor Ḥāmid's house. They told him about what our Shaikh had entrusted them with and gave him a letter from our Shaikh to be delivered to Sudan's president, Omar al-Bashir, asking for permission to build a Kasnazānī takya in Sudan. The purpose of the letter was to introduce the Ṭarīqa to the president and to prevent any misunderstanding about what the Ṭarīqa wanted in establishing itself in Sudan, especially since the Ṭarīqa's Shaikhs were from another country. The unexpected visit stunned Professor Ḥāmid because that morning, before the three dervishes arrived, his sister-in-law, who was living with his family, had told him that she had had a dream that night where she saw that a messenger had left Baghdad three days earlier and was headed towards him. Professor Ḥāmid sent for his sister-in-law and told her that her dream had come true. The messenger she had seen in her dream was the caliph who was sent by Shaikh Muḥammad al-Muḥammad al-Kasnazān. He noted, however, that the messenger had arrived the same day he left Baghdad, not three days after, as she had seen in the dream. The caliph interjected here, giving another detail about his trip that confirmed the vision's accuracy. He left Baghdad for Amman on Sunday 30th/October, but he had to stay in Amman for two days, waiting for the only weekly trip from Amman to Khartoum, on Tuesday. Indeed, his trip took three days, not one day as Professor Ḥāmid thought!

The next morning, Professor Ḥāmid took the three dervishes on a tour of the al-Ṣāfiya neighbourhood where he lived, searching for a building that could be rented as a place for a takya, after which they would then send our Shaikh's letter to the president to obtain the state's approval. After several hours in which they visited many places, they did not find a suitable building. When they returned to the house around three in the afternoon for lunch, Ṭāhā remembered a dream he had seen the night before about the takya's location. He saw a big mosque wherein there was a tall minaret. Next to it, there were simple, old, terraced houses. On the other side of the side street, there was a yard in front of the mosque the size of a football pitch. In the middle of it, there is a very large house, so it was isolated from any other structure. In that house, there was one very tall tree that had many branches. When the caliph recounted his dream, Professor Ḥāmid was surprised, and said: "It seems like you know the area better than me"! He went on to say that the big house belonged to a someone called Muḥammad al-Ṭayyib, and that the mosque was well known, named Ummat al-Ijāba. They were located in Shambāt al-Ḥilla, which was about a kilometre away from al-Ṣāfiya.

On their way to visit the site, Professor Ḥāmid explained that Muḥammad al-Ṭayyib had registered a mosque with the office of religious endowment that he wanted to build on that large expanse of land. However, he built a big house with an area of about a thousand metres that no one lived in. It was used from time to time as a secluded area to memorize the Qur'an. As for the tree, it was a doum palm tree that had grown over the years in a place where water that students used for ablution ran. Another distinguishing feature of the tree is that it was the only tree in the area, as the small houses in that residential neighbourhood had no gardens. After arriving at the house, they all noted the dream's accurate description of it. Professor Ḥāmid agreed that it would make for a suitable takya. They met al-Ṭayyib who agreed to rent out the house as a takya. This was how the first Kasnazānī takya in Sudan was established. Our Shaikh appointed Professor Ḥāmid, who became a member of the Islamic jurisprudence council, as his deputy in Sudan. Afterwards, many takyas were opened in various cities in Sudan.

13.4.3 The Bangalore Takya in India

We have mentioned the great preaching achievements of our Shaikh in India, where about thirty small takyas were established over the years in buildings that were not dedicated to them. However, the lack of a takya in a dedicated, separate building limited the Ṭarīqa's ability to spread. Launching a new preaching campaign in India in 2011, our Shaikh sent caliph ʿImād ʿAbd al-Ṣamad and advised him as follows: "We have been wanting to establish a takya in Bangalore for about twenty years. Your goal is to preach and establish a takya". The first specialised takya was established in India, in the city of Bangalore, through an amazing karāma whose events began on June 2012. This is its story, as told by caliph ʿImād:

> Carrying out my Shaikh's order, during my preaching tour I searched for a suitable plot of land to establish a takya. Whenever I found a place, I would tell the honourable Shaikh about it, but he did not want any of these places because they were far from where caliphs and dervishes lived.
>
> I then had a dream where I saw the honourable Shaikh driving his old red Landcruiser and I was sitting beside him. He said to me: "My son, do you see that yellow-lighted lamp?" I said: "Yes". He said: "I want you to get land in this area". I said: "With the spiritual influence of the Shaikhs, I will do so". Then he said: "My land is there. There are documents that show that it is in my name. Try to find these documents". I promised him that I would, then we left the place with him driving the car. While we were going back, I saw a train pass near the place. Then I woke up. I began to ask if there was a railroad nearby whenever I was shown a plot of land, searching for that sign.
>
> A while later, I had a second dream. The honourable Shaikh was sitting in a car and I was standing next to it. He asked me from the car window: "My son, have you found the place?" I told him that I was still searching, then I woke up. When I told the honourable Shaikh about the two dreams, he commented: "Allah willing, the Shaikhs will give you what you have seen".
>
> About a week later, I was in Shadab Nagar in the centre of Bangalore,

close to where all the caliphs lived, when a Muslim real estate agent came to me with documents for a plot of land that was on sale in Saraipalya. I told him that it was very small, as I needed a tract of land that had an area of no less than one thousand metres squared because it would be a takya. He had other small portions of land neighbouring that land, so I told him that I needed between eighteen to twenty of those small adjoining plots. The agent said that they would be costly. At the time, I didn't have any money, but I put my trust in Allah.

I asked him what his name was and he said: "Muḥammad Irshād". When I heard his name, I felt a fluttering in my chest. I saw in the name the first sign from my Master that this was the land for the takya. His first name, "Muḥammad", was the honourable Shaikh's name, and his last name, "Irshād" (preaching), was what the takya would do. Caliphs Zakariyyā Ibrāhīm Shaikh, Fayrūz Khān ʿAzīz, and Jaʿfar Muḥammad Ḥanīf, who live in Bangalore, witnessed this and the wonders that followed.

It was afternoon when we went to inspect the land. An indescribable feeling came over me. It was as if I had entered Paradise because we had passed by a railway. Then I saw the streetlight that I saw in my dream. I told my companions that this was the yellow-lighted lamp, and I told them about the two dreams. I told them that the two signs in the dream that we saw on the land and the fact that the agent's name was Muḥammad Irshād constituted a definitive indication that this was indeed the takya's land.

The area had a Hindu majority. There were two or three Muslim households and they had a small mosque made of mud. After we performed Wird al-ʿAṣr, I told the caliphs that we would stay until darkness fell so that they could see the yellow light with their own eyes. The area was filled with mosquitoes, so the caliphs tried to dissuade me from staying, but I insisted on waiting for darkness to descend.

After we performed the sunset prayer, we kept waiting for streetlights to light up so that we could see the colour of that streetlamp. About half an hour passed and the streetlights were still dark. I asked Fayroz and Jaʿfar to ask the Hindu owner of a small shop under the streetlamp why the streetlights did not light up and what colour that streetlamp was. He told them that the power was out until nine o'clock and that the colour of the light was white. When they told me what he said, I swore a serious oath that it was yellow. They were taken aback by my insistence, as the shopkeeper must know better the colour of the streetlight whose light fell on his shop every night!

I asked my companions to stay there until power was restored so that we could determine the light's colour. We were there at the mercy of the mosquitoes for another hour and a half. A while after we performed the night prayer and its dhikr, the power came. Zakariyyā noted that the light was white. I swore a second time that it was yellow. He started to laugh hysterically when he saw the resoluteness of my belief, despite it being contradicted by what the shopkeeper had said and what the eye saw. While Zakariyyā was laughing, he was soon baffled when the white light began to turn yellow. It became apparent that the bulb was a halogen bulb. I asked the caliphs to go back to the shopkeeper and ask him why he had said that the light was white. The man came out of his shop to look at the light. When he saw that it was yellow, he also seemed astonished. He told them that he was prepared to swear that the light was white and that he was absolutely sure of this since he had owned this shop for many years.

Another wondrous thing in what happened, which was the secret behind the honourable Shaikh mentioning that the colour of that streetlight was yellow in the dream, was that all the other streetlights were white; this was the only streetlamp that was yellow! The caliphs wept because of the karāma they had seen. I restated what I said earlier, that this land definitely belonged to the Ṭarīqa. We began to pursue the process of purchasing the land.

Two days later, Muḥammad Irshād came to me with a man he introduced as a mediator between us and the landowners. I asked him what his name was, and he said Aḥmad Irshād. Thus, the signs kept coming. After we paid the down payment, we went to an office where we met a person named ʿAbbās, who represented the landowners. When I greeted ʿAbbās, he began kissing my hands and feet and delighted me by surprising me with the fact that, for more than fifteen years, his late mother had been a disciple of the honourable Shaikh ʿAbd al-Karīm al-Kasnazān. She had taken the pledge at the hand of caliph ʿAbd al-Razzāq Sharīf, a caliph of the honourable Shaikh ʿAbd al-Karīm. Expressing his desire to serve the Ṭarīqa, ʿAbbās said that he would try to secure a reduction of the land's square foot price.

He took us to meet a Muslim individual who was the senior person responsible for a large amount of land, including the plot that we wanted to buy. This man said that he also wished to serve the takya project since it belonged to the honourable Shaikh ʿAbd al-Qādir al-Gaylānī's Ṭarīqa. He offered to bear the cost of the takya's opening ceremony. I thanked him and asked him what his name was. He stunned me by replying that his name was "Irshād".

When I informed the honourable Shaikh that the name of the first individual was Muḥammad Irshād, the second, Aḥmad Irshād, and the third, Irshād, he commented: "Your Shaikh is the Quṭb al-Irshād (axis of preaching), Allah be praised, and the Ṭarīqa is a Ṭarīqa of irshād (preaching). This takya is for you, Allah willing, by the spiritual influence of our Master al-Gaylānī,

> may Allah sanctify his innermost being, and by the spiritual influence of Shāh al-Kasnazān, may Allah sanctify his innermost being".
>
> Indeed, we purchased the land and built a takya on it, just as the honourable Shaikh said and as the chain of astounding karāmas indicated.[272]

Construction of the takya began at the end of 2013.

This was an intricately detailed type of karāma that included various people, places, and times. It demonstrates the tremendous divine force that is behind every muʿjiza and karāma.

---

[272] Fatoohi, *The Wonders of Ṭarīqa Kasnazāniyya Brought to India*, pp. 79-83.

Photo 28: Shaikh Muḥammad al-Muḥammad, middle, in a session of songs of praise in the mosque of the takya in Baghdad (the 1990s).

Photo 29: Shaikh Muḥammad al-Muḥammad in a dhikr circle at the beginning of the construction of the main takya in Basra (1992).

"If you abandon dervishhood, if you abandon dhikr, if you abandon your wirds, the Shaikhs abandon you. Wirds and dhikrs are the disciples' shields. Our weapons, our tanks, our fighter planes, are Allah's dhikr (exalted and high is He). We die on Allah's dhikr. We live on Allah's dhikr. We die for the sake of Allah's dhikr (exalted and high is He). We live for the sake of Allah's dhikr (exalted and high is He). Our food, the soul's food, is Allah's dhikr (exalted and high is He). Do not forget your dhikrs and your wirds".

Shaikh Muḥammad al-Muḥammad al-Kasnazān
(Sermon, 7th/January/2010)

14

Dhikrs

Shaikh Muḥammad al-Muḥammad al-Kasnazān introduced new dhikrs to the Ṭarīqa and altered some of those that were from before he assumed the Ṭarīqa's Shaikhdom. In this chapter, we will discuss these alterations after a short preface on the importance of dhikr and an introduction to the Ṭarīqa Kasnazāniyya dhikrs.

14.1 The Means to Reach Allah

Dhikr is the foundation of reaching Allah, as Allah linked His remembering of His servant to His servant's remembering of Him: "Remember Me; I will remember you" (al-Baqara 152). In His noble Book, He commanded that it be done in abundance: "O you who have believed, remember Allah with much remembrance (41) and exalt Him morning and afternoon" (al-Āḥzāb 41-42). Even prayer, which the Messenger (PBUH) described as the "pillar of the religion"[273], is a type of dhikr, as illustrated by Allah in His noble Book: "Establish prayer for My remembrance" (Ṭāhā 14). Prayer is dhikr performed at a specific time with specific conditions: "Indeed, prayer has been decreed upon the believers, a decree of specified times" (al-Nisā` 103). Let us also reflect on His noble words:

> "O you who have believed, when it is called for the prayer on Friday, then proceed to the remembrance of Allah and leave trade. That is better for you, if you only knew. When the prayer has been concluded, disperse within the land and seek from the bounty of Allah, and remember Allah often that you may succeed". (al-Jumu'a 9-10)

Evidently, the purpose of the Friday prayer is remembering Allah. The Friday prayer, just like all prayers, has a specific time and specific conditions. Allah's dhikr, in general, however, has no specific time, nor does it have any limit. Hence, Allah ordered believers to persist in

---

[273] Bayhaqī, *Shu'ab al-'Īmān*, III, no. 2807, p. 39.

remembering him with abundance after they finished the Friday prayer and dispersed to their various matters. The essence of prayer is dhikr, so dhikr encompasses prayer and prayer is one form of dhikr. This is why Allah describes dhikr as being greater:

"Recite [O Muḥammad] what has been revealed to you of the Book and establish prayer. Indeed, prayer prohibits immorality and wrongdoing, and the remembrance of Allah is greater. Allah knows that which you do". (al-'Ankabūt 45)

This is another verse that shows that dhikr in general, i.e excluding the prayers and dhikrs with specific conditions, can be performed any time, anywhere, and in whatever state the person is in:

Those who remember Allah while standing, sitting or [lying] on their sides and reflect on the creation of the heavens and the earth, [saying], "Our Lord, You have not created this in vain; exalted are You [above such a thing]; protect us from the punishment of the Fire" (3.191).

This is what Allah says in a Qudsī ḥadīth about the unique role of dhikr in connecting the servant with Allah and drawing his closer to Him:

"I am as My servant thinks of Me, and I am with him when he remembers Me. If he remembers Me within himself, I remember him within Myself. If he remembers Me in a gathering, I remember him in a better gathering. If he approaches Me by a hand's span, I approach him by an arm's length; if he approaches Me by an arm's length, I approach him by a fathom. Anyone who approaches Me walking, I come rushing towards him".[274]

The following are some of the Prophet's (PBUH) ḥadīths on the merits of dhikr:

"No group of people sits to remember Allah (mighty and sublime is He) except that the angels surround them, mercy envelops them, tranquillity descends upon them, and Allah remembers them before those who are with Him".[275]

"Everything has its own polish, and the heart's polish is the remembrance of Allah (mighty and sublime is He)".[276]

---

[274] Bukhārī, *Al-Jāmi' al-Ṣaḥīḥ*, III, no. 7129, p. 693.
[275] Muslim, *Ṣaḥīḥ Muslim*, IV, no. 2700, p. 2074.
[276] Bayhaqī, *Shu'ab al-Īmān*, I, no. 523, p. 396.

"The example of one who remembers his Lord and one who does not remember his Lord is that of the living and the dead".[277]

"Remember Allah excessively, until they say [that you have gone] 'mad'".[278]

There are many noble Ḥadīths regarding the status of dhikr, its importance, and the merits of various dhikrs.

In his description of the people of dhikr's preoccupation with Allah, Shaikh ʿAbd al-Qādir al-Gaylānī says about the correlation between Allah's remembering of a servant with that servant's remembering of his Lord:

"They joined Him and those who love Him. They travelled with Him in their hearts until they reached Him, and they attained the Companion before the way. They opened the door between them and Him with their remembrance (dhikr). They continued remembering Him until remembrance relieved them of their burdens. They are inexistent when they are with other than Him, and they exist when with Him. They heard His words (Almighty and Glorious is He): 'Remember Me; I will remember you. Be grateful to Me and do not deny Me' (al-Baqara 152). They adhered to His remembrance, hoping for His remembrance of them. They heard the words He (Almighty and Glorious is He) spoke, in one of his utterances: 'I accompany the one who remembers Me'.[279] They abandoned people's gatherings and contented themselves so that they receive His company".[280]

He (may Allah sanctify his noble innermost being) also described the state of a servant engrossed with dhikr: "His limbs may rest, but his heart never rests. The eyes of his head may sleep, but the eyes of his heart never sleep. With his heart, he works unceasingly. He remembers Allah even while asleep".[281]

Dhikr is a dervish's spiritual link to his Master, who connects him to the chain of Shaikhs, to the Messenger (PBUH), connecting to Allah. Every blessing, spiritual state, and spiritual station that comes to him from Allah through his Shaikh do so because of dhikr. Hence, our Master constantly calls for disciples to heed the Great Ghawth's words:

---

[277] Bukhārī, *Al-Jāmiʿ al-Ṣaḥīḥ*, III, no. 6180, p. 474.

[278] Bayhaqī, *Shuʿab al-Īmān*, I, no. 526, p. 397.

[279] Bayhaqī, *Shuʿab al-Īmān*, I, no. 680, p. 451.

[280] Shaikh ʿAbd al-Qādir al-Gaylānī, *Al-Fatḥ al-Rabbānī wal-Fayḍ al-Raḥmānī*, p. 22.

[281] Shaikh ʿAbd al-Qādir al-Gaylānī, *Jilā' al-Khāṭir*, p. 45.

"Whoever cuts off wirds, spiritual support is cut off him". In other words, the spiritual blessing from his Shaikh is cut off from him. A seeker must remember Allah continuously, which is why Ṭarīqa has wirds for all times of day and night, as we will see later. Our Master says:

> "If you did not have daily wirds, you would not have daily spiritual support. This is why they (the Ṭarīqa's Shaikhs) have given disciples dhikrs: daily dhikrs, perennial dhikrs, the Wird al-ʿAsr, and so on. This is so that you can always be in Allah's presence, always present with Allah".[282]

He says that the spiritual plant that a seeker receives from the Messenger (PBUH) when he takes the Ṭarīqa's pledge from the Shaikh must be watered with the light of dhikr until it grows like the tree that Allah described in this Qur'anic analogy: "Like a good tree, whose root is firmly fixed and its branches [high] in the sky (24). It produces its fruit all the time, by permission of its Lord" (Ibrāhīm 24-25).[283]

One condition of dhikr is that the heart of the one performing the dhikr must not be concerned with anything else besides Allah. Giving an example to describe this isolation with Allah, our Shaikh likens the person who performs dhikr to the person who dips his head into the water so he no longer hears any sound that would occupy him. Shaikh Muḥammad al-Muḥammad frequently reminds people of the distinction the Messenger (PBUH) makes between an accepted and an unaccepted prayer, that is, his distinguishing between the presence and absence of the heart during dhikr. The heart's presence in dhikr is a state that a person must strive to achieve while making dhikr. One should not stop making dhikr and wait for this state to come first, as Shaikh Ibn ʿAṭāʾ Allah al-Sakandarī said:

> "Do not abandon dhikr because you lack a presence with Allah therein. Your heedlessness *of* remembering Him is worse than your heedlessness *in* remembering Him. Perhaps He raises you from making dhikr with heedlessness to making dhikr with attentiveness, from making dhikr with attentiveness to making dhikr with presence, and from making dhikr with presence to making dhikr with a state of being absent from everything besides the One being remembered: 'And that is not difficult for Allah' (Ibrāhīm

[282] Shaikh Muḥammad al-Muḥammad al-Kasnazān, *sermon*, 19th/September/2012.
[283] Shaikh Muḥammad al-Muḥammad al-Kasnazān, *sermon*, last third of October/2013.

20)".[284]

Since dhikr is the means to reach Allah, the Shaikhs of Ṭarīqa have placed great importance on it and have made it a seeker's main concern.

14.2 Specific Dhikrs

The dhikr of Allah polishes and enlivens the heart, as the Prophet (PBUH) has said. Just as every bodily illness in a diseased person's body has chemical or herbal treatments, there are special dhikrs for every spiritual malady to medicate the heart. Numerous Prophetic Ḥadīths confirm the speciality of particular dhikrs. They even specify reciting these dhikrs a certain number of times: "Everything with Him is by due measure" (al-Ra'd 8). In one of these Ḥadīths, a few poor people visited the Messenger (PBUH) and told him: "The wealthy pray as we pray, they fast as we fast, and they have money to free slaves and give away as charity". He replied: "When you pray, say '*subḥān Allah* (exalted is Allah)' thirty-three times, '*alḥamdu lillāh* (praise be to Allah)' thirty-three times, '*Allāhu akbar* (Allah is greater)' thirty-four times, and '*lā ilāha illā Allāh* (there is no god but Allah)' ten times. With that, you will have caught up with those who went ahead of you and will go ahead of those who come after you". He (PBUH) also said: "Two traits that are not kept by a Muslim man except that he enters Paradise: he *yusabbiḥ* (exalts) Allah ten times at the end of every prayer, *yaḥmaduhu* (praises) Him ten times, *yukabbiruhu* (says '*Allāhu akbar*') ten times, *yusabbiḥ* (exalts) Allah when he goes to bed thirty-three times, *yaḥmaduhu* (praises) Him thirty-three times, and *yukabbiruhu* (says '*Allāhu akbar*') thirty-four times".[285]

One of the dhikrs that the Prophet (PBUH) especially highlighted the merits of in many Ḥadīths is the dhikr of Oneness: "*Lā ilāha illā Allāh* (There is no god but Allah)" (Muḥammad 19). He (PBUH) has described the dhikr of "*lā ilāha illā Allāh waḥdahu lā sharīka lah* (there is no god but Allah, alone, He has no partner)" as: "The best thing that I and the prophets before me have ever said".[286] he (PBUH) has also said about this noble dhikr: "Truly, Allah has forbidden the Fire from [consuming] one

[284] Sakandarī, *Ḥikam Ibn 'Aṭā' Allah*, pp. 87-89.
[285] Tirmidhī, *Al-Jāmi' al-Kabīr*, I, no. 410, p. 435-436.
[286] Mālik, *Muwaṭṭa' al-Imām Mālik*, II, no. 726, p. 300.

who has said '*lā ilāha illā Allāh* (There is no god but Allah)' seeking Allah's Face by [uttering] this".[287]

This is a karāma that demonstrates the blessing of this dhikr. Shaikh Ḥusayn al-Kasnazān told the disciples that were in a spiritual retreat with him, who numbered between forty or fifty, that that night, they would see the light of *lā ilāha illā Allāh.* They were occupied with their dhikrs at night when they suddenly saw a minaret of light moving towards them from the direction of the Ka'ba. When it reached them, it passed by them, one by one, before leaving in the direction of Sulaymāniyya. Even the people of Karbchna, meaning those who were not in the retreat, saw the minaret of the light of *lā ilāha illā Allāh.*[288]

Shaikh Muḥammad al-Muḥammad al-Kasnazān relates a vision that he saw about the blessing of this dhikr:

> "They took me to see a dead man buried in the earth that had completely turned into dust. While I was looking at him, I saw a weak light flowing through the arteries and veins, but it retreated before reaching the entire body. They told me that this was the light of infancy, the light of innocence. Then this simple light receded and was replaced by an ugly red fire that spread throughout the entire body. They told me that this was the fire of Satan. After that, I saw a white light, whose beauty and brilliance are indescribable, originate from the head and spread through the body's circulatory system and extinguish the ugly red fire. They told me that this beautiful light was the light of *lā ilāha illā Allāh.* When a person performs this dhikr, it spreads throughout his body and protects him from the Fire".[289]

This vision is an embodiment of the Messenger's (PBUH) description of the dhikr of *lā ilāha illā Allāh*, in that it repels the Fire from the one who performs the dhikr. The dhikr of *lā ilāha illā Allāh* is one of the wirds of the Ṭarīqa Kasnazāniyya, and our Shaikh describes it as "the master of dhikrs".[290]

14.3 Kasnazānī Dhikrs

A diseased person's body needs a doctor who is a master of medicine to

---

287 Bukhārī, *Al-Jāmi' al-Ṣaḥīḥ*, I, no. 419, p. 158.

288 Shaikh Muḥammad al-Muḥammad al-Kasnazān, *sermon*, 14th/September/2016.

289 Shaikh Muḥammad al-Muḥammad al-Kasnazān, *sermon*, 12th/May/2000.

290 Shaikh Muḥammad al-Muḥammad al-Kasnazān, *sermon*, 2nd/February/2018.

diagnose its malady and prescribe the suitable medication for it. Similarly, spiritual diseases of the heart require a doctor who is experienced with diagnosing spiritual maladies and who knows the dhikrs that cure each of them. The Shaikh of Ṭarīqa is the soul's doctor, and the Ṭarīqa's dhikrs are remedies for a seeker's spiritual diseases. While the physical body's doctor obtains his medical knowledge through academic study and then the experience he gains by practising medicine, the Shaikh of Ṭarīqa obtains his spiritual knowledge through the Messenger (PBUH) and the Ṭarīqa's Shaikhs, and by drawing near to Allah (mighty and sublime is He) through worship. Our Shaikh explains that only grand walīs, specifically those who have obtained the rank of "ghawth", can introduce wirds. The Shaikhs of Ṭarīqa do not come up with dhikrs arbitrarily, nor do their dhikrs stem from transmitted knowledge they read in books or heard by word of mouth. The Shaikh only orders disciples to recite a given dhikr when he is ordered to do in a spiritual revelation. Our Master emphasizes that it is impermissible for any person to prescribe any given dhikr to anyone unless he is authorised to do so. The Shaikh of Ṭarīqa is authorised by the Ṭarīqa's Shaikhs to give dhikrs: "One who invites to Allah, by His permission, and an illuminating lamp" (al-Āḥzāb 46).

Likewise, no one other than the Shaikh of Ṭarīqa can alter any of its wirds. In his first spiritual retreat, our Shaikh read and directed all the dervishes that were with him to read the following dhikr aloud one hundred times after the sunset prayer: "*Ṣalla Allāhu subḥānahu wa-t'ālā ʿalayka wa-sallam yā rasūla Allāh* (May Allah (exalted and high is He) bless and send peace upon you, O Messenger of Allah)". One day, he heard a dervish named Maḥmūd replace the word "*rasūla* (messenger)" with "*ḥabība* (beloved)". This is the same disciple who, after seeing Shaikh ʿAbd al-Qādir al-Gaylānī in the retreat, decided that he would no longer seek spiritual support from our Shaikhs, but he would rather seek it directly from Shaikh ʿAbd al-Qādir (see §3.7). Our Master sent for him and explained to him that every Muslim believes that the Prophet Muḥammad (PBUH) is Allah's Beloved, but there are secrets known to the Shaikhs of Ṭarīqa that in this particular dhikr, the Prophet (PBUH) is specifically addressed by the title of "Messenger", rather than any of his many other noble titles. He warned him against trying to alter this dhikr or any of the Ṭarīqa's dhikrs.

A seeker reads the dhikrs of his Ṭarīqa because his Shaikh has authorised him to do so. This also means that a seeker must suffice himself with the dhikrs that his Shaikh has authorised him to read and not to turn to other dhikrs, whether they be from books or from what other people read. A dhikr's benefit comes from the Shaikh's being authorised to read it, who in turn authorises his disciples to read it. Hence, a seeker does not benefit from reading wirds that his Shaikh has not permitted him to read. This correlation becomes evident in Shaikh ʿAbd al-Qādir al-Gaylānī's saying that when a seeker abandons wirds, spiritual support is cut from him. The dhikrs that the Shaikh has authorised a seeker to read are the means of communication between them and, consequently, they are the vehicle through which spiritual support from the Shaikh reaches a seeker.

Allah has awarded many dhikrs to the Masters of Ṭarīqa Kasnazāniyya, which they introduced at different times. In the next section, we will see what our Shaikh has added to the Kasnazāni dhikrs and which ones he has changed. The Kasnazāniyya dhikrs are divided into three main groups: daily dhikrs, perennial dhikrs, and the dhikr circle.

Daily dhikrs consist of five sets each of which is read after one of the daily prayers, another set that is read one hour before the sunset prayer, and a particular formula of prayers of peace and blessings upon the Prophet (PBUH) that is read throughout the day.

As for the perennial dhikrs, there are nineteen of them. They are read sequentially, each one hundred thousand times. After completing the nineteenth dhikr, the seeks starts a new cycle of the nineteen dhikrs with the first one, and so on. The perennial dhikrs are not associated with any particular daily prayers or specific times.

The Ṭarīqa Kasnazāniyya also has a dhikr circle that consists of a large number of dhikrs and is formed in the takya every Monday and Thursday. Participants stand in concentric circles and the dhikr is led by a caliph (photo 39). The dhikr circle has two parts, the first is only vocal whereas the second is accompanied by special rhythms of both tambourines and drums. It is well known that the first Islamic use of the tambourine was when the people of Yathrib were welcoming the migrating Messenger (PBUH) by the timeless ode "*Ṭalʿa al-Badru ʿAlaynā* (the full moon has risen over us)".[291] As for the drum, Shaikh ʿAbd al-Qādir al-Gaylānī introduced it to the dhikr circle, which is why it is

---

[291] Bayhaqī, *Dalāʾil al-Nubuwwa wa-Maʿrifat Aḥwāl Ṣaḥib al-Sharīʿa*, II, pp. 506-507.

known as "Gaylānī's drum" or "the Falcon's drum", after Shaikh ʿAbd al-Qādir's title "the White Falon".

There is also a blessing from the grand Shaikh Aḥmad al-Rifāʿī in the Ṭarīqa Kasnazāniyya dhikrs. One afternoon, Shaikh ʿAbd al-Karīm Al-Kasnazān was sitting near Shāh al-Kasnazān's reservoir in Karbchna when Shaikh Aḥmad ar-Rifāʿī came to him from the direction of the Kaʿba. Shaikh ʿAbd al-Karīm stood and greeted him. Shaikh Aḥmad al-Rifāʿī asked him if he recognized him, and Shaikh ʿAbd al-Karīm answered in the affirmative. Shaikh al-Rifāʿī presented a ring to Shaikh ʿAbd al-Karīm and asked him to take it. Shaikh ʿAbd al-Karīm, however, said that whatever he had was already enough. Shaikh al-Rifāʿī repeated his request, and Shaikh ʿAbd al-Karīm repeated his response. Shaikh Aḥmad al-Rifāʿī reached out and placed the ring in Shaikh ʿAbd al-Karīm's pocket and told him that this was an "order", meaning he was ordered to give the ring to Shaikh ʿAbd al-Karīm. After this incident, Shaikh ʿAbd al-Karīm added a new dhikr to the dhikr circle, which used to end with the chanting of the dhikr "dā`im, dā`im". He added the dhikr "*ḥayy, ḥayy, ḥayy, Allāh*" after Shaikh al-Rifāʿī's gift to the Ṭarīqa Kasnazāniyya, and he added a second section of the dhikr "*dā`im, dā`im*" after the new dhikr to keep "*dā`im*" as the dhikr with which the dhikr circle is concluded.

The merits of dhikr circles are mentioned in several Prophetic Ḥadīths, including this: "When you pass by the gardens of Paradise, revel [in them]". When he was asked about what these gardens were, he replied: "Dhikr circles".[292] Our Shaikh relates a spiritual unveiling that he experienced while attending a dhikr circle in Baghdad's main takya:

> "One night, I was standing outside the dhikr circle when I saw — Allah knows [the truth of what I'm saying], and He is present, watching, and seeing us right now — a streak like a white rope descend from the sky and land on each disciple's head in the dhikr circle. After that, they (the Shaikhs) showed me a large board in front of the takya's yard where the dhikr was. There were circular rings on this board with a name inside each one. They told me that the name of each disciple who was present in the dhikr was written in on this board".[293]

---

[292] Tirmidhī, *Al-Jāmiʿ al-Kabīr*, V, no. 3510, p. 488.

[293] Shaikh Muḥammad al-Muḥammad al-Kasnazān, *sermon*, 27th/September/2012.

The Ṭarīqa's Shaikhs gave the glad tidings to our Master during Eid al-Fitr of August 2012 that when a Kasnazāni dervish attends the dhikr circle on Monday or Thursday, he leaves purified from sins.[294]

In addition to the Ṭarīqa's permanent dhikrs — daily, perennial, and dhikr circle — the Ṭarīqa's Shaikhs have given temporary wirds for various purposes. Sometimes, they are given to all dervishes; in other cases, to a particular group of them; and at other times, to individual dervishes.

14.4 Kasnazānī Dhikrs in the Era of Shaikh Muḥammad al-Muḥammad

Allah has conferred on our Master many unveilings that made him change some of the dhikrs that he inherited from the Shaikhs of the Ṭarīqa and introduce new ones. These changes included the daily, perennial, and circle dhikrs. He also introduced temporary dhikrs. Allah has also honoured our Shaikh with a great dhikr called "Ḥizb al-Wāw".

14.4.1 Perennial Dhikrs

There were 19 perennial dhikrs in the era of Shaikh ʿAbd al-Karīm al-Kasnazān, and this has not changed in the time of our Shaikh. Each dhikr was read 82,000 times except "*ya wadūd*", which was read 65,000 times. After coming out of his first seclusion, which he entered about six months after assuming the Shaikhdom of Ṭarīqa, our Master changed these numbers to 100,000. This number is known in the terminology of Ṭarīqa Kasnazāniyya as "*khatma*", which is derived from an Arabic root that means "complete" or "conclude". In 1996, he also replaced the dhikr of "*Allāhumma ṣallī ʿalā sayyidinā Muḥammadi wa-ʿalā `ālihi wa-ṣaḥbihi wa-sallim taslīmā* (O Allah! Send prayer on our Master and on his lineage and companions and salute him with a perfect salutation)" with "*Allāhumma ṣallī ʿalā sayyidinā Muḥammadi `l-waṣfi wal-waḥyi war-risālati wal-ḥikmati waʿalā `ālihi wa-ṣaḥbihi wa-sallim taslīmā* (O Allah! Send prayer on our Master whose quality, revelation, message, and wisdom are most praised (Muḥammad), and on his lineage and companions, and salute him with a

[294] Shaikh Muḥammad al-Muḥammad al-Kasnazān, *sermon*, 28th/September/2012; 5th/December/2012.

perfect salutation)".

These are the 19 perennial dhikrs:

1) *Lā ilāha illā Allah* (There is no god save Allah).

2) *Allah.*

3) *Yā Hū* (O He!).

4) *Yā Ḥay* (O Ever-living One!).

5) *Yā Wāḥid* (O One!).

6) *Yā ʿAzīz* (O Invincible One!).

7) *Yā Wadūd* (O Loving One!).

8) *Yā Raḥmān* (O Gracious One!).

9) *Yā Raḥīm* (O Merciful One!).

10) *Subḥāna Allah* (exalted be Allah), *wal-ḥamdu li-Llāh* (and praise be to Allah), *wa-lā ilāha illā Allāh* (and there is no god save Allah), *wa-Llāhu Akbar* (and Allah is Greater).

11) *Allāhumma ṣallī ʿalā sayyidinā Muḥammadi `l-waṣfi wal-waḥyi war-risālati wal-ḥikmati waʿalā `ālihi wa-ṣaḥbihi wa-sallim taslīmā* (O Allah! Send prayer on our Master whose quality, revelation, message, and wisdom are most praised (Muḥammad), and on his lineage and companions, and salute him with a perfect salutation).

12) *Bismi Allāhi ar-Raḥmāni ar-Raḥīm* (In the name of Allah, the Gracious, the Merciful), *wa-lā ḥawla wa-lā quwwata illā bi-Llāh* (and there is no might nor strength but by Allah) *al-ʿAlī al-ʿAẓīm* (the High, the Great).

13) *Bismi Allāhi ar-Raḥmāni ar-Raḥīm* (In the name of Allah, the Gracious, the Merciful). *Qul Huwa Allāhu Aḥad* (Say, He, Allah, is One), *Allāhu aṣ-Ṣamad* (Allah the Self-Sustained), *lam yalid wa-lam yūlad* (He begets not, nor is He begotten), *wa-lam yakun lahu kufuwan aḥad* (and there is no peer to Him).

14) *Lā ilāha illā Allah* (There is no god save Allah), *al-Maliku al-Ḥaqqu al-Mubīn* (the manifestly True King). *Muḥammadun rasūlu Allāh* (Muḥammad is the Messenger of Allah), *ṣallā Allah taʿālā ʿalayhi wa-sallam* (prayer and peace of Allah (high is He) be upon him), *ṣādiqu al-waʿdi al-āmīn* (the truthful in (his) promise, the trustworthy one).

15) *Ṣallā Allāhu subḥānahu wa-taʿālā ʿalayka wa-sallam yā rasūla Allāh* (prayer and peace of Allah (exalted and high is He) be upon you, O Messenger of Allah!).

16) *Lā maqṣūda illā Allāh* (There is no destination save Allah).

17) *Lā mawjūda illā Allāh* (There is no one save Allah).
18) *Lā maṭlūba illā Allāh* (There is no one sought after save Allah).
19) *Lā murāda illā Allāh* (There is no one wanted save Allah).

14.4.2 Daily Dhikrs

Our Shaikh added new dhikrs the daily dhikrs and changed the numbers of some that he inherited from Shaikh ʿAbd al-Karīm al-Kasnazān. We will mention here some of these changes.

In the 1980s, our Shaikh added the recitation of the Qur'anic Chapter of Īkhlāṣ, along with the basmala, 200 times. Consisting of 4 verses, reciting this chapter with the basmala 200 times a day is equivalent to reading 1,000 verses. This brings to mind this ḥadīth of the Messenger (PBUH): "Anyone who reads one thousand verses for Allah's sake, Allah writes his name alongside the prophets, the truthful, martyrs, and the righteous".[295]

In the early 1990s, our Shaikh introduced the recitation of the following dhikr three times after each of the five obligatory prayers: "*Allahu ḥādirī* (Allah is present with me), *Allahu nāẓirī* (Allah sees me), *Allahu shāhidun ʿalay* (Allah is a witness on me). *Allahu maʿī* (Allah is with me), *Allahu muʿīnī* (Allah is my helper), *wa-huwa bi-kulli shay'in muḥīṭ* (and He encompasses everything)". This is a wird of Shaikh ʿAbd al-Qādir al-Gaylānī that he received from Shaikh Maʿrūf al-Karkhī. Our Master says that this dhikr embodies Iḥsān,[296] religion's third pillar, which the Prophet (PBUH) described as follows: "to worship Allah as if you see Him; and if you cannot see Him, then verily He sees you".[297] One can only reach this level of awareness of Allah by way of divine unveilings that draw a person closer to the spirit world while he is in this world.

In March 2016, our Shaikh added one recitation of the following dhikr after every prayer: *Astaghfiru Allah* (I seek forgiveness from Allah), *al-ladhī Lā ilāha illā Huwa* (whom there is no god besides), *ar-Raḥmān ar-Raḥīm* (the Gracious, the Merciful), *al-Ḥayyu al-Qayyūm* (the Ever-living, the Sustainer of Existence) *al-ladhī lā yamūt* (who never

---

[295] Bayhaqī, *Al-Sunan al-Kubrā*, IX, no. 18575, p. 291.
[296] Shaikh Muḥammad al-Muḥammad al-Kasnazān, *sermon*, 22nd/January/2010; 4th/August/2013.
[297] Bukhārī, *Al-Jāmiʿ al-Ṣaḥīḥ*, I, no. 50, p. 65.

dies), *wa-atūbu 'ilayhi* (and I repent to Him). *Rabbī ighfir lī* (My Lord, forgive me!)

He introduced three alterations to Wird al-ʿAṣr, which is performed an hour before the sunset prayer. This blessed wird goes back to the latter days of Shaikh ʿAbd al-Qādir al-Kasnazān when he was a migrant in Iran. One night, a caliph named Mullā Muḥammad Imām had a vision where he saw Shaikh ʿAbd al-Qādir al-Gaylānī give him this wird and order him to communicate it to Shaikh ʿAbd al-Qādir al-Kasnazān. The wird contained nine dhikrs that were each read 33 times.

In the morning, Mullā Muḥammad went to visit Shaikh ʿAbd al-Qādir. When the Shaikh saw him, he laughed and said: "My son, my time is up. Let this communication be for the one who comes after me". Then, he asked him to tell him what he saw. When the caliph saw his Shaikh get ahead of him by referring to the matter before he even told him about it, he jokingly answered that there was no need to tell him what had happened since it was obvious that he already knew! Sulṭān Qādir reiterated what he had said before, that his time was almost up, and he ordered him to communicate this dhikr to the Shaikh of Ṭarīqa after him. Shortly after that, Shaikh ʿAbd al-Qādir al-Kasnazān departed to the spirit world, and his son, Shaikh Ḥusayn, assumed the Ṭarīqa's Shaikhdom after him, so he added Wird al-ʿAṣr to the Ṭarīqa's dhikrs.

This karāma illustrates that Wird al-ʿAṣr is a gift from Shaikh ʿAbd al-Qādir al-Gaylānī to the Ṭarīqa Kasnazāniyya Shaikhs and that there are spiritual secrets behind adding any dhikr to the Ṭarīqa's dhikrs or altering them. The following karāma about this specific dhikr confirms that the Shaikh of Ṭarīqa only introduces a dhikr when spiritually instructed to do so. Shaikh Musṭafā Aḥmad, one of Shāh al-Kasnazān's grandsons, was visiting his cousin Shaikh Ḥusayn when he said that the Ṭarīqa already has many dhikrs, so Wird al-ʿAṣr has become a burden to the disciple. Shaikh Ḥusayn replied that this dhikr's introduction came by way of order and that it was not his own decision. Shaikh Musṭafā restated his argument, but Shaikh Ḥusayn replied with the same answer. Shortly after, the time had come to perform Wird al-ʿAṣr. The Shaikh and disciples sat in the yard in front of Karbchna's mosque facing the Kaʿba and began the dhikr. While chanting the first dhikr of Wird al-ʿAṣr, "*Yā Allāhu Yā Ḥayyu Yā Qayyūm* (O Allah, O Ever-living, O Sustainer of Existence)", they saw a falcon come from the direction of the Kaʿba and land on the edge of the mosque's roof, just above Shaikh Ḥusayn's sitting place. The direction of the Ka'ba in Karbchna is in the direction of Baghdad — Shaikh 'Abd al-Qādir al-Gaylānī's resting place. The falcon was rocking its head back and forth. When bending forward, it would reach the Shaikh's head, and when raising its head, it would transcend high into the sky. The falcon stayed there until the last dhikr of Wird al-'Aṣr, "*Yā Raḥīm* (O Merciful One)", was completed, and it disappeared after that. After the dhikr ended, Sulṭān Ḥusayn turned to Shaikh Musṭafā and said: "What do you now have to say"? The latter acknowledged his mistake.

The first time the Wird al-'Aṣr was added to the Ṭarīqa's dhikrs in the time of Sulṭān Ḥusayn, each one of its nine dhikrs was read 33 times. This number remained the same in the time of Shaikh 'Abd al-Karīm, then our Master increased it to 50 after he assumed the Ṭarīqa's Shaikhdom. In 2005 or 2006, he increased the number a second time to 66. In early October 2010, he added "*Yā Arḥam ar-Rāḥimīn* (O Most Merciful of the merciful)" to the end of Wird al-'Aṣr, which our Shaikh has described as a "supplication", distinguishing it from the nine dhikrs.

On the evening of 28th/January/2018, a Sunday, after a celebration of the Prophet's (PBUH) birth, because of Shaikh Nahro's return from the USA, our Shaikh instructed that Wird al-'Aṣr be performed. The performing of this dhikr at night is a rare occurrence, if not unprecedented. After those performing the dhikr reached the final dhikr of "*Yā Raḥīm*", our Shaikh began the dhikr of "*lā ilāha illā Allāh*" 100 times. He named this addition to Wird al-'Aṣr the "Victory Dhikr". As for the supplication of "*Yā Arḥam ar-Rāḥimīn*", a seeker may read it as many times as he likes after "*lā ilāha illā Allāh*".

The spiritual benefits of Wird al-'Aṣr are so great that our Shaikh has even advised those who are not able to perform it at its designated time to make it up, just as obligatory prayers are made up when they are missed. Even when our Shaikh is away from the takya — for example, in a car — he performs Wird al-'Aṣr alone.

These are the current daily dhikrs:

(1) The Dhikr After the Dawn Prayer

(a) *Lā ilāha illā Allah* (There is no god save Allah). [300 times]

(b) *Lā ilāha illā Allah* (There is no god save Allah) *Muḥammadun rasūlu Allah* (Muḥammad is the Messenger of Allah) *ṣallā Allah ta'ālā 'alayhi wa-*

sallam (prayer and peace of Allah (high is He) be upon him), *fī-kulli lamḥatin wa-nafas* (with every look and breath), *'adada mā wasi'ahu 'ilmu Allah* (as many times as Allah's knowledge encompasses). [100 times]

(c) Allah. [300 times]

(d) The Chapter of Fātiḥa. [30 times]

(e) *Astaghfiru Allah al-'Aẓīm* (I ask Allah the Great for forgiveness). [100 times]

(2) The Dhikr After the Midday Prayer

(a) *Lā ilāha illā Allah* (There is no god save Allah). [165 times]

(b) The Chapter of Fātiḥa. [25 times]

(c) *Astaghfiru Allah al-'Aẓīm* (I ask Allah the Great for forgiveness). [100 times]

(3) The Dhikr After the Afternoon Prayer

(a) *Lā ilāha illā Allah* (There is no god save Allah). [165 times]

(b) The Chapter of Fātiḥa. [20 times]

(c) *Astaghfiru Allah al-'Aẓīm* (I ask Allah the Great for forgiveness). [100 times]

4) Wird al-'Aṣr (one hour before the sunset prayer)

(a) *Yā Allāhu Yā Ḥayyu Yā Qayyūm* (O Allah, O Ever-living, O Sustainer of Existence) [66 times].

(b) *Yā Allah mawlāy Allah* (O Allah, Allah is my Master!) [66 times].

(c) *Yā Hū* (O He!) [66 times].

(d) *Yā Ḥay* (O Ever-living One!) [66 times].

(e) *Yā Wāḥid* (O One!) [66 times].

(f) *Yā 'Azīz* (O Invincible One!) [66 times].

(g) *Yā Wadūd* (O Loving One!) [66 times].

(h) *Yā Raḥmān* (O Gracious One!) [66 times].

(i) *Yā Raḥīm* (O Merciful One!) [66 times].

(j) *Lā ilāha illā Allah* (There is no god save Allah). [100 times].

(5) The Dhikr After the Sunset Prayer

(a) *Lā ilāha illā Allah* (There is no god save Allah). [165 times]

(b) The Chapter of Fātiḥa. [15 times]

(c) *Astaghfiru Allah al-'Aẓīm* (I ask Allah the Great for forgiveness). [100 times]**

6) The Dhikr After the Night Prayer

(a) *Lā ilāha illā Allah* (There is no god save Allah). [300 times]

(b) *Lā ilāha illā Allah* (There is no god save Allah) *Muḥammadun rasūlu*

Allah (Muḥammad is the Messenger of Allah) *ṣallā Allah taʿālā ʿalayhi wa-sallam* (prayer and peace of Allah (high is He) be upon him), *fī-kulli lamḥatin wa-nafas* (with every look and breath), *ʿadada mā wasiʿahu ʿilmu Allah* (as many times as Allah's knowledge encompasses). [100 times]

(c) Allah. [300 times]

(d) The Chapter of Fātiḥa. [10 times]

(e) *Astaghfiru Allah al-ʿAẓīm* (I ask Allah the Great for forgiveness). [100 times]

(f) *Allāhumma ṣallī ʿalā sayyidinā Muḥammadi `l-waṣfi wal-waḥyi war-risālati wal-ḥikmati waʿalā `ālihi wa-ṣaḥbihi wa-sallim taslīmā* (O Allah! Send prayer on our Master whose quality, revelation, message, and wisdom are most praised (Muḥammad), and on his lineage and companions, and salute him with a perfect salutation). [100 times]

(g) The Chapter of Ikhlāṣ. [200 times]

(7) The Dhikr After Every Obligatory Prayer

(a) *Allahu ḥādirī* (Allah is present with me), *Allahu nāẓirī* (Allah sees me), *Allahu shāhidun ʿalay* (Allah is a witness on me). *Allahu maʿī* (Allah is with me), *Allahu muʿīnī* (Allah is my helper), *wa-huwa bi kulli shay`in muḥīṭ* (and He encompasses everything). [3 times]

(b) *Astaghfiru Allah* (I seek forgiveness from Allah), *al-ladhī Lā ilāha illā Huwa* (whom there is no god besides), *ar-Raḥmān ar-Raḥīm* (the Gracious, the Merciful), *al-Ḥayyu al-Qayyūm* (the Ever-living, the Sustainer of Existence) *al-ladhī lā yamūt* (who never dies), *wa-atūbu ʿilayhi* (and I repent to Him). *Rabbī ighfir lī* (My Lord, forgive me!) [1 time]

8) The "Ṣalāt Waṣfiyya" (Descriptive Prayer)

"*Allāhumma ṣallī ʿalā sayyidinā Muḥammadi `l-waṣfi wal-waḥyi war-risālati wal-ḥikmati waʿalā `ālihi wa-ṣaḥbihi wa-sallim taslīmā* (O Allah! Send prayer on our Master whose quality, revelation, message, and wisdom are most praised (Muḥammad), and on his lineage and companions, and salute him with a perfect salutation)" [1,000 times]

14.4.3 Prayers of Peace and Blessings Upon the Prophet (PBUH)

Our Shaikh continuously emphasizes the importance of reading prayers upon and greetings to the Messenger (PBUH) and urges seekers to recite them. He describes them as "the greatest gift to the Messenger's nation

(PBUH)".[298] Reading prayers upon the Messenger (PBUH) turns into love for him (PBUH) in a seeker's heart, and this love, in turn, develops into love for Allah (mighty and sublime is He).[299] He constantly cites the noble verse, "Indeed, Allah and His angels read prayers upon the Prophet. O you who have believed, read prayers upon him and send greetings of peace" (al-Āḥzāb 56), indicating that sending prayers upon the Prophet (PBUH) is a "trait of Allah". He comments that "the divine order in this noble verse came to us in a new Qur'anic formula that is distinguished and differs from the other formats of divine orders in the noble Qur'an" that begin with the order directly, such as: "O you who have believed, decreed upon you is fasting as it was decreed upon those before you that you may become righteous" (al-Baqara 183). He goes on to explain:

> "However, when the order was to read prayers upon the Messenger of Allah (PBUH), it came in another formula. Allah (mighty and sublime is He) began this noble verse with the words: 'Indeed, Allah and His angels read prayers upon the Prophet', to indicate that the station of reading prayers upon the Prophet (PBUH) is a station of honour for servants in addition to being a station of obligation that's meant to demand that action. Reading prayers upon the Prophet (PBUH) is a station of honour and obligation simultaneously. It's as if Allah (mighty and sublime is He) is saying to his servant: 'I send prayers upon My beloved, and My angels send prayers upon My beloved, so when you send prayers on him, you become present with Me and My angels in this lofty station'".[300]

Shaikh Muḥammad al-Muḥammad frequently mentions noble Ḥadīths about the merits of the prayers upon the Messenger (PBUH), such as: "Whoever reads one prayer upon me, Allah reads prayer upon him ten times".[301] In regards to the greatness of prayers upon the Prophet (PBUH), our Master says: "No one knows the secrets of this prayer besides Allah, the Messenger (PBUH), and those firmly rooted in the knowledge of the spirit". He also stresses that any supplication must be preceded by, infused with, and end with prayers so that it may be accepted. In other words, the supplication must be "wrapped" with

---

[298] Shaikh Muḥammad al-Muḥammad al-Kasnazān, *sermon*, 12th/September/2013.
[299] Shaikh Muḥammad al-Muḥammad al-Kasnazān, *sermon*, 3rd/September/2017.
[300] Shaikh Muḥammad al-Muḥammad al-Kasnazān, *Al-Ṭarīqa al-ʿAliyya al-Qādiriyya al-Kasnazāniyya*, pp. 14-15.
[301] Muslim, *Ṣaḥīḥ Muslim*, I, no. 408, p. 306.

reading prayers upon the Prophet (PBUH).[302]

Just before three o'clock in the morning on 11th/August/2017, our Shaikh was given the glad tidings that as soon as a person intends to read prayers upon the Messenger (PBUH) and prepares himself and his prayer beads for it, Allah Almighty forgives him of his sins by the Messenger's (PBUH) blessing. He confirms that reading prayers upon the Prophet (PBUH) realises one's wishes and solves various problems. He often advises dervishes who consult him about difficulties and problems that they have to read prayers upon the Messenger (PBUH) in abundance. In his sermons, he always talks about the special quality of reading prayers upon the Prophet (PBUH), such as this:

> "Always perfume your worshipping, sleeping, eating, drinking, working, coming and going, praying — perfume all of them with reading prayers on the honourable Messenger (PBUH). The key to everything, all spiritual matters, which descend from Allah (exalted and high is He), is reading prayers upon the honourable Messenger (PBUH). It is the key to everything: the key to this world and the hereafter, the key to Paradise, the key to heaven, the key to the earth, the key to the acceptance of supplication, the key to the acceptance of worship, the key to dhikr. Reading prayers upon the honourable Messenger (PBUH) is the core of all forms of worship in Islam because it is Allah's trait, as he commanded: 'Indeed, Allah and His angels read prayers upon the Prophet'. He ordered the people of Islam, the people of Īmān: 'O you who have believed, read prayers upon him and send greetings of peace'. Therefore, always enlighten your hearts, deeds, sleep, wakefulness, eating, drinking, and every move — enlighten them with reading prayers and you will see what is unveiled to you. Allah willing, you will always be under the protection of the Most Merciful, under the protection of the honourable Messenger (PBUH)".[303]

Countless karāmas have shown the blessing of reading prayers upon the Prophet (PBUH). One night, Shaikh ʿAbd al-Karīm saw light rising from a house opposite his home in Kirkuk. The light ascended to heaven and stayed there until dawn. In the morning, he sent for the house's resident, who was a dervish named ʿAbd Allah (may Allah have mercy on him). When he asked him what he had been doing the night before, the question made the dervish worry, thinking that he was being accused of

[302] Shaikh Muḥammad al-Muḥammad al-Kasnazān, *sermon*, 3rd/October/2013.

[303] Shaikh Muḥammad al-Muḥammad al-Kasnazān, *sermon*, 20th/March/2014

something. He denied having done anything wrong. Reassuringly repeated his question, Shaikh 'Abd al-Karīm asked 'Abd Allah if he had been sitting, or if he had been praying, or doing something in particular. The dervish answered that he had been reading the *Dalā'il al-Khayrāt*, a book wherein Muḥammad Ibn Sulaymān al-Jāzūlī compiled many formulas of reading prayers upon the Messenger (PBUH). Shaikh 'Abd al-Karīm had authorised dervishes to read this book. The dervish's reading of prayers upon the Prophet (PBUH) caused that continuous light that ascended from his house to the sky. As we have mentioned, Shaikh Muḥammad al-Muḥammad has also compiled different formulas of reading prayer upon the Messenger of Allah (PBUH) in a book entitled *al-Ṣalawāt Kasnazāniyya* that was published in 1990. Collecting various such formulas is an ongoing project of our Shaikh.

Our Shaikh's love for the Messenger (PBUH) is unparalleled. It is a love that manifests itself in his words, on his face, in his movements, and in his deeds. Signs of this ardent love are seen even when he hears the name of our Master Muḥammad (PBUH) or one of his epithets in a book title. He consistently reminds disciples of the importance of love for the Messenger (PBUH) and continuously reading prayers upon him because he is the gateway to reaching Allah (exalted and high is He): "Say [O Muḥammad]: 'If you love Allah, then follow me, [so] Allah will love you and forgive you your sins. Allah is forgiving and merciful'" ('Āl 'Imrān 31).

One dhikr that our Shaikh introduced, in the 1980s, is a formula of reading prayers upon the Prophet (PBUH). In 2013, in Amman, our Shaikh referred to this prayer in his following talk about reading prayers upon the Prophet (PBUH) in general:

> "In our Ṭarīqa 'Aliyya Qādiriyya Kasnazāniyya, we have the greatest khatma, which is '*lā ilāha illā Allah* (there is no god save Allah) *Muḥammadun rasūlu Allah* (Muḥammad is the Messenger of Allah) *ṣallā Allah ta'ālā 'alayhi wa-sallam* (prayer and peace of Allah (high is He) be upon him)'. Look at the greatness that Allah conferred on the honourable Messenger (PBUH). After the declaration of oneness comes honouring the Messenger (PBUH), reading prayers upon the honourable Messenger (PBUH). He orders us by this: 'Indeed, Allah and His angels read prayers upon the Prophet. O you who have believed, read prayers upon him and send greetings of peace' (al-Āḥzāb 56). He has given us a gift. Reading prayers is a gift, reading prayers is mercy, reading prayers is a blessing, reading prayers is a treasure, reading prayers is sustenance, reading prayers is this life and the Day of Resurrection, reading

prayers is Paradise, reading prayers is light, reading prayers draws one closer to Allah and to the honourable Messenger: 'If he [My servant] comes one span nearer to Me, I go one cubit nearer to him. If he comes one cubit nearer to Me, I go a distance of two outstretched arms nearer to him'.[304] When you send prayers upon the honourable Messenger (PBUH), you draw nearer to Allah. We have this khatma, the greatest khatma in Islamic Sufism, the greatest khatma in Islam, the greatest khatma in our Ṭarīqa. Whoever wants to test it out may try. This khatma is not found in other Ṭarīqas; you may search if you want to! I have perhaps thousands of Sufi books. No Shaikh has this khatma besides your Kasnazāni Shaikhs. This happened by an order. By Allah, by Allah, by Allah, the dhikr of '*lā ilāha illā Allah Muḥammadun rasūlu Allah*' came by an order. This order came to me when I was in Baghdad. This dhikr was conveyed to me by an order. Undoubtedly, all Sufi matters are from Allah (exalted and high is He) to the honourable Messenger to the Shaikhs".[305]

Our Shaikh has included the recitation of this formula one hundred times in the daily dhikr after the dawn and night prayers. In January 2006, he added the phrase, "*fī-kulli lamḥatin wa-nafas* (with every look and breath), *ʿadada mā wasiʿahu ʿilmu Allah* (as many times as Allah's knowledge encompasses)" to this dhikr. The formula of the prayer thus became: "*Lā ilāha illā Allah* (There is no god save Allah), *Muḥammadun rasūlu Allah* (Muḥammad is the Messenger of Allah) *ṣallā Allah taʿālā ʿalayhi wa-sallam* (prayer and peace of Allah (high is He) be upon him), *fī-kulli lamḥatin wa-nafas* (with every look and breath), *ʿadada mā wasiʿahu ʿilmu Allah* (as many times as Allah's knowledge encompasses)".

In July 1996, our Shaikh was also honoured with a second formula of reading prayers upon the Prophet (PBUH). One afternoon, after coming out of his resting room, he told dervishes that he had been gifted a new formula of reading prayers upon the Messenger (PBUH) that had not been granted to anyone before. This is it: "*Allāhumma ṣallī ʿalā sayyidinā Muḥammadi `l-waṣfi wal-waḥyi war-risālati wal-ḥikmati waʿalā `ālihi wa-*

[304] This is the full text of the Qudī ḥadīth that the Messenger (PBUH) conveyed from Allah: "'I am just as My slave thinks I am, and I am with him if He remembers Me. If he remembers Me in himself, I too remember him in Myself; and if he remembers Me in a group of people, I remember him in a group that is better than them. If he comes one span nearer to Me, I go one cubit nearer to him. If he comes one cubit nearer to Me, I go a distance of two outstretched arms nearer to him. If he comes to Me walking, I go to him running" (Bukhārī, *Al-Jāmiʿ al-Ṣaḥīḥ*, III, no. 7129, p. 693).

[305] Shaikh Muḥammad al-Muḥammad al-Kasnazān, *sermon*, 12th/September/2013.

ṣaḥbihi wa-sallim taslīmā (O Allah! Send prayer on our Master whose quality, revelation, message, and wisdom are most praised (Muḥammad), and on his lineage and companions, and salute him with a perfect salutation)". Our Shaikh described it at the time as the "seal of Kasnazāni readings of prayers)". He also described it as being "authored" by the Messenger (PBUH):

> "This formula of reading prayers (on the Prophet (PBUH)) is not from me. Rather, it was communicated to me. Look at how blessed al-Ṣalāt Waṣfiyya is. It is from him, from the light, from the honourable Messenger (PBUH). In the past, we did not have this formula of reading prayers (on the Prophet (PBUH)). This is very blessed, as it is from him. He is the one who has informed us [of it]. This is why we read it continuously. This formula of reading prayers (on the Prophet (PBUH)) did not exist in any book. It is from him, from the honourable Messenger. He communicated it, so we communicated it…how beautiful and how blessed it is. He himself granted this formula of reading prayers (on the Prophet (PBUH)), it was authored by him. How beautiful it is. Try as you may, your mind would not comprehend the blessing of al-Ṣalāt Waṣfiyya because it came about by his wish, by his order, and by the order of Allah (exalted and high is He)".[306]

One thing that distinguishes this ṣalawāt from others is that it does not include the Prophet's (PBUH) name explicitly. This is made clear when we understand the word "Muḥammad" as a "descriptor" of his creation and his manners, of the revelation that was sent down to him, of the message he conveyed, and of the wisdom he came with. This is the explanation of why our Shaikh named this formula as the "Ṣalāt Waṣfiyya (the Descriptive Ṣalawāt)". This formula indirectly refers to our Master Muḥammad (PBUH) by mentioning his four praiseworthy gifts: "praiseworthy attributes", "praiseworthy revelation", "praiseworthy message", and "praiseworthy wisdom". We also find the adjective of "Muḥammad (praiseworthy)", but preceded by the definite article, in the name "Muḥammad al-Muḥammad", which the Messenger (PBUH) conferred on our Shaikh. As we explained in §9.1, "al-Muḥammad" is a title of the Prophet (PBUH) that emphasizes that he is the most receiving of praise.

Our Shaikh added the recitation of Ṣalāt Waṣfiyya one hundred times

---

[306] Shaikh Muḥammad al-Muḥammad al-Kasnazān, *sermon*, 1st/May/2018.

to the daily dhikr after the night prayer. Ṣalāt Waṣfiyya also replaced this formula of reading prayers upon the Prophet (PBUH), which is read at least one thousand times every day at any time of the day: "*Allāhumma ṣallī 'alā sayyidinā Muḥammadi wa'alā `ālihi wa-ṣaḥbihi wa-sallim taslīmā* (O Allah! Send prayer on our Master Muḥammad and on his lineage and companions, and salute him with a perfect salutation)". Ṣalāt Waṣfiyya also took its place in the perennial dhikrs.

As a result of the special spiritual power of Ṣalāt Waṣfiyya, Shaikh Muḥammad al-Muḥammad sometimes orders dervishes in certain circumstances to perform a khatma of it. Before receiving Ṣalāt Waṣfiyya, our Shaikh would direct disciples in such circumstances to read the renowned formula of reading prayers upon the Messenger (PBUH) known as "Ṣalāt Nāriyya" (Fiery Prayer):

> *Allahumma ṣalli ṣalātan kāmila, wa-sallim salāman tāmman 'alā sayyidina Muḥammad al-laththī tanḥallu bihi al-'uqad, wa-tanfariju bihi al-kurab, wa-tuqdhā bihi al-ḥawā`ij, wa-tunālu bihi al-raghā`ib, wa-ḥusnu al-khawātim, wa-yustasqā al-ghamāmu biwajhihi al-karīm, wa'alā `ālihi wa-ṣaḥbihi, fikulli lamḥatin wanafa, bi'adadi kulli ma'lumin laka* (O Allah, read complete prayers and salute with a perfect salutation our Master Muḥammad, by whom all difficulties are solved, all calamities go away, all needs fulfilled, all cherished desires obtained, and good ends to life achieved; and rain-showering clouds are requested by means of his noble countenance; and on his family and companions in every moment and every breath, as many times as is in Your knowledge.

Our Shaikh may advise Ṣalāt Nāriyya be read under certain circumstances, but in most cases, he advises that Ṣalāt Waṣfiyya be read.

14.4.4 Dhikr Circle

Shaikh Muḥammad al-Muḥammad introduced many alterations to the dhikr circle. It now begins with the following supplication:

> *Yā dā`ima l-faḍli 'alā al-bariyya, yā bāsiṭa l-yadayni bil-'aṭiya, yā ṣāḥib al-mawāhib as-saniyya, ṣalli 'alā Muḥammadin khayri l-bariyya, waghfir lanā yā Rabbanā fī-hādhihi al-'ashiyya* (O You of permanent favour on the creation! O You whose hands are outstretched with gifts, O You of brilliant attributes, read prayers on Muḥammad, the best of creation, and forgive us, our Lord, on this night).

He also changed the formulas of seeking spiritual support from the

Prophet (PBUH) and Imām ʿAlī Ibn Abī Ṭālib (may Allah ennoble his face) by adding to them words of Shaikh Muḥyiddīn Ibn ʿArabī.[307] This is the formula of seeking support from the Messenger (PBUH), with the addition beginning from the phrase "*alḥamdu lillāhi rabbi l-ʿālamīn*" (Praise be to Allah, Lord of the worlds) and extending to the end of the phrase "*wal-mubarqaʿi bi l-ʿamāʾ* (the one veiled by heavy clouds)". The addition consists of a supplication in praise of Allah followed by a formula for reading prayers upon the Prophet (PBUH) that includes many of his spiritual attributes and titles (PBUH):

> *Madad yā sayyidanā wa-nabiyyanā wa-shafīʿa dhunūbinā. Yā ṣāḥiba l-āyāt wal-muʿjizāt, wa-yā ṣāḥiba dalāʾili l-khayrāt wa-khawāriqi l-ʿādāt, wa-yā sayyida s-sādāt, ḥabība rabbi l-ʿālamīn, wa-khātima n-nabiyyīn wa-sayyida l-mursalīn. Al-ḥamdu lillāhi rabbi l-ʿālamīn, ḥamdān azaliyyan bi abadiyyatihi wa-abadiyyan bi azaliyyatihi, sarmadan bi iṭlāqih, mutajalliyan fī-marāyā āfāqih, ḥamda l-ḥāmidīn wa-dahra d-dāhirīn. Ṣalawātu Allahi wa-malāʾikatihi wa-ḥamalati ʿarshihi wa-jamīʿi khalqihi min arḍihi wa-samāʾihi ʿalā sayyidinā wa-nabiyyinā, aṣli l-wujūdi wa-ʿayni sh-shāhidi wal-mashhūd, wa-awwali al-awāʾil, wa-adalli ad-dalāʾil, wa-mabdaʾi l-anwāri al-azalī wa-muntahā al-ʿurūji l-kamālī. Ghāyati l-ghāyāt, al-mutaʿayyin bi n-nashaʾāt. Abi l-akwān bi fāʿiliyyatihi, wa-ummi l-imkān bi qābiliyyatihi. Al-mathali l-aʿlā l-ilāhī, hayūlī l-ʿawālimi ghayri l-mutanāhī. Rūḥi l-arwāḥ wa-nūri l-ashbāḥ, fāliqi iṣbāḥi l-ghaybi wa-rāfiʿi ẓulmati r-rayb. Muḥtadi t-tisʿati wat-tisʿīn. Raḥamatin lil-ʿālamīn. Sayyidina fīl-wujūd, ṣāḥib liwāʾi l-ḥamdi wal-maqāmi l-maḥmūd, wal-mubarqaʿi bi l-ʿamāʾ, ḥabīb Allah Muḥammad al-Muṣṭafā ṣallā Allah taʿāla ʿalayhi wa-sallim* (Grant us support, O our Master, our Prophet, and intercessor of our sins! O possessor of signs and miracles. O possessor of waymarks of goodness and paranormal occurrences. O Master of Masters, Beloved of the Lord of the worlds, Seal of Prophets and Master of Messengers. Praise be to Allah, Lord of the worlds, everlasting praise with His eternality and eternal praise with His everlastingness, perpetual praise with His absoluteness, manifest praise in the mirrors of His horizons, praise of those who praise, lasting throughout all time. Prayers of Allah, His angels, the bearers of His throne, and all of His creation from His earth and His sky, be upon our Master and Prophet, the source of existence, the essence of the witness and what is witnessed, foremost of the foremost, the greatest of proofs, the beginning of pre-eternal lights and

[307] These words of Shaikh Ibn ʿArabī are quoted by Marʿashī in *Mulḥaqāt al-ʾIhqāq*, who in turn quoted it from Shaikh Iṣbahānī's *Faḍl Allah Ibn Rūzbhān. Sharḥ Ṣalawāt Chharda Maʿṣūm – Wasīlat al-Khādim ilā al-Makhdūm*, p. 293.

end of perfected ascension, the destination of all destinations, the establisher of what is established, the father of the universes by his action, the mother of all ability by his capability, the highest divine example, the endless fabric of the universe, the soul of souls and light of spirits, the cleaver of the dawn of the unseen and lifter of the darkness of doubt, the origin of the ninety-nine, mercy to all the worlds, our Master in existence, the bearer of the standard of praise and the station of praiseworthiness, and the one veiled by heavy clouds, Allah's Beloved, Muḥammad, the Chosen One, Allah Almighty's prayers and peace be upon him).

The following is the formula of seeking spiritual support from Imām ʿAlī. Our Master's addition begins from the phrase "*wa-ʿalā sirri l-asrār* (and on the secret of secrets)" and ends at the phrase "*imāmi l-a`imma* (Imām of imams)", and it contains spiritual titles and attributes of the Imām:

"*Madad yā sayyidī wa-sanadī wa-murshidī wa-tāja ra`sī wa-nūra ʿaynī. Fārisa l-mashāriqi wal-maghārib, ṣāḥib muẓhiri l-ʿajā`ib wal-gharā`ib, asad Allahi l-ghālib. Wa-ʿalā sirri l-asrāri wa-mashriqi l-anwār, al-muhandisi fil-ghuyūbi l-lāhūtiyya. Unmūdhaji l-wāqiʿi wa-shakhṣi l-iṭlāqi, al-munṭabiʿi fī-marāyā l-anfusi wal-āfāq. Sirri l-anbiyā'i wal-mursalīn, sayyidi l-awṣiyā'i waṣ-ṣiddīqīn. Ṣūrati l-ilāhiyya, māddati l-ʿulūmi l-ghayri l-mutanāhiyya, aẓ-ẓāhiri l-burhān, al-bāṭini bi l-qadri wal-sha`n, basmalati kitābi l-wujūd, ḥaqīqati n-nuqṭati l-bā`iyya, al-mutaḥaqqiqi bi l-marātibi l-insāniyya. Ḥaydari ājāmi l-ibdāʿ, al-karrāri fī-maʿāriki l-ikhtirāʿ, as-sirri l-jalī wan-najmi th-thāqib, Imāmi l-a`immati ʿAlī Ibn Abī Ṭālib ʿalayhi ṣ-ṣalāti was-salām.* (Grant us support, O my Master, my supporter, my guide, the crown of my head and light of my eye, the knight of the east and the west, the companion of the manifester of wonders and marvels, the victorious lion of Allah! And on the secret of secrets and source of lights, the architect of divine unseen. The paradigm of reality and absolute man, he who is printed on the mirrors of selves and horizons, the secret of the prophets and messengers, the master of guardians and the truthful. The Divine picture, the unending essence of knowledge, the one whose proof is apparent, the one whose rank and stature are hidden, the basmalah of the scripture of existence, the reality of the dot of the letter bā`, the one who realized the levels of humanity, the brave lion of the forts of ingenuity, the ferocious fighter in battles of contrivance, the manifest secret and the penetrating star, the Imām of all Imams, ʿAlī Ibn Abī Ṭālib, prayers and blessings be upon him)".

The dhikr circle came to end with the recitation of this ṣalāt:

"*Allahumma ṣalli was sallim wa-bārik 'alā an-nabī Muḥammad wa-`āli Muḥammad, sayyidi ar-rijāli al-mufaḍḍal, yā baḥra al-kamāl yā Muhamamd* (O Allah, send prayers, peace, and blessings upon the Prophet Muḥammad and the family of Muḥammad, the preferred one, Master of men, O sea of perfection, O Muḥammad!", followed by Ṣalāt Waṣfiyya. The sessions of praise and sermons are also sealed by these two formulas of prayers on the Prophet (PBUH).

Shaikh 'Abd al-Karīm al-Kasnazān used to attend the final portion of the dhikr circle, which is accompanied by drums and tambourines. He would stand for a short while outside the circle without entering it, before going to sit on his chair in front of the circle while dervishes complete the dhikr. Our Shaikh also used to attend the same part of the dhikr circle, but he would enter the circle's centre (photos 30, 39). One day he commented on this, saying that "Shaikh 'Abd al-Karīm knew why he did not enter the circle and I know why I enter it".

While standing in the circle, our Master would sometimes correct the way some dervishes would stand or their dhikr movements. Nearing the end of the dhikr, when dervishes sit on the ground, our Shaikh leaves the circle and goes to sit on his chair in front of the circle, where dervishes visit him after the dhikr ends. He may deliver a sermon, then a session of praise would be held.

At times, our Master raises his foot during the dhikr and moves it slightly so that he stays leaning on his other foot and his cane. This is a gesture of humility and subservience to grand Shaikhs when their spirits attend the dhikr circle. As we have mentioned before, as a result of his health, he has stopped attending the dhikr circle, except on some special occasions.

14.4.5 Temporary Dhikrs

In addition to the established Ṭarīqa's established dhikrs, that is, the daily, perennial, and dhikr circle, our Shaikh sometimes instructs dervishes to perform certain dhikrs temporarily. The reason behind these wirds may or may not be disclosed. Often, the dhikr is limited to a certain number, although some wirds end after a certain time or with the ending of an event. The instruction is often to read these instead of the perennial dhikrs. Disciples return to complete the perennial wirds from where they left off after completing the temporary wirds. As an example of a temporary dhikr, on 10th/February/2017, our Master instructed disciples to read the dhikr "*lā ilāha illallāh*" one hundred thousand times and the dhikr "*lā ilāha illallāh, Muḥammad rasūl Allāh, ṣallallāhu taʿālā ʿalayhi wa-sallam* (there is no god but Allah, Muḥammad is the Messenger of Allah, Allah's peace and blessings be upon Him)" one hundred thirty-five thousand times. The reward for reciting the dhikrs is to be gifted to the Ṭarīqa's Shaikhs. The dhikrs were to be read with the intention of whatever was in our present Shaikh's heart, i.e. the purpose he had in his heart.

14.4.6 Individual Dhikrs

Our Shaikh often instructs a disciple to perform a special dhikr a certain number of times or for a specific period. This is usually for a need that the disciple seeks his help in fulfilling, such as increasing sustenance, removing harm, or curing an illness. He sometimes prescribes a particular dhikr to a dervish or a group of dervishes for matters related to Ṭarīqa that he knows.

14.4.7 Ḥizb al-Wāw

While the term "wird" refers to a dhikr that the person recites regularly, a "ḥizb" is a dhikr that the person reads when he likes, such as when he has a specific need. Our Shaikh says that the thought came to him that many Shaikhs have ḥizbs that are particular to them, but he did not have one. In 2013, Allah Almighty granted him a special ḥizb called "Ḥizb al-Wāw". He described this ḥizb as an "order from Allah to the honourable Messenger (PBUH), to the Shaikhs, and the Shaikhs conveyed it to me".[308] This ḥizb consists of every Qur'anic verse that begins with the letter "wāw", totalling 2,128 verses, sequentially ordered as they appear in the muṣḥaf. The first verse is "Those who believe in what has been revealed to you [O Muḥammad] and what was revealed before you and of the Hereafter, they are certain [in faith]" (al-Baqara 4), and the last verse is "From the evil of an envier when he envies" (al-Falaq 5). Our Shaikh has described Ḥizb al-Wāw as "a tremendous thing". He has printed this unique ḥizb but has not permitted it to be read without his permission. The best time to read it is during the last third of the night, and a person may complete its

[308] Shaikh Muḥammad al-Muḥammad al-Kasnazān, *sermon*, 12th/September/2013.

recitation in more than one night.

14.5 The Shaikh's Dhikrs

The Ṭarīqa Kasnazāniyya Shaikhs customarily join dervishes in performing Wird al-ʿAṣr and the dhikr circle. However, since Shaikhhood is a unique and special spiritual rank, the Shaikh has dhikrs that are particular to him that differ from those of the disciples. For example, our Shaikh has wirds that, when reading them, he does not speak to anyone except by gesture. At times, he performs such dhikrs from after the sunset prayer until the time of the night prayer. When a person does not understand what he wants by way of his gesturing, our Shaikh waits until he finishes that dhikr, and then speaks to him about what he wanted. Shaikh ʿAbd al-Karīm would also devote himself to worship after the sunset prayer. His personal assistant would leave him alone and would not return until the Shaikh nears the end of his wirds.

Our Shaikh also has special wirds that he reads after the dawn prayer until sunrise, walking while reading them, sometimes from his bedroom to an adjacent yard if available, or simply to the bedroom's entrance, even if it is a short distance. It seems that walking while reciting these dhikrs is one of their requirements: "Who remember Allah while standing or sitting or [lying] on their sides and give thought to the creation of the heavens and the earth" (`Āl ʿImrān 191).

Another special worship of our Shaikh, which he had early in his Shaikhdom when was living in Kirkuk, was to perform four cycles of prayer one hour before the call to the noon prayer. The time for the prayer was very precise. He would stand on the prayer rug a minute or two before the time for this prayer, and he would look at his watch until it was exactly one hour before the noon prayer, at which point he would begin praying. Whenever there was someone in his assembly that did not know of this daily practice of his, he would inform them before the prayer that the time for the noon prayer had not yet arrived, so that they would not think that he was performing the noon prayer.

Shaikh Sāmān, who was sometimes forced to sleep in the Shaikh's bedroom in his house in Karbchna, relates that our Master habitually read the Qur'anic chapter of Yā Sīn when he went to bed. One of the astonishing things he noticed is that sometimes our Shaikh would doze off while reading Yā-Sīn, but when wakes up, he goes back to completing the chapter from the verse he had been reading before he fell asleep!

Even though in his eighties, our Shaikh performs optional worships in the last third of the night. After departing from his public assembly, usually before midnight, he goes to his private room, where he sleeps for a while. He then wakes up and remains in worship until sunrise. He goes back to sleep for two or three hours before waking up to begin his worship and to tend to his daily responsibilities in managing the Ṭarīqa's affairs. The condition of his health now determines what he can do in this regard.

The following is a special spiritual experience that demonstrates the fusion of remembering Allah with our Master internally and externally. When he decided to have a kidney transplant in 2010 in the USA, before the procedure, the Ṭarīqa's Shaikhs told him that they had performed the surgery for him in their spiritual hospital, so the operation in the hospital of the world of appearances would be successful. This symbolic language meant that the success of the procedure was guaranteed, which is what indeed happened. After waking up from the anaesthesia, he found his external existence reading the last two verses of the chapter of al-Tawba: "There has certainly come to you a Messenger from among yourselves. Grievous to him is what you suffer; [he is] concerned over you and to the believers is kind and merciful. If they turn away [O Muḥammad], say: 'Sufficient for me is Allah; there is no deity except Him. On Him I have relied, and He is the Lord of the Great Throne'" (al-Tawba 128-129), while he found his internal existence reading the two verses of Prophet Jonah's supplication and Allah's answering his call: "'There is no deity except You; exalted are You. Indeed, I have been of the wrongdoers.' We responded to him and saved him from distress. And thus do We save the believers" (al-Ānbiyā` 87-88). Prophet Jonah called out by this supplication when he was in the whale's belly, while our Shaikh's internal existence was reading these two verses while he was under the effects of the anaesthesia. There seemed to be an element of similarity in the Prophet Jonah's being in the whale's depths, temporarily isolating him and his senses from his natural surroundings, and our Shaikh's being anaesthetised, temporarily isolating his external existence from the world.

Photo 30: Shaikh Muḥammad al-Muḥammad in the dhikr circle in the takya of Kirkuk (27th/August/1993).

"Compete in preaching; compete in opening takyas; compete in having good manners; compete in doing more dhikr; compete in worshipping at night; compete in fasting often; compete in performing seclusion and spiritual exercises. Do not compete in chasing after this world. This world is carrion and those who seek it are dogs. This world seeks those who run away from it and runs away from those who seek it".

Shaikh Muḥammad al-Muḥammad al-Kasnazān
(Sermon, 22nd/December/2005)

15

Riyāḍa (Spiritual Exercising)

The word "riyāḍa" in Sufism means "cultivating", "disciplining", and "training" the self and "controlling" it, so it may be translated as "spiritual exercising". It refers to forms of internal discipline that a person voluntarily adheres to for a period. The taming of the self is brought about by denying it materialistic pleasures it likes and combining that denial with a focus on worship. This way, a disciple's heart is illuminated and cleansed, and he begins to taste the unique spiritual experiences in the Ṭarīqa.

Taming the self to bring it closer to Allah takes various forms. The Muslim may choose the practices that are within his capability. Accordingly, practising riyāḍa does not special permission from the Shaikh. The Ṭarīqa Kasnazāniyya Shaikhs urge disciples to practice riyāḍa.

Riyāḍa includes various spiritual exercises. For instance, fasting for a day in a month other than Ramadan, in which fasting is obligatory, is a form of riyāḍa. But Ṭarīqa Kasnazāniyya has also a specific approach of riyāḍa developed by the Ṭarīqa's Shaikhs. It includes the following:

- Refraining from consuming animal products and their derivatives.
- Gradually reducing the consumption of bread because it has a similar effect on the self that meat has.
- Drinking less water, especially cold water, because it leads to heedlessness and sleep.
- Speaking less of worldly matters.
- Performing dhikr of Allah in abundance.
- Ensuring that all food and drink are undoubtedly halal because that is better for keeping the heart conscious.

The duration of a course of riyāḍa is usually forty days divided into four equal parts of ten days each. Each part increases the efforts made therein. Unlike seclusion, which we will talk about in the next chapter, a dervish does not need special permission from the Shaikh of Ṭarīqa to practice riyāḍa. He is always permitted by his Shaikh to practice it.

A seeker must always hide, as much as he can, his being in a state of riyāḍa, saving his heart from any negative effects that might be caused by people's knowledge of his condition. All of his actions may then be for Allah, not for showing off to people. Shaikh ʿAbd al-Karīm al-Kasnazān once practised riyāḍa for six months without anyone being aware of it. He would go out to hunt during this period. When they would hunt birds and animals, he would ask that some are grilled and others are fried, and he would prepare himself to eat with people and sit with them, but he would avoid eating the meat without anyone noticing that he was doing so. He did not disclose this matter until later, to teach disciples the importance of concealing their worship so that it does not attract people's attention, so it may be purely for Allah.

All Ṭarīqa Shaikhs practised riyāḍa. We have discussed briefly Sulṭān Ḥusayn al-Kasnazān's spiritual exercises, which are almost unparalleled. Just as the spiritual exercises of disciples are directed by the Ṭarīqa's Shaikhs, those of the Shaikhs, as is the case with their actions in general, are guided by orders from the Messenger (PBUH). One instructive occurrence is that Sulṭān Ḥusayn often practised his worship at night in an underground pit in front of the mosque that adjoins the Shaikhs' shrines in Karbchna (photo 31). A dervish named ʿAbd al-Karīm would stand at his service, staying near the Shaikh until around midnight, awaiting his request for a final cup of tea. After bringing it, he would leave him to complete his worship alone and go to sleep in his house, which was about a hundred metres away from the place of seclusion. Sulṭān Ḥusayn would drink tea sweetened with honey instead of sugar.

One night, Shaikh Ḥusayn remained completely engrossed with his worship until the time when he would usually ask for a final cup of tea passed. While ʿAbd al-Karīm awaited the Shaikh's request, he began to feel blessings and mercy fill the place. He saw small glimmering things falling from the sky onto Sulṭān Ḥusayn, who was too preoccupied with his worship to notice them. It was getting very late, so the dervish felt fatigued and sleepy. It seemed that the Shaikh would remain like this, immersed in his dhikr and prayer, so he would not ask for a cup of tea. ʿAbd al-Karīm quietly sneaked away, careful not to disturb the Shaikh, and went to his house.

He went straight to bed and wrapped himself in sheets. Suddenly, he heard Sulṭān Ḥusayn's voice in the house, calling him: "Uncle 'Abd al-Karīm". The caliph answered: "Yes, my beloved", and got up from the bed. He looked around, but the Shaikh was nowhere to be seen in the house, so he headed for his place of seclusion. He found Sulṭān Ḥusayn still sitting in the same position that he had left him in. This time, he looked at him and gestured with his hand, asking for a cup of tea.

While preparing the tea, 'Abd al-Karīm called to his Shaikh in his heart: "My beloved, you are fasting from food, and this honey has a sharp taste that would harm your stomach. It is better to sweeten the tea with sugar instead". Sulṭān Ḥusayn immediately looked at him and said: "Uncle 'Abd al-Karīm, by Allah, there is no barrier between me and the honourable Messenger (PBUH)". He stretched his hand out, opening it, indicating the inexistence of any barrier, before adding: "He commands me and says: 'Ḥusayn, drink this, eat this, do this dhikr'. I do not do anything of my own accord — only by order of the honourable Messenger (PBUH)". The caliph understood that this was in response to his request to use sugar instead of honey in the tea. Even the method of sweetening the tea that Shaikh Ḥusayn drank was by an order from the Messenger (PBUH).

As for Shaikh Muḥammad al-Muḥammad, he began practising riyāḍa before he became Shaikh of the Ṭarīqa. He would be in a state of riyāḍa several times a year. All of his spiritual exercises, as is the case with his dhikrs, were by direct instruction from Shaikh 'Abd al-Karīm, his spiritual teacher. This is always the case of the Ṭarīqa's Shaikhs with their deputies because this direct instruction is one of the Shaikh of Ṭarīqa's duties in training the person who will succeed him. Similarly, our present Shaikh is the one who directs his General Deputy and son, Shaikh Nahro, in regards to any riyāḍa or dhikrs.

After becoming Shaikh of the Ṭarīqa, our Master would sometimes practise riyāḍa during the blessed month of Ramadan. When breaking his fast, he would abstain from consuming certain kinds of food, such as meat. He would sometimes abstain from drinking cold water, even when it was hot out, and would not drink it until it had warmed.

Photo 31: The mosque in Karbchna; in front of it is the underground seclusion place of Shāh al-Kasnazān and Shaikh Ḥusayn. Shaikh Muḥammad al-Muḥammad has built a protective structure on it (19th/March/2016).

Photo 32: Shaikh Muḥammad al-Muḥammad in a session of songs of praise in the courtyard of the takya in Baghdad (1996).

"If you exploit this world for purposes of the hereafter, to serve Sharia and the Ṭarīqa, to serve Islam, to serve mankind, to serve humanity, then it is mercy because this world is the hereafter's farm. In this world, you act and do things for Allah's sake: 'and spend out of what We have provided for them' (al-Baqara 3). One of the pillars of Islam is spending for Allah's sake. A seeker wants [something], and Allah (exalted and high is He) wants [something] from the seeker; what does He want from the seeker? He wants obedience: 'Obey Allah and obey the Messenger and those in authority among you' (al-Nisā` 59). When you use this world to serve the hereafter, this is excellent, this is necessary, as we do not abandon this world: 'Work for your world as if you were to live forever, and work for your hereafter as if you were to die tomorrow'.[309] This world and the hereafter, these words; when you use this world for the hereafter, this is the best thing, a blessed thing. We do not say 'O Seeker, abandon this world!' No, we rather, say: 'Do [as you will], for Allah will see your deeds, and His Messenger and the believers' (al-Tawba 105), meaning righteous deeds: 'Indeed, those who have believed and done righteous deeds — they will have the Gardens of Paradise as a lodging" (al-Kahf 107).

Shaikh Muḥammad al-Muḥammad al-Kasnazān
(Sermon, 29th/January/2010)

[309] Our Shaikh has said that some claim that this is a Prophetic ḥadīth, while others attribute it to Imām ʿAlī Ibn Abī Ṭālib.

16

Khalwa (Seclusion)

"Khalwa", or seclusion, is a unique form of riyāḍa that combines several kinds of struggle, worship, and isolation from people and being alone with Allah. The Prophet (PBUH) was wont to seclude himself with his Lord, far away from people, in the Cave of Ḥirā` for lengthy periods. Sayyida ʿĀ`ishā said: "The love of seclusion was bestowed on him. He would seclude himself in the Cave of Ḥirā` and devote himself to worship there for nights before going back to his family. He would gather the necessary supplies for this. He would return to Khadīja to gather supplies again for another stay. He did this until the Truth came to him while he was in the Cave of Ḥirā`".[310] In another narration about the first revelation, he (PBUH) says: "I stayed in Ḥirā` for a month. When my stay was completed, I came down and went to the heart of the valley".[311] Seclusion is a form of worship in the Ṭarīqa because it is a sunna of the Prophet (PBUH). As is the case with riyāḍa, khalwa is aimed at cultivating the self, taming it, distancing it from worldly pleasures, and causing it to draw near to its Lord. Hence, it has much hardship for the self, such as limiting the kinds and amounts of food it is allowed, lessening sleep, and increasing worship.

Muḥammad (PBUH) would seclude himself to worship and contemplate, far from worldly preoccupations. His seclusions, even before the Qur'an was revealed to him, were filled with spiritual experiences, which are some of the fruits of that isolation with Allah. This spiritual outpouring from Allah is what made him return, repeatedly and frequently, to more seclusions. This is some of what Shaikh ʿAbd al-Qādir al-Gaylānī says about khalwa and the secrets that appear in it:

> "How could the righteous not love seclusion when their hearts are filled with intimacy with their Lord (mighty and sublime is He)? How could they

[310] Bukhārī, *Al-Jāmiʿ al-Ṣaḥīḥ*, I, no. 3, p. 50.

[311] Muslim, *Ṣaḥīḥ Muslim*, I, no. 161, p. 144.

not flee from creation when their hearts cannot see their benefit and harm, as they see the harm and benefit coming from their Lord (mighty and sublime is He)? The drink of nearness revives them, whereas soberness kills them. The speech of yearning draws them near and being acquainted with secrets is their Paradise".[312]

Despite the difficulty of seclusion, the righteous find solace in and cherish it. Later in this chapter, we will look at some spiritual experiences that Shaikh Muḥammad al-Muḥammad al-Kasnazān has had during his seclusions.

16.1 Al-Kasnazāniyya Khalwa

In the Ṭarīqa Kasnazāniyya, one seclusion lasts for forty days. It has a special system designed by the Ṭarīqa's Shaikhs that must be followed to the letter by anyone who goes into seclusion. A seeker begins the seclusion in the afternoon by intending to enter it. During the seclusion, the seeker fasts like the fast of Ramadan but with additional strict limitations regarding food because the seeker remains in a state of riyāḍa for the duration of the khalwa. The khalwa is divided into four parts, each of which lasts for ten days. The one in seclusion eats one naan a day, which he may choose to eat in its entirety once the fast is broken or divide into meals during the period when the fast is broken. In addition to the naan, the seeker eats a little bit of fruit and vegetables, or a cup of fat- and salt-free lentil soup, in addition to tea. Then, the naan becomes half a naan in the second ten days and a quarter of a naan in the third ten.

There is no naan in the last ten days. For the first week, the seeker's daily food includes three dates or the equivalent quantity of raisins, that is, less than ten, while the seeker is sufficed in the final three days with water and tea.[313] The seeker is blessed with the spiritual presence of the Ṭarīqa's Shaikhs during the seclusion, as well as other spiritual experiences. This spiritual feeling multiplies in the last three days when the dervish does not taste any food.

Smokers are allowed to smoke when the fast is broken, on the

[312] Shaikh 'Abd al-Qādir al-Gaylānī, *Jilā' al-Khāṭir*, p. 76.

[313] Shaikh Muḥammad al-Muḥammad al-Kasnazān, *Al-Ṭarīqa al-'Aliyya al-Qādiriyya al-Kasnazāniyya*, p. 183.

condition that they do not use manufactured cigarettes, but rather natural tobacco, meaning unprocessed. Our Shaikh has never smoked and detests smoking, but he has not declared it haram.

As for worship, the seeker continues to perform the daily and perennial dhikrs while in seclusion. In addition to the obligatory prayers, he must offer sunna prayers. He must refrain from thinking about worldly affairs and must be completely preoccupied with worship. The seeker must combine with the paucity of food and abundance of dhikr significant reduction in sleep. Night sleep is not allowed, so he must stay awake, busy with his worship until sunrise. Afterwards, he can sleep for a short while. In any case, the plentitude of dhikr necessitates that sleep is kept to a minimum anyway.

Khalwa is the most difficult of all spiritual exercises because it represents the greatest striving against the self. It contains the abandoning of food, drink, speech, sleep, people, and the world in general and complete preoccupation with Allah's dhikr. However, the human body and mind are not naturally prepared for such harsh conditions. Without supernatural intervention protecting the person in seclusion, his body and mind would certainly be harmed. Our Shaikh recounts that five or six days after his first seclusion, some dervishes who accompanied him were suffering greatly as a result of the little food they were eating. He was worried about their ability to complete the khalwa. He then underwent a spiritual experience that dismissed his anxiety and improved the dervishes' condition. He saw Shaikh ʿAbd al-Karīm carry a small pepper in his hand, point to it, and say that should the Shaikhs tell a dervish that this small pepper would be enough food for him for the whole day, then the dervish's heart should believe that this is true and not be worried. He asked him to convey this message to the dervishes.[314] Our Shaikh felt assured, informed the disciples of what Shaikh ʿAbd al-Karīm said, and advised them to engross themselves in dhikr and forget about hunger. Their feeling of hunger went away and they completed the khalwa.

Shaikh ʿAbd al-Karīm's words show that the Shaikh spiritually intervenes to help a disciple carry the physical and psychological hardships of the khalwa. Rationing food or limiting sleep to this extent,

---

[314] Shaikh Muḥammad al-Muḥammad al-Kasnazān, *sermon*, 21st/November/2018.

let alone combining the two, is not within the natural capabilities of the human body. There is a need for supernatural intervention to help a disciple and protect him from harm. One critical requirement for successfully completing a khalwa is trust in Allah and absolute confidence that the Shaikh of Ṭarīqa does not order except what he is instructed to do and what will benefit disciples. Trusting in Allah and obedience that is built on perfectly good thoughts about the Shaikh are the bases of a seeker's spiritual development in his Ṭarīqa journey.

Entering seclusion leaves the person vulnerable to exceptional targeting of attacks by evil beings, from both jinns and devils, that want to make him abandon his worship. These attempts are aimed at his body, his mind, and even his life. These attempts intensify when the secluding dervish is not in a state of dhikr, such as when he is sleeping or taking care of other bodily needs. When he is not in a state of worship, the dervish is in a weak spiritual state. Evil beings find it easier to approach him and try to cause him harm. As a result of this danger, a disciple in Ṭarīqa Kasnazāniyya must not enter a khalwa without permission from the Shaikh, because he knows his spiritual state, the extent of his eligibility to enter a khalwa, and the spiritual care he needs. When the Shaikh permits a seeker to enter a khalwa, he is responsible for his spiritual protection against evil spirits that try to affect him, externally and internally, while awake and asleep. Shaikh Muḥammad al-Muḥammad al-Kasnazān says:

> "There are many Sufis who enter a khalwa as believers and come out as unbelievers. Anyone who does not have a Shaikh, who does not have someone instructing him, does not have the allegiance of Ṭarīqa, does not have the spiritual touch and the power of the Shaikhs of Ṭarīqa, who does not have with him these pure spirits, the guiding spirits — the spirits of Shaikhs leading to the honourable Messenger (PBUH) — Satan harms him with whispers, while he is in the state of silent dhikr and in other states. He harms him and tempts him, so he slips. He leaves religion, Īmān, and sound belief in one place and ends up in another.
>
> This happened to many Sufis who did not have a Shaikh. They start to gradually practise Sufism, then they decide to enter a khalwa. They enter into isolation, and they get affected. Sometimes, they get afflicted with diseases that they cannot be rid of until they die. At others, they stray from the path and head towards Satanic directions. They abandon praying and fasting, begin to make false claims about themselves, describe themselves as having

ḥāl, and participate in other falsehoods and satanic deeds. Thus, Satan tempts them and takes them to the abyss".[315]

A seeker also needs the Shaikh's spirituality to protect him from other dangers. Dervishes who entered the khalwa with our Shaikh often saw scorpions and serpents in their places of seclusion. They did not go near them, however, nor did they try to harm them. The dervishes also did not try to harm them. The need for the person in seclusion for the Shaikh is an obvious application of the well-known saying, "the person who has no Shaikh has Satan as his Shaikh". Our Shaikh emphasizes that only the person who has reached the level of wilāya can complete a khalwa without needing a Shaikh to protect him.[316]

When a person enters a khalwa, he must also carry a dagger or sword with him. It is needed to scare off, or, if the situation so requires, strike the evil spirits that appear in physical bodies, human and animal, and come to harm him. It seems that when a jinn assumes a physical body, he becomes vulnerable to whatever harms that being, including bodily injuries.

A seeker may find himself incapable of completing a khalwa for one reason or another, so he asks the Shaikh for permission to leave it. In our Shaikh's first khalwa, four dervishes left at the beginning. A day later, after the sunset prayer, our Shaikh told the dervishes that the Shaikhs told him that a fifth disciple would leave. He said that that dervish had a right to take permission to leave the khalwa at the end of that day and that he was not responsible for any consequences resulting from the dervish leaving the khalwa after that time. After the night prayer, a dervish came to ask permission to leave the khalwa, and he was permitted to do so. At that time, our Shaikh said that the number of the khalwa's dervishes was now complete. All remaining disciples completed the khalwa.

The great struggle against the self that the person in seclusion experiences is what made Shāh al-Kasnazān enter forty khalwas, including two consecutive years, in the Cave of Gaylān Āwā on Mount Sagarma. His food there was limited to what looked like clay mixed with tree leaves. As we have mentioned, no human being can live on this food, let alone for such a long time. He was, obviously, enveloped by divine

---

[315] Shaikh Muḥammad al-Muḥammad al-Kasnazān, *sermon*, 25th/May/2000.
[316] Shaikh Muḥammad al-Muḥammad al-Kasnazān, *sermon*, 16th/April/2016.

care during the khalwa. Some of Shāh al-Kasnazān's seclusions were in a cave underneath Mount Sagarma, and others were in an underground cave in front of the mosque that he built in Karbchna. His grandson Sulṭān Ḥusayn used these two caves for his many seclusions, and he also retreated to Gaylān Āwā for one summer. In his last years, Shaikh Ḥusayn was in a virtually perpetual khalwa until he became known by the title of "Shāh al-Khalwa".

While Shāh al-Kasnazān, Sulṭān Ḥusayn, and our present Shaikh entered seclusions, Sulṭān ʿAbd al-Qādir and Sulṭān ʿAbd al-Karīm were not ordered to enter a khalwa. All of our Shaikhs, however, practised various spiritual exercises. One feat of Shaikh ʿAbd al-Qādir al-Kasnazān's asceticism was revealed one day when he passed by the takya's bakery. He took a piece of hot bread in his hand then put it back in its place. He turned to a dervish walking behind him and said: "For seven years my self has been asking me for hot bread, but by Allah, I won't give it any".[317]

16.2 Shaikh Muḥammad al-Muḥammad al-Kasnazān's Seclusions

Our Shaikh entered three seclusions in three consecutive years, all after he became Shaikh of the Ṭarīqa. They were in the same cave that Shāh al-Kasnazān and Sulṭān Ḥusayn secluded themselves in at the foot of the mountain (photo 33). The first khalwa was in the year in which he received the Shaikhdom, 1978 (photo 34), and the second and third were in the following two years. Each khalwa began ten days before the month of Ramadan and continued throughout the month of fasting to complete forty days. According to the Gregorian calendar, the first khalwa began around the 26th/July and ended on 3rd/September. Each of the following two seclusions began and ended eleven days before the one that preceded it, as the Hijri year is shorter than the Gregorian year by eleven days. The third khalwa differed from the first two in that he did not spend all of his time in the cave. He would remain inside it from the morning prayer until the night prayer and then return to the takya, probably because of his need to closely manage the Ṭarīqa's affairs and the impossibility of

[317] Shaikh Muḥammad al-Muḥammad al-Kasnazān, *sermon*, 25th/May/2000.

postponing everything for forty days.

Before he entered his first seclusion, our Shaikh visited the shrines of the Shaikhs in Karbchna. When he was about to enter the cave, he read the basmala, then followed it with the following noble verse: "Retreat to the cave. Your Lord will spread out for you of His mercy and will make easy for you your affair" (al-Kahf 16). This noble verse is Allah's order to those converted youths to enter the cave that witnessed the miracle of their lengthy slumber and then waking up.

This natural cave faces the Ka'ba, and its walls and ceiling are made up of huge rocks. It is about three metres deep, and it is more than two metres high in most places, so it is possible to stand at its entrance, but it gradually narrows on some of its sides. When inside the cave, the person is completely isolated from the outside world. In this way, it is reminiscent of Cave of Ḥirā`, where the Prophet (PBUH) would seclude himself. Since our Shaikh's three seclusions were in the heat of summer, he would stay inside the cave during the day, and when the temperature would cool at night, he would go out and sit on the roof of the cave.

The Kasnazāni khalwa diet, which we have already explained, is very difficult to adhere to, yet our Shaikh subjected himself to a far more strict diet as Shaikh of the Ṭarīqa. In the first thirteen days of his first khalwa, in a single day, he would consume a quarter of a ruqāq bread prepared without any salt or sugar. Ruqaq bread is extremely thin: when our Shaikh would break off a piece of a loaf in his palm before eating it, it would not fill his palm. After that, he completely stopped eating bread for the rest of that khalwa and in the following two khalwas, limiting his diet to fruit, such as melons. He could only eat a few kinds of fruit since they would cause discomfort as a result of eating them without any other food. He would also eat a few pieces of boiled okra that have been cooked without fat or salt because it helps in softening the stomach as a result of its abundant fibre. A few days after no longer eating food, however, water and tea started to cause acidity in the stomach.

Our Shaikh also put himself through additional struggles during his khalwa. In the first khalwa, he asked his brother in law, Sāmān, to accompany him in the khalwa without being in a state of seclusion himself, meaning without abiding by its conditions. Our Shaikh would ask for the best, most delicious kinds of food for his companion at the time of breaking the fast, so the latter would eat in front of him. Shaikh

Sāmān relates that as soon as the khalwa ended, he realized very clearly that our Shaikh was subjecting himself to additional struggle by allowing him to eat these delicious foods in front of him. Sāmān cannot hide his amazement about the fact that he never thought about this matter at all during the khalwa. It was as if the Shaikh had thrown a veil over him that prevented him all that time from realizing that he served him as an additional means of causing himself to struggle. While our Shaikh would watch his companion eating as much as he liked of the tastiest of foods, what he would eat of very limited foods throughout the entire day would not fill the palm of one hand. Commenting on the difficulty of this struggle against the self, our Shaikh says: "There are times when one wishes he could give everything he owns for a piece of bread".[318] This emphasizes the magnitude of spiritual influence that helps the one in seclusion withstand its difficulties.

Before entering the khalwa, our Shaikh delivered a sermon to those entering it about its rules and etiquettes. About thirty-five dervishes from different cities in Iraq and some from Iran entered the first khalwa with him. Before the khalwa began, he determined the area of seclusion for the dervishes, on the same mountain, close to the cave of his place of seclusion. Each disciple chose a small, natural place suitable for seclusion or prepared a suitable place using branches and shrubs as roofs and walls. It was incumbent upon the one in seclusion to stay within the limits of the khalwa area even when leaving his place of seclusion for whatever reason. Some disciples secluded themselves on an individual basis, while the rest were in pairs. Our Shaikh cautioned the dervishes that were near one another to not busy themselves with talking instead of worship. He and the dervishes refrained from shaving their beards during the khalwa.

In every khalwa, the first dhikr that our Shaikh and the disciples would perform was the first khatma of the perennial dhikrs, "*lā ilāha illallāh*", and they would also complete a khatma of each of the other eighteen perennial wirds during the khalwa. Dervishes were not allowed to sleep at night and spent it instead purely in worship. A dervish could sleep for a while after finishing his dhikrs that follow the dawn prayer.

The disciples spent most of their time alone performing their devotional duties, but they would come together at certain times of the

---

[318] Shaikh Muḥammad al-Muḥammad al-Kasnazān, *sermon*, 25th/May/2000.

day for congregational dhikrs. They would also recite Imām al-Būṣīrī's *Qaṣīdat al-Burda* (The Ode of the Mantle) every night as a group. Also, after praying and breaking the fast, our Shaikh and the dervishes would stand in the direction of the Ka'ba to recite the dhikrs "*Yā Khabīr* (O All-Aware One!)" and "*ṣalallāhu subḥānahu wa-ta'ālā 'alayka wa-sallam yā rasūlallāh* (may Allah (high is He) send prayers upon you, O Messenger of Allah!)" one hundred times.

In the morning, the dervishes taking part in the khalwa would gather in front of the Shaikh's cave to hear a sermon from him, any instructions or remarks he had, and the answers to questions related to the seclusion. When a disciple had a question or a particular issue he wanted to present to the Shaikh outside the group meeting time, for example, a private matter, he would inform the person standing at the Shaikh's service for him to arrange a meeting. Dervishes outside the khalwa would also sometimes visit our Shaikh for a short visit.

16.3 Supernatural and Spiritual Experiences

Entering seclusion makes a person go through various spiritual experiences, from divine unveilings and visitations from good spirits to vexations from evil spiritual creatures trying to stop him from this devotion to Allah at any cost and to harm him. In this section, we will mention some of the spiritual experiences that our Shaikh experienced during his seclusions.

Our Shaikh says that during the three seclusions, whenever he closed his eyes, without sleeping or entering into a state of spiritual meditation, whether by night or by day, he would see his Master, Shaikh 'Abd al-Karīm, and his Master's Master, Shaikh Ḥusayn, standing at the entrance of the place of seclusion.[319] Their spiritual presence was to protect their caliph and deputy, the present Shaikh of the Ṭarīqa. In one of the seclusions, devils disseminated for a period an extremely foul odour, like that of a rotting corpse, at the time of breading the fast, and the odour would persist until approximately the time of the night prayer. It made it difficult for our Master to eat or drink.

One day, he was lying down in the place of seclusion and had closed

[319] Shaikh Muḥammad al-Muḥammad al-Kasnazān, *sermon*, 25th/May/2000.

his eyes in a state of dhikr when his heart suddenly received an inspiration to order the dervish standing in his service, who was sitting nearby, to immediately get up and leave his post. As soon as he left his place, a massive rock fell from the cave's roof onto the spot where he had been seated, which would have undoubtedly killed him had he remained in his place.

One night, a snake dangled from the roof of the place of seclusion towards our Shaikh's assistant in the khalwa. As soon as our Shaikh drew his sword, the snake fled. In another incident, he asked his assistant to clean his pillow, and when he lifted it, he found a very large scorpion underneath it.

Here is one occurrence that all the dervishes in seclusion witnessed. At times, after the night prayer but before midnight, the part of the sky facing the opening of our Shaikh's cave would transform into something like a battlefield because of the abundance of meteors shooting across it. This indicates an abnormal level of presence and activity, on the one hand, of devils and evil jinns who try to negatively impact the divine atmosphere that the khalwa creates and, on the other, good spirits that undo their efforts. This phenomenon is a confirmation of what Allah Almighty says in the Qur'an:

> "We have placed within the heaven mansions and beautified it for observers. We have protected it from every cursed devil, except one who steals a hearing so and is pursued by a clear burning flame". (Al-Ḥijr 16-18)
>
> "Indeed, We have adorned the nearest heaven with an adornment of stars and as protection against every rebellious devil. They may not listen to the exalted assembly [of angels] and are pelted from every side, repelled; and for them is a constant punishment, except one who snatches [some words] by theft, but they are pursued by a burning flame, piercing [in brightness]". (Al-Ṣāffāt 6-10)

The following noble verse mentioned by a jinn spokesperson explicitly mentions the increase of guards in the heavens at certain times when special spiritual activities take place:

> "We have sought [to reach] heaven but found it filled with powerful guards and burning flames. We used to sit therein in positions for hearing, but whoever listens now will find a burning flame lying in wait for him". (Al-Jinn 8-9)

This is another example of how Ṭarīqa transforms Īmān from being "traditional" to "authentic" by causing a devoted dervish to see spiritual proofs and from the unseen, which are unattainable otherwise. There is no doubt that the dervishes in seclusion had complete faith in Allah's words, including verses that describe pelting the devils who try to infiltrate the good spirits' world. However, their witnessing of the phenomenon of the abundance of meteors with their own eyes drew them closer to the level of Iḥsān. Karāmas are the means of crossing over from "believing" in the Qur'an's truthfulness to "witnessing" it.

After reading, with the disciples, "*Yā Khabīr*" and "*Ṣalla Allāhu subḥānahu wa-t'ālā 'alayka wa-sallam yā rasūla Allāh*" one hundred times after the sunset prayer while standing and facing the Ka'ba, he would proceed with his personal wirds afterwards. At that time, all the dervishes would begin to hear what sounded like the chirping of thousands of crickets. The sound would continue until he finished those dhikrs at the time of the night prayer, at which point it would disappear. At times, the sound would be loud to the point where our Master would have to raise his voice when speaking, even when speaking to those near him. One astonishing aspect of this phenomenon is its happening at night in an isolated, mountainous area, where stillness is almost ubiquitous. This phenomenon sometimes recurs even outside of the khalwa. At times, our Shaikh goes out to walk in Amman. At the end of the path he walks on, there is a grove wherein there are tall pine trees. In a spot there, he would perform the sunset prayer and the sunna prayers and read his special wirds. Sometimes, the same sounds are heard until he finishes his wirds.

In seclusion, many spiritual unveilings and visitations from Shaikhs and good spirits occur. The following is one such karāma that happened to our Shaikh in his second seclusion, which he disclosed in a speech to dervishes who were visiting him:

> A moment ago, Shaikh 'Abd al-Karīm came and called me: "Muḥammad". I answered: "Yes, my beloved". He said: "Look at my hand". There was a wire in his hand that looked like a radio antenna. He shook the wire, and a tremendous fire broke out from the city of Penjwin (in northern Iraq, on the border with Iran) to the city of Abadan (in southern Iran, on the border with Iraq). Shaikh 'Abd al-Karīm said: "Do you see that"? I answered in the affirmative. Shaikh 'Abd al-Karīm shook the wire again, and the fire spread as had happened the first time. Shaikh 'Abd al-Karīm said: "Tell your dervishes that we sat you in the Shaikhs' place and put the Ṭarīqa's staff in your hand.

The one who sticks to you is safe, and the one who does not is responsible for that".

This unveiling happened in mid-1979. A little more than a year later, the devastating war between Iraq and Iran that lasted eight years broke out.

A karāma that illustrates the spiritual benefits of seclusion happened three days before the end of our Shaikh's third khalwa, i.e. on the twenty-seventh night of the month of Ramadan. This is the night that many consider "*Laylat al-Qadr*" (the Night of Power). The Ṭarīqa's Shaikhs told our Master to inform the dervishes in seclusion that the Messenger (PBUH) was telling them to submit all of their requests that night. They told him that a sign of the truth of this message is that when he would inform the dervishes, one of them would be struck with an intense ḥāl that would cause him to go to the mountain. The next day, after breaking the fast, our Shaikh stood atop the cave that he was secluded in, which overlooked all the dervishes' places of seclusion, and informed them of the Messenger's order (PBUH) to present their requests to Allah (exalted and high is He) after the night prayer. An Iranian dervish named sayyid ʿAbd al-Raḥmān was struck with a ḥāl that caused him to go to the mountain. The following day, our Shaikh had to send someone to bring him back. Late in the night of the notification, a dervish called Mullā Muḥammad, a cousin of our Shaikhs, came having experienced a ḥāl that made him cry and laugh. The dervish asked our Shaikh for permission to speak. He agreed and told him that he knew what he would say. The dervish said that, while awake, he saw every disciple present his requests in the form of a scroll. He saw the honourable Messenger's hand (PBUH) take every request and raise them to Allah (mighty and sublime is He).[320]

Several deceased walīs who were disciples of Shaikh ʿAbd al-Karīm visited our Shaikh in his khalwa. Among them were some who passed away in Shaikh ʿAbd al-Karīm's time, some when our Shaikh was young, and others who had died during our present Master's Shaikhhood. These visitors from the spirit world would ask him what he wanted from them in the way of service to the Ṭarīqa, but he would dismiss them without asking for anything.

---

[320] Shaikh Muḥammad al-Muḥammad al-Kasnazān, *sermon*, 30th/June/2000; 4th/December/2013.

The following is another karāma that happened in our Shaikh's khalwa. He would suffer from the intense mid-summer heat during the day inside the cave, so the Shaikhs made an opening in the cave through which a cool breeze, like that of an electric air conditioner, would come to him.

Many dervishes witnessed karāmas of our Shaikh that revealed the spiritual support of the Shaikhs to him in his seclusion. In our Shaikh's second seclusion, his nephew, Shaikh ʿAlī Ḥusayn, who was not in the khalwa, had a particular dream twice. He saw Imām ʿAlī (may Allah ennoble his face) descend from a rope from the sky and to the place of seclusion.

These paranormal occurrences are just the tip of the iceberg of what happened during our Shaikh's khalwas. Most karāmas are secrets that cannot be divulged.

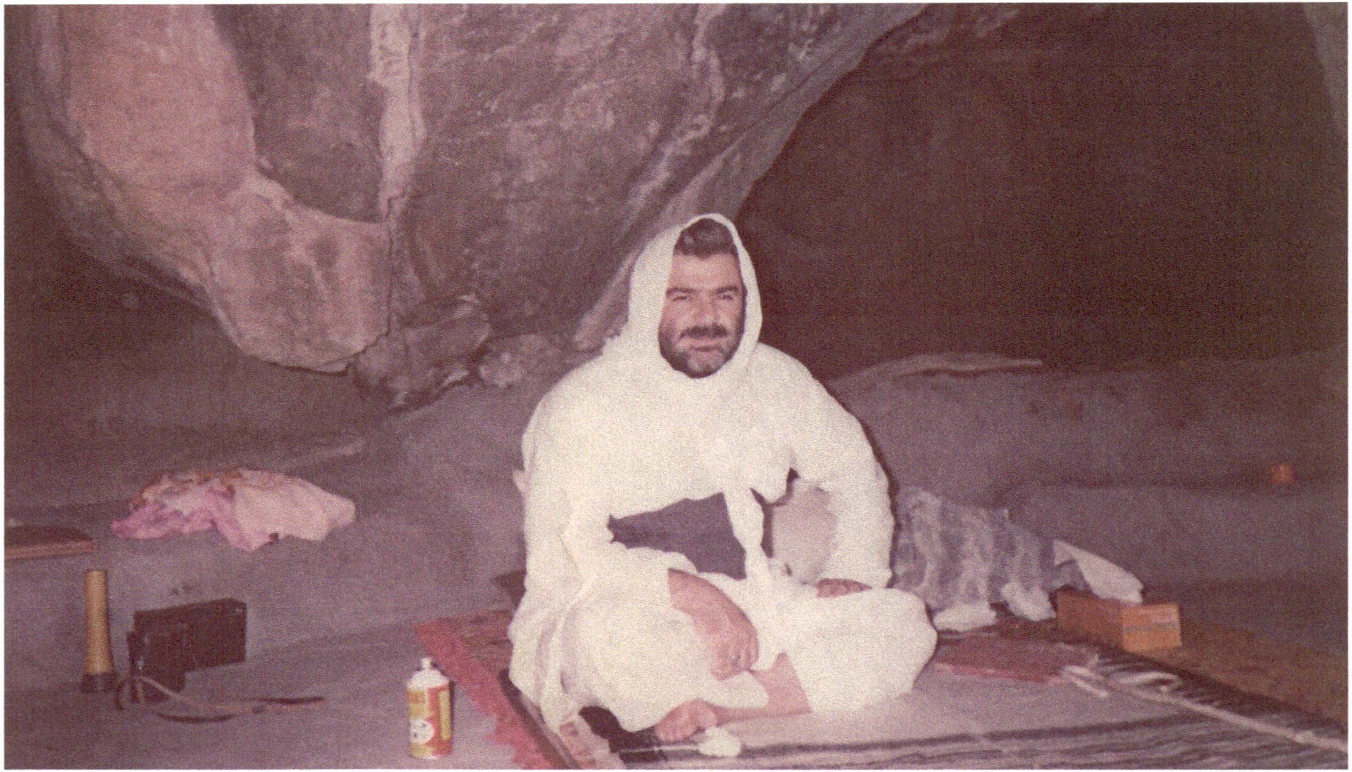

Photo 33: The first seclusion of Shaikh Muḥammad al-Muḥammad in a cave at the foot of Mount Sagarma, which Shāh al-Kasnazān and Shaikh Ḥusayn also used for seclusion (1978).

Photo 34: Shaikh Muḥammad al-Muḥammad immediately after completing his first seclusion in Karbchna, followed by his assistant Ḥājj Muḥammad Maḥmūd (September/1978).

"'Indeed, those who believe and do righteous deeds' (al-Baqara 277). Righteous deeds include dhikrs, wirds, repentance, truthfulness, and consuming what is permissible. It is distancing oneself from lying, that which is prohibited, spying, destruction, killing, stealing, and thievery. Above all, you must be a righteous member of society: 'The best of people are those who benefit people'.[321] If you hurt people, you are not a seeker. If you commit oppression, treachery, or anything that contradicts the Messenger's Sharia, then you are a contravener and would not benefit from your worship. This is what Allah said about prayer through the Messenger: 'Indeed, prayer prohibits immorality and wrongdoing' (al-ʿAnkabūt 45). O my brother! Even if you are not a seeker, but a believer who prays — whether you are a farmer, an officer, an employee, a merchant, or a believing worker — the sign of Īmān is staying away from violating Sharia. Otherwise, how can you be a believer? How can you have Īmān when you cheat? How can you have Īmān when you consume what is prohibited; have Īmān and spy on your country; have Īmān and sabotage your country; have Īmān and, God forbid, wreak havoc on your country, community, and people? Is this Islam? Islam has conditions: 'A Muslim is one whose tongue and hand Muslims are safe from'.[322] [You must meet these conditions] for you to call yourself a Muslim, before you can be a seeker".

Shaikh Muḥammad al-Muḥammad al-Kasnazān
(Sermon, 12th/September/2013)

---

[321] Bayhaqī, *Shuʿab al-Īmān*, VI, no. 7658, p. 117. This ḥadīth also occurs in the form "the best of people are those who are most beneficial to people" (Ṭabarānī, *Al-Muʿjam al-Āwsaṭ*, VI, no. 5787, p. 58).
[322] Bukhārī, *Al-Jāmiʿ al-Ṣaḥīḥ*, I, no. 10, p. 55.

17

Political Persecution Against the Ṭarīqa in Iraq

In Chapter 7, we discussed the political and military activities of Shaikh Muḥammad al-Muḥammad al-Kasnazān with the Kurdish movement in northern Iraq from the end of the 1950s until he retired from these activities in the mid-1960s. After assuming the Ṭarīqa's Shaikhdom in early February/1978, he carried on in the way of his Master, Shaikh 'Abd al-Karīm, of peaceful coexistence with the governing political authorities. He would always order dervishes to refrain from clashing with the government and to not put the Ṭarīqa into conflict with it. He preferred using peaceful dialogue in influencing political decisions in Iraq for the public's and the Ṭarīqa's best interests. As we will see later, when Iraqi authorities persecuted our Shaikh personally, he preferred migrating from the country over abandoning his peaceful approach, preserving peace and security, and protecting the Ṭarīqa. The Shaikh puts the Ṭarīqa's best interests before his own because his position, which the Prophet (PBUH) and Ṭarīqa's Shaikhs placed him in, requires the Ṭarīqa's best interests to be his one concern.

There was an exceptional need for this approach during the reign of the Arab Socialist Ba'ath Party in Iraq, which came to power in mid-1968 after a coup that overthrew 'Abd ar-Raḥmān 'Ārif's administration. Like any one-party political system — which sees the multiplicity of parties and perspectives, and democracy in general, as a threat — the Ba'ath authorities looked with suspicion and fear at any institution, organization, or large movement, whether political, religious, social, or cultural. It would see in them a possible threat to its existence, even if these kinds of institutions and movements had no political dimension whatsoever, as is the case with the Ṭarīqa. Throughout history, our Ṭarīqa's Shaikhs absolutely refused to politicise religion and inject religion into politics. Since the Shaikh of Ṭarīqa's primary duty is to call people to Allah and to facilitate their travelling on the Ṭarīqa's path, maintaining its ability to operate openly and freely, even if not completely, is essential. Our Master would avoid any conflict with the authoritarian government that could affect the Ṭarīqa's ability to carry out its mission.

Naturally, the government's first instinct was to try and control the Ṭarīqa and politicise it for its own interests. The first move came as early as the second year after becoming the Master of the Ṭarīqa, that is, before he moved from Kirkuk to Baghdad and the Ṭarīqa began to spread widely in the capital of Baghdad and other cities of Iraq. Nūrī Fayṣal Shāhir, who served as the Director of the North Office of Ba'ath, asked to meet our Shaikh. He wanted him to help the government build good relations with tribal elders in the northern region, in return for allocating a monthly salary to the Ṭarīqa. Our Shaikh smiled and asked Shāhir how much the sum would be. He replied that it would be a thousand dinars, which was an impressively large sum at the time. Our Shaikh replied: "A thousand dinars is not enough to buy the meat we cook for dervishes in the takya". Shāhir suspiciously suggested that our Shaikh must have a very generous source of money. Our Shaikh confirmed that he had a source from which he got a lot of money. Shāhir got even more interested, so he asked him, with intrigue, about this source. Our Shaikh answered: "The source of my money is Allah (mighty and sublime is He), al-Ghawth al-Āʿẓam, Shaikh ʿAbd al-Qādir al-Gaylānī, and the Master of the Ṭarīqa. My sustenance is from them, and they do not leave me in need, which is why I do not need financial assistance". Shāhir understood that the matter was not about the amount and an increase in the offer; it was clear that our Shaikh would not take payment from the government as a matter of principle. Shāhir showed a mix of amazement and admiration at our Shaikh's refusal of his offer, especially given that he had already made these kinds of deals with influential religious clerics and clan leaders. Our Shaikh added that part of his duties as Master of the Ṭarīqa was to help the government in its duties in improving social conditions for the people and to be just, and he did not want payment for that. He never moved away from this principled position. Even in a one-party state, he often criticised religious clerics who sold their consciences, becoming government mouthpieces, instead of saying what is right and advising rulers to look objectively and humanely at what they do and its positive or negative effect on the people they govern.

In attempting to grant the Ṭarīqa financial assistance, the government wanted to buy it out and make it one of its instruments. This thinking, in and of itself, reflects the ignorance of the politicians involved of the Ṭarīqa and its Shaikh's role. The Shaikh manages the Ṭarīqa according to the instructions of the Messenger (PBUH) and the Shaikhs, not as worldly people, politicians or otherwise, wish. Our Shaikh says that he hears the opinions of experts and knowledgeable people in matters of this world, but he only listens to his Shaikhs in matters of the Ṭarīqa.

Although there is nothing within the spiritual objectives and activities of the Ṭarīqa that represents any sort of threat to the ruling authorities, diverting the attention of single-party politicians away from the Ṭarīqa and removing their doubts about it and its Shaikh is not easy, as a result of the political and security authorities' ignorance of the Ṭarīqa's mission and objectives. This ignorance led the authorities to view the large number of dervishes and their loyalty to the Shaikh as a potential danger to its existence. This sense of danger was increased by its suspicion of the Ṭarīqa's sources of funding. The security forces' fears of the Ṭarīqa was further exacerbated by the way some dervishes spoke at times, saying things that the government saw as threatening or hostile. Even though these statements were individual actions that did not reflect the Shaikh of Ṭarīqa's directives, they often reflected on the Shaikh of Ṭarīqa and its dervishes in general.

17.1 The Spread of the Ṭarīqa and the Obedience of Dervishes to the Shaikh

Despite being the most widespread Ṭarīqa in Iraq and having many takyas and followers in different cities in Iraq, including a particularly large presence in the al-Ānbār governorate in western Iraq, the Ṭarīqa Kasnazāniyya was primarily based in northern Iraq before our Master's Shaikhhood. The Ṭarīqa's Shaikhs lived in Karbchna before Shaikh ʿAbd al-Karīm moved to Kirkuk at the end of 1965. Shaikh ʿAbd al-Karīm's large public funeral in 1978 was an indication of the Ṭarīqa Kasnazāniyya's popularity. Among the first things that Shaikh Muḥammad al-Muḥammad did after becoming Master was to direct the building of a grand takya in Baghdad. Construction began in 1980, and he moved from Kirkuk to live there permanently in 1982. Preaching is the Shaikh of Ṭarīqa's main duty and sole preoccupation, and our Shaikh saw this change in the location of the Shaikh's takya as necessary for the Ṭarīqa to spread more.

Moving the main takya from a secondary city to the capital led to the Ṭarīqa very quickly spreading in various regions inside and outside Iraq. Large numbers of people started to take the Ṭarīqa's pledge every day. The main takya began to be filled with dervishes who attended the dhikr circles on Monday and Thursday nights. During religious celebrations, such as the Prophet's (PBUH) birthday and Eids, even streets surrounding the takya would be filled with visitors. The number of those outside the takya would exceed the number of those inside it.

The main takya in Baghdad did not only attract large numbers of ordinary people, but it also became a place frequented by many famous and learned individuals, including scholars, writers, artists, media professionals, and others. Many VIPs, military officials, ambassadors, and diplomats also visited the takya, with many taking the pledge. Foreign TV stations and media visited the takya to document the Ṭarīqa's activities, including dhikr and darbāsha, and air programs about the Ṭarīqa. The number of takyas in Baghdad and other cities in Iraq began to increase drastically.

This expansion of the Ṭarīqa brought a great and yet anticipated challenge with it, which was a negative reaction from government authorities and security agencies. Dealing with the growing suspicion, harassment, and restrictions of the government, while simultaneously preserving the Ṭarīqa's ability to preach and the freedom of dervishes, required tremendous wisdom.

The concerns of government authorities, particularly security agencies, with the fast spread of the Ṭarīqa was exacerbated by the level of loyalty, love, and obedience that disciples had toward the Shaikh. A seeker loves his Shaikh ardently and obeys him because he is the guide who orders him to obey Allah and remember Him, and to obey His commands and to refrain from what He has prohibited. The Shaikh is a teacher who teaches a seeker how to worship Allah and attain His pleasure in this life and the next, and he is a reminder who reminds him of Allah and the perfect Muslim, our Master Muḥammad (PBUH). The Shaikh does not promise to make a seeker a successful merchant, appoint him to a lofty position in the state, grant him political power, or provide him with any other worldly benefits. Following the Shaikh with sincerity causes the Ṭarīqa's blessing to touch various aspects of a seeker's life, but the goal of the journey of the Ṭarīqa is drawing near to Allah, not acquiring pleasures of this world. The ignorance of the government and the security authorities of this reality, due to their misunderstanding of or refusal to believe it, caused them to see a great danger in the Ṭarīqa due to the absolute loyalty of disciples to the Shaikh.

We see this ignorance in the interrogation by security officials of a dervish about the cause of the love disciples have towards the Shaikh. They told him that working for President Saddam Hussein, meaning by joining the security agencies, grants a person rewarding salaries and new cars and makes his life in general much better-off. The Shaikh, conversely, did not give them anything besides the takya's soup! The disciple answered by saying that the Shaikh owned the dervishes' hearts because he guides them to Allah and His Messenger (PBUH). The security officers did not understand the disciple's love for the person who leads him on the path to Allah because it differs from all the kinds of love that they were familiar with. Explaining this love by way of an example, our Shaikh says that the Ṭarīqa's Shaikhs leave the container of their honey with the present Shaikh of Ṭarīqa, so disciples become attracted to him: "I bestowed love upon you from Me" (Ṭāhā 39).

Later in this chapter, we will see how harassment from authorities forced our Shaikh to migrate more than once.

17.2 The Ṭarīqa's Sources of Income

Some of what Nūrī Fayṣal Shāhir said to our Shaikh revealed that the government's ignorance of the Ṭarīqa's sources of income was another issue that aroused its concern. No doubt its failure to buy out the Ṭarīqa increased its suspicion of the existence of anti-government sources funding the Ṭarīqa. This, in turn, meant that the government believed that these sources could use the Ṭarīqa against the ruling party. The large number of the dervishes combined with their great love and loyalty to the Shaikh could only increase this concern.

There are two sources of the Ṭarīqa's income: the zakāt and charity that the dervishes give for Allah's sake, and whatever the Shaikh's agriculture and trade brings in. The Ṭarīqa, in turn, utilises this income in the best interests of Muslims and people in general, so Allah blesses it: "Who is it that would loan Allah a goodly loan so He may multiply it for him many times over? It is Allah who withholds and grants abundance, and to Him you will be returned" (al-Baqara 245). In the Ṭarīqa, some of this increase comes from the blessing that Allah placed in its Shaikhs: "He has made me blessed wherever I am" (Maryam 31).

Numerous karāmas have shown the role of the Ṭarīqa's blessing in increasing its funds. A dervish called Muḥammad Majīd, who was in charge of shopping for the takya and Shaikh ʿAbd al-Karīm's house in Kirkuk, asked the Shaikh for money to buy necessities for the kitchen of the takya and the house. The Shaikh told him that there was no money. The dervish noticed that the door of the small safe in which the Shaikh kept money was open and the safe was empty. While Muḥammad was talking to Shaikh ʿAbd al-Karīm, nervous about what he would do without money, the Shaikh reached out and closed the safe. Then he told the dervish that there was the buzz of a fly coming from inside the safe, and he asked him to step forward to open it. When he opened it, he found two wads of cash, each containing a thousand dinars. He told him to spend this money until Allah brought new income. This karāma does not mean that the Ṭarīqa's Shaikhs rely on this blessing whenever they need money. Rather, as with all karāmas of the Ṭarīqa's Shaikhs, there are reasons behind it. The Shaikh of the Ṭarīqa refrains from performing karāmas for personal gain.

Anyone who does not have enough knowledge about the Ṭarīqa, its conduct, and its blessing, cannot understand how it can sustain its financial resources for its spending in Allah's way. While every business enterprise focuses all its human resources on its commercial objectives to succeed and make abundant profits, the Ṭarīqa's business is Allah's dhikr and donating in Allah's way: "Indeed, Allah has purchased from the believers their lives and their properties [in exchange] for that they will have Paradise" (al-Tawba 111). Dervishes do not gather in the takya for business, but they reserve this time, and other times, for worship, instead of utilising it in making more money. When an authoritarian government fails to comprehend the Ṭarīqa's source of income, it looks at it with doubt and suspicion. A tyrannical government would not feel safe until it has control over everything, big or small, in the country. It was not uncommon for high-security officials to visit the takya in Baghdad and ask our Shaikh, Shaikh Nahro, others who are close to our Shaikh, about the Ṭarīqa's sources of income and how it spends it. At times, they would enquire directly or indirectly through dervishes who have certain positions in the state. Security officials have always had suspicions that the Ṭarīqa receives outside assistance, despite the absence of any proof of this. These suspicions have caused them to see the Ṭarīqa as a possible danger to the government.

In a particularly instructive karāma, a man who frequently visited Shaikh ʿAbd al-Karīm al-Kasnazān always wondered to himself about the source of the Shaikh's income. One day, he and others accompanied Shaikh ʿAbd al-Karīm on a hunting trip to a mountain. While atop the mountain, in an area where people usually seldom went to, about fifteen male and female dervishes suddenly came to greet the Shaikh and gave him a sum of cash, as a gift for the takya. When the man saw this situation, he was moved, so he addressed the Shaikh: "Glory be to Allah, you are on a hunting trip atop a rock on a mountain summit, yet people come to you to gift you money? You are right, O Shaikh, that the Ṭarīqa's sustenance comes from Allah".

One day in 1973/1974, when the Ṭarīqa was experiencing financial hardship as a result of the siege imposed by Kurdish rebels on the Ṭarīqa's agricultural sources of income, Shaikh ʿAbd al-Karīm was told that there was no longer any money in the takya. He reminded them of Allah's generosity and told them to wait until the afternoon and see what Allah would do for them. In the afternoon, a dervish came with two individuals from Pakistan who wanted to visit the takya and the Shaikh. They donated a bundle of Pakistani money. Shaikh ʿAbd al-Karīm sent someone to convert the money into Iraqi currency, which came to around five hundred dinars, which was a large amount at the time.

Here is one lesson about putting one's trust in Allah that Shaikh Muḥammad al-Muḥammad taught us. He once travelled from Kirkuk to stay for a while in Baghdad, carrying with him eight thousand dinars to cover building costs of the main takya that was being built at the time and other expenses. During the first ten days of his stay, not a single donation from dervishes came to the takya, which was utterly unusual and unexpected. At the end of the tenth day, he sent for the engineer responsible for building the takya, opened a money bag in front of him, and told him: "These five dinars are all that is left. For this visit, I brought eight thousand dinars in preparation for any costs, so no money came to the takya! The reason behind the cutting off of income is my having relied on myself, instead of trusting [that Allah would take care of it]!" He went on to say that whatever was in his possession had run out, gesturing with his hand that he no longer had anything. The next morning, after the cash that our Shaikh had brought with him had finished, money started flowing into the takya from every direction.

The takya's money is particularly inviolable because it comes from zakāt and charity, and the takya is a treasury for Muslims. The Shaikhs always remind dervishes and those responsible for managing this money of the importance of not using it for personal gain and not misusing it. An instructive lesson of Shaikh ʿAbd al-Karīm's is that he sent caliph Mīnā Karam (may Allah have mercy on him), who possessed ḥāls and was close to the Shaikh, with some dervishes to preach in villages in Shahrizor. Many people took up the pledge of Ṭarīqa, especially when they would see darbāsha and other karāmas of the Shaikhs that would happen at the hands of dervishes and preachers. After they returned from the preaching trip, Mīnā visited Shaikh ʿAbd al-Karīm in Kirkuk and informed him of the mission's achievements, the karāmas that took place, the number of people who took up the Ṭarīqa, as well as the number of takyas that they established in the villages they visited. Then he took donations that he had been collecting from dervishes out of his pocket, close to five hundred dinars, and put the money in front of the Shaikh. The Shaikh looked at the cash and asked Mīnā if this was all the money. The caliph was surprised by the Shaikh's question but he answered in the affirmative. The Shaikh then repeated his question, which shook and saddened the caliph, as it seemed as if the Shaikh was questioning whether he had given him all of the money. Mīnā slowly withdrew from the room, hurt and astounded by the Shaikh's question. Before reaching the outside gate, he suddenly remembered a twenty-five fils piece that an old woman had given him, which he had forgotten to add to the cash that he presented to the Shaikh because it was such a small amount. He quickly returned to the Shaikh's place and told him: "This is twenty-five fils that an elderly lady gave me. I forgot to add it to the amount". The Shaikh answered: "Yes, I want this twenty-five fils"! It is clear that Shaikh ʿAbd al-Karīm was not interested in this money for its value, but that he wanted to give a lesson about the sanctity of the takya's money. He might have also seen special significance in this negligible amount of money because it was from an elderly lady who was of limited means.

17.3 Harassment From the Authorities[323]

The last few of the eighteen years during which our Shaikh lived in Baghdad until his migration from it at the end of 2000 were the most difficult for the Ṭarīqa Kasnazāniyya in terms of harassment and pressure from the regime. This is not surprising since this period witnessed an unprecedented spread of the Ṭarīqa in the one-party country. This harassment caused various problems, some of which we touched on above, and here we will mention others.

The Ṭarīqa was always under observation by security agencies, but the main takya, in particular, was under intense and constant surveillance because it was the residence of the Shaikh of Ṭarīqa, making it the takya of the largest gatherings of dervishes. One could always find secret security members pretending to be dervishes, whose mission was to listen to our Shaikh's sermons, note what dervishes talked about, and observe what took place in the takya in general. To avoid problems, our Shaikh would leave these spies to their business and order the caliphs likewise. However, in his sermons, he would often mention that the goal of dervishhood was to draw near to Allah and that the takya was a place for remembering Allah, and not for pursuing worldly purposes, including political ones.

For whatever reason, our Shaikh would sometimes take a completely different stand, exposing spies who had infiltrated the dervishes' community. We have already seen the incident when a staff member of the National Command of the Ba'ath Party visited Karbchna on a spying mission and hid among the dervishes who were visiting our Master. After our Shaikh exposed him, he took up the Ṭarīqa and became a dervish, and even helped facilitate obtaining building permits for the main takya in Baghdad. In another karāma of this kind, our Master was preaching in

---

[323] My main source of the details of the persecution of Shaikh Muḥammad al-Muḥammad and the Ṭarīqa in Baghdad and how he migrated to Sulaymāniyya is Shaikh Ghāndī, the second-eldest son of our Shaikh.

the main takya in Baghdad when he stopped his speech and pointed to someone in the sitting crowd, telling him: "My brother, why are you recording what I am saying? What do you see me talking about? Go to the people who sent you and tell them that all this man speaks about is what Allah (mighty and sublime is He) has said and what His Messenger (PBUH) has said". The person pretended not to realize that our Shaikh was speaking about him, so he pointed to him for emphasis: "Yes, you. Go back to whoever sent you". The man stood and was extremely embarrassed. Some caliphs who manage the affairs of the takya came and asked him about the recording device that our Shaikh had referred to, so he took it out of his pocket. Our Shaikh asked them not to harass him, and he asked him to approach and gave him the Ṭarīqa's pledge. He told him to return to those who sent him and tell them that he did not find the Shaikh say or do anything that would be cause for concern or suspicion.

Spying on the Ṭarīqa did not begin at the time of our present Shaikh, but its spread and the political conditions in Iraq in the 1980s and 90s drastically increased these occurrences, until the Ṭarīqa was under constant surveillance by security agencies. It seems that spying on the Ṭarīqa was not limited to domestic agents. One day, a little before the sunset prayer, three Arabic-speaking men visited Shaikh ʿAbd al-Karīm al-Kasnazān in Kirkuk. One of them appeared to be of African descent, the second was wearing European clothing, while the third wore the garb of a religious cleric and had a small turban on his head. From his features, he appeared to be from China or Japan. Shaikh ʿAbd al-Karīm asked caliph Yāsīn Ṣūfī to take care of the visitors, making sure that they had dinner in the takya and staying in their company for the duration of their stay. The night prayer was followed by a dhikr circle, then Shaikh ʿAbd al-Karīm gave a talk, and then songs of praise were sung. The visitors were sitting on a sofa. The man wearing European clothing was constantly moving his lips, but with an inaudible voice, as if he were reading something. Suddenly, caliph Yāsīn felt prompted to go to the religious cleric and present him a tambourine and ask him to sing a song in praise of the Messenger (PBUH). The visitor replied in classical Arabic: "I do not know", so the caliph repeated his request, but the answer did not change. Shaikh ʿAbd al-Karīm called Yāsīn to his side and whispered in his ear, telling him that this was a fake religious cleric and that he was not even Muslim, but rather a spy. Were he not a guest of his, he would throw him out.

A few minutes later, the African-looking man pointed to Yāsīn, indicating that he wanted to tell him something. When the caliph approached him, the visitor told him that he wanted to speak and that he wanted him to translate what he said into Kurdish because there were Kurds in attendance who did not know Arabic. The caliph replied that, following the Ṭarīqa's etiquettes, he first needed to ask Shaikh ʿAbd al-Karīm for permission. The Shaikh asked the caliph what the visitor wanted, and when told, he answered indicating that he preferred that the man did not speak, but he also did not want to embarrass him, so he permitted him to speak. The man spoke to the dervishes in Arabic, and the caliph translated into Kurdish:

> I am from Senegal, and I work as a translator for the state. I took leave to visit the city of Medina. When I was there, I received an order to visit Shaikh ʿAbd al-Karīm in Kirkuk. Do not say that Shaikh ʿAbd al-Karīm is only in Kirkuk or Iraq, as there are takyas in Senegal and we have given the pledge of Ṭarīqa in Shaikh ʿAbd al-Karīm's name. Do not say that you truly know Shaikh ʿAbd al-Karīm.

Shortly after the man finished speaking, the caliph asked him why he had come with the man disguised in the garb of a cleric. He said that he met him and the other man at the prophetic Rawḍa. When he was instructed to visit Shaikh ʿAbd al-Karīm, he told them, and they asked to accompany him. When Yāsīn and the man were talking, Shaikh ʿAbd al-Karīm asked that a locked guest room be opened, then he called the Senegalese man and entered the guest room with him. He asked the caliph to stand by the room's door so that no one else could enter. After about ten minutes, Shaikh ʿAbd al-Karīm and the Senegalese man came out. As soon as he stepped outside the guest room, the Shaikh uttered the well-known saying: "Whoever knows himself has known his Lord". He turned to the caliph and said, in Kurdish, that he had made the Senegalese man understand that he was not to accompany the false religious cleric. Then he added, referring to the man in European clothing, that he had not stopped reading prayer upon the Prophet (PBUH) throughout his stay in the takya. This karāma of Shaikh ʿAbd al-Karīm shows that spying on the Ṭarīqa did not begin in our Shaikh's time.

Coming back to our present Shaikh's time, the security agencies' suspicion and harassment increased over time as a result of the increasing spread of the Ṭarīqa in Baghdad and other cities in Iraq. But there was another factor that directly contributed to the authorities' escalation of their constraints on our Shaikh and the Ṭarīqa's activities. At times, some caliphs and dervishes engaged in talking against the government and the Ba'ath Party. This sometimes included a disregard for the government and threats, such as referring to how our Shaikh and the Ṭarīqa represented greater and stronger spiritual power than Saddam Hussein and his administration. This violated our Master's orders not to attack the government and to avoid triggering the fear, anger, and concern of security agencies, which would cause them to look at dervishes with more suspicion. The worsening consequences of the economic blockade that followed the occupation of Kuwait and the political isolation of Iraq made the regime increasingly feel under constant threat from outside powers that wanted to remove it. It was only natural that the Ṭarīqa would be a target of the authorities' suspicion and apprehension.

In addition to the harassment from authorities in general, some high-ranking and influential officials have shown exceptional hostility to the Ṭarīqa for one reason or another. These include Hussein Kamel, the husband of one of Saddam Hussein's daughters, Raghad. In the second half of 1995, when Hussein Kamel was Minister of Military Manufacturing with very wide-ranging powers, he sent for Shaikh Nahro. A close associate of Kamel disclosed to Shaikh Nahro that he intended him harm, so he told our Master about the matter. Our Shaikh told him to go to the meeting and not to fear. While sitting in Kamel's office waiting to be called to the meeting, Shaikh Nahro noticed unusual movements, with office staff coming in and going out in haste. A staff member came to him and told him that the meeting had been postponed. When asking about the reason, the staff member told him that Kamel felt a pain in the head, after which he lost consciousness and collapsed on the ground, and he had been taken to the hospital! A short while after this incident, specifically on the night of 8th/August, Kamel, with his wife and brother Saddam and his wife, Ranā, Saddam's second daughter, and their children, fled Iraq to Jordan, where he announced his dissent from Saddam Hussein's administration. It is worth noting that Kamel and his brother returned with their families to Iraq in February 1996, having been reassured that they had been forgiven and would be spared any revenge. However, as soon as they entered Iraq, they were forced to divorce their wives and their relatives were ordered to kill them three days later, at the instruction of the president.

One limitation our Shaikh's freedom of movement by the regime was placed after his return from visiting the holy sites in Najaf and Karbala in 1995, where the Sultan of Bohra Dr Mohammed Burhanuddin welcomed him. Four individuals, among them Nūrī Fayṣal Shāhir, from the National Command and Regional Command of the Ba'ath Party came to meet him. They told him to stop visiting Najaf and Karbala. In line with our Shaikh's approach of avoiding confrontations, this was indeed his last visit to the two holy cities. The authorities' decision reflects their fear of convergence between the Ṭarīqa and the centre of Shia religious leadership in Najaf and Karbala, especially since our Shaikh would get a grand reception on his visits. Even before this prohibition, our Master was cautious when on visits to holy sites that could rouse the concern of security agencies. For example, he would only visit the shrine of his grandfather Imām Mūsa al-Kāẓim once a year, even though he frequented the area intending to visit but without entering the shrine to avoid provoking security agencies. 'Izzat al-Dūrī, vice president and second-in-command after Saddam Hussein, who had taken the Ṭarīqa al-Kasnazāniyya's pledge from Shaikh 'Abd Al-Karīm, also openly told our Shaikh that he did not want the Ṭarīqa to preach to Shia Muslims. However, he ignored al-Dūrī, and caliphs and dervishes continued to speak about the Ṭarīqa with everyone who wanted to learn about the spiritual side of Islam and offer them its pledge.

Another unjust decision regarding the Ṭarīqa by the authorities that demonstrated the nature of their concern was prohibiting our Shaikh from using the title "Ra`īs al-Ṭarīqa", which means "head of the Ṭarīqa", which is the title that had since he became Master of the Ṭarīqa. The reason is that "Ra'īs" also means "president", which was Saddam Hussein's title. Their thinking is that there must not be two "heads" in Iraq!

If security authorities saw whatever threat in the title "Ra`īs al-Ṭarīqa", then their decision to ban the Ṭarīqa from using drums and tambourines in dhikr could only have come about to harass it, limit its activities, and exercise control over what it does, especially given that the decision singled out takyas in the capital of Baghdad. This is also the only explanation for the security authorities' decision to prohibit the main takya from sending food to the mental health hospital, whose patients were malnourished and neglected.

Suspicion of the Ṭarīqa reached such a level that monitoring its Shaikh and dervishes became the responsibility of the "Hostile Activity Division" in the notorious Intelligence Service, "Mukhābarāt". This unit was responsible for combatting espionage, such as Israeli-backed activities and those of the Iranian-backed Islamic Dawa Party. Not content with constantly sending spies in the form of dervishes to the takya, in mid-2000, security agencies escalated matters by imposing a permanent public security presence inside the takya in Baghdad to monitor our Shaikh, his family, and dervishes, as was the case with the Scientific Seminary in Najaf, where the most senior Shia clerics lived and taught, which was under constant security surveillance.

When state and security authorities would impose a new restriction on the freedom of the Ṭarīqa, our Shaikh would first try to convince them to reverse their decision, by talking to them directly or by seeking the help of influential individuals who were on good terms with the Ṭarīqa. If such attempts failed, he was always prepared to make compromises by tolerating the restrictions that the authorities imposed, instead of entering into a confrontation with them that would lead to the Ṭarīqa being completely banned. With his cautious approach and focus on avoiding problems with the authorities, our Shaikh's principle was to "sacrifice a part for the sake of the whole". However, harassment from security authorities against the Ṭarīqa persistently increased with the increase of its popularity and its number of dervishes until it reached the level of persecution. Indeed, the harassment became open, rather than subtle. Unfortunately, the government's oppression of the Ṭarīqa was getting worse, directly affecting our Shaikh's family.

17.4 Personal Persecution

In June 1998, the Interior Minister, Muḥammad Zumām ʿAbd ar-Razzāq, visited our Shaikh and delivered a message to him he described as needing to be kept secret but he did not declare its origin. The message included the following commands: the Ṭarīqa was not to celebrate the birth of the Prophet (PBUH), which occurred early the following month; army officers were prohibited from going to the takya; the Ṭarīqa was not to send out dervishes preach to people; there would not be but ten takyas in Baghdad, and the tens other takyas would be closed; and the Ṭarīqa's activities in Baghdad would be confined to the main takya. Our Shaikh replied that he would first inquire whether these decisions of the Interior Ministry were supported by higher authorities in the country.

He sent his eldest son, Nahro, to meet ʿIzzat al-Dūrī to ask whether the Interior Ministry's orders were issued from the county's highest command, meaning Saddam Hussein and the Revolutionary Command Council. He instructed Shaikh Nahro that if he found the matter to be so, he was to tell al-Dūrī that these demands meant that the Ṭarīqa could not coexist with the regime and to then request that the authorities grant our Shaikh a grace period of six months to arrange migration from Iraq to another country, even if the situation necessitated migrating to a non-Arabic Islamic state. Our Shaikh did not consider Kurdistan in northern Iraq an option, even though it was the easiest and most suitable, because it was outside the control of the government of Baghdad and under Kurdish rule. Going there would cause Baghdad to see this as his standing with the Kurds, which could cause the central government to crack down on dervishes in Baghdad and other cities.

Al-Dūrī said that he did not know of the Interior Minister's message but that it was unlikely to reflect Saddam Hussein's stance. He promised to inquire about the truth of the matter. After about ten days, al-Dūrī got in touch, confirming that the Interior Minister's notifications were all personal and they were not issued by Saddam Hussein. He stressed that our Shaikh could stay in Baghdad, that the Ṭarīqa would not be harassed, and that there was no justification whatsoever for not celebrating the honourable Prophetic birth. It is possible that behind al-Dūrī's response was the reasoning by the state's leadership that our Shaikh's migration from Iraq could make him more influential and dangerous to the country because he would be far from its control. The same misguided fears and doubts that reflected the authorities' misunderstanding of the Ṭarīqa were behind their harassment of it. However, even if al-Dūrī's response reflected the true stance of the highest authority, it was clear that there were people in very high positions of power, such as the Interior Minister, who harboured much suspicion and enmity towards the Ṭarīqa, treated it unjustly, and looked for opportunities to harm it.

Our Shaikh was concerned that security authorities would see the

Ṭarīqa's annual celebration of the noble Prophetic birth as a challenge to it. He felt reassured after he saw the Messenger (PBUH) in a dream, as we explained in detail in Section 3.9. Our Shaikh celebrated the noble birth at the end of the first week of July 1998 in his orchard in Dōra, Baghdad, as the main takya could not accommodate all attendees. This was the grandest celebration of the birth of the Prophet (PBUH) that the Ṭarīqa hosted, indeed, the largest in Iraq, where thousands attended.

Several ministers and eminent individuals attended, in response to our Shaikh's invitation. He wanted to reassure authorities that this large gathering had come together solely to celebrate the Messenger (PBUH) and that there was nothing in it that could rouse the concern of security agencies. Some ambassadors and diplomats also attended. When our Shaikh went out of the resting house and up to the podium with the Minister of Endowments, ʿAbd al-Munʿim Aḥmad Ṣāliḥ, the minister witnessed the enormous gathering of the Ṭarīqa's disciples. Surprised, he turned towards our Shaikh and said that his ministry's celebration of the noble birth was not attended by more than 150 people. He asked how our Shaikh could gather all these people. Our Shaikh handled the situation with wisdom and diplomacy, replying with a smile: "Please take your seat, your excellency. It is the spiritual influence of the Messenger (PBUH), of Shaikh ʿAbd al-Qādir al-Gaylānī, that brought them here".

The Minister of Endowments asked with even more amazement if all these thousands of attendees would be fed, and our Shaikh answered affirmatively. After dinner was served, a dervish in charge of serving food to attendees called out in a loud voice near the place where our Shaikh was sitting whether any dervishes had not eaten yet, perhaps because they had arrived late. Our Master gestured to the minister to point out how that massive crowd was fed.

Our Shaikh attempted to anticipate adversaries of the Ṭarīqa among the regime who would want to stir problems and incite the government because of its organization of the Prophetic birth celebrations. The following morning, he sent a video recording of the celebration to President Saddam via caliph Aḥmad Jāsim, who had personal connections with the president's personal secretary, ʿAbd Ḥmūd al-Tikrītī. When the latter came to know of what the caliph came with, he rudely and admonishingly replied that the Ṭarīqa was prohibited from organizing the celebration and that this was a challenge to the state. This animosity towards the Ṭarīqa was a new attitude that the caliph had previously not heard from Ḥmūd. He had clearly adopted the stance of the Interior Minister and other authorities who harboured enmity against the Ṭarīqa.

Saddam watched the video in the presence of ʿAbd Ḥmūd, and one of the ways of pitting the president against the Ṭarīqa was telling him that one of the people who served the dervishes in the birth celebration was a major-general in the army and that there were high-ranking officers among the dervishes who were kissing the Shaikh's hand. The reality is that the presence and behaviour of the officers and leaders at the celebration had nothing to do with their official positions. They were there as Muslims celebrating the birth of their Prophet (PBUH) with their Shaikh and spiritual guide. Also, the officers were dressed in civilian clothing, not in their military suits. Nonetheless, Saddam was successfully agitated, so he commented, "This is a state within a state", and that this situation could not be allowed to continue.

The lie that played the biggest role in personally prodding Saddam to be hostile to the Ṭarīqa was the falsification, done by some with malicious intent, of the meaning of some of what was contained in Shaikh Nahro's speech at the celebration. Specifically, they picked up on his saying that the Ṭarīqa's objective was to deliver the message of the Prophet (PBUH) to humanity everywhere. Although this sort of talk was nothing new, since our Shaikh always reiterates that the primary duty of the Ṭarīqa's Shaikh and its dervishes is to guide people to true Islam, some provocateurs claimed that Shaikh Nahro's speech was referring to political ambitions tantamount to threatening the regime, which was something that Saddam would not tolerate. Thus, the state's persecution of the Ṭarīqa became directed by its highest authority, its dictator with absolute power. It also turned into persecution of our Shaikh's family.

A month after the birth celebration, specifically at on 6th/August/1998, security authorities arrested Shaikh Nahro. He was accused, with others, of forging President Saddam Hussein's signature to authorise the granting of rights to export and sell a quantity of Iraqi gas outside the country. He was transferred to a prison run by the notorious Special Security Organisation and located in the headquarters of the equally infamous Intelligence Service. Shaikh Nahro came to know that the authorities intended to arrest his brother Malās. The next day, with the help of a guard, he called home to deliver an encrypted message asking him to join his brothers ʿAbd al-Karīm and Brīsh in Sulaymāniyya before the authorities arrested him.

Two days later, before Shaikh Malās left Baghdad, the security authorities arrested him. They did not detain him with his brother but transferred him to solitary confinement in the General Security Directorate for forty days. He lost a lot of weight during solitary confinement, to the point that when Shaikh Nahro saw him after they were transferred to the same prison, he was worried that he would not survive because of the degree of emaciation he had experienced. He took him under his care until he regained his natural weight and health.

About a month later, on 3rd/September, the authorities arrested another of our Shaikh's sons, Ghāndī, who at the time held the position of "Secretary-General of Endowments and Religious Matters". Several dervishes were also arrested under the same charge. The three brothers were placed in a prison belonging to the Special Security Organisation in the Republican Palace. This was exclusively for political prisoners and those considered dangerous to the state. Shaikh Nahro and Shaikh Malās were in one prison cell and their brother was in another. Meanwhile, the United States of America and Britain were escalating their accusations towards Iraq for a lack of cooperation with the weapons of mass destruction inspection teams. When it became likely that they would attack Iraq, on 11th/November, the Special Security Organisation transported its prisoners in the Republican Palace to another secret prison inside Abu Ghraib prison, west of Baghdad. Unlike Abu Ghraib prison, which belonged to the Ministry of Justice, this secret prison was run directly by the Special Security Organisation, and its inmates were not disclosed to the Abu Ghraib prison management. On 16th-19th/December/1998, the United States and Britain launched operation "Desert Fox", fiercely bombarding Iraq. These conditions increased the inclination of Iraqi authorities to cast various accusations of threatening the state's security on individuals and groups in the country.

The three brothers stayed in prison for more than eight months without trial. In May/1999, they were finally put on trial in a court that did not belong to Ministry of Justice but was exclusive to the Interior Ministry that dealt with cases affecting state security, including cases related to political prisoners. Its judgement was absolute and could not be appealed. After a mock trial in one hearing, before which the verdicts had already been decided, the judge released Shaikh Ghāndī but sentenced his two brothers to ten years in prison. This sentence included another defendant, while other defendants were sentenced to six years in prison.

A significant irony is that the lawyer Khalīl ad-Dalīmī, who our Shaikh hired to defend his sons, and whose defence did not succeed in the sham trial, was hired later by Saddam to defend him after the fall of his regime, and he failed to defend him as well! It was as if history was saying that the harm that Saddam intended for our Shaikh and his children turned on him.

Our Shaikh was deeply grieved by his sons' imprisonment, which greatly affected his health, including his being afflicted with diabetes. His grief peaked after the court sentence. Two days later, he began to bleed from his eye, marking the beginning of the deterioration of his eyesight and the multiple operations that followed. Despite our Shaikh's trust that Allah would safely return his sons to him, especially since the elder of the two was destined to be his spiritual caliph and Shaikh of the Ṭarīqa after him, this did not prevent him from grieving. This is similar to how the knowledge of Prophet Jacob that Allah would one day join him with his son Joseph did not prevent him from grieving over him and temporarily losing his eyesight because of that grief: "[Jacob] said, 'Rather, your souls have enticed you to something, so total patience [is my choice]. May Allah bring them to me altogether. Indeed it is He who is the Knowing, the Wise'. He turned away from them and said, 'Oh, my sorrow over Joseph', and his eyes became white from grief, for he was [of that] a suppressor" (Yūsuf 83-84). During the detention and imprisonment of his children, our Shaikh would send them instructions regarding special dhikrs that they would read, which included "Ṣalawāt Nāriyya".

Some people tried to persuade our Master to ask to meet Saddam to request that he pardons his sons, but he refused, despite the devastating pain he was in. He did not even try to contact ʿIzzat al-Dūrī to ask him to intercede for the release of his sons. He would say: "The One who gave them to me will be able to bring them back to me". A while after the children were in prison, al-Dūrī sent an associate of his to inform our Shaikh that he did not interfere because the matter was out of his hands. This could only mean that what had happened was personally ordered and overseen by Saddam Hussein.

Our Shaikh's sister, sayyida ʿĀʾisha, decided to meet Saddam to ask him to pardon the two prisoners. Despite his personal refusal to meet Saddam for that purpose, our Shaikh did not stand in the way of his sister's attempt. She submitted her request for a meeting by the name of 'Ā'isha 'Abd al-Karīm 'Abd al-Qādir, without using the title "al-Kasnazān", so those in charge in the president's office did not know who she was. The request was approved and a date for the meeting was set for 12th/January/2000. When she met Saddam and told him that she was Shaikh Muḥammad al-Muḥammad al-Kasnazān's sister, he welcomed her and unhesitatingly approved her request to pardon Shaikh Nahro and Shaikh Malās. He delivered a verbal message to our Shaikh that to limit Shaikh Nahro's actions, which meant that he saw some sort of threat in Shaikh Nahro. The proceedings were quickly completed and they were released on 15th/January/2000. It is well known that Saddam would sometimes grant requests to pardon prisoners when their family members directly appealed to him. This sort of exercising authority seemed to fulfil a psychological need he had. He would use this practice to gain popularity. No question, he knew that many of those in his prisons for political reasons were there unjustly.

Shaikh Nahro and Shaikh Malās' stay in prison lasted about a year and four months, while Shaikh Ghāndī spent more than eight months incarcerated. Meanwhile, prison officials and guards would ask our Shaikh for large amounts of money to provide care for them in those harsh circumstances.

Shaikh Nahro's release was coupled with conditions, including open surveillance of the movements of our Shaikh and his children. For example, our Shaikh and Shaikh Nahro were not allowed to leave Baghdad without first informing the authorities. Security agencies stepped up their monitoring of the takya and increased the number of spies disguised as dervishes in the takya. Government authorities also transferred every dervish working in sensitive government positions, including those that were in the president's special guards, to other jobs with no responsibility that would rouse the authorities' concern.

A short while later, our Shaikh submitted a request to travel with his eldest son to Britain to treat his eyes. They reached London in March 2000 and stayed until September. In addition to receiving medical treatment, during these six months our Shaikh gave many talks at his residence to dervishes and lovers of Sufism who visited him. He gave the pledge of the Ṭarīqa to a large number of people (photo 26). He also designated several caliphs to continue preaching and giving the pledge in Britain. As already mentioned, almost every morning, he would spend a few hours in the British Library to review its collection of Sufi manuscripts (photo 27).

There was an incident that shows the extent of the surveillance and the controlling of movement the regime placed the Ṭarīqa under. Months before our Shaikh's decision to visit Britain, I had planned to organise a celebration for Shaikh ʿAbd al-Qādir al-Gaylānī in London on 7th/May/2000. It was serendipitous that this celebration coincided with his visit to London, so I asked Shaikh Nahro to participate by giving a speech. Before the celebration, however, a security officer visited Shaikh Ghāndī in Baghdad and told him that Shaikh Nahro intended to deliver a speech in a celebration of Shaikh ʿAbd al-Qādir al-Gaylānī and warned him that it would make matters worse for our Shaikh and his family. Our Shaikh decided that Shaikh Nahro would not attend the celebration to avoid escalating the situation and asked me to deliver Shaikh Nahro's speech in his place. Delivering a speech in that religious celebration would not have affected Iraq's security in any way whatsoever, but this attitude of the security authorities reflects their continued and growing suspicion about everything our Shaikh and Shaikh Nahro did and their fear that they were working against the regime in one way or another.

It should be noted that the poetic verses that are at the front of this book were written for that celebration. A few days earlier, our Shaikh contacted the poet, caliph ʿAlī Fāyiz, in Baghdad and asked him to compose a poem in praise of Shaikh ʿAbd al-Qādir al-Gaylānī to be read at the celebration. The caliph wrote it in about four hours and sent it to our Shaikh in London by fax on 3rd/May. This is why the poet started the poem with this verse:

> Write for the people of piety in the farthest cities,
> about the Quṭb of Baghdad ʿAbd al-Qādir al-Ḥasanī.

17.5 Migration from Baghdad

Our Shaikh's extreme caution and prudence did not prevent the regime from going too far in exposing him, his family, and the Ṭarīqa to further persecution and injustice. The official attitude towards our Shaikh and the Ṭarīqa was going from bad to worse. Even the relatively small celebration of the birth of the Prophet (PBUH) organised by the Ṭarīqa after our Shaikh's return from the trip for medical treatment in London was a source of concern for the security authorities. The enemies of our Shaikh and the Ṭarīqa also fabricated news of anti-government political activities by our Shaikh and Shaikh Nahro in London, claiming that this was the real reason they stayed in Britain's capital for six months.

Our Shaikh returned to Iraq from London via Turkey, the same way he had left it. Due to the air embargo on Iraq at the time, he entered Iraq by land from Turkey through the Ibrāhīm Khalīl border crossing. He was welcomed in Iraq by many disciples, in addition to his family. Shaikh Ghāndī accompanied our Shaikh and Shaikh Nahro in the car on the way to Baghdad. He mentioned that our Shaikh's house in the main takya in Baghdad had been renovated. Our Shaikh surprised him by retorting: "Who asked you to renovate it? How do you know that I will live in it?" This was the first sign from our Shaikh his stay in Baghdad was nearing its end.

About two months after his return from London, ʿIzzat al-Dūrī asked our Shaikh to visit him in his on his farm in the city of Dōr. He took his sons Nahro and Ghāndī and met al-Dūrī on 27th/November/2000, which coincided with the first days of the blessed month of Ramadan. Shaikh Nahro diplomatically thanked al-Dūrī for helping release him and his brother. He responded by saying that there was nothing to thank him for because he had no hand in the matter. But what al-Dūrī added, addressing our Shaikh, was truly astonishing: "Shaikh Nahro and his brother's coming out safe and sound from prison is one of the greatest karāmas of Shāh al-Kasnazān". He explained that the Revolutionary Command Council had decided to execute them and that he himself was surprised when he learned that Saddam had pardoned and released them. He starkly added that the Ṭarīqa should not expect to have good fortune with the regime in the future. Clearly, the regime's lack of trust in our Shaikh and Shaikh Nahro was now irreversible.

Al-Dūrī went on to reveal why he had asked our Shaikh to visit him. He first dismissed his personal guards and took our Shaikh and Shaikh Nahro on a walking tour in the farm, so that no one else could hear what he would reveal. He informed our Shaikh that it was in Shaikh Nahro's best interests to go somewhere out of reach of the government, as the authorities were planning a new plot against him. The secrecy with which al-Dūrī spoke and his urging of Shaikh Nahro to quickly flee showed the seriousness of what the government was preparing for Shaikh Nahro. Perhaps the authorities had decided to permanently eliminate him this time. Our Master decided that Shaikh Nahro would leave Baghdad for Sulaymāniyya in secret that night without delay.

About three weeks later, on Monday 18th/December/2000, while attending the dhikr circle at night, our Shaikh felt that he was about to fall to the ground had he not been leaning on his staff. After the dhikr, he told some of those who were close to him that the regime was something bad for him and his family, so he decided to leave Baghdad for Sulaymāniyya. Even though Kurdistan had been outside the jurisdiction of Baghdad's government since 1991, when the Iraqi army withdrew from it after the first Gulf War, the central government had issued directives about a week before stating that the authorities would not prevent anyone wanting to leave other Iraqi cities for Kurdistan from doing so. Because of his position, our Shaikh wanted to avoid provoking the authorities by suddenly leaving Baghdad without their knowledge, which may make them think he had left it to ally with opposing Kurdish forces in Kurdistan. This would be very detrimental to the Ṭarīqa and its dervishes. Accordingly, he asked his son Ghāndī to submit an official request on his behalf to approve his trip to Kurdistan. The request included approval to travel by private car because the departure of private cars from areas that the government had control over and to enter into Kurdistan also needed special approval.

The next morning, Shaikh Ghāndī submitted the request to the intelligence officer in charge of monitoring the takya. Due to our Shaikh's status and the fact that he was under surveillance, approval was the responsibility of Director of the Intelligence Service. The request stated that our Shaikh had not visited Sulaymāniyya for about ten years and that he wanted to spend the final days of the month of Ramadan and Eid there, and potentially the month after it. The request did not disclose his intention to migrate from Baghdad.

The officer told Shaikh Ghāndī that the Director of the Intelligence Service would review the request the same day, but this did not happen because of latter was busy and did not check his mail. While this was transpiring, our Shaikh would regularly ask Shaikh Ghāndī about any news of the approval. During this time, Shaikh Ghāndī did not go to work in order to stay by the phone at home, as there were no mobile phones in Iraq at the time, to receive the response to the request as soon as it came. Despite not receiving the approval, our Shaikh asked his wife to prepare the luggage for travel on Thursday. On Thursday morning, he once again asked whether there was any news about the request, but there was none. The problem was that the delay of the approval until after Thursday afternoon would likely mean that it would not be issued until after the weekend, on or after Saturday, but our Sheikh had already decided to travel. At about four o'clock in the afternoon, however, the intelligence officer contacted Shaikh Ghāndī to tell him that the Director of had finally checked his mail and approved the travel request.

The night of Thursday 21st/December/2000 coincided with "*Laylat al-Qadr*" (the Night of Power), 27th/Ramadan. Religious scholars and judges were going to visit our Shaikh in the main takya to celebrate the blessed night, so he asked Shaikh Ghāndī to receive the guests in his place and to apologize to them for having to travel.

Our Shaikh left Baghdad on a cold and rainy night. He arrived at his house in Kirkuk at about ten o'clock at night, having attended the funeral gathering of an acquaintance. He told Shaikh Ghāndī that he would leave Kirkuk for Sulaymāniyya in the morning. When Shaikh Ghāndī informed the intelligence officer, he replied that this was not possible because a telegram of approval had not yet been sent to the security authorities in Kirkuk. As the following day was Friday, which is the weekend, our Shaikh had to postpone his travel to Saturday or Sunday. When Shaikh Ghāndī informed our Master, he was amazed by his response, that if he did not leave the next day he would not be able to leave after that! Once again, Shaikh Ghāndī contacted the officer, who managed to send the necessary telegram to the sentry officer in Kirkuk. Our Shaikh's driver went to receive the authorization to pass through government checkpoints. On Friday morning, 22nd/December/2000, our Shaikh headed for the city of Sulaymaniya. Surprisingly, no checkpoint asked the driver for authorization. Since entering Sulaymāniyya, our Shaikh has not returned to Baghdad or any other city in Iraq outside of Kurdistan. It did not become clear to the government of Baghdad that he had permanently migrated from Baghdad until more than a year later, when Shaikh Ghāndī also left to join his father and his brothers.

Our Shaikh always dealt cautiously, patiently, and diplomatically with the authorities and did everything in his power to prevent the Ṭarīqa from clashing with them. He would always follow the principle of "sacrificing a part for the sake of the whole" in addressing restrictions and harassment by authorities, as any escalation and confrontation would have serious consequences for the Ṭarīqa in general. Even this policy, however, has its limits, as some encroachments and restrictions are impossible to accept and to live with. In the end, he was forced to leave Baghdad.

In Sulaymāniyya, Shaikh Nahro supported the efforts to end Saddam Hussein's dictatorial regime and replace it with a democratic system. The new system would treat all segments of Iraqi society with equality and grant them the human rights that the dictatorship had denied them. After the fall of the one-party regime in 2003, the door was opened for political pluralism. Many parties with various agendas and goals appeared. Yet this golden opportunity to build the positive political environment that Iraq had been crying out for for decades gradually and rapidly took a dangerous turn because most of these parties adopted sectarian or nationalist goals and programs that only created discord and led to the division of Iraq. Rather than the newly gained freedom uniting Iraqis in building their country on humanitarian principles, political parties, each of which adopted the interests of a certain group at the cost of others, divided them. Iraq was transformed from a single-party country into a country plagued by many parties, each of which worked like a single-party autocracy.

Amid this political chaos, the Ṭarīqa's dervishes wondered about the Ṭarīqa's position, especially since there were dervishes who wanted to enter the political arena. Shaikh Nahro decided to found a party that focuses on the best interests of Iraq and Iraqis in general, contrary to the majority of parties that promoted policies that divided the country's population and, directly or indirectly, called for its division. Shaikh Nahro announced the formation of the "Coalition for Iraqi National Unity", a party that believes in the unity of the land and peoples of Iraq, just as Shaikh ʿAbd al-Karīm and our present Shaikh were always against the attempts to divide Iraq. Among our Shaikh's words that reflect his desire for a united Iraq is that he would not accept a separation between Shaikh ʿAbd al-Qādir al-Gaylānī, Shaikh ʿAbd al-Karīm Shāh al-

Kasnazān, and Shaikh Ḥasan al-Baṣrī. These three of the Ṭarīqa's Masters have their shrines in Baghdad, Karbchna, and Baṣra, respectively, thus representing Iraq's centre, north, and south. Although the founder of the party is the deputy of the Ṭarīqa al-Kasnazāniyya Shaikh, the party has no relation to the Ṭarīqa and is not exclusive to the Ṭarīqa's dervishes. The Ṭarīqa is a spiritual path in which there is no place for politics. As we have mentioned before, the Ṭarīqa al-Kasnazāniyya Shaikhs were always against politicising religion and religionising politics.

17.6 Migration from Sulaymāniyya

Three days after arriving in Sulaymāniyya, our Shaikh had a cholecystectomy at Shoresh Hospital. Many Iranian dervishes came to visit him when they heard that he was in Sulaymāniyya. One manifestation of the regime's surveillance of our Shaikh is that it sent three of its agents to visit him in the hospital to make sure he had indeed undergone an operation.

The concern about the Ṭarīqa and the harassment it suffered in Baghdad is bound to occur wherever there is no true democracy and full respect for human rights. Political authorities and security agencies in such states would always see any organization, let alone the Ṭarīqa with its enormous number of followers and their absolute devotion in loving the Shaikh, as a source of concern for its monopoly on power. After our Shaikh moved to Sulaymāniyya, some Iranian officials came to inquire about his reasons for leaving Baghdad and settling in Sulaymāniyya. They were trying to deduce whether this was a political move that could affect the Tarīqa's dervishes in Iran most of whom are Kurds. Our Shaikh asked Shaikhs Sāmān and ʿAlī Ḥusayn to meet the officials and reassure them that his move to Sulaymāniyya was due to the authorities in Baghdad persecuting him and that this would not affect Iran at all. The representatives told the delegation that the Shaikh's instructions to Iran's dervishes had not changed, which is that they were to focus their activities on the Ṭarīqa and to avoid engaging in things that worried Iranian authorities. They also conveyed the Shaikh's request that the Iranian authorities to not harass dervishes and to permit them to practice the Ṭarīqa's activities.

The Tarīqa then began to suffer harassment from the authorities in

Sulaymāniyya, whose local government was independent of the central government in Baghdad. Our Shaikh decided to hold a celebration of the birth of Messenger (PBUH) in the takya in Sulaymāniyya and wanted Iranian disciples who wanted to come to do so, but this led to all Kurdistan security departments being put on alert. Indeed, even Iranian security agencies in Iranian Kurdistan were also put on alert. This is reminiscent of how the enormous turnout at the celebration of the birth of the Prophet (PBUH) in 1998 in Baghdad exacerbated the security authorities' fear, contributing to his migration eighteen months later.

There was also an attempt on our Shaikh's life. The takya was teeming with hundreds of dervishes, a large number of whom were lined up to visit and greet the Shaikh, among them dervishes who had come from Iran. An intruder who had come with the visitors from Iran presented him with a staff. Usually, when our Master receives a gift from a visitor, he hands it over to a personal assistant standing near him. This time, however, he kept the staff in his hand, making sure it did not touch the ground. After dervishes finished visiting him, he handed it to one of his assistants and asked him to send it to be examined. He made it clear that it must be handled with extreme caution and not let it touch the ground. The examination revealed that the staff contained explosive substances that would have exploded if it touched the ground. This was not the first time that our Shaikh had exposed and escaped an assassination attempt. In the first half of the 1990s, when he was in Baghdad, someone presented to his family a poisoned cake as a gift. By the grace of Allah, our Shaikh became alert of the situation and ordered the family not to touch the cake. A later examination confirmed that the cake contained lethal poison.

After the explosive staff incident, our Shaikh began to take precautions in his movements. He no longer followed a fixed timetable for when he would leave his home for the takya and attend dhikr circles with disciples. Rather, the time he would attend was unknown and was decided at the moment.

The harassment of the authorities in Kurdistan continued to worsen until they sent an envoy to a close associate of our Shaikh to inform him of their desire for him to leave Kurdistan. On 2nd/August/2007, he left Kurdistan and moved to Amman, Jordan, returning a few times to visit Sulaymāniyya.

Photo 35: Shaikh Muḥammad al-Muḥammad before entering the hall of the shrine of Shaikh ʿAbd al-Qādir al-Gaylānī in Baghdad (1990s).

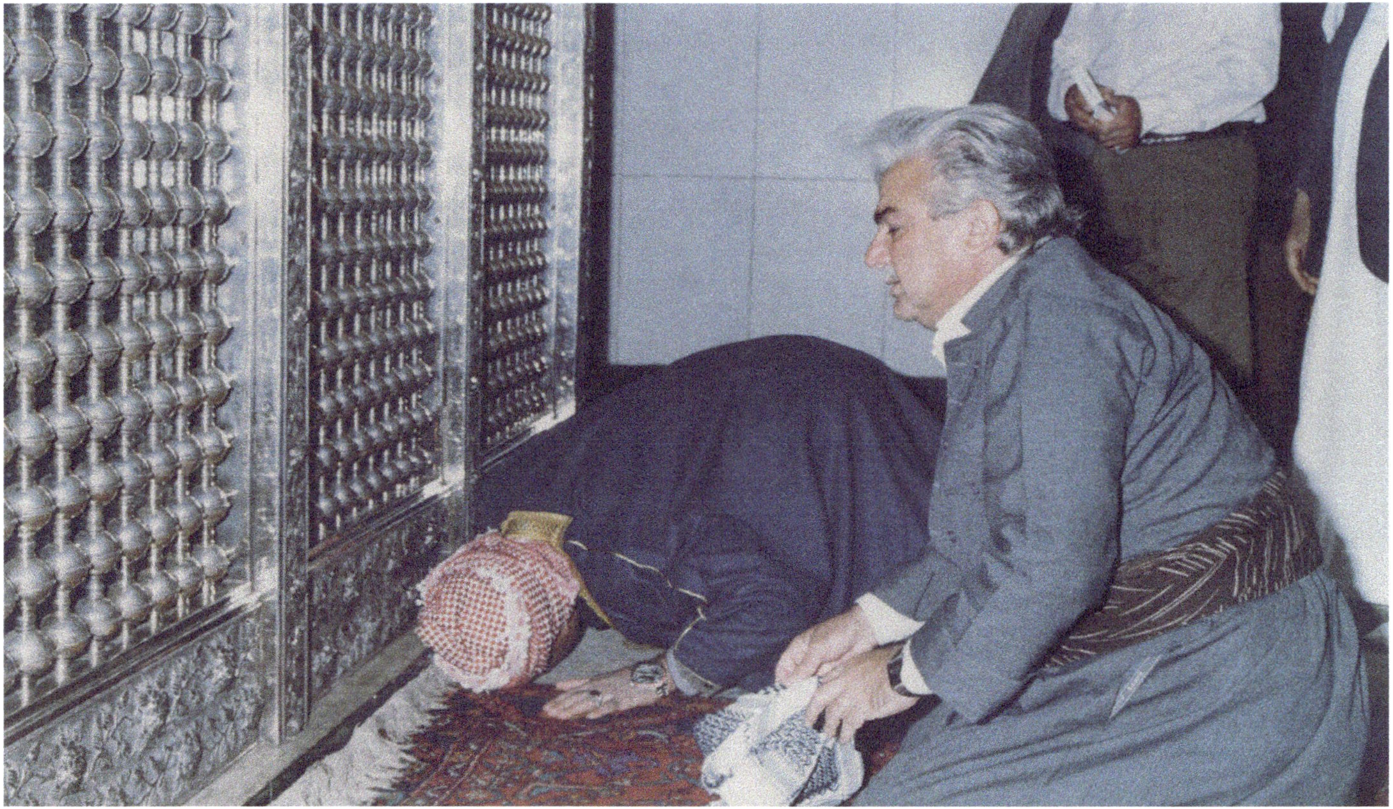

Photo 36: Shaikh Muḥammad al-Muḥammad in front of the shrine of Shaikh ʿAbd al-Qādir al-Gaylānī in Baghdad (1990s).

"O Kasnazāni dervishes! What is incumbent upon you is incumbent upon me; obedience is incumbent upon us: 'Obey Allah and obey the Messenger and those in authority among you' (al-Nisā` 59). The seeker must obey the Shaikh because the Shaikh obeys Allah (exalted and high is He), obeys the honourable Messenger, and obeys the Shaikhs. From a spiritual standpoint, I and you are connected from Shaikh to Shaikh, to the honourable Messenger, to Allah (exalted and high is He). Dervishhood is not merely taking the pledge, then you go away and that's all. No! Dervishhood is spiritually connecting to the Ṭarīqa. You are spiritually connected to your Shaikh's soul, from Shaikh to Shaikh, to the honourable Messenger, to Allah (exalted and high is He)".

Shaikh Muḥammad al-Muḥammad al-Kasnazān
(Sermon, 27th/September/2012)

18

Achievements

Our Shaikh has many many social, cultural, and religious achievements and contributions. We have discussed some of them, such as his exceptional effort in making people aware of Islam's spiritual side and its humanitarian values, authoring the first encyclopedia of Sufism, establishing hundreds of takyas, and helping the needy and weak in society. Here, we will focus on some achievements that we did not mention earlier.

18.1 Reconstruction of Holy Sites

The shrines of Imams and Shaikhs are especially sacred to Sufis because they are blessed places visited and inhabited by righteous souls and angels. There are innumerable karāmas that confirm the sanctity of these places, and we have mentioned some of these miracles. Our Shaikh has looked after the renovation of holy sites, overseeing the work himself. His efforts in this field started before he received the Ṭarīqa's Shaikhdom. In 1977, Shaikh ʿAbd al-Karīm obtained the Ministry of Endowments' agreement to help financially with the renovation of the shrines in Karbchna, supervised by the Ministry's regional office in Kirkuk. Shaikh ʿAbd al-Karīm designated his deputy Shaikh Muḥammad al-Muḥammad as the one in charge of the project.

Our Shaikh wanted to use stone from Karbchna to build the exterior of the mosque, takya, and shrines. The Ministry engineer argued that this would increase the project's cost, but our Shaikh insisted on it and assured him that he would be responsible for obtaining the approval for the additional cost. Stone was not used in construction in Karbchna, so this was an innovative idea of our Shaikh's. The stone was brought from a quarry behind Shāh al-Kasnazān's reservoir. He used the same stone to build his house in Kirkuk. He brought marble from Mount Sagarma and used it to build the flooring of both his house in Kirkuk and the main takya in Baghdad. The use of stone and marble from Karbchna is intended to seek the blessings of this village. In one of his sayings about the virtues of this blessed village, our Shaikh has said: "The light of the Messenger (PBUH) has shone a thousand times on Karbchna's shrines, its mountain, and the village in its entirety. Everything in Karbchna is blessed".

Skilled engravers and carvers from Kirkuk carved the exterior of the building. A few months after starting the renovation of the mosque and the shrines, Shaikh ʿAbd al-Karīm passed away. Our Shaikh then completed the reconstruction before the late Shaikh's forty-day death anniversary. The tombs of Shāh al-Kasnazān and Sulṭān ʿAbd al-Qādir were in one room and the tombs of Sulṭān Ḥusayn and Sulṭān ʿAbd al-Karīm were in another, but the four tombs are now housed in one hall topped by a large dome (photos 4, 6).

Our Shaikh also decided to place a golden crown, two meters high, on each tomb and build a large new door for the entrance of the hall (photo 5). He sent for caliphs from Sanandaj, Iran, who were skilled in designing with gold, and for caliphs from Isfahan, who were deft engravers. He met them in Karbchna at Shaikh ʿAbd al-Karīm's forty-day death anniversary. He would discuss his designs with them, they would sketch them out and present them to him, and he would approve them or ask for changes to be made. The inscriptions and ornamentations our Shaikh settled on were of the kind known as "Karbalā`iyya" (in the style of patterns found in Karbala). After the designs were completed, our Shaikh paid the craftsmen who went back to Iran and began work.

After obtaining land for the main takya in Baghdad, our Shaikh asked that the door of the takya's mosque be of the same design as the door to the hall of the shrines in Karbchna. The symbolic meaning of his decision is that the door of the takya's mosque in Baghdad is the door to the hall of the shrines of the Shaikhs in Karbchna, as he is their caliph and successor as Master of the Ṭarīqa.

It took four years and three months to manufacture the tombs' crowns and the two doors because it was precise manual work. The work was completed in mid-1982. Amazingly, as the pieces could not be transported by car because of the closed borders between Iraq and Iran due to the ongoing war between the two countries, dervishes carried them on their heads and transported them on foot from Isfahan in Iran to

Karbchna! The hall's door, in particular, was very heavy, with each side needing to be carried by more than ten men. The area through which the cargo had to be transported was rugged and mountainous. It was sometimes difficult to walk in even without a load, let alone carrying such a very heavy and large load. The transporting required crossing snow-covered mountains. The crossing road of Mount Sūrīn, in particular, was very narrow, even for a person walking alone without carrying anything. Also, crossing the border in secret and without approval forced the dervishes to avoid well-known paths and, instead, take secret, rugged roads to cross over the no-man's land between the two countries, which was about ten kilometres deep. They would only travel at night to prevent army troops from seeing them. The transporting process took eleven days. Despite this, army troops discovered them more than once and opened fire at them. One karāma that happened to them was that the bullets would sometimes hit them but would not harm them. The transporting of the tombs' crowns and the hall's door, each section of which required several dervishes to carry, was extremely difficult and dangerous.

Our Shaikh refurbished Karbchna's hall of shrines from the inside. Its flooring is made of precious marble, and its ceiling is ornamented with beautiful patterns, beautiful and unique chandeliers were placed inside it, and the walls were decorated with pieces of ceramic with beautiful inscriptions and a blue stripe with the noble lineage inscribed on it. The hall has a dome plated from inside with reflective mirrors that give the hall a brilliant lustre. It has a door leading to the front yard and another leading to the adjacent mosque.

On the forty-day death anniversary of Shaikh ʿAbd al-Karīm, the walī Kāka ʿAzīz, who we previously mentioned in Section 2.1, was sitting with caliph Yāsīn Ṣūfī in the corner of the wall that separates the mosque from the shrines, and behind them was Shāh al-Kasnazān's tomb. Kāka ʿAzīz suddenly said that he saw Shaikh ʿAbd al-Qādir al-Kasnazān demolish the wall of the mosque that was in front of them, that is, the wall facing the valley, which had just been constructed. Thinking that the demolition would be ordered by our Shaikh, the caliph remarked that the construction had taken a long time and great effort to complete, so it was inconceivable that it would be torn down. Kāka ʿAzīz replied that he only said what had been revealed to him, which was that Shaikh ʿAbd al-

Qādir demolished that wall but not the others. When Yāsīn asked just exactly what would happen to the wall, Kāka ʿAzīz answered that the wall and its roof would suffer damage. During the Iraq-Iran war, which began about two and a half years after this incident, the Iraqi army targeted Karbchna in a campaign that destroyed many villages, including mosques and shrines, in Kurdistan that the government suspected contained some inhabitants that were collaborating with the Peshmerga. Some of the destruction damaged the buildings of the hall of the shrines and the mosque, but the walls and roofs were not affected, except for the wall that Kāka ʿAzīz saw Shaikh ʿAbd al-Qādir al-Kasnazān's hand demolish, which collapsed. The government also blew up the living halls of the dervishes. Later, our Shaikh renovated them completely, and he installed a dome at the centre of the mosque standing on four concrete columns and used Islamic arabesque to beautify it, inside and out, in addition to refurbishing its furniture.

At the same time, our Shaikh decided that the door of the takya's mosque in Baghdad would have an identical design to the door of the hall of the Shrines in Karbchna, he also decided to replace the crown of Shaikh ʿAbd al-Qādir al-Gaylānī's tomb. He obtained the approval of the official authorities, and the crown was completed in 1983. Dervishes sent it to Kirkuk, where our Shaikh was at the time. It was then transported to the main takya in Baghdad because he wanted to keep it there for one night to seek its blessings. The following day, it was moved to Shaikh ʿAbd al-Qādir's shrine in Baghdad. Surprised, having noticed that the crown was from Iran, one of the people in charge of the shrine asked our Shaikh how this was possible. The borders between the two countries were closed and monitored on both sides by armies prepared to open fire on anyone who crossed them. He answered, "How did our Master al-Gaylānī throw his wooden shoe from Baghdad to India?", citing a karāma of al-Ghawth al-Āʿẓam. A disciple from today's Pakistan came to visit him. When the disciple was in Baghdad, someone tried to assault his daughter in Pakistan, so the Shaikh threw his wooden shoe from Baghdad, hitting the assaulter and saving the young woman from harm. One of the karāmas that happened while the crown was being transported from Iran was that the dervishes who were carrying it did not feel the cold when they had to sleep in rugged snow-covered areas. Instead, they would feel hot to the point of sweating!

The old crown was transported and placed atop Shaikh Junayd al-Baghdādī's tomb. The following is a karāma that accompanied the replacing of the crown. After the dervishes removed the old crown to place the new one in its place, caliph Yāsīn Ṣūfī, who was among those charged with replacing the crown, took a palm-sized piece of silver from the old crown. He wanted to have six or seven rings made of it because of its blessings. He would keep one for himself and gift the others to certain dervishes who possessed ḥāls. After the work was completed, he went back to his family in Erbil and asked his cousin, who worked as a jeweller, to transform the piece of blessed silver into rings. However, the jeweller apologised because he did not have a mould for rings and offered, instead, to make it into circles. Yāsīn agreed and emphasized to his relative the importance of using up the entire silver piece when making the circles so that no waste was left because it was from the blessed tomb of Shaikh ʿAbd al-Qādir. The caliph kept the matter secret and told no one about it.

After he returned to Ramādī, where he lived to preach, a dervish named Aḥmad Sūr (may Allah have mercy on him), who was a walī, visited him in the takya. Hajj Aḥmad surprised the caliph by saying:

> Last night, Shaikh ʿAbd al-Qādir informed me of the following: "Yāsīn has taken fifteen circles from my tomb. Tell him to give you one".

The caliph answered:

> O Hajj Aḥmad! I took a piece of silver to make rings from it. It could produce six or seven, but it could not produce fifteen. I also had the intention to give you one of them even before this message had come.

Hajj Aḥmad replied:

> O dervish! I am only telling you what Shaikh ʿAbd al-Qādir al-Gaylānī has told me. Otherwise, was I with you that I should know about this matter? He is the one who said that you had taken fifteen circles from his tomb and ordered me to tell you to give me one of them.

About a week later, caliph Yāsīn's nephew visited his uncle and gave him an enclosed package that his mother asked him to deliver to him. When he opened it, he found that it contained the circles. There were fourteen of them, so he told his nephew that one ring is missing. The latter laughed in surprise and said that when his mother knew that the circles were made from a piece of Shaikh ʿAbd al-Qādir's tomb, she kept one for herself for the blessing. So, the total number of circles was fifteen, just as Shaikh ʿAbd al-Qādir had informed Hajj Aḥmad Sūr in the vision.

Later on, those in charge of the shrine replaced the crown that our Shaikh had made with another made out of silver, produced in India. When our Shaikh came to know of this, he said that he had done his duty in service to the shrine and refurbished its crown. Whatever those in charge of the shrine did was up to them. The crown our Shaikh made was transferred from Baghdad and placed on the tomb of Shaikh ʿAbd al-ʿAzīz, son of Shaikh ʿAbd al-Qādir al-Gaylānī, in the city of ʿAqra in the governorate of Nineveh in northern Iraq. Our Shaikh also redid the patio that surrounds Shaikh ʿAbd al-Qādir's shrine, inlaying it with high-quality marble.

Our Master rebuilt Shaikh Ismāʿīl al-Wilyānī's shrine in ʿAqra and clothed it in a gold shroud. This project took more than five months to complete, during which time the finest calligrapher of Baghdad penned Qur'anic verses, prayers on the Prophet (PBUH), dhikrs, and poetry. The most brilliant craftsmen of Isfahan crafted the golden shroud. The noble shrine was erected on the birthday of Shaikh ʿAbd al-Qādir al-Gaylānī on 11th/Rabiʿ al-Thānī/1427 Hijri, 9th/May/2006 CE.

Among our Shaikh's accomplishments with respect to rebuilding holy sites is that he funded and implemented the project of delivering water and electricity to Prophet Jonah's (peace be upon him) mosque in Mosul.

18.1.1 Visiting Holy Sites

Naturally, our Shaikh loves to visit holy sites and shrines, Karbchna in particular. When he was in Baghdad, he would regularly visit Shaikh ʿAbd al-Qādir al-Gaylānī's shrine, as well as other shrines of Shaikhs of Ṭarīqa, such as Maʿrūf al-Karkhī, Sarī al-Saqaṭī, and Junayd al-Baghdādī. As we have mentioned, our Master stopped visiting the holy shrines in Karbala and Najaf after his final visit to them in 1995, when Baghdad's government told him to do so because of its fear of any convergence between the Ṭarīqa and Shia religious leaders. He would also visit the shrines of Imām Mūsa al-Kāẓim and his grandson Imām Muḥammad al-Jawād in Baghdad once a year. At other times, he would frequent the area near the shrines without entering, avoiding problems with the authorities.

There were periods when our Shaikh could not visit Karbchna due to military operations between government and Kurdish forces in northern Iraq and, later, as a result of the Iran-Iraq war. He would send dervishes who lived in nearby areas to visit the shrines on his behalf. He would also sometimes send someone to visit other holy places in his place.

The Shaikh of Ṭarīqa has his reasons for deciding to visit certain holy sites at specific times. At times he would disclose those reasons and at others he would not. For example, one morning in 1993, before going out for his daily visit to a manuscript house in Baghdad, he informed some caliphs in the takya that a man with black skin would come. He instructed them to ask the visitor to wait for him until he returned, as he was his guest. He also asked caliph Majīd Ḥamīd, who would accompany him in his daily visit to manuscript houses, to stay in the takya to wait for the man's arrival.

A dark-skinned Sudanese man with a limp came and sat in the room where dervishes rest and sleep. Caliph Majīd saw him when he entered the takya, but he did not think that he was the man that our Shaikh referred to. Given his simple and plain clothing and undistinguished condition in general, the caliph did not see anything in him that could interest our Shaikh and make him a special guest among the many visitors to the takya every day. When our Master returned to the takya, before going to his house, he asked about the man. Majīd told him about the arrival of a man with black skin, but he did not know if he was the man he was waiting for. Instead of our Shaikh sending for him, as is the custom when he wants to speak with a dervish, he went to see him in the dervishes' resting room. There, he initiated the conversation by saying that Shaikh Junayd al-Baghdādī had visited him the night before and told him that he would send him a man who had an affliction and would ask for his help. The Shaikh asked him if he had visited Shaikh Junayd al-Baghdādī. Amazed, he answered that he had indeed visited him the day before. He added that in the morning, he felt a strong desire to visit the Kasnazānī takya. Then he asked him about his affliction. He answered that while working, hot tar fell on his foot and severely burned it. Hot tar can penetrate deep into the body and may even cause permanent disability. Our Shaikh reassured the man and told him that he would remain under his care until he was cured. He asked some dervishes to take the man to a doctor to receive treatment. He remained in the takya until he was completely cured. When he returned to Sudan, he founded a Kasnazānī takya there. Our Master was happy with the man's visit, whom he described as "a gift from our Master Junayd al-Baghdādī". As a result, he went to visit his shrine. Our Master's visits to the shrine of Shaikh ʿAbd al-Qādir were mostly due to visions that he saw or in response to a call from the Shaikh to visit him.

Our Shaikh shows the utmost reverence and respect in his visits to holy sites. When he visits Shaikh ʿAbd al-Qādir, he always kisses the gate's threshold (photos 35, 36). He would never turn his back to the noble tomb during the visit. The following is an instance that illustrates the level of reverence and veneration that he demonstrates when he visits his Master Shaikh ʿAbd al-Qādir al-Gaylānī. One morning at the end of the 1990s, he decided to visit the shrine and permitted some dervishes who were in the takya at the time to accompany him on the visit. On the way to the shrine, he told Shaikh Sāmān, was accompanying him, that Shaikh ʿAbd al-Qādir had summoned him and honoured him that night. He did not disclose the nature of this honour. When the car arrived on the shrine's street, he disembarked before it reached the shrine to walk to it, one of his etiquettes in visiting the blessed shrine. The caliphs and dervishes were following him. However, instead of crossing the outside patio that separates the street from the building hosting the shrine to enter the noble courtyard, he headed towards a dog sitting in the shade on the outside patio in front of the shrine. He addressed him gently, asking him to allow him to stand in his place to greet Shaikh ʿAbd al-Qādir from there! Dervishes who were with him experienced various ḥāls when they witnessed this tremendous scene of his humility. The dog left its place, so our Shaikh stood on that spot. He faced the noble shrine and addressed its owner (may Allah sanctify his innermost being). Although dervishes who were near to him heard his speech, they did not understand anything he said.

What our Master did with the dog in this visit was not unprecedented. In another visit to the shrine of Shaikh ʿAbd al-Qādir, he was only accompanied by Shaikh Sāmān and the chauffeur. When they arrived at the patio in front of the building hosting the shrine, he turned towards his companion and told him that he would stand a little with a friend of his. Shaikh Sāmān did not understand what he meant given that the place was empty, as it was about two o'clock in the afternoon on a very hot summer day. Our Shaikh walked towards a dog, reddish in colour, that was taking shade near a wall. He stood next to it and lifted one of his feet a little above the ground and started to move it, balancing himself on his other foot and his staff. He makes this symbolic gesture to humble himself in front of great Shaikhs out of respect to them, including when Shaikhs' souls attend the dhikr circle. He remained standing there for a short while then headed to visit the honourable shrine. This dog was the friend our Master had referred to!

That night at the takya, our Shaikh told Shaikh Sāmān to ask some dervishes to wash the takya's yard and the front patio all the way to the street, the next morning, before our Shaikh leaves his house for the takya. In the morning, after the dervishes finished cleaning, our Master left for the takya. Not long after, the dog that was outside the shrine of Shaikh ʿAbd al-Qādir the day before came from the street and headed towards the takya's door, crying with visible tears and an audible voice. When our Shaikh saw the dog, he asked the caliph to tell dervishes in the takya that the takya's dog was not impure, so that they would not stop him from entering. The dog went to the kitchen and sat under a table while his weeping sound was still being heard. After a while, a dervish gently picked him up and took him out from under the cooker so it left the takya. Evidently, this is not normal behaviour for a dog. Allah knows that creature's reality and affair.

Our Master's behaviour on his visit was striving against his self so that no pride would come to it because of the blessings he received from Shaikh ʿAbd al-Qādir and the Ṭarīqa's Shaikhs. This action of his reminds us of a saying that he frequently reiterates, that a true dervish is in his loyalty and obedience to his Master like a dog to his owner.

The following is an instructive lesson of our Master's to dervishes regarding imitating a dog in its loyalty. He was in the main takya in Basra when he saw a child outside throwing stones at a dog that was following him. The dog dodged the stones and continued to accompany the child. He asked those in attendance to call the child to him. When he came, he asked him why he was throwing stones at the dog. The child answered that he wanted to stop it from walking behind him, but to no avail. He then asked him why the dog was following after him, and the child replied that the dog loved him. Our Shaikh nodded his head in agreement and said to the present dervishes: "This is how a seeker must be with his

Shaikh. He must not get angry with his Shaikh and must come to him as soon as he beckons to him". In this regard, Shaikh ʿAbd al-Qādir al-Gaylānī has said:

> "O young man, when the servant comes to know the True One (mighty and sublime is He), He draws his heart with complete proximity, grants him everything, confers ultimate intimacy on him, and honours him with all honour. Once he gets used to this, He takes it away from him, leaves him empty-handed, sends him back to his self, and establishes a veil between Himself and him to test him and see what he does: Does he run away? Does he deviate or remain steadfast? If he stands firm, He removes the veil from him and returns him to how he was. Have you not seen how a father puts his son to the test? He sends him out of his house, locks the door in his face, and waits to see what he does. If he finds that his son kept to the doorstep, did not go to his neighbour, did not complain about him, and did not abandon polite behaviour, he reopens the door, allows him in, embraces him, and honours him more than before".[324]

18.2 The Muḥammadī Calendar

For the Shaikh of Tarīqa, the birth of Muḥammad (PBUH) has a unique sacred status among Islamic events because he is the Prophet of Islam, the one to whom the Qur'an was revealed, and the means of guiding people. His birth represents the descent of Allah's light among people: "There has come to you from Allah a light and a clear Book" (al-Māʾida 15). It is also the date of Allah's sending of mercy to people: "We have not sent you except as a mercy to the worlds" (al-Ānbiyāʾ). Several miracles accompanied this unique universal event, including the shaking of the mansion of the Persian empire and the fall of fourteen of its terraces, the extinguishing of the temple fire that was worshipped in Persia, the subsiding of the waters of the lake of Sāwa, and others.[325]

Celebrating the Prophetic birth is one of the greatest religious practices in the Tarīqa. The Prophet (PBUH) is the door to Allah, remembering and reading prayers on him is to remember Allah, and loving him takes the person to love Allah. This is why Allah said that a Muslim must give precedence to the Messenger (PBUH) over everyone

---

[324] Shaikh ʿAbd al-Qādir al-Gaylānī, *Jilā' al-Khāṭir*, pp. 52-53.
[325] Aṣbahānī, *Dalāʾil al-Nubuwwa*, p. 399.

else and anything:

> Say [O Muḥammad]: "If your fathers, your sons, your brothers, your wives, your relatives, wealth which you have obtained, commerce wherein you fear decline, and dwellings with which you are pleased are more beloved to you than Allah and His Messenger and jihad in His cause, then wait until Allah executes His command. Allah does not guide the defiantly disobedient people". (Al-Tawba 24)

A Muslim who does celebrate the birth of the Messenger (PBUH) should not celebrate anyone else or anything. This celebration is an acknowledgement of Allah's favour to people having sent His noble Prophet (PBUH) and obeying His order. Shaikhs of the Tarīqa and scholars have said so much about the virtue of celebrating the noble Prophetic birth, such as Shaikh Ḥasan al-Baṣrī's words: "I wish I had as much gold as Mount Uḥud so that I can spend it on reading [in praise of] the birth of the Messenger (PBUH)".[326]

On the night of 12th/Rabīʿ al-Āwwal/144 Hijrī, which corresponds to 19th/September/1991, Shaikh Muḥammad al-Muḥammad Muḥammad put forward an initiative that represents a permanent celebration of the Prophetic birth and reveres and venerates the noble Messenger (PBUH). He proposed the introduction of a new lunar calendar that dates events relative to the birth of the Prophet (PBUH).

This calendar does great service to the study of Islamic history because it dates events relative to its real beginning. It, thus, presents an effective solution to one barrier to the study of early Islamic history. Historians usually indirectly divide Islamic history into three periods that are dated using three different reference years. The first period is from the birth of the Messenger (PBUH) to the beginning of the revelation of the glorious Qur'an. For instance, biographical works of the Messenger (PBUH) state that he married sayyida Khadīja when he was "twenty-five years old"[327], and that he was "thirty-five years old"[328] when he wisely advised the tribes of the Quraysh about how to place the Black Stone in the Kaʿba, sparing them a potential war among themselves. The reference year for this period is his birth year.

---

[326] Bakrī, *Iʿānat al-Ṭālibīn*, III, p. 364.
[327] Ibn Hishām, *Sīrat al-Nabī*, I, p. 242.
[328] Ibn Hishām, *Sīrat al-Nabī*, I, p. 248.

The second period extends from the first revelation of the Qur'an to the Prophetic migration, which is dated relative to the revelation year. For example, the first group of Muslims who migrated from Mecca, going to Abyssinia, is said to have happened in "the month of Rajab of the fifth year after prophethood was conferred on the Messenger of Allah (PBUH)"[329] and that he travelled to Ṭā'if "in the last few nights of the month Shawwal when of the eleventh year after prophethood was conferred on the Messenger of Allah (PBUH)".[330]

The third period is the one that followed the migration of the Prophet (PBUH) from Mecca to Medina. Its reference year is the year of migration. Accordingly, early Islamic history has been dated using three different reference years, which is the equivalent of using three different calendars.

The "Mīlādī Muḥammadī", or "Muḥammadī" for abbreviation, is not a replacement for the Hijrī calendar. In addition to its religious significance, it can have practical benefits because of its use of the year of noble Prophetic birth as a common reference year for all periods of Islamic history.

The Muḥammadī year consists of twelve months, each of which starts when its respective lunar crescent becomes visible, as is the case in the Hijrī calendar. As this calendar celebrates the birth of the Prophet (PBUH), its first month and year are the birth's first month and year, respectively. Accordingly, the date of the noble birth according to the Muḥammadī calendar is 1st/1/12. The Muḥammadī year begins two months after the beginning of the Hijrī year because the Hijrī month of the noble birth, Rabīʿ al-Āwwal, is the third month of the Hijrī year. Our Shaikh called the first year of the Muḥammadī calendar the "year of light", after Allah's description of the Prophet Muḥammad (PBUH) as "light" in this verse: "There has come to you from Allah a light and a clear Book" (al-Mā`ida 15).

Intended to commemorate Islam's main symbol, the Messenger Muḥammad (PBUH), and Islam in general, the months of the Muḥammadī calendar have been named after great Islamic characters, symbols, and events. For the month names to have historical significance,

---

[329] Ibn Saʿad, *Kitāb al-Ṭabaqāt al-Kabīr*, I, p. 173.
[330] Ibn Saʿad, *Kitāb al-Ṭabaqāt al-Kabīr*, I, p. 180.

they were chosen to celebrate events that happened in their respective months. These are the names of the Muḥammadī months and why they have been chosen:

1) Al-Nūr (the light): This is the birth month of the Messenger (PBUH). In the same way that our Shaikh called the year of the noble birth "the year of light", this month derived its name from the Qur'anic description of the Prophet (PBUH).

2) Al-Quds (Jerusalem): This is one of Islam's most sacred cities, embracing the Aqṣā Mosque to which the Messenger (PBUH) was first transported at night before being taken to the heavens. In this month, the leader Saladin liberated Jerusalem in the famous battle of Hittin (637 M / 583 H).

3) Al-Karrār (the attacker): In this month the conquest of Khaybar took place (71 M / 7 H). After a 15-day siege, the Muslim army attacked this fortified city for two days but without success. When the army came back on the second unsuccessful day, the Messenger made his well-known declaration: "By Allah, I will give the standard tomorrow to a man who loves Allah and who Allah and His Messenger love, who is an attacker (karrār), not one who flees, and who will conquer it by force".[331] Next day, he called for Imam ʿAlī Ibn Abī Ṭālib and tasked him with the responsibility of conquering the fort, which he did.

4) Al-Zahrā` (the brilliant one): This is the title of sayyida Fāṭima, daughter of the Messenger (PBUH). She was born on 20th of this month (38 M / 17 H). The Prophet said about the virtues of sayyida Fāṭīma al-Zahrā`: "Fāṭīma is a part of me; anything that hurts her hurts me too".[332]

5) Al-Isrā` (the night journey): This is the month in which Allah (exalted and high is He) took the Messenger at night from the Ḥarām Mosque in Mecca to the Aqṣā Mosque in Jerusalem (52 M / 3 BH): "Exalted is He who took His Servant by night from the Ḥarām Mosque to the Aqṣā Mosque, whose surroundings We have blessed, to show him of Our signs. Indeed, He is the Hearing, the Seeing" (al-Isrā` 1).

6) Al-Qādisiyya: This month witnessed the battle of Qādisiyya (69

---

[331] Abū al-Fidā`, *Al-Mukhtaṣar fī-Akhbār al-Bashar*, I, p. 140.

[332] Muslim, *Ṣaḥīḥ Muslim*, IV, no. 2449, p. 1903.

M / 15 H) in which the Muslims defeated the army of the Persian Sasanian empire and that led to the conquest of Iraq.

7) Ramadan: This is the name of this month in the glorious Qur'an: "The month of Ramadan [is that] in which was revealed the Qur'an, a guidance for the people and clear proofs of guidance and criterion" (al-Baqara 185).

8) Al-Naṣr (the victory): In this month, the Muslims defeated an alliance involving the tribe of Quraysh in the battle of the Trench (59 M / 5 H).

9) Al-Bay'a (the pledge): This is the month of the pledge of Riḍwān (60 M / 6 H), which the Qur'an mentioned: "Certainly Allah was pleased with the believers when they pledged allegiance to you [O Muḥammad] under the tree, and He knew what was in their hearts, so He sent down tranquillity upon them and rewarded them with an imminent conquest" (al-Fatḥ 18).

10) Al-Ḥajj (the pilgrimage): This is the month in which Muslims perform pilgrimage to the Ḥarām Mosque in Mecca.

11) Al-Hijra (the migration): The first month of the Hijrī year.

12) Al-Futūḥ (the conquests): In this month, the conquest of Nahawand (74 M / 21 H) took place. This is also known as the "conquest of conquests" because it was a decisive battle in the ultimate conquest of Muslims of the Persian empire. There were also other important battles in this month, such as the raid of Abwā` or Waddān (55 M / 2 H), the first Muslim raid, and the conquest of Ctesiphon (69 M / 16 H), the imperial capital of the Sassanid empire.

Table 2: The Muḥammadī Months and Their Hijrī Equivalents

Muḥammadī		**Hijrī**	
No.	Month	No.	Month
1	Al-Nūr	3	Rabī' al-Āwwal
2	Al-Quds	4	Rabī' al-thānī
3	Al-Karrār	5	Jamādā al-Uwlā
4	Al-Zahrā`	6	Jamādā al-`Ākhira
5	Al-Isrā`	7	Rajab
6	Al-Qādisiyya	8	Sha'bān
7	Ramadan	9	Ramadan
8	Al-Naṣr	10	Shawwāl

9	Al-Bay'a	11	Dhū al-Qi'da
10	Al-Ḥajj	12	Dhū al-Ḥijja
11	Al-Hijra	1	Muḥarram
12	Al-Futūḥ	2	Ṣafar

The Muḥammadī calendar is 53 years and 10 months ahead of the Hijrī calendar. This is the period between the start of the first Muḥammadī year, that is, "the year of the light", and the start of the first Hijrī year. The days of the month in both calendars are the same because both follow the lunar month, which starts with the first visibility of the lunar crescent. But the months and years differ. We will now discuss the conversion between Hijrī and Muḥammadī dates.

18.2.1 Converting Hijrī to Muḥammadī Dates

The general formula for converting a Hirjī date into its Muḥammadī equivalent is as follows:

- Muḥammadī date = Hijrī date + 53 years + 10 months ...... (1)

A) Calculating the Month

A Hijrī month is converted into its Muḥammadi equivalent as follows:
For Hijrī months 1-2:

- Muḥammadī month = Hijrī month + 10 ...... (1-1)

For Hijrī months 3-12:

- Muḥammadī month = Hijrī month - 2 ...... (1-2)

One of these two formulas should be used regardless of the year.

B) Calculating the Year

Calendars do not use year zero. The first Hijrī year, that is, 1 H, is preceded by year 1 before Hijrī, which may be numerically represented as -1. Similarly, the first Muḥammadī calendar is preceded by year -1 M. Accordingly, there are two different pairs of formulas for converting Hijrī years into Muḥammadī years, depending on the Hijrī date.

These two formulas are used for calculating the year for any date except for the period from 2/54 BH to 12/1 BH:

For Hijrī months 1-2:

- Muḥammadī year = Hijrī year + 53 ...... (1-3)

For Hijrī months 3-12:

- Muḥammadī year = Hijrī year + 54 ...... (1-4)

Example: Muslims conquered Mecca peacefully on 20th of Ramadan in the eighth Hirjī year, i.e. 20th/9/8 H. The equivalent Muḥammadī date is as follows:

- The day is the same in the two calendars, so the Muḥammadī day is 20th.

Given that the Hijrī month is number 9, formulas 1-2 and 1-4 should be used:

- Muḥammadī month = 9-2 = 7
- Muḥammadī year = 8+54 = 62

The date of the conquest of Mecca according to the Muḥammadī calendar is 20th/7/62, that is 20th/Ramadan/62.

If the Hijrī date is between month 2 of year 54 BH and month 12 of year 1 BH, then formulas 1-3 and 1-4 must be replaced with the following two formulas for calculating the Muḥammadī year:

For Hijrī months 1-2:

- Muḥammadī year = Hijrī year + 54 ...... (1-5) instead of (1-3)

For Hijrī months 3-12:

- Muḥammadī year = Hijrī year + 55 ...... (1-6) instead of (1-4)

Example: The night journey of the Prophet (PBUH) from the Ḥarām Mosque to the Aqṣā Mosque happened on 27th/Rajab of year three before Hijra. This is how to convert it to the corresponding Muḥammadī date:

- The day is the same in the two calendars, so the Muḥammadī day is 27th.

Given that the Hijrī month is number 7 and the date is in the period 2/54 BH – 12/1 BH, formulas 1-2 and 1-6 should be used:

- Muḥammadī month = 7-2 = 5
- Muḥammadī year = -3+55 = 52

The Muḥammadī date of the night journey is 27th/5/52, that is 27th/al-Isrā`/52.

18.2.2 Converting Muḥammadī to Hijrī Dates

The general formula for converting Muḥammadī dates into Hirjī dates is as follows:

- Hijrī date = Muḥammadī date - 53 years - 10 months...... (2)

A) Calculating the Month

A Muḥammadi month is converted into the corresponding Hijrī date as follows:

For Muḥammadi months 11-12:

- Hijrī month = Muḥammadi month + 10 ...... (2-1)

For Muḥammadi months 1-10:

- Hijrī month = Muḥammadi month + 2 ...... (2-2)

B) Calculating the Year

The following two formulas are used for calculating the year for any date except the period 1/1-10/54 M:

For Muḥammadi months 11-12:

- Hijrī year = Muḥammadī year - 53 ...... (2-3)

For Muḥammadi months 1-10:

- Hijrī year = Muḥammadī year - 54 ...... (2-4)

Example: The Muslims conquered Mecca on 20th/Ramadan/62 M. This date can be converted to its Hijrī equivalent as follows:

- The day is the same in the two calendars, so the Muḥammadī day is 20th.

Given that the Muḥammadī month is 7, we must use formulas 2-2 and 2-4:

- Hijrī month = 7-2 = 5
- Hijrī year = -3+55 = 52

The date of the conquest of Mecca according to the Hijrī calendar is 20th/Ramada/8.

If the Muḥammadī date is between month 1 of year 1 and month 10 of year 54, which is before the first Hijrī year, then formulas 2-3 and 2-4 must be replaced with the following formulas to calculate the Hijrī year:

For Muḥammadī months 11-12:

- Hijrī year = Muḥammadī year - 54 ...... (2-5) instead of (2-3)

For Muḥammadī months 3-12:

- Muḥammadī year = Hijrī year + 55 ...... (2-6) instead of (2-4)

Example: The Prophet (PBUH) was born on 12th of the first month, that is the month of the light, of the first Muḥammadī year, i.e. 12/1/1 M. The equivalent Hijrī date is calculated as follows:

- The day is the same in the two calendars, so the Hijrī day is 12th.

Given that the Muḥammadī month is 1, we must use formula 2-2 to calculate the Hijrī month:

- Hijrī month = 1+2 = 3

As the Muḥammadī month is 1 and the date is in the period 1/1-10/54, formula 2-6 must be used to find the Hijrī year:

- Hijrī year = 1-55 = -54

The date of the noble Prophetic birth according to the Hijrī calendar is 12th/3/-54, i.e. 12th/Rabīʿ al-Āwwal/54 BH.[333]

18.3 The Solar Date of the Birth of the Prophet (PBUH)

Our Shaikh's introduction of the Muḥammadī calendar was accompanied by another initiative to calculate the date of the birth of the Messenger (PBUH) according to the Gregorian calendar, i.e. the ubiquitous Western calendar. There is a consensus that the Hijrī day and month of the birth are known to be 12th of Rabīʿ al-Āwwal, which correspond to 12/al-Nūr in the Muḥammadī calendar, and the year of birth is the "year of the elephant", which corresponds to 570 CE. This means that it is possible to calculate the Gregorian date of the birth of the Prophet

---

[333] For more information, see Fatoohi, "Nahjun Jadīdun Naḥwa Ta`rīkhin Daqīqin Lil-Sīra al-Nabawiyya wal-ʿAṣr al-Islāmī al-Awwal".

(PBUH).[334] This date was accurately calculated to be Friday 2nd/May/570. Our Master celebrates this date every year in the same way he commemorates its Hijrī equivalent.

18.4 The Muḥammadī Shamsī Calendar

The solar calendar is not less important than the lunar one in the Islamic world. In fact, the official calendar in many Islamic countries is the Gregorian one, which is a solar calendar that reckons time from the hypothetical date of the birth of Jesus (PBUH). The Qur'an points out the benefits of using the sun and the moon in the reckoning of time:

> [He is] the cleaver of daybreak and has made the night for rest and the sun and moon for calculation. That is the determination of the Impregnable, the Knowing. (Al-Ān'ām 96)
>
> It is He who made the sun a shining light and the moon a derived light and determined for it phases - that you may know the number of years and account [of time]. Allah has not created this except in truth. He details the signs for a people who know. (Yūnus 5)

Less than three years after introducing the Muḥammadī calendar, our Shaikh initiated another project to celebrate the birth of the Prophet (PBUH). On the anniversary of the noble birth according to the Gregorian calendar on 2nd/May/1994, he proposed a new solar calendar that reckons time from the month of the birth. To distinguish it from the lunar "Muḥammadī" calendar, this calendar was called "Muḥammadī Shamsī", where "Shamsī" means "solar". The first Muḥammadī Shamsī month, which is the birth month, corresponds to the fifth month in the Gregorian calendar. Accordingly, the Muḥammadī Shamsī calendar starts four months after the start of the Gregorian year. In other words, the Gregorian date of the noble birth on 2nd/5/570 CE converts to 2nd/1/1 in the Muḥammadī Shamsī calendar.

Most months of this calendar were named after weather and seasonal changes that happen in those months in the Arabian peninsula where

---

334 This calendar used to be called the "Julian" calendar after the Roman general Julius Caesar, who proposed it in 46 BCE. It took effect from the first of January, which is the first month of the Roman year, 45 BCE. Due to the Julian year being shorter than the solar year, Pope Gregory XIII amended this calendar in 1582, so it became known as the "Gregorian" calendar.

Prophet Muḥammad (PBUH) was born and from where Islam spread. These are the names of the months:

1) Al-Raḥma (the mercy): This is the month of the birth of the Messenger whom the Qur'an described with this quality: "We have not sent you [O Muḥammad] except as a mercy to the worlds" (al-Ānbiyā` 107).

2) Al-Firdaws (paradise): Fields are full of fruits, vegetables, and seeds in this month.

3) Al-Shams (the sun): This is the first month of the hot summer.

4) Al-Ruṭab (dates): In this month, dates ripen. Date palm is considered to be a blessed tree in Islam.

5) Al-Riḥla (the journey): The migration of the Messenger (PBUH) took place in this month. He left Mecca on 8th and arrived at Medina two weeks later, on 22nd.

6) Al-Ghayth (rain): Rain starts falling in this month.

7) Al-Bard (cold): This is the first month of winter.

8) Al-Thalj (snow): Snow starts falling in this month.

9) Al-Rīḥ (wind): This month usually has strong winds.

10) Al-Zar' (planting): The first month of planting the summer plants.

11) Al-Burāq (the Burāq): The Messenger's (PBUH) ascension to the heavens was in this month. Burāq is the name of the means that he used in his journey.

12) Al-Rabī' (spring): The first month after the vernal equinox.

Table 3: The Muḥammadī Shamsī Months and Their Gregorian Equivalents

Muḥammadī Shamsī		**Gregorian**	
No.	Month	No.	Month
1	Al-Raḥma	5	May
2	Al-Firdaws	6	June
3	Al-Shams	7	July
4	Al-Ruṭab	8	August
5	Al-Riḥla	9	September
6	Al-Ghayth	10	October
7	Al-Bard	11	November

8	Al-Thalj	12	December
9	Al-Rīḥ	1	January
10	Al-Zarʿ	2	February
11	Al-Burāq	3	March
12	Al-Rabīʿ	4	April

The Muḥammadī Shamsī calendar lags 569 years and 4 months behind the Gregorian calendar. This is the time between the beginning of the first Gregorian year, which is the hypothetical year of the birth of Jesus (PBUH), and the beginning of the first Muḥammadī Shamsī year, that is the year of the birth of Prophet Muḥammad (PBUH). The days in both calendars are the same, as they both follow the solar month, but the months and years differ. We will see now how to convert dates between the Muḥammadī Shamsī and Gregorian calendars.

18.4.1 Converting Gregorian to Muḥammadī Shamsī Dates

The general formula for converting Gregorian dates into Muḥammadī Shamsī dates is as follows:

- Muḥammadī Shamsī date = Gregorian date - 569 years - 4 months ...... (3)

A) Calculating the Month

A Gregorian month is converted into its Muḥammadi Shamsī equivalent as follows:

For Gregorian months 5-12:

- Muḥammadī Shamsī month = Gregorian month - 4 ...... (3-1)

For Gregorian months 1-4:

- Muḥammadī Shamsī month = Gregorian month + 8 ...... (3-2)

B) Calculating the Year

The following formulas are used for converting Gregorian years into Muḥammadī Shamsī years, except for dates in the period 1/1-4/570 CE:

For Gregorian months 5-12:

- Muḥammadī Shamsī year = Gregorian year - 569 ...... (3-3)

For Gregorian months 1-4:

- Muḥammadī Shamsī year = Gregorian year - 570 …… (3-4)

Example: The night journey of the Messenger (PBUH) was on 6th/3/620 CE. The corresponding Muḥammadī Shamsī date is as follows:

- The day is the same in the two calendars, so the Muḥammadī Shamsī day is 6th.

Given that the Gregorian month is number 3, formulas 3-2 and 3-4 must be used:

- Muḥammadī Shamsī month = 3+8 = 11
- Muḥammadī Shamsī year = 620-570 = 50

The Muḥammadī Shamsī date of the night journey is 6th/11/50, which is 6th/al-Burāq/50.

If the Gregorian date is between month 1 of year 1 CE and month 4 of year 570 CE, then formulas 3-3 and 3-4 must be replaced with the following two formulas to calculate the Muḥammadī Shamsī year:

For Gregorian months 5-12:

- Muḥammadī Shamsī year = Gregorian year - 570 …… (3-5) instead of (3-3)

For Gregorian months 1-4:

- Muḥammadī Shamsī year = Gregorian year - 571 …… (3-6) instead of (3-4)

18.4.2 Converting Muḥammadī Shamsī to Gregorian Dates

The general formula for converting Muḥammadī Shamsī dates into Gregorian dates is as follows:

- Gregorian date = Muḥammadī Shamsī date + 569 years + 4 months …… (4)

A) Calculating the Month

A Muḥammadī Shamsī month is converted into its Gregorian equivalent as follows:

For Muḥammadī Shamsī months 1-8:

- Gregorian month = Muḥammadī Shamsī month + 4 ...... (4-1)

For Gregorian months 12-9:

- Gregorian month = Muḥammadī Shamsī month - 8 ...... (4-2)

B) Calculating the Year

The following formulas are used for converting Muḥammadī Shamsī years into Gregorian years, except for dates in the period 9/570-1/12 before Muḥammadī Shamsī:

For Muḥammadī Shamsī months 1-8:

- Gregorian year = Muḥammadī Shamsī year + 569 ...... (4-3)

For Muḥammadī Shamsī months 9-12:

- Gregorian year = Muḥammadī Shamsī year + 570 ...... (4-4)

Example: The Prophet (PBUH) arrived at Medina having migrated from Mecca on 22nd/5/53 MS. The Gregorian date is calculated as follows:

- The day is the same in the two calendars, so the Gregorian day is 22nd.

Given that the Gregorian month is number 5, formulas 4-1 and 4-3 must be used to calculate the Gregorian year:

- Gregorian month = 4+5 = 9
- Gregorian year = 569+53 = 622

The Gregorian date of the arrival of the Messenger (PBUH) to Medina is 22nd/September/622.

If the Muḥammadī Shamsī date is between month 9 of year 570 BMS and month 12 of year 1 BMS, then formulas 4-3 and 4-4 must be replaced with the following formulas for calculating the Gregorian year:

For Muḥammadī Shamsī months 1-8:

- Gregorian year = Muḥammadī Shamsī year + 570 ...... (4-5) instead of (4-3)

For Gregorian months 9-12:

- Gregorian year = Muḥammadī Shamsī year + 571 ...... (4-6) instead of (4-4)

18.5 Al-Salām University College

As we explained in Chapter 6, our Shaikh accords great import to knowledge and science and always reiterates the saying, "knowledge is light". He urges disciples to seek as much education as possible and to obtain the highest academic degrees. One manifestation of our Shaikh's promotion of knowledge and his urging disciples and people, in general, to obtain the greatest amount of it his establishment in 2003 in Baghdad of a private university-level educational institution. It was first named "Shaikh Muḥammad al-Kasnazān University College" but was later renamed the "Al-Salām University College".

The college opened in 2004 with four departments: Computer Science, Law, English, and Interfaith and Intercivilization Dialogue. To encourage students to enter the latter, tuition in this department continued to be free for several years.

At present, the institution includes science and humanities departments. Specifically, it has the following departments: Computer Engineering, Computer Science, Law, English, Banking and Finance, Pathology, Islamic Studies, and Interfaith and Intercivilization Dialogue. The college grants baccalaureate degrees in these subjects.

Our Shaikh intends to make this institution the seed of a university that teaches various sciences and grants baccalaureate and post-graduate degrees.

18.6 Prophetic Odes

The nature and impact of any statement on the listener is not determined solely by its words. Other factors, such as the identity of the speaker, his manner of speech, and his voice also have an effect on the listener. When a speaker wants to intimidate listeners, he speaks in a manner that increases a listener's sense of intimidation, and when he wants to earn his affection, he addresses him in a gentle, calm tone, and so on. We see the importance of such factors even when reading Allah's Book. Reciting the Qur'an in a beautiful voice and with melodies that touch the innermost corners of the heart increases the impact of Allah's Word on the listener. Hence, the Messenger of Allah (PBUH) said: "Beautify the Qur'an with your voices, for a beautiful voice increases the Qur'an's beauty".[335] It is in the nature of the human being to be influenced by beautiful sounds and melodies. This natural phenomenon can be seen even in small children. Indeed, it is scientifically proven that even animals and plants respond to music, as it has been shown to aid in their growth and accelerate their recovery from injuries.

For centuries, Sufis have attached importance to composing and singing odes in praise of the Messenger (PBUH) and the Shaikhs of Ṭarīqa. Mentioning the Prophet (PBUH) and the Shaikhs of Ṭarīqa and remembering their qualities and deeds are two factors that affix their love and consequently plant Allah's love in the heart, because they are His callers and special servants. Songs of praise have a special role in reminding the traveller on the path to Allah of the First Guide (PBUH) and of those who walked on his noble way, increasing the love for them in his heart, and affecting it through their remembrance. A song of praise emanates from love and inspires love. When a beautiful voice sings it to a nice rhythm, its effect multiplies. This is why the throats of the people of Medina launched the first ode of praise in Islam, "Ṭalaʿa al-Badru ʿAlaynā (The Full Moon Rose Upon Us)", when they welcomed the Light of Islam (PBUH) when he arrived as a migrant from Mecca.

The Ṭarīqa Kasnazāniyya has a large heritage of brilliant odes, in Arabic, Kurdish, and Persian. In Shaikh ʿAbd al-Karīm al-Kasnazān's time, most odes were in Kurdish because the Ṭarīqa was mainly spread in Kurdish areas. In our Master's time, the Ṭarīqa's base changed to Baghdad, and the number of Arabic-speaking dervishes surpassed the number of those who spoke Kurdish, so Arabic became the language of the majority of new odes. Encouraged by our Shaikh, a number of the Ṭarīqa's writers authored dozens of poems, in both classical Arabic and the Iraqi dialect, in praise of the Messenger (PBUH) and the Shaikhs of Ṭarīqa. After setting a special melody to each poem, the Ṭarīqa's singers everywhere begin to sing them.

Excluding some famous songs of praise of the Prophet (PBUH) that are not particular to the Ṭarīqa Kasnazāniyya, such as al-Būṣīrī's "Burda (the Mantle)", the odes that our Shaikh and the dervishes of our Ṭarīqa listen to are authored by Kasnazāni dervishes and exclusively focus on the

---

[335] Dārimī, *Musnad al-Dārimī*, IV, no. 3544, p. 2194.

feats and karāmas of the Ṭarīqa Kasnazāniyya Shaikhs. The benefit of odes for a seeker is growing love for the Prophet (PBUH) and the Shaikhs of his Ṭarīqa's chain in his heart and increasing his belief that they are his means to reach Allah.

Usually, two or three odes are sung after dhikr circles on Monday and Thursday nights. Songs of praise are also performed in religious celebrations, such as the celebration of the honourable Prophetic birth and the birth of Shaikh ʿAbd al-Qādir al-Gaylānī. Dervishes also like to sometimes sing odes in takyas at other times.

When our Shaikh's health allowed him to attend dhikr circles, he would stay for the session of songs of praise that follows the dhikr. He still calls for the singing of odes in his assembly and calls dervishes present in the takya to attend it (photos 1, 2, 14, 28, 32). He also attends every celebration that the main takya hosts.

Our Master is greatly moved by odes, with his tears often expressing what his heart harbours. He is particularly affected when the Prophet (PBUH) is mentioned. Mention of Imām Ḥusayn and the suffering he went through also particularly affects him. He commemorates his martyrdom every year.

Sometimes, our Shaikh orders that a word or phrase in an ode is changed into something better. For instance, one poem started with the phrase "ṣāla ʿalā al-fursān jaddī Ḥaydara (my grandfather Ḥaydara attacked the knights)", where "Ḥaydara", which means "lion", is a title of Imām ʿAlī Ibn Abī Ṭālib. It is a title that the Imām himself mentioned when he fought and defeated the bravest warriors of Khaybar when Muslims conquered it. Our Shaikh pointed out that the word "fursān (knights)" is a flattering description that indicates bravery that should not be used for those who fought Imām ʿAlī. He changed it to the word "kuffār (disbelievers)", so the beginning of the poem became: "ṣāla ʿalā al-kuffār jaddī Ḥaydara (my grandfather Ḥaydara attacked the disbelievers)".

In 2015, our Master received a gift from the Ṭarīqa's Shaikhs, the following couplet of poetry in Kurdish in praise of the Messenger (PBUH):

Aḥmad Muḥammad har du yak nāwa
Ṣalawāt ladyār aw chūta chāwa

It means:

Aḥmad, Muḥammad, the two names are one
Praise and blessings upon the two eyes

It is well known that "Aḥmad" and "Muḥammad" are names of the Messenger (PBUH). "Aḥmad" is the superlative of "Ḥāmid", so it means "most-praising", meaning most in praise of Allah. As for "Muḥammad", it is the superlative of "Maḥmūd", meaning "much-praised".

Our Shaikh asked a caliph, Dr 'Abd al-Salām al-Ḥadīthī, to compose a poem in Arabic that had this couplet as its refrain. This poem became one of the most often-sung odes. When singers begin to perform this poem, our Shaikh often stands out of respect for this ode of the Prophet (PBUH), which he received from the Ṭarīqa's Shaikhs.

Photo 37: Shaikh Muḥammad al-Muḥammad on his farm in Dōra. The building behind him is today part of the al-Salām University College (1995/1996).

Photo 38: A page from the first printout of the Muḥammadī calendar, which was printed in its year of introduction (1991).

"Allah (exalted and high is He) says: 'Indeed, I will make upon the earth a successive authority (caliph)' (al-Baqara 30). Allah's caliph is the Shaikh who enjoins good and forbids evil. You pledged, you promised the Shaikh of Ṭarīqa that you would be a seeker, meaning a person who is righteous, a believer, and has faith in Allah (exalted and high is He). [You promised] that you would be the best person in society; that you would be a just person, an honest person, far from lying; [that you would] consume what is permissible, speak according to what is permissible, walk towards what is permissible, expel what is forbidden, not consume what is forbidden, not speak of forbidden things, eschew lying, and be a good member of society, so that anyone who looks at you knows that you are a person who was taken the pledge, meaning that you are a human being signed to Allah (exalted and high is He) to be good in society so that people point to you [and say]: this is a caliph or dervish".

Shaikh Muḥammad al-Muḥammad al-Kasnazān
(Sermon, 27th/September/2012)

19

Interests

Reading has always been one of our Shaikh's main hobbies (photos 12, 13, 27). After assuming the Ṭarīqa's Shaikhdom, he focused his reading on books of Sufism, and he also became interested in Sufi manuscripts, supplications, and dhikrs. In addition to reading books and manuscripts, he cares a lot about collecting these sources and has an invaluable personal library. His library contains a huge number of printed books, and he has also collected a very large number of manuscripts, including ancient and rare ones, in addition to photocopies of manuscripts.

His interest in manuscripts has led him to discover unknown, important ones. For example, there is an ancient manuscript of the magnificent Qur'an penned by Mullā Ibrāhīm Marwī, who mentions it has nine marvels that reveal aspects of the miraculousness of the Qur'an. More specifically, the manuscript proves that the order of chapters and verses in the muṣḥaf was inspired by Allah to the Prophet (PBUH). This confirms the consensus that the order of verses goes back to the Prophet (PBUH), while also refuting the opinion of some scholars who claim that the order of chapters was wholly or partly the work of the Companions.[336] One of these astonishing marvels is that each page of this muṣḥaf begins with the beginning of a verse and ends with the ending of another. Another is that each page contains fifteen lines. Third, the first and fifteenth lines begin with the same letter, the second and fourteenth lines with the same letter, the third and thirteenth lines with the same letter, and so on. There is a unique symmetry between the beginning of the first seven lines and the last seven on each page. The fourth amazing feature is that the eighth line, which halves the page, begins with the same letter that the eighth line on the opposite page begins with! The repetition of this extraordinary symmetry on every page of the muṣḥaf, let alone being something that no one could have

[336] Zarkashī, *Al-Burhān fī-'Ulūm al-Qur'an*, pp. 256-260.

thought of, means that it must be a Qur'anic miracle. Similarly, its discovery by Mullā Marwī was no doubt by spiritual revelation.

It is not surprising that our Shaikh keeps ancestral heirlooms of the Ṭarīqa Kasnazāniyya Shaikhs, from Shāh al-Kasnazān to the Ṭarīqa's Master before him, Shaikh ʿAbd al-Karīm, such as dhikr beads, staffs, swords, daggers, and others. He is also interested in collecting belongings of Shaikhs of Ṭarīqa in general. He has an ablution water jug that belonged to Shaikh ʿAbd al-Qādir al-Gaylānī, a staff of Kāka Aḥmad al-Shaikh, Shaikh Ḥasan al-Qarachwārī's ring, and other blessed belongings of great walīs. On our Master's estate, there is also the belt of the Prophet (PBUH) that he gifted to Imām ʿAlī Ibn Abī Ṭālib.

Agriculture is a major interest for our Master, and it is also his trade. Since the time of his father, Shaikh ʿAbd al-Karīm, he was in charge of the Ṭarīqa's agricultural lands and often directly oversaw the planting and harvesting work. As we mentioned before, one of the times he was honoured to meet the Messenger (PBUH) took place in a period when he was supervising his farm in Qaradagh in 1957. After moving to Kirkuk, he established a farm in Bānī Maqān, which is five kilometres away from Chamchamāl. We referred earlier to his farm in Dora in Baghdad, which is about 180 acres in size, where the 1998 celebration of the birth of the Prophet (PBUH) was held after the main takya could not accommodate the number of attendees.

Our Shaikh's talent and creativity in agriculture are especially evident at the farm he set up in Qūpī in Sulaymāniyya. When construction began at the end of 2003, the land, which is 650 acres in size, was completely bereft of trees, and it seemed very difficult to use this rocky, high-altitude land that is located between two mountains in a successful commercial agricultural project. The project required overcoming challenges such as identifying a close natural water source and designing water storage and transport methods, in addition to the preparation of roads for the transport of agricultural equipment. When our Shaikh lived in Sulaymāniyya, he would directly supervise the work done on the farm and discuss details, big and small, with the engineer in charge. Even after moving to Amman, he continued to constantly follow up on news of the farm, sometimes daily.

A manifestation of our Shaikh's acumen and intelligence is that he often alerts those in charge of the farm to details they missed, despite his physical distance from the farm and the limited time that he can devote to think about it due to his many responsibilities. This is another exhibition of his extraordinary multitasking ability. One of his karāmas in this regard is that he once called the farm engineer from Amman to ask him if an insect had attacked the Euphrates poplar trees, known locally as "qogh". The engineer replied that he had not noticed this but promised to make sure. In a later telephone call, he asked the engineer the same question. The latter confirmed that the last time he asked him, he examined the trees and found no trace of any insect. The following day, however, when the engineer was walking between some Euphrates poplar trees, he suddenly noticed that an insect, locally known as "ḥaffār", had spread on those trees. He immediately remembered our Shaikh's words and combatted the insects.

The farm now consists of about 40,0000 trees, including 25,000 trees of various kinds of pistachios, in addition to many other kinds of plant, including walnuts, almonds, oak, chestnuts, pomegranates, apricots, grapes, quince, tomatoes, okra, laurels, and persimmons, which are new to that area. Our Shaikh also installed artesian wells to supply water when it is scarce. A commentator was spot on when he praised the farm's role in serving the environment, noting that "the Shaikh has built an oxygen factory that suffices all the cities of Sulaymāniyya", in reference to the role of plants in the process of photosynthesis, where they absorb carbon dioxide from the atmosphere and release oxygen.

Our Shaikh's focus on plant quality is no less than his interest in its types and quantities, using the best cuttings and seeds in agriculture. We see his tendency to be creative in his particular interest in introducing new agricultural products that do not exist in the region, many of which are brought from outside Iraq. To this end, he established a special nursery on the farm for the cultivation of experimental new plants. After successfully cultivating a new species in the nursery, it is planted on the farm. Out of generosity, he gifts about half of what the nursery succeeds in planting to other farmers so that they may benefit from growing these new crops in their fields. For example, he succeeded in cultivating a type of Indian berry that was not available in Iraq that is now widespread in many farms in northern Iraq.

Our Shaikh is also interested in herbal medicine, often prescribing herbal treatments for certain diseases. He uses honey in many of his medical prescriptions, and he sometimes prescribes certain herbal remedies along with a special dhikr for a patient. He also often prescribes patients only dhikrs. It is important to emphasize here that he does not use these treatments as an alternative to conventional medical treatment. He respects sciences that serve people, and he even urges dervishes to obtain the most academic learning that they can. He also especially likes medicine and encouraged his children to study it, with four of them completing university studies in medicinal fields. He considers practising medicine as a form of worship because it benefits people.

Shaikh Muḥammad al-Muḥammad has an experimental approach to herbal medicine. When he discovers a certain treatment for a particular disease and prescribes it to an individual who suffers from that disease, he follows up the patient's condition to ascertain the effectiveness of the drug. Reading and talking to people with experience and expertise in this area are sources of our Shaikh's information about herbal remedies. However, there are also remedies that he spiritually received the knowledge of, as the Ṭarīqa's Shaikhs informed him of them.

One hobby that our Shaikh used to practice in the past, before he stopped due to old age, was hunting animals on prairies and in the mountains using a shotgun. He was a skilled huntsman, and the years he spent in the Kurdish movement polished his skills with various kinds of weapons. Even when he moved to Baghdad, he would often go to the wilderness to hunt rabbits. This is where his interest in hound dogs comes from.

Our Shaikh has a special love for dhikr beads, precious stones, and rings decorated with Qur'anic verses and dhikrs. He regularly buys and gifts them, which is one sign of his generosity and his love for presenting gifts. He also cares for antiques and has a longstanding interest in horses.

Photo 39: Shaikh Muḥammad al-Muḥammad in the middle of the dhikr circle in the takya in Baghdad (the 1990s).

"The Shaikh is a medium for good. The Shaikh enjoins good and forbids evil. The Shaikh directs you towards Allah, so he is a medium for good. You do not worship the Shaikh, I seek forgiveness from Allah. No! You worship Allah (exalted and high is He) with knowledge through the Shaikh's words, through the Shaikh's orders. The Shaikh enjoins good and forbids evil: good as described in the Book and the Sunna; good as described in texts found in the Islamic religion. The Shaikh orders you to follow the Ṭarīqa, the Ṭarīqa that the Shaikhs have decreed. This way is not of Shaikh Muḥammad al-Muḥammad's innovation. This way is decreed from Allah (exalted and high is He): 'Hold firmly to the rope of Allah all together and do not become divided' (`Āl 'Imrān 103), 'Indeed, those who pledge allegiance to you [O Muḥammad] are pledging allegiance to Allah. The hand of Allah is over their hands' (al-Fatḥ 10)".

Shaikh Muḥammad al-Muḥammad al-Kasnazān
(Sermon 30th/January/2013)

Epilogue

It is not easy to write a biography of a great walī of Allah, and it is even more difficult to summarise it. Shaikh Muḥammad al-Muḥammad al-Kasnazān's life is rich with countless achievements, sermons, legacies, and karāmas that a writer cannot familiarize themselves with, nor can a book compile. This is why this biography has focused on listing major incidents in his life, introducing his thought through his words and writings, and relating some of his karāmas in the context of related topics.

For this biography to be comprehensive, we did not limit it to Shaikh Muḥammad al-Muḥammad's history after assuming the Ṭarīqa's Shaikhdom. Rather, we also followed his life before that, including events that predated his birth that are important in realizing and understanding his spiritual role. The biography illustrates how being honoured and obligated by the duty of leading the Ṭarīqa transformed him completely. Each of his movements and non-movements came under the command and direction of the Ṭarīqa's Shaikhs, reflecting the great spiritual responsibilities that they placed on him when they made him their deputy and representative among the people.

We followed the noble Qur'an's style of storytelling when our recounting this blessed biography. We related it using two approaches at the same time: history and thought. While we recounted major events in chronological order, at the same time, we were keen to introduce our Shaikh's thought. The more informed the reader becomes of our Master's life, the more familiar he grows with his thoughts on various aspects of Sufism in particular, and Islam in general. The biography of our perfected Sufi Shaikh is the best explanation of Islam and Sufism.

I pray that this book will be a preamble to other books about the life of a full moon that has adorned the sky of Islamic Sufism, our Master sayyid Shaikh Muḥammad al-Muḥammad al-Kasnazān, and about the lives of the other Shaikhs of the Ṭarīqa ʿAliyya Qādiriyya Kasnazāniyya, may Allah sanctify all of their innermost beings.

Photo 40: Shaikh Muḥammad al-Muḥammad during the construction of the main takya in Baghdad (1981).

Appendix A

Biographical Timeline

We have compiled in this table major events in the life of Shaikh Muḥammad al-Muḥammad al-Kasnazān in chronological order.

Event	Date
Birth in the village of Karbchna in the city of Sulaymāniyya	15th/April/1938
His first marriage	Late 1957
Leaving Karbchna to live in the village of Būbān in the province of Penjwin	February/1959
Meeting Prime Minister 'Abd al-Karīm Qāsim in Baghdad	1960
Divorce from his first wife	1961
Leading an attack on a police station on the Penjwin- Darbandikhān road and the start of the Kurdish revolution	7th/September/1961
Retiring from political and military involvement with the Kurdish revolution	1966
His second marriage, to sayyida Kažāl	Early 1969
The birth of his first son, Nahro	12th/December/1969
Shaikh 'Abd al-Karīm's announcement that Shaikh Muḥammad al-Muḥammad is his General Deputy	January/1971
Settling in Kirkuk	1971
Performing pilgrimage to Mecca	January/1973
Travelling to Cairo to enrol in al-Āzhar University	Late 1977
Assuming the Shaikhdom of the Ṭarīqa	4th/February/1978
Performing 'umrah	The first half of 1978
Starting his first seclusion in Karbchna	26th/July/1978
Increasing the number of perennial dhikrs to one hundred thousand	The second half of 1978
Starting his second seclusion in Karbchna	15th/July/1979

Starting his third seclusion in Karbchna	4th/July/1980
Completion of the construction of the main takya in Baghdad and moving to live there	1982
Renovation of the shrines in Karbchna	Middle of 1982
Replacing the crown of the shrine of Shaikh 'Abd al-Qādir al-Gaylānī	1983
Publication of the book *Al-Ānwār al-Raḥmāniyya fīl-Ṭarīqa al-'Aliyya al-Qādiriyya al-Kasnazāniyya*	The first half of 1988
Publication of the book *Jilā' al-Khāṭir*	1989
Publication of the book *Al-Ṣalawāt al-Kasnazāniyya*	1990
Proposing the concept of the Muḥammadī calendar and starting its implementation	19th/September/1991
Sending the first caliph to India to preach	1994
Proposing the concept of the Muḥammadī Shamsī calendar and starting its implementation	2nd/May/1994
Adding the Ṣalāt Waṣfiyya to the dhikrs of the Tarīqa	July/1996
Publication of the book *Al-Ṭarīqa al-'Aliyya al-Qādiriyya al-Kasnazāniyya*	1998
The arrest and imprisonment of Shaikh Nahro by the Iraqi regime	6th/August/1998
Release of Shaikh Nahro from prison	15th/January/2000
Travel to London, UK, for medical treatment	March/2000
Migration from Baghdad to Sulaymāniyya	21st/December/2000
Travel to the USA for medical treatment	2003
Founding the "Shaikh Muḥammad al-Kasnanza University College" (al-Salam University College)	2003
Travel to the USA for medical treatment	2004
Pulication of *Mawsū'at Al-Kasnazān Fīmā Aṣṭalaḥa 'Alayhi Ahl Al-Taṣṣawuf wal-'Irfān*	2005
Renovation of the shrine of Shaikh Ismā'īl al-Wilyānī in 'Aqra and clothing it in a gold shroud	9th/May/2006
Being awarded the "Arab Historian Medal" and the "Arab History Certificate" by the Union of Arab Historians.	July/2006

Migration from Sulaymāniyya to Amman, Jordan.	2nd/August/2007
Travel to the USA for a kidney transplant	2010
Receiving the Ḥizb al-Wāw	2013
Travel to the USA for medical treatment	2014
Adding this dhikr to the daily wirds: *Astaghfiru Allah al-ladhī Lā ilāha illā Huwa ar-Raḥmān ar-Raḥīm al-Ḥayyu al-Qayyūm al-ladhī lā yamūt wa-atūbu 'ilayhi Rabbī ighfir lī*	March/2016
The Prophet (PBUH) added his name to the name of our Shaikh, making it "Muḥammad al-Muḥammad"	18th/May/2016
Being awarded the title of "caliph" by the Shaikhs of the Tarīqa	22nd/June/2016
Travel to the USA for medical treatment	24nd/July/2016
Adding one hundred times to the dhikr of lā ilāha illā Allah to the Wird al-'Aṣr	28th/January/2018
Travel to the USA for medical treatment	24th/June/2019

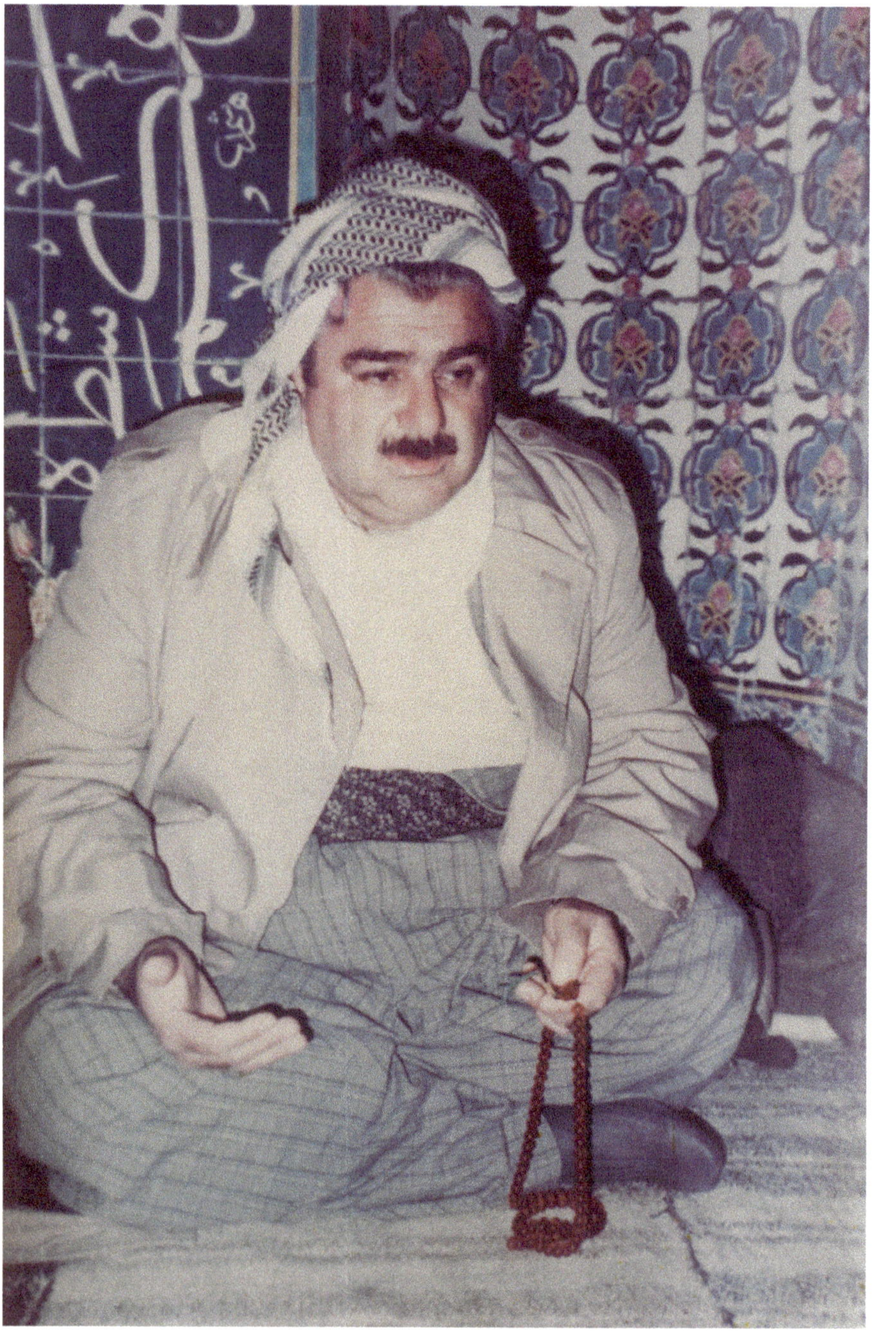

Photo 41: Shaikh Muḥammad al-Muḥammad in the mosque of Karbchna (early 1980s).

Appendix B

Glossary

These are Arabic terms that are used in the book and their meanings. At times, we have used an Arabic term without translation, as in the case of "dhikr", while at others we alternated between an Arabid term and its translations, as in the case of "khalwa (seclusion)".

Term	Meaning
Basmala	The Qur'anic verse: "Bismi Allāhi ar-Raḥmāni ar-Raḥīm"
Bāṭin	Inward
Dhikr	The act of remembering Allah and any specific form of remembrance of Allah.
Ḥadīth	When written with a "Ḥ", it refers to the corpus of sayings that are attributed to the Prophet (PBUH). When written with a "ḥ", it denotes any one of those sayings.
Ḥadīth Qudsī	A saying whose meaning is from Allah but whose wording is from the Prophet (PBUH)
Ḥāl	Any of countless spiritual states that the Shaikh bestows on a dervish
Ḥizb	A type of dhikr that is not read regularly
Irshād	Preaching
Karāma	A paranormal feat of a walī
Kasnazānī	Related to Tarīqa Kasnazāniyya
Khalwa	Seclusion
Khatma	One-hundred thousand recitations of a particular dhikr
Madad	Spiritual support and help
Muʿjiza	A paranormal feat of a prophet
Muṣḥaf	A copy of the written Qur'an
Riyāḍa	Spiritual practices of striving against

	one's self, such as fasting, that the person adheres to for a period
Nafs	Self
Sayyid	A male descendant of the Prophet (PBUH)
Sayyida	A female descendant of the Prophet (PBUH)
Subhānahu wa-ta'ālā	A form of glorifying Allah that may be translated as "exalted and high is He"
Ṣuḥba	Companionship, fellowship
Sunna	When written with an "S", it refers to the sayings, practices, and lifestyle of the Prophet (PBUH). When written with an "s", it denotes any one of these sayings, practices, or lifestyle aspect.
Walī	A "walī" is someone near to Allah on whom He has conferred spiritual blessings that at times are manifested in supernatural feats
Wilāya	The state of being a "walī"
Wird	A type of dhikr that is read regularly

References

This is a listing of the classical and old works and another of the modern works that are cited in this book. Except for three in English and two in Kurdish, all sources are in Arabic.

A) Classical and Old Works

ʿAbd al-Razzāq, Abū Bakr. *Al-Muṣannaf*, edited by Ayman Naṣr al-Dīn al-Āzharī, 10 vols, Beirut: Dār al-Kutub al-ʿIlmiyya, 2000.

ʿAbd Ibn Ḥamīd, Abū Muḥammad. *Al-Muntakhab min Musnad ʿAbd Ibn Ḥamīd*, edited by Abū ʿAbd Allah Muṣṭafā Ibn al-ʿAdawī, 2 vols, Riyadh: Dār Bilnisya Lil-Nashr wal-Tawzīʿ, 2002.

Abū al-Fidāʾ, ʿImād al-Dīn Ismāʿīl. *Al-Mukhtaṣar fī-Akhbār al-Bashar*, 4 vols, Egypt: al-Maṭbaʿa al-Ḥusayniyya, 1907.

Abū Dāwūd, Abū Dāwūd Sulaimān al-Sajistānī. *Sunan Abī Dāwūd*, edited by Shuʿaib al-Ārnaʾūṭ and Muḥammad Qaraballī, 7 vols, Damascus: Dār al-Risāla al-ʿĀlamiyya, 2009.

Aḥmad Ibn Ḥanbal. *Musnad al-Imām Aḥmad Ibn Ḥanbal*, edited by Shuʿaib al-Ārnaʾūṭ et al., 50 vols, Beirut: Muʾassasat al-Risāla, 1995–2001.

ʿAlī Ibn Abī Ṭālib, Imām. *Nahj al-Balāgha*, edited by al-Sharīf al-Raḍī, Beirut: Al-Maʿārig, 1990.

Al-Āṣbahānī, Abū Naʿīm. *Akhlāq al-Nabī wa-ʾĀdābuh*, edited by Ṣāliḥ al-Wanyān, 4 vols, Riyadh: Dār al-Muslim, 1998.

Al-Āṣbahānī, Abū Naʿīm. *Dalāʾil al-Nubuwwa*, edited by Muḥammad Rawās Qalʿa Jī and ʿAbd al-Barr ʿAbbas, 2 vols, Beirut: Dār al-Nafāʾis, 1986.

Al-ʿAsqalānī, Aḥmad Ibn ʿAlī Ibn Ḥajar. *Al-Iṣāba fī-Tamyīz al-Ṣaḥāba*, Beirut: Al-Maktaba Al-ʿAṣriyya, 2012.

Al-Bakrī, Abū Bakr. *Iʿānat al-Ṭālibīn*, 4 vols, Egypt: Dār Iḥyāa al-Kutub al-ʿArabiyya, 1300 H.

Al-Bayhaqī, Aḥmad Ibn al-Ḥusayn. *Al-Sunan al-Kubrā*, edited by Muḥammad ʿAṭā, 11 vols, Beirut: Dār al-Kutub al-ʿIlmiyya, 2003.

Al-Bayhaqī, Aḥmad Ibn al-Ḥusayn. *Al-Zuhd al-Kabīr*, edited by ʿĀmir Aḥmad Ḥaydar, Beirut: Dār al-Jinān, 1987.

Al-Bayhaqī, Aḥmad Ibn al-Ḥusayn. *Dalā`il al-Nubuwwa wa-Maʿrifat Aḥwāl Ṣaḥib al-Sharīʿa*, edited by ʿAbd al-Muʿṭī Qalʿachī, Beirut: Dār al-Kutub al-ʿIlmiyya, 1988.

Al-Bayhaqī, Aḥmad Ibn al-Ḥusayn. *Shuʿab al-`Īmān*, 7 vols, Beirut: Dār al-Kutub al-ʿIlmiyya, 2000.

Al-Bukhārī, Muḥammad. *Al-Jāmiʿ al-Ṣaḥīḥ, edited by ʿAbd al-Qādir al-Ḥamad*, 3 vols, Riyadh: ʿAbd al-Qādir al-Ḥamad, 2008.

Al-Dārimī, ʿAbd Allāh. *Musnad al-Dārimī*, edited by Ḥusain al-Dārānī, 4 vols, Riyadh: Dār al-Maghnī lil-Nashr wal-Tawzīʿ, 2000.

Al-Dhahabī, Shams al-Dīn Muḥammad. *Siyar Aʿlām al-Nubalā`*, edited by Shuʿayb al-Ārna`ūṭ and Muḥammad Naʿīm al-ʿArqsūsī, 20 vols, Beirut: Mu`ssasat al-Risāla, 1996.

Al-Gaylānī, Shaikh ʿAbd al-Qādir. "Al-Ghawthiyya", *Dīwān ʿAbd al-Qādir Al-Jīlānī*, edited by Yūsuf Zaydān, Beirut: Dār al-Jīl, pp. 203-230, undated.

Al-Gaylānī, Shaikh ʿAbd al-Qādir. *Al-Fatḥ al-Rabbānī wal-Fayḍ al-Raḥmānī*, Egypt: Dār al-Rayyān Lil-Turāth, undated.

Al-Gaylānī, Shaikh ʿAbd al-Qādir. *Jilā` al-Khāṭir*, edited by Khālid Al-Zarʿī and ʿAbd al-Nāṣir Sirrī, Damascus: Dār Ibn Qayyim, 1994.

Al-Gaylānī, Shaikh ʿAbd al-Qādir. *Jilā` al-Khāṭir*, edited by Shaikh Muḥammad al-Muḥammad al-Kasnazān, Baghdad: Sharikat ʿIshtār Lil-Ṭibāʿa wal-Nashr, 1988.

Al-Hītamī, Aḥmad Shihā al-Dīn. *Al-Fatāwā al-Ḥadīthiyya*, Beirut: Dār al-Maʿrifa, undated.

Ibn ʿAbd al-Birr, Yūsuf. *Al-Istīʿāb fi-Maʿrifat al-Āṣḥāb*, edited by ʿAlī al-Bijjāwī, Beirut: Dār al-Jīl, 1992.

Ibn ʿAjība, Aḥmad Ibn Muḥammad. *`Īqāẓ al-Himam fi-Sharḥ al-Ḥikam*, edited by Muḥammad Aḥmad Ḥasab Allah, Cairo: Dār al-Maʿārif, 1984.

Ibn ʿArabī, Muḥyyī al-Dīn. *Al-Risāla al-Wujūdiyya fi-Maʿnā Qawlihi (PBUH) Man ʿArafa Nafsahu faqad ʿArafa Rabbāhu*, edited by ʿĀṣim al-Kayyālī, Beirut: Dār al-Kutub al-ʿIlmiyya, 2007.

Ibn Hishām, ʿAbd al-Malik. *Sīrat al-Nabī*, edited by Fatḥī al-Dābūllī, 4 vols, Tanta: Dār al-Ṣaḥāba lil-Turāth, 1995.

Ibn Qayyim al-Jawzīyya, Muḥammad. *Zād al-Maʿād fī-Hadyī Khayri al-ʿIbād*, edited by Shuʿayb al-Ārnaʾūṭ and ʿAbd al-Qādir al-Ārnaʾūṭ, Beirut: Muʾassat al-Risāla, 1998.

Ibn Rajab, ʿAbd al-Raḥmān. *Al-dhayl ʿalā Ṭabaqāt al-Ḥanābila*, edited by ʿAbd al-Raḥmān al-ʿUthaymīn, Mecca: Maktabat al-ʿUbaykān, 1425 H.

Ibn Saʿad, Muḥammad. *Kitāb al-Ṭabaqāt al-Kabīr*, edited by ʿAlī Muḥammad ʿUmar, Cairo: Maktabat al-Khānijī, 2001.

Ibn Taymiyya, Aḥmad. *Majmūʿ Fatāwā*, compiled and edited by ʿAbd al-Raḥmān Ibn Qāsim, vol. 1, Medina: King Fahd Complex for the Printing of the Holy Quran, 2004.

Al-Jīlī, Shaikh ʿAbd al-Karīm. *Al-Nādirāt al-ʿAyniyya*, edited by Yūsuf Zaydān, Cairo: Dār al-Āmīn, 1999.

Al-Lālikkāʾī, Hibatu Allah Ibn al-Ḥasan. *Karāmāt Awliyāʾ Allah ʿAzza wa-Jall*, edited by Aḥmad Ḥamdān, Riyadh: Dār Ṭība, 1992.

Mālik Ibn Anas, Abū ʿAbd Allāh. *Muwaṭṭaʾ al-Imām Mālik (Narrated by Yaḥyā Ibn Yaḥyā al-Laithī)*, edited by Muḥammad al-Āʿẓamī, 6 vols, Abu Dhabi: Muʾassasat Zāyid Ibn Sulṭān ʾĀl Nhayyān al-Khairiyya, 2004.

Muslim, Abū al-Husain. *Ṣaḥīḥ Muslim*, edited by Muḥammad ʿAbd al-Bāqī, 5 vols, Cairo: Dār al-Ḥadīth, 1991.

Al-Najafī, Muḥammad. *Baḥr al-Ānsāb (al-Mushajjar al-Kashshāf Li-Uṣūl al-Sāda al-Āshrāf)*, edited by Anas al-Ḥasanī, Medina: Dār al-Mujtabā Lil-Nashr wal-Tawzīʿ, 1999.

Al-Nawawī, Abū Zakariyyā Muḥyī al-Dīn. *Ṣaḥiḥ Muslim bi-Sharḥ al-Nawawī*, 18 vols, Cairo: Al-Maṭbaʿa al-Maṣriyya bil-Azhar, 1930.

Al-Qāḍī, Ḥusayn. *Sirāj al-Sālikīn*, Manuscript mentioned by Muḥammad Amīn Zakī in *Tārīkh al-Sulaymāniyya*, p. 217.

Al-Qādiri, Ismāʿīl. *Al-Fiyūḍāt al-Rabbāniyya fil-Maʾāthir wa-Wird al-Qādiriyya*, Egypt: Maṭāʿat Muṣṭafā al-Bābī al-Ḥalabī wa-Awlādih, 1353 H.

Al-Qurṭubī, Muḥammad. *Al-Āsnā fī-Sharḥ Asmāʾ Allah al-Ḥusnā*, edited by Muḥammad Ḥasan Jabal and Ṭāriq Aḥmad Muḥammad, 2 vols, Tanta: Dār al-Ṣaḥaba Lil-Turāth bi-Ṭanta, 1995.

Al-Rāzī, Fakhr al-Dīn. *Mafātīḥ al-Ghaib: Al-Tafsīr al-Kabīr*, 32 vols, Beirut: Dār al-Fikr lil-Ṭibāʿa wal-Nashr wal-Tawzīʿ, 1981.

Al-Sakandarī, Ibn ʿAṭāʾ Allah. *Ḥikam Ibn ʿAṭāʾ Allah*, commentary by Shaikh Aḥmad Zarrūq, edited by ʿAbd al-Ḥalīm Maḥmūd, Cairo: Muʾassat Dār al-Shaʿb, 1985.

Al-Sakandarī, Ibn ʿAṭāʾ Allah. *Laṭāʾif al-Minan*, edited by ʿAbd al-Ḥalīm Maḥmūd, Cairo: Muʾassat Dār al-Maʿārif, 1999.

Al-Shaʿrānī, ʿAbd al-Wahhāb. *Al-Ṭabaqāt al-Kubrā*, edited by Aḥmad al-Sāʾiḥ and Tawfīq Wahba, Cairo: Maktabat al-Thaqāfa al-Dīniyya, 2005.

Al-Shaṭnūfī, ʿAlī Ibn Yūsuf. *Bahjat al-Āsrār wa-Maʿdan al-Ānwār*, Fez: Al-Muhaẓẓama al-Maghribiyya lil-Tarbiyya wal-Thaqāfa wal-ʿUlūm, 2013.

Al-Suyūṭī, Jalāl al-Dīn. "Al-Qawl al-Āshbah fī-Ḥadīth Man ʿArafa Nafsahu faqad ʿArafa Rabbah", *Majmūʿat Rasāʾil ʿAshra*, Lahore: Al-Maṭbaʿ al-Muḥammadī, undated.

Al-Ṭabarānī, Sulaymān Ibn Aḥmad. *Al-Muʿjam al-Āwsaṭ*, edited by Ṭāriq ʿAwaḍ Allah and ʿAbd al-Muḥsin Ībrāhīm, Cairo: Dār al-Ḥaramayn lil-Ṭibāʿa wal-Nashr, 1995.

Al-Ṭabarānī, Sulaymān Ibn Aḥmad. *Al-Muʿjam al-Kabīr*, edited by Ḥamdī al-Salafī, Cairo: Maktabat Ibn Taymiyya, undated.

Al-Ṭabarānī, Sulaymān Ibn Aḥmad. *Al-Muʿjam al-Ṣaghīr*, edited by Muḥammad Amrīr, Beirut: Al-Maktab al-Islāmī, 1985.

Al-Ṭabarī, Muḥammad Ibn Jarīr. *Jāmiʿ al-Bayān fī Tafsīr ʾĀy al-Qur'an*, edited by ʿAbd Allah ʿAbd al-Muḥsin al-Turkī, Giza: Hajr lil-Ṭibāʿa wal-Nashr wal-Iʿlān, 2001.

Al-Tādifī, Muḥammad Ibn Yaḥyā. *Qalāʾid al-Jawāhir*, Cairo: al-Maṭbaʿa al-Ḥamīdiyya, 1356 H.

Al-Tirmidhī, Muḥammad. *Al-Jāmiʿ al-Kabīr*, edited by Bashshār Maʿrūf, 6 vols, Beirut: Dār al-Gharb al-Islāmī, 1996.

Al-ʿUlaymī, Mujīr al-Dīn. *Al-Manhaj al-Āḥmad fī-Tarājim Aṣḥāb al-Imām Aḥmad*, edited by Shuʿaib al-Ārnaʾūṭ and Muḥyī al-Dīn Najīb, 6 vols, Beirut: Dār Ṣādir, 1997.

Al-Yāfiʿī, ʿAbd Allah. *Khulāṣat al-Mafākhir fī-Manāqib al-Shaikh ʿAbd al-Qādir*, edited by Aḥmad al-Muzīdī, Maryland: Dār al-ʾĀthār al-Islāmiyya, 2006.

Al-Zarkashī, Badr al-Dīn. *Al-Burhān fī-ʿUlūm al-Qur'an*, edited by Muḥammad Ibrāhīm, 4 vols, Cairo: Maktabat Dār al-Turāth, 1984.

B) Modern Works

ʿAbd al-Raḥmān, Saʿīd. *Shuyūkh al-Āzhar*, vol. 5, Cairo: Al-Sharika Al-ʿArabiyya Lil-Nashr wal-Tawzīʿ, undated.

ʿAlī, ʿUthmān. *Al-Ḥaraka al-Kurdiyya al-Muʿāṣira: Dirāsa Taʾrīkhiyya wathāʾiqiyya 1833-1946*, Erbil: Maktab al-Tafsīr Lil-Nashr wal-Iʿlān, 2011.

Al-ʿAnqarī, ʿAbd Allah. *Karāmāt al-Āwliyāʾ: Dirāsa ʿAqadiyya fī-Ḍawʾ Ahl al-Sunna wal-Jamāʿa*, Riyadh: Dār al-Tawḥīd Lil-Nashr, 2012.

Aḥmad, Kamāl Muẓhir. *Kurdistan fī-Sanawāt al-Ḥarb al-ʿĀlamiyya al-ʾUlā*, Beirut: Al-Fārābī, 2013.

Aḥmad, Maḥmūd Razūq. *Al-Ḥaraka al-Kurdiyya fīl-ʿIrāq: Dawr al-Barazāniyyīn fī-Ṭarīq al-Ḥukm al-Thātī 1918-1968*, Amman: Dār al-Muʿtazz lil-Nashr wal-Tawzīʿ, 2014.

Barazānī, Ayyub. *Al-Ḥaraka al-Taḥarruriyya al-Kurdiyya wa-Ṣirāʿ al-Qiwā al-Iqlīmiyya wal-Duwaliyya 1958-1975*, Geneva: Dār Nashr Ḥaqāʾiq al-Mashriq, 2011.

Barazānī, Masʿūd. *Al-Barazānī wal-Ḥaraka al-Taḥarruriyya al-Kurdiyya 2*, Beirut: Kāwā lil-Thaqāfa al-Kurdiyya, 1997.

Bell, Gertrude. *Review of the civil administration of Mesopotamia*, His Majesty's Stationery Office, 1920.

Bruinessen, Martin Van. "The Qadiriyya and the lineages of Qadiri shaykhs in Kurdistan". *Journal of the History of Sufism*, 1991, 213-229.

Daza yī, Muḥsin. *Aḥdāth ʿĀṣartuhā, al-Juzʾ al-Thānī 1961-1975*, Erbil: Dār ʾĀrās lil-Ṭibāʿa wal-Nashr, 2002.

Edmonds, C. J. *Kurds, Turks and Arabs: Politics, travel and research in North-Eastern Iraq 1919-1925*, London: Oxford University Press, 1957.

Fatoohi, Louay et al. "Nahjun Jadīdun Nḥwa Taʾrīkhin Daqīqin Lil-Sīra al-Nabawiyya wal-ʿAṣr al-Islāmī al-Āwwal", *Dirāsat ʿArābiyya*, number 1/2, 1994.

Fatoohi, Louay. "Mafhūm 'Ladun' fīl-Qur'ān al-ʿAẓīm", *Al-Manhal*, vol. 61, no. 560, pp. 26-29, 1999.

Fatoohi, Louay. *Ṣifāt Qiyādiyya Lil-Nabī Muḥammad (PBUH)*, http://www.louayfatoohi.com/2014/01/islam/leadership-qualities-of-prophet-muhammad/, 1st/January/2014.

Fatoohi, Louay. *The Prophet Joseph in the Qur'an, the Bible, and History*. Kuala Lumpur: Islamic Book Trust, 2005.

Fatoohi, Louay. *The Wonders of Ṭarīqa Kasnazāniyya Brought to India*, Birmingham: The Way Publishing, 2015.

Al-Gaylānī, ʿAbd al-Razzāq. *Al-Shaikh ʿAbd al-Qādir: Al-Imām al-Zāhid al-Qudwa*, Damascus: Dār al-Qalam, 1994.

Al-Gaylānī, Mājid ʿArsān. *Hākathā Ẓahara Jīl Ṣalāḥ al-Dīn wa-Hākathā ʿĀdat al-Quds*, Virginia: Al-Maʿhad al-ʿĀlamī Lil-Fikr al-Islāmī, 1981.

Al-Iṣbahānī, Faḍl Allah Ibn Rūzbhān. *Sharḥ Ṣalawāt Chharda Maʿṣūm – Wasīlat al-Khādim ilā al-Makhdūm*.

Jab Allah, Ṭayyib. "Dawr al-Ṭuruq al-Ṣūfiyya fil-Mujtamaʿ al-Jazāʾirī", *Maʿārif*, year 8, no. 14, pp. 133-150, 2013.

Juwayda, Wadīʿ. *Al-Ḥaraka al-Qawmiyya al-Turkiyya wa-Nashʾatuhā wa-Taṭawwuruhā*, Beirut: Dār al-Fārābī, 2013.

Karīm, ʿUmar Sharīf. *Sha Ri Qāta Kānī Kifrī*, Sulaymāniyya, 2010. (In Kurdish)

Al-Kasnazān, Alī Ḥusayn. *Al-Mujāhid al-Ākbar al-Shaikh ʿAbd al-Qādir al-Kasnazān*, unpublished article shared by the author, 2017.

Al-Kasnazān, Shaikh Muḥammad al-Muḥammad. *Al-Ānwār al-Raḥmāniyya fil-Ṭarīqa al-ʿAliyya al-Qādiriyya al-Kasnazāniyya*, Baghdad: Sharikat ʿIshtār Lil-Ṭibāʿa wal-Nashr, 1988.

Al-Kasnazān, Shaikh Muḥammad al-Muḥammad. *Al-Ṭarīqa al-ʿAliyya al-Qādiriyya al-Kasnazāniyya*, Baghdad: Al-Ṭarīqa al-Kasnazāniyya, 1998.

Al-Kasnazān, Shaikh Muḥammad al-Muḥammad. *Mawsūʿat Al-Kasnazān Fīmā Aṣṭalaḥa ʿAlayhi Ahl Al-Taṣṣawuf wal-ʿIrfān*, 24 vols, Beirut: Dār ʾĀya, 2005.

Mankūrī, Mīrzā. *Bah Sah Rhātī Syāsī Kūrd*, Sulaymāniyya: Markaz Glāwīj al-Thaqāfiyya al-Ādabiyya, 1999. (In Kurdish)

Al-Marʿashī, Shihāb al-Dīn, *Mulḥaqāt al-ʾIhqāq*, edited by Maḥmūd Al-Marʿashī, vol 33, Qom: Manshurāt Maktabat ʾĀyat Allah al-ʿUẓmā Al-Marʿashī al-Najafī, 1957.

Mcdowall, David. *A Modern History of The Kurds*, London: I.B.Taurus, 2005.

Al-Mudarris, ʿAbd al-Karīm. *ʿUlamāʾunā fi-Khidmat al-ʿIlm wal-Dīn*, Baghdad: Dār al-Ḥurriya Lil-Ṭibāʿa, 1983.

Muḥammad, Samar. *Akrād al-'Iraq Tahta Ḥukm 'Abd al-Karīm Qāsim 1958-1963*, MA dissertation, Zagazig University, Egypt, undated.

Al-Ṣallābī, 'Alī Muḥammad. *Al-Dawla al-Zangiyya wa-Najāḥ al-Mashrū' al-Islāmī biqiyādat Nūr al-Dīn Maḥmūd al-Shahīd fī-Muqawamt al-Taghalghul al-Bāṭinī wal-Ghazū al-Ṣalībī*, Beirut: Dār al-Ma'rifa, 2007.

Al-Ṭalabānī, Jalāl. Newspaper Interview, *al-Ḥayāt*, number 358, date 7th/December/1998.

Zakī, Muḥamamd Amīn. *Khulāṣat Tārīkh al-Kurd wa-Kurdistan min Aqdam al-'Uṣūr al-Tārīkhiyya ilā al-`Ān*, Egypt: Al-Sa'āda, 1936.

Zakī, Muḥamamd Amīn. *Tārīkh al-Sulaymāniyya*, Baghdad: Sharikat al-Nashr wal-Ṭibā'a al-'Irāqiyya al-Maḥdūda, 1951.

Zaydān, Yūsuf. *'Abd al-Qādir al-Jīlānī: Bāz Allah al-Āshhab*, Beirut: Dār al-Jīl, 2001.

www.ingramcontent.com/pod-product-compliance
Lightning Source LLC
Chambersburg PA
CBHW041310240426
43661CB00064B/2881
* 9 7 8 1 9 0 6 3 4 2 2 5 8 *